THE

COMMON SCHOOL SYSTEM

OF THE

STATE OF NEW-YORK,

COMPRISING

THE SEVERAL GENERAL LAWS RELATING TO COMMON SCHOOLS, TOGETHER WITH FULL EXPOSITIONS, INSTRUCTIONS AND FORMS FOR THE USE OF THE SEVERAL SCHOOL OFFICERS AND INHABITANTS OF DISTRICTS, A COMPLETE DIGEST OF THE DECISIONS OF THE STATE SUPERINTENDENT, AND THE SEVERAL LOCAL PROVISIONS FOR THE SUPPORT OF COMMON SCHOOLS IN THE CITIES AND VILLAGES OF THE STATE.

TO WHICH IS PREFIXED

A HISTORICAL SKETCH

OF THE

ORIGIN, PROGRESS AND PRESENT OUTLINE

OF THE SYSTEM.

Prepared in Pursuance of an Act of the Legislature,

UNDER THE DIRECTION OF THE

HON. CHRISTOPHER MORGAN,

SUPERINTENDENT OF COMMON SCHOOLS.

BY SAMUEL S. RANDALL,

DEP. SUP'T COMMON SCHOOLS.

TROY, N. Y.:

JOHNSON AND DAVIS, STEAM PRESS PRINTERS.

1851.

PREFACE.

In submitting the following work to the inhabitants and officers of school districts, the various town and county officers charged with the local administration of the common school system in its several departments, and the public generally, the compiler has been actuated by an earnest desire to diffuse as widely as possible, a more thorough and accurate knowledge of the history and details of that system than has hitherto appeared. Having been connected with the department of Common Schools, with a slight interval, for the past fourteen years, during which period five successive Superintendents have been in office, and the system has undergone numerous important modifications, the necessary materials for a complete digest of its various provisions, as well as for the requisite adaptation of the numerous expositions, decisions, and instructions of the department, to the present state of the law, were probably more fully within his reach than that of any other individual.

The volume of Laws and Decisions prepared and published by Gen. Dix in 1837, however valuable for its intrinsic interest, and for its clear and lucid exposition of the fundamental principles of our system of public instruction, has become to a very great extent inapplicable to the existing details of that system; and where relied upon as a guide, by officers of districts, of towns and counties, must necessarily embarrass and mislead. The compiler of the present work has therefore deemed it his duty to obviate this result so far as may be in his power, by giving first, a general abstract of the existing provisions of the law in reference to the powers, duties and liabilities of each class of officers connected with the administration, of the system, and of the inhabitants of the several school districts; and secondly, a digested view under each head, of the various instructions, expositions, and decisions of the department, or rather of the *principles* of such instructions and decisions, in their application to the law as it now stands: preceded by the general laws and the various local provisions applicable to the several cities and larger towns.

A historical sketch of the origin and progress of the system from its inception to the present period, accompanied by a brief exposition of its present condition, has been annexed to the work, with the design of rendering it more acceptable as well to our own citizens as to those of other portions of the Union, who may feel an interest in tracing the gradual advancement of our legislation on this important subject, and in ascertaining the prominent features of our system, as moulded by the successive improvements consequent upon an experience of nearly forty years.

The importance of an uniform and enlightened administration of a system embracing so great a variety of interests and forming so material an ingredient in the intellectual, moral, and social civilization of the community, has not been one of the least among the considerations which have led to the publication of this work: and if through its means any facilities shall have been afforded for the accomplishment of this desirable result, the time and pains spent in its preparation will not have been regretted. That it is free from imperfections and errors it would be presumptuous to assert; but in commending it to those for whose use it is specially designed, and to the friends of popular education generally, the compiler can accompany it with the assurance that no efforts on his part have been spared to render it worthy of their attention and regard.

Albany, *May*, 1851.

SECRETARY'S OFFICE,
Department of Common Schools.

Albany, May 15, 1851.

Having examined the following "Digest of the Common School System of the State of New York," I take pleasure in saying that it is a full and correct exposition of that system; and entitled to the confidence of officers and inhabitants of school districts, Town Superintendents of common schools, and others interested in the cause of popular education.

CHRISTOPHER MORGAN,
Sup't of Common Schools.

PART I.

ORIGIN, PROGRESS, AND PRESENT CONDITION

OF THE

COMMON SCHOOL SYSTEM OF NEW YORK,

From the Origin of the State Government to the Year 1851.

At the first meeting of the State Legislature after the adoption of the Constitution, the governor, Geo. Clinton, called the attention of that body to the subject of education. The following is an extract from his speech:

"Neglect of the education of youth is one of the evils consequent upon war. Perhaps there is scarce any thing more worthy your attention than the revival and encouragement of seminaries of learning; and nothing by which we can more satisfactorily express our gratitude to the Supreme Being for his past favors; since piety and virtue are generally the offspring of an enlightened understanding."

In this year, the act incorporating the Regents of the University was passed.

In 1789 an act was passed, requiring the surveyor-general, to set apart two lots in each township, of the public land thereafter to be surveyed, for gospel and school purposes.

The following is an extract from the report of the Regents of the University, for 1793:

"On this occasion we cannot help suggesting to the legislature the numerous advantages which we conceive would accrue to the citizens in general, from the institution of schools in various parts of the state, for the purpose of instructing children in the lower branches of education, such as reading their native language with propriety, and so much of writing and arithmetic, as to enable them when they come forward into active life, to transact with accuracy and dispatch, the business arising from their daily intercourse with each other. The mode of accomplishing this desirable object, we respectfully submit to the wisdom of the legislature.

"The attention which the legislature has evinced to promote literature, by the liberal provision heretofore made, encourages, with all deference, to suggest the propriety of rendering it permanent by setting apart for that salutary purpose some of the unappropriated lands. The value of these will be enhanced by the increase of population. The state will thus never want the means of promoting useful science; and will thereby secure the rational happiness, and fix the liberty of the people on the most permanent basis—that of knowledge and virtue."

At the opening of the session of the legislature in 1795, Gov. Clinton thus again alluded to the subject:

"While it is evident that the general establishment and liberal endowment of academies are highly to be commended, and are attended with the most beneficial consequences, yet it cannot be denied that they are principally confined to the children of the opulent, and that a great portion of the community is excluded from their immediate advantages. The establishment of common schools throughout the state, is happily calculated to remedy this inconvenience, and will therefore engage your early and decided consideration."

On the 11th of January, the Assembly appointed a committee consisting of JONATHAN NICOLL HAVENS, of Suffolk, as chairman; DAVID BROOKS, of Dutchess, DAVID PYE, of Orange, EBENEZER PURDY, of Westchester, DANIEL GRAY, of Rensselaer, ADAM COMSTOCK, of Saratoga, and RICHARD FURMAN, of New York, to take into consideration that portion of the Governor's Message relating to the establishment of Common Schools throughout the state. Mr. HAVENS, from this committee, reported on the 19th of February "An Act for the encouragement of schools," which passed the House on the 4th, and the Senate on the 22d of March, and became a law on the 9th of April 1795. By this act the sum of £20,000 or $50,000 was annually appropriated for five years, "for the purpose of encouraging and maintaining schools in the several cities and towns in this state, in which the children of the inhabitants residing in the state, shall be instructed in the English language, or be taught English grammar, arithmetic, mathematics, and such other branches of knowledge as are most useful and necessary to complete a good English education." This sum was at first apportioned to the several counties according to their representation in the legislature, and afterwards according to the number of electors for members of assembly; and to the several towns according to the number of taxable inhabitants of each. The boards of supervisors were *required* to raise by tax upon each town, a sum equal to one-half of that appropriated by the state, to be applied in like manner. While this bill was under discussion in the assembly, a motion to add a proviso, "that no town after receiving for one year its proportion of the moneys appropriated by the act, shall be entitled in any year thereafter to receive its proportion of the same, unless the freeholders and inhabitants of such town, should, at their next preceding town-meeting, have voted a sum for the use of schools in such town, equal to at least one-half of the proportion of the moneys to which such town shall have been entitled by this act in the preceding year; and in case such sum shall not have been voted to be raised as aforesaid by any town, the supervisors of the county should apportion the moneys to which such town would otherwise have been entitled, among the other towns in such county, which should have voted for such sum" was rejected, by a vote of 30 to 27. The adoption of this proviso, would have left it discretionary with the inhabitants of any town to comply with the requisitions of the act, and thereby entitle itself to receive its proportion of the public money; a measure subsequently resorted to, as will hereafter be seen, but speedily abandoned on experience of its effects.

The prominent features of the act of 1795, were the following: Not less than three, nor more than seven commissioners, were annually to be chosen by the electors of the respective towns, to whom were to be committed the supervision and direction of the schools, and the apportionment of public money among the several districts. The inhabitants residing in different sections of each town, were authorized "to associate together for the purpose of procuring good and sufficient schoolmasters, and for erecting and maintaining schools in such and so many parts of the town where they may reside, as shall be most convenient," and to appoint two or more trustees, who were directed to "confer with the commissioners concerning the qualification of the master or masters that they may have employed, or may intend to employ in their schools; and concerning every other matter which may relate to the welfare of their school, or to the propriety of erecting or maintaining the same, to the intent that they may obtain the determination of the said commissioners whether the said school will be entitled to a part of the moneys allotted to or raised in that town by virtue of this act, and whether the abilities and moral character of the master or masters employed, or intended to be employed therein, are such as will meet with their approbation." The share of public money to be paid to each district, was to be apportioned by the commissioners, "according to the number of days for which instruction shall appear, by the annual report of the trustees, to have been given in each of the said schools, in such manner that the school in which the greater number of days of instruction shall appear to have been given, shall have a proportionably larger sum. And if it shall at any time appear to the said commissioners, that the abilities or moral character of the master or masters of any schools, are not such that they ought to be entrusted with the education of the youth, or that any of the branches of learning taught in any school, are not such as are intended to receive encouragement from the moneys appropriated by this act, the said commissioners shall notify in writing the said trustees of such school thereof; and to the time of such notification, and no longer, shall any allowance be made to such school unless the same thereafter be conducted to the approbation of the said commissioners." The commissioners were required to give to the trustees of each district, an order on the county treasurer for the sum to which the district was entitled. Provisions were also made for annual returns from the several districts, towns and counties. An abstract of these returns, from sixteen out of the twenty-three counties of the state, for the year 1798, shows a total of 1,352 schools, organized according to the act, in which 59,660 children were taught.

In the year 1799 an act was passed directing the raising, by means of four successive lotteries, of the sum of one hundred thousand dollars, $12,500 of which, were to be paid to the Regents of the University, to be by them distributed among the Academies in such manner as they shall deem most proper, and the residue, $87,500 was to be paid into the treasury, to be appropriated for the encouragement of common schools, as the legislature should thereafter direct. This bill probably grew out of a project proposed by the Hon. Jedediah Peck, of Otsego. "It is due" observes Judge Hammond, in his Political History, "to this plain, unlettered farmer, to add that he was intent upon making some permanent provisions for these institutions, and that he formed the project of establishing a common school fund in pursuance of the example then lately furnished by Connecticut, the state from whence he emigrated: that he never lost sight of it; and that to his indefatigable and persevering efforts, aided by Mr. Adam Comstock, of Saratoga, another uneducated and plain, but clear sighted and patriotic man, we are principally indebted for our school fund and common school system. What military chieftain —what mere conqueror by brute force, has conferred so deep, so enduring an obligation upon posterity?"

At the opening of the Session of the Legislature in 1800, Gov. Jay called the attention of both Houses to the subject of Common Schools, in the following language:

"Among other objects which will present themselves to you, there is one which I earnestly recommend to your notice and patronage. I mean our institutions for the education of youth. The importance of common schools is best estimated by the good effects of them, where they most abound and are the best regulated."

On the 25th of March of the same year, the Assembly, by a vote of fifty-seven to thirty-six, adopted the following resolution, offered by Mr. Comstock, of Saratoga:

"*Resolved*, That the 'Act for the Encouragement of Schools,' passed the 9th day of April, 1795, ought to be revised and amended; and that out of the annual revenue arising to this State from its stock and other funds, the sum of $50,000 be annually appropriated for the encouragement of schools, for the term of five years."

On the 3d of April, subsequently, a clause to this effect was inserted in the annual supply bill, on Mr. Comstock's motion, by a vote of fifty-one to thirty-five. The Senate, however, by a vote of nineteen to sixteen, struck out the clause. The house, on the return of the bill, at first refused to concur with the Senate in this amendment, by a vote of forty-two to forty-one; but subsequently reconsidered its vote, and assented to the amendment, on the last day but one of the Session.

By an act passed on the 3d of April, 1801, the sum of $100,000 was directed to be raised by lottery, of which one-half was ordered to be paid into the Treasury for the use of Common Schools; leaving to future legislatures the discretion of making such application of it as they might judge most conducive to the end in view. In order to promote so laudable an object, the Legislature of 1803, by an act passed on the 6th of April. directed the Comptroller to invest in good real estate, all such sums of money as had been, or should thereafter be received from the proceeds of each lottery, for the term of two years.

In 1802, the Governor (GEO. CLINTON,) again called the attention of the Legislature to the subject of Common Schools. He observes, "The system of Common Schools having been discontinued, and the advantage to morals, religion, liberty and good government, arising from the general diffusion of knowledge being universally admitted, permit me to recommend this subject to your deliberate attention. The failure of one experiment for the attainment of an important object, ought not to discourage other attempts." No legislative action however, in reference to the subject, was had during the session of that year.

In 1803, Gov. Clinton renewed his recommendation in the following energetic terms: "The establishment of common schools has, at different times, engaged the attention of the Legislature; but although its importance is generally acknowledged, a diversity of sentiment respecting the best means, has hitherto prevented the accomplishment of the object. The diffusion of knowledge is so essential to the promotion of virtue and the preservation of liberty, as to render arguments unnecessary to excite you to a perseverance in this laudable pursuit. Permit me only to observe, that education, by correcting the morals and improving the manners, tends to prevent those evils in society which are beyond the sphere of legislation."

On the 21st of February of that year, Mr. Peck, of Otsego, from the joint committee of both houses on this portion of the governor's speech, reported a bill authorizing the several towns to organize their schools, and to raise money to support the same. No definite action, however, took place upon it during the session of that year.

In 1804, the governor again called the attention of the legislature to the subject. On the 3d of March, in that year, Mr. Peck, from the committee on that portion of the speech, again made a favorable report, accompanied by a bill, which, however, shared the fate of its predecessor.

At the extra session of the legislature, in November, 1804, Gov. LEWIS brought the subject before that body, in the following language:

"I cannot conclude, gentlemen, without calling your attention to a subject which my worthy and highly respected predecessor in office had much at heart, and frequently, I believe, presented to your view—the encouragement of literature. In a government, resting on public opinion, and deriving its chief support from the affections of the people, religion and morality cannot be too sedulously inculcated. To them, science is an handmaid; ignorance, the worst of enemies. Literary information should then be placed within the reach of every description of citizens, and poverty should not be permitted to obstruct the path to the fane of knowledge. Common schools, under the guidance of respectable teachers, should be established in every village, and the indigent be educated at the public expense. The higher seminaries also, should receive every patronage and support within the means of enlightened legislators. Learning would thus flourish, and vice be more effectually restrained than by volumes of penal statutes."

On the 4th of February, 1805, Gov. Lewis transmitted a special message to the legislature in reference to this subject, in which he recommended the application of all the state lands for the benefit of colleges and schools; the whole fund and entire management of the system to be confided to the Regents of the University, under such regulations as the legislature might prescribe; the Regents to have the power of appointing three trustees for each district; who should be authorized to locate the sites for school houses, and to erect such houses wherever necessary, employ teachers, apply the funds of the district, and levy taxes on the inhabitants, for such further sums as might be required for the support of the school and the education of indigent children. None of these suggestions, however, with the exception of the first, seem to have met with any favor at the hands of the legislature.

On the 2d of April, the legislature passed an act providing that the nett proceeds of 500,000 acres of the vacant and unappropriated lands of the people of this state, which should be first thereafter sold by the surveyor-general, should be appropriated as a permanent fund for the support of common schools; the avails to be safely invested until the interest should amount to $50,000; when an annual distribution of that amount should be made to the several school districts. This act laid the foundation of the present fund for the support of common schools.

By the act to incorporate the Merchants' Bank in the city of New-York, passed the same year, the state reserved the right to subscribe for three thousand shares of the capital stock of that institution, which, together with the accruing interest and dividends, were appropriated as a fund for the support of common schools, to be applied in such manner as the legislature should from time to time direct.

By acts passed March 13, 1807, and April 8, 1808, the comptroller was authorized to invest such moneys, together with the funds arising from the proceeds of the lotteries authorized by the act of 1803 in the purchase of additional stock of the Merchants' Bank, and to loan the residue of the fund.

No determinate action on the part of the legislature, in reference to the establishment of a system of common schools, was had during the years, 1806–7–8–9 or 10. At the opening of the session in the latter year, Gov. Tompkins thus alludes to the subject.

"I cannot omit this occasion of inviting your attention to the means of instruction for the rising generation. To enable them to perceive and duly to estimate their rights, to inculcate correct principles and habits of morality and religion, and to render them useful citizens, a competent provision for their education is all-essential. The fund appropriated for common schools already produces an income of about $26,000 annually, and is daily becoming more productive. It rests with the legislature to determine whether the resources of the state will justify a further augmentation of that appropriation, as well as to adopt such plan for its application and distribution, as shall appear best calculated to promote the important object for which it was originally designed."

On the 28th of February, of that year, the comptroller, in obedience to a resolution of the legislature, calling upon him for information as to the condition of the school fund, reported that the amount of receipts into the treasury up to that period, of moneys belonging to the fund, was $151,115.69, of which $29,100 had been invested in the capital stock of the Merchants' Bank, $114,600 loaned in pursuance of law, and the residue remained in the treasury.

In 1811, Gov. Tompkins again called the attention of the legislature to this subject; and a law was passed, authorizing the appointment by the governor, of five commissioners, to report a system for the organization and establishment of common schools. The commissioners appointed under this act were Jedediah Peck, John Murray, Jr., Samuel Russell, Roger Skinner, and Samuel Macomb. On the 14th of February, 1812, they submitted a report, accompanied by the draft of a bill, comprising substantially the main features of our common school system, as it existed up to the year 1838. In the bill, as it originally passed, the electors of each town were authorized to determine at their annual town meeting, whether they would accept their shares of the money apportioned by the state, and direct the raising of an equal amount on their taxable property. So embarrassing, however, was the practical operation of this feature of the system, that on the recommendation of the superintendent, Gideon Hawley, Esq., it was stricken out; and each county required to raise by tax an amount equal to that apportioned by the state.

The following are extracts from the report of the commissioners:

"Perhaps there never will be presented to the legislature a subject of more importance than the establishment of common schools. Education, as the means of improving the moral and intellectual faculties, is, under all circumstances, a subject of the most imposing consideration. To rescue man from that state of degradation to which he is doomed, unless redeemed by education; to unfold his physical, intellectual, and moral powers; and to fit him for those high destinies which his Creator has prepared for him, cannot fail to excite the most ardent sensibility of the philosopher and philanthropist. A comparison of the savage that roams through the forest, with the enlightened inhabitant of a civilized country, would be a brief but impressive representation of the momentous importance of education.

"It were an easy task for the commissioners to show, that in proportion as every country has been enlightened by education, so has been its prosperity. Where the heads and hearts of men are generally cultivated and improved, virtue and wisdom must reign, and vice and ignorance must cease to prevail. Virtue and wisdom are the parents of private and public felicity: vice and ignorance, of private and public misery.

"If education be the cause of the advancement of other nations, it must be apparent to the most superficial observer of our peculiar political institutions, that it is essential, not to our prosperity only, but to the very existence of our government. Whatever may be the effect of education on a despotic or monarchical government, it is not absolutely indispensable to the existence of either. In a despotic government, the people have no agency whatever, either in the formation or in the execution of the laws. They are the mere slaves of arbitrary authority, holding their lives and property at the pleasure of uncontrolled caprice. As the will of the ruler is the supreme law; fear, slavish fear, on the part of the governed, is the principle of despotism. It will be perceived readily, that ignorance on the part of the people can present no barrier to the administration of such a government; and much less can it endanger its existence. In a monarchical government, the operation of fixed laws is intended to supersede the necessity of intelligence in the people. But in a government like ours, where the people is the sovereign power; where the will of the people is the law of the land; which will is openly and directly expressed; and where every act of the government may justly be called the act of the people; it is absolutely essential that that people be enlightened. They must possess both intelligence and virtue: intelligence to perceive what is right, and virtue to do what is right. Our republic, therefore. may justly be said to be founded on the intelligence and virtue of the people. For this reason, it is with much propriety that the enlightened Montesquieu has said, 'in a republic the whole force of education is required.'

"The commissioners think it necessary to represent in a stronger point of view, the importance and absolute necessity of education, as connected either with the cause of religion and morality, or with the prosperity and existence of our political institutions. As the people must receive the advantages of education, the inquiry naturally arises, how this end is to be attained. The expedient devised by the legislature, is the establisment of common schools; which being spread throughout the state and aided by its bounty, will bring improvement within the reach and power of the humblest citizen. This appears to be the best plan that can be devised to disseminate religion, morality, and learning throughout a whole country. All other methods, heretofore adopted, are partial in their operation and circumscribed in their effects. Academies and universities, understood in contradistinction to common schools, cannot be considered as operating impartially and indiscriminately, as regards the country at large. The advantages of the first are confined to the particular districts in which they are established; and the second, from causes apparent to every one, are devoted almost exclusively to the rich. In a free government, where political equality is established, and where the road to preferment is open to all, there is a natural stimulus to education; and accordingly we find it generally resorted to, unless some great local impediments interfere. In populous cities, and the parts of the contry thickly settled, schools are generally established by individual exertion. In these cases, the means of education are facilitated, as the expenses of schools are divided among a great many. It is in the remote and thinly populated parts of the state, where the inhabitants are scattered over a large extent, that education stands greatly in need of encouragement. The people here, living far from each other, makes it difficult so to establish schools, as to render them convenient or accessible to all. Every family, therefore, must either educate its own children, or the children must forego the advantages of education.

"These inconveniences can be remedied best by the establishment of common schools, under the direction and patronage of the state. In these schools should be taught, at least, those branches of education which are indispensably necessary to every person in his intercourse with the world, and to the performance of his duty as a useful citizen. Reading, writing, arithmetic, and the principles of morality, are essential to every person, however humble his situation in life. Without the first, it is impossible to receive those lessons of morality, which are inculcated in the writings of the learned and pious; nor is it possible to become acquainted with our political constitutions and laws; nor to decide those great political questions, which ultimately are referred to the intelligence of the people. Writing and arithmetic are indispensable in the management of one's private affairs, and to facilitate one's commerce with the world. Morality and religion are the foundation of all that is truly great and good, and are consequently of primary importance. A person provided with these acquisitions, is enabled to pass through the world respectably and successfully. If, however, it be his intention to become acquainted with the higher branches of science, the academies and universities established in different parts of the state are open to him. In this manner, education in all its stages is offered to the citizens generally.

"In devising a plan for the organization and establishment of common schools, the commissioners have proceeded with great care and deliberation. To frame a system which must directly affect every citizen in the state, and so to regulate it, as that it shall obviate individual and local discontent, and yet be generally beneficial, is a task, at once perplexing and arduous. To avoid the imputation of local partiality, and to devise a plan, operating with equal mildness and advantage, has been the object of the commissioners. To effect this end, they have consulted the experience, of others, and resorted to every probable source of intelligence. From neighboring states, where common school systems are established by law, they have derived much important information. This information is doubly valuable, as it is the result of long and actual experience. The commissioners by closely examining the rise and progress of those systems, have been able to obviate many imperfections otherwise inseparable from the novelty of the establishment, and to discover the means by which they have gradually risen to their present condition.

"The outlines of the plan suggested by the Commissioners are briefly these: that the several towns in the State be divided into school districts, by three commissioners, elected by the citizens qualified to vote for town officers: that three trustees be elected in each district, to whom shall be confided the care and superintendence of the school to be established therein: that the interest of the school fund be divided among the different counties and towns, according to their respective population, as ascertained by the successive census of the United States: that the proportions received by the respective towns be subdivided among the districts into which such towns shall be divided, according to the number of children in each, between the ages of five and fifteen years: that each town raise by tax annually, as much money as it shall have received from the school fund: that the gross amount of moneys received from the State and raised by the towns, be appropriated exclusively to the payment of the wages of the teachers: and that the whole system be placed under the superintendence of an officer appointed by the Council of Appointment.

* * * * * * * *

"Let us suppose that the school fund were arrived at that point where by law it is to be divided. There will then be $50,000 of the public money to be distributed among the schools; and as by the contemplated plan a sum is to be raised annually by tax, equal to the interest of the school fund, the gross amount of moneys which the schools will receive will be $100,000. There are in this State forty-five counties, comprising, exclusively of the cities, four hundred and forty-nine towns. It will be very evident, therefore, that the proportion of each town must be necessarily small. As, however, the school districts are authorized to raise by tax a sum sufficient to purchase a lot, on which the school house is to be built, to build the school house and keep the same in repair, and as the school moneys are devoted exclusively to the payment of the teachers' wages, the sum, however small, which each district will be entitled to, will be from these considerations so much the more efficacious. It will, however, be evident to the Legislature, that the funds appropriated from the State for the support of the common school system, will, alone, be very inadequate. And the commissioners are of opinion that the fund, in any stage of it, even when the residue of the unsold lands shall be converted into money, bearing an interest, never will be, alone, adequate to the maintenance of common schools; as the increase of the population will probably be in as great if not a greater ratio than that of the fund. But it is hardly to be imagined that the Legislature intended that the State should support the whole expense of so great an establishment. The object of the Legislature, as understood by the commissioners, was to rouse the public attention to the important subject of education, and by adopting a system of common schools, in the expense of which the State would largely participate, to bring instruction within the reach and means of the humblest citizen. And the commissioners have kept in view the furtherance of this object of the Legislature; for by requiring each district to raise by tax a sum sufficient to build and repair a school house, and by allotting the school moneys solely to the payment of the teachers' wages, they have in a measure supplied two of the most important sources of expense. Thus every inducement will be held out to the instruction of youth." * * * *

"The Legislature will perceive in the system contained in the bills submitted to their consideration, that the commissioners are deeply impressed with the importance of admitting, under the contemplated plan, such teachers only as are duly qualified. The respectability of every school must necessarily depend on the character of the master. To entitle a teacher to assume the control of a school, he should be endowed with the requisite literary qualifications, not only, but with an unimpeachable character. He should also, be a man of patient and mild temperament. 'A preceptor,' says Rousseau, 'is invested with the rights, and takes upon himself the obligations of both father and mother.' And Quintillion tells us, 'that to the requisite literary and moral endowments, he must add the benevolent disposition of a parent.'" * * * *

"When we consider the tender age at which children are sent to school; the length of the time they pass under the direction af the teachers; when we consider that their little minds are to be diverted from their natural propensities to the artificial acquisition of knowledge; that they are to be prepared for the reception of great moral and religious truths—to be inspired with a love of virtue and a detestation of vice; we shall forcibly perceive the absolute necessity of suitable qualifications on the part of the master. As an impediment to bad men getting into the schools, as teachers, it is made the duty of the town inspectors strictly to inquire into the moral and literary qualifications of those who may be candidates for the place of teacher. And it is hoped that this precaution, aided by that desire which generally prevails, of employing good men only, will render it unnecessary to resort to any other measure.

"The commissioners, at the same time that they feel impressed with the importance of employing teachers of the character above described, cannot refrain from expressing their solicitude, as to the introduction of proper books into the contemplated schools. This is a subject so intimately connected with a good education, that it merits the serious consideration of all who are concerned in the establishment and management of schools. Much good is to be derived from a judicious selection of books, calculated to enlighten the understanding, not only, but to improve the heart. And as it is of incalculable consequence to guard the young and tender mind from receiving fallacious impressions, the commissioners cannot omit mentioning this subject as a part of the weighty trust reposed in them. Connected with the introduction of suitable books, the commissioners take the liberty of suggesting that some observations and advice touching the reading of the Bible in the schools might be salutary. In order to render the sacred volume productive of the greatest advantage, it should be held in a very different light from that of a common school book. It should be regarded as a book intended for literary improvement, not merely, but as inculcating great and indispensable moral truths, also. With these impressions, the commissioners are induced to recommend the practice introduced into the New York Free School, of having select chapters read at the opening of the school in the morning, and the like at the close in the afternoon. This is deemed the best mode of preserving the religious regard which is due to the sacred writings. * * * * *

"The commissioners cannot conclude this report without expressing once more their deep sense of the momentous subject committed to them. If we regard it as connected with the cause of religion and morality merely, its aspect is awfully solemn. But the other views of it already alluded to, is sufficient to excite the keenest solicitude in the legislative body. It is a subject, let it be repeated, intimately connected with the permanent prosperity of our political institutions. The American empire is founded on the virtue and intelligence of the people. But it were irrational to conceive that any form of government can long exist without virtue in the people. Where the largest portion of a nation is vicious, the government must cease to exist as it loses its functions. The laws cannot be executed where every man has a personal interest in screening and protecting the profligate and abandoned. When these are unrestrained by the wholesome coercion of authority, they give way to every species of excess and crime. One enormity brings on another, until the whole commuuity, becoming corrupt, bursts forth into some mighty change or sinks at once into annihilation. 'Can it be,' said Washington, 'that Providence has not connected the permanent felicity of a nation with its virtue.' The experiment, at least, is recommended by every sentiment which ennobles human nature.

"And the commissioners cannot but hope that that Being who rules the universe in justice and in mercy, who rewards virtue and punishes vice, will most graciously deign to smile benignly on the humble efforts of a people, in a cause purely his own, and that he will manifest this pleasure in the lasting prosperity of our country."

We cannot deem any apology necessary for the space occupied by these extracts from this admirable report: shadowing forth as it does, the great features of that system of public instruction subsequently adopted, and successfully carried into execution; and laying down in language at once eloquent and impressive, those fundamental principles upon which alone any system of popular education, in a republic like ours, must be based. The leading features of the system proposed by the commissioners, were adopted and passed into a law by the Legislature, during the session of 1812, with the exception of leaving it discretionary with the electors of the several towns, after the first distribution of public money, to receive their share and to raise an equal amount by tax, or to dispense alike with the burthen and the benefits of the legal provisions, by vote at their annual town meetings.

Administration of GIDEON HAWLEY, *Superintendent of Common Schools*—1813 to 1821.

On the organization of the system, GIDEON HAWLEY, Esq., then of the county of Saratoga, was appointed by the Council of Appointment, Superintendent of Common Schools.

On the fourth day of February, 1814, the first annual report of Mr. Hawley, as Superintendant of Common Schools, was transmitted to the Legislature; in which he informs that body that, in pursuance of the act for the establishment of common schools, passed on the 19th of June, 1812, he had at the commencement of the preceding year given due notice of an intended distribution of the interest of the school fund, and that by means of such notice, that act had been carried into operation so far as depended on him: that although no official returns had been received from which an estimate might be formed of the beneficial operation of the act, yet that satisfactory evidence had been obtained, that in many cases its operation had been prevented by the refusal or neglect of towns to comply with its provisions; and that in other cases where such compliance had been made, and the act thereby carried into effect, its operation had been much embarrassed by difficulties, arising, as was believed, from the imperfection of its provisions; that notwithstanding these obstacles and embarrassments, its influence had already proved very salutary, and that with the aid of legislative amendment, it promised to yield all that encouragement to common schools which it was designed to give. "It was not to be expected," continues the Superintendent, "that any system for the establishment of common schools could be devised, which in its first form should be wholly free from imperfections; and accordingly it has been found that the existing law for the establishment of such a system is, in some respects, defective in its provisions, and obscure and doubtful in its meaning." The report goes on to suggest such amendments as were deemed requisite in various particulars, not necessary to enumerate here. The operation, however, of that portion of the law which left it optional with the several towns to comply with its conditions and participate in its benefits, or not, as the inhabitants at their annual town meeting might determine, is worthy of special notice. We quote from that portion of the report which examines this feature of the system.

"The fifth section of the act provides that such towns in every county as shall have complied with the law, by directing their Supervisors to levy on them the sum required by the act to entitle them to their proportion of the public money, shall receive by appointment, from the board of supervisors, the whole dividend of the county, according to their respective population, to the exclusion of such towns as shall not have complied with the law. By a subsequent part of the same section, it is further provided that the sum required to be raised on each town, to entitle it to a share of the public money, must be equal to the sum apportioned to such town by the board of supervisors. By the operation of these several provisions in the act, the case may be that a single town in a county shall be entitled to receive the whole dividend for such county; and although this sum shall be more than sufficient, (as in ordinary cases it will be,) to support all its schools, it must nevertheless be subjected by tax to the payment of an additional sum equal in amount to the sum it is entitled to receive; and this additional sum must, in law, be applied to the support of its schools, which may have had (and in ordinary cases will have had) an excess of support already. Although the case here supposed has not yet occurred, to the knowledge of the Superintendent, there is nevertheless good reason to believe it will occur; satisfactory evidence having been obtained, that in some counties but few towns have complied with the law, or shown any disposition to comply therewith. The mischief herein complained of, may be remedied by providing that the board of supervisors shall not, in any case, raise by tax on any town, a sum exceeding the sum which such town shall be entitled to receive out of the county dividend, if all the towns in the county had complied with the law."

"It will be found by inspection of the act, that one of its principal features is the provision which gives every town an election, either to comply with the act and receive its benefits, and bear its burdens, or to refuse such compliance, and thereby forego its benefits and avoid its burdens. In the exercise of this choice, it has already been observed that many towns have refused to comply with the act, and it is believed they will generally persist in such refusal, and that some other towns which have already complied with the law, will endeavor to retract their compliance. By allowing such an option to every town, the operation of the act depending on the pleasure, and not unfrequently the caprice of a few individuals, will be always partial and fluctuating; it will, moreover, be embarrassed by all the difficulties which are naturally connected with instability of system and intricacy of form. It is therefore submitted whether this provision in the act may not be so amended as to make it obligatory on towns to comply with the act, and also on the board of supervisors of the several counties to levy on their respective towns, a sum equal to the sum which shall be apportioned to such towns out of the public money to be distributed."

This suggestion was adopted by the legislature, and the act amended in this and various other respects, in conformity to the recommendation of the Superintendent.

On the 11th of February, 1815, Mr. Hawley transmitted to the legislature his second annual report as Superintendent. The returns which had been made to him from the several counties were, however, so few in number, and in general so extremely defective in substance, and inartificial in form, that he did not deem it advisable to communicate them to the legislature, preferring to defer the performance of the duty required of him in this respect until more perfect returns, in accordance with forms and instructions to be prepared by him, should enable him to discharge it more beneficially to the public.

On the first day of April, 1816, the Superintendent transmitted his third annual report, from which it appeared that returns relative to the condition of the schools had been made to him from 338 towns in thirty-six of the forty-six counties then in the State; that the whole number of districts from which reports had been received by the commissioners, in conformity to law, was 2,631; that the whole number of children between the ages of five and fifteen in said districts was 176,449; and that 140,106 had been under instruction during a portion of the year reported, in the common schools. The Superintendent, however, observes:

"The returns not being complete, and many of them being defective in some one or more of their necessary requisites, it is difficult to form any certain estimate from them. Taking, however, the most correct and full returns for a criterion, it would appear that there are within the state about five thousand districts in which common schools are established; that the number of children taught in them is at least two hundred thousand; and that the number of children between the ages of five and fifteen years, residing in those districts, is about two hundred and fifty thousand. The city of Albany and the city and county of New York, not being divided into school districts under the act are not included in this estimate." These being the first statistical returns under the act of 1812, it may not be uninteresting to contrast them with those for the year 1849, after a lapse of thirty-nine years. The whole number of school districts is now eleven thousand four hundred; the number of children between the ages of five and sixteen is about seven hundred and fifty-thousand and not less than eight hundred thousand are under instruction during the whole or a portion of the year in common schools.

But to resume our quotation from Mr. Hawley's report:—

"The Superintendent has also had the satisfaction to learn from other sources, that the establishment of common schools by law has already produced many great and beneficial results. The number of schools has been increased; many school houses have been built; more able teachers employed, and much of that interest which ought to be felt in behalf of common schools, has been generally excited. The beneficial operation of the act has also been visible in the pecuniary aid which many schools have derived from it. A perpetual annuity of twenty dollars, which is the average sum received by each district, under the act, ought not to be considered a trifle unworthy of any account. It has been very sensibly felt, especially in those districts where, from the inability of the inhabitants, or from any other cause, common schools have not been kept open for the whole year, and when the revenue of the fund shall have attained its full growth, the distributive share of each district will be so much more considerable, that the munificence of the legislature cannot fail to be more gratefully acknowledged.

"But the great benefit of the act does not lie in any pecuniary aid which it may afford. The people of this state are, in general, able to educate their children without the aid of any public gratuity, and if they fail in this respect, it is owing more to their want of proper schools than of sufficient means. The public gratuity is important, as it tends to excite an interest in the affairs of common schools which might not otherwise be felt, and is also beneficial in many other respects. But the great benefit of the act consists in securing the establishment of common schools, wherever they are necessary; in organizing them on a suitable and permanent foundation, and in guarding them against the admission of unqualified teachers. These were the great ends proposed in the establishment of common schools by law, and under the wise and liberal policy of the legislature, these ends have been so far accomplished as to warrant full faith in their final complete attainment."

On the 12th of March, 1817, Mr. HAWLEY transmitted to the Legislature his fourth annual report, in which he states that "the returns which have been made to him during the last year, from most of the counties of the State, afford satisfactory evidence of a progressive increase in the number of common schools, and a corresponding improvement in their condition. It is ascertained with sufficient certainty, that there are within the State, exclusive of the city and county of New York, at least five thousand common schools, which have been organized and kept up under the act for their establishment; and that the number of children annually taught in them exceeds two hundred thousand."

In his fifth annual report, under date of March 16, 1818, the Superintendent informs the Legislature, that from the returns made to him during the preceding year, it appeared that there were more than five thousand common schools, in which were annually taught upwards of two hundred thousand children, the returns not being sufficiently full and definite to enable him to speak with more precision. "On comparing the returns of common schools, however for different years, it appeared that in almost every district a greater proportion of the children between the ages of five and fifteen years, have been taught, and a regular school supported for a longer time in every succeeding year, than in the preceeding one. To this result, so favorable to the establishment of common schools by law, it may be added—and it has not escaped the most transient observer—that under the operation of this system, better teachers have been employed, a new and more respectable character given to our common schools, and a much greater interest excited in their behalf."

"It is now more than five years," continues the Superintendent, "since common schools were established by law. The first act of the legislature was passed in 1812. Soon after this act was carried into operation, it was discovered to be defective in many of its provisions. To supply this defect, and to add some provisions which were deemed necessary, a new act was passed in 1814. This act was also found on trial to be imperfect, and in the following year it underwent sundry amendments. Since that time, the system founded on the act of 1814 and the amendments of 1815, has remained unaltered; nor has a practice of three years under it discovered any very great defects. It was not, however, to be expected, even after the amendments of 1815, that the system would be found complete and perfect in all its details; on the contrary, it was to be expected of this as of every other new and untried system, that time would develope many imperfections which had not been foreseen." The Superintendent proceeds to suggest several particulars of the system which, in his judgment, required amendment, and adds, "although when a system is once established it is not advisable to subject it to frequent revision and amendment, without urgent cause—yet as the system of common schools might be improved in these and other respects not adverted to, and it will be necessary, at least, to consolidate the different acts on the subject, the propriety of revising the whole system and amending it in some of its subordinate parts, is respectfully submitted." The residue of the report is devoted to a consideration of the Lancasterian system of education, the introduction of which into the common schools had been strongly recommended by the governor, (De Witt Clinton,) in his speech at the opening of the session. The peculiar excellencies of this system were clearly and distinctly pointed out by the Superintendent, and its adoption, especially in all the larger schools in cities and villages, urgently and ably enforced. Under the impetus thus given, Lancasterian schools were established in many portions of the State, and societies incorporated, some of which are still in existence, having for their object the introduction and promotion of the system of Bell and Lancaster, then at its zenith of popularity. Experience, however, failed to realize the sanguine anticipations of those friends of education who saw in the general adoption of this system the commencement of a new and brighter era in the science of elementary instruction; and after an ephemeral and sickly existence, these institutions, from which such favorable results were expected, languished, and with few exceptions, disappeared. Whether the failure of this experiment resulted from inherent defects in the monitorial system of instruction, from its want of adaptation to the peculiar genius of our people, or from an inability on the part of those to whom its administration was committed, to carry into effect the plan of its founders and the views of its advocates, is still an unsettled question.

On the 17th of February, 1819, the Superintendent transmitted to the Legislature his sixth annual report. From the returns which had been made to him during the preceding year, it appeared that the whole number of common schools in this State, organized and permanently established under the act of the Legislature, may be estimated at nearly six thousand; and the number of children annually taught in them, in the various branches of elementary education, at nearly two hundred and fifty thousand. "This great increase and prosperity of our common schools," continues the Superintendent, "is evidently the result of the wise and liberal policy adopted by the legislature for their encouragement and support. On comparing the returns of schools made for different years since their first establishment by law, it appears that they have increased in a much greater ratio than the increase of population, and that their condition, which was before stationary, has, under the salutary operation of the law for their establishment, been rapidly and substantially improved.

"The same data also afford evidence that common schools have risen in public estimation, and received a degree of care and attention to their concerns, corresponding with their increase and prosperity. If these results were the only evidence of a beneficial operation in the system of common schools provided by law, they would be sufficient to establish the public confidence in the policy of that system, and to secure it a permanent duration. But it is well known, although it does not appear from any data in the returns, that the system has produced other results not less in magnitude or merit. It has secured our schools against the admission of unqualified teachers, by requiring them to submit to examination before a public board of inspectors, and to obtain from them a certificate of approbation, before they can legally be employed. It has imparted to common schools a new and more respectable character, by making them a subject of legal notice, and investing them with powers to regulate their own concerns. It has corrected many evils in the discipline and government of schools, not only by excluding unqualified teachers but by subjecting the schools and course of studies in them to the frequent inspection of public officers. It has founded schools in places where, by conflicting interests or want of concert in the inhabitants, none had been before established; and it has, by its pecuniary aid, enabled many indigent children to receive the benefits of education which would not otherwise have been within their reach. The system having already fulfilled so many of the beneficial ends of its institution, and it being now only six years since it was first organized and carried into operation, it is warrantable to infer that all the expectations of its founders will in due time be realized.

The Superintendent renews his recommendation for a revision and consolidation of the several enactments relating to common schools. His suggestions in this respect were adopted by the legislature, and on the 19th of April following, the "Act for the support of Common Schools" was re-enacted, with the various amendments which had from time to time been made, and such as were suggested by Mr. Hawley in his reports for the two preceding years. The publication of the revised act was accompanied by an able exposition of its various provisions, from the pen of Mr. Hawley, and with complete forms for the several proceedings required under it by the several officers connected with its administration.

On the 21st of February, 1820, Mr. Hawley transmitted to the legislature his seventh annual report. He states "that the returns of common schools for the last year are much more full and satisfactory than any before received;" that from these returns it appeared that in 515 towns there were

5,763 common schools, organized according to law, and that in 5,118 of these schools, from which only particular district returns had been received, there had been taught during the year, in the various branches of elementary education, 271,877 children. The number of children between the ages of five and fifteen years, residing in the districts from which returns had been received, was 302,703, making the number of children taught equal to nine-tenths of the whole number between the ages of five and fifteen.

On the 21st of February, 1821, Mr. Hawley transmitted to the Legislature his eighth and last annual report as Superintendent; from which it appeared that in 545 towns from which returns had been received, there were 6,323 school districts organized according to law, from 5,489 of which particular district reports had been made, showing that of 317,633 children between the ages of five and fifteen years, residing in those districts, 304,-549 had been under instruction during portions of the year in the common schools. "The proportion," observes the Superintendent, "which, from the present returns, the number of children taught bears to the number between the ages of five and fifteen years is much greater than at any former period. In about one half of the towns in the state, the number taught exceeds the number between the ages of five and fifteen years; and taking the whole state together, the number taught is more than nineteen-twentieths of the number between these ages.

"The average length of time for which schools have been kept for the last year, has also increased in about the same ratio as the number of children taught. There is now, therefore, reason to believe that the number of children in the state who do not attend any school, and who are not otherwise in the way of receiving a common education, is very small. The public bounty is sufficient to defray the expense of most schools for about three months in the year; and where that is expended in different parts of the year, so as not to defray the whole expense of the school for any particular part, it is understood that in most districts poor children have been permitted to attend the district school free of expense, under that provision in the school act which empowers districts to exonerate those children from the payment of teachers' wages. The readiness with which such permission has been generally granted, wherever it has been deserved, is very creditable to the public spirit and liberality of the inhabitants of school districts, and it is considered proper on this occasion, to bring the fact to the notice of the legislature. From these circumstances, in connection with the friendly disposition every where manifested in the cause of education, it is considered warrantable to infer, that of the rising generation in this state, very few individuals will arrive to maturity without the enjoyment and protection of a common education."

To no individual in the state, are the friends of common school education more deeply indebted for the impetus given to the cause of elementary instruction in its infancy, than to Gideon Hawley. At a period when every thing depended upon organization; upon supervision; upon practical acquaintance with the most minute details; and upon a patient, persevering, laborious process of exposition, Mr. Hawley united in himself all the requisites for the efficient discharge of the high functions devolved upon him by the legislature. From a state of anarchy and confusion, and complete disorganization, within a period of less than eight years, arose a beautiful and stately fabric, based upon the most impregnable foundations, sustained by an enlightened public sentiment, fortified by the best and most enduring affections of the people, and cherished as the safeguard of the state —the true palladium of its greatness and prosperity. Within this brief period the number of school districts had more than doubled, and the proportion of children annually participating in the blessing of elementary instruction, increased from four-fifths to twenty-four twenty-fifths of the whole number residing in the state of a suitable age to attend the public schools. When we take into view the disadvantages under which every new and untried system must, of necessity, labor, before it can be commended to general adoption, and consider the immense variety of interests which were, to a greater or less extent, affected by the stringent provisions of the act of 1812, and its subsequent amendments, we cannot fail of being surprised at the magnitude of the results which developed themselves under the administration of Mr. Hawley. The foundations of a permanent and noble system of popular education were strongly and securely laid by him, and we are now witnessing the magnificent superstructure, which, in the progress of a quarter of a century, has been gradually upbuilt on these foundations. WELCOME ESLEECK, of the city of Albany, was named as his successor in office, but the legislature saw fit to abolish the office as a separate department of the government, and to devolve its duties upon the secretary of state.

Administration of JOHN VAN NESS YATES, *Secretary of State and Superintendent ex officio of common Schools*, 1821 to 1826.

By the Constitution of 1821, the proceeds of all lands thereafter to be sold, belonging to the state, with the exception of such as might be reserved for public use or ceded to the United States, together with the existing school fund, were declared to constitute "a perpetual fund, the interest of which shall be invioably appropriated and applied to the support of common schools throughout this state."

In his speech at the opening of the legislature, at its session of 1822, the governor (De Witt Clinton) refers to the condition of the system of public intruction, in the following terms:

"The excellent direction which has been given to the public bounty, in appropriations for common schools, academies and colleges, is very perceptible in the multiplication of our seminaries of education, in the increase of the number of students, and in the acquisition of able and skilful teachers. The Lancasterian or monitorial system is making its way in the community, by the force of its transcendant merits. Our common schools have flourished beyond all former example." * * * * * * *

"I am happy to have it in my power to say that this state has always evinced a liberal spirit in the promotion of education; and I am persuaded that no considerations short of total inability will ever prevent similar demonstrations. The first duty of a state is to render its citizens virtuous, by intellectual instruction and moral discipline, by enlightening their minds, purifying their hearts, and teaching them their rights and their obligations. Those solid and enduring honors which arise from the cultivation of science, and the acquisition and diffusion of knowledge, will outlive the renown of the statesman and the glory of the warrior; and if any stimulus were wanting in a case so worthy of all our attention and patronage, we may find it in the example before our eyes of the author of the Declaration of Independence, who has devoted the evening of his illustrious life to the establishment of an university in his native state."

In connection with this subject the governor also transmitted the proceedings of the legislatures of the several states, relative to the appropriation of a portion of the national domain to the purposes of education; by which it appeared that in eleven of the new states and territories, the general government had appropriated one thirty-sixth part of the public land for common schools, and one fifth part of that thirty-sixth part for colleges and academies; and while it was admitted that this disposition was in all respects proper and laudable, it was contended that the other members of the confederacy were entitled to a correspondent benefit out of the same common fund. "This claim," observes his Excellency, "appears to be sustained by the most conclusive reasoning; and it is believed to be impossible for congress to resist an application so just and beneficial. If, however, this measure were calculated to embarrass the financial arrangements of the national government, to make a serious inroad on the national domain, or to disparage the interests of the states which have already been benefitted, I should be entirely unwilling to press it. Whatever ratio of distribution may be adopted, the quantum of population, or the extent of territory of each state, the deduction from the landed estate of the empire, would be so small as scarcely to be felt. In either case it would not exceed ten millions out of five hundred millions of acres owned by the United States. It is our duty to co-operate in obtaining justice for our sister states as well as for ourselves. If we were willing to waive the benefit which might be derived from the success of this application, it would furnish no just ground of hostility to the claim in general; and indeed in such case it would entirely correspond with the dictates of magnanimity, to advocate it with all our might and influence. This state, on the basis of appropriation originally adopted, would be entitled to 800,000 acres for our common schools, and 160,000 for our colleges and academies; which, with proper management, and in connection with existing funds, would answer all the requisitions of education."

By the annual report of the acting Superintendent of Common Schools (JOHN VAN NESS YATES, Esq., Secretary of State) it appears that the total number of school districts in the state was 6,865, from 5,882 of which reports in accordance with law had been received; that the total number of children between the ages of five and sixteen years residing in the several districts, was 380,000; and the total number of children of all ages taught in the common schools during the year reported, was 342,479; and that the average number of months during which the schools were kept open in the several districts was eight. Several amendments in the details of the system were suggested, most of which were adopted by the legislature; including, for the first time, the provision investing the Superintendent with appellate jurisdiction over all controversies arising under the school laws, and declaring his decision thereon final. In pursuance of a provision contained in this act, the act of 1819, with all the subsequent amendments, was republished by the Superintendent, accompanied by an exposition of its various provisions, and an abstract of the decisions which had been pronounced, during the period which had elapsed since the adoption of the appellate system.

On the 3d of February, 1823, Mr. Yates transmitted to the legislature his second annual report as Superintendent of Common Schools; from which it appeared that returns had been received during the preceding year from all the counties in the State, fifty-two in number, comprising 649 towns and wards; that the whole number of school districts in the state exceeded 8,000; from 6,255 of which, only, reports in accordance with law had been received, in which the number of children between the ages of five and fifteen was about 357,000; that for the term of eight months during the year reported, 351,173 children were receiving a common school education in the several districts from which reports had been received—being 18,194 more than were educated the preceding year. The Superintendent adds: "Even in Connecticut, which possesses a larger school fund than we do, and where the school system was established and in successful operation long before it was here introduced, the number of children educated in common schools is far less in proportion to its population than it is in this state." He complains of the "want of uniformity in the course of studies pursued, and the books and treatises now used in common schools. A great diversity of opinion has long existed and still continues to exist as to the proper books to be introduced into these schools; and teachers and parents are not unfrequently at a loss to select among the great variety of treatises on education recommended by their authors, the most suitable and best adapted for the use of the student. Whether this evil could be remedied by directing some judicious and appropriate work to be prepared in the nature of a 'Common School Instructor,' and to be recommended to the public under the immediate sanction and approbation of the legislature, is respectfully submitted."

The annual appropriation from the funds of the state, at this period, for the benefit of common schools, was fixed by the act of 1819, at $80,000.—These funds consisted of the loan of 1792, then amounting to $500,000; of that of 1808, amounting to $449,000; of stock in the Merchant's Bank of the city of New York, the par value of which amounted to $180,000, and on which annual dividends of nine per cent. were regularly made; of one half the quit-rents, estimated at $100,000; and the fees of the supreme court, then producing an annual income of about $7,000. The revenues arising from these several sources were estimated at $80,000 per annum at least. But in consequence of a reduction of the fees of the supreme court, and a diversion of those fees from the school fund—together with a commutation for quit-rents, and a temporary suspension of dividends by the Merchant's Bank, growing out of frauds to a large amount which had been practised on that institution—an annual deficiency, varying from $13,000 to $7,000, had occurred during the preceding four years, which the legislature, considering the faith of the State pledged to keep up the appropriation directed by the act of 1819, had supplied by special grants from the general funds. A continuance of this deficiency being probable, the governor (Joseph C. Yates) had recommended, in his annual message at the commencement of the session of 1823, "the sale of the whole or a part of the public lands appropriated to the school fund, for the purpose of raising a productive capital, yielding an interest sufficient to make good the annual deficiency in the school revenue."

On the 7th of January, 1824, the acting Superintendent, Mr. Yates, transmitted his third annual report to the legislature, from which the following results were shown:

1. That all the counties, fifty-four in number, and all the towns and wards, being 684 in number, had, with the exception of twenty-seven towns presented their reports for the preceding year.

2. That there were in the state 7,382 school districts, from 6,705 of which reports had been received in accordance with law:

3. That 331 new school districts had been organized during the year.

4. That upwards of 377,000 children had been instructed in the districts from which reports had been received, for an average period of eight months during the preceding year; and 23,500 more were estimated to have been under instruction during the same period in the non-reporting districts, making a grand total of upwards of 400,500 children thus under instruction in all the common schools of the state, exceeding by nearly 26,000 the number under instruction during the preceding year:

5. That the whole number of children between the ages of five and fifteen years, residing in the several districts from which reports were received, was about 373,000:

6. That the sum of $182,802.25 of public money had been expended during the year reported, in the payment of the wages of duly qualified teachers; and it was estimated by the Superintendent that in addition to this amount more than $850,000, from the private funds of individuals, were appropriated in like manner during the same period; making a grand total of upwards of ONE MILLION of dollars. "These facts," observes the Superintendent, "require no comment. They demonstrate the signal success which has attended the exertions made from time to time by the legislature to disseminate useful knowledge among every class of the community; and it must also be gratifying to perceive that our sister states, animated with a like zeal for ameliorating the condition of society, are introducing and supporting among them institutions similar to our own." Among other recommendations and suggestions, the Superintendent recommends the establishment of schools in cities and villages exclusively for the benefit of *colored children.* He also suggests the consolidation and revision of the several acts relating to common schools, and concludes as follows:

"The funds provided and secured by the Constitution for the support of common schools have become only in part productive, as will be seen from the operations of the treasury department for the past year. By far the largest portion of those funds is still inactive, and must continue so, until advantageous sales can be made of nearly a million of acres of land, appropriated to the use of common schools. It is not extravagant to predict that when that period shall arrive, the anticipations of the patriot and philanthropist with regard to the still more extensive operation of our school system, and its favorable effects upon the condition of society, will be fully realized. Indeed, what has education not already effected! It has given man dominion, not only over the elements, but it has enlarged his capacity and faculties beyond the sphere in which he moves. It has shown him that intellectual wealth is national wealth, and that it lies at the foundation of all that is useful in the arts; that its influence extends to the narrower path of private virtue and daily duty; and that while it strengthens the tie between parent and child, husband and wife, citizen and citizen, it secures from the rude and withering hand of oppression, and from the iron grasp of despotism, those valuable institutions of government, which it is no less the pride than it is the duty of freemen to maintain pure and inviolate. Common schools, supported by law and open alike to the poor and to the rich, (as they emphatically are in this State,) together with the higher seminaries of learning, are those monuments which render the glory of a nation imperishable; and while this state is engaged in the great works of canals and other internal improvements, she shows the boundless extent of her resources and the energies of her character, by supporting at the same time, upon a basis equally broad and enduring, a plan of education unequalled in its operations and effect, by that of any other country in the civilized world."

On the 12th of January, 1825, Mr. Yates transmitted to the legislature his fourth annual report, from which it appeared that the number of children taught, for an average period of nine months, in the common schools during the preceding year, was 402,940; being nearly 26,000 more than the number taught in 1823. The number of school districts was 7,642 from 6,936 of which reports had been received. The aggregate amount of public money received and expended in the payment of teacher's wages in the reporting districts, during the year, was $182,741.61.

In August of the preceding year, the Superintendent had issued a circular recommending *school celebrations* in the several towns of the state, from which the following are extracts: "The object in view is extremely important, for it is addressed as well to the affections of the parent as the feelings and interests of the citizen. The happiness of society and the freedom of our country mainly depend upon the general diffusion of knowledge, and it is our duty to devise the best means for attaining and securing that very desirable end. In a few years, the children that now sit upon our knees, or play around the room, will fill our places and become the future legislators, magistrates and judges of our country, while we are silently descending to the tomb. How consoling then the reflection will be, that those objects of our affection are about to realize our fondest hopes and do honor to our memories? Even now, when we hear recounted the sage deliberations of the statesman, or the gallant achievements of the warrior, or the brilliant and still more useful attainments of the scholar, or the sacred and impressive eloquence of the divine, or the profound arguments of the lawyer, or the useful inventions and experiments of the philosopher, farmer and mechanic, do not our bosoms burn with admiration, and do not the eyes and hearts of each of us exclaim, 'Would that he were my son?'

"If then, these are the delightful emotions excited in us from the mere relation of the grand effects which knowledge and virtue produce, can we refuse yielding our best exertions to realize them in the persons of our children? The means, under Providence, are fully within our power, and painful will be our reflections, if we neglect them.

"The plan suggested for the improvement of our common schools, by instituting celebrations, promises, I am convinced, far more beneficial and important consequences than any other hitherto devised. The experiment is neither doubtful nor difficult; and its benefits are certain, and their extent beyond calculation. Indeed when, we see the flourishing condition of our colleges and academies, and know that much is attributable to their public anniversaries, and commencements, why should we hesitate to believe that the same means when used in support of our common schools, will produce the same end? And why, permit me to ask, should not our common schools be placed on a footing as respectable as any other seminaries of learning? Are they not as useful? and is not their influence more generally felt and acknowledged? When we consider also the high character which our common schools have so deservedly maintained—whenwe find other states and countries imitating their example and quoting their success, should we not feel the strongest desire to render them still more worthy of this distinction, and still more useful to ourselves and to posterity?"

Administration of A. C. Flagg—1826 *to* 1833.

In his message to the legislature, at the opening of the session of 1826, the Governor (De Witt Clinton) thus adverts to the subject of education:

"The first duty of government, and the surest evidence of good government, is the encouragement of education. A general diffusion of knowledge is the precursor and protector of republican institutions; and in it we must confide as the conservative power that will watch over our liberties, and guard them against fraud, intrigue, corruption and violence. In early infancy, education may be usefully administered. In some parts of Great Britain, infant schools have been successfully established comprising children from two to six years of age, whose tempers, hearts and minds are ameliorated, and whose indigent parents are enabled by these means to devote themselves to labor, without interruption or uneasiness. Institutions of this kind are only adapted to a dense population, and must be left to the guardianship of private benevolence. Our common schools embrace children from five to fifteen years old and continue to increase and prosper. The appropriation for the school fund for the last year, amounted to $80,670, and an equivalent sum is also raised by taxation in the several counties and towns, and is applied in the same way. The capital fund is $1,333,000, which will be in a state of rapid augmentation from sales of the public lands and other sources; and it is well ascertained that more than 420,000 children have been taught in our common schools during the last year. The sum distributed by the state is now too small, and the general fund can well warrant an augmentation to $120,000 annually.

"Our system of instruction, with all its numerous benefits, is still, however, susceptible of improvement. Ten years of the life of a child may now be spent in a common school. In two years the elements of instruction may be acquired, and the remaining eight years must either be spent in repetition or in idleness, unless the teachers of common schools are competent to instruct in the higher branches of knowledge. The outlines of geography, algebra, mineralogy, agricultural chemistry, mechanical philosophy, surveying, geometry, astronomy, political economy and ethics, might be communicated in that period of time by able preceptors, without essential interference with the calls of domestic industry. The vocation of a teacher, in its influence on the character and destinies of the rising and all future generations, has either not been fully understood or duly estimated. It is, or ought to be, ranked among the learned professions. With a full admission of the merits of several who now officiate in that capacity, still it must be conceded that the information of many of the instructors of our common schools does not extend beyond rudimental education; that our expanding population requires constant accessions to their numbers; and that to realize these views, it is necessary that some new plan for obtaining able teachers should be devised. I therefore recommend a *seminary for the education of teachers*, in the monitorial system of instruction, and in those useful branches of knowledge which are proper to engraft on elementary attainments. A compliance with this recommendation will have the most benign influence on individual happiness and social prosperity. To break down the barriers which poverty has erected against the acquisition and dispensation of knowledge, is to restore the just equilibium of society, and to perform a duty of indispensable and paramount obligations; and under this impression I also recommend that provision be made for the gratuitous education, in our superior seminaries, of indigent, talented, and meritorious youth.

"I consider the system of our common schools as the palladium of our freedom; for no reasonable apprehension can be entertained of its subversion, as long as the great body of the people are enlightened by education. To increase the funds, to extend the benefits, and to remedy the defects of this excellent system, is worthy of your most deliberate attention. The officer who now so ably presides over that department is prevented by his other official duties from visiting our schools in person, nor is he indeed clothed with this power. A visitorial authority for the purpose of detecting abuses in the application of the funds, of examining into the modes and plans of instruction, and of suggesting improvements, would unquestionably be attended with the most propitious effects."

It will be perceived that the governor here shadows forth two of the greatest features of public instruction subsequently engrafted upon our system; the establishment of institutions for the education of teachers; and the appointment of visitors.

On the 4th of February subsequently, Mr. John C. Spencer, from the literature committee of the senate, to which this portion of the message of the governor had been referred, made an able report, in the course of which he distinctly suggests the expediency and practicability of a plan of county supervision, without however, going into any specific details. Thus it will be perceived, that as early as 1826, several of the prominent features of the admirable system which has since prevailed, were brought to the notice and attention of the legislature, by two of our most distinguished and eminent statesmen; one of whom, (Mr. Spencer) fifteen years afterwards, aided in carrying into practical and successful operation, the very plan in substance, which he had suggested at this early period. In the mean time, however, a similar suggestion had been earnestly and urgently pressed upon the public consideration by another distinguished friend of the common school system—the Hon. Jabez D. Hammond; who in 1837 published a series of numbers in the Cherry-Valley Gazette, from whence they were transferred to other periodicals, showing as well the practicability as the expediency of the adoption of the system of county supervision and inspection, and urging the abolition of the office of town inspector. Judge Hammond's plan was the appointment by the governor and senate, or by the State Superintendent, of a County Inspector of Common Schools, in each county, with power to license teachers and visit schools, and who should be required to report periodically to the Superintendent. This was, in substance, the plan afterwards recommended to the legislature by Mr. Spencer.

The following extracts from the report of Mr. Spencer in 1826, to which allusion has above been made, will be found interesting:

"The committee concur entirely in the sentiments expressed by the governor in relation to the importance of the vocation of a teacher, and to the propriety of occupying the time of the young in the higher branches of knowledge. The progress of improvement in the great business of education, must necessarily be slow and gradual. Our common school system is itself but of recent origin; and during the few years in which it has been in operation, incalculable good has been effected, particularly in causing the establishment of schools where none existed before, and where none would have existed but for its provisions. We cannot expect to make it at once perfect, but must content ourselves with remedies for the most obvious and important defects as they are discovered. From the observation of the committee, and from the best information they can obtain, they are persuaded that the greatest evils now existing in the system are the want of competent teachers, and the indisposition of the trustees of districts to incur the expense of employing those who are competent, when they can be obtained. It is a lamentable fact that from a mistaken economy, the cheapest teachers, whether male or female, and generally the latter, are employed in many districts for three-fourths of the year, and a competent instructor is provided for only one-quarter, and sometimes not at all, during the year. The state is thus made to contribute almost wholly to the support of teachers. This is a perversion of the public bounty; and its effect on the children, who ought to be provided with the means of instruction during the whole year, is most disastrous: for those above five or six years old are thus excluded from school three-fourths of their time, which must be spent in mental idleness, and thus the most precious time for education is utterly thrown away. The present arrangement of the authority to license and employ teachers, contributes to this result. Teachers are licensed by town inspectors, themselves generally and necessarily incompetent to determine upon the qualifications of candidates, and willing to sanction such as the trustees feel able or disposed to employ. This is essentially wrong; and the state, which contributes so large a portion of the compensation of the teacher, has a right to direct its application in such a way as to effect the object of procuring useful instruction. The remedy must be found in the organization of some local board, vested with the authority of licensing teachers and of revoking the license, and charged with a general superintendence of the schools within the prescribed limits. The division of the state into counties affords a convenient distribution of territory for these purposes. And if it be made a condition of receiving the public donation, that teachers thus authorized shall have been employed for a portion of the year, it is believed that the sure and inevitable consequence would be the employment of instructors much more competent than the average of the present teachers. In those counties where the population is small and scattered, the standard of competency will necessarily be low; but it will advance with the means of the districts and with the prosperity and intelligence of the counties. In other counties, where candidates were more numerous, the qualifications, would be higher. The teachers would become emphatically a profession; men would devote themselves to it as the means of livelihood, and would prepare themselves accordingly. Their character would advance, and with it their usefulness and the respect of their fellow-citizens. Such is an outline of the first efforts, which, in the opinion of the committee, should be made to obtain able teachers.

"The next object is to provide the means of qualifying the necessary number of teachers. By the report of the Superintendent of Common schools made in January, 1825, it appears there were then in this state 7,642 school districts. That, then, is the number of teachers now required; the best evidence that can be adduced to show that there must always be a sufficient demand for those who are qualified. It is obvious that the suggestion of the governor, in his message respecting the establishment of an institution especially for the purpose of educating teachers, will not answer the exigencies of the case. It is entitled to much weight, however, as a means, in conjunction with others, to effect the object. But in the view which the committee have taken, our great reliance for nurseries of teachers must be placed on our colleges and academies. If they do not answer this purpose they can be of very little use. That they have not hitherto been more extensively useful in that respect, is owing to inherent defects in the system of studies pursued there. When the heads of our colleges are apprised of the great want of teachers which it is so completely in their power to relieve,if not supply it, is but reasonable to expect that they will adopt a system by which young men whose pursuits do not require a knowledge of classics, may avail themselves of the talent and instruction in those institutions suited to their wants, without being compelled also to receive that which they do not want, and for which they have neither time nor money.

"Our academies also have failed to supply the want of teachers, to the extent which was within their power; although it is acknowledged that in this respect they have been eminently useful. But instead of being incited to such efforts, they are rather restrained by the regulations adopted by the Regents of the University for the distribution of the literary fund placed at their disposal. The income of that fund is divided among the academies in proportion to the number of classical students in each, without reference to those who are pursuing the highest and most useful branches of an English course. With such encouragement, how could it be expected of trustees of academies that they should prefer a pupil disposed to study the Elements of Euclid, surveying, or Belles-lettres, to a boy who would commit the Latin grammar, while the latter would entitle them to a bounty which was refused to the former? The committee are not disposed to censure the Regents; they have merely followed the fashion of the times; and it is believed that they are themselves alive to the importance of extending the usefulness of the institutions under their care, by adapting them more to the wants of the country and the spirit of the age. But if they should not be willing to extend the benefits of the fund under their control beyond classical students, still it will be in the power of the legislature, and within the means of the state, to appropriate a capital sum that will yield a sufficient income to compensate for this inequality, and to place the English student on the same footing with the others, and thus make it the interest of the academies to instruct them. And if this bounty be distributed in reference to the number of persons instructed at an academy who shall have been licensed as teachers of common schools by the proper board, it is believed the object of obtaining able instructors will soon be accomplished.

"The committee have not been able to discover why, upon every principle of justice and of public policy, seminaries for the education of females in the higher branches of knowledge should not participate equally with those for the instruction of males, in the public bounty.

"In connection with these, the committee admit that the establishment of a separate institution for the sole purpose of preparing teachers, would be a most valuable auxiliary, especially if they were to be prepared to teach on the monitorial plan. They hesitate to recommend its adoption now, chiefly because the other measures which they intend to submit, and which they conceive to be more immediately necessary, will involve as much expense as ought now to be incurred. But they fondly anticipate the time when the means of the state will be commensurate with the public spirit of its legislature, and when such an institution will be founded on a scale equal to our wants and our resources."

The committee, after adverting to the embarrassments caused by the prevalent diversity of text books in the several schools of the state, recommend an appropriation for "the printing of large editions of such elementary works as the spelling book, an English dictionary, a grammar, a system of arithmetic, American history and biography, to be used in schools, and to be distributed gratuitously, or sold at cost." "There can be no doubt," says the committee, "that a selection of such works as have been enumerated could be made by a competent board, excluding all sectarian views and tenets, as would be entirely satisfactory to the citizens of this state."

On the 14th of February, 1826, Azariah C. Flagg, of the county of Clinton, was appointed secretary of state; and the administration of the common school system consequently devolved upon him. The interests of public instruction had been ably and faithfully guarded by Mr. Yates, who seems to have united to eminent talents as an executive and administrative officer, a lively zeal for the promotion of education and the diffusion of knowledge among the great body of the people. His various reports exhibit an accurate practical knowledge of the working of the common school system, in all its departments; his decisions on the numerous appeals which were from time to time brought before him, were characterized by a sound discrimination; and his efforts for the improvement and advancement of the schools were earnest and indefatigable.

The first annual report of Mr. Flagg as Superintendent of Common Schools was transmitted to the legislature on the 13th of March, 1826, from which it appeared that 425,350 children had been taught in the common schools during the year; being 22,410 more than were taught the preceding year, and exceeding by 29,764 the number between the ages of five and fifteen residing in the state. The whole number of organized school districts in the state was 7,773. The Superintendent alludes to the necessity of "some provision which should have a tendency to increase the number of qualified instructors," and adds:

"It might be beneficial to offer facilities for the special education of common school teachers; and as the districts progress in wealth, and the donation of the state is increased, inducements will be furnished for a greater number of persons of competent talents, to engage in the business of teaching, as a profession."

At the opening of the session of 1827, Gov. Clinton thus eloquently alluded to the subject of popular education:

"The great bulwark of republican government is the cultivation of education; for the right of suffrage cannot be exercised in a salutary manner without intelligence. It is gratifying to find that education continues to flourish. We may safely estimate the number of our common schools at 8,000; the number of children taught during the last year, on an average of eight months, at 430,000; and the sum expended in education at 200,000 dollars. It is, however, too palpable that our system is surrounded by imperfections which demand the wise consideration and improving interposition of the legislature. In the first place, there is no provision made for the education of competent instructors. Of the eight thousand now employed in this state, too many are destitute of the requisite qualifications, and perhaps no considerable number are able to teach beyond rudimental instruction. Ten years of a child's life, from five to fifteen, may be spent in a common school; and ought this immense portion of time to be absorbed in learning what can be acquired in a short period? Perhaps one-fourth of our population is annually instructed in our common schools; and ought the minds and the morals of the rising, and perhaps the destinies of all future generations, to be entrusted to the guardianship of incompetence? The scale of instruction must be elevated; the standard of education ought to be raised, and a central school on the monitorial plan ought to be established in each county for the education of teachers, and as exemplars for other momentous purposes connected with the improvement of the human mind. * * * * Small and suitable collections of books and maps, attached to our common schools, and periodical examinations to test the proficiency of the scholars and the merits of the teachers, are worthy of attention. When it is understood that objects of this description enter into the very formation of our characters, control our destinies through life, protect the freedom and advance the glory of our country, and when it is considered that seminaries for general education are either not provided in the old world, or but imperfectly supplied by charity and Sunday schools, and that this is the appropriate soil of liberty and education, let it be our pride, as it is our duty, to spare no exertion and to shrink from no expense in the promotion of a cause consecrated by religion and enjoined by patriotism; nor let us be regardless of ample encouragement of the higher institutions devoted to literature and science. Independently of their intrinsic merits and their diffusive and enduring benefits, in reference to their appropriate objects, they have in a special manner, a most auspicious iufluence on all subordinate institutions.

"They give to society men of improved and enlarged minds, who, feeling the importance of information in their own experience, will naturally cherish an ardent desire to extend its blessings. Science delights in expansion, as well as in concentration; and after having flourished within the precincts of academies and universities, will spread itself over the land, enlightening society and ameliorating the condition of man. The more elevated the tree of knowledge, and the more expanded its branches, the greater will be its trunk and the deeper its root."

On the 21st of February, Mr. Spencer, from the literature committee of the senate, to which had been referred that portion of the message of the governor relating to common schools and the providing of competent teachers, brought in a bill, entitled, "An act to provide permanent funds for the annual appropriation to common schools, to increase the literature fund, and to promote the education of teachers," which, with some slight amendments, became a law on the 13th of April following. This bill transferred to the common school fund the balance due on the loan of 1786, together with $100,000 of bank stock owned by the state: and to the literature fund, from the canal fund, the sum of $150,000; the income of which, together with that of the $95,000 formerly belonging to the fund, was required to be annually distributed by the Regents of the University "among the incorporated academies and seminaries of this state, other than colleges, which are subject to the visitation of the said Regents, &c., in proportion to the number of pupils instructed in each academy or seminary for six months during the preceding year, who shall have pursued classical studies, *or the higher branches of English education, or both.*" From the report accompanying the bill the following extracts are taken, with the view of showing the design of the legislature in thus increasing the literature fund.

"Another object of still greater importance is the furnishing of competent teachers for the instruction of common schools. In vain will you have established a system of instruction; in vain will you appropriate money to educate the children of the poor, if you do not provide persons competent to execute your system, and to teach the pupils collected in the schools. The message of the governor and the report of the Superintendent concur in pressing this subject upon our attention with the most anxious solicitude; and every citizen who has paid attention to it, and become acquainted practically with the situation of our schools, knows that the incompetency of the great mass of teachers is a radical defect, which impedes the whole system, frustrates the benevolent designs of the legislature, and defeats the hopes and wishes of all who feel an interest in disseminating the blessings of education. There are 8,114 organized school districts in this state; and if there be added the schools in the city of New-York, in Albany, Troy and Hudson, not included in the returns, and the private schools which are established in almost every county, we shall be justified in estimating the number of teachers required to carry on the business of instruction, at not far from ten thousand. This result places in a strong view the vast importance of the subject. From what sources can this supply of teachers be obtained? And how can the great body of this multitude be rendered competent to their stations? In a free government resting upon the intelligence of its citizens, these questions are of vital importance.

"The governor has recommended the establishment of central schools upon the monitorial plan for the instruction of teachers. From the best consideration which the committee have been able to bestow upon the subject, and from all the information which they can collect, a doubt is entertained whether the monitorial plan is adapted to small schools in the country, or to the higher branches of education. The means of instruction in the ordinary mode must be provided. The colleges and academies ought to furnish competent instructors, and indeed to them we are indebted, but chiefly to the academies, for the qualified instructors now employed. While academies are instituted, and by proper encouragement may supply our wants, the committee would doubt the policy of establishing central schools in their vicinity, which would necessarily divert from them much of their present support." After referring to the location of the several academies in different parts of the state, with the view of showing that in this respect they were capable of meeting the wants of the community, and that but few portions of the state were not adequately supplied with these institutions, provided they were suitably encouraged, the report proceeds to recommend a different standard of apportionment than the one in operation, and an increase of the fund, specifically for the purpose of encouraging the preparation of a class of students, who might serve as teachers of the common schools. "The income derived from the literature fund, they propose in the bill herewith reported, shall be distributed among the academies in proportion to the number of students pursuing the classical studies and the higher branches of an English education; and their object is to promote the education of young men in those studies which will prepare them for the business of instruction, which it is hoped may be accomplished to some extent, by offering inducements to the trustees of academies to educate pupils of that description." "These are the considerations which have guided the committee in preparing the bill now presented. They have only further to say, that if any confidence can be reposed in the official communications of those officers of the government whose duty it is to give the legislature information on this subject, if the concurring testimony of all who have spoken or written concerning it can be relied upon, there is a radical, deep, and extensive defect in our common school system, which deprives it of much of its value; and that defect consists in the want of competent instructors. From six to ten years of the most valuable portion of human life—of that very period when instruction is most easily imparted and most firmly retained, is absolutely wasted and thrown away. Every one in the least acquainted with the subject knows that a boy, under proper instruction, can, and ought to know as much at seven or eight years old, as he acquires under the present system at fourteen or sixteen. Having undertaken a system of public instruction, it is the solemn duty of the legislature to make that system as perfect as possible. We have no right to trifle with the funds of our constituents by applying them in a mode which fails to attain the intended object. Competent teachers of common schools must be provided: the academies of the state furnish the means of making that provision. There are funds which may be safely and properly applied to that object; and if there were none, a more just, patriotic, and in its true sense, popular, reason for taxation cannot be urged. Let us aid the efforts of meritorious citizens, who have devoted large portions of their means to the rearing of academies; let us reward them by giving success to their efforts; let us sustain seminaries that are falling into decay; let us revive the drooping and animate the prosperous by the cheering rays of public beneficence; and thus let us provide nurseries for the education of our children, and for the instruction of teachers who will expand, and widen, and deepen the great stream of education, until it shall reach our remotest borders, and prepare our posterity for the maintenance of the glory and prosperity of their country."

From the annual report of the Superintendent for this year, it appeared that there were 8,114 organized school districts in the state—341 new districts having been formed during the preceding year; that returns had been received from 7,544 of these districts, in which 431,601 children had been taught during the year reported, being an increase over the number so taught the preceding year, of 13,864; the whole number of children residing in the state, between the ages of five and fifteen, was 411,256.

Speaking in reference to the practical operation of the existing system of visitation and inspection of the common schools, the Superintendent holds the following language: "The system of inspection might be improved, by the appointment of competent persons to visit the schools of a county, or larger district; to investigate the mode of instruction, the qualifications of teachers, the application of the public money, and to inquire into all the operations of the school system. Such inspectors would aid the schools by their advice, and add to the stock of intelligence on the subject of education, by collecting information in relation to the condition of the schools, and the manner in which they are conducted; and these inspections would be the means of more effectually ascertaining what the common schools now effect, and what they may be made to accomplish." The results of the subsequent adoption of this plan, in substance, has effectually vindicated the prescience of the Superintendent, in this respect. The report goes on to recommend, first, "the establishment of schools in the several counties for the education of teachers;" and second, "the gradual introduction of the system of mutual instruction." The improvement of the system of female education is also adverted to, as well as the propriety of furnishing the schools with a judicious selection of text books. "The course of instruction in the common schools ought to be adapted to the business of life, and to the actual duties which may devolve upon the person instructed. In a government where every citizen has a voice in deciding the most important questions, it is not only necessary that every person should be able to read and write, but that he should be well instructed in the rights, privileges and duties of a citizen. Instruction should be co-extensive with universal suffrage."

The sum of $100,000 was this year apportioned by the Superintendent among the several school districts, in pursuance of the provisions of an act passed the preceding year, authorizing the annual distribution of this amount from the common school fund. The several laws relating to common schools were also revised by the legislature and republished, with the necessary expositions and instructions from the department.

Gov. Clinton, in his message at the opening of the session of 1828, again adverts to the subject of common school education, in the following terms:

"That part of the revised laws relative to common schools is operative on this day, and presents the system in an intelligible shape, but without those improvements which are requisite to raise the standard of instruction, to enlarge its objects, and to elevate the talents and qualifications of the teachers. It is understood that Massachusetts has provided for these important cases; but whether the experiment has, as yet, been attended with promising results, is not distinctly known. It may, however, be taken for granted, that the education of the body of the people can never attain the requisite perfection without competent instructors, well acquainted with the outlines of literature and the elements of science. And after the scale of education is elevated in common schools, more exalted improvements ought to be engrafted into academical studies, and proceed in a correspondent and progressive ascent to our colleges.

"In the meantime I consider it my duty to recommend a law authorizing the supervisors of each county to raise a sum, not exceeding two thousand dollars, provided the same sum is subscribed by individuals, for the erection of a suitable edifice for a monitorial high school in the county town. I can conceive of no reasonable objection to the adoption of a measure so well calculated to raise the character of our schoolmasters, and to double the powers of our artizans, by giving them a scientific education."

From the annual report of the Superintendent, it appeared that the number of school districts had increased to 8,298, from 7,806 of which returns had been received, showing that the whole number of children between the ages of five and fifteen, in the districts, was 419,216; and that the whole number taught in the common schools during the year reported, was 441,-856; being an increase of 10,225 since the preceding year, and of 301,750 since 1816. The aggregate amount of public money received and expended by the several districts, in the payment of the wages of duly qualified teachers, was $222,995.77; of which $100,000 was paid from the state treasury, $110,542.32 raised by tax upon the several towns and counties, and $12,453.-45 derived from local funds.

The productive capital of the school fund was increased during the year reported, $256,121.50, by the transfer of $33,616.19, the balance due on the loan of 1786 to this fund; and of $100,000 of bank stock owned by the state; by the avails of the premiums received on the sale of the stock of the Hudson and Delaware canal company, amounting to $31,156.50; and by the sale of lands owned by the state at Oswego, by which $91,349 were realized for the benefit of the fund.

The Superintendent recommends the affording additional facilities for common school instruction to children engaged in manufacturing establishments; and suggests the appropriation by the commissioners of common schools, of a portion of public money to each such establishment, according to the number of children to be benefitted by instruction.

In 1829 the number of common schools had increased to 8,609, from 8,104 of which returns were received by the Superintendent. The number of children be tween five and sixteen years, residing in the several districts from which reports had been received, was 440,113; and the number of children taught during the year reported, was 468,205; being an excess of 26,349 over the preceding year.

In 1830 the number of districts was 8,872; reporting, 8,292; in which were 468,257 children between the ages of five and sixteen; and 480,041 children taught; being an increase of 11,836 during the year reported. The Superintendent, in his annual report, adverts to the "serious deficiency in the supply of competent teachers," as "the great obstacle which it is necessary to remove before we can reasonably expect to accomplish the great result, and confer the enduring benefits which were anticipated by those who founded and those who have fostered our system of common school instruction." "Those who have turned their attention to the subject of giving a higher character to the common schools, in this, as well as in other states," he continues, "have recommended the establishment of seminaries for the exclusive education of teachers. This would serve to multiply the number of those who would be qualified to teach; but after being thus qualified at the public expense, what guaranty would there be that such persons would follow the business of teaching, unless they could be as liberally compensated in a district school as in the other pursuits of life? If the inhabitants of the districts were resolved to have none other than teachers of the highest grade, and would pay the highest premium for talent, our academies and high schools would be thronged by persons fitting themselves for the business of teaching; and all these institutions would practically become schools for the education of teachers. If the districts could be induced to give an adequate compensation, and constant employment to first rate instructors, then it would be eminently useful to establish seminaries for the special purpose of training persons as professional instructors." "To secure permanent teachers, it is indispensable that the inhabitants of the districts should afford such reasonable compensation and constant employment as will induce persons of good talents to devote themselves to the business of teaching as a profession." "If the intelligent farmers in the districts would apply a small share of their attention and practical common sense to this subject, a revolution in the character of the schools would soon be effected."

The Superintendent also adverts to the multiplicity of text books in use in the several schools, but expresses the opinion that the designation of any particular work or series of works, to the exclusion of all others, would be attended with injurious consequences, not only to the schools themselves, but to the cause of education generally. He remarks that "great improvements are constantly going on in the character of school books; the greatest experience and much of the best talent of the country is enlisted in this business; and the fruits of their labors are constantly giving them new claims to the approbation of the public. The adoption of a particular book would amount to a prohibition upon all improvements, and would subject the inhabitants to a loss of the prohibited books then on hand. The interests of the common schools may be seriously injured, and cannot be essentially benefitted by the adoption by law of any book or set of books."

The following is the earliest specific suggestion, looking to the establishment of district libraries, which I have been able to find. It is contained in Mr. Flagg's report for this year, (1830.)

"A society has been established in England, for the purpose of imparting useful information to all classes of community, particularly to such as are unable to avail themselves of experienced teachers. To effect this object, treatises on the various sciences, and books of practical utility have been published at such moderate prices as to bring them within the reach of all classes. A small sum applied to the publication and distribution among the several school districts, of similar works, would have the most favorable influence."

It will have been perceived, however, that Gov. Clinton, in his message at the opening of the session of 1827, called the attention of the legislature to the expediency of providing "small and suitable collections of books and maps," to be attached to the common schools.

Gov. Throop, in his message to the legislature at the opening of the session of 1831, thus alludes to this great interest of the state:

"There is no one of our public institutions of more importance, or which has better fulfilled public expectation, than that providing for instruction in common schools. The large fund appropriated to that object has produced a complete organization throughout the state; and although the system has had to encounter all the obstacles to a new enterprize of such magnitude in its operations and objects, yet it has been well seconded by public zeal and liberality. Its imperfections may receive some correction from legislation, yet more is to be hoped from individual exertions to carry the design of the legislature into effect within the several districts."

From the annual report of the Superintendent for this year it appears that the whole number of districts was 9,062, from 8,630 of which reports had been made in accordance with law; that the number of children between the ages of five and sixteen residing in the several districts from which such reports had been received, was 497,503; and the number of children taught therein during the year reported, 499,434, being an increase of 19,333 over the number so taught the preceding year. The aggregate amount of public money received and expended in the several districts for the payment of the wages of duly qualified teachers, was $239,713.00; of which $100,000 was paid by the State from the common school fund; and the residue derived from a tax on the several towns, and from local funds. In addition to the public money, there was paid by the inhabitants of the several districts, on rate bills for teachers' wages, $346,807, making a total of $586,520 paid for teachers' wages alone. The average annual increase of the number of scholars instructed in the common schools, during the preceding eleven years was 20,000.

The productive capital of the common school fund amounted at this time to $1,696,743.66; and the revenue actually received into the treasury on account of this fund, during the year 1830, exceeded the sum required for apportionment among the several districts by $678.60, it being the first year in which the revenue had produced the sum requisite for this purpose.

The Superintendent, in this report, examines and discusses at considerable length the various plans for the education of teachers, and recommends the conversion of the several academies, equal in number at that period to the counties in the state, into seminaries for training teachers. On this subject he remarks: "The state has done much for these schools, and something in aid of the cause of the common schools may reasonably be expected from them; and if the required information to fit a person for teaching can be obtained in the present institutions, sound policy and good economy are in favor of relying upon them for the training of teachers." He adverts in this connection to the proposition presented to the legislature at its preceding session, by a committee of the citizens of Rochester, for the establishment of a state seminary for the education of teachers, and a town central school in each town in the state, as a document exhibiting "much research and attention to the subject of common school instruction." In this memorial (legislative documents, 1830, volume iv. no. 387,) the committee, (Messrs. Penney, Comstock, Brown, Ward and Norton,) after recapitulating the prominent defects in the existing condition of common school education submits a plan, designed

"1. To furnish a competent supply of well qualified teachers.

"2. To diffuse the benefits of good teaching, at an early period, through all the districts in the state, and to accomplish the intention of the law as to an efficient inspection.

"3. To secure such a degree of respect and compensation to teachers, as to induce men of good talents and qualifications to make teaching a profession for life, and

"4. So to organize and govern the whole system of common school education as sufficiently to protect this great interest from every kind of abuse, and to cherish it for the various useful ends it may be made to serve.

"It is proposed to effect the first of these objects by the establishment of say three state seminaries, for the education of teachers; the second, by promoting the erection of one central school of the most approved description in each town, having the duties and services of its teacher so connected with all the other districts of the town, as to secure the object of good teaching to all, and gradually to qualify good teachers for the whole." The particular details of the plan were also presented under the five following general heads:

"1. Of the proper qualifications of a teacher.

"2. Of a state seminary for educating teachers—its government—its course of instruction—admission of students—their diplomas and privileges.

"3. Of the town central schools—their government, &c.

"4. Of an annual meeting of the faculties, and report on school boooks, &c.

"5. Of the government and general superintendence of the whole."

The great length of this document precludes its insertion here. It is, however, well worthy of a deliberate and attentive examination, in the present advanced stage of educational science; and its sound suggestions and practical views commend it to the favorable regards of all desirous of elevating and expanding to their utmost practicable limits the capabilities of our unrivalled system of public instruction. The condition of the common school fund at the period when these views were presented, interposed an insuperable obstacle to the adoption of the plan proposed. This objection has now to a great extent disappeared; and it is believed that a sound and enlightened public sentiment will sustain the public authorities in carrying into execution, with such modifications and improvements as experience has subsequently brought to light, the recommendations and suggestions of the memorialists, at least so far as a state seminary for the preparation of teachers is concerned. The Superintendent, in his report for the present year, also examines and discusses the question, how far the expenses of supporting and maintaining the common schools, and supplying them with competent teachers, may advantageously be provided from the public funds of the state, and to what extent they may safely and successfully be committed immediately to the inhabitants of the several districts. He compares the operation of our system in this respect with those of Pennsylvania, Virginia, Connecticut and other states, in the two former of which the public funds were exclusively appropriated to the benefit of the children of indigent inhabitants of the several districts, and in Connecticut, were lavished with an indiscriminate profusion, furnishing ample means for the gratuitous instruction of all classes.

"Our system" he observes, "is well calculated to awaken the attention of all the inhabitants to the concerns of the district school. The power given to district meetings to levy a tax, to a limited extent, upon the property of the district, excites a direct interest with all the taxable inhabitants to attend the district meetings, whether they have children requiring school accommodations or not. The wealthy are thus prompted to act as trustees, and to watch over the concerns of the district, in order to see that its affairs are conducted with care and economy; and much of the intelligence of the district is put in requisition by the peculiarity of our plan, which might be wholly lost to the districts if the whole expense of the tuition was provided by a state fund." "It has been urged," he remarks, in another place, "that the amount distributed from our fund is too small, and that an increase of the fund would, of itself, raise the standard of the common school; but an increase of the school moneys would be much more likely to decrease the contributions of individuals, than to elevate the standard of the common schools." At this period the amount of public money apportioned by the state for the payment of teachers' wages in the several districts, was $100,000; while the amount raised on rate bills was $346,807. The annual report of the Superintendent for 1844 shows that while the amount of public money received from the state treasury applicable to the same purpose, was $220,000, the amount paid on the rate bills was $509,-376.97 only; being $254,000 less than a proportionate amount under the increased fund contributed by the state.

On the subject of a proposed uniformity of text books in the several schools, the Superintendent remarks, "no man or set of men could make out a list of class books for the instruction of half a million of scholars, which would give general satisfaction; and there is great reason to believe that the experiment to produce uniformity would do more harm than it promises to do good. In view of all the difficulties which surround the subject, the Superintendent believes that it is best to leave the selection of class books to the intelligence of the inhabitants of the districts and towns." In support of these views he refers to a very able report of the literature committee in the assembly, made the preceding year, and which will be found in the fourth volume of the legislative documents of that year, (No. 431,) of 1830.

In conclusion, the Superintendent observes:

"The immense importance of elevating the standard of education in the common schools is strongly enforced by the fact, that to every ten persons receiving instruction in the higher schools, there are at least five hundred dependent upon the common schools for their education. In urging the importance of common schools, it is not designed to depreciate the great utility of those of a higher grade. In the discussions on the subject of popular education, it has in some cases been urged that academies and high schools were injurious to the common schools, by withdrawing from the aid of the latter, the patronage and care of those who are able to send to the former schools. There is nothing in our experience which should induce us to look with disfavor upon the higher schools, and the patriot and philanthropist, in estimating the means which are to contribute to the perpetuity of our happy form of government, will regard all our schools and seminaries as parts of the same useful and valuable system, from the university to the infant school."

In 1832, the number of school districts had increased to 9,333, from 8,835 of which reports were received. The whole number of children between five and sixteen years of age residing in the several reporting districts, was 504,685; and the number taught during the preceding year, was 497,257; being an increase of 7,463 since the last report.

"The school system of New-York," remarks the Superintendent, "has been formed by combining the advantages of the different plans of supporting common schools which prevail in the New-England states. Connecticut has a large fund which produces nearly or quite the amount paid for teachers' wages, and they have no local tax. Massachusetts and Maine have no public fund, and the wages of teachers are provided by a town tax. Our system happily combines the principles of a state fund and a town tax; enough is apportioned from the state treasury to invite and encourage the co-operation of the districts and towns; and not so much as to induce the inhabitants to believe that they have nothing more to do than to hire a teacher to absorb the public money. The tax authorized upon the property of the town and district has a most salutary effect in awakening the attention of the inhabitants to the concerns of the common schools. The power of district meetings to raise money by tax, induces the inhabitants to attend the meetings, and to overlook the interest and proceedings of the district; when, if the whole expense was provided by a state fund, they would allow the trustees to receive and expend the money, as if it was a matter which did not interest the great body of the inhabitants of the district. Whatever differences of opinion may exist as to the best mode of providing for the expense of giving instruction to all the children of the state, the success which has attended our system warrants the conclusion that a public fund may be made eminently useful in organizing a system of universal instruction. The apportionment of a few dollars is often the immediate inducement for neighborhoods to establish schools where none existed before, and for prompting new settlements to erect school houses, at an earlier period than they otherwise would have done, in order to participate in a fund, however small, which they know is enjoyed by other districts in their towns."

In relation to the "vexed question" of text books, the Superintendent renews the expression of his opinion "that the adoption of a particular set of class books could be of no advantage except to the favored authors, to whom the monopoly of supplying the scholars should be given. Towards all other authors, who have devoted their time and talents to the preparation of books, as well as publishers who have embarked their fortunes in particular works, *it* would operate proscriptively and with manifest injustice."

Administration of JOHN A. DIX—1833 *to* 1839.

In his message at the opening of the session of 1833, Gov. MARCY thus adverts to the subject of common schools:

"Of all institutions, there is none that presents such strong claims to the patronage of the government as our system of common schools; and it is gratifying to know that these claims have been recognized, and to a very considerable extent, satisfied. The wisdom and providence of our legislation appears perhaps no where so conspicuously, as in the measures which have been adopted, and the means which have been provided for the general diffusion of primary education among the children of all classes of our citizens." After adverting to the information contained in the annual report of the Superintendent, relative to the condition and prospects of the common schools, the governor proceeds: "An active and adventurous spirit of improvement characterizes the present age. Its best direction would seem to be towards multiplying the facilities, and consequently abridging the time and labor of acquiring knowledge. I indulge the hope that much may yet be done in this respect for primary education. One of the most obvious improvements in relation to common schools, would be a plan for supplying them with competent teachers. Under present circumstances, the remedy of the evils resulting from the employment of persons not properly qualified, can only be applied by the trustees and inspectors; and I am not apprised that any further direction for regulating their duties in this respect, could be usefully presented to the legislature."

From the annual report of the Superintendent it appeared that in 1833, the number of school districts had increased to 9,600; from 8,941 of which reports were received, in which there were 508,878 children between five and sixteen years of age; and 494,959 children taught during the year reported; being a decrease of 2,146 since the preceding year. The Superintendent renews the expression of his conviction that the academies are adequate to the supply of competent teachers for the common schools. He also again calls the attention of the legislature to the expediency of making some suitable provision for the education of the children of persons engaged in the various manufacturing establishments of the state.

"The policy of all our laws," he observes, "is to secure a good common school education to every child in the state; and the condition of the children who are employed in the manufactories, as to their means of instruction, ought to be carefully inquired into and provided for. The diffusion of education among all classes of our population is deemed of such vital importance to the preservation of our free institutions, that if the obligations which rest upon every good citizen in this particular are disregarded, the persons having the custody of such children ought to be visited with such disabilities as will induce them, from interest if not from principle, to cause the children to be instructed, at least in reading, writing and arithmetic. Intelligence has been regarded as the vital principle of a free government, and every parent, guardian or master, who neglects or refuses to give the children under his charge the advantages of a common school education, particularly in cases where the instruction is offered "without money and without price," is as much an offender against the state, as the man who refuses to perform any other duty which is deemed essential to the preservation of our liberties."

On the 15th day of January, 1833, JOHN A. DIX was appointed secretary of state and Superintendent of Common Schools, Mr. Flagg having been promoted to the office of comptroller. During the administration of the latter, a period of seven years, the number of school districts in the state had increased from 7,773 to 9,600 ; the number of children instructed in them, from 425,586 to 494,959, and the proportion of the number of children taught to the whole number residing in the several districts, from 100 to 93, to 250 to 249. The amount of public money annually appropriated for the payment of the wages of approved teachers, had increased from $182,790.09 to $305,582.78. The external organization and internal details of the system had received the fostering care and enlightened attention of the most practical and discriminating minds of the state ; and the unequalled rapidity with which districts sprung up in every section of the state, and children of all ages and classes were gathered into the common schools, sufficiently indicate the general appreciation of the advantages and merits of the system, on the part of the people generally. To untiring industry and great efficiency, Mr. Flagg united an eminently practical mind, which enabled him, in the midst of numerous and plausible projects for the elevation and improvement of the system of popular education, to select and recommend those only which promised the realization of the hopes and aspirations of the sound and judicious friends of the common schools ; and accordingly, while steadfastly setting his face against the adoption of an uniform series of text books, and of a state seminary for the instruction of teachers, as impracticable in the existing state of things, he strongly urged the adoption of a more efficient and vigorous system of inspection and supervision, and several years in advance of any direct movement on the subject, recommended the publication and distribution of suitable books for the diffusion of useful knowledge, among the several school districts of the state.

During his administration of the common school department, the foundations were laid of those equitable principles upon which the various controversies growing out of the several school laws, were adjusted by the decisions of the Superintendent. Up to this period, no records of the adjudications of this officer had been kept ; and the various questions almost daily presented for settlement had been determined upon their specific merits, without apparently any attempt to reduce the system to unity and harmony, or to establish and maintain general principles of interpretation and decision. The decisions of Mr. Flagg, and his successor, Gen. Dix, were in 1837, collected by the latter and published, for the benefit of the several officers connected with the administration of the system throughout the state ; and they have not only served as a basis for the determination of the numerons and complicated questions which have since arisen, but have exercised a highly beneficial influence upon the councils and proceedings of the officers and inhabitants of the several districts, by repressing litigation, by defining the powers, privileges and responsibilities of those called to the performance of any duty in relation to the common schools, and by the introduction and settlement of fixed principles of interpretation, applicable to almost every emergency likely to arise in the practical operation of the system.

From the annual report of Gen. Dix, as Superintendent of Common Schools, made on the 8th of January, 1834, it appeared that there were 9,690 school districts in the state, from 9,107 of which reports had been made in accordance with law. The number of children between the ages of five and sixteen, residing in the several districts from which reports were received, was 522,618; and the whole number of children taught in the several district schools, was 512,475; being an increase of 17,516 over the number thus instructed during the preceding year. In reference to the amount of the public funds provided for the support of common schools, the Superintendent expresses his opinion that the sum ($100,000) distributed among the several districts, was as great as was necessary to accomplish every object of such a distribution. "Experience in other states," he observes, "has proved what has been abundantly confirmed by our own, that too large a sum of public money distributed among the common schools has no salutary effect. Beyond a certain point, the voluntary contributions of the inhabitants decline in amount with almost uniform regularity as the contributions from a public fund increase." "Should the general fund at any future day be recruited so as to admit of an augmentation of the capital or revenue of the common school fund, or both, the policy of increasing the sum annually distributed to the common schools, beyond an amount which shall, when taken in connection with the number of children annually taught in them, exceed the present rate of apportionment, would be in the highest degree questionable."

With respect to the preparation of teachers for the common schools, the Superintendent concurs generally in the views of his predecessor, that the several academies in the state, aided by liberal appropriations for this purpose from the literature fund, are abundantly adequate to the accomplishment of the object in view; that the establishment of one or more teachers' seminaries, devoted exclusively to this subject, would be impracticable without requiring the districts not only to employ such teachers when prepared, but to provide them with an adequate compensation—neither of which measures would for a moment be tolerated; and that the demand on the part of the districts for teachers of a higher degree of qualification will be met by a corresponding supply from the academies, whenever sufficient inducements are held out to the latter to devote a large portion of their attention to the preparation of such teachers. An enlightened appreciation, on the part of inhabitants of districts generally, of the functions and responsibilities of teachers—a determination to secure the highest order of talent, and to provide an adequate compensation—and a disposition to elevate the character and advance the social rank of the teacher, by assigning him that station in the regards of the community which is due to the dignity and utility of his profession; these are regarded as indispensable pre-requisites to the success of any system which contemplates the specific preparation of teachers.

On the subject of the adoption of a uniform series of text books for the use of schools, the Superintendent also adopts the views of his predecessors, discountenancing such a measure as impracticable and unjust.

In reference to the establishment of District Libraries, the Superintendent observes:

"If the inhabitants of school districts were authorized to lay a tax upon their property for the purpose of purchasing libraries for the use of the district, such a power might with proper restrictions become a most efficient instrument in diffusing useful knowledge, and in elevating the intellectual character of the people. A vast amount of useful information might in this manner be collected, where it would be easily accessible, and its influence could hardly fail to be in the highest degree salutary, by furnishing the means of improvement to those who have finished their common school education, as well as to those who have not. The demand for books would ensure extensive editions of works containing matter judiciously selected, at prices which competition would soon reduce to the lowest rate at which they could be furnished. By making the imposition of the tax wholly discretionary with the inhabitants of each district, and leaving the selection of the works under their entire control, the danger of rendering such a provision subservient to the propagation of particular doctrines or opinions would be effectually guarded against by their watchfulness and intelligence."

By an act of the legislature passed this year, the surplus income of the literature fund, beyond the sum of $12,000, was placed at the disposal of the Regents of the University, to be by them distributed to such of the academies subject to their visitation as they might select, and to be devoted exclusively to the education of common school teachers. The funds thus appropriated were estimated at about $3,000 per annum.

At the opening of the session of 1835, Gov. Marcy, in his message, commended to the special attention of the legislature, the adoption of "a provision for supplying competent teachers, improvements in the method of instruction, and the faithful and economical application of the funds to such objects and in such a manner as will insure the best results." He observes: "In regard to the common schools, considering their great importance in a political and moral point of view, the efforts of the legislature should not be intermitted until the system shall be so improved as to secure to the children of all classes and conditions of our population, such an education as will qualify them to fulfil in a proper manner, the duties appertaining to whatever may be their respective pursuits and conditions of life."

The number of school districts at this period had increased to 9,865; the whole number of children between the ages of five and sixteen to 534,000, and the number taught in the several districts from which reports had been received to 521,240, or 18,256 more than were so instructed during the preceding year.

The following extract from the annual report of the Superintendent, transmitted to the legislature on the 7th of January of this year, will exhibit the views of that officer in reference to the adequacy of the academies to furnish the common schools with a competent supply of duly qualified teachers, and also in reference to the relations which the various institutions for the promotion of public instruction should sustain to each other:

"If the foundations of our whole system of public instruction were to be laid anew, it would, perhaps, be advisable to create separate seminaries for the preparation of teachers, although from the nature of our institutions, it might be deemed arbitrary, if indeed it were practicable, to compel the school districts to employ them. It would be equally difficult, without a great augmentation of the school fund, to present to the districts a sufficient pecuniary inducement to engage the individuals thus prepared; and it may be safely assumed that nothing short of a thorough conviction in the public mind, that common school teachers are in general incompetent to the proper fulfilment of their trusts, and that the standard of education is extremely imperfect, would accomplish the object. If that conviction can now be created, the existing evils may be readily redressed. Our common school system is so perfectly organized, and administered throughout with so much order and regularity, and so many academies under able management are already established, that it would seem the part of wisdom to avail ourselves of these institutions, to the extent of their capacity, for the purpose of training teachers for the common schools. Their endowments, their organization, the experience and skill of their instructors, and their whole intellectual power, may be made subservient to the public purpose in view, and with the aid which the state can lend, much may be effected. But, whatever differences of opinion may prevail with regard to the foundation of this plan, in sound policy, the question has been settled by the legislature, and it remains only to carry it into execution with proper energy.

Should it prove inadequate to the ends proposed, a change of plan may then be insisted on, without being open to the objection of abandoning a system which has not been fairly tested.

"It may not be improper to remark in this place that the necessary connexion which exists between our common schools and the literary institutions of the state, including those of the highest grade, has been too frequently overlooked. The academies have already been, in effect, without receiving from the state any direct pecuniary aid for the purpose, nurseries for common school teachers. The great body of those who have either temporarily or permanently devoted themselves to teaching, have been prepared at the academies with a view to that occupation, or to some professional employment. The instructors in the academies have in their turn been educated in the colleges; and but for the latter or some other system of classical and scientific education, as a substitute for the course of training pursued in the colleges, the academies would obviously be destitute of the necessary supply of tutors. Thus all our incorporated literary institutions minister to the improvement of the common school system, on which the great body of the people are dependent for their education."

The Superintendent, after adverting to the defective state of the systems of instruction in common schools, proceeds at considerable length to combat the idea that "the education which an individual receives, should be designed exclusively to fit him for the particular employment which he is destined to pursue." "The attention of the great body of the people" he justly remarks, "should be directed to objects beyond the sphere of the employments on which they depend for their support." "Knowledge carries with it influence over the minds of others, and this influence is power. In free governments—what is of more vital concern—it is political power." And he illustrates these views by a reference to the range and importance of the duties devolving upon every American citizen.

On the 8th of January, 1835, Gen. Dix, as chairman of a committee of the Regents of the University, appointed to prepare and report a plan for the better education of teachers of common schools, submitted an elaborate and able report recommending the establishment and organization of a teachers' department, to be connected with one academy to be designated by the Regents, in each of the eight senatorial districts of the state; indicating the course of study to be pursued in such departments; and suggesting for the consideration of the Regents the academies to be selected for this purpose, which should each receive annually the sum of $400 from the fund applicable to this object. The report was agreed to by the Regents, and Erasmus Hall Academy in Kings county, Montgomery Academy, Orange county, Kinderhook, St. Lawrence, Fairfield, Oxford, Canandaigua, and Middlebury Academies were designated for the establishment of these institutions, on the basis and subject to the restrictions and regulations indicated in the report.

On the 13th of April of this year, the foundations of the District School Library were laid by an act authorizing the taxable inhabitants of the several school districts to impose a tax not exceeding twenty dollars for the first year, and ten dollars for each succeeding year, "for the purchase of a district library, consisting of such books as they shall in their district meeting direct."

This bill was ably advocated in the Senate by Col. Young of Saratoga, and the Hon. Levi Beardsley of Otsego; and its friends were indebted for its success, in great part, to the untiring exertions and extensive influence of James Wadsworth of Geneseo; an eminent philanthropist, who lost no opportunity to aid, by his ample wealth and enlightened intellect, every means by which the mental and moral advancement of the youth of the state might be promoted.

On the 6th of May, Mr. Wetmore, of New York, chairman of the literature committee of the house, made a very able report, concluding with a recommendation for the establishment of a separate "Department of Public Instruction," under the superintendence of an officer to be known as "Secretary of

Public Instruction," to be appointed by the legislature triennially, in the same manner with other state officers; who should possess the powers and discharge the duties of Superintendent of Common Schools, and be ex-officio Chancellor of the Regents of the University, &c. The several colleges and academies of the state were to be subject to his visitation; and he was required particularly to visit and inspect those academies in which departments for the education of teachers were established. No definite action was however had on this proposition, by the legislature.

The following is an extract from Gov. Marcy's message at the opening of the session of 1836:

"In a government like ours, which emanates from the people, where the entire administration, in all its various branches, is conducted for their benefit and subject to their constant supervision and control; and where the safety and perpetuity of all its political institutions depend upon their virtue and intelligence, no other subject can be equal in importance to that of public instruction, and none should so earnestly engage the attention of the legislature. Ignorance, with all the moral evils of which it is the prolific source, brings with it also numerous political evils, dangerous to the welfare of the state. It should be the anxious care of the legislature to eradicate these evils by removing the causes of them. This can be done effectually, only by diffusing instruction generally among the people. Although much remains here to be done in this respect, the past efforts of legislation upon the subject merit high commendation. Much has been already accomplished for the cause of popular education. A large fund has been dedicated to this object, and our common school system is established on right principles. But this is one of those subjects for which all cannot be done that is required, without a powerful co-operation on the part of the people in their individual capacity. The providing of funds for education is an indispensable means for attaining the end; but it is not education. The wisest system that can be devised cannot be executed without human agency. The difficulty in the case arises, I fear, from the fact that the benefits of general education can only be fully appreciated by those who are educated themselves. Those parents who are so unfortunate as not to be properly educated, and those whose condition requires them to employ their time and their efforts to gain the means of subsistence, do not, in many instances, sufficiently value the importance of education. Yet it is for their children, in common with all others, that the common school system is designed; and until its blessings are made to reach them, it will not be what it ought to be. If parents generally were sensible of the inestimable advantages they were procuring for their children by educating them, I am sure the efforts and contributions which are required to give full efficiency to our present system would not be withheld. If I have rightly apprehended the indications of public opinion on this subject, a more auspicious season is approaching. At this time, a much larger number of individuals than heretofore are exerting their energies and contributing their means, to impress the public mind with the importance of making our system of popular instruction effective in diffusing its benefits to all the children of the state. I anticipate much good from the prevalence of the sentiment that the efforts of individuals must co-operate with the public authorities to ensure success to any system of general education."

From the annual report of the Superintendent, it appeared that the number of districts had increased to 10,132; the number of children between the ages of five and sixteen, to 543,000; and the number taught in the several districts from which reports had been received, to 541,400, being an increase of over 10,000 from the preceding year. The Superintendent repeats the expression of his conviction, "that a school fund so large as to admit of a distribution of money to the common schools in any degree approaching the amount expended for their support, would be likely to be injurious rather than beneficial. A school fund," he observes, "can only be useful when its revenue is sufficient, and no more than sufficient, to operate as an inducement to the inhabitants of school districts to contribute liberally to their support." "It is, from the nature of the subject, impossible to fix the exact limit, below which a reduction of the sum distributed (including the amount raised by taxation in the several towns) would cease to operate as an inducement to the inhabitants to assume the residue of the expenses of maintaining the schools, or beyond which its increase would render their burdens so light as to create inattention to the concerns of the districts. It may, however, be safely assumed, that, at any point between forty and fifty cents per scholar, it is not probable that either of these evils would be felt; and that its augmentation above the maximum, on the one hand, or its reduction on the other, below the minimum above named, ought to be avoided, if practicable." The effect of the subsequent increase of the sum so distributed during the past few years, has certainly, it may here be remarked, by no means impeached the soundness and accuracy of this proposition; the extent to which the schools have improved being clearly attributable to other and more potent influences than the augmentation of the public funds applicable to their support.

At the opening of the session of 1837, Gov. Marcy again brought the subject of common school education before the legislature, in connection with the act of congress of the preceding year, authorizing the deposit of the share belonging to this state, of the surplus revenue of the United States, with the state for safe keeping, until required by the general government. He recommended the appropriation from the income of this fund, of an amount equal to the sum annually distributed to the common schools, to be applied to the same purpose, viz. the payment of the wages of duly qualified teachers; making the annual distribution for this purpose, $220,000—a liberal appropriation to the academies, "having in view principally the design of rendering them more efficient as seminaries for educating common school teachers—and the addition of the residue of such income to the capital of the common school fund. He also recommended the transfer of the general superintendence and supervision of the several academies of the state, from the Regents of the University to the secretary of state in his capacity of Superintendent of Common Schools, disapproving of the proposed erection of a separate department of public instruction, and suggesting the appointment of an additional deputy to aid the secretary in the performance of this portion of his official duties. He commends the efforts in progress for the promotion of popular instruction by the diffusion of education through all ranks of the people, and the devotion of talents and wealth to this great cause; and expresses his conviction, that aided by the powerful co-operation of the legislature, its advancement may confidently be anticipated.

The sum of $110,000 was this year apportioned among the several school districts, the number of which had augmented to 10,207. The number of children between five and sixteen residing in the several districts from which reports had been received, was 538,398; and the number instructed within the year, 532,167; being a diminution of 9,234 from the number instructed the preceding year. This diminution is accounted for by the Superintendent, "by the prevalence of an absorbing attention, in a considerable portion of the community, to their pecuniary interests rather than to the interests of education." "Strong excitements in the community," he observes, "especially when continued for a length of time, are in their nature unfriendly to the cause of education; and of such excitements none is perhaps so much so as that which is characteristic of periods when fortunes are amassed without effort and by the mere chances of speculation." "In the year 1834," he continues, "the common schools were in better condition, in all respects, than they had been at any previous time; and, as is well known, that year was distinguished by a serious depression in the business affairs of the country. The interests of education seem never to be better secured than in seasons when individuals are compelled to husband their resources, and when the highest as well as the most certain rewards are those which are the fruits of patient industry. No period seems less propitious to the promotion of those interests, than that season of delusive prosperity in which multitudes are tempted by a few instances of wealth suddenly acquired, to lay aside their accustomed avocations, and embark in the precarious pursuits of fortune."

In his message at the opening of the session of 1838, Gov. Marcy repeats his recommendations of the previous year, in reference to the proper disposition of the revenue of the United States deposit fund, with the additional suggestion that a portion of this fund be devoted to the purchase of District Libraries, in such of the several school districts of the state as should raise by taxation an equal amount for that object. In reference to the departments for the education of teachers connected with the respective academies designated by the Regents of the University, he expresses the opinion, that however ably conducted, they must of necessity be inadequate to the supply of the requisite number of teachers for the common schools, and suggests the establishment of county normal schools, "on principals analogous to those on which our system of common shools is founded." An increase of the number of academies provided with teachers' departments, is also suggested, the additional expense to be defrayed from the revenue of the deposit fund.

The number of school districts had now increased to 10,345: the number of children between five and sixteen residing in the several districts from which reports were received, to 536,882 and the number taught was 524,188; showing a still further diminution of nearly 8,000 from the preceding year.

During this session the sum of $160,000 was added from the annual revenue of the United States deposit fund, to the amount to be apportioned among the several school districts of the state; of which $55,000 was is required to be expended by the trustees in the purchase of suitable books for a district library, and the residue for the payment of the wages of duly qualified teachers. An equal amount was also required to be raised by taxation on the several counties and towns, and applied to the same purpose. The residue of the income, after making certain appropriations to the colleges and academies, was added to the capital of the common school fund.

On the 7th of March, the Hon. Daniel D. Barnard, from the literature committee of the house, submitted a masterly and eloquent report upon the general subject of public instruction, to which we regret that our limits compel us only to advert. Many important and valuable suggestions for the extension and greater efficiency of our systems of popular education will be found embraced in this document. No specific action, however, in accordance with the recommendations of the report was had.

At the opening of the session of 1839, Gov. Seward called the attention of the legislature, in an especial manner, to the interests of elementary public instruction; expressing his conviction of the paramount necessity of elevating the standard of education; recommending legislative co-operation in the furtherance of the effort to engraft the system of normal schools upon our institutions for education, through the agency of the academies; strongly commending the district library system; and urging the indispensable necessity of a more thorough and efficient visitation and supervision of our common schools.

By the annual report of the superintendent, it appeared that the number of organized school districts in the state was, at this period, 10,583; the number of children between the ages of five and sixteen years, residing in the several districts from which reports had been received, 539,749; and the number of children under instruction, 528,913; exceeding by 4,725 the number instructed the preceding year.

In reference to the act of April, 1838, appropriating the income of the U. S. Deposit Fund to the purposes of education, the Superintendent observes:

"The acts of April last, after making certain appropriations for the support of colleges, academies and common schools, from the income of the United States Deposit Fund, provides that the residue of that income shall be added annually to the capital of the common school fund. The income of the former fund will amount to nearly $260,000 per annum, and the appropriations referred to amount to $208,000, viz.: to the common schools, to be applied to the payment of teachers, $110,000, and $55,000 to the purchase of school district libraries; to the literature fund $28,000, and to colleges $15,000; leaving a balance of about $50,000 to be applied to the increase of the last mentioned fund. Should this appropriation continue undisturbed, the capital of the common school fund will, by the year 1850, amount to about $3,000,000, without any further provision for its increase; as the sales of lands belonging to it may be expected to yield two or three hundred thousand dollars."

On the subject of moral and religious instruction in the several schools, the Superintendent has the following sensible and judicious remarks:

"However desirable it may be to lay the foundation of common school education in religious instruction, the multiplicity of sects in this state would render the accomplishment of such an object a work of great difficulty. In the state of Massachusetts it is provided by law that no school books shall be used in any of the schools 'calculated to favor any religious sect.' In this state no such legal provision has been made; but the natural desire of every class of Christians to exclude from the schools instruction in the tenets of other classes has led to the disuse, by common consent, of religious books of almost every description, excepting the Bible and New Testament, which are used in more than one hundred towns as reading books. The spirit of jealousy by which the schools are surrounded, regarded as they are as most efficient instruments in the formation of opinions, will probably render this state of things perpetual; and it is of the greater importance, therefore, that moral instruction and training should constitute a principal branch of the system of education. No teacher can receive a certificate of qualification from the inspectors, unless they are satisfied as to his moral character. In this respect the inspectors cannot be too rigid in their scrutiny. A teacher whose moral sentiments are loose, or whose habits of life are irregular, is an unfit instructor for the young, whatever may be his intellectual acquirements, or his skill in communicating knowledge. The lessons of moral truth which are taught at the domestic fireside and the examples of moral rectitude and purity which are there displayed, will be in danger of losing all their benefit, if the school room does not reinforce them by its sanctions. If neither the atmosphere of the family circle, nor of the school, is free from impurity, to what other source can the young resort for those principles of morality which shall render their intellectual improvement subservient to useful purposes, and without which it might become an instrument to be wielded for the annoyance of their fellows and for their own destruction? Though moral principles may have their origin in the heart, it is not to be expected that their proper development can be effected amid the perpetual counteraction of hostile influences. Moral cultivation should, therefore, be one of the first objects of common school instruction. The great doctrines of ethics, so far as they concern the practical rules of human conduct, receive the intuitive assent of all; and with them may be combined instruction in those principles of natural religion, which are drawn from the observation of the works of nature, which address themselves with the same certainty to the conviction, and which carry to the minds of all observers irresistible evidence of the wisdom, the beneficence and the power of their divine author. Beyond this, it is questionable whether instruction in matters of religious obligation can be carried, excepting so far as the school districts may make the Bible and New Testament class books; and there can be no ground to apprehend that the schools will be used for the purpose of favoring any particular sect or tenet, if these sacred writings, which are their own safest interpreters, are read without any other comment than such as may be necessary to explain and enforce, by familiar illustration, the lessons of duty which they teach.

"In connexion with this subject, it is highly gratifying to consider that the religious institutions of the country, reaching, as they do, the most sequestered neighborhoods, and the sabbath schools, which are almost as widely diffused, afford ample means of instruction in the principles and practice of the Christian faith. In countries where ecclesiastical affairs are the subject of political regulation, there is no difficulty in making religious instruction the foundation of education, by arrangements independent of the action of those whom it immediately concerns. But the policy of our law is to leave the subject, where it may be most properly left, with the officers and inhabitants of the school districts."

In passing from the administration of Gen. Dix to that of his successor, it is scarcely necessary to observe that the exertions of the former, during the six years in which the interests of the common schools were committed to his charge, to elevate and expand the system of popular education, were unsurpassed by any of his predecessors. The impress of his clear, discriminating and cultivated mind, was stamped upon every feature of that system, and the order, arrangement and harmony which pervaded all its parts, were due not less to the ceaseless vigilance of its supervision than to the symmetry and beauty of the system itself. In 1837 Gen. Dix, under the authority of the legislature, collected together and published a volume of the decisions of his predecessor and himself, embracing an exposition of nearly every provision of the school act, and establishing, upon a permanent basis, the principles of future interpretation and decision, in reference to those provisions. The system of district school libraries was also organized and put into successful operation under his immediate auspices; and to his clear and convincing exposition of the principles upon which this great institution was based, the ends it was designed to subserve, and the objects it was capable of accomplishing, a large share of the success which has attended its establishment thus far, is unquestionably due.

Administration of John C. Spencer—*County Superintendents*—1839 *to* 1842.

On the 4th of February, 1839, the Hon. John C. Spencer was appointed secretary of state and Superintendent of Common Schools. Deeply impressed with the necessity of a more thorough and efficient supervision and inspection of the several schools, his first measure was to procure the passage of a law authorizing the appointment of a County Board of Visitors, whose duty it should be gratuitously to visit the common schools of their county, and to report to him the results of such examination, together with such suggestions for the improvement of these institutions as they might deem expedient. These visitors were selected from among the most intelligent citizens of the several counties, without distinction of party; and under specific instructions from the department, most of the common schools of the state were visited by them, and a mass of valuable information respecting their condition and prospects, accompanied by suggestions for their improvement, obtained and communicated to the legislature. With great unanimity the plan of a county supervision through the medium of an officer to be appointed either by the Superintendent or by some local board, was urged upon the department and the legislature; and under the strong recommendation of the Superintendent, backed by the exertions of several of the most eminent friends of popular education, among whom may be enumerated the Hon. Jabez D. Hammond, who as early as 1835 had given to the public the details of a plan essentially similar; the Rev. Dr. Whitehouse, of Rochester; Francis Dwight, Esq., editor of the District School Journal, then of Geneva; Professor Potter, of Union College, and James Wadsworth, Esq., of Geneseo, this project became, in 1841, by the nearly unanimous action of the legislature, incorporated with our system of common schools.

In his message at the opening of the session of 1840, Gov. Seward thus adverts to the subject of elementary education:

"Although our system of public education is well endowed, and has been eminently successful, there is yet occasion for the benevolent and enlightened action of the legislature. The advantages of education ought to be secured to many, especially in our large cities, whom orphanage, the depravity of parents or some form of accident or misfortune seems to have doomed to hopeless poverty and ignorance. Their intellects are as susceptible of expansion, of improvement, of refinement, of elevation and of direction, as those minds which, through the favor of Providence, are permitted to develop themselves under the influence of better fortunes; they inherit the common lot to struggle against temptations, necessities and vices; they are to assume the same domestic, social and political relations, and they are born to the same ultimate destiny.

"The children of foreigners, found in great numbers in our populous cities and towns, and in the vicinity of our public works, are too often deprived of the advantages of our system of public education, in consequences of prejudices arising from difference of language or religion. It ought never to be forgotten, that the public welfare is as deeply concerned in their education as in that of our own children. I do not hesitate, therefore, to recommend the establishment of schools in which they may be instructed by teachers speaking the same language with themselves, and professing the same faith. There would be no inequality in such a measure, since it happens from the force of circumstauces, if not from choice, that the responsibilities of education are, in most instances, confided by us to native citizens, and occasions seldom offer for a trial of our magnanimity, by committing that trust to persons differing from ourselves in language or religion. Since we have opened our country and all its fulness to the oppressed of every nation, we shall evince wisdom equal to such generosity by qualifying their children for the high responsibilities of citizenship."

From the annual report of the Superintendent it appeared that the whole number of organized school districts in the state was 10,706; the number of children between the ages of five and sixteen, residing in the several districts from which reports had been received, 564,790, and the number of children taught during the year reported, 557,229—showing an increase of 28,316 over the preceding year.

On the 13th of April, 1840, the Superintendent transmitted to the legislature the reports of the several Visitors of Common Schools appointed by him under the act of the preceding session, accompanied by a condensed abstract of their views and suggestions, together with a full exposition of his own, in reference to the various proposed improvements and modifications of the system. In relation to the inspection of the schools the Superintendent observes:

"It has already been shown to the legislature, from the official returns, that at least one half of all the schools in the state are not visited at all by the inspectors. The reports of the Visitors show that the examinations of the inspectors are slight and superficial, and that no benefit is derived from them. Many of the Boards unhesitatingly recommend the abolition of the office." "The Superintendent is constrained to express his concurrence in the opinion expressed by several of the boards of visitors, that the office of town inspector of schools is unnecessary, and rather an incumbrance on the administration of the system." He recommends the appointment of Deputy Superintendents of common schools for each county and expatiates upon the signal advantage to be secured to the interests of the common schools by the adoption of a system of visitation at once so comprehensive and efficient. He dissents from the views of the visitors in reference to the expediency of establishing normal schools in each county for the instruction of teachers; being of the opinion that, the existing system of academical departments for this purpose was preferable; and he accordingly concurs in the recommendation of his predecessor to increase the number of those departments. He strongly urges the establishment, under the patronage of the state, of a journal to be exclusively devoted to the promotion of education; the attainment, if practicable, through the organization of some general society of an uniformity of text books for the use of schools; some adequate provision for the vaccination of children attending the common schools; the introduction of vocal music as a branch of elementary instruction; the extension of the official term of office of the trustees of the several districts, and of commissioners of common schools, and the election of one annually: the voluntary organization of county boards of education, and of town, county and state associations for the improvement of common school education; the establishment in cities and populous places of schools of different grades under the charge of a local Superintendent; and the denial of costs to plaintiffs in suit commenced against school officers in cases where the court shall certify that the act complained of was performed in good faith and in the discharge of official duty.

On the subject of the proper preparation of teachers for the common schools, the Superintendent holds the following language:

"The common school system of the state is comparatively of recent origin. The first law authorizing the establishment of common schools was passed about 26 years ago. In the management of the pecuniary and economical affairs of the districts there is nothing to be desired. Greater regularity in the administration of this part of the system cannot well be fancied. But its defects become apparent the moment we enter the schools. All these defects centre in a common deficiency under which the Russian schools languished so long—the want of efficient and well qualified teachers. One of the principal improvemenients which have occupied the attention of the legislature and the friends of education during the last six years has been to supply this defect; but in the pursuit of this common objeet some diversity of opinion has prevailed with regard to the measures best calculated to accomplish it. Some distinguished advocates of the cause of popular education (and among these are found several of the chief magistrates of the state) have recommended the establishment of teachers' seminaries on the Prussian plan. The prevailing opinion, however, has been in favor of departments for the education of teachers, engrafted upon the incorporated academies of the state, with such endowments as to render them adequate to the object in view."

"Although the proper objects of popular instruction are better understood than they have been at any previous time, the importance of the reform now in progress is not, perhaps, so generally appreciated as it deserves to be. It is but a few years since common school instruction was ordinarily limited to a knowledge of reading, writing and arithmetic. The acquisitions which are now regarded as the means of education, were then sought as its objects and end.—No plan of education can now be considered complete, which does not embrace a full development of the intellectual faculties, a systematic and careful discipline of the moral feelings, and a preparation of the pupil for the social and political relations which he is destined to sustain in manhood. It must be conceded that the standard of common school education in this state falls far short of the attainment of these objects. But the aim of its friends is to introduce into the established system such improvements as shall ultimately secure their accomplishment. Is this a visionary hope? Those who are most familiar with the practical workings of the system, believe that it is not. The whole reform will be accomplished by furnishing each school district with a competent teacher. The application of the remedy is certainly surrounded with difficulties. It must be accomplished by the gradual progress and influence of opinion. The Prussian system not only prepares the teachers, but compels the school districts to employ them. Our whole system proceeds upon the principle of accomplishing by persuasion what the Prussian effects by force."

"There is reason to hope and believe that opinion will gradually accomplish what it seems difficult, if not impossible, to secure by compulsory measures.—No people are more quick sighted as to their true interests than the inhabitants of this state. They cannot fail to see that the education of their children will be best secured by employing competent teachers, and that the avenues to wealth and distinction, though open to all, are beset with difficulties for those who enter them without the mental preparation which is necessary to enable them to contend successfully against more favored competitors. These convictions may and doubtless will be, the fruit of time; for they are to take the place of long established opinions, which are not often hastily eradicated. The reform of the Prussian system, as has already been observed, was gradual.—The teachers' seminaries were, for many years, few in number, and were altogether inadequate to supply the schools. Our departments for the education of teachers have been in operation but little more than three years; and there is certainly much ground for encouragement in the fact that the demands of the school districts upon these departments, for teachers, have been greater than they have been able to supply."

In reference to the plan of county supervision through the medium of local superintendents, he observes: "A regular supervision is indispensable to the success of every public or private undertaking. There is not a department of the government which is not subject to some direct and immediate control, and no individual appoints an agent for the management of any business, without reserving and exercising a superintendence over him. Conscious of the absolute necessity of such a provision in the common school system, the framers of the law endeavored to secure it by the election of town inspectors. But the object has not been obtained. The official reports show to what extent even the duty of simple visitation has been neglected. And when the nature of these visitations is considered, it will be obvious that if they were as frequent as might be desired, they could not accomplish the great purpose in view. To be of any avail, the inspection of schools must be conducted by those who are competent to judge of the qualifications of the teacher, and of the progress of the pupils, by examinations in the different studies pursued, and to suggest such improvements and modifications as will enable the student to derive the greatest amount of benefit from the schools. And time must be devoted not only to the schools and their masters, but to the trustees and inhabitants." "All writers on public education concur in the unanimous and decided opinion, that effectual inspection and supervision are more essential to the proper management of schools, and more indispensable to their improvement than any other agency or all other agencies combined; and the Superintendent does not hesitate to express his conviction that until they are provided, all efforts to improve the condition of the schools, to extend the range and elevate the character of the instruction in them, will be utterly hopeless. M. Cousin, the celebrated author on popular education, attributes the success of the schools in Holland almost enirely to the constant and unremitting inspection to which they are continually subjected, and demonstrates that wherever schools have failed, in other countries, to meet the public expectation in the degree and amount of instruction, it has been owing to the want of such supervision."

On the 15th of April, John A. King, Esq., from the committee on colleges, academies and common schools, of the assembly, submitted an elaborate report, accompanied by a bill embracing substantially the improvements and modifications of the system recommended by the Superintendent. This bill passed the assembly on the 12th of May subsequently, by a vote of fifty-eight to forty-seven; but no definitive action was had upon it in the senate, for want of time.

The following are extracts from the message of Gov. Seward, at the opening of the session of 1841:

"The number of children attending the common schools is about 570,000; and the whole number of children between five and sixteen years of age, as nearly as can be ascertained, is about 600,000. There are about eleven thousand common school districts in the state, in all of which schools are maintained during an average period of eight months in the year. Of these school districts there are very few which have not complied with the act providing for the establishment of school district libraries. * * * Although an injudicious choice of books is sometimes made, these libraries generally include history and biography, voyages and travels, works on natural history and the physical sciences, treatises upon agriculture, commerce, manufactures and the arts, and judicious selections from modern literature. Henceforth no citizen, who shall have improved the advantages offered by our common schools and the district libraries, will be without some scientific knowledge of the earth, its physical condition and its phenomena, the animals that inhabit it, the vegetables that clothe it with verdure, and the minerals under its surface; the physiology and the intellectual powers of man; the laws of mechanics and their practical uses; those of chemistry and their application to the arts, the principles of moral and political economy; the history of nations, and especially that of our own country; the progress and triumph of the democratic principle in the governments on this continent, and the prospects of its ascendency throughout the world; the trials and faith, valor and constancy of our ancestors; with all the inspiring examples of benevolence, virtue and patriotism, exhibited in the lives of the benefactors of mankind. The fruits of this enlightened and beneficent enterprise are chiefly to be gathered by our successors. But the present generation will not be altogether unrewarded. Although many of our citizens may pass the district library, heedless of the treasures it contains, the unpretending volumes will find their way to the fireside, diffusing knowledge, increasing domestic happiness, and promoting public virtue."

"When the census of 1850 shall be taken, I trust it will show, that within the borders of the state of New York, there is no child of sufficient years who is unable to read and write. I am sure it will then be acknowledged, that when ten years before, there were thirty thousand children growing up in ignorance and vice, a suggestion to seek them, wherever found, and win them to the ways of knowledge, and virtue by pursuasion, sympathy and kindness, was prompted by a sincere desire for the common good. I have no pride of opinion concerning the manner in which the education of those whom I have brought to your notice shall be secured; although I might derive satisfaction from the reflection. that amid abundant misrepresentations of the method suggested, no one has contended that it would be ineffectual, nor has any other plan been proposed. I observe, on the contrary, with deep regret, that the evil remains as before, and the question recurs not merely how, or by whom shall instruction be given, but whether it shall be given at all, or be altogether withheld. Others may be content with a system that erects free schools, and offers gratuitous instruction; but I trust I shall be allowed to entertain the opinion, that no system is perfect that does not accomplish what it proposes; that our system is therefore deficient in comprehensiveness, in the exact proportion of the children that it leaves uneducated; that knowledge, however acquired is better than ignorance; and that neither error, accident, nor prejudice, ought to be permitted to deprive the state of the education of her citizens. Cherishing such opinions, I could not enjoy the consciousness of having discharged my duty, if any effort had been omitted which was calculated to bring within the schools all who are destined to exercise the rights of citizenship; nor shall I feel that the system is perfect, or liberty safe, until that object be accomplished. Not personally concerned about such misapprehensions as have arisen, but desirous to remove every obstacle to the accomplishment of so important an object, I very freely declare, that I seek the education of those whom I have brought before you, not to perpetuate any prejudices or distinctions which deprive them of instruction, but in disregard of all such distinctions and prejudices. I solicit their education less from sympathy than because the welfare of the state demands it, and cannot dispense with it. As native citizens they are born to the right of suffrage. I ask that they may at least be taught to read and write; and in asking this, I require no more for them than I have dilligently endeavored to secure to the inmates of our penitentiaries, who forfeited that inestimable franchise by crime; and also to an unfortunate race, which having been plunged by us into degradation and ignorance, has been excluded from the franchise by an arbitrary property qualification incongruous with all our institutions. I have not recommended, nor do I seek, the education of any class in foreign languages, or in particular creeds or faiths; but fully believing, with the author of the Declaration of Independence, that even error may be safely tolerated where reason is left free to combat it, and therefore indulging no apprehensions from the influence of any language or creed among an enlightened people, I desire the education of the entire rising generation in all the elements of knowledge we possess, and in that tongue which is the universal language of our countrymen. To me, the most interesting of all our republican iustitutions is the common school. I seek not to disturb, in any manner, its peaceful and assiduous exercises, and least of all with contentions about faith or forms. I desire the education of all the children in the commonwealth in morality and virtue, leaving matters of conscience where, according to the principles of civil and religious liberty established by our constitution and laws, they rightfully belong."

In his annual report for the present year, the Superintendent strongly urges the continuance of the departments for the instruction of teachers connected with the academies, and the increase of the number of the institutions required to maintain such departments. "Normal Schools," he observes, "which are so strongly urged by some, must, after all, be essentially like these departments and the academies in which they are established. There must be a board of managers or trustees, teachers, a building, books and apparatus. These are already furnished by the existing academies, and there can be no intrinsic defect in them which should prevent their being made as useful as any normal schools. The change of name will not change the real nature of the institution. The sum of money which would be requisite to purchase ground, erect buildings for one normal school, and fit them for the purpose, would enable at least ten academies to maintain similar schools in buildings already prepared, and under managers already organized. The Superintendent does not mean to under-rate those schools, nor to depreciate the benevolent motives of those who recommend them. He acknowledges, and indeed earnestly urges, the inestimable value and absolute necessity of institutions in which our youth may be prepared for the business of teaching. But he would use the means we already have at hand for the purpose without incurring what seems to him the needless expense of providing others of a similar character. He would respectfully recommend the extension of the public patronage to all the academies in the state, to enable them to establish teachers' departments, and in those counties where there are no academies, the establishment of normal schools. For the latter purpose there might be a provision, authorizing the boards of supervisors in such counties to raise the necessary sums to procure suitable grounds and erect proper buildings; and upon their being completed appropriating from the funds of the state a sufficient sum to employ competent teachers." He, however, remarks in conclusion, "One model school or more might be advantageously established in some central part of the state, to which teachers and those intending to become such might repair, to acquire the best methods of conducting our common schools."

Professor Potter, of Union College, who, at the request of the department, had visited and personally inspected during the year 1840, several of the teachers' departments connected with the academies, submitted a very able report of the result of his examination closing with the following suggestion: "I would suggest whether some means might not be adopted for training a class of teachers with more especial reference to country common schools, and to primary schools in villages and cities—teachers whose attainments should not extend much beyond the common English branches, but whose minds should be awakened by proper influences—who should be made familiar by practice with the best modes of teaching, and who should come under strong obligations to teach for at least two or three years. In Prussia and France normal schools are supported at the public expense; most of the pupils receive both board and tuition gratuitously; but at the close of the course they give bonds to refund the whole amount received, unless they teach, under the direction of the government, for a certain number of years. That such schools, devoted exclusively to the preparation of teachers, have some advantages over any other method, is sufficiently apparent from the experience of other nations; and it has occurred to me that as a *supplementary* to our present system, the establishment of one in this state might be eminently useful. If placed under proper auspices, and located near the capitol, where it could enjoy the supervision of the Superintendent of Common Schools, and be visited by the members of the legislature, it might contribute in many ways to raise the tone of instruction throughout the state."

The Superintendent renewed his recommendation of such a modification of the common school system, as was suggested in his report of the preceding year. He contrasts the present situation of the schools with their condition in 1815, the number of organized and reporting districts having increased from 2,631 to 10,397; the number of children instructed from 140,706 to 572,995; and the amount paid from the treasury towards defraying the compensation of teachers from $46,398 to $220,000; and after referring to the fact that $275,000 were annually distributed in taxes, and nearly $500,000 on rate-bills, for the support of the schools, observes, " A people who have thus freely expended their money and appropriated their private means for the education of their children, to an amount nearly double the expense of administering the government cannot with any truth or justice, be said to be indifferent to the subject. And when we find thirty thousand trustees of school districts gratuitously rendering their services, and making their returns with order, regularity and promptitude, we ought not to deny their appreciation of the value of the labor in which they engage, nor their merit in performing it. It is no slight proof of the value of a system which is thus administered without compulsion. Its fruits are seen in the education of one-fourth of an entire population, and of nearly every child of a proper age for the primary schools; in the advance of the wages paid to teachers, a clear indication that a higher degree of talent is employed and appreciated; and in the interest almost universally excited among our fellow-citizens of every class, in the success of the effort. Still, like every other human institution, it is susceptible of constant improvement. This is not to be accomplished by sudden changes which derange the machinery, and which, when effected, will probably be found to require alteration; and least of all by those schemes which are so comprehensive as to be incapable of practical execution. Amendments, when experience has indicated their necessity, may be gradually incorporated in the system, without obstructing it. And the introduction of new elements to aid, invigorate and sustain what we have, and in keeping with it, will be more likely to accomplish their purpose than if they were antagonistic to what is already established."

On the 26th of May, 1841, the legislature, by a nearly unanimous vote, passed the act drawn up by Mr. Spencer, and reported by the literature committees of the two houses, providing for the appointmeut by the board of supervisors of each county, biennially, of a County Superintendent of common schools, charged with the general supervision of the interests of the several schools under his jurisdiction. The various powers, functions and duties of this officer, will hereafter be more particularly adverted to. The number of town inspectors of schools was reduced to two; the qualifications of voters at school district meetings, specifically defined; provisions made for the establishment of schools for the instruction of colored children; a subscription for so many copies of a monthly periodical exclusively devoted to the cause of education, as should supply each district in the state, authorized; and various minor amendments in the details of the system made.

Under this act, County Superintendents were appointed in the various counties of the state; and under full and ample instructions from the Superintendent, entered in the succeeding winter upon the discharge of their official duties. S. S. Randall, then a clerk in the department, was appointed by Mr. Spencer, general Deputy Superintendent, in accordance with one of the provisions of the act.

By an ordinance of the Regents of the University, of the 4th of May, 1841, the sum of $300 was directed to be annually apportioned to *two* academies in each of the Senate districts, for the maintenance of the departments for the education of teachers of common schools; in addition to which seven other academies were provided with similar departments, under the act of 1838, requiring their establishment in every institution receiving a share of the literature fund equal to $700 per annum. In October of this year Mr. Spencer was transferred to a seat in the Cabinet, as Secretary of War; and by a provision in the act of 1841, above referred to, the duties of Superintendent of Common Schools devolved upon his general deputy, until the vacancy was filled by the legislature in the month of February ensuing.

Of the energy, ability and transcendent success with which the brief administration of Mr. SPENCER was conducted, it would be superfluous here to speak. The value and importance of the reform effected under his auspices, and chiefly through his indefatigable exertions, in the system of common schools, by the adoption of the plan of local supervision through the agency of County Superintendents, will be best appreciated by the fact that every successive legislature since convened, through every mutation of party, has, with unexampled unanimity, sanctioned and sustained the system so devised and matured: that the practical operation of that system has immeasurably elevated the condition of the common schools throughout the state, advanced the standard of popular educatiou, enlisted the efficient co-operation of an enlightened public sentiment, and laid the foundations for that universal diffusion of knowledge, which under the guidance of sound moral and religious principles, is destined to sustain, and we would fain hope, to perpetuate, the fabric of our free institutions.

On the 5th of January, 1842, the acting Superintendent, (S. S. RANDALL) transmitted to the legislature the annual report required from the department, from which it appeared that the whole number of school districts in the state was 10,886; the number of children between the ages of five and sixteen, residing in the several districts from which reports had been received (exclusive of the city of New York,) 583,347, and the number of children under instruction 603,583, being an increase of 30,588 over that of the preceding year.

Administration of SAMUEL YOUNG—*Town Superintendents, Normal School and Teachers' Institutes*—1842 *to* 1846.

On the 7th of February succeeding, the Hon. SAMUEL YOUNG, of Saratoga, wa s appointed Secretary of State and Superintendent of Common Schools; and in May following he met the several county superintendents in convention at Utica, and possessed himself of a thorough acquaintance with the details and practical operations of the system whch he had been called upon to supervise. In his first annual report, (Jan. 12, 1843) he recommended the reduction of the academical departments for the education of teachers of common schools to four, and the appropriation of a sufficient sum to establish and maintain a normal school at the seat of government, where it might be subjected to the immediate supervision as well of the department as of the representativesof the people during the sessions of the legislature; the abolition of the offices of commissioner and inspector of common schools, and the substitution of a town superintendent; the extension of the official term of trustees of school districts to three years, one to be elected annually; the vesting of appellate powers in the first instance in the several county superintendents; the perpetuation of the district library system, with suitable modifications and restrictions, and various other incidental and minor reforms of the system: most of which, with the exception of that portion relating to a normal school, in pursuance of his suggestions, and on an able and argumentative report from Mr. HULBURD, of St. Lawrence, chairman of the committee on colleges, academies and common schools, of the assembly, were incorporated by the legislature in the act of April 16, 1843. At this period the number of school districts had attained the number of 10,893; the number of children between 5 and 16, residing in the several reporting districts, was 601,765, and the whole number under instruction 598,749. The Superintendent acknowledges a "decided predisposition" on his accession to office, "to exercise whatever influence he might possess" for the abolition of the system of county supervision. But after attending the convention of county superintendents, and possessing himself of a thorough acquaintance with the previous defects and present advantages of that system, he thus sums up the conclusions to which he had arrived:

"Deputy Superintendents properly qualified for the discharge of their functions, possessing a competent knowledge of the moral, intellectual, and physical sciences, familiar with all the modern improvements in elementary instruction, and earnestly intent on elevating the condition of our common schools, can do much more to accomplish this desirable result, than all the other officers connected with the system. Acting on a broader theatre, they can perform more efficiently all that supervision which has heretofore been so deplorably neglected, or badly executed. The system of deputy superintendents is capable of securing, and can be made to secure, the following objects:

"It can produce a complete and efficient supervision of all the schools of the state, in reference as well as to their internal management, as to their external details:

"It can be made to unite all the schools of the state into one great system; making the advancement of each the ambition of all; furnishing each with the means of attaining the highest standard of practical excellence, by communicating to it every improvement discovered or suggested in every or any of the others:

"It can do much towards dissipating the stolid indifference which paralyses many portions of the community, and towards arousing, enlightening and enlisting public sentiment, in the great work of elementary instruction, by systematic and periodical appeals to the inhabitants of each school district, in the form of lectures, addresses, &c.

"It can be made to dismiss from our schools all immoral and incompetent teachers, and to secure the services of such only as are qualified and efficient, thereby elevating the grade of the schoolmaster, and infusing new vitality into the school.

"An attentive examination of the interesting reports of the deputy superintendents will clearly show that the accomplishment of several of the most important of these objects is already in a state of encouraging progression.

"In these times of commercial paralysis, monetary pressure and impending taxation, superinduced by causes which were clearly foreseen, and might easily have been obviated, it is very far from the intention of the Superintendent to advocate any system which shall add weight to the existing burdens of the community. Instead of this, it will be manifest that the system of deputy superintendents can be made to supersede official duty heretofore badly performed, and taxation heretofore imposed with little resulting utility, to an amount greatly exceeding the expenses of this system."

Gov. Bouck, in his annual message to the legislature of 1844, thus alludes to the condition and prospects of the common schools:

"No interest of the State is entitled to a more favorable regard, or a greater share of attention at the hands of the legislature, than that of public instruction. The intellectual and moral culture of the six or seven hundred thousand children who are speedily to succeed the generation now on the stage of active life, and to assume the duties and responsibilities, as well of government as of society, in all its departments, involves, in its consequences, the existence and destinies of the Republic itself, and cannot be neglected without danger to the vital interests of free institutions. The elementary education of the youth of the state has attracted the attention, and occupied a prominent position in the policy of, the executive and legislative departments, from a very early period of our existence as a state. A perpetual fund, the revenue of which, for several years past, has secured an annual apportionment from the the treasury, for the benefit of the common schools, of $110,000, has been specifically appropriated, by a provision of the constitution, to this object; and since the year 1839, the additional amount of $165,000 has annually been appropriated, by the liberal and enlightened policy of the state, from the revenue of the United States Deposite Fund, to the same object, and to the procurement of common school libraries in the several school districts of the state. An amount in the aggregate equal to these two sums ($275,000) is required to be annually raised upon the taxable property in the several towns; and the proceeds of this fund, augmented by nearly an equal amount, contributed by the inhabitants of the several districts, on rate bills, by various local funds, and by sums voluntarily raised for this purpose by the inhabitants of the towns, are applied exclusively to the payment of the wages of competent and approved teachers, and to the purchase of suitable books for the school district libraries.

"The substitution of a single officer, charged with the supervision of the common schools of each town, for the Board of Commissioners and inspectors formerly existing, in connection with the supervisory and appellate powers of the several county Superintendents, as defined by the law of the last session, seems to have met with the general approbation and concurrence of the people. Conventions and associations of the friends of education have, during the past year, been held in almost every section of the state, indicating a concentration of interest, and a direction of effort to this great subject, which cannot fail of producing the most salutary results. The standard of qualification of teachers has been materially advanced; parents and the people generally manifest an increased interest in the welfare and prosperity of these elementary institutions of learning; and there are the most abundant reasons for anticipating a steady and continued improvement in all the elements of our extended system of common school education."

There were in the state, as appears by the annual report of the Superintendent, (Jan. 13, 1844) 10,875 organized school districts, 670,995 children between the ages of five and sixteen, exclusive of those residing in the city of New York; and 657,782 children taught during the year. "We may reasonably," observes the Superinteodent, "congratulate ourselves upon the accession of a new order of things, in relation to the practical workings of our system. Through the medium of an efficient county and town supervision, we have succeeded not only in preparing the way for a corps of teachers thoroughly competent to communicate physical, intellectual and moral instruction—themselves enlightened and capable of enlightening their pupils—but also in demolishing the numerous barriers which have hitherto prevented all intercommunication between the several districts. An extended feeling of interest in the condition and progress of the school has been awakened; and in addition to the periodical inspection of the county and town superintendendents, the trustees and inhabitants are now, in many portions of the state, beginning to visit the schools of their districts; striving to ascertain their advancement; to encourage the exertions of teachers and pupils, and to remove every obstacle resulting from their previous indifference. Incompetent teachers are beginning to find the avenues to the common school closed against them; and the demand on the part of the districts for a higher grade of instructors, is creating a supply of enlightened educators, adequate to the task of advancing the youthful mind in its incipient efforts to acquire knowledge. The impetus thus communicated to the schools of one town and county, is speedily diffused to those of others. Through frequent and periodical meetings of town and county associations of teachers and friends of education, the improvements adopted in any one district are made known to all; and the experience, observations and suggestions of each county Superintendent, annually communicated through their reports, to all. By these means the stream of popular education, purified at its source and relieved from many of its former obstructions, is dispensing its invigorating waters over a very considerable portion of the state.

"The reports of the several county Superintendents exhibit unequivocal evidence of effiicent exertions on their part, in the performance of the responsible duties assigned them by law and by the instructions of this department. To their efforts is to be attributed, to a very great extent, the revolution in public sentiment, by which the district school from being the object of general aversion and reproach, begins to attract the attention and regard of all. To their enlightened labors for the elevation and advancement of these elementary institutions, we owe it in a great measure, that new and improved modes of teaching, of government and of discipline have succeeded in a very large proportion of the districts, to those which have hitherto prevailed; that a higher grade of qualifications for teachers has been almost universally required; that parents have been induced to visit and take an interest in the schools; that private and select schools have been to a considerable extent discountenanced, and the entire energies of the inhabitants of districts concentrated on the district school; and that the importance, the capabilities and extended means of usefulness of these nurseries of knowledge and virtue, are beginning to be adequately appreciated in nearly every section of the state. Collectively considered, these officers have well vindicated the confidence reposed in them by the legislature and the people. and justified the anticipation of the friends of edution."

The attention of the friends of Common School Education was now powerfully and systematically directed to the subject of a State Normal School for the proper instruction and preparation of teachers. To this end, Mr. Hulburd, of St. Lawrence, who was again at the head of the Assembly Committee on Colleges, Academies and common schools, visited, during the early part of the session, the several Normal Schools of Massachusetts, observed their parctical working, made himself thoroughly acquainted with the principles upon which they were founded, and collected a valuable body of information in regard to the general history and specific operations of similar institutions in Europe.

On the 22d of March, he submitted an elaborate and eloquent report, embracing the entire subject, reviewing the legislation of the State in reference to the various appropriations made from the literature fund, to the several Academies, for the purpose of organizing and establishing Teachers Departments; showing that these institutions were wholly incomptent to supply the demand for competent teachers, throughout the state; giving a concise history of the origin and progress of Normal Schools in Europe and America, with a detailed account of their operations in Massachusetts; and strongly recommending the appropriation from the income of the literature fund of $9,600 for the establishment, and $10,000 annually thereafter for the support and maintenance of a State Normal School, to be located in the city of Albany, for the education and proper preparation of teachers of common schools, of both sexes, and to be composed of pupils selected from the several counties of the state in proportion to the representation of such counties in the popular branch of the Legislature.

After a full recapitulation of the previous legislation of the state, in reference to Academical Departments for the instruction of teachers the committee observe:

"It will appear that the principal reliance of the friends and supporters of the common schools for an adequate supply of teachers has, from a very early period, been upon the academies—that the inability of the latter to supply this demand, induced, in 1827 an increase of $150,000 of the fund applicable to their support, and this for the express purpose of enabling them to accomplish this object: that the Regents of the University, the guardians of these institutions, characterized this increase of the fund as an unwonted and extraordinary act of liberality on the part of the state towards them—explicitly recognized the condition, or rather the avowed expectations on which it was granted—accepted the trust, and undertook to perform those conditions and to fulfil those expectations: that, to use the language of one of the Superintendents, "the design of the law was not sustained by the measures necessary to give it the form and effect of a system;" that to remedy this evil, one academy was specially designated in each Senate district, with an endowment of $500 to provide the necessary means and facilities of instruction, and an annual appropriation of $400 for the maintenance of a department for the education of teachers, and soon afterwards the sum of $28,000 added to the literature fund from the avails of the U. S. Deposit fund while eight additional academies were required to organize and maintain similar departments: that finally the number of these departments was augmented to twenty-three, and every exertion put forth to secure the great results originally contemplated in their establishment; and that in the judgment of successive Superintendents of common schools, the Regents of the University, and the most eminent and practical friends of education throughout the state, these institutions, whether considered in the aggregate or with reference to those specially designated from time to time, for the performance of this important duty of supplying the common schools with competent teachers, have not succeeded in the accomplishment of that object. Having, therefore, to revert again to the language of the Superintendent before referred to, "proved inadequate to the ends proposed;" may not now "a *change of plan* be insisted on, without being open to the objection of abandoning a system which has not been fairly tested?" And have the academies any just reason to complain if they are not longer permitted to enjoy undiminished the liberal appropriation conferred upon them by the state *for a specific object*—an object which they have not been able satisfactorily to accomplish?"

The committee then proceed minutely to trace the origin, progress and practical operation of Normal Schools in Europe and in this country, and after a general discussion of their applicability and expediency under the peculiar circumstances which exist in our own state, and the recommendation of an appropriation for the organization and support of a Normal School at the seat of government, for the education and training of teachers, observe:

"It will be noticed that the committee speak of the establishment of one Normal School: Did our present means seem to warrant it, the committee would, with confidence, recommend the immediate establishment of *at least one in each of the eight Senatorial districts*. If one is now established, and that is properly endowed and organized, there cannot be a doubt that not only one will be called for in each of the eight Senatorial districts, but in a brief period very many of the large counties will insist upon having one established within their limits. The establishment of *one* is but an experiment—if that can be called an experiment, which for more than a century has been in operation, without a known failure—which, if successful, will lead the way for several others. It is believed that several of the Academies now in operation can and will be converted into Normal Seminaries, when the period arrives for the rapid improvement of education; in this way there will be no loss of academic investment, and the great interest of the public will be as well or better subserved than they are at present.

"The committee believe the experiment should be tried at the Capital; if it cannot be tested in the presence of all the people, it should be before all the representatives of the people. As a government measure, it is untried in this state; the result, therefore, will be of deep interest. Here at each annual session of the legislature, can be seen for what and how the public money is expended; here can be seen the exhibition of the pupils of the Seminary and of the Model School; here, if unsuccessful no report of interested officials can cover up its failure, or prevent the abandonment of the experiment; here citizens from all parts of the state, who resort to the Capital during the session of the legislature, the terms of the courts, &c., can have an opportunity of examining the workings of the Normal school system, of learning the best method of teaching, and all the improvements in the science and practice of the art; those who in the spring and autumn, pass through the city, and to and from the Great Metropolis, and those who from all parts of the union make their annual pilgrimage to the Fountain of Health, will pause here to see what the Empire State is doing to promote the education of her people."

On the seventh of May, succeeding, the bill reported by the Committee was passed into a law, by which the sum of $9,600 was appropriated for the first year, and $10,000 annually for five years thereafter and until otherwise directed by law, for the establishment and support of a Normal school to be located at Albany, and to be under the supervision, management and direction of the Superintendent of common schools and the Regents of the University, who were authorized and required, from time to time, to make all needful rules and regulations; to fix the number and compensation of teachers and others to be employed therein; to prescribe the preliminary examination and the terms and conditions on which the pupils should be received and instructed; to apportion such pupils among the respective counties, conforming as nearly as might be to the ratio of population; and generally, to provide in all things for the good government and management of the school. They were also required to appoint an executive committee, consisting of five persons, one of whom should in all cases be the State Superintendent of common schools, to whom the immediate government and direction of the institution should be committed, subject to such general rules as the Regents might prescribe, and whose duty it should be to make full and detailed reports from time to time to the Superintendent and Regents, and to recommend such rules and regulations as they might deem proper for the school. The Superintendent and Regents were likewise required annually to transmit to the legislature, an account of their proceedings and expenditures.

In pursuance of this act, the Regents of the University, proceeded on the 1st of June thereafter, to the appointment of an Executive Committee, consisting of the Superintendent of common schools (Col. Young) Rev. Alonzo Potter, Rev. William H. Campbell, Hon. Gideon Hawley and Francis Dwight, Esq., who held their first meeting on the 20th of June. Having obtained from the corporation of the city of Albany, the lease for five years of a commodious building for the use of the school, they adopted the necessary measures for its organization and establishment, by requesting the Board of Supervisors of the several counties, to appoint on the nomination of the county Superintendents, a number of pupils, corresponding to their respective representation in the Assembly; by the appointment of David P. Page, of Newburyport, Mass., as Principal, George R. Perkins, of Utica, as Professor of Mathematics, Frederick I. Ilsley, of Albany as teacher of Music, and J. B. Howard, of Rensselaer, as teacher of Drawing; and by making such general rules and regulations as they deemed expedient and necessary, in reference to the course of study, management and discipline of the school. On the 18th of December, the school was opened, by a public address from the Superintendent of common schools. Twenty-nine pupils only were in attendence; this number, however, speedily increased to upwards of one hundred; and an experimental or model school was at the commencement of the second term, attached to the institution, comprising upwards of a hundred children of both sexes,

At the opening of the session of the legislature of 1845, Gov. Wright, in his annual message to both Houses, thus adverted to the subject of common school education:

"No public fund of the state is so unpretending, yet so all pervading—so little seen, yet so universally felt—so mild it its exactions, yet so bountiful in its benefits—so little feared or courted, and yet so powerful, as this fund for the support of common schools. The other funds act upon the secular interests of society, its business, its pleasures, its pride, its passions, its vices, its misfortunes. This acts upon its mind and its morals. Education is to free institutions what bread is to human life, the staff of their existence. The office of this fund is to open and warm the soil, and sow the seed from which this element of freedom must grow and ripen into maturity; and the health or sickness of the growth will measure the extent and security of our liberties. The thankfulness we owe to those who have gone before us, for the institution of this fund, for its constitutional protection, and for its safe and prudent administration hitherto, we can best repay by imitating their example and improving upon their work, as the increased means placed in our hands shall give us the ability.

"Few, if any instances, are upon record in which a fund of this description has been administered, and its bounties dispensed through a period of forty years, with so few suspicions, accusations, or complaints of the interference of either political or religious biases to disturb the equal balance by which its benefits should be extended to our whole population. This should continue as it has been. Our school fund is not instituted to make our children and youth either partizans in politics, or sectarians in religion ; but to give them education, intelligence, sound principles, good moral habits, and a free and independent spirit ; in short, to make them American freemen and American citizens, and to qualify them to judge and choose for themselves in matters of politics, religion and government. Such an administration of the fund as shall be calculated to render this qualification the most perfect for the mature minds, with the fewest influences tending to bias the judgment or incline the choice, will be the most consonant with our duties, and with the best interests of our constituents. Under such an administration, education will flourish most and the peace and harmony of society be best preserved."

From the annual report of the Superintendent, (Col. YOUNG) it appeared that the whole number of school districts in the state, was 10,990 ; the whole number of children between the ages of five and sixteen, was 696,548 ; the number of children of all ages, actually taught in the common schools during the year reported, 709,156, or more than 50,000 beyond the number taught during the preceding year ; the amount paid for teachers' wages $992,222 ; of which $447,566 was raised on rate-bills ; the amount paid for library purposes $94,950.54 ; and the number of volumes in the several district libraries 1,038,396.

"A more just appreciation on the part of the public," observes the Superintendent, in concluding his report, "not only of the importance of adequate intellectual and moral culture in our common schools, but of the responsibilities of teachers, is beginning to prevail. There is much in the prospect thus opened to us, cheering and encouraging to the friends of free institutions, to the friends of education, and of civil, social and moral progress. The great idea of education, in its most comprehensive acceptation, consists in that development, culture and discipline of all the faculties of our nature, which shall fit us for the highest sphere of usefulness, and the highest degree of enjoyment of which that nature, in the circumstances by which we are surrounded, is susceptible.

"This conception of that preliminary training which is to give us the complete and efficient control of the energies, physical and moral, of our common humanity, has at length, it is to be hoped, assumed its place as the foundation of the science of elementary instruction. Institutions for the preparation of teachers upon the most approved models, are already diffusing far and wide, a more enlightened and practical system of mental culture, by furnishing to the schools instructors of a high grade of qualifications, intellectual and moral ; and these instructors, in their turn, communicate elements of knowledge and the means of self-improvement, to the pupils committed to their charge. The general substitution of *knowledge* for the parrot-like rote, by which a vigorous and retentive *memory* was made the principal test of mental capacity, may be regarded as one of the strongest indications of the prevalence of sounder principles, and of a progressive revolution in the theory and practice of education.

"These are the principal agencies through whose united influence our common schools have imbibed that spirit of improvement which is perceptible in nearly every section of the state, and which must ultimately renovate our entire system of public education, and exert a beneficial influence upon all our institutions, civil, social and political. In the late strongly contested election for the chief magistrate of the United States, the result was determined for good or for evil, by 237,600 votes cast in this state ; and the result will, doubtless, eventuate in a course of measures which will affect, beneficially or otherwise, the interests of some twenty millions of human beings, for a series of years to come. The whole number of children now under the course of instruction in the common schools of this state, exceeds

700,000; estimating one-half of this number as females, and making a still farther deduction of 100,000, or one-seventh of the whole, for removal from the state, death, or inability from any other cause, to discharge the duties appertaining to the citizen—and we have remaining 250,000, who, upon a reasonable estimate will, within a less period than fifteen years, emerge from our common schools invested with all the functions of popular sovereignty; a number exceeding by upwards of 12,000 that which has recently given to the Union a Chief Magistrate.

"On the flourishing condition of our schools repose the hopes of the present and the destinies of the future. Without a sound, moral and intellectual education, the functions of self government can neither be duly appreciated nor successfully maintained. The constitution of several of the South American Republics appeared theoretically to secure human liberty. But paper provisions are powerless unless they are also impressed on the hearts, and combined with the intelligence of the people. Without an accurate knowlede of their rights and duties, and a determination to maintain them, no community can long be free; and the melancholy truth that the South American Republics have fallen into revolutionary decrepitude, and degenerated into military despotisms, affords to us an impressive admonition. Indeed without going beyond our own borders, premonitious of an anti-social spirit—of insubordination to the law—of combining to perpetrate violence, riot, incendiarism and murder—are sufficiently alarming in their rapid increase during the last few years. If the same spirit pervaded the majority of the community, the existing government would be at an end; and as human society cannot exist without a superintending power of protection, the aid of some more energetic and despotic form of government would necessarily be invoked to administer justice, to maintain order, and to shield the poor from the exactions of the rich,—the weak from the aggressions of the strong.

"The great extent of the American Republic—its rapidly increasing population—the diversity of habits, pursuits, productions, and interests, some of which are regarded as hostile to others—render necessary at all times, the cultivation of a liberal spirit of forbearance and conciliation. Without the diffusion of education, such a spirit, in sufficient strength to maintain harmony, cannot exist. It may be safely affirmed, that there is now no people of equal numbers on the face of the earth, who, if placed uuder such institutions as ours, would maintain the government for a single year. And unless moral and intellectual culture, shall at least keep pace with the increase of numbers, this republic will assuredly fall. On the careful cultivation in our schools, of the minds of the young, the entire success or the absolute failure of the great experiment of self government is wholly dependent; and unless that cultivation is increased, and made more effective than it has yet been, the conviction is solemnly impressed by the signs of the times, that the American Union, now the asylum of the oppressed and "the home of the free," will ere long share the melancholy fate of every former attempt of self government. That Union is and must be sustained by the moral and intellectual powers of the community, and every other power is wholly ineffectual. Physical force may generate hatred, fear and repulsion; but can never produce Union. The only salvation for the republic is to be sought for in our schools. It is here that the seeds of liberty are sown, and made to germinate and grow, and produce rich fruit in abundance. Every improvement that can be given to these primary institutions, affords an additional guaranty for the permanent maintenance of rational freedom.

"The duration of the life of man should be estimated, not by the years of his physical existence, which would degrade him to the level of the brute—but by the period of the expansion and enjoyment of his moral and intellectual faculties. Thence it has been affirmed with philosophic truth, that "he who shortens the road to human knowledge lengthens life." The cradle and the grave are in such close proximity, even when the interval is most extended, that human existence may be regarded as nearly a blank, unless the early portion of the brief space by which they are separated is seduously devoted to the developement of the mind. The undying part of our nature has been impressed by its creator with an unconquerable desire for knowledge, not that limited acquaintance with the external forms of things which is bestowed upon the animals by instinct—but a knowledge vastly more minute and exclusive, which embraces within its scope, all the properties and laws, both of mind and matter. The earth itself with all its appendages, is much too small a theatre, to satiate the inquisitiveness, even of children; and if human power were commensurate with human aspirations, the daring ken of man would be thrown through the abyss of Heaven, to the *ultima thùle* of the works of God—to the farthest verge in fathomless space, in which the energies of creative power have yet been consummated—to regions where the embryon *nebulae* of unformed worlds are in the transition or the quiescent state, obedient to the primeval fiat of the Almighty."

The introduction of *Teachers' Institutes* as an elementary portion of the system of Public Instruction, which was effected at about this period, constitutes an important feature in the progress of improvement, with reference to the practical qualification of teachers of common schools. The subject was first brought to the attention of the friends of education, by a series of resolutions submitted to the Tompkins County Teachers' Association, in October 1842, by J. S. DENMAN, the County Superintendent of Tompkins, setting forth the necessity of united and efficient action on the part of teachers to elevate their profession and the standard of common school education generally, and recommending the establishment, in that County of a Teachers' Institute, where all the teachers might meet semi-annually in the spring and fall, preparatory to the commencement of the respective summer and winter terms: and spend from two to four weeks, in receiving instruction from efficient instructors, in listening to lectures from scientific men, and in the discussion of plans for the improvement of schools. The first Teachers' Institute was opened at Ithaca, on the 4th day of April 1843, under the management and direction of Mr. Denman, who had engaged the services of Salem Town Esq., the Rev. David Powell and Prof. James Thompson, of Auburn, as instructors and lecturers. Twenty eight teachers were in attendance, and instruction was given daily for a term of two weeks in the best mode of Governing and teaching common schools, including a critical analysis and review of the various elementary branches; and sundry advanced branches not heretofore in use in the Schools generally. During the Autumn of the same year, several similar institutions were opened in different sections of the State; and in the succeeding year their operations were greatly enlarged and extended. In his annual report for 1845 the State Superintendent thus alludes to them:

"In no less than seventeen of the largest counties, Teachers' Institutes have been established during the past two years, in which upwards of one thousand teachers have been instructed during periods varying from two to six or eight weeks, immediately preceding the commencement of their respective terms of instruction, by the most competent and experienced educators whose services could be procured, in conjunction with the county Superintendent. These associations are wholly voluntary, and the expenses, including board, tuition, and the use of convenient rooms, apparatus, &c., have hitherto been defrayed exclusively by the teachers. The course of instruction consists generally of a critical and thorough review of all the elementary branches required to be taught in the common schools, full expositions and illustrations of the most approved methods of communicating knowledge to the young, and of the proper government and discipline of schools, and a mutual interchange of views and opinions among the teachers, instructors and Superintendent. Among the numerous improvements which the experience of past imperfections has introduced into the practical operation of our common schools, there is none which combines so much utility and value as these local and temporary institutions; and in the judgment of the Superintendent they are highly deserving of legislative aid. A concise exposition of their general features, the mode of instruction adopted, and its effects not only upon the teachers, but upon the whole character of the schools under their charge, and upon the public sentiment generally, has, it is understood, been prepared by Mr. SALEM TOWN, of Cayuga, a veteran teacher, who has himself most ably and efficiently contributed to the establishment and success of this species of instruction."

In reviewing the administration of the common school system, by Col. YOUNG, it is impossible not to perceive the vast impulse which was given to all its varied operations by the efficiency, energy and public spirit of that distinguished statesman. Bringing to the discharge of the peculiar duties of the office of Superintendent no previous experience, and strong prejudices against some of the most cherished features of the system of public instruction, he not only speedily rendered himself familiar with all its details, but divesting himself of all these unfavorable pre-conceptions which had obtained possession of his mind, dispassionately surveyed the entire bearings of the whole system, and having convinced himself of its value and utility, devoted his best energies and all his powerful influence to its advancement and improvement. The plan of county and town supervision, the Normal school and Teachers' Institutes, and District Libraries, were cherished and strengthened by his exertions; and the impress of his vigorous mind and strong understanding will long remain upon the common school system of our State.

Upon his retirement from the office of Secretary of state, Col. YOUNG received from the Regents of the University, the appointment of member of the Executive Committee of the Normal School, in the place of Dr. POTTER, who had been elected Bishop of the diocese of Pennsylvania and had removed to that State. HARMANUS BLEEKER, Esq., of the city of Albany was also appointed a member of the Executive Committee to fill the vacancy occasioned by the death of FRANCIS DWIGHT, Esq., which took place on the 18th of December, 1845.

The removal from the State of Dr. POTTER, and the death of Mr. DWIGHT in the fulness of his faculties and the apparent meridian of his usefulness, were deeply and extensively felt by the friends of common school education. In all the measures which had been canvassed and adopted for the improvement and elevation of our systems of public instruction, both these gentlemen had borne a conspicuous and an efficient part; and to their constant and uniform co-operation with the legislature and the executive authorities of the state charged with the general supervision of these great interests, the success of those measures is to a very considerable extent due. As the conductor of the District School Journal, as County Superintendent and member of the Board of Education of the city of Albany, and as a member of the Executive Committee of the State Normal School, Mr. DWIGHT essentially contributed to the advancement of popular education, and to the general diffusion of sound principles of elementary instruction throughout the state.

Administration of NATHANIEL S. BENTON—*Failure of the effort to ingraft the Free School System on the Constitution—Abolition of the office of County Superintendent.*

On the 3d day of February, 1845, the Hon. NATHANIEL S. BENTON, of Herkimer, was appointed by joint ballot of both Houses of the Legislature, Secretary of State and Superintendent of Common Schools: and entered upon the discharge of his duties on the 6th of the same month.

From his first annual report, bearing date on the 15th of January, 1846, it appeared that the whole number of school districts in the state, on the first day of July preceding, was 11,018; the number of children between the ages of five and sixteen, residing in the state, on the first day of January, 1845, 690,914; the whole number of children of all ages, taught in the common schools during the year 1844, 736,045; the amount of public money applied to the payment of teachers' wages, $629,856.94; the amount raised on rate-bills, $458,127.78, making an aggregate of $1,088,084.72, and the amount of public money applied to library purposes and school apparatus, $95,159.25. The number of volumes in the several district libraries was 1,145,250, being an increase, during the year reported, of 106,854 volumes.

In reference to the fund applicable to the support of district libraries, the Superintendent observes:

"It is not proposed to take from the inhabitants of the school districts the power of controlling the direction that shall be given to that part of the fund denominated library money; but leave them to make such application thereof, either to the purchase of books, or the apparatus before named, or apply the whole or a part of it to the payment of teachers; subject, however, to the approval of the department. After the districts have been supplied with a given number of books, in proportion to the children in them, and after the appropriate school apparatus and maps shall have been obtained, it is believed that in many instances, it would prove highly salutary, to authorize the inhabitants of such districts to apply this money to the payment of teachers' wages generally, or of the rate-bills of exempted scholars. To ensure a faithful compliance with the conditions required, it may be necessary in all cases, to vest in the department a supervision over this expenditure. This will incite an interest in the district and its officers, where it is desired to make this application to preserve their libraries, maps, globes, black-boards and other apparatus, with the best possible care."

On the subject of teachers' institutes, the Superintendent says:

"Teachers' Institutes" and "teachers' drills," have been held during the the last year, in nearly thirty counties in the state, and were attended by more than three thousand school teachers, for periods varying from two to to four and eight weeks of continued session. These voluntary associations are rapidly spreading over our entire state, and are destined soon, to occupy much of the public attention. An ardent desire for improvement is seated in the minds of professional teachers; "the school-master is abroad," in search of that educational knowledge which will qualify him to discharge the important duties of his profession, and elevate him and his vocation in public esteem. The Principal of the State Normal School, and the Professor of Mathematics, attended a number of these county "Institutes" during the last autumn, and several of its graduates were called upon to preside over their proceedings and conduct the courses of instruction pursued in them. The pertinent and instructive lectures of the former, and the eminently successful efforts of the latter, have been duly appreciated by the members of the institutes where these services were performed, and that appreciation has been manifested in the most decided terms of approval.—It may not be out of place to remark here, that the expense of the "associations" are paid by the teachers themselves, which is somewhat burthensome to those who are females, and to others possessing limited means of support. In answer to a suggestion that some pecuniary aid and encouragement should be granted to the members attending these "institutes" by the legislature, it has been remarked that these teachers are only fitting themselves to pursue a profession for mere private gain or personal advantage, and why should this particular class more than any other, be selected as the recipients of legislative bounty and favor? But does this objection present a full and fair statement of all the facts bearing upon this subject? Our laws require that a school shall be taught in a district, at least four months in the year by a *licensed teacher*, to entitle such district to a participation in the public moneys devoted to the maintenance of the schools; recognizing no act of this kind as legal, where the instructor does not possess *in form*, the evidence of full qualification; and hence it becomes a matter of the highest import to the state, and every member of the community, that these qualifications should, "in respect to moral character, learning and ability" and aptness to teach, be possessed by every instructor of youth.—

The general enquiry is more as to the amount of the teacher's *wages* than in regard to *fitness*; and competition serves rather to cheapen the rewards of this employment, than to encourage an emulation to excel among the teachers. Whether these considerations should justify any pecuniary relief, and to what extent, must depend upon the view taken of the magnitude of the inconveniences to be overcome or removed, and the extent to which the welfare of the state may be involved by permitting their continuance."

The progress of the Normal School, during the preceding year was eminently gratifying and satisfactory. At the close of the second term thirty four of the pupils received their diplomas as teachers. During its third term, commencing on the 15th of October 1845, the number of its pupils had increased to nearly two hundred, embracing a representation from fifty eight of the fifty-nine Counties The board of instruction was increased and strengthened by the appointment of Darwin G. Eaton, as teacher of Mathematics, in conjunction with Prof. Perkins, Sumner C. Webb, as Teacher of Arithmetic and Geography, Silas T. Bowen, of Grammar, William W. Clark, of Natural Philosophy and Chemistry, William F. Phelps, as Permanent Teacher of the Model or Experimental School, and Miss Elizabeth C. Hance, as Teacher of Reading and History.

"The end proposed in the establishment of the Normal School" observe the Executive Committee in the Annual report for the present year "was to educate teachers for our common schools; to send forth those to take charge of the susceptible minds of the children of this commonwealth, who, together with high moral principles, should possess the requisite knowledge of the branches to be taught, and withal be "apt to teach." The school was designed to educate the moral qualities of the instructor—to impress him with the solemn responsibilities of his work—so that he might feel the blessedness of being patient, longsuffering and unwearied in his efforts for the good of his pupils. It was intended to teach its students, and by their precept and example to impress all who aspired to the honor of instructing, that the work of teaching was so important that no labor of preparation could be too great, since the good that could be accomplished was vast, beyond the powers of human conception. Hence a stimulus was to be imparted to the teacher, which should never be spent, but be continually operative, urging him to the acquisition of higher attainments in virtue, knowledge and aptness to teach. This, it is conceived, was the philanthropic end which the legislature of 1844 had in view, when they established the Normal School."

On the first day of June of this year, a Convention of Delegates from the several Counties of the State met at Albany for the revision of the Constitution. On the 5th Mr. Bowdish, of Montgomery, moved for the appointment of a committee to inquire into the expediency of the establishment of a system of Free Schools for the State. On the 12th, a standing committee, consisting of Mr. Nicoll of New-York, as chairman, Messrs. Munro, of Onondaga; Bowdish, of Montgomery; A. W. Young, of Wyoming; Tuthill, of Orange; Willard, of Albany; and Hunt of New-York, was appointed by the President, (the Hon John Tracy, of Chenango,) on the subject of education, common schools and their appropriate funds. On the 15th Mr. R. Campbell, of Otsego offered a resolution of inquiry as to the propriety of a "constitutional provision for the security of the common school, literature deposit and other trust funds, from conversion or destruction by the legislature, and the establishment of such a system of common schools as will, by taxation, bestow the facility of acquiring a good education on every child in the State," which was adopted by the Convention, and referred to the Committee. On the 18th, the President presented to the Convention a communication from S. S. Randall, President of the State Convention of County Superintendents of common schools, held at Albany, in April preceding, transmitting a preamble and resolutions in favor of the Free School System.

On the 22d of July, Mr. Nicoll, from the committee, reported for the consideration of the Convention, a series of propositions designed to be incorporated as a part of the new constitution, declaring the proceeds of all lands belonging to the state, except such parts thereof as might be reserved, or appropriated to public use, or ceded to the United States, which shall hereafter be sold or disposed of, together with the fund denominated the Common School fund, and all moneys heretofore appropriated by law for the use and benefit of said fund, should be and remain a perpetual fund, the interest to be inviolably appropriated and applied to the support of common schools throughout the state; that the net revenues of the U. S. Deposit Fund, should likewise be inviolably applied to the same purpose, after meeting all existing appropriation; and that the legislature should, at its first session after the adoption of the proposed constitution, and from time to time thereafter as should be necessary, provide by law *for the free education and instruction of every child between the ages of four and sixteen years, whose parents, guardians or employers, shall be resident in the state, in the Common Schools now established, or which should thereafter be established therein*—the expense of such education and instruction after applying the public funds as above provided, to be defrayed by taxation, at the same time and in the same manner as provided by law for the liquidation of town and county charges. This latter provision, relating to the establishment of free schools, the committee proposed to submit separately to the people of the state, for their sanction.

On the 1st day of October, Mr. BOWDISH, of Montgomery, made a powerful and eloquent appeal to the Convention in behalf of this great measure of Free Schools, in which he was sustained by Mr. NICOLL, of New York, Mr. WORDEN, of Ontario, Mr. PATTERSON, of Chautauque, Mr. RUSSELL, of St. Lawrence, and others; and on the 8th of October, the day preceding the adjournment of the Convention, the first section reported by the committee permanently appropriating the proceeds of State lands and the Common School fund, to the support of common schools, was after some discussion adopted by a vote of 104 to 3. Mr. NICOLL then moved the adoption of the following section, to be separately submitted to the people, viz:

"§ 6. The Legislature shall provide for the free education and instruction of every child of the State in the common schools, now established, or which shall hereafter be established therein."

This section was *adopted* by a *vote* of 57 to 53, on a call for the ayes and noes; and a provision added on motion of Mr. RUGGLES, of Dutchess, by a vote of 82 to 26, directing the legislature to provide for raising the necessary taxes in the several school districts, to carry out the intention of the section. As thus modified, the entire ninth article of the proposed constitution, as reported by the committee, was agreed to by the convention and ordered to be engrossed. The convention then took a recess for dinner.

On the assembling of the Convention in the afternoon, Mr. ARPHAXED LOOMIS, of Herkimer, offered a resolution *to refer the article to a committe of* ONE *with instructions to strike out the two last sections, relating to the establishment of Free Schools, and report the same as amended to the Convention* INSTANTER. Mr. TAGGART, of Genesee. sustained, and Mr. TOWNSEND, of New York, opposed this motion; but under the operation of the previous question, it prevailed by a vote of 61 to 27; and Mr. LOOMIS being appointed the committee, immediately reported as instructed, and his report being agreed to by the Convention, the provision for the establishment of Free Schools, as a portion of the Constitution was finally defeated.

The ninth article as adopted is as follows:

"The Capital of the Common School Fund; the capital of the Literature Fund, and the capital of the United States Deposit Fund, shall be respectively preserved inviolate. The revenue of the said common school fund shall be applied to the support of common schools; the revenue of the said literature fund shall be applied to the support of academies; and the sum of $25,000 of the revenues of the United States Deposit fund shall each year be appropriated to and made a part of the capital of the said common school fund"

On the 1st of October, of this year, SAMUEL L. HOLMES, Esq., of the County of Westchester, received the appointment of State Deputy Superintendent of common schools, to supply the vacancy occasioned by the resignation and retirement on account of ill health of the then incumbent S. S. Randall, who had held the office during the two preceding administrations, and up to the present period.

From the annual report of the Superintendent for 1847, it appeared that the number of organized school districts in the state, on the first of July preceding, was 11,008; the number of children between the ages of 5 and 16, 704,000; the number of children of all ages under instruction in the common school during the year 1845, 742,433; the amount of public money applied during the same year to the payment of teachers wages, $635,051.15; the amount contributed on rate bills for the same purpose $460,764.78 making an aggregate of $1,095,815.93; the amount of public money expended in the purchase of libraries and school apparatus in the several districts, $95,881.86, and the number of volumes in the several District Libraries, 1,203,139, being an increase during the year reported of 57,889 volumes.

"A successful administration of the school laws of the State," observes the superintendent "requires an intelligent and active local, as well as general supervision; and without the former it is believed the present organization must eventually be abandoned, and one less complex in its details and arrangements and less stringent in its requirements, adopted in the place of it. Numerous plans, no doubt, might be suggested on paper, giving promise of great excellence if adopted; but when brought to the test of actual experiment they will entirely fail to accomplish the object designed. Radical changes in any system of public instruction, perfected by years of trial, and accommodated to the habits and inclination of the community, will be found a hazardous expedient. After struggling through a long series of years to elevate our schools, to infuse a greater zeal and excite a higher interest in regard to them, without advancing one step in attaining these objects, actual visitation and inspection were provided as a substitute for an inefficient local supervision; and this duty was enjoined upon officers designated by law. The results of this change have been and now are seen and deeply felt in our own state and by our people, and have justly excited commendation and approval wherever they are known in other states of the Union.

"The actual external and internal condition of our common schools, always a subject intensely interesting to the philanthropist, and the patriotic statesman, is such in the judgment of the Superintendent as will afford much satisfaction in regard to the present, and allow high hopes for the future. That more might have been accomplished since the establishment of our system, and under other and more favorable circumstances, is quite probable; but that we now see upwards of seven hundred and forty thousand of the youth of our state resorting to the common schools in pursuit of knowledge, should excite in us profound gratitude to the All-wise disposer of national events, and the highest respect for the founders of the system."

The Superintendent also renewed his recommendation of the preceding year in relation to the appropriation of the whole or a portion of the Library money of the several districts, to the payment of teachers' wages, under a vote of the district subject to the approbation of the department.

Under the provisions of an act passed in 1846, schools for the instruction of Indian children were organized on the Onendaga, Cattaraugus, Allegany and St. Regis reservations, under circumstances eminently favorable to the intellectual and moral improvement of this class of the population.

Gov. Young, in his annual message to the legislature, for the present year, thus alluded to the Normal School:

"The State Normal School continues to advance in public estimation and public usefulness. Its only object is to improve the teachers of common schools, and any progress in the advancement of that object, it quite apparent, must exert a salutary influence on the cause of education throughout the state."

The Executive Committee, in their annual report, stated that the number of pupils in attendance during the fourth term of the school, commencing in May, and closing in September, 1846, was 205, and that every county, with a single exception, was represented. The number of graduates, at the close of the third term, was 47, and of the fourth, 63. "It is found," observe the committee, "upon examination of the school register, that since Dec. 18, 1844, 508 students have attended the school for a longer or a shorter period. Of this number 178 are now in the school; 6 have died; 14 were found to be incompetent for teaching, and were at an early day advised to engage in other pursuits; 11 left on account of ill health, unfitting them alike for study or teaching; and 29 left at an early period of their connection with the school, relinquishing for various reasons the purpose of teaching. If these numbers be added, their sum will be found to be 238; and if this last number be subtracted from the whole number on the register, the remainder to be accounted for is 270. Of these 270, 144 are graduates of the school, and the committee *know* that 129 of them have been engaged in teaching since their graduation; and of the remaining 15 graduates one has died, and the rest, with the exception of four, are *believed* to be teaching, though no definate knowledge of their pursuits has been obtained. It may also be proper to state, that those persons who have not been heard from, were graduates of last term, and sufficient time has hardly elapsed to afford an opportunity of learning their pursuits. Of the remainder of the 270, numbering 126, who left the school prior to graduation, nearly all, on leaving, declared that it was their intention to teach. 84 are *known* to have taught since they left, and but few of the others have been heard from. Thus, it appears that the school has sent out 213 persons, who, when heard from, were actually engaged in teaching. In many instances, also, accounts have been received of the manner in which these students were acquitting themselves as teachers, and the committee are happy to say, that as far as heard from, they are giving great satisfaction."

On the 13th of November, 1847, the legislature passed an act abolishing the office of County Superintendent of Common Schools, and directing that all appeals authorized by law, to be brought to them, should be made directly to the State Superintendent, and that the annual reports heretofore made to them by the Town Superintendents, should be made to the County Clerks, respectively, and condensed statements thereof by them, be transmitted to the department.

For this measuse the friends of the system, although they had, with great unanimity, resisted it for a series of years, were prepared, from the great unpopularity of the office, growing out of the mode of appointment and of the compensation of this class of officers. Their selection had been, very injudiciously, confided to the Boards of Supervisors of the respective counties, whose functions, however useful and important in other respects, had no particular reference to the educational wants and interests of the community; and who were, besides, to a great extent, divided into political parties, upon the varying supremacy of which, the choice of County Superintendents was, too generally made to depend, without especial regard to the intellectual and moral qualifications of the candidate for the important and responsible station he was destined to fill. While, therefore, far the greater number of officers appointed by them, were men eminently qualified for the discharge of their duties, there were some who were justly obnoxious to the charge, not only of incapacity, but of a perversion of the high functions devolved upon them to sinister personal and political ends; and the indignation excited by these instances of disregard of duty and moral obliquity, gradually extended itself to other localities where no reasonable grounds for suspicion existed. The pecuniary burden likewise, of defraying one-half the salary of these officers from the county treasuries, was magnified and dwelt upon by the interested and designing; and the legislature was annually flooded with petitions for the abolition of the office, as unnecessary, oppressive and improperly administered. Committee after committee, to whom these petitions were referred, reported against the adoption of the measure desired; and the ablest and soundest arguments were brought to bear upon the great and manifest utility of the office. It was clearly and repeatedly shown that the abuses complained of were such as admitted of an easy and practical remedy, while the advantage secured by the retention of this class of officers could be obtained through no other agency. Public clamor, however, persisted in demanding the repeal of the obnoxious act; and notwithstanding the avowed and strong opposition of the successive heads of the department, of the several committees of both houses of the legislature, charged with the supervision of the interests of public instruction, and of the great body of the most enlightened friends of education throughout the state, the measure was finally carried through at the extra session, convoked for the purpose of enacting the several new laws rendered necessary by the adoption of the amended constitution.

The effect of this measure upon the prosperity of the common school system was, in many essential respects, most disastrous. During a period of nearly forty years its progress had been uninterruptedly onward; and a succession of wise enactments had strengthened and matured its foundations and expanded its usefulness in every direction. The abolition of that feature, which, more, perhaps, than any other, constituted its distinguishing characteristic, and gave to it its peculiar symmetry and power, was the first retrograde step in its history. Its immediate consequences were felt in the comparative inefficiency and inutility of the local and general supervision of the schools—in the absence of any connecting link between the department and the several town and district officers, and the inhabitants of the districts—in the discontinuance of a local appellate tribunal, where the numerous controversies constantly springing up, relative to the external arragements of the various districts, might be equitably adjusted by an officer on the spot—and in the utter impossibility of obtaining with any accuracy, those statistical details in reference to the practical operation of the system, of so great value to the department, the legislature, and the public. Town Superintendents, however well qualified for the specific discharge of the duties devolved upon them, were, for obvious reasons, wholly incapable of supplying the place in the system, which had been assigned to this higher class of officers. Their jurisdiction was strictly local—their peculiar duties circumscribed—their influence necessarily confined to their respective towns—and their powers limited; while the county Superintendents were in constant and regular communication, not only with the head of the department, but with their colleagues throughout the state—their influence extensive—and their means of usefulness unrestricted.

At the same time, the legislature passed the "Act for the establishment of Teachers' Institutes," by which the sum of sixty dollars was appropriated annually from the income of the United States Deposit Fund, payable on the order of the several county treasurers, to be expended for the use and benefit of teachers' institutes, in each of the counties of the state where a majority of the town superintendents shall unite in desiring its expenditure for this purpose, and file a certificate thereof with the county clerk. An advisory committee, consisting of three of such town Superintendents, is required to be appointed by the counly clerk, to make the necessary arrangements for organizing and managing such institute, and public notice is to be given by him to teachers and others who may desire to become such, specifying the time and place of meeting of such institute. The advisory committee are also authorized to procure the services of suitable lecturers and teachers for such institute. Whenever the county treasurer shall receive satisfactory evidence, that not less than fifty, or in counties whose population is under thirty thousand, not less than thirty teachers, or individuals intending to become such within one year, shall have been in regular attendance on such institute for ten days, he is authorized and required to audit and allow the accounts of such advisory committee, not exeeeding the sum of sixty dollars, for the expenses of such institute.

On the 15th of December, the various statutes relating to common schools were combined and consolidated into one act, with such alterations and amendments as were deemed expedient. Town Superintendents were authorized to hold their offices for two years; and to enter upon the discharge of their duties respectively on the first Monday of November, subsequent to their election or appointment: and the library law was so modified as to authorize the expenditure of the whole or any portion of the public money received by the respective districts for that purpose, with the approbation of the state Superintendent, in the payment of teachers wages wherever the number of volumes in districts numbering over fifty children between the age of 5 and 16 exceeded one hundred and twenty-five, or one hundred in districts with a less number of children than fifty and where the district was supplied with maps, globes, black boards and the requisite scientific apparatus for the use of the school. Several other alterations of minor importance were made in the details of the system; and the Superintendent of common schools was authorized to cause the amended act to be published and generally distributed throughout the state.

In his annual Message to the Legislature at the opening of the Session of 1848, Gov. Young, thus adverted to the subject of education:

"In our country, for reasons that have been so often and so well stated, that I need not repeat them, the education of its children has been, and I trust will continue to be, matter of the deepest solicitude. Common schools, from their universality, reaching every neighborhood, and shedding their influence upon every family and into every mind, expelling the primary causes of vice and crime, and erecting altars to patriotism and virtue, have justly been considered the peculiar objects of legislative care.

"The practical importance of the State Normal School for the education of teachers is begining to be felt; and in the tone, strength and vigor given to common schools by distributing through the State, teachers who shall have been thoroughly instructed, it is believed will be found most convincing arguments in defence of reasonable, but liberal appropriations by the State to this object."

From the annual report of the Superintendent, it appeared that the number of school districts in the state, on the first of July 1847, was 11,052; number of children between the ages of five and sixteen, 700,443; whole number, of all ages instructed in the common schools of the state during the year 1846, 748,387; amount of public money expended in the payment of teachers wages, $595,974,20; amount raised on rate bill for the same purpose $462,840,44 making an aggregate of $1,058,814,64; amount of public money expended in the purchase of libraries and school apparatus $93,791,-29; and the number of volumes in the several district libraries 1,310,986, being an increase of 107,847, during the year reported.

In reference to the establishment of free schools, the Superintendent holds the following language:

"The extension of free schools in the state is progressing moderately; and laws are passed nearly every session of the Legislature, providing for their establishment in populous and wealthy villages; while the poorer and less populous districts, in the same towns, are left to struggle on, from year to year, in the best way they can—sustaining a school perhaps only four months in the year, to secure the next apportionment of the public moneys. Is this policy just?—is it right to discriminate in this manner, between the school children of the state? Why should ample provision be made for the children residing in particular localities, and others turned over to the naked bounties of the state; which, although munificent in the aggregate, are only sufficient to pay a few weeks tuition for each child? This great and essential question turns simply on the mode of taxation; by changing this and requiring the boards of supervisors, to raise upon the counties respectively, a sum equal to the amount apportioned from the treasury to each county for the support of schools, and upon the towns another sum equal to the apportionment of such town from the school fund, which would increase the local taxation upon the counties, not to exceed five-tenths of a mill on the valuation in any county, and our schools might be rendered nearly *free* to every child in the state.

"Our fellow citizens have heretofore cheerfully acquiesced in the imposition of a tax to support the government and *sustain* the *credit* of the state, of more than twice the amount proposed to be raised in the plan suggested. What improvement, internal or external, is more worthy of the fostering care of the legislature or of greater importance to the community, than the *mental* improvement of those who are soon to exercise all the privileges of citizens, and wield the destinies of the state. It would be an unjust impeachment of the patriotism and good sense of the people, to suppose they would not cheerfully embrace and cordially approve any reasonable measures which will reflect so much honor on the present, and confer such enduring benefits on the future."

In reference to the abolition of the office of county Superintendent, he observes:

"The act abolishing the office seemed to be in accordance with the public will, and should be cheerfully obeyed; but the wisdom and expediency of the measure must be tested by the experience of the future. The labor and expense thrown upon this office, in consequence of this legislative act, cannot justly and therefore does not form any ground of complaint with the undersigned. With the other official duties devolved upon the incumbent of this office, a personal supervision and inspection of the schools, if in any way desirable, is wholly impracticable. This question is then presented to the grave consideration of the legislature and the people of the state—are we to dispense entirely with all personal visitation, inspection and supervision, except what may be performed by the local town officers? and are we not hereafter to have any statistical information of the relative condition of our school houses? and of the condition of the winter and summer schools from year to year, showing the number of schools visited and pupils in attendance at the time? the course and extent of the studies pursued, with the ages, sex and time of the employment of the teachers, and the compensation paid? To repeat the just encomiums bestowed upon our system in all its parts, as it recently existed, and which distinguished educators and philanthropists in other states have urged upon the consideration of their legislatures, as worthy of being incorporated into their own systems, might seem disrespectful." * * * * * *

"Other plans might be suggested that would, no doubt, if adopted, greatly add to the efficiency of our local supervision and inspection, and take the place of that which has recently been abolished; but whether, at this time, any suggestions of this sort would be likely to meet with public favor, may well be questioned. From actual official information, obtained during the year 1846, the undersigned believed that the amount of compensation paid to town Superintendents and town officers for services connected with the schools, amounted to about $35,000 annually. It is not supposed that this amount exceeds the sums actually paid by the towns that year; nor will it cover the expenses of 1848, by $10,000. The duties of the town Superintendents must now necessarily be extended, and their services increased; and the aggregate annual compensation paid to these officers will, it is believed, on a careful examination, exceed $45,000. Without any material increase of expense, provision might be made by law for the election by the people of inspectors of schools, in each Assembly district, whose compensation should be limited, and who could conveniently perform many of the duties of town Superintendents; and thus, by dividing the labor and compensation between these officers, the aggregate expenses of both would not exceed the compensation of the latter officers."

It is due to Mr. Benton, to say that in his official capacity as Superintendent he resisted to the utmost extent of his power and influence, the retrograde movements of the legislature in reference to the supervision of the schools: that he was a firm and devoted advocate of the introduction of the free school principle as a part of our system of public instruction; and that his administration of that system was characterised by an enlightened and discriminating regard to the public interests and welfare.

The operations of the Normal School during the year 1847, tended to strengthen the confidence of the people in this Institution and to realize the expectations of the friends of education generally throughout the state. The number of pupils varied from 200 to 220; and the semi-annual graduating classes from 45 to 65. The whole number of graduates up to the 1st of January 1848, was 234; of whom 222 were actually engaged in teaching the common schools of the state, and the whole number of pupils entered upon the register of the Institution was 537, of whom 421 were then employed in the district schools. TRUMAN H. BOWEN had been appointed Teacher of Vocal Music, in place of Prof. ILSLEY, and Miss ANN MARIA OSTROM, Teacher of Drawing, in place of Prof. Howard.

The institution at this period however, received a severe blow, and the friends of education sustained an irreparable loss, by the death of Mr. PAGE the Principal of the school, which took place on the 1st day of January 1848. Although still in the prime of life, Mr. PAGE had attained a reputation and standing as a teacher, not surpassed in the Union. To intellectual qualifications of the highest order, he added all those moral virtues and christian graces which are so indispensably requisite to the instructor of youth. He was in all respects admirably adapted to the performance of the high functions which had been devolved upon him: and to the perfect order, system and harmony which he infused into all its departments, and his luminous exposition of the duties, obligations and responsibilities of the pupils under his charge, a large share of the prosperity, and success of the Normal School was preeminently due. Fortunately for the interests and advantage of his numerous pupils and admirers, and the profession of teachers generally throughout the State and Union, he had completed the preparation and publication of his admirable course of Lectures annually delivered before the school, on the "Theory and Practice of Teaching"—a work which embraces a comprehensive view of the whole subject and is in all respects worthy of its distinguished author and of the great cause to which he had, too assiduously, devoted his entire energies.

The Executive Committee with great unanimity designated Prof. PERKINS to supply the station rendered vacant by the death of Mr. PAGE. To an intimate acquaintance with the plans and general policy of his predecessor in the conduct and discipline of the school, Prof. PERKINS added all the intellectual and moral qualifications requisite to its successful administration; and under his supervision and direction the institution has continued to maintain its high reputation, and to dispense its blessing over every section of the state.

Administration of CHRISTOPHER MORGAN—*Adoption of the Free School System*—1848 to 1851.

On the first day of January, 1848, the Hon. CHRISTOPHER MORGAN, of Cayuga entered upon the discharge of the duties of the office of Secretary of State and Superintendent of common schools, to which he was elected in November preceding. A. G. JOHNSON, Esq., of Rensselaer, was in March thereafter appointed by him Deputy Superintendent, in place of Mr. Holmes.

On the 12th of April, the legislature passed the "*Act for the permanent establishment of the Normal School*" by which the sum of fifteen thousand dollars (afterwards extended to $25,000) was appropriated for the erection of a suitable building for its accommodation, and the previous provision of law applicable to its supervision, mangement and government, were made permanent. Under this act the Executive Committee have erected a spacious and convenient Hall, in a commodious location in the neighborhood of the Capitol, and of the State Geological and Agricultural Rooms, in the city of Albany, where the school is now insuccessful operation.

At the opening of the session of the legislature of 1849, GOV. FISH, in his annual message expresses his belief "that the restoration of the office of County Superintendent would be productive of good to the school system." In reference to the Normal School he observes, "This school is doing a great and good work. It has ceased to be an experiment, and under its present judicious management, it is growing in the confidence of its friends, and attracting the interest of many who once doubted its practicability or its usefulness."

From the annual report of the Superintendent, it appeared that the number of school districts in the state on the first day of July preceding was 10,621: the number of children between the ages of 5 and 16, 718,123; the number, of all ages under instruction during the year 1847 in the common schools of the state 775,723; the amount of public money expended in the payment of teachers wages during the same year $639,008, and the amount contributed on the rate bills for this purpose 466,674, amounting in the aggregate to $1,105,682; the amount of public money expended in the purchase of libraries and school apparatus $81,624,00 and the number of volumes in the several district libraries 1,338,848, showing an increase of 27,862 volumes since the preceding year.

Schools for colored children had been kept in fifteen counties of the state, at which 4,741 children were in attendance, being an increase of 877, since 1846, and of 2,185 since 1845: and the amount of public money apportioned to such schools was $16,926.68. In a large number of the counties, however, no effort had been made to collect accurate statistics in reference to these schools; the number of colored children between the ages of 5 and 16 residing in the state being estimated at not less than 11,000.

"The colored population," observes the Superintendent, "is enumerated in the census of the State, and is a part of the basis of the distribution of the School Fund. Colored children are enumerated by the trustees in their annual reports, they draw public money for the district in which they reside, and are equally entitled with white children to the benefit of it. In the rural districts of the State, colored children are generally admitted into the Common Schools.

"If unreasonable prejudice exclude colored children from the village schools, the trustees are empowered to establish separate schools for them. The children attending draw the public money to which they are entitled, and the trustees can exempt those parents who are unable to pay a rate-bill, the exemptions becoming a charge upon the whole district. A special appropriation for incorporated villages, only excites prejudice and parsimony. The trustees of the village will, generally, expend the special appropriation for the colored children, and the public money drawn by them will be shared among the white children of the village.

"There seems to be no satisfactory reason for this special appropriation. It cannot be justly urged that negroes are an especial burden to incorporated villages any more than to cities, or rural districts, and that they are, therefore, entitled to an extraordinary allowance of money to educate them."

Schools for the instruction of Indian children had been established upon the St. Regis, the Onondaga, the Cattaraugus and Allegany, and the Shinecock Indian Reservations. In that of the St. Regis 50 children had attended school during a period of nine months, the average daily attendance being 35; in that of the Onondaga 61 children for 11 months, in those of the Allegany and Cattaraugus, 229 children; and in that of the Shinecocks 40.

The superintendent informs the legislature that about four hundred applications had been made to him for his official approbation to the diversion of the whole or portions of the Library money to the payment of teachers wages, under the provisions of the act of 1847. "He has withheld it, *in all cases*, believing that every volume of a well selected library is a perpetual teacher to all who will go to it for instruction." He expresses his belief "that the district libraries *cannot be too large* and that *the people are in no danger of learning too much.*

"Selections for the district libraries, are made from the whole range of literature and science, with the exception of controversial books, political or religious; history, biography, poetry, philosophy, mental, moral and natural, fiction; indeed every department of human knowledge contributes its share to the district school library. The object of this great charity was not merely to furnish books for children, but to establish in all the school districts, a miscellaneous library suited to the tastes and characters of every age. By means of this diffusive benevolence, the light of knowledge penetrates every portion of the State, and the sons of our farmers, merchants, mechanics and laborers, have daily access to many well selected books, of which, but for this sagacious policy of our State, a majority of them would have never heard. If knowledge is power, who can calculate the energy imparted to the people of this State by the district school, and the district library?"

Teachers's Institutes had been held under the provision of the act of 1847, in sixteen counties, at which 1096 teachers had been in attendance. The Superintendent recommends a considerable increase in the appropriation to this object.

In reference to the abolition of the office of County Superintendent, the Superintendent observes:

"It is believed that the friends of the Common School system in the State, very generally desired the continuance of the office. It was, however, abolished, without petitions from any considerable number of citizens, and without even proposing a substitute.

"There is now no immediate officer between this Department and the town officers. Such an office is needed as the medium of communication between this Department and the nine hundred town superintendents, and eleven thousand school districts. The territory is too large; its subdivisions too many; its relations too diverse; the local officers too numerous; and the interval between the Department and them too wide, to permit that actual and minute supervision which is necessary to an efficient administration of the School laws.

"The undersigned would, therefore, recommend to the Legislature two measures, either of which, in his opinion, will be approved by the friends of the Common School system, and will supply a want daily felt in this Department.

"1st. A repeal of chap. 358, Laws of 1847, restoring the office of County Superintendent, and making it elective by the people.

"2d. The election of a Superintendent in every Assembly district, except in the city of New York, and the cities which now have, or shall hereafter have a city Superintendent, or Board of Education, to manage their school affairs.

"If the latter measure should be adopted, I would recommend that the salary of such officer be fixed at not less than $200 per year, in each Assembly district, composed of towns and that the same be a county charge; that the salary of City Superintendents be fixed by the civil authorities thereof, as shall be provided in their several charters or city laws and ordinances; and that not less than $200 of such salary be a county charge. Among the powers and duties of such District Superintendent should be the following:—To make the abstract of the reports of Town Superintendents in his district, at the same time and in the same manner now required of the County Clerks; to recommend persons from his district as pupils in the State Normal School; to recommend each year two teachers in his district as worthy to receive a State certificate; to visit each school in his district at least twice a year, once in the summer and once in the winter, to make such report of his visitation as may be required by the State Superintendent; to hear and determine all the controversies arising in his district under the school laws, an appeal being allowed from his decision to this Department. The Superintendent makes these suggestions with diffidence, and only from a sense of their necessity."

The superintendent then proceeds to examine the present condition of the school law, in reference to the provision for the support of schools, upon which he bases a recommendation for the adoption of the Free School system:

"The mode of supporting a school under the present system," he observes, "is as follows:"

"The Trustees employ a qualified teacher for stipulated wages. At the close of his term, they give him an order upon the town superintendent for such portion of the public money, as may have been voted by the district for the term, or in case no vote has been taken, for such portion as they think proper. But in no case can the Trustees legally draw for more money than is due the teacher at the date of the order. If the public money is not sufficient to pay the teacher's wages, the trustees proceed to make out a rate-bill for the residue, charging each parent or guardian, according to the number of days' attendance of his children. Under the present law, the trustees have power to exempt indigent persons, and the amount exempted is a charge upon the district, and may be immediately collected by tax, or added to any tax thereafter levied. After the rate-bill is completed, thirty days' notice of its completion is given by the trustees, one of whom must be in attendance, on a day and place appointed in said notice, once a week for two successive weeks, to receive payment; and during the whole of the said thirty days any person may pay to either of the trustees, or to the teacher, the sum charged to him upon the rate-bill. At the expiration of the thirty days, if all the persons named in the rate-bill, have not voluntarily paid, the trustees put it with their warrant, into the hands of the district collector, who has the same authority to collect it by levy and sale of goods and chattels, as a town collector. The collector is also authorized to collect fees, not only upon the money paid to him, but upon that paid voluntarily to the trustees and teacher, and he is allowed thirty days to make his return to the trustees.

"A more troublesome or vexatious system could not well be devised.

"A teacher having performed his contract, is yet obliged, unless the trustees advance the money, to wait thirty, or sixty days for his pay. The first thirty days' delay under the notice is no advantage to any one. The time of the trustees is spent uselessly.

"Nothing is gained by payment to the trustees. Is there any other instance upon the Statute book in which legislation compels a man to wait sixty days for his wages after he has completed his work? In the absence of any contract, the wages of the laborer are due and payable, when his work is done. In the case of the teacher, the payment of his wages is postponed for sixty days after his school is closed, for payment from trustees cannot be enforced, until the time fixed by law for collection has expired.

"A slight error in the apportionment of the rates, or in the legal forms of making it, subjects the trustees to a suit by any one of whom a few cents may have been illegally collected; and, unfortunately, there are not wanting in every town persons ready to avail themselves of such errors.

"The trustees can, if they choose, make out a tax for the amount of exemptions, and the collector is bound to collect it for the trifling fees, upon a five, or ten dollar tax-list.

"A law has been passed, authorizing courts to deny costs to a plaintiff in a suit against the trustees, and also authorizing boards of supervisors to order a tax to be assessed upon a district to refund costs and expenses incurred in suits by, or against them, on account of the discharge of their official duties.—But the law allows them nothing for their responsibility and labor, either in the discharge of their duties, or in the prosecution, or defence of suits.

"Now, a free school system may be devised that shall relieve trustees from the duty of making out rate-bills, or tax-lists, in any case and from all litigation arising therefrom, and which shall secure to the teacher his pay when his work is done.

"It may be made applicable only to the towns, requiring the cities, however, to make their schools free, but leaving them to adopt such an organization as shall be suited to their peculiar wants.

"Teachers complain of the rate-bill system, not only because it improperly withholds their wages, but because the trustees find great difficulty in exercising with fidelity, and at the same time satisfactorily the power of exemption.—While the cupidity of the tax-payer is excited, the pride of men of moderate means is aroused, and their sense of independence revolts at being certified and put upon the record as indigent persons.

"The rate bill system requires every person to pay in proportion to the attendance of his children. How strong then is the inducement of many parents, to wink at absence, and truancy, and how little are they inclined to second by parental authority the efforts of the teacher to enforce punctuality and regularity of attendance. The fact that the number of children attending school less than four months, uniformly exceeds the number attending a longer time, furnishes strong evidence for believing that the rate bill system is the principal cause of the irregular attendance of scholars.

"Letters have been addressed to the Superintendent from various parts of the State, urging him to recommend to the Legislature the free school system, and assuring him that the people are ready to sustain the Legislature."

"It is urged by the opponents of the system that those who have property are taxed to educate their own, as well as the children of the poor; and that those who are blessed with property, but denied children, are also obliged to contribute something for the education of the indigent. Those who have omitted their duty, or are more fortunate than their neighbors in the possession of property have no reason to complain of the trifling burthen which good fortune imposes upon them.

"Are property holders wronged or injured by this system of taxation?

"Property is the creature of law. Its ownership is regulated by law. Even the income of some kinds of property is limited by law. Human beings are property in South Carolina; and the taxes assessed upon them, and paid out of the earnings of their labor, go to the support of free schools, while in this state there can be no property in man.

"Land is property, and in civilized countries it constitutes the bulk of all property; yet it is not property in the absence of law. What idea of property in land has a Camanche Indian, or a Calmuck Tartar? To him the land is as free for his roaming, as the air for his breathing; or the water for his drink. The wild Bedouin will guard as his own, his tent, his camel, his wife; but his laws are the keenness of his scimetar, and the fleetness of his steed.

"The security of property is one of the paramount objects of government; but how shall that security be attained? By the stern restraints and crushing force of military power?

"The experience of the last year, in Europe and America, has proven that there is greater security for persons and property, in the general intelligence and education of the people, than in an overawing soldiery.

"Europe has been convulsed—cities have been the scenes of fearful and mortal strife—fields have been laid waste by contending armies—governments have been overthrown—revolution has followed revolution—uncertainty and insecurity are stamped upon all things—political changes have been effected only by civil war and commotion.

"The people of the United States have effected the choice of a Chief Magistrate, involving a change in the policy of the government. It was accomplished in a day, with the cheerful and peaceful acquiescence of the Union.

"These are the results of the intelligence and moral elevation of the American people.

"There is a moral and intellectual power in the universal education of the people which furnishes more abiding security for persons and property than disciplined armies.

Property must be taxed to support a soldiery. Why should it not then contribute to a system of protection which may preclude the necessity of armies?

"Crime and pauperism are too often the results of ignorance. The detection and punishment of the one and the support of the other, are mainly effected by the imposition of taxes upon property.

"Is it not wise, then, to establish a system of education, universal and complete, which may in a great measure, prevent the commission of crime and avoid the evils of pauperism?"

On the 26th of March, 1849, the legislature passed the "*Act establishing Free Schools throughout the State.*" Its prominent provisions were the following:

Common schools in the several school districts in this state were declared free to all persons residing in the district over five and under twenty-one years of age. Persons not residents of a district were to be admitted into the schools kept therein with the approbation in writing of the trustees thereof, or a majority of them.

It was made the duty of the several boards of supervisors, at their annual meetings, to cause to be levied and collected from their respective counties, in the same manner as county taxes, a sum equal to the amount of state school moneys apportioned to such counties and to apportion the same among the towns and cities in the same manner as the moneys received from the State are apportioned. They were also to cause to be levied and collected from each of the towns in their respective counties, in the same manner as other town taxes, a sum equal to the amount of state school moneys apportioned to said towns respectively.

The trustees of each school district within thirty, and not less than fifteen days preceding the time for holding the annual district meeting in each year, were directed to prepare an estimate of the amount of money necessary to be raised in the district for the ensuing year, for the payment of the debts and expenses to be incurred by the district for fuel, furniture, school apparatus, repairs, and insurance of school house, contingent expenses, and teachers wages exclusive of the public money and the money required by law to be raised by the counties and towns and the income of local funds, and to cause printed or written notices thereof to be posted for two weeks previous to said meeting, upon the school house door, and in three or more of the most public places in said district. The trustees were directed to present such estimate to such meeting, and the voters present of full age residing in such school district and entitled to hold land in the state, who own or lease real property in such district, subject to taxation for school purposes, or who may have paid any district tax within two years preceding, or who own any personal property liable to be taxed for school purposes in such district, exceeding fifty dollars in value, exclusive of such as is exempt from execution, and no others, were entitled to vote thereon for each item separately, and so much of said estimate as shall be approved by a majority of such voters present, was required to be levied and raised by tax on said district, in the same manner as other district taxes are now by law levied and collected.

Whenever the voters of any district at their annual meeting refuse or neglect to raise by tax a sum of money, which added to the public money, and the money raised by county and towns will support a school in said district for at least four months in a year, keep the school house in proper repair and furnish the necessary fuel, then it was made the duty of said trustees to repair the school house, purchase the necessary fuel, and employ a teacher for four months, and the expense was directed to be levied and collected in the manner above provided.

Free and gratuitous education was to be given to each pupil, in each of the common, public, ward and district schools in the respective cities of this State, now incorporated or hereafter to be incorporated, including the schools of the public school society in the city of New York, according to any law now in force in said cities. And by each city, where such free and gratuitous education is not already established, laws and ordinances were without delay, to be passed, providing for, and securing and sustaining the system in each of their common, public, ward or district schools.

All laws and parts of laws inconsistent with the provisions of the act, other than those relating to free schools in any cities in this state, were repealed.

The electors of the State were to determine by ballot at the annual election to be held in November following, whether this act should or should not become a law.

In case a majority of the votes cast were found to be against such law, the act was to be null and void; otherwise to take effect immediately.

At the annual state election, held on the 6th of November, the whole number of votes cast for the New School Law was 249,872, and the whole number against it 91,951, being a majority in its favor of 157,921. Four counties only, viz: Tompkins, Chenango, Cortland and Otsego, giving majorities against it, amounting in the aggregate, to 1,257, while the aggregate majorities in its favor, cast in the remaining fifty-four counties was 158,181. Mr. MORGAN was re-elected Secretary of state and Superintendent of Common Schools.

The following is a statement of the votes of the several counties, showing the whole number of votes given, and the majorities in each for and against the act:

COUNTIES.	For the New School Law.	Against the New School Law.	Majority for.	Major ag'st.
Albany,	8604	1806	6798	......
Allegany,	3840	1669	2171	......
Broome,	2584	1554	1030	......
Cattaraugus,	4003	1303	2700	......
Cayuga,	5419	3056	2373	......
Chatauque,	4648	2550	2098	......
Chemung,	2799	812	1987	......
Chenango,	3079	3511	....	432
Clinton,	2855	747	2108	......
Columbia,	5476	987	4489	......
Cortland,*	1316	925	391	......
Delaware,	2789	2663	120	......
Dutchess,	7606	1279	6327	......
Erie,	8800	1542	7258	......
Essex,	2633	854	1779	......
Franklin,	1838	460	1378	......
Fulton and Hamilton,	2270	1133	1137	......
Genesee,	2758	1254	1504	......
Greene,	2935	2140	795	......
Herkimer,	3393	1461	1932	......
Jefferson,	5997	3312	2685	......
Kings,	8549	159	8390	......
Lewis,	1961	1206	755	......
Livingston,	3851	1791	2060	......
Madison,	3912	2268	1644	......
Monroe,	7541	2323	5218	......
Montgomery,	4222	785	3437	......
New York,	21052	1313	19739	......
Niagara,	2853	1881	972	......
Oneida,	8506	2911	4595	......
Onondaga,	7940	2002	5938	......
Ontario,	4611	1683	2928	......
Orange,	4448	2288	2160	......
Orleans,	2804	1334	1470	......
Oswego,	5474	2350	3124	......

*Including the votes given for and against the "Free School Law," and for and against the "School Law," the majority *against* the law in this county was 80.

COUNTIES.	For the New School Law.	Against the New School Law.	Majority for.	Major ag'st.
Otsego,	4009	4019	....	10
Putnam,	1211	277	934	......
Queens,	2652	396	2256	......
Rensselaer,	7254	978	6276	......
Richmond,	1437	22	1415	......
Rockland,	1117	414	703	......
St. Lawrence,	4997	2546	2451	......
Saratoga,	4749	2110	2639	......
Schenectady,	2304	304	2000	......
Schoharie,	2751	2674	77	......
Seneca,	2799	886	1913	......
Steuben,	5714	2321	3393	......
Suffolk,	2479	938	1541	......
Sullivan,	2421	499	1922	......
Tioga,	2343	837	1506	......
Tompkins,	2459	3177	....	718
Ulster,	5688	1182	4506	......
Warren,	1708	679	1029	......
Washington,	4109	2298	1811	......
Wayne,	4277	2619	1658	......
Westchester,	4554	982	3572	......
Wyoming,	3000	1652	1348	......
Yates,	2480	829	1651	......
	249,872	91,951	158,181	1240

On the 10th of December, 1849, Samuel S. Randall was re-appointed Deputy Superintendent of Common Schools, in the place of Mr. Johnson, appointed Deputy Secretary.

Notwithstanding the almost unanimous vote of the electors of the state in favor of the act of 1849,it was met at the outset of its practical administration by a violent and wide spead hostility. In nearly half the counties of the state, the Board of Supervisors had adjourned their sessions, before the official annunciation of its adoption, and consequently without making provision for the additional county tax required by the second section. The heavy deficiency of funds thus occasioned was left to be supplied by a district tax; and the great inequality in the taxable property of the several districts was severely felt, and contributed to a very great extent, to render the practical operation of the new law, burdensome and oppressive. Many of the heaviest tax payers had no direct interest in the schools; and in general wherever they constituted a majority of the legal voters of the district, they refused all appropriations for the support of the school beyond the four months required by law. Petitions for a repeal or modification of the law, were forwarded in great numbers from every section of the state: and a very general disaffection existed towards the new system.

By an act passed on the 30th of March, the sum of $250 was appropriated, annually for three years to the Trustees of such Academies as the Regents of the University, should designate for that purpose, on condition that at least twenty individuals in such Academies should be instructed in the science of common school teaching for at least four months during each of said years.

On the first day of January, 1850, the Superintendent forwarded to the legislature his annual report, by which it appeared that the number of school districts in the state, was 11,191, the number of children between five and sixteen 739,655 and the whole number of children taught during the year 1848, 778,309. The recommendation to restore the office of county Superintendent, or to create that of assembly district Superintendent, was renewedly urged upon the legislature, together with several other important modification, of the existing law.

Several bills were brought forward in each branch of the legislature, in accordance with these recommendations, and with the object of removing the obnoxious features of the new law. Able reports were made by Mr. BEEKMAN of New York, Chairman of the Literature Committee of the senate, and by Mr. KINGSLEY of Cortland from a select Committee of the assembly, to whom the various petitions for a repeal or modification of the law, were referred. Mr. BURROUGHS of Orleans, the Chairman of the Committee on colleges, academies and common schools, brought forward a bill, providing for the levying of a general state tax of $800,000 annually, for the support of the schools, in conjunction with the annual revenue of the school fund.

This bill passed the Assembly by a vote of 70 in the affirmative to 30 in the negative; but no action was had on it in the Senate. In that body a bill was introduced by Mr. MANN, of Oneida, referring the question of repeal of the act of 1849, to the decision of the people at the ensuing election, which passed the Senate, and received the assent of the House, after midnight of the last day of the session.

The friends of Free Schools, after the most strenuous and persevering though ineffectual efforts to obtain such amendments or modification of the law as might render its provisions generally acceptable, determined, under these circumstances, to oppose its unconditional repeal. They united, with great unanimity, in the call for a State Convention at Syracuse, which was held on the 10th day of July, the Superintendent of Common Schools, Mr. MORGAN, presiding; at which, resolutions were adopted in favor of the principle of Free Schools, and recommending the friends of education generally throughout the State, to oppose the repeal of the existing law with the view of amending and perfecting its details. An animated and vigorous canvass ensued—the opponents of the law insisting upon its unconditional repeal, without regard to the principle involved, and the friends of Free Schools, while conceding to the fullest extent the objections urged against the existing law, insisting upon its retention on the Statute book, for the sake of that principle, and pledging themselves to unite with its opponents in such amendments and modifications of the law itself, as public opinion should demand, and the best interests of education require. So obnoxious, however, were the main features of the law to the inhabitants of the several districts generally, that an aggregate majority of 46,874 was obtained, at the annual election in the fall of 1850, in forty-two of the fifty-nine counties of the State, in favor of its repeal. In the remaining seventeen counties, including the City and County of New York, the aggregate majority against repeal amounted to 71,912. The whole number of votes cast on this question (exclusive of imperfect and scattering ballots) was 393,654; of which 184,308 were given for, and 209,346 against the repeal of the law; leaving a majority of 25,038 against such repeal.

The following Statement of the vote in the several Counties of the State, for and against the Repeal of the Free School Law, is derived from the official returns to the Secretary of State's Office:

COUNTIES.	For Repeal of the new School Law	Against Repeal of the new School Law.	Majority for Repeal.	Majority against Repeal.
Albany,	3310	8582		5272
Allegany,	3787	2161	1626	....
Broome,	3021	1846	175	....
Cattaraugus,	3175	2196	979	....
Cayuga,	3639	3409	230	....
Chautauque,	4724	3094	1630	....
Chemung,	2315	2135	180	....
Chenango,	4828	2358	2470	....

COUNTIES.	For Repeal of the new School Law	Against Repeal of the new School Law.	Majority for Repeal.	Majority against Repeal
Clinton,	1963	1893	70	....
Columbia,	2566	4394		1828
Cortland,	3150	1153	1997	....
Delaware,	4068	2040	2028	....
Dutchess,	2841	6764		3923
Erie,	4672	6415		1743
Essex,	2138	1559	579	....
Franklin,	1664	1221	443	....
Fulton & Hamilton,	2510	1537	973	....
Genesee,	2830	1698	1132	....
Greene,	3217	1847	1379	....
Herkimer,	3588	3038	50	....
Jefferson,	6064	3958	2106	....
Kings,	1060	11136		10076
Lewis,	1709	455	964	....
Livingston,	3599	2548	1051	....
Madison,	3896	3254	642	....
Monroe,	5099	5031	68	....
Montgomery,	2253	3295		1042
New York,	987	38816		37827
Niagara,	3461	2169	1292	....
Oneida,	7414	6517	897	....
Onondaga,	4657	6583		1926
Ontario,	3712	2970	742	....
Orange..	4183	3274	909	....
Orleans,	2835	1523	1312	....
Oswego,	4241	3770	471	....
Otségo,	3816	2096	1720	....
Putnam,	845	959		114
Queens,	1542	2050		508
Rensselaer,	3370	7176		3806
Richmond,	351	1212		861
Rockland,	826	948		112
St. Lawrence,	4628	3549	1069	....
Saratoga	4211	3077	1134	....
Schenectady,	1365	1417		52
Schoharie,	4159	1611	2548	....
Seneca,	1810	2113		303
Steuben,	5377	4016	1361	....
Suffolk,	2252	1884	368	....
Sullivan,	1748	1475	273	....
Tioga,	2784	1130	1654	....
Tompkins,	4441	1924	2517	....
Ulster,	3826	4063		237
Warren,	1806	1102	704	....
Washington,	3726	2718	1008	....
Wayne,	4742	2605	2137	....
Westchester,	2164	4436		2272
Wyoming,	3155	1610	1545	....
Yates,	2186	1525	661	....
	184308	209316	46874	71912

Majority against repeal, 25,038.

In his annual message at the opening of the Legislature of 1851, Governor HUNT thus adverted to the subject:

"The operations of the act of 1849, establishing free schools, have not produced all the beneficial effects, nor imparted the general satisfaction anticipated by the friends of the measure. It has been the policy of our State from an early period, to promote the cause of popular education by liberal and enlightened legislation. A munificent fund created by a series of measures, all aiming at the same great result, has been dedicated by the Constitution to the support of common schools, and the annual dividend from this source will gradually increase. The duty of the State to provide such means and facilities as will extend to all its children the blessings of education, and especially to confer upon the poor and unfortunate a participation in the benefits of our common schools, is a principle which has been fully recognized and long acted upon by the Legislature and the people.

"The vote of 1849, in favor of the free school law, and the more recent vote by a reduced majority against its repeal, ought doubtless to be regarded as a re-affirmation of this important principle, but not of the provisions of the bill, leaving it incumbent upon the Legislature, in the exercise of a sound discretion, to make such enactments as will accomplish the general design, without injustice to any of our citizens. An essential change was made by the law under consideration, in imposing the entire burthen of the schools upon property, in the form of a tax, without reference to the direct benefits derived by the tax payer. The provisions of the act for carrying this plan into effect, have produced oppressive inequalities and loud complaints.

"In some districts the discontent and strife attendant upon these evils, have disturbed the harmony of society. An earnest effort should be made to reconcile differences of opinion, to remedy the grievances arising from the imperfect operation of the law, and to equalize the weight of taxation by such principles of justice and equity as will ensure popular sanction. The success of our schools must depend, in a great degree, upon the united counsels and friendly co-operation of the people in each small community composing a district, and nothing can be more injurious to the system of common school education than feuds and contentions among those who are responsible for its healthful action and preservation.

"It cannot be doubted that all property, estates, whether large or small, will derive important advantages from the universal education of the people. A well considered system, which shall ensure to the children of all, the blessings of moral and intellectual culture, will plant foundations broad and deep, for public and private virtue; and its effects will be seen in the diminution of vice and crime, the more general practice of industry, sobriety and integrity, conservative and enlightened legislation, and universal obedience to the laws. In such a community the rights of property are stable, and the contributions imposed on it are essentially lightened. But I entertain a firm conviction that the present law requires a thorough revision, and that an entire change in the mode of assessment is indispensable."

On the 7th of January, 1851, Mr. MORGAN transmitted to the Legislature his third annual report as Superintendent, from which it appears that the whole number of districts in the State was 11,397; the number of children between five and sixteen, on the 31st of December, 1849, 735,188; and the number of children taught during the preceding year in the several common schools of the State, 794,500—being an excess of 59,312 over the number between the ages of five and sixteen, and of 16,191 over the whole number previously taught. The entire expenditure for school purposes, during the year reported, was $1,766,668.24. The number of volumes in the several district libraries was about 1,500,000. The Superintendent again urged upon the Legislature the importance of a more thorough and efficient local supervision, through the agency of a County or Assembly District Superintendent; alluded to the increased usefulness and flourishing prospects of the Normal School in which, in addition to the usual course of instruction, a limited number of Indian youth had been received as pupils during the preceding year; and concluded by strongly urging upon the attention of the legislature the expediency and necessity of such an amendment of the existing law, establishing Free Schools throughout the State, as was demanded by an enlightened public sentiment. "The history of the past year," he observes, "in reference to this great enterprise, has been one of mingled triumph and disaster, The principle incorporated in the 'Act for the establishment of Free Schools throughout the State' has been again subjected to the test of public opinion. In their almost unanimous approval of that *principle* in the canvass of 1849, the electors very generally overlooked the specific details of the bill submitted to their sanction, confiding in the disposition of the Legislature to modify such of its features as might be practically objectionable. Serious obstacles to the successful operation of the law presented themselves almost upon the threshold of its administration. The boards of supervisors in more than one-half of the counties of the State had adjourned their annual sessions before the act took effect, without making the appropriations required by its provisions, leaving the several school districts to sustain a most unequal and oppressive burden of taxation for the support of their schools.

"Inequalities in the valuations of taxable property contributed, in many localities, greatly to aggravate this burden, and a spirit of opposition to the new law, inflamed by its determined opponents, manifested itself at the primary district meetings, and too often resulted in the entire rejection of the estimates prepared by the trustees, and the limitation of the term of school to the lowest possible period authorized by law. Appeals were assiduously made to the cupidity of the heavy tax-payers—their interests sought to be arrayed against that of their less favored brethren, and against the interests of their children; their passions stimulated by the real inequalities as well as fancied injustice of the burdens imposed by the new law, were readily enlisted against every attempt to carry it into operation. Numerous petitions were sent to the Legislature, praying for its repeal, or for such amendments as might render it more generally acceptable.

"It was obvious that the law was liable to just and serious objections, and it did not meet with that general approval which was necessary to ensure its success. Under these circumstances, the friends of the new system were among the first to concede the defects of the bill, and while urging the preservation of the fundamental principle which it involved, were anxiously solicitous so to modify the details of the measure, as to obviate all its obnoxious features. At their suggestion and with their co-operation, bills were introduced into both branches of the Legislature, providing for a general and equitable system of State or county taxation, for the purpose of rendering the common schools free to all, dispensing with the necessity of a district assessment, out of which the principal embarrassment had originated. In the Assembly, the measures thus proposed were approved by a large majority; the Senate did not concur in the action of the House, but sent to the House a bill proposing a re-submission of the law to the people. At the close of the session, and when it became evident that no modification of the obnoxious law could be obtained, this bill received the assent of the House.

"By the adoption of this measure, the friends of free schools found themselves in a very embarassing position; they were compelled either to give their votes and influence in favor of the continuance of a law, some of the distinctive feature of which were at variance both with their wishes and judgment, or, by sanctioning its repeal, hazard the principle which had been deliberately adopted by the Legislature, and approved by the emphatic expression of the public will. The issue thus presented could not fail of being greatly misapprehended. While the electors secured the renewed triumph of the principle involved, there can be no doubt that thousands of votes were cast for the repeal of the law, by citizens who desired only its amendment, and who would have recorded their suffrages in favor of a system of free-schools properly guarded, had the form of the ballot permitted them to do so.

"It remains then for the Legislature to give efficacy to this renewed expression of the popular will, by the enactment of a law which shall definitively engraft the free school principle upon our existing system of primary education, and at the same time remove all just cause of complaint as to the inequality of taxation. District taxation has been found to be unjust, unequal and oppressive. It should therefore at once be abandoned, so far as the ordinary support of the schools is concerned. The funds necessary for payment of teachers' wages, in addition to the amount received from the State Treasury, should be provided either by a State tax equitably levied on real and personal property according to a fixed and uniform valuation, by a county and town tax, levied and assessed in the same manner, or by such a combination of these three modes as might be deemed most expedient and judicious.

"The common schools of the State should be declared free to every resident of the respective districts, of the proper age to participate in their benefits; and their support should be made a charge upon the whole property, either of the state at large, or of the respective counties and towns in which they are situated.

"The bill which passed the Assembly at its last session, provided for the levying of an annual tax of $800,000 on the real and personal property of the state according to the assessed valuation of such property, and for the distribution of the aggregate amount so to be raised, among the several counties and towns of the state, according to the number of children, of proper school age, residing in each. This sum, together with the amount annually apportioned from the revenue of the common school fund, would, it was supposed, be sufficient for the support of the several schools of the state,during an average period of eight months in each year. The whole amount expended for teachers' wages, during the year 1849, was $1,322,-696 24, to which is to be added an aggregate amount of $110,000 for library purposes, making in the whole $1,432,696 24. The superintendent, however, entertains no doubt that the amount proposed to be raised by the bill referred to, in conjunction with the State appropriation, the revenue for which is rapidly and steadily increasing, will be amply adequate to the payment of teachers' wages for the average length of time during which the schools have heretofore been taught, and to the annual and adequate replenishment of the libraries and necessary apparatus in the schools.

"Under the present defectively administered system of assessment, however, such a tax will operate very unequally in different sections of the State. The standard of valuation, both of real and personal property, varies, as is well known, in nearly every county of the State; while in some it is estimated at its fair and market value, in others it is assessed at three-fourths, two-thirds and sometimes as low as one-half its actual value. If, therefore the existing standard of valuation is to be made the basis of the apportionment of the proposed tax, it is manifest that a very unjust and oppressive burden will be cast upon those counties where the assessment is in strict accordance with the provisions of law, for the benefit of those sections in which its requirements are evaded by an arbitrary standard of valuation.

"The distribution of money when raised, serves likewise to render this disproportion still more manifest, that being based upon the population according to the last preceding census of the respective counties."

"Should the legislature deem it expedient to charge the annual support of the schools, over and above the revenue of the school fund, upon the taxable property of the State, and to retain the existing mode of distribution, the necessity of devising some mode by which the standard of valuation should be as nearly as practicable uniform thoughout the state, will be apparent. If this can be accomplished, or if the distribution of the funds raised were directed to be made upon the same basis with the apportionment of the tax, there can be no doubt,in the judgment of the Superintendent, that a state tax for the support of our common schools will prove the simplest, most efficient and beneficial mode of providing for the object in view: the establishment and maintenance of a system of free school education, in accordance with the expressed wishes of the inhabitants of the State.

"If, however, this were found impracticable, the same result may be obtained by requiring the board of supervisors of each county of the State to raise *twice* the amount apportioned to the county, as a county tax, and levy an equal amount as a town tax, in the mode prescribed by the existing law, which requires only an *equal* amount to be levied as a county and town tax respectively. This provision would simply increase the amount of school money now by law required to be raised, one-third, while it would entirely dispense with district taxation, for the current support of the schools. Inequalities in the standard of valuation adopted by the respective counties, would in this case prove unjust and burdensome to none; as the existing law has made complete provision for the adjustment of such inequalities in the case of joint districts formed from parts of two or more counties or towns. The whole amount of taxable property of each county would contribute in equal and fair proportions to the support of the schools located in its territory; and the angry dissensions growing out of the necessity of district taxation, the fruitful source of nearly all the opposition which has been made to the existing law, would be averted.

"In apportioning the public money, and the money raised by a county or State tax among the several school districts, the Superintendent is of opinion that some more effectual provision than now exists, should be made for the smaller and weaker districts, upon whom the burden of supporting a school for any considerable length of time during the year, is peculiarly oppressive. If a specified amount, say for instance fifty dollars, were required to be apportioned to every duly organized district whose report for the preceding year shall be found in accordance with law, leaving the balance to be apportioned according to the number of children between the ages of four and twenty-one years residing in the district, the necessary encouragement would be afforded to every district, however limited its means, or however sparse its population, while ample resources would be left for larger and more populous districts. The several districts being thus furnished with adequate funds for the maintenance of efficient schools during an average period of eight months in each year, the trustees should be peremptorily required to expend the moneys thus placed at their disposal, in the employment of suitably qualified teachers for such a length of time as those means may justify.

"Such an arrangement would, it is believed, prove almost universally acceptable to the people of the State. The principle involved has repeatedly received the sanction of public sentiment. It is in accordance with the enlightened spirit of the age. It is the only system compatible with the genius and spirit of our republican institutions. It is not a novelty, now for the first time sought to be engrafted upon our legislation, but a principle recognized and carried into practical operation in our sister State of Massachusetts from the earliest period of its colonial history—indentified with her greatness and prosperity, her influence and her wealth, and transplanted from her soil to that of some of the younger States of the Union.

"In each of our own cities, and in many of our larger villages, it has been established and successfully sustained by the general approval of their citizens, and wherever it has obtained a foothold it has never been abandoned. It is only requisite to adjust the details of the system equitably and fairly, to commend it to the approbation of every good citizen as the noblest palladium and most effectual support of our free institutions.

"The existing law has excited a degree of opposition which was not anticipated, but it is believed that it has grown out of the defects of the law, rather than from any prevailing hostility to the principle of free schools.

"No law can be successfully and prosperously administered under our government, which does not receive the general approval of the people. It is the earnest desire, therefore, of the Superintendent, that the present law should be so amended as to produce greater equality—to remove all reasonable ground of complaint, and to render our great system of education more efficient and useful.

"The idea of universal education is the grand central idea of the age. Upon this broad and comprehensive basis, all the experience of the past, all the crowding phenomena of the present, and all our hopes and aspirations for the future, must rest. Our forefathers have transmitted to us a noble inheritance of national, intellectual, moral and religious freedom. They have confided our destiny as a people to our own hands. Upon our individual and combined intelligence, virtue and patriotism, rests the solution of the great problem of self-government. We should be untrue to ourselves, untrue to the cause of liberty, of civilization and humanity, if we neglected the assiduous cultivation of those means, by which alone we can secure the realization of the hopes we have excited. Those means are the *universal education of our future citizens*, without discrimination or distinction. Wherever in our midst a human being exists, with capacities and faculties to be developed, improved, cultivated and directed, the avenues of knowledge should be freely opened, and every facility afforded to their unrestricted entrance. Ignorance should no more be countenanced than vice and crime. The one leads almost inevitably to the other. Banish ignorance, and in its stead introduce intelligence, science, knowledge and increasing wisdom and enlightenment, and you remove, in most cases, all those incentives to idleness, vice and crime, which now produce such a frightful harvest of retribution, misery and wretchedness. Educate every child, 'to the top of his faculties,' and you not only secure the community against the depredations of the ignorant and the criminal, but you bestow upon it, instead, productive artisans, good citizens, upright jurors and magistrates, enlightened statesmen, scientific discoverers and inventors, and the dispensers of a pervading influence in favor of honesty, virtue and true goodness. Educate every child physically, morally and intellectually, from the age of four to twenty-one, and many of your prisons, penitentiaries and alms-houses will be converted into schools of industry and temples of science, and the immense amount now contributed for their maintenance and support will be diverted into far more profitable channels. Educate every child—not superficially—not partially—but thoroughly—develope equally and healthfully every faculty of his nature—every capability of his being—and you infuse a new and invigorating element into the very life blood of civilization—an element which will diffuse itself throughout every vein and artery of the social and political system, purifying, strengthening and regenerating all its impulses, elevating its aspirations, and clothing it with a power equal to every demand upon its vast energies and resources.

"These are some of the results which must follow in the train of a wisely matured and judiciously organized system of universal education. They are not imaginary, but sober inductions from well authenticated facts—deliberate conclusions from established principles, sanctioned by the concurrent testimony of experienced educators and eminent statesmen and philanthropists. If names are needed to enforce the lesson they teach, those of Washington, and Franklin, and Hamilton, and Jefferson and Clinton, with a long array of patriots and statesmen, may be cited. If facts are required to illustrate the connection between ignorance and crime, let the official return of convictions in the several courts of the State for the last ten years be examined, and their instructive lessons be heeded. Out of nearly 28,000 persons convicted of crime, but 128 had enjoyed the benefits of a *good* common school education; 414 only had what the returning officers characterize as a 'tolerable' share of learning; and of the residue, about one-half only could either read or write. Let similar statistics be gathered from the wretched inmates of our poor house establishments, and similar results would undoubtedly be developed. Is it not, therefore, incomparably better, as a mere prudential question of political economy, to provide ample means for the education of the whole community, and to bring those means within the reach of every child, than to impose a much larger tax for the protection of that community against the depredations of the ignorant, the idle and the vicious, and for the support of the imbecile, the thoughtless and intemperate?

"Every consideration connected with the present and future welfare of the community—every dictate of an enlightened humanity—every impulse of an enlarged and comprehensive spirit of philanthropy, combine in favor of this great principle. Public sentiment has declared in its favor. The new States which, within the past few years, have been added to the Confederacy, have adopted it as the basis of their system of public instruction; and the older States, as one by one they are reconstructing their fundamental laws and constitutions, are engrafting the same principle upon their institutions. Shall New York, in this noble enterprise of education, retrace her steps? Shall she disappoint the high hopes and expectations she has excited, by receding from the advanced position she now occupies in the van of educational improvement? Her past career, in all those elements which go to make up the essential wealth and greatness of a people, has been one of progress and uninterrupted expansion. Her far-seeing legislators and statesmen, uninfluenced by the skepticism of the timid, the ignorant and the faithless, and unawed by the denunciations of the hostile, prosecuted that great work of internal improvement which will forever illustrate the pride and glory of her political history. The rich results of the experiment thus boldly ventured upon have vindicated their wisdom. Is the development of the intellectual and moral resources of her millions of future citizens an object of less interest, demanding a less devoted consecration of the energies of her people, and worthy of a less firm and uncompromising perseverance?

"Disregarding the feelings of the present hour, and looking only to the future, will the consciousness of having laid the foundation for the universal education of our people be a less pleasing subject of contemplation than that of having aided in replenishing the coffers of their wealth?

"In conclusion, the Superintendent cannot feel that he has fully met the responsibility devolved upon him by his official relations to the schools of the State, were he to fail in again urging upon the Legislature the definite adoption of this beneficent measure. Let its details be so adjusted as to bear equally upon all, oppressively upon none. Let every discordant element of strife and passion be removed from the councils of the districts, let the necessary assessment for the great object in view be diffused over the vast aggregate of the wealth and property of the State. Then let teachers, worthy of the name, teachers intellectually and morally qualified for the discharge of their high and responsible duties, dispense the benefits and riches of education, equally and impartially, to the eight hundred thousand children who annually congregate within the district school room.

"The children of the rich and the poor, the high and the low, the native and the foreigner, will then participate alike in the inexhaustible treasures of intellect, they will commence their career upon a footing of equality, under the fostering guardianship of the State, and will gradually ripen into enlightened and useful citizens, prepared for all the varied duties of life, and for the full enjoyment of all the blessings incident to humanity."

Numerous petitions were forwarded to the legislature from different sections of the state, for the repeal or amendment of the act of 1849. On the 6th day of February, Mr. T. H. Benedict, of Westchester, from the majority of the Assembly committee on colleges, academies and common schools, presented an elaborate and able report, accompanied by a bill "to establish Free Schools throughout the State." This bill declared common schools free to every child between the ages of five and twenty-one years; directed the levying of an annual state tax of $800,000 for their support, in addition to the funds already provided by the constitution; and provided for any balance that might be necessary for the payment of teachers' wages by a poll tax to be levied by the trustees on the inhabitants of the respective districts. Mr. Burroughs, of Orleans from the minority of the committee, reported a bill entitled "An act in relation to Common Schools," directing the sum of $800,000 to be annually levied by a state tax, one-fourth of the avails of which together with one-fourth of all other monies applicable to the support of common schools was directed to be equally divided among the several school districts, and the residue to be apportioned according to the number of children residing in each between the ages of five and twenty-one; and any balance requisite to be raised by rate bill.

After a protracted discussion of several weeks the bill entitled "AN ACT TO ESTABLISH FREE SCHOOLS THROUGHOUT THE STATE," was passed by a vote of 72 to 21. By this act the several common schools of the state was declared free to all persons residing in the several districts over five and under twenty-one years of age, as thereinafter provided; an annual state tax of $800,000 was directed to be levied for their support, *one-third* of which and of all other monies applicahle to the support of common schools, was directed to be equally divided among the several districts, and the residue to be apportioned according to the number of children between the ages of five and twenty-one; and any balance required for the payment of teachers' wages, to be provided for by a rate-bill, exempting all indigent persons. All property exempt by law from levy and sale on execution was declared to be exempt from the operation of the collectors warrant, on such rate bills. On the 10th of April, this bill passed the Senate without amendment, by a vote of 22 to 4, and on the 12th of April, was signed by the Governor and became a law.

Among those who by their exertions and influence, contributed materially to the final establishment and recognition of the Free School principle, and its incorporation as a fundamental portion of our Common School System, we may be permitted without disparagement to others less prominently connected with this important movement, to enumerate Governors SEWARD and HUNT, Superintendents YOUNG, BENTON and MORGAN, JAMES W. BEEKMAN, HORACE GREELEY and HENRY J. RAYMOND of New York; THOMAS LEGGETT, Jr. of Queens; Hon. FRANKLIN TUTHILL of Suffolk, A. W. LEGGETT, CALEB ROSCOE and THEODORE H. BENEDICT of Westchester: ALEXANDER G. JOHNSON, HENRY B. HASWELL, JOHN O. COLE, FRANKLIN TOWNSEND, JOHN V. L. PRUYN, BRADFORD R. WOOD, Rev. HENRY MANDEVILLE, FRIEND HUMPHREY, J. N. T. TUCKER, J. W. BULKLEY and WILLIAM F. PHELPS of Albany, Gen. JOHN E. WOOL, Prof. BAERMAN and GEORGE M. TIBBITTS of Rensselaer; JOHN BOWDISH of Montgomery; HALSEY R. WING of Warren; WILLIAM L. CRANDALL, editor of the Free School Clarion; HARVEY BALDWIN, CHARLES B. SEDGWICK, Rev. SAMUEL J. MAY, E. W. CURTIS, BENJAMIN COWLES, and the members of the Teachers Association of Onondaga; O. B. PIERCE, of Oneida; Dr. JOHN MILLER, SAMUEL B. WOOLWORTH and LEWIS KINGSLEY of Cortland; ALANSON HOLLEY of Wyoming; Gen. W. S. HUBBELL and DAVID MCMASTER of Steuben; CALEB LYON of Lewis; Dr. H. D. DIDAMA of Seneca; SALEM TOWN of Cayuga; JABEZ D. HAMMOND of Otsego; President NOTT of Union College; O. G. STEELE and Messrs STARR & RICE of Erie; SILAS M. BUROUGHS of Orleans; O. ARCHER of Wayne and CHARLES R. COBURN of Tioga. There were numerous other active and influential friends of education, in different sections of the state, whose services and exertions in behalf of this great measure, are none the less appreciated, although the limited space at our disposal does not permit us to give their names in this connection.

GENERAL OUTLINES OF THE SYSTEM.

The entire territory of the state, comprising, exclusively of the waters of the great lakes, an area of 45,658 square miles has been subdivided into about eleven thousand and four hundred school districts, averaging somewhat more than four square miles each—seldom, in the rural districts, varying materially from this average—and bringing the remotest inhabitants of the respective districts within a little more than one mile of the school house.

Common schools in the several districts of the state are free to all residents of the districts between the ages of four and twenty-one years, and non-residents of the district may be admitted into the school of any district with the written consent of the trustees.

Every male person of the age of twenty-one years and upwards, residing in any school district, (including aliens entitled by law to hold real estate) who owns or hires real property in such district subject to taxation for school puposes, or who is a legal voter at town meetings, and is the owner of personal property liable to taxation in the district for school purposes, exceeding fifty dollars in value, beyond such as is exempt from execution, is entitled to vote at any school district meeting held in such district.

An annual meeting of the inhabitants of each district entitled to vote therein, is to be held, after the first organization of the district, at the time and place designated at the first and at each subsequent meeting; and special meetings are to be held whenever called by the trustees.

When legally assembled in any district meeting, the inhabitants of each district, so entitled to vote, are authorized by a majority of the votes of those present, either by ballot or otherwise as they may determine, to choose three trustees, a district clerk, collector, and librarian. The trustees chosen at the first legal meeting of the district, are to be divided by lot into three classes, and the term of office of the first is to be one year; of the second, two, and of the third, three years; and one trustee, only is thereafter annually to be elected, who holds his office for three years. The clerk, collector and librararian are annually elected. In the event of a vacancy happening in the office of trustee, by death, refusal to serve, removal out of the district, or incapacity to act, such vacancy may be supplied by the district, and if more than a month is permitted to elapse, without filling it, the town Superintendent is authorized to appoint; and the person so chosen or appointed holds only for the unexpired term of the office whose place he fills. A similar vacancy in the offices of clerk, collector, or librarian, is to be supplied by appointment of the trustees or a majority of them. The town Superintendent, on good cause shown, is authorized to accept the resignation of any district officer.

The inhabitants of the several districts, in district meeting assembled are also authorized to designate a site for a schoolhouse,or(with the consent of the town superintendent)for two or more school houses for the district,and to vote such an amount as they may deem sufficient to purchase or lease such a site or sites and to build hire or purchase a school house or houses, keep the same in suitable repair,and furnish them with the necessary fuel and appendages; and may, in their discretion vote a tax not exceeding twenty dollars in any one year for the purchase of maps, globes, black-boards and other school apparatus. No tax, however, for building, hiring or purchasing a school house can exceed the sum of $400, unless the town Superintendent of the town in which such house is to be situated, shall certify that a larger sum, specifying the same, ought to be raised; and when the site for the school house has once been fixed, it cannot be change, while the district remains unaltered, but by the written consent of the town Superintendent, and by the vote ayes and noes of a majority of the inhabitants of the district, at a special meeting called for that purpose. In this case the inhabitants may direct the sale of the former site or lot, together with the buildings and appertenances on such terms as they may deem most advantageous to the district, and the trustees, or a majority of them are empowered to effect such sale and to execute the necessary conveyances. The proceeds are to be applied to the purchase of a new site, and to the removal, erection or purchase of new houses.

The general administration of the affairs of the several districts, devolves principally upon the trustees, who have the custody of all the district property; contract with, employ and pay the teachers; assess all district taxes, following the valuations of the town assessor, so far as they afford a guide, and make out the necessary tax lists and warrants for their collection; call the annual and special meetings of the inhabitants; purchase or lease sites for the school house, as previously designated by the district, and build, hire or purchase, keep in repair and furnish such school house with necessary fuel and appendages, out of the funds provided by the district for that purpose;

purchase suitable books for the district library, which is specially committed to their care, and procure all such school apparatus as the district may direct; and on the first of January in each year make their report of the condition of the district, in the form prescribed by law, to the Town Superintendent.

The productive capital of the Common School Fund is at this time,...	$2,243,563 36
The capital of that portion of the U. S. Deposite Fund, the interest of which is annually appropriated to the support of Common Schools, is..	2,750,000 00
To which may be added a sum that will annually produce an income of $25,000, reserved by the constitution to be added to the capital of the school fund, viz :.................	416,666 67
Making an aggregate of..	$5,400,230 03

The annual interest on this sum, at 6 per cent., is $324,000.00 ; of which $300,000 is annually appropriated to the support of Common Schools, including $55,000 for the purchase of District Libraries and school apparatus.

The sum of eight hundred thousand dollars is annually required to be levied on the real and personal property of the State, and when collected to be paid over to the several County Treasurers, subject to the order of the State Superintendent of Common Schools, who is to ascertain the proportion of such sum to be assessed and collected in each county, according to the valuation of real and personal estate therein, and to certify the same to the several County Clerks, to be laid before the boards of Supervisors, whose duty it is to levy such amount upon the County. On or before the first day of January in each year, the State Superintendent is required to apportion two-thirds of the amount so raised, together with all other monies appropriated to the support of Common Schools among the several counties, cities and towns of the State, according to the population of such counties, cities and towns, and to divide the remaining third equally among the several districts.

Under these provisions, the aggregate amount of public money annually apportioned by the State Superintendent, and raised upon the taxable property of the several counties, is $1,100,000.00 ; of which, $1,045,000 is applicable exclusively to the payment of teachers' wages, and the support of the school, and the remaining $55,000 to the purchase of school libraries and apparatus.

In addition to this, the inhabitants of each town of the State are authorized to raise an additional amount, equal to their share of the state fund, to be appropriated exclusively to the support of schools ; and many of the towns are in possession of local funds applicable to this object, derived from the sale of lands originally set apart in each township, by the State, for this purpose.

Town superintendents are biennially elected by the inhabitants and legal voters of the several towns, at their annual meetings in March and April of each alternate year, and enter upon the execution of the duties devolved upon them, on the first Monday of November succeeding their election, holding for the term of two years thereafter. They are required to execute to the supervisor of their town a bond with sufficient sureties, with a penalty in double the amount of all the school money received by the town, conditioned for the faithful application and legal disbursement of all the school money which may come into their hand during their term of office, and for the faithful discharge of all their duties. They are authorized to form, regulate and alter the boundaries of school districts, when applied to for that purpose, or when in their judgment necessary and expedient, associating with them the supervisor and town clerk of their town, whenever requested by the trustees of any district interested in any proposed alteration;

and it is their duty to apply for and receive from the county treasurer and town collector respectively, all school money apportioned or belonging to their town; and on or before the first Tuesday in April of each year to apportion the same among the several districts of their town, according to the number of children between the ages of four and twenty-one, residing in each, as reported to them by the trustees, provided such districts have in all respects complied with the directions of law during the preceding year, and made the annual report required of them.

No district, without the special permission of the state superintendent can participate in such apportionment, which has not had a school taught within it for at least six months during the year reported, by a duly qualified teacher; which has not faithfully expended all its public money in the mode prescribed by law; or in which a school has been taught for a period exceeding one month by an unqualified teacher.

In making such apportionment, the town Superintendents designate the respective sums applicable to the payment of teachers, and to the purchase of libraries and school apparatus; and hold the former subject to the order of the trustees, or of a majority of them, in favor of the teachers employed by them and duly qualified according to law; paying over the library money directly to the trustees. They are also to examine candidates for teachers and to grant certificates of qualification, which are valid for one year only, and may at any time be annulled by them, on notice to the teacher holding such certificate; and to visit and inspect the several schools of their town at least twice in each year, and oftener if they deem it necessary. On the first day of July of each year, they are to make and file with the county clerk, a report in the form prescribed by the State Superintendent and containing such information in reference to the condition of the schools in their town, as he may from time to time direct. At the expiration of their term of office they are to account to their successors for all the school moneys received and disbursed by them, and to pay over any balance remaining in their hands. For their services they are entitled to receive $1,25 per day for every day actually devoted by them to the discharge of their official duties.

At the seat of government, the State Normal School semi-annually receives under its instruction from two hundred to two hundred and fifty pupils of both sexes, selected by the Board of Town Superintendents of the respective counties, each county being entitled to two pupils for each member of Assembly. After spending from two to three years in the institution, the graduates return to their respective counties, and enter upon the active discharge of their duties as teachers; communicating, as often as may be practicable, through the agency of the Teachers Institutes, in the spring and fall of each year, a general knowledge of the modes of teaching, government and discipline attained by them in the Normal School. These Institutes, under the supervision and general direction of the most experienced guides, enable every teacher to acquaint himself practically and familiarly with the duties devolving upon him, and secure to each one of the eleven thousand districts of our State, a faithful and efficient teacher.

At the head of the whole system—controlling, regulating, and giving life and efficiency to all its parts is the state Superintendent. He apportions the state tax of $800,000, and the public money among the several counties and towns,—distributes the laws, instructions, decisions, forms &c., through the agency of the town Superintendents to the several districts, —has final jurisdiction, on appeal, from all the acts and proceedings of the inhabitants of the several districts and their officers, as well as of Town Superintendents, keeps up a constant correspondence with the several officers connected with the administration of the system in all its parts, as well as with the inhabitants of districts seeking aid, counsel or advice; exercises a liberal discretionary power, on equitable principles, in all cases of inadvertent, unintentional, or accidental omissions to comply with the strict requisitions of the law; grants state certificates of qualification to such teachers as he deems worthy: reports annually to the legislature respecting the condition, prospects and resources of the Common Schools, and the management of the School fund, together with such suggestions for the improvement of the system as may occur to him; and vigilantly watches over, encourages, sustains, and expands to its utmost practicable limit, the vast system of common school education throughout the state.

Such is a condensed view of our present system of COMMON SCHOOL EDUCATION;—a system elaborated and matured to its present state, by the exertions of the highest minds among us, during a period of forty years; a system comprehending the best and dearest interests present and prospective of an enlightened and free people—full of promise for the future, and containing within itself, the germs of the most extended individual, social and national prosperity; a system identified with the highest hopes and interests of all classes of the community, and from which are destined to flow those streams of intelligence and of public and private virtue which alone can enable us worthily to fulfil the noble destinies involved in our free institutions.

But in this country, no systems, however perfect, no enactments, however enlightened, and no authority, however constituted, can attain to the full accomplishment of their object, however praiseworthy and laudable, without the hearty and efficient co-operation of public sentiment. Aided by this co-operation, the most important results may be anticipated from the most simple organization. The repeated and solemn recognition by the representatives of the people, of the interests of popular education and public instruction; the nearly unanimous adoption of a system, commended to the public favor as well by practical experience, as by the concurring testimony of the most enlightened minds of our own and other countries; and the simplification of much of the complicated machinery which served only to encumber and impede the operation of that system; these indications afford the most conclusive evidence not only of the importance which the great mass of our fellow citizens attach to the promotion of sound intellectual and moral instruction, but of their determination to place our common schools, where this instruction is chiefly dispensed to the children of the state, upon a footing which shall enable them most effectually to accomplish the great objects of their institution.

It is upon the extent and permanency of this feeling, that the friends of education rely; and this spirit to which they appeal, in looking forward to the just appreciation and judicious improvement of those means of moral and mental enlightenment which the beneficent policy of the state has placed at the disposal of the inhabitants of the several districts. The renovation of our common schools, distributed as they are, over every section of our entire territory, their elevation and expansion to meet the constantly increasing requirements of science and mental progress, and their capability of laying broad and deep the foundations of character and usefulness, must depend upon the intelligent and fostering culture which they shall receive at the hands of those to whose immediate charge they are committed. There is no institution within the range of civilization, upon which so much, for good or for evil depends—upon which hang so many and such important issues to the future well being of individuals and communities, as the common district school. It is through that alembic that the lessons of the nursery and the family fire-side, the earliest instructions in pure morality, and the precepts and examples of the social circle are distilled; and from it those lessons are destined to assume that tinge and hue which are permanently to be incorporated into the character and the life. Is it too much then, to ask or to expect of parents, that laying aside all minor considerations, abandoning all controversies and dissentions among themselves in reference to local, partisan and purely selfish objects, or postponing them at least, until the interests of their children are placed beyond the influence of these irritating topics, they will consecrate their undivided energies to the advancement and improvement of these beneficent institutions. Resting as it does upon their support, indebted to them for all its means of usefulness, and dependent for its continued existence upon their discriminating favor and efficient sanction, the practical superiority of the existing system of public instruction, its comprehensiveness and simplicity—its abundant and unfailing resources—and its adaptation to the educational wants of every class of community, will prove of little avail without the invigorating influences of a sound and enlightened public sentiment, emanating from, and pervading the entire social system. The district school must become the central interest of the citizen and the parent, the clergyman, the lawyer, the physician, the merchant, the manufacturer and the agriculturist. Each must realise that there, under more or less favoring auspices, as they themselves shall determine, developments are in progress which are destined, at no distant day to exert a controlling influence over the institutions, habits, modes of thought and action of society in all its complicated phases; and that the primary responsibility for the results which may be thus worked out, for good or for evil, rests with them. By the removal of every obstacle to the progressive and harmonious action of the system of popular education, so carefully organized and amply endowed by the state, by a constant, and methodical and intelligent co-operation with its authorized agents, in the elevation and advancement of that system in all its parts, and especially by an infusion into its entire course of discipline and instruction of that high moral culture which can alone adequately realize the idea of sound education, results of inconceivable magnitude and importance to individual, social, and moral well being may confidently be anticipated. These results can only be attained by an enlightened appreciation and judicious cultivation of the means of elementary instruction. They demand and will amply repay the consecration of the highest intellectual and moral energies, the most comprehensive benevolence, and the best affections of our common nature.

COMPARATIVE STATEMENT

Of the condition of the Common Schools, from 1815, *the period of the first Statistical Report, to* 1850.

Date of report of trustees	Whole No. of Districts in the towns from which reports were made.	Number of Districts from which returns were rec'd.	No. of children taught in said Districts.	No. of children between the ages of 5 & 16 years residing in said distr's.	Sum annually paid from State Treasury.	Amount of money rec'd by the Districts.	Amount paid by individuals on rate bills.
May 1, 1815	2,755	2,631	140,106	176,449	$48,376	$55,720 98	....
" 1816	3,713	2,873	170,385	198,440	46,398	64,834 88	....
" 1817	3,264	3,228	183,253	218,969	54,799	73,235 42	....
" 1818	4,614	3,844	210,316	235,871	59,933	93,010 54	....
" 1819	5,763	5,118	271,877	302,703	59,968	117,151 07	....
Jan. 1, 1820	6,332	5,489	304,559	317,633	59,930	146,418 08	....
" 1821	6,659	5,882	332,979	339,258	79,957	157,195 04	....
" 1822	7,051	6,255	351,173	357,029	80,104	173,420 60	....
" 1823	7,382	6,705	377,034	373,208	80,000	180,820 25	....
" 1824	7,642	6,876	402,940	383,500	80,000	182,741 61	....
" 1825	7,773	7,117	425,566	395,586	80,000	182,790 09	....
" 1826	8,114	7,550	431,601	411,256	80,000	185,720 46	....
" 1827	8,298	7,806	441,856	419,216	80,000	222,995 77	....
" 1828	8,609	8,164	468,205	449,113	100,000	232,343 21	....
" 1829	8,872	8,292	480,041	468,257	100,000	214,840 14	$297,048 44
" 1830	9,063	8,631	499,424	497,503	100,000	238,640 36	346,807 20
" 1831	9,339	8,841	507,105	509,967	100,000	244,998 85	374,001 54
" 1832	9,600	8,941	494,595	508,878	100,000	305,582 78	358,320 17
" 1833	9,690	9,107	512,475	522,618	100,080	307,733 08	369,696 36
" 1834	9,865	9,392	531,240	534,002	100,080	316,153 93	398,137 04
" 1835	10,132	9,676	541,401	540,285	100,080	312,181 20	419,878 69
" 1836	10,207	9,696	532,167	538,398	100,000	313,376 91	425,560 86
" 1837	10,345	9,718	224,188	536,882	100,000	335,895 10	436,346 46
" 1838	10,583	9,830	528,913	539,747	110,000	335,882 92	477,848 27
" 1839	10,706	10,127	557,229	564,790	113,793	374,411 61	521,477 49
" 1840	10,769	10,397	572,995	592,564	*275,000	633,685 94	476,443 27
" 1841	10,886	10,588	603,583	583,347	*275,000	658,954 70	483,479 54
" 1842	10,893	10,645	598,749	601,765	*285,000	676,086 07	468,688 22
" 1843	10,875	10,656	667,782	677,995	*275,000	660,727 41	509,376 97
" 1844	10,990	10,357	709,156	696,548	275,000	639,606 60	447,565 97
" 1845	11,018	10,812	736,045	690,914	275,000	725,066 19	458,127 78
" 1846	11,008	10,796	742,423	703,399	275,000	772,578 02	460,764 78
" 1847	11,052	10,859	748,387	700,443	275,000	829,802 83	462,840 44
" 1848	10,621	10,494	475,723	718,123	275,826	858,594 84	466,674 44
" 1849	11,191	10,928	778,309	739,655	284,902	846,710 45	489,696 63
" 1850	11,397	11,173	794,506	735,188	285,000	767,389 20	508,724 56

*Including revenue from United States Deposit Fund.

AN ACT TO ESTABLISH FREE SCHOOLS THROUGHOUT THE STATE.

Passed April 12, 1851.

The People of the State of New York, represented in Senate and Assembly, do enact as follows:

§ 1. Common schools in the several school districts in this State shall be free to all persons residing in the district, over five and under twenty-one years of age, as hereinafter provided. Persons not resident of a district may be admitted into the schools kept therein, with the approbation, in writing, of the trustees thereof, or a majority of them.

§ 2. There shall hereafter be raised by tax, in each and every year, upon the real and personal estate within this state, the sum of eight hundred thousand dollars, which shall be levied, assessed and collected in the mode prescribed by chapter thirteen, part first of the revised statutes, relating to the assessment and collection of taxes, and when collected shall be paid over to the respective county treasurers, subject to the order of the state superintendent of common schools.

§ 3. The state superintendent of common schools shall ascertain the portion of said sum of eight hundred thousand dollars to be assessed and collected in each of the several counties of this state, by dividing the said sum among the several counties, according to the valuation of real and personal estate therein, as it shall appear by the assessment of the year next preceding the one in which said sum is to be raised, and shall certify to the clerk of each county, before the tenth day of July in each year, the amount to be raised by tax in such county; and it shall be the duty of the several county clerks of this state to deliver to the board of supervisors of their respective counties, a copy of such certificate, on the first day of their annual session, and the board of supervisors of each county shall assess such amount upon the real and personal estate of such county, in the manner provided by law for the assessment and collection of taxes.

§ 4. The state superintendent of common schools shall, on or before the first day of January in every year, apportion and divide, or cause to be apportioned and divided, one third of the sum so raised by general tax, and one third of all other moneys appropriated to the support of common schools, among the several school districts, parts of districts, and separate neighborhoods in this state, from which reports shall have been received in accordance with law in the following manner, viz: to each separate neighborhood belonging to a school district in some adjoining state, there shall be apportioned and paid a sum of money equal to thirty-three cents for each child in such neighborhood (between the ages of four and twenty-one); but the sum so to be apportioned and paid to any such neighborhood, shall in no case exceed the sum of twenty-four dollars, and the remainder of such one-third shall be apportioned and divided equally among the several districts; and the state superintendent of common schools shall, by proper regulations and instructions to be prescribed by him, provide for the payment of such moneys to the trustees of such separate neighborhoods and school districts.

§ 5. It shall be the duty of the state superintendent of common schools, on or before the first day of January in every year, to apportion and divide the remaining two-thirds of the said amount of eight hundred thousand dollars, together with the remaining two-thirds of all other moneys appropriated by the state for the support of common schools among the several counties, cities and towns of the state, in the mode now prescribed by law for the division and apportionment of the income of the common school fund; and the share of the several towns and wards so apportioned and divided shall be paid over on and after the first Tuesday in February, in each year, to the several town superintendents of common schools, and ward or city officers, entitled by law to receive the same, and shall be apportioned by them among the several school districts and parts of districts in their several towns and wards, according to the number of children between the ages of four and twenty-one years, residing in said districts and parts of districts, as the same shall have appeared from the last annual report of the trustees; but no moneys shall be apportioned and paid to any district or part of a district, unless it shall appear from the last annual report of the trustees, that a school has been kept therein for at least six months during the year ending with the date of such report, by a duly qualified teacher, unless by special permission of the state superintendent of common schools; excepting, also, that the first apportionment of money under this act shall be made to all school districts which were entitled to an apportionment of public money in the year eighteen hundred and forty-nine.

§ 6. Any balance required to be raised in any school district for the payment of teachers' wages, beyond the amount apportioned to such district by the previous provisions of this act, and other public moneys belonging to the district applicable to the payment of teachers' wages, shall be raised by rate-bill, to be made out by the trustees against those sending to school, in proportion to the number of days and of children sent, to be ascertained by the teacher's list; and in making out such rate-bill, it shall be the duty of the trustees to exempt, either wholly or in part, as they may deem expedient, such indigent inhabitants as may in their judgment be entitled to such exemption; and the amount of such exemption shall be added to the first tax list thereafter to be made out by the trustees for district purposes, or shall be separately levied by them, as they shall deem most expedient.

§ 7. The same property which is exempt by section twenty-two, of article two, title five, chapter six, part three of the revised statutes, from levy and sale under execution, shall be exempt from levy and sale under any warrant to collect any rate-bill for wages of teachers of common schools.

§ 8. Nothing in this act shall be so construed as to repeal or alter the provisions of any special act relating to schools in any of the incorporated cities or villages of this state, except so far as they are inconsistent with the provisions contained in the first, second, third and fourth sections of this act.

§ 9. Chapter one hundred and forty of the session laws of one thousand eight hundred and forty-nine, entitled "An act establishing free schools throughout the state," and chapter four hundred and four of the session laws of one thousand eight hundred and forty-nine, entitled "An act to amend an act establishing free schools throughout the state," and sections sixteen, seventeen and eighteen of the revised statutes relating to common schools, requiring the several boards of supervisors to raise by tax, on each of the towns of their respective counties, a sum equal to the school moneys apportioned to such towns, and providing for its collection and payment, and all other provisions of law incompatible with the provisions of this act are hereby repealed.

§ 10. The state superintendent of common schools shall cause to be prepared, published and distributed among the several school districts and school officers of the state, a copy of the several acts now in force relating to common schools, with such instructions, digest and expositions as he may deem expedient; and the expense incurred by him therefor shall be audited by the comptroller and paid by the treasurer.

§ 11. All the moneys received or appropriated by the provisions of this act shall be applied to the payment of teachers' wages exclusively.

§ 12. It shall be the duty of the trustees of the several school districts in this state, to make out and transmit to the town superintendent of the town in which their respective school houses shall be located, on or before the first day of September next, a correct statement of the whole number of children residing in their district on the first day of August preceding the date of such report, between the ages of four and twenty-one; and such town superintendent shall embody such statement in a tabular form, and transmit the same to the county clerk in sufficient season to enable the latter to incorporate the information thus obtained in the annual report required by him to be made to the state superintendent of common schools for the present year.

§ 13. It shall also be the duty of the trustees of the several school districts, in their annual reports thereafter to be made, to specify the number of children, between the aforesaid ages, residing in their respective districts on the last day of December in each year, instead of the number of such children between the ages of five and sixteen.

§ 14. This act shall take effect on the first day of May next; but nothing herein contained shall be so construed as to affect provisions already made in the several school districts for the support of schools therein under existing laws for the current year.

PART II.

STATUTES

RELATING TO

COMMON SCHOOLS,

INCLUDING

TITLE II. CHAPTER XV. PART I. REVISED STATUTES.

[Pursuant to the directions of the 10th section of the act of chap. 151 of the laws of 1851, there are inserted in this publication of the second title of chapter 15, all acts and parts of acts connected with the subjects of the said title, which are now in force; and where the provisions of that title have been altered by subsequent acts, such provisions have been varied in order to conform them to such alteration. The original number of each section is in all cases retained, whether it was a part of the Revised Statutes or was taken from some session law passed since 1828. In the latter case, there is a reference to a note at the foot of the page, which gives the particular chapter from which the section is taken, and its number is enclosed within brackets, in order to designate it more distinctly from the sections of the Revised Statutes, which are printed with the section mark only.

To facilitate references to them, the sections in this edition are also numbered continuously from the first to the last, without regard to the statutes from which they are taken. The index at the end refers to these numbers.]

TITLE II.

OF COMMON SCHOOLS.

ART. 1.—Of the powers and duties of the superintendent of common schools, and of the apportionment of school moneys.

ART. 2.—Of the distribution of the common school fund.

ART. 3.—Of the powers and duties of town superintendents of common schools.

ART. 4.—Of inspection and supervision by town superintendents.

ART. 5.—Of the formation and alteration of school districts; the powers of school district inhabitants; of the choice, duties and powers of school district officers; the assessment and collection of school district taxes; the annual reports of trustees; school district libraries.

ART. 6.—Of certain duties of the county clerk.

ART. 7.—Miscellaneous provisions.

ARTICLE FIRST.

Of the Powers and Duties of the Superintendent of Common Schools, and of the Apportionment of School Moneys.

No. 1—§ 1. There shall continue to be a superintendent of common schools, whose duty, among other things, it shall be, to prepare and submit an annual report to the legislature containing,

1. A statement of the condition of the common schools of the state:

2. Estimates and accounts of expenditures of the school moneys:

3. Plans for the improvement and management of the common school fund, and for the better organization of the common schools; and,

4. All such matters relating to his office, and to the common schools, as he shall deem expedient to communicate.

No. 2—[§ 41.] The superintendent of common schools may designate and appoint any one of the clerks employed by him to be his general deputy, who may perform all the duties of the superintendent in case of his absence or a vacancy in his office.[1]

No. 3—[§ 8.] The superintendent of common schools may appoint such and so many persons as he shall from time to time deem necessary, to visit and examine into the condition of the common schools in the county where such persons may reside, and report to the superintendent on all such matters relating to the condition of such schools, and the means of improving them, as he shall prescribe; but no allowance or compensation shall be made to the said visitors for such services.[2]

No. 4—[§ 10.] The superintendent of common schools, on such evidence as may be satisfactory to him, may grant certificates of qualification under his hand and seal of office, which shall be evidence that the holder of such certificate is well qualified in respect to moral character, learning and ability, to teach any district school within this state; which certificate shall be valid until duly revoked by the superintendent.[3]

(1.) Laws of 1841, chap. 260, § 41. (2.) Laws of 1839, chap. 330, §8. (3.) Laws of 1843, chap. 133, §10.

No. 5—[§ 7.] Copies of papers deposited or filed in the office of the superintendent of common schools, and all acts and decisions by him, may be authenticated under the seal of the office of secretary of state, and when so authenticated shall be evidence equally, and in like manner as the originals.[4]

No. 6—[§2 & 3.] The superintendent shall apportion the school moneys to be annually distributed amongst the several counties of the state, and the share of each county, amongst its respective towns and cities. Such apportionment shall be made among the several towns and cities of the state, according to the ratio of their population respectively, as compared with the population of the whole state, according to the last preceding census.

No. 7—[§ 6.] When the census or returns, upon which an apportionment is to be made, shall be so far defective, in respect to any county, city or town, as to render it impracticable for the superintendent to ascertain the share of school moneys, which ought then to be apportioned to such county, city or town, he shall ascertain, by the best evidence in his power, the facts upon which the ratio of such apportionment shall depend, and shall make the apportionment accordingly.

No. 8—[§ 2.] There shall hereafter be raised by tax, in each and every year, upon the real and personal estate within this state, the sum of eight hundred thousand dollars, which shall be levied, assessed and collected in the mode prescribed by chapter thirteen, part first, of the revised statutes, relating to the assessment and collection of taxes, and when collected shall be paid over to the respective county treasurers, subject to the order of the state superintendent of common schools.[1]

No. 9—[§ 3.] The state superintendent of common schools shall ascertain the portion of said sum of eight hundred thousand dollars to be assessed and collected in each of the several counties of this state, by dividing the said sum among the several counties, according to the valuation of real and personal estate therein, as it shall appear by the assessment of the year next preceding the one in which said sum is to be raised, and shall certify to the clerk of each county, before the tenth day of July in each year, the amount to be raised by tax in such county; and it shall be the duty of the several county clerks of this state to deliver to the board of supervisors of their respective counties, a copy of such certificate, on the first day of their annual session, and the board of supervisors of each county shall assess such amount upon the real and personal estate of such county, in the manner provided by law for the assessment and collection of taxes.[1]

No. 10—[§ 4.] The State superintendent of common schools shall, on or before the first day of January in every year, apportion and divide, or cause to be apportioned and divided, one third of the sum so raised by general tax, and one third of all other

---

(4.) Laws of 1839, chap. 330, § 7. (1.) Laws of 1851, chap. 151, § 1,2.

monies appropriated to the support of common schools, among the the several school districts, parts of districts and separate neighborhoods in this state, from which reports shall have been received in accordance with law, in the following manner, viz: to each separate neighborhood, belonging to a school district, in some adjoining state, there shall be apportioned and paid a sum of money equal to thirty three cents for each child in such neighborhood, between the ages of four and twenty-one; but the sum so to be apportioned and paid to any such neighborhood shall in no case exceed the sum of twenty-four dollars, and the remainder of such one-third shall be apportioned and divided equally among the several districts; and the state superintendent of common schools shall by proper regulations and instructions to be prescribed by him, provide for the payment of such monies to the trustees of such separate neighborhoods and school districts. [1]

No. 11—[§ 5.] It shall be the duty of the state superintendent of common schools, on or before the first day of January in every year, to apportion and divide the remaining two thirds of the said amount of eight hundred thousand dollars, together with the remaining two-thirds of all other moneys appropriated by the state for the support of common schools, among the several counties, cities and towns of the state, in the mode now prescribed by law for the division and apportionment of the income of the common school funds; and the share of the several towns and wards so apportioned and divided, shall be paid over on and after the first Tuesday of February in each year, to the several town superintendents of common schools, and ward or city officers, entitled by law to receive the same, and shall be apportioned by them among the several school districts and parts of districts in their several towns and wards, according to the number of children between the ages of four and twenty-one years, residing in said districts and parts of districts, as the same shall have appeared from the last annual report of the trustees; but no monies shall be apportioned and paid to any district or part of a district, unless it shall appear from the last annual reports of the trustees that a school has been kept therein for at least six months during the year ending with the date of such report, by a duly qualified teacher, unless by special permission of the state superintendent of common schools; excepting also that the first apportionment of money under this act shall be made to all school districts which were entitled to an apportionment of public money, in the year eighteen hundred and forty-nine. [1]

No. 12—[§ 11.] All the monies received or appropriated by the provisions of this act shall be applied to the payment of teachers' wages exclusively. [2]

No. 13—[§7.] Whenever, in consequence of the division of a town, or the erection of a new town, in any county, the apportion-

---

(1) Laws of 1851, chap. 151, § 3, 4. (2.) Laws of 1851, chap. 151, § 11.

ment then in force shall become unjust, as between two or more of the towns of such county, the superintendent shall make a new apportionment of the school moneys next to be distributed amongst such towns, ascertaining by the best evidence in his power, the facts upon which the ratio of apportionment as to such towns, shall depend.

No. 14—[§8.] The superintendent shall certify each apportionment made by him, to the comptroller, and shall give immediate notice thereof, to the clerk of each county interested therein, and to the clerk of the city and county of New York; stating the amount of moneys apportioned to his county, and to each town and city therein, and the time when the same will be payable to the treasurer of such county, or to the chamberlain of the city of New York.

No. 15—[§3.] It shall be the duty of the clerk of the board of supervisors in each county in this state, on the last day of December in each year, to transmit to the superintendent of common schools certified copies of all resolutions and proceedings of the board of supervisors, of which he is clerk, passed or had during the preceding year, relating to the raising of any money for school or library purposes, and in case it shall not appear that the amount required by law to be raised for school and library purposes has been directed to be raised during the year by the board of supervisors of any county, the superintendent of common schools and the comptroller may direct that the money appropriated by the state and apportioned to such county, be withheld until the amount that may be deficient shall be raised, or that so much only of the money apportioned to such county be paid to the treasurer thereof, as shall be equal to the amount directed to be raised therein by the supervisors of such county; and in such case the balance so withheld shall be added to the principal of the common school fund.

No. 16—[§9.] The superintendent shall prepare suitable forms and regulations for making all reports, and conducting all necessary proceedings under this Title, and shall cause the same, with such instructions as he shall deem necessary and proper, for the better organizations and government of common schools, to be transmitted to the officers required to execute the provisions of this Title throughout the state.

No. 17—[§10.] He shall cause so many copies of the first six Articles of this Title, with the forms, regulations and instructions prepared by him, thereto annexed, to be, from time to time, printed and distributed amongst the several school districts of the state, as he shall deem the public good to require.

No. 18—[§11.] All moneys reasonably expended by him, in the execution of his duties, shall upon due proof, be allowed to him by the comptroller, and be paid out of the treasury.

No. 19—[§13.] Whenever any money is paid into the treasury of the State for or on account of the common school fund, it shall be the duty of the comptroller to credit the common school fund with interest on the sum so paid in, at the rate of six per cent per annum, for the time the same shall remain in the Treasury.[1]

ARTICLE SECOND.

Of the distribution of the Common School Fund.

No. 20—[§12.] The sum annually to be distributed for the encouragement of common schools, shall be paid on the first day of February, in every year, on the warrant of the comptroller, to the treasurers of the several counties, and the chamberlain of the city of New York.

No. 21—[§13.] The treasurer of each county, and the chamberlain of the city of New York, shall apply for and receive the school moneys apportioned to their respective counties, as soon as the same become payable.

No. 22—[§14.] Each treasurer receiving such moneys, shall give notice in writing, to the town superintendent or to some one or more of the commissioners of common schools of each town or city in his county, of the amount apportioned to such town or city, and shall hold the same subject to the order of such town superintendent or commissioners.

No. 23—[§15.] In case the commissioners or town superintendent of any such city or town shall not apply for and receive such moneys, or in case there are no commissioners or town superintendent appointed in the same, before the next receipt of moneys apportioned to the county, the moneys so remaining with the treasurer shall be retained by him, and be added to the moneys next received by him, for distribution from the superintendent of common schools, and be distributed therewith, and in the same proportion.

No. 24—[§16.] Whenever the clerk of any county shall receive from the superintendent of common schools notice of the apportionment of moneys to be distributed in the county, he shall file the same in his office, and transmit a certified copy thereof to the county treasurer, and to the clerk of the board of supervisors of the county; and the clerk of the board of supervisors shall lay such copy before the supervisors at their next meeting.

Of the Election and Powers of Town Superintendents.

No. 25—[§1.] There shall continue to be elected in each of the towns in this State, at the same time, and in the manner now provided by law for the election of other town officers, an officer to be denominated "town superintendent of common schools," who shall possess all the powers, perform all the duties, and be subject to all the restrictions, liabilities and penalties conferred and imposed by this act.[2]

---

(1) Laws of 1849, chap. 382, § 13.
(2) This and the following sections, except where altered by subsequent enactments, were taken from the act chapter 480 of Laws of 1847.

No. 26—[§3.] The town superintendents of common schools hereafter to be elected in conformity with the provisions of this act, shall, each of them, on or before the first Monday of November succeeding such election, execute to the supervisor of his town and file with the town clerk, a bond with one or more sufficient sureties to be approved by the said supervisor by endorsement over his signature on said bond, with a penalty in double the amount of all the school moneys received by his town from all sources during the preceding year and conditioned for the faithful application and legal disbursement of all the school money coming into his hands during his term of office, and for the faithful discharge of all the duties of said office; and in case such bond shall not be executed, filed and approved within the time herein prescribed, the office of such town superintendent shall be deemed vacant; and any such or any other vacancy that may occur in said office, shall be filled by any three justices of the peace of the same town by a warrant under their hands and seals, who are hereby authorized to make such appointments; and the persons so appointed shall hold their respective offices until others are elected or appointed in their places, and shall have the same powers and be subject to the same duties and penalties as if they had been duly chosen by the electors.

No. 27—[§4.] The justices making the said appointment shall forthwith cause the said warrant to be filed in the office of the town clerk of the town, and give immediate notice to the person appointed.

No. 28—[§5.] Every town superintendent elected after this act takes effect shall on executing the bond as before provided, enter upon the duties of his said office on the first Monday of November succeeding his election, and shall hold his office for two years thereafter, and until a successor who shall have been duly elected, shall have taken the oath of office and filed an official bond pursuant to the provisions of this act.

No. 29—[§14.] Any person appointed to the office of town superintendent by the justices of the peace, shall hold his office till the first Monday of November following the next annual town meeting, and whenever the office of town superintendent shall be vacant for any cause, or before the time of the annual town meeting, shall be held by a person so appointed, the electors of the town at such town meeting shall choose a town superintendent to fill such vacancy or to supercede such appointee; and the person so elected shall enter upon the duties of the office on the first Monday of November following his election, and shall hold his office for the term of two years.[2]

No. 30—[§6.] No town superintendent of a town shall hold the office of trustee of a school district, nor shall a person chosen a

(2) Laws of 1849, Chap. 382, §14.

trustee, hold the office of district clerk, and no town superintendent shall hold the office of either supervisor or town clerk.

No. 31—[§1.] The office of trustees of the Gospel and school lots in the several towns in this state, is hereby abolished; and the powers and duties now by law conferred and imposed upon said trustees, shall hereafter be exercised by the town superintendent of common schools.[1]

ARTICLE THIRD.

The powers and duties of the town superintendent of common schools.

No. 33—§ 8. It shall be the duty of the town superintendent of common schools in each town,

1. To divide the town into a convenient number of school districts, and to regulate and alter such districts as hereinafter provided:

2. To set off by itself any neighborhood in the town adjoining to any other state of this Union where it has been usual or shall be found convenient for such neighborhood to send their children to school in such adjoining state:

3. To describe and number the school districts, and to deliver the description and numbers thereof, in writing, to the town clerk, immediately after the formation or alteration thereof:

4. To deliver to such town clerk a description of each neighborhood, adjoining to any other state, set off by itself:

5. To apply for and receive from the county treasurer all moneys apportioned for the use of common schools in his town:

6. To apportion the school moneys received on the first Tuesday of April, in each year, among the several school districts, parts of districts and neighborhoods separately set off, within the town, in proportion to the number of children residing in each, over the age of four and under that of twenty-one years, as the same shall have appeared from the last annual report of their respective trustees.

7. If the town superintendent shall have received the school moneys of the town, and all the reports from the several school districts therein, before the first Tuesday of April, he shall apportion such moneys as above directed, within ten days after receiving all of the said reports and the said moneys:

8. To sue for and collect, by his name of office, all penalties and forfeitures imposed in this title, and in respect to which no other provision is made, which shall be incurred by any officer or inhabitant of his town, and after deducting his costs and expenses, to add the sums recovered to the school moneys received by him, to be apportioned and paid in the same manner.

No. 34—§ 9. In making the apportionment of moneys among

---

(1) Laws of 1846, Chap. 86, §1.

the several school districts, no share shall be allotted to any district, part of a district or separate neighborhood, from which no sufficient annual report shall have been received for the year ending on the last day of December immediately preceding the apportionment.

No. 35—[§10.] In making the apportionment of public money, it shall be duty of the town superintendent to designate the respective proportions of teachers' and library money belonging to each district, and to pay over as much as is designated teachers' money, on the written order of a majority of the trustees of each district, to the teachers entitled to receive the same.

No. 36—[§11.] No moneys shall be apportioned and paid to any district or part of a district, except by special permission of the state superintendent of common schools, unless it shall appear by such report that a school had been kept therein for at least six months during the year ending at the date of such report, by a qualified teacher;[1] that no other than a duly qualified teacher had at any time during the year for more than one month been employed to teach the school in said district; and that all moneys received during that year have been applied to the payment of the compensation of such teacher; and no portion of the library money shall be apportioned or paid to any district or part of a district, unless it shall appear from the last annual report of the trustees that the library money received at the last preceding apportionment was duly expended according to law, on or before the first day of October subsequent to such apportionment.

No. 37—[§ 11.] Every teacher shall be deemed a qualified teacher who shall hold a certificate dated within one year from the superintendent of common schools for the town in which such teacher shall be employed, or who shall have in possession a state or county certificate of qualification or a diploma from the state normal school.[2]

No. 38—[§ 13.] No part of such moneys shall be apportioned or paid to any separate neighborhood adjoining another state, unless it shall appear from the report of its trustees that all moneys received by them during the year ending at the date of such report have been faithfully applied, in paying for the instruction of children residing in such neighborhood.

No. 39—[§ 14.] Whenever an apportionment of the public money shall not be made to any school district, in consequence of any accidental omission to make any report required by law, or to comply with any other provision of law, or any regulation, the state superintendent may direct an apportionment to be made to such district, according to the equitable circumstances of the case, to be paid out of the public money on hand; or if the same shall have been distributed, out of the public money to be received in a succeeding year.

No. 40—[§ 15.] If after the time when the annual reports are required to be dated, and before the apportionment of the school

---

(1) Laws of 1851, chap. 151, § 5. (2) Laws of 1849, chap. 382, § 11.

moneys shall have been made, a district shall be duly altered, or a new district be formed in the town, so as to render an apportionment founded solely on the annual reports, unjust, as between two or more districts of the town, the town superintendent shall make an apportionment among such districts, according to the number of children in each, over the age of four, and under twenty-one years, ascertaining that number by the best evidence in his power.

No. 41—[§ 16.] The provisions of the foregoing section shall extend to all cases where a school district shall have been formed at such time previous to the first day of January, as not to have allowed a reasonable time to have kept a school therein for the term of six months, such district having been formed out of a district or districts in which a school shall have been kept for six mouths by a teacher duly qualified, during the year preceding the first day of January.

No. 42—[§ 17.] All moneys apportioned by the town superintendent, to the trustees of a district, part of a district, or separate neighborhood, which shall have remained in the hands of the town superintendent for one year after such apportionment, by reason of the trustees neglecting or refusing to receive the same, shall be added to the moneys next thereafter to be apportioned by the town superintendent, and shall be apportioned and paid therewith in the same manner.

No. 43—[§ 18.] In case any school moneys received by the town superintendent cannot be apportioned by him, for the term of two years, after the same are received, by reason of the non-compliance of all the school districts in his town with the provisions of this title, such moneys shall be returned by him to the county treasurer, to be by him apportioned and distributed, together and in the same manner with the moneys next thereafter to be received by him for the use of common schools.

No. 44—[§ 19.] It shall be the duty of the town superintendent in each town, between the first day of July and the first day of August in each year, to make and transmit to the county clerk a report in writing, bearing date on the first day of July, in the year of its transmission, and stating,

1. The whole number of school districts and neighborhoods separately set off within the town:

2. The districts, parts of districts and neighborhoods from which reports shall have been made to him, or his immediate predecessor in office, within the time limited for that purpose:

3. The length of time a school shall have been kept in each of such districts or parts of districts, distinguishing what portion of that time the school shall have been kept by qualified teachers:

4. The amount of public moneys received in each of such districts, parts of districts and neighborhoods:

5. The number of children taught in each, and the number of children over the age of four and under twenty-one years, residing in each:

6. The whole amount of moneys received by him, or his predecessor in office, during the year ending at the date of such report, and since the date of the last preceding report; distinguishing the amount received from the county treasurer, and from any other and what source:

7. The manner in which such moneys have been expended, and whether any, and what part remains unexpended, and for what cause:

8. The amount of money paid for teachers' wages, in addition to the public money paid therefor, the amount of taxes levied for purchasing school-house sites, for building, hiring, purchasing, repairing and insuring school-houses, for fuel and supplying deficiencies in rate bills, for district libraries, or for any other purposes allowed by law, in the districts, parts of districts and neighborhoods from which reports shall have been received by him or his immediate predecessor in office, with such other information as the state superintendent may from time to time require, in relation to the districts and schools within his town.

No. 45—[§ 20.] Town superintendents who neglect to furnish the information required by the last preceding section, shall severally forfeit to the town for the use of the commom schools therein, the sum of ten dollars, to be sued for by the supervisor of the town.

No. 46—[§ 21.] In case the town superintendent in any town shall not, on or before the first day of August, in any year, make such report to the clerk of the county, it shall be his duty to give immediate notice of such neglect to the clerk of such town.

No. 47—[§ 22.] The town superintendent neglecting to make such report within the limited period, shall forfeit to the town, for the use of the common schools therein, the sum of ten dollars; and the share of school moneys apportioned to such town for the ensuing year, may, in the discretion of the state superintendent be withheld, and be distributed among the other towns in the same county, from which the necessary reports shall have been received.

No. 48—[§ 23.] When the share of school moneys apportioned to a town, shall thus be lost to the town, by the neglect of its town superintendent, the town superintendent guilty of such neglect, and his sureties shall be liable for the full amount so lost with interest.

No. 49—[§ 24.] It shall be the duty of the supervisor of the town, upon notice of such loss, from the state superintendent or county treasurer, to prosecute without delay, in the name of the town, for such forfeiture; and the moneys recovered shall be distributed and paid by such supervisor to the several districts, parts of districts, or separate neighborhoods of the town, in the same manner as it would have been the duty of the town superintendent to have distributed and paid them, if received from the county treasurer.

No. 50—[§ 25.] The town superintendent in each town, shall keep a just and true account of all school moneys received and expended by him during each year for which he shall have been chosen, and shall lay the same before the board of auditors of town accounts at the annual meeting of such board, in each year.

No. 51—[§ 26.] The town superintendent of common schools in each town shall, within fifteen days after the termination of his office, render to his successor in office, a just and true account, in writing, of all school moneys by him received, before the time of rendering such account, and of the manner in which the same shall have been appropriated and expended by him; and the account so rendered shall be delivered by such successor in office to the town clerk, to be filed and recorded in his office.

No. 52—[§ 27.] On rendering such account, if any balance shall be found remaining in the hands of the town superintendent, the same shall immediately be paid by him to his successor in office.

No. 53—[§ 28.] If such balance, or any part thereof, shall have been appropriated by the town superintendent to any particular school district, part of a district or separate neighborhood, and shall remain in his hands for the use thereof, a statement of such appropriation shall be made in the account so to be rendered, and the balance paid to such successor in office, shall be paid over by him, according to such appropriation.

No. 54—[§ 29.] Such successor in office may bring a suit in his name of office for the recovery, with interest, of any unpaid balance of school moneys, that shall appear to have been in the hands of any previous town superintendent on leaving his office, either by the accounts rendered by such town superintendent, or by other sufficient proof, and in case of the death of such town superintendent, such suit may be brought against his representatives.

No. 55—[§ 30.] The town superintendent in each town, shall have the powers and privileges of a corporation, so far as to enable him to take and hold any property transferred to him, for the use common schools in such town.

No. 56—[§ 10.] Town superintendents are hereby authorised to administer oaths in all cases relating to school district affairs and controversies, but shall not be entitled to charge any fees therefor.[1]

No. 57—[§ 31.] The town superintendent shall be entitled to receive one dollar and twenty-five cents per day for every day actually and necessarily devoted by him in his official capacity, to the service of the town for which he may be chosen, the same to be paid in like manner as other town officers are paid.

Of the duty of Town Clerks.

No. 58—[§ 32.] It shall be the duty of the Town Clerk of each town,

1. To receive and keep all reports made to the town superintendent from the trustees of school districts, and all the books anp

(1) Laws of 1849, chap. 382, § 10.

papers belonging to the town superintendent, when required, and to file them in his office:

2. To receive all his estimates and apportionments of school money, and to record the same in a book to be kept for that purpose:

3. To notify the town superintendent, upon receiving notice from the county clerk that he has not made his annual report, for the purpose of making such report.

ARTICLE FOURTH.

Of Inspection and Supervision by Town Superintendents.

No. 59—[§ 33.] The town superintendent in each town shall be the inspector of common schools therein, and every town superintendent, during his continuance in office, shall be deemed a qualified teacher.[1]

No. 60—[§ 34.] It shall be his duty to examine all persons offering themselves as candidates for teaching common schools in such town.

No. 61—[§ 35.] In making such examination, it shall be the duty of the town superintendent to ascertain the qualification of the candidate, in respect to moral character, learning and ability.

No. 62—[§ 36] If he shall be satisfied in respect to the qualifications of the candidate, he shall deliver to the person so examined, a certificate signed by him, in such form as shall be prescribed by the state superintendent.

No. 63—[§ 37.] The town superintendent may annul any such certificate given by him or his predecessors in office, when he shall think proper, giving at least ten days' previous notice in writing to the teacher holding it, and to the trustees of the district in which he may be employed, of his intention to annul the same.

No. 64—[§ 38.] The town superintendent, whenever he shall deem it necessary, may require a re-examination of all or any of the teachers in his town, for the purpose of ascertaining their qualifications to continue as such teachers.

No. 65—[§ 39.] The annulling of a certificate shall not disqualify the teacher to whom it was given, until a note in writing thereof, containing the name of the teacher, and the time when his certificate was annulled, shall be made by the town superintendent, and filed in the office of the town clerk.

No. 66—[§ 40.] When any school district shall be composed of parts of two or more towns, the town superintendent of the town in which the school house of such district may be situated, shall examine into and certify the qualifications of any teacher offering to teach in such district, in the same manner as is provided by the preceding sections of this article, and may also in the same manner annul the certificate of such teacher; and no school-

(1) Laws of 1849, chap. 382, § 9.

house shall be erected so as to stand on the division lines of any two or more towns.

No. 67—[§ 41.] It shall be the duty of the town superintendent to visit all such common schools, within his town, as shall be organized according to law, at least twice a year, and oftener if he shall deem it necessary.

No. 68—[§ 42.] At such visitation, the town superintendent shall examine into the state and condition of such schools, both as respects the progress of the scholars in learning, and the good order of the schools; and may give his advice and direction to the trustees and teachers of such schools as to the government thereof, and the course of studies to be pursued therein.

ARTICLE FIFTH.

Of the Formation and Alteration of School Districts.

No. 69—[§ 43.] In the erection or alteration of a school district, the trustees of any district to be affected thereby, may apply to the supervisor and town clerk to be associated with the town superintendent; and their action shall be final unless duly appealed from; the compensation of the supervisor and town clerk when thus associated, shall be the same as that of the town superintendent.

No. 70—[§ 44.] Whenever it may become necessary or convenient to form a district out of two or more adjoining towns, the town superintendent of each of such adjoining towns, or the major part of them, may form, regulate and alter such district.

No. 71—[§ 45.] No alteration of any school district, made without the consent of the trustees thereof, shall take effect until three months after notice, in writing, shall be given by the town superintendent, to some one or more of such trustees; nor shall any alteration or regulation of an organized school district be made to take effect between the first day of December in any one year, and the first day of May following.

No. 72—[§ 46.] If the town supeintendent in any town, shall require by notice in writing, the attendance of the town superintendents of any other town or towns, at a joint meeting for the purpose of altering a school district formed from their respective towns, and a major part of the town superintendents notified shall refuse or neglect to attend, the town superintendents attending, by a majority of votes, may call a special district meeting of such district, for the purpose of deciding on such proposed alteration; and the decision of such meeting shall be as valid as if made by the town superintendents of all the towns interested, but shall extend no further than to dissolve the district formed from such towns.

No. 73—[§ 50.] When two or more districts shall be consolidated into one, the new district shall succeed to all the rights of property possessed by the districts of which it shall be composed, and when a district is annulled and portions thereof are annexed to other districts, the property of the district so annulled shall be sold by the town superintendent of the town in which the school house is located, at public auction to the highest bidder therefor, after at least five days public notice by notices posted in three or more public places in said town, one of which shall be within the district so annulled, and the proceeds of such sale shall be first applied so far as requisite, to the payment of any just debts due from the district so annulled, and the residue thereof shall be apportioned among the taxable inhabitants of the district so annulled in the ratio of their several assessments upon the last corrected assessment roll of the town or towns within which such district is located.[1]

No. 74—[§ 52.] When there shall be any moneys in the hands of the officers, of a district that is or may be annulled, or belonging to such district, the town superintendent of the town may demand, sue for and recover the same, in his name of office, and shall apportion the same equitably between the districts to which the several portions of such annulled district may have been annexed, to be held and enjoyed as district property.

No. 75—[§ 53.] Whenever a school district shall be dissolved by consolidation, or otherwise, it shall be the duty of the trustees of such district to make out all the necessary ratebills and tax-lists, and issue their warrants according to law, for the collection of all such sums of money as shall be necessary to discharge all legal liabilities of such district so dissolved or consolidated, and to call special meetings of the legal voters of such district, if it be necessary, to raise money by tax, to discharge such demands, and the collector to whom any such rate-bill or tax-list and warrant shall be delivered for collection, shall have power to execute the same in the same manner and with like authority as though such district had not been dissolved or consolidated.

Of the powers of school district inhabitants, and of the choice, duties and powers of school district officers.

No. 76—[§54.] Whenever any school district shall be formed in any town, it shall be the duty of the town superintendent, within twenty days thereafter, to prepare a notice in writing, describing such district, and appointing a time and place for the first district meeting, and to deliver such notice to a taxable inhabitant of the district.

No. 77—[§ 55.] It shall be the duty of such inhabitant to notify every other inhabitant of the district, qualified to vote at district meetings, by reading the notice in the hearing of such inhabitant, or in case of his absence from home, by leaving a copy thereof, or of so much thereof as relates to the time and place of such meeting, at the place of his abode, at least six days before the time of the meeting.

(1) Laws of 1849, Chap. 382, §2.

No. 78—[§ 56.] In case such notice shall not be given, or the inhabitants of a district shall refuse or neglect to assemble, or form a district meeting, when so notified; or in case any such district, having been formed and organized in pursuance of such notice, shall afterwards be dissolved, so that no competent authority shall exist therein, to call a special district meeting in the manner hereinafter provided; such notice shall be renewed by the town superintendent, and served in the manner above prescribed.

No 79—[§ 57.] Every taxable inhabitant to whom a notice of a district meeting shall have been properly delivered for service, who shall refuse or neglect to serve the notice in the manner above in this article enjoined, shall for every such offence forfeit the sum of five dollars.

No. 80—[§ 58.] Whenever any district meeting shall be called, in the manner prescribed in the preceding sections of this article, it shall be the duty of the inhabitants of the district, qualified to vote at district meetings, to assemble together at the time and place mentioned in the notice.

No. 81—[§ 59.] Every male person of full age, residing in any school district, and entitled to hold lands in this state, who owns or hires real property in such district subject to taxation for school purposes, and every resident of such district authorized to vote at town meetings of the town in which such district or part of district is situated, and who has paid any rate-bill for teachers' wages in such district, within one year preceding, or who owns any personal property liable to be taxed for school purposes in such districts, exceeding fifty dollars in value, exclusive of such as is exempt from execution, and no others, shall be entitled to vote at any school district meeting held in such district.

No. 82—[§ 60.] If any person offering to vote at any school district meeting, shall be challenged as unqualified by any legal voter in such district, the chairman presiding at such meeting shall require the person so offering, to make the following declaration: "I do declare and affirm that I am an actual resident of this school district, and that I am qualified to vote at this meeting." And every person making such declaration shall be permitted to vote on all questions proposed at such meeting, but if any person shall refuse to make such declaration, his vote shall be rejected.

No. 83—[§ 61.] Every person who shall wilfully make a false declaration of his right to vote at a district meeting, upon being challenged as herein before provided, shall be deemed guilty of a misdemeanor, and punishable by imprisonment in the county jail for a term not exceeding one year, nor less than six months, at the discretion of the court; and any person voting at any school district meeting without being qualified, shall, on conviction, be subject to a fine of ten dollars, to be sued for and recovered by the trustees of the district for its use, and with costs of suit, before any justice of the peace.

No. 84—[§ 62.] The inhabitants so entitled to vote, when so assembled in such district meeting, or when lawfully assembled at any other district meeting, shall have power, by a majority of the votes of those present:

1. To appoint a chairman for the time being:
2, To adjourn from time to time, as occasion may require:
3. To chose a district clerk, three trustees, a district collector, and a librarian at their first meeting, and as often as such offices or either of them become vacated:
4. To designate a site for a district school house:
5. To lay such tax on the taxable inhabitants of the district, as the meeting shall deem sufficient to purchase or lease a suitable site for a school house, and to build, hire or purchase such school house, and to keep in repair and furnish the same with the necessary fuel and appendages:
6. To alter, repeal and modify their proceedings from time to time as occasion may require:
7. To vote a tax for the purchase of a book for the purpose of recording the proceedings in their respective districts:
8. With the consent of the town superintendent of the town, to designate sites for two or more school houses, for such district, and lay a tax on the taxable property in such district, to purchase or lease such sites, and to hire, build or purchase such school houses, and to keep in repair, and furnish the same with necessary fuel and appendages, and may also in their discretion lay a tax, not exceeding twenty dollars in any one year, to purchase maps, globes, black-boards, and other school apparatus.

No. 85—[§ 63.] The trustees chosen at the first legal meeting of any school district, shall be divided by lot into three classes, to be numbered, one, two and three; the term of office of the first class shall be one year, of the second, two, of the third, three; and one trustee only shall thereafter annually be elected, who shall hold his office for three years, and until a successor shall be duly elected or appointed. In case of a vacancy in the office of either of the trustees, during the period for which he or they shall have been respectively elected, the person or persons chosen or appointed to such vacancy shall hold the office only for the unexpired term.

No. 86—[§ 64.] Every notice of a district meeting called in pursuance of this act shall state the purpose for which such meeting is called.

No. 87—[§. 65.] In each school district an annual meeting shall be held at the time and place previously appointed; and at the first district meeting, and at each annual meeting, the time and place of holding the next annual meeting shall be fixed.

No. 88—[§ 66.] Whenever the time for holding annual meetings in a district for the election of district officers shall pass without such election being held, a special meeting shall be notified by the clerk of such district to choose such officers; and if no such notice be given by him or the trustees last elected or appointed, with twenty days after such time shall have passed, the town superintendent or town clerk may order any inhabitant of such district qualified to vote at district meetings, to notify such meeting in the manner provided by law in case of the formation of a new district; and the officers chosen at any such special meeting, shall hold their office until the time for holding the next annual meeting.

No. 89—[§ 67.] When the clerk and all the trustees of a school district shall have removed or otherwise vacated their office, and where the records of a district shall have been destroyed or lost, or where trustees neglect or refuse to call meetings to choose trustees, the superintendent shall have authority to order such meetings, and the same shall be notified in the manner provided by law in the case of the formation of new districts.

No. 90—[§ 68.] When in consequence of the loss of the records of a school district, or the omission to designate the day for its annual meeting, there shall be none fixed, or it cannot be ascertained, the trustees, of such district may appoint a day for holding the annual meeting of such district.

No. 91—[§ 69.] A special meeting shall be held in each district whenever called by the trustees; and the proceedings of no district meeting, annual or special, shall be held illegal for want of a due notice to all the persons qualified to vote thereat, unless it shall appear that the omission to give such notice was wilful and fraudulent.

No. 92—[§ 70.] No tax to be voted by a district meeting for building, hiring or purchasing a school house, shall exceed the sum of four hundred dollars, unless the town superintendent of the town in which the school house is to be situated, shall certify in writing his opinion that a larger sum ought to be raised, and shall specify the sum; in which case, a sum not exceeding the sum so specified, shall be raised; and in districts composed of parts of several towns, the certificate of a major part of the superintendents of said towns shall be necessary for such purpose.

No. 93—[§ 71.] Whenever a majority of all the taxable inhabitants of any school district, to be ascertained by taking and recording the ayes and noes of such inhabitants attending at any annual, special or adjourned school district meeting legally called or held, shall determine that the sum proposed and provided for in the next preceding section, shall be raised by instalments; it shall be the duty of the trustees of such district, and they are hereby authorized to cause the same to be levied, raised and collected, in equal annual instalments, in the same manner, and with the like authority that other school district taxes are raised, levied and collected, and to make out their tax list and warrant, for the collection of such instalments as they become payable according to the vote of the said inhabitants; but the payment or collection of the last instalment shall not be extended beyond five years from the time such vote was taken; and no vote to levy any such tax shall be reconsidered except at an adjourned general or special meeting to be held within thirty days thereafter, and the same majority shall be required for reconsideration as is required to levy such tax.

No. 94—[§ 72.] In every case where a district embraces a part of more than one town, the town superintendents of the towns so in part embraced, upon application of the trustees of such districts, or of those persons liable to pay taxes upon real property therein, shall proceed to enquire and determine whether the valuation of real property upon the several assessment rolls of said towns are substantially just as compared with each other, so far as such district is concerned, and if determined not to be so, they shall determine the relative proportion of taxes that ought to be assessed upon the real property of the parts of such districts so lying in different towns, and the trustees of such district shall thereupon assess the proportion of any tax thereafter to be raised according to the determination of said superintendents until the same shall be altered by said superintendents upon like application, using the assessment rolls of the several towns to distribute the said proportion among the persons liable to be assessed for the same. In cases where two superintendents shall be unable to agree, they shall summon a superintendent from some adjoining town, who shall unite in such inquiry and determination.

No. 95—[§ 73.] Whenever a school house shall have been built or purchased for a district, the site of such school house shall not be changed, nor the building thereon be removed, as long as the district shall remain unaltered, unless by the consent, in writing, of the town superintendents of common schools, of the town or towns within which such districts shall be situated, stating that in their opinion such removal is necessary; nor then, unless a majority of all the taxable inhabitants of said district to be ascertained by taking and recording the ayes and noes, at a special meeting, called for that purpose, shall be in favor of such new site.

No. 96—[§ 74.] Whenever the site of a school house shall have been changed as herein provided, the inhabitants of the district entitled to vote, lawfully assembled at any district meeting, shall have power by a majority of the votes of those present, to direct the sale of the former site or lot, and the buildings thereon, and appurtenances, or any part thereof, at such price, and upon such terms as they shall deem most advantageous to the district; and any deed duly executed by the trustees of such district, or a majority of them, in pursuance of such direction, shall be valid and effectual to pass all the estate or interest of such school district in the premises intended to be conveyed thereby, to the grantee named in such deed; and when a credit shall be directed to be given upon such sale, for the consideration money, or any part thereof, the trustees are hereby authorized to take in their corporate name, such security by bond and mortgage, or otherwise, for the payment thereof, as they shall deem best, and shall hold the same as a corporation, and account therefor to their successors in office and to the district, in the manner they are now required by law to account for moneys received by them; and the trustees of any such district for the time being, may in their name of office, sue for and recover the moneys due and unpaid upon any security so taken by them, or their predecessors in office, with interest and cost.

No. 97—[§ 75.] All moneys arising from any sale made in pursuance of the last preceding section, shall be appropriated to the payment of the expenses incurred in procuring a new site, and in removing or erecting a school house, or either of them, so far as such application thereof shall be deemed necessary.

No. 98—[§ 77.] In case the office of trustee shall be vacated by the death, refusal to serve, removal out of the district, or incapacity of any such officer, and the vacancy shall not be supplied by a district meeting within one month thereafter, the town superintendent of the town may appoint any person residing in such district to supply such vacancy.

No. 99—[§ 78.] In case of a vacancy in the office of school district clerk, collector or librarian, for any of the causes mentioned in the next preceding section, such vacancy may be supplied by appointment under the hands of the trustees of the district or a majority of them, and the persons so appointed shall hold their respective offices until the next annual meeting of the district, and until others are elected in their places.

No. 100—[§ 79.] Every person duly chosen or appointed to any such office, who, without sufficient cause, shall refuse to serve therein, shall forfeit the sum of five dollars; and every person so chosen or appointed, and not having refused to accept, who shall neglect to perform the duties of his office, shall forfeit the sum of ten dollars.

No. 101—[§ 80.] Any person chosen or appointed to any such office, may resign the same by presenting his resignation to the town superintendent of the town where such officer shall reside, who is authorised for sufficient cause shown to him, to accept the same, and the acceptance of such resignation shall be a bar to the recovery of either of the penalties mentioned in the preceding section. The town superintendent accepting the resignation shall give notice thereof to the clerk, or to one of the trustees of the school district, to which the officer resigning shall belong.

No. 102—[§ 81.] It shall be the duty of the clerk of each school district,

1. To record the proceedings of his district in a book to be provided for that purpose by the district, and to enter therein true copies of all reports made by the trustees of his district, to the town superintendent.

2. To give notice of the time and place for special district meetings, when the same shall be called by the trustees of the district, to each inhabitant of such district liable to pay taxes, at least five days before such meeting shall be held, in the manner prescribed in the fifty-fifth section of this act:

3. To affix a notice in writing of the time and place for any adjourned district meeting, when the same shall be adjourned for a longer time than one month, in at least four of the most public places of such district, at least five days before the time appointed for such adjourned meeting:

4. To give the like notice of every annual district meeting:

5. To keep and preserve all records, books and papers, belonging to his office, and to deliver the same to his successor in office; and in case of his neglect or refusal so to do, he shall be subject to a fine of not exceeding fifty dollars.

Of the duty of trustees of school districts.

No. 103—[§ 82.] It shall be the duty of the trustees of every school district, and they shall have power,

1. To call special meetings of the inhabitants of such districts liable to pay taxes, whenever they shall deem it necessary and proper:

2. To give notice of special, annual and adjourned meetings in the manner prescribed in the last preceding section, if there be no clerk of the district, or he be absent or incapable of acting:

3. To make out a tax list of every district tax, voted by any such meeting, containing the names of all the taxable inhabitants residing in the district at the time of making out the list, and the amount of tax payable by each inhabitant, set opposite to his name:

4. To annex to such tax list a warrant, directed to the collector of the district, for the collection of the sums in such list mentioned:

5. To purchase or lease a site for the district school house, as designated by a meeting of the district, and to build, hire or purchase, keep in repair, and furnish such school house with necessary fuel and appendages, out of the funds collected and paid to them for such purposes:

6. To have the custody and safe-keeping of the district school-house:

7. To contract with and employ all teachers in the districts:

8. To pay the wages of such teachers when qualified, by giving them orders on the town superintendents for the public money belonging to their districts, so far as such moneys shall be sufficient for that purpose; and to collect the residue of such wages from all persons liable therefor:[1]

9. To divide the public moneys received by them, whenever authorized by a vote of their district, into not exceeding two portions for each year; to assign and apply one of such portions to each term during which a school shall be kept in such district, for

(1) Laws of 1849, chap. 382, § 12

the payment of teacher's wages during such term; and to collect the residue of such wages, not paid by the proportion of public money allotted for that purpose, from the persons liable therefor, as above provided:

10. To exempt from the payment of the wages of teachers, either in part or wholly, such indigent persons within the district as they shall think proper, in any one quarter or term, and the same shall be a charge upon such district:

11. To certify such exemptions and deliver the certificate thereof to the clerk of the district to be kept on file in his office:

12. To ascertain by examination of the school lists kept by such teachers, the number of days for which each person not so exempted, shall be liable to pay for instruction, and the amount payable by each person:

13. To make out a rate-bill containg the name of each person so liable, and the amount for which he is liable; and to annex thereto a warrant for the collection thereof:

14. To deliver such rate-bill, with the warrant annexed, after the same shall have been made out and signed by them, to the collector of the district, who shall execute the same in like manner with other warrants directed by such trustees to such collector for the collection of district taxes, except as hereinafter provided; and the collector to whom any such rate-bill and warrant shall be delivered for collection, shall possess the same power, be entitled to the same fees, and subject to the same restrictions and liabilities with their bail and sureties, except as hereinafter provided, as by this title is provided in proceedings to collect school district taxes. [1]

No. 104—[§ 9.] The trustees of any school district may expend in the repair of the school house a sum not exceeding ten dollars in any one year, and the same may be levied and collected by a separate tax, or added to any tax authorized to be levied and collected. [2]

No. 105—[§ 84.] Where by reason of the inability to collect any tax or rate-bill, there shall be a deficiency in the amount raised, the inhabitants of the district in district meeting shall direct the raising of a sufficient sum to supply such deficiency by tax, or the same shall be collected by rate-bill, as the case may require.

No. 106—[§ 6.] Any balance required to be raised in any school district for the payment of teachers' wages, beyond the amount apportioned to such district by the previous provisions of this act, and other public moneys belonging to the district, applicable to the payment of teachers' wages, shall be raised by rate-bill to be made out by the trustees, against those sending to school, in proportion to the number of days and of children sent, to be ascertained by the teachers' list; and in making out such rate-bill, it shall be the duty of the trustees to exempt, either wholly or in part, as they may deem expedient, such indigent inhabitants as may, in

(1) Laws of 1849, chap. 382, §6, as amended by chap. 151 laws of 1851, §7.
(2) Laws of 1849, chap. 382, §9

their judgment, be entitled to such exemption, and the amount of such exemption shall be added to the first tax list thereafter to be made out by the trustees for district purposes, or shall be separately levied by them as they shall deem most expedient. [1]

No. 107—[§ 7.] The same property which is exempt by section twenty-two, of article two, title five, chapter six, part three, of the revised statutes, from levy and sale under execution, shall be exempt from levy and sale under any warrant to collect any rate-bill for wages of teachers of common schools. [2]

Of the Assessment and Collection of District Taxes.

No. 108—[§ 85.] In making out a tax list the trustees of school districts shall apportion the same on all the taxable inhabitants of the district, or corporations holding property therein, according to the valuation of the taxable property which shall be owned or possessed by them, at the time of making out such list within such district, or partly within such district and partly in an adjoining district, and upon all real estate lying within the boundaries of such district, the owners of which shall be non-residents, and which shall be liable to taxation for town or county purposes, and shall be situated within three miles of the site of the school-house in such district. But when it shall be ascertained that the proportion of any tax upon any lot, tract or parcel not occupied by any inhabitant would not amount to fifty cents, the trustees in their discretion may omit such lot, tract or parcel from the tax list.

No. 109—[§ 86.] Any person working land under a contract for a share of the produce of such land, shall be deemed the possessor, so far as to render him liable to taxation therefor, in the district where such land is situate.

No. 110—[§ 87.] Every person owning or holding any real property within any school district, who shall improve and occupy the same by his agent or servant, shall, in respect to the liability of such property to taxation, be considered a taxable inhabitant of such district, in the same manner as if he actually resided therein.

No. 111—[§ 88.] Where any district tax for the purpose of purchasing a site for a school-house, or for purchasing or building, keeping in repair, or furnishing such school-house with necessary fuel and appendages, shall be lawfully assessed and paid by any person, on account of any real property, whereof he is only tenant at will, or for three years, or for a less period of time, such tenant may charge the owner of such real estate with the amount of the tax so paid by him, unless some agreement to the contrary shall have been made by such tenant.

No. 112—[§ 89.] When any real estate within a district, so liable to taxation, shall not be occupied and improved by the owner, his servant or agent, and shall not be possessed by any tenant, the trustees of any district, at the time of making out any tax list by which any tax shall be imposed thereon, shall make and insert in

(1) Laws of 1851, chap. 151, §6–7. (2) Laws of 1751, chap. 151, §7.

such tax list, a statement and description of every such lot, piece or parcel of land so owned by non-residents therein, in the same manner as required by law from town assessors in making out the assessment roll of their towns; and if any such lot is known to belong to an incorporated company, liable to taxation in such district, the name of such company shall be specified, and the value of such lot or piece of land shall be set down opposite to such description, which value shall be the same that was affixed to such lot or piece of land in the last assessment roll of the town; and if the same was not separately valued in such roll, then it shall be valued in proportion to the valuation which was affixed in the said assessment roll to the whole tract, of which such lot or piece shall be a part.

No. 113—[§90.] If any tax on the real estate of a non-resident mentioned in the tax list delivered to the collector shall be unpaid at the time he is required by law to return his warrant, he shall deliver to the trustees of such district an account of the taxes so remaining due, containing a description of the lots and pieces of land upon which any taxes were imposed as the same were stated in his tax list together with the amount of the tax assessed on each, and upon making oath before any justice of the peace or judge of any court of record that the taxes mentioned in such account remain unpaid, and that after diligent efforts he has been unable to collect the same, he shall be credited by said trustees with the amount thereof.

No. 114—[91.] Whenever the trustees of any school district shall receive such an account of unpaid taxes from any collector, they shall compare the same with the original tax list, and if found to be a true transcript, they shall add to such account a certificate to the effect that they have compared the same with the original tax list and found it to be correct, and shall immediately transmit such account, with the affidavit of the collector, and their certificate to the treasurer of the county.

No. 115—[§ 92.] Out of any moneys in the county treasury, raised for contingent expenses, the county treasurer shall pay to the trustees of the school district in which such taxes were imposed, the amount thereof so returned as unpaid.

No. 116—[§ 93.] Such account, affidavit and certificate shall be laid, by the county treasurer, before the board of supervisors of the county, who shall cause the amount of such unpaid taxes, with seven per cent of the amount in addition thereto, to be levied upon the lands of non-residents on which the same were imposed, and if imposed upon the lands of any incorporated company, then upon such company, in the same manner that the contingent charges of the county are directed to be levied and collected, and when collected the same shall be returned to the county treasury to reimburse the amount so advanced, with the expense of collection.

No. 117—[§ 94.] Any person whose lands are included in any such account may pay the tax assessed thereon to the county treasurer, at any time before the board of supervisors shall have directed the same to be levied.

No. 118—[§ 95.] The same proceedings in all respects shall be had for the collection of the amount so directed to be raised by the board of supervisors as are provided by law in relation to county taxes; and upon a similar account as in the case of county taxes of the arrears thereof uncollected, being transmitted by the county treasurer to the comptroller, the same shall be paid on his warrant to the treasurer of the county advancing the same; and the amount so assumed by the state shall be collected for its benefit, in the manner prescribed by law in respect to the arrears of county taxes upon land of non-residents; or if any part of the amount so assumed consisted of a tax upon any incorporated company the same proceedings may also be had for the collection thereof as provided by law, in respect to the county taxes assessed upon such company.

No. 119—[§ 96.] The valuations of taxable property shall be ascertained so far as possible, from the last assessment roll of the town; and no person shall be entitled to any reduction in the valuation of such property, as so ascertained unless he shall give notice of his claim to such reduction, to the trustees of the district, before the tax list shall be made out.

No. 120—[§ 97.] In every case where such reduction shall be duly claimed, and in every case where the valuation of taxable property cannot be ascertained, from the last assessment roll of the town, the trustees shall ascertain the true value of the property to be taxed, from the best evidence in their power, giving notice to the persons interested, and proceeding in the same manner as the town assessors are required by law to proceed, in the valuations of taxable property.

No. 121—[§ 98.] Every taxable inhabitant of a district, who shall have been, within four years, set off from any otherdistrict without his consent, and shall, within that period have actually paid in such other district, under a lawful assessment therein, a district tax for building a school-house, shall be exempted by the trustees of the district where he shall reside, from the payment of any tax for building a school house therein.

No. 122—[§ 99.] Every district tax shall be assessed, and the tax list therefor be made out by the trustees, and a proper warrant attached thereto, within thirty days after the district meeting in which the tax shall have been voted.

No. 123—[§ 100.] It shall be the duty of the said trustees, after the expiration of the said thirty days, to deliver the said tax list and warrant to the collector of the district, and such collector is hereby authorised and directed, upon receiving his warrant, for two successive weeks, to receive such taxes as may be voluntarily paid to him; and in case the whole amount shall not be so paid in, the collector shall proceed forthwith to collect the same. He shall receive for his services, on all sums paid in as aforesaid, one per cent, and upon all sums collected by him after the expiration of the time mentioned, five per cent; and in case a levy and sale shall be necessarily made by such collector, he shall be entitled to travelling fees at the rate of six cents per mile, to be computed from the school house in such district.[1]

No. 124—[§ 101.] If by the neglect of any collector, any school moneys shall be lost to any school district, which might have been collected within the time limited in the warrant delivered to him for their collection, he shall forfeit to such district the full amount of the moneys thus lost, and shall account for and pay over the same to the trustees of such district, in the same manner as if they had been collected.

No. 125—[§ 102.] For the recovery of all forfeitures, and of balances in the hands of a collector which he shall have neglected to pay over, the trustees of the district may sue in their name of office, and shall be entitled to recover the same with interest and costs; and the moneys recovered shall be applied by them in the same manner as if paid without suit.

No. 126—[§ 103.] Any collector to whom any such tax list and warrant may be delivered for collection, may execute the same in any other district or town in the same county, or in any other county, where the district is a joint district, and composed of territory from adjoining counties, in the same manner, and with the like authority as in the district in which the trustees issuing the said warrant may reside, and for the benefit of which said tax is intended to be collected, and the bail or sureties of any collector given for the faithful performance of his official duties, are hereby declared and made liable for any moneys received or collected on any such tax list and warrant, and may be prosecuted for the recovery thereof.

No. 127—[§ 104.] It shall be the duty of the trustees of school districts, to procure for the use of their district, two bound blank books from time to time, as shall be necessary, in one of which the accounts of all moneys received and paid by the trustees, and a statement of all moveable property belonging to the district, shall be entered at large, and signed by such trustees, at or before each annual meeting in such district. In the other of the said books, the teachers shall enter the names of the scholars attending school, and the number of days they shall have respectively attended, and also the days on which such school shall have been inspected by the town superintendent; which entries shall be verified by the oath or affirmation of the teachers. The said books shall be preserved by the trustees as the property of the district, and shall be delivered to their successors.

No. 128—[§ 105.] When the necessary fuel for the school of any district shall not be provided, by means of a tax on the inhabitants of the district or otherwise, it shall be the duty of the trustees of the district to provide the necessary fuel, and levy a tax upon the inhabitants of the district to pay for the same.[2]

No. 129—[§ 109.] When the trustees of any school district are required or authorized by law, or by vote of their district, to

(1) Laws of 1849, chap. 382, §5. (2) Laws of 1849, chap. 382, §7.

incur any expense for such district, and when any expenses incurred by them are made by express provision of law a charge upon such district, they may raise the amount thereof by tax in the same manner as if the definite sum to be raised had been voted by a district meeting, and the same shall be collected and paid over in the same manner.

No. 130—[§ 110.] The warrant issued and annexed to any tax list or rate bill, shall be under the hands of the trustees of the district or a majority of them, and it shall not be necessary for the said trustees to affix their seals to any such warrant.

No. 131—[§ 111.] The warrants issued by the trustees of school districts for the collection of any district tax authorized to be levied, raised and collected by this title, or for the collection of any rate bill shall have the like force and effect, [except as herein before provided in respect to rate bills,] as warrants issued by boards of supervisors of counties to collectors of taxes in towns; and the collector to whom any such warrant may be delivered for collection is hereby authorized and required to collect from every person in such tax list or rate bill named, the sum therein set opposite to his name, or the amount due from any person or persons specified therein, in the same manner that collectors are authorized to collect town and county charges, [except as aforesaid.]

No. 132—[§ 112.] If the sum or sums of money, payable by any person named in such tax list or rate bill, shall not be paid by him, or collected by such warrant within the time therein limited, it shall and may be lawful for the trustees to renew such warrant in respect to such delinquent person; or in case such person shall not reside within their district, at the time of making out a tax list or rate bill, or shall not reside therein at the expiration of such warrant, and no goods or chattels can be found therein whereon to levy the same; the trustees may sue for and recover the same, in their name of office.

No. 133—[§ 113.] Whenever the trustees of any school district shall discover any error in a tax list or rate bill made out by them, they may with the approbation and consent of the state superintendent, after refunding any amount that may have been improperly collected on such tax list or rate bill, if the same shall be required, amend and correct such tax list or rate bill, in conformity to law; and whenever more than one renewal of a warrant for the collection of any tax list or rate bill, may become necessary in any district, the trustees may make such further renewal, with the written approbation of the town superintendent of the town in which the school house of said district shall be located, to be endorsed upon such warrant.

No. 134—[§ 114.] If the moneys apportioned to a district by the town superintendent shall not have been paid, it shall be the duty of the trustees thereof, to bring a suit for the recovery of the same, with interest, against the town superintendent in whose hands the same shall be, or to pursue such other remedy for the ecovery thereof, as is or shall be given by law.

Of the annual reports of trustees, their duties and liabilities.

No. 135—[§ 115.] The trustees of each school district shall, between the first and fifteenth days of January, in every year, make and transmit a report, in writing, to the town superintendent for such town, dated on the first day of January, in the year in which it shall be transmitted.

No. 136—[§ 116.] Every such report, signed and certified by a majority of the trustees making it, shall be delivered to the town superintendent, and shall specify,

1. The whole time any school has been kept in their district during the year ending on the day previous to the date of such report, and distinguishing what portion of the time such school has been kept by qualified teachers:

2. The amount of moneys received from the town superintendent during such year, and the manner in which such moneys have been expended:

3. The number of children taught in the district during such year.[1]

4. The number of children residing in the district on the last day of December previous to the making of such report, over the age of four years, and under twenty-one years of age, (except Indian children otherwise provided for by law,) and the names of the parents or other persons with whom such children shall respectively reside, and the number of children residing with each:[1]

5. The amount of money paid for teachers' wages, in addition to the public money paid therefor, the amount of taxes levied in said district for purchasing school-house sites, for building, hiring, purchasing, repairing and insuring school-houses, for fuel, for supplying deficiencies in rate bills, for district libraries, or for any other purpose allowed by law, and such other information in relation to the schools and the districts as the superintendent of common schools may from time to time require.

No. 137—[§ 117] It shall not be lawful for the trustees of any school district to include in their annual returns the names of any children who are supported at a county poor-house, or orphan asylum.

No. 138—[§ 118.] The annual reports of trustees of school districts, of children residing in their district, shall include all over four and under twenty-one years of age, who shall, at the date of such report, actually be in the district, composing a part of the family of their parents or guardians, or employers, if such parents, guardians, or employers reside at the time in such district, although such residence be temporary, but such report shall not include children belonging to the family of any person who shall be an inhabitant of any other district in this state, in which such children may be law be included in the reports of its trustees.

(1) Laws of 1849, chap. 382, § 8.

No. 139—[§ 119.] The trustees of school districts shall not enumerate and include in their annual reports any Indian children residing on Indian reservations where schools are taught.

No. 140—[§ 120.] All children included in the reports of the trustees of any school district shall be entitled to attend the schools of such district; and whenever it shall be necessary for the accommodation of the children in any district, the trustees thereof may hire, temporarily, any room or rooms for the keeping of schools therein, and the expense thereof shall be a charge upon such district.

No. 141—[§ 121.] Where a school district is formed out of two or more adjoining towns, it shall be the duty of the trustees of such district to make and transmit a report to the town superintendent for each of the towns out of which such district shall be formed, within the same time, and in the same manner, as is required by sections one hundred and fifteen, and one hundred and sixteen of this act; distinguishing the number of children over the age of four and under twenty-one years, residing in each part of a district which shall be in a different town from the other parts, and the number of children taught, and the amount of school moneys received from each part of the district.

No. 142—[§ 122.] Where any neighborhood shall be set off by itself, the inhabitants of such separate neighborhood shall annually meet together and chose one trustee; whose duty it shall be every year, within the time limited for making district reports, to make and transmit a report in writing, bearing date on the first day of January, in the year in which it shall be transmitted, to the town superintendent of the town from which such neighborhood shall be set off, specifying the number of children over the age of four and under twenty-one years, residing in such neighborhood, the amount of moneys received from the town superintendent since the date of last report, and the manner in which the same has been expended.

No. 143—[§ 123.] Every trustee of a school district, or separate neighborhood, who shall wilfully sign a false report to the town superintendent of his town, with the intent of causing such town superintendent to apportion and pay to his district or neighborhood, a larger sum than its just proportion of the school moneys of the town, shall for each offence, forfeit the sum of twenty-five dollars, and shall also be deemed guilty of a misdemeanor.

No. 144—[§ 124.] All property now vested in the trustees of any school district, for the use of schools in the district, or which may be hereafter transferred to such trustees for that purpose, shall be held by them as a corporation.

No. 145—[§ 125.] The trustees of each school district shall, once in each year render to the district, at its annual district meeting, a just and true account in writing, of all moneys received by them respectively for the use of their district; and of the manner in which the same shall have been expended, which account shall be delivered to the district clerk, and be filed and recorded by him.

No. 146—[§ 126.] Any balance of such moneys, which shall appear from such account to remain in the hands of the trustees, or either of them, at the time of rendering the account, shall immediately be paid to some one or more of their successors in office.

No. 147—[§ 127.] Every trustee who shall refuse or neglect to render such account, or to pay over any balance so found in his hands, shall for each offence forfeit the sum of twenty-five dollars.

No. 148—[§ 128.] It shall be the duty of his successors in office to prosecute, without delay, in their name of office, for the recovery of such forfeiture; and the moneys recovered shall be applied by them to the use and benefit of their district schools.

No. 149—[§ 129.] Such successors shall also have the same remedies for the recovery of any unpaid balance in the hands of a former trustee, or his representatives, as are given to the town superintendent againt a former town superintendent and his representatives; and the moneys recovered shall be applied by them to the use of their district, in the same manner as if they had been paid without suit.

No. 150—[§ 130.] Every trustee of a school district who shall, while in office, neglect or refuse annually to render an account of the moneys received by him as such trustee, shall for each offence forfeit the sum of twenty-five dollars; and it shall be the duty of the town superintendent of the town in which such trustee may reside, to prosecute, without delay, in his name of office, for the recovery of such forfeiture; and the moneys recovered shall be applied by such superintendent to the use and benefit of the district school of the district to which such defaulting trustee shall belong.

No. 151—[§ 131.] Such town superintendent shall also have the same remedies for the recovery of any unpaid balance of moneys, in the hands of such delinquent trustee, in office, as are given to the town superintendents in office, against a former town superintendent; and the moneys recovered shall be applied by such town superintendent to the use of the district to which the same may belong, and be paid over to the trustee or trustees of such district, who are not in default.

No. 152—[§ 132.] Any person conceiving himself aggrieved in consequence of any decision made,

1. By any school district meeting.

2. By the town superintendent in the forming or altering, or in refusing to form or alter any school district, or in refusing to pay any school moneys to any such district:

3. By the trustees of any district, in paying any teacher, or refusing to pay him, or in refusing to admit any scholar gratuitously into any school:

4. Or concerning any other matter under the present title may appeal to the superintendent, who is hereby authorized and required to examine and decide the same, and the decision of the state superintendent shall be final and conclusive.

Of school district libraries.

No. 153—[§ 133.] The taxable inhabitants of each school district in the state, shall have power when lawfully assembled at any district meeting, to lay a tax on the district not exceeding ten dollars in any one year, for the purchase of a district library, consisting of such books as they shall in their district meeting direct, and such further sum as they may deem necessary for the purchase of a book case: The intention to propose such tax, shall be stated in the notice required to be given of such meeting.

No. 154—[§ 135. The taxes authorized by the foregoing section to be raised, shall be assessed and collected in the same manner as a tax for building a school house.

No. 155—[§ 136.] The sum of fifty-five thousand dollars, directed to be distributed to the several school districts of this state, by the fourth section of chapter two hundred and thirty-seven of the laws of eighteen hundred and thirty-eight shall continue to be applied to the purchase of books for a district library, until otherwise directed; but whenever the number of volumes in the district library of any district, numbering over fifty children between the ages of five and sixteen years, shall exceed one hundred and twenty-five; or of any district numbering fifty children or less, between the said ages, shall exceed on hundred volumes, the inhabitants of the district qualified to vote therein, may, at a special or annual meeting duly notified for that purpose, by a majority of votes, appropriate the whole, or any part of the library money belonging to the district for the current year, to the purchase of maps, globes, black boards,or other scientific apparatus, for the use of the school: And in every district having the required number of volumes in the district library, and the maps, globes, black-boards, and other apparatus aforesaid, the said moneys, with the approbation of the state superintendent, may be applied to the payment of teachers' wages.

No. 156—[§ 137.] The trustees of every school district shall be trustees of the library of such district; and the property of all books therein, and of the case and other appurtenances thereof, shall be deemed to be vested in such trustees, so as to enable them to maintain any action in relation to the same: It shall be their duty to preserve such books and keep them in repair; and the expenses incurred for that purpose, may be included in any tax list to be made out by them as trustees of a district, and added to any tax voted by a district meeting, and shall be collected and paid over in the same manner: The librarian of any district library shall be subject to the directions of the trustees thereof, in all matters relating to the preservation of the books and appurtenances of the library, and may be removed from office by them for wilful disobedience of such directions, or for any wilful neglect of duty.

No. 157—[§ 138.] Trustees of school districts shall be liable to their successors for any neglect or omission, in relation to the care and superintendence of district libraries, by which any books therein are lost or injured, to the full amount of such loss or injury in an action on the case, to be brought by such successors in their name of office.

No. 158—[§ 139.] A set of general regulations respecting the preservation of school district libraries, the delivery of them by librarians and trustees to their successors in office, the use of them by the inhabitants of the district, the number of volumes to be taken by any one person at any one time or during any term, the periods of their return, the fines and penalties that may be imposed by the trustees of such libraries for not returning, for losing or destroying any of the books therein, or for soiling, defacing, or injuring them, and the conditions upon which any school district may apply the library money to the payment of teachers' wages, may be framed by the state superintendent, and printed copies thereof shall be furnished to each school district of the state; which regulations shall be obligatory upon all persons and officers having charge of such libraries, or using or possessing any of the books thereof. Such fines may be recovered in an action of debt, in the name of the trustees of any such library, of the person on whom they are imposed, except such person be a minor; in which case they may be recovered of the parent or guardian of such minor, unless notice in writing shall have been given by such parent or guardian to the trustees of such library, that they will not be responsible for any books delivered such minor: And persons with whom such minors reside shall be liable in the same manner and to the same extent, in cases where the parent of such minor does not reside in the district.

No. 159—[§ 140.] Any person conceiving himself aggrieved by any act or decision of any trustees of school districts, concerning district libraries, or the books therein, or the use of such books, or of any librarian, or of any district meeting in relation to their school library, may appeal to the state superintendent in the same manner as provided by law.

No. 160—[§ 141.] The legal voters in any two or more adjoining districts may, in such cases as may be approved by the town superintendent, unite their library moneys and funds as they shall be received or collected, and purchase a joint library for the use of the inhabitants of such districts, which shall be selected by the trustees thereof, or by such persons as they shall designate, and shall be under the charge of a librarian to be appointed by them; and the foregoing provisions of this act shall be applicable to the said joint libraries, except that the property in them shall be deemed to be vested in all the trustees, for the time being, of the districts so united. And in case any such district shall desire to divide such library, such division shall be made by the trustees of the two districts whose libraries are so united, and in case they cannot agree, then such division shall be made by the town superintendent.

No. 161—[§ 142.] Where, by reason of the non-compliance with the conditions prescribed by law, the library money shall be withheld from any school district, the same may be distributed among other districts complying with such conditions, or may be retained and paid subsequently to the district from which the same was withheld, as shall be directed by the state superintendent according to the circumstances of the case.

No. 162—[§ 143.] The state superintendent whenever requested by the trustees of a school district, under the directions of the legal voters of such district, may select a library for their use, and cause the same to be delivered to the clerk of the county in which such district is situated, at its expense.

ARTICLE SIXTH.

Of certain duties of the county clerks.

SEC. 172.—County clerk to report to the superintendent of common schools; what, and when.

SEC. 173.—Forfeiture for neglecting it.

SEC. 174.—Who to prosecute for it, and where paid when recovered.

SEC. 175.—Duty of county clerk when commissioners [town superintendents] do not report.

No. 163—§ 172. [§ 112.] It shall be the duty of each county clerk, between the first day of August and the first day of October, in every year, to make and transmit to the superintendent of common schools, a report in writing, containing the whole number of towns in his county, distinguishing the towns from which the necessary reports have been made to him by the town superintendent of common schools, and containing abstracts of all such reports in such form as the state superintendent shall direct.

No. 164—§ 173. [§ 113.] Every clerk who shall refuse or neglect to make such report, within the period so limited, shall, for each offence, forfeit the sum of one hundred dollars to the use of the school fund of the state.

No. 165—§ 174. [§ 114.] It shall be the duty of the superintendent of common schools to prosecute without delay, in his name of office, for such forfeiture, and to pay the moneys recovered, into the treasury of the state, to the credit of the school fund.

No. 166--[§ 144.] It shall be the duty of each county clerk, immediately after the first day of August in every year, in case the town superintendent of any town in his county shall have neglected to make to him his annual report, to give notice of such neglect to the clerk of the town, who shall immediately notify such town superintendent for the purpose of making his report.[1]

Miscellaneous provisions connected with the foregoing articles.

No. 167—[§ 1.] Common schools in the several school districts in this state shall be free to all persons residing in the district over five and under twenty-one years of age, as herein [before] provided. Persons not resident of a district may be admitted into the schools kept therein, with the approbation in writing of the trustees thereof, or a majority of them.[2]

No. 168--[§ 145.] Town superintendents, trustees, collectors and clerks of school districts, refusing or wilfully neglecting to make any report, or to perform any other duty required by law, or by regulations or decisions made under the authority of any statute, shall severally forfeit to their town, or to their district as the case may be, for the use of the common schools therein, the sum of ten dollars for each such neglect or refusal, which penalty shall be sued for and collected by the supervisor of the town, and paid over to the proper officers to be distributed for the benefit of the common schools in the town or district to which such penalty belongs; and when the share of school or library money apportioned to any town or district, or school, or any portions thereof, or any money to which a town or district would have been entitled, shall be lost in consequence of any wilful neglect of official duty by any town superintendent or trustees or clerks of school districts, the officers guilty of such neglect shall forfeit to the town or district the full amount, with interest, of the moneys so lost; and they shall be jointly and severally liable for the payment of such forfeiture.

No. 169—[§ 146.] In any suit which shall hereafter be commenced against town superintendents or officers of school districts, for any act performed by virtue of, or under color of their offices, or for any refusal or omission to perform any duty enjoined by law, and which might have been the subject of an appeal to the superintendent, no costs shall be allowed to the plaintiff in cases where the court shall certify that it appeared on the trial of the cause that the defendants acted in good faith. But this provision shall not extend to suits for penalties, nor to suits or proceedings to enforce the decisions of the superintendent.

No. 170--[§ 1.]*a* Whenever a suit shall have been commenced or shall hereafter be commenced against the trustees of a

---

(1) Laws of 1847, chap. 480, § 144. (2) Laws of 1851, chap. 151, § 1.
(*a*) Laws of 1847, chap. 172, § 1, 2, 3, 4. Laws of 1849, chap. 388.

school district in consequence of acts by them performed in pursuance of and by the direction of such district, for any act performed by virtue of, or under color of their office, and such suit shall have been finally determined, or whenever, after the final determination of any suit commenced by or against any trustees or other officers of a school district, a majority of the taxable inhabitants of any school district shall so determine, it shall be the duty of the trustees to ascertain in the manner hereinafter described, the actual amount of all the costs, charges and expenses paid by such officer, and to cause the same to be assessed upon and collected of the taxable inhabitants of said district in the same manner as other taxes of said district are by law assessed and collected, and when so collected, to pay the same over to the officer by virtue of this act entitled to receive the same; but this provision shall not extend to suits for penalties, nor suits or proceedings to enforce the decisions of the superintendent.

No. 171—[§ 2.] Whenever any person mentioned in the first section of this act shall have paid any costs, charges or expenses as mentioned in said first section, he shall make out an account of such charges, costs and expenses so paid by him, giving the items thereof, and verify the same by his oath or affirmation; he shall serve a copy of said account so sworn to, upon the trustees of the district against which such claim shall be made, together with a notice in writing that on a certain day therein specified, he will present such account to the board of supervisors of the county in which such school district shall be situated, for settlement at some legal meeting of such board; and it shall be the duty of the officer upon whom such copy, account and notice shall be served, to attend at the time and place in such notice specified, to protect the rights and interests of such district upon such settlement.

No. 172—[§ 3.] Upon the appearance of the parties, or upon due proof of service of the notice and copy of account mentioned in the second section of this act, if the said board shall be of opinion that such account or any portion thereof ought justly to be paid to the claimant, such board may by an order to be made by a majority of all the members elected to the same, and to be entered in its minutes, require such account or such part thereof as such board shall be of opinion ought justly to be paid to the claimant, by such district to be so paid; but no portion of such account shall be so ordered to be paid which shall appear to the said board to have arisen from the wilful neglect or misconduct of the claimant. The account, with the oath of the party claiming the same, shall be prima facie evidence of the correctness thereof. The board may adjourn the hearing from time to time as justice shall seem to require.

No. 173—[§ 4.] It shall be the duty of the trustees of any school district, within thirty days after service of a copy of such order upon them to cause the same to be entered at length in the book of records of said district, and to issue to the collector of said district a warrant for the collection of the amount so directed to be paid, in the same manner and with the like force and effect as upon a tax voted by said district.

No. 174—[§ 1.]*b* No person shall wilfully disturb, interrupt or disquiet any assemblage of persons met at any school district, with the assent of the trustees of the school district, for the purpose of receiving instruction in any of the branches of education usually taught in the common schools of this state, or in the science of music.

No. 175—[§ 2.] Whoever shall violate the provisions of the foregoing section, may be tried before any justice of the peace of the county, or any mayor, alderman, recorder, or other magistrate of any city where the offence shall be committed ; and upon conviction, shall forfeit a sum not exceeding twenty-five dollars, for the use and benefit of the school district in which such offence shall be committed.

No. 176—[§ 3.] It shall be the duty of the trustees of any school district in which any such offence shall be committed, to prosecute such offender before any officer having cognizance of such offence.

No. 177—[§ 4.] If any person convicted of the offence herein prohibited, shall not immediately pay the penalty incurred, with the costs of conviction, or give security, to the satisfaction of the officer before whom such conviction shall be had, for the payment of the said penalty and costs within twenty days thereafter, he shall be committed by warrant to the common jail of the county, until the same be paid, or for such term, not exceeding thirty days, as shall be specified in such warrant.

No. 178—[§ 5.] It shall and may be lawful for any person who may be complained of for a violation of the provisions of this act, to demand of such magistrate that he may be tried by a jury. Upon such demand, it shall be the duty of such officer to issue a venire to the proper officer, commanding him to summon the same number of jurors, and in the same manner, and the said court shall proceed to empannel a jury for the trial of said cause, in the same manner and subject to all the rules and regulations prescribed in the act providing for the trials by jury in courts of special sessions.

No. 179—[§ 147.] A school for colored children may be established in any city or town of this state, with the approbation of the commissioners or town superintendent of such city or town, which shall be under the charge of the trustees of the district in which such school shall be kept ; and in places where no school districts exist, or where from any cause it may be expedient, such

(*b*) Laws of 1845, chap. 228, § 1, 2, 3, 4, 5.

school may be placed in charge of trustees to be appointed by the commissioners or town superintendent of common schools of the town or city, and if there be none, to be appointed by the state superintendent. Returns shall be made by the trustees of such school to the town superintendent at the same time and in the same manner as now provided by law in relation to districts; and they shall particularly specify the number of colored children over four and under twenty-one years of age, attending such school from different districts, naming such districts respectively, and the number from each. The town superintendent shall apportion and pay over to the trustees of such schools, a portion of the money received by them annually, in the same manner as now provided by law in respect to school districts, allowing to such schools the proper proportion for each child over four and under twenty-one years, who shall have been instructed in such school at least four months by a teacher duly licensed, and shall deduct such proportion from the amount that would have been apportioned to the district to which such children belong; and in his report to the state superintendent, the town superintendent shall specially designate the schools for colored children in his town or city.

No. 180—[§ 15.] Whenever it shall be satisfactorily proven to the state superintendent that any county or town superintendent or other school officer, has embezzled the public money, or any money coming into his hands for school purposes, or has been guilty of the wilful violation of any law, or neglect of any duty, or of disobeying any decision, order or regulation of the department of common schools, the state superintendent is hereby anthorized to remove such officer from such office, by an order under the seal of office of the secretary of state.[1]

No. 181.—[§148.] The state superintendent may cause to be printed a sufficient number of forms of reports by trustees of school districts and town superintendents and of lists of pupils attending schools, and cause them to be transmitted to the several county clerks, for the use of those officers and of teachers of schools; and he shall cause title second of chapter fifteen and part first of the Revised Statutes to be printed, and shall insert therein all acts and parts of acts which have been passed by the legislature, connected with the subjects of the said title, which are now in force; and where any provisions of the said title have been altered by the subsequent acts, such provisions shall be varied so as to make them conformable to such alterations; but the original numbers of the sections shall be indicated in such mode as he shall judge proper, except as herein amended or altered. Copies of the said title so amended shall be transmitted to the town superintendent, and all other officers charged with the performance of any duty under its provisions, with such explanations and instructions as may be deemed expedient.

---

(1) Chap. 382, Laws of 1849, §15.

No. 182—[§150.] All such provisions of law as are repugnant to or inconsistent with the provisions of this title, are hereby repealed; but nothing herein contained shall be so construed as to impair or affect any of the local provisions respecting the organization and management of schools in any of the incorporated cities or villages or towns of this state, except as the same are affected by the preceding sections of this act.

Town School Funds.

The acts passed in 1789 for the sale of lands belonging to the people of this State, required the Surveyor General to reserve in each township, one lot for the support of the gospel, and one lot for the use of schools in such township.

The following is a list of the principal reservations of this nature, viz:

One lot of 550 acres, in each of the twenty-eight townships in the Military tract.

Forty lots of 250 acres each, in each of the twenty townships west of the Unadilla river, being ten thousand acres.

One lot of 640 acres each, in each of the townships of Fayette, Clinton, Greene, Warren, Chenango, Sidney and Hampden, then in the counties of Broome and Chenango.

Ten lots of 640 acres each, in the townships along the St. Lawrence.

Sixteen lots of 640 acres each in Totten and Crossfield's purchase.

In the township of Plattsburgh 400 acres were reserved for the use of a minister of the gospel, and 460 acres for the use of a public school or schools in the said township.

In the township of Benson 640 acres were reserved for gospel and schools.

By an act passed in 1798, in relation to gospel and school lots, it is provided "that the moneys arising from the leasing of the said lots of land as aforesaid, and from the trespasses aforesaid, shall be applied to the use of schools or support of the gospel, in the original townships, as surveyed, in which such lots shall be respectively situated, and for no other purpose; which said application shall be made, either for schools or gospel or both, and in such way and manner as the freeholders and inhabitants of the towns in which the same lands shall lie, shall in legal town meeting, from time to time direct, order and appoint."

By an act passed in 1808, the act of 1798 was extended to all the townships where lots of land are reserved for the support of gospel and schools, and the following provision was added:

"§ 1. *Be it enacted, &c.,* That the moneys arising from the annual rents and profits of the gospel lots in each township, shall be equally divided by the supervisor and commissioners appointed in each township, between the several religious societies legally organized in such township, and that the money arising from the annual rents and profits of the several school lots shall be distributed among the schools kept in each respective township, by teachers to be approved of by the supervisor and commissioners constituted by the act to which this is an amendment, or a majority of them in said township, in proportion to the aggregate number of days which the scholars in each respective school shall have respectively attended such schools in the year immediately preceding such division."

The fourth section of an act concerning the gospel and school lots passed in 1813, is as follows:

"*And be it further enacted,* That the rents, issues, and profits of the aforesaid lands, and the annual interest of the moneys arising from the sale thereof, shall be applied by the said trustees for the time being, to the support of the gospel and schools in their several towns in such manner, as the freeholders and inhabitants of the towns respectively, at their annual town meeting, shall order and direct, or as the legislature shall prescribe by law." Session Laws of 1813, p. 157.

In 1819, an act was passed in relation to the gospel and school lots which contains the following section:

"§ 2. *And be it further enacted,* That all moneys now due or hereafter to become due, and which shall have come into the hands of the aforesaid commissioners of public lots, and have not been applied and paid over to religious societies, shall be apportioned among the several school districts in the several towns of the aforementioned counties, [Onondaga, Cayuga and Seneca] anything in the acts heretofore passed to the contrary notwithstanding."

By section first of chapter 186, Laws of 1846, (No. 31 ante) "the office of trustees of the gospel and school lots in the several towns in this state is hereby abolished; and the powers and duties now by law conferred and imposed upon said trustees, shall hereafter be exercised by the town superintendent of common schools."

By the provisions of chapter XV, Title IV, of Part I of the Revised Statutes, the trustees of the several Gospel and school lots were authorized and required,

"1. To take and hold possession of the gospel and school lot of their town:

"2. To lease the same for such time not exceeding twenty-one years, and upon such conditions as they shall deem expedient:

"3. To sell the same with the advice and consent of the inhabitants of the town, in town meeting assembled, for such prices and upon such terms of credit as shall appear to them most advantageous:

"4. To invest the proceeds of such sales in loans secured by bond and mortgage upon unincumbered real property of the value of double the amount loaned.

"5. To purchase property so mortgaged upon a fore-closure, and to hold and convey the property so purchased, whenever it shall become necessary.

"6. To release the amount of such loans repaid to them, upon the like security.

"7. To apply the rents and profits of such lots, and the interest of the money arising from the sale thereof, to the support of the gospel and schools, or either, as may be provided by law, in such manner as shall be thus provided.

"8. To render a just and true account of the proceeds of the sales, and the interest on the loans thereof, and of the rents and profits of such gospel and school lots, and of the expenditure and appropriation thereof, on the last Tuesday next preceding the annual town meeting in each year, to the board of auditors of the accounts of other town officers.

"9. To deliver over to their successors in office, all books, papers and securities relating to the same, at the expiration of their respective offices: and

"10. To take therefor a receipt, which shall be filed in the clerk's office of the town.

"§ 4. The board of auditors in each town shall annually report the state of the accounts of the trustees of the gospel and school lots in that town, to the inhabitants thereof, at their annual town meeting.

"§ 5. Whenever a town having lands assigned to it for the support of the gospel or of schools, shall be divided into two or more towns, or shall be altered in its limits by the annexing of a part of its territory to another town or towns, such lands shall be sold by the trustees [town superintendent] of the town in which such lands were included immediately before such division or alteration; and the proceds thereof shall be apportioned between the towns interested therein in the same manner as the other public moneys, of towns, so divided or altered, are apportioned.

"§ 6. The shares of such moneys to which the towns shall be respectively entitled, shall be paid to the trustees of the gospel and school lots [Town Superintendents] of the respective towns, and shall thereafter be subject to the provisions of this Title.

"§ 7. If in either of such towns, trustees of gospel and school lots [Town Superintendents] shall not have been chosen, or there be none in office, the share of such town shall be paid to the supervisor."

An Act relative to moneys in the hands of Overseers of the Poor.

PASSED April 27, 1829.

§ 1. It shall be lawful for the inhabitants of any town, in such counties as have abolished the distinction between county and town paupers, and in such counties as may hereafter abolish such distinction, at any annual or special town meeting, to appropriate all or any part of the monies and funds remaining in the hands of the overseers of the poor of such town, after such abolition, to such objects and for such purposes as shall be determined at such meeting.

§ 2. If any such meeting shall appropriate any such money or funds for the benefit of common schools in their town, the money so appropriated shall be denominated "the Common School Fund of such town," and shall be under the care and superintendence of the [Town Superintendent] of Common Schools of said town.

§ 3. If any such meeting shall appropriate such money or funds for the benefit of common schools, after such appropriaticn shall have been made, and after the town superintendent of common schools shall have taken the oath of office, the overseers of the poor of such towns shall then pay over and deliver to the said town superintendent such moneys, bonds, mortgages, notes and other securities remaining in their hands as such overseers of the poor, as will comport with the appropriation made for the benefit of common schools of their town.

§ 4. The said town superintendents of common schools may sue for and collect, in their name of office, the money due or to become due on such bonds, mortgages, notes or other securities, and also all other securities by them taken under the provisions of this act.

§ 5. The monies, bonds, mortgages, notes and other securities aforesaid shall continue and be a permanent fund, to be denominated the common school fund of the town appropriating the same, the annual interest of which shall be applied to the support of common schools in such towns, unless the inhabitants of such town, in annual town meeting, shall make a different disposition of the whole of the principal and interest, or any part thereof, for the benefit of the common schools of such town.

§ 6. The said town superintendents of common schools, whenever the whole or any part of the principal of said fund shall come to their hands, shall loan the same on bond, secured by a mortgage on real estate of double the value of the monies so loaned, exclusive of buildings or artificial erections thereon.

§ 7. The said town superintendents of common schools may purchase in the estate on which the fund shall have been secured, upon the foreclosure of any mortgage, and may hold and convey the same for the use of said fund.

§ 8. The said town superintendents of common schools shall retain the interest of said common school fund, which shall be distributed and applied to the support of common schools of such town, in like manner as the public money for the support of common schools shall be distributed by law·

§ 9. The said town superintendents of common schools shall account annually, in such manner and at such times as town officers are required by law to account, and shall deliver to their successors in office all moneys, books, securities and papers whatsoever relating to said fund, and shall take a receipt therefor, and file the same with the town clerk.

Lewiston School Fund.

[Laws of 1826, p. 239. 1 Rev. Stat. 614.]

§ 1. The property now belonging to the Lewiston School Fund shall remain a continual fund, the interest of which shall be inviolably appropriated to the support of common schools in the village of Lewiston, under the direction of the commissioners of the Lewiston school fund for the time being.

§ 2. The commissioners of the Lewiston school fund shall not exceed three in number, and shall hold their offices for two years, and until others shall be appointed. In case of vacancies in the office of such commissioners, the vacancies shall be filled and all appointments hereafter be made by the governor and senate, in the same manner that other appointments are made.

§ 3. All such commissioners hereafter to be appointed, shall continue in office for two years and until others shall be appointed, unless in cases of appointment to fill vacancies, where the term shall expire with that of the other commissioners.

§ 4. Every person hereafter appointed a commissioner of the Lewiston school fund shall, before he enters on the duties of his office, give to the trustees of the corporation of the village of Lewiston, a bond in the penalty of fifteen thousand dollars, with two or more sureties, conditioned that he shall faithfully execute the duties of his office—which bond shall be deposited with the clerk of the said corporation.

§ 5. The commissioners of the Lewiston school fund shall have power and it shall be their duty,

1. To sell or lease the lots of land in the village of Lewiston, belonging to the said fund, on such terms as they may judge most conducive to the interests of the fund:

2. To certify to the commissioners of the Land office, on receiving payment for such sales, a description of the land sold, the price, the time when sold, the name of the purchasers, and that the consideration money and interest has been fully paid:

3. To loan all moneys which may come to their hands, belonging to the fund:

4. To take a bond on making such loans to themselves as such commissioners, secured by a mortgage on unincumbered real property, of at least double the value of the sum loaned, exclusive of buildings:

5. To collect all bonds and mortgages or other debts due to the fund:

6. To pay over to the trustees of common schools in the said village, all moneys received by the commissioners for interest on loans or rents of lands belonging to said fund:

7. To keep suitable books and accounts of all matters relating to the management of said fund, which shall be open to the inspection of the inhabitants of the village at all reasonable times: and—

8. To deliver, at the expiration of their several offices, to the remaining commissioners or their successors in office, all the books and papers relating to said fund.

§ 6. Before the trustees of common schools in said village shall be entitled to receive such moneys from the commissioners, the trustees shall execute a bond to the supervisors of the town of Lewiston, in such penalty and with such sureties as the supervisor shall approve, conditioned that the trustees shall faithfully apply such moneys towards the support of schools in the village of Lewiston, for the benefit of such of its inhabitants as shall have resided in the village at least six months; and shall render a just aud true account of the expenditure of such moneys to the supervisor, when required.

§ 7. It shall be the duty of the trustees of the corporation of the village of Lewiston, in case of any breach of the conditions of the bond given by such commissioners, and of the supervisor of the town of Lewiston, in case of any breach of the conditions of the bond given by the trustees of common schools for the village of Lewiston, to sue for and receive on said bonds all damages which may have accrued by such breaches for the use of said schools.

PART III.

INSTRUCTIONS, DIGEST & EXPOSITION

OF THE

GENERAL LAWS

RELATING TO

COMMON SCHOOLS.

WITH FORMS, &c., FOR THE USE OF SCHOOL OFFICERS.

CHAPTER I.

OF THE SCHOOL FUND AND STATE TAX, AND THEIR APPORTIONMENT AND DISTRIBUTION AMONG THE SEVERAL COUNTIES, CITIES AND TOWNS.

COMMON SCHOOLS in the several school districts of this state are FREE to all persons residing in the district, over four and under twenty-one years of age; and all children enumerated in the annual reports of the trustees of the several districts are legally ENTITLED to attend the schools of such district. Children whose parents or guardians are non-residents of the district in which they may desire to attend school, may be admitted into such school, with the approbation in writing of the trustees thereof, or of a majority of them. If any terms of admission are intended to be imposed, other than those common to resident children of the district, such terms must be distinctly specified at the time of such admission: otherwise it will be presumed that the non-resident children so admitted are to share in all the privileges of the school with resident children of the district.

The capital of the common school fund, consisting of the proceeds of the sales of all lands belonging to the state, is, by the constitution, to be "preserved inviolate," and its revenues to be applied to the support of common schools. This fund amounted on the 30th of September last, to $2,243,563.36; consisting of bonds for lands sold, and for loans, bank stock, state stock, &c., yielding an annual revenue of about $135,000 for distribution among the several school districts.

By chapter 237 of the Laws of 1838, the sum of $110,000 was annually appropriated from the revenue of the United States Deposite Fund, together with an additional amount of $55,000 for the purchase of district libraries. The aggregate amount therefore to be annually apportioned and distributed from the common school fund is $300,000. The constitution also provides that "the sum of twenty-five thousand dollars of the revenues of the United States Deposite Fund shall each year be appropriated to and made a part of the capital of the said common school fund;" and by § 13 of chapter 382 of the laws of 1849, "whenever any money is paid into the treasury of the state for or on account of the common school fund, it shall be the duty of the comptroller to credit the common school fund with interest on the sum so paid in, at the rate of six per cent. per annum, for the time the same shall remain in the treasury."

By the "Act to establish Free Schools throughout the State," it is provided that there shall hereafter be raised by tax, in each and every year, upon the real and personal estate within this state, the sum of eight hundred thousand dollars, to be levied, assessed and collected in the mode prescribed by the revised statutes, relating to the assessment and collection of taxes, and when collected be paid over to the respective county treasurers, subject to the order of the state superintendent of common schools, who is required to ascertain the portion of said sum to be assessed and collected in each of the several counties of this state, by dividing the said sum among the several counties, according to the valuation of real and personal estate therein, as it shall appear by the assessment of the year next preceding the one in which said sum is to be raised, and to certify to the clerk of each county, before the tenth day of July in each year, the amount to be raised by tax in such county; and it is made the duty of the several county clerks to deliver to the board of supervisors of their respective counties, a copy of such certificate, on the first day of their annual session, and of the board of supervisors to assess such amount upon the real and personal estate of such county, in the manner provided by law for the assessment and collection of taxes.

The state superintendent of common schools is required on or before the first day of January in every year, to apportion and divide, one-third of the sum so raised by general tax, and one-third of all other moneys appropriated to the support of common schools, among the several school districts, parts of districts, and separate neighborhoods in this state, from which reports shall have been received in accordance with law, in the following manner, viz: to each separate neighborhood belonging to a school district in some adjoining state, a sum of money equal to thirty-three cents for each child in such neighborhood (between the ages of four and twenty-one); but the sum so to be apportioned and paid to any such neighborhood, is in no case, to exceed the sum of twenty-four dollars, and the remainder of such one-third is to be apportioned and divided equally among the several districts; and the state superintendent of common schools is, by proper regulations and instructions to be prescribed by him, is to provide for the payment of such moneys to the trustees of such separate neighborhoods and school districts. It is also the duty of the state superintendent of common schools, on or before the first day of January, in every year, to apportion and divide the remaining two-thirds of the said amount of eight hundred thousand dollars, together with the remaining two-thirds of all other moneys appropriated by the state for the support of common schools among the several counties, cities and towns of the state, in the mode now prescribed by law for the division and apportionment of the income of the common school fund; and the share of the several towns and wards so apportioned and divided, is to be paid over, on and after the first Tuesday in February, in each year, to the several town superintendents of common schools, and ward or city officers, entitled by law to receive the same.

When the census, or returns, upon which an apportionment is to be made, shall be so far defective, in respect to any county, city, or town, as to render it impracticable for the superintendent to ascertain the share of school moneys, which ought then to be apportioned to such county, city, or town, he is required to ascertain, by the best evidence in his power, the facts upon which the ratio of such apportionment shall depend, and to make the apportionment accordingly; and whenever, in consequence of the division of a town, or the erection of a new town, in any county, the apportionment then in force shall become unjust, as between two or more of the towns of such county, he is required to make a new apportionment of the school moneys next to be distributed amongst such towns, ascertaining by the best evidence in his power, the facts upon which the ratio of apportionment as to such towns, shall depend. He is also to certify each apportionment made by him, to the comptroller.

Under these provisions the sum of $1,100,000 is annually to be apportioned by the state superintendent among the several counties, cities and towns, for the support of common schools; of which the sum of $55,000 is to be applied to library purposes, and the residue exclusively to the payment of the wages of duly qualified teachers, in the mode prescribed by law.

Treasurers of counties have no right to deduct from the amount of the school moneys apportioned to each town a commission of one per cent. They are unquestionably *entitled* to such a commission under § 26, 1 R. S. 370 on the moneys received and paid by them for the use of the common schools; but they have no right to diminish the amount of the moneys placed in their hands for distribution, under an apportionment by the superintendent. Their commission is a charge upon the county, and not upon the common school fund.—*Com. School Dec.* 279.

In addition to the funds thus provided by the general law, a large proportion of the towns are annually in the receipt of local funds, arising from the proceeds of the sales or leases of gospel and school lots belonging to such towns, reserved under an act passed in 1789, by the surveyor-general in the original allotment of townships; from the appropriation of moneys remaining in the hands of the overseer of the poor of towns in those counties in which the distinction between town and county paupers has been abolished, to the support of the schools, by a vote of the inhabitants at their annual town meeting; and in some instances from testamentary bequests and voluntary donations, for the benefit of common schools. In most of the cities of the state, too, as will be seen hereafter, large sums are directed by special acts to be raised for the support of the public schools.

CHAPTER II.

TOWN SUPERINTENDENTS OF COMMON SCHOOLS.

By the first section of chap. 133, Laws of 1843, the offices of Commissioners and Inspectors of common schools were abolished; and by the first section of chap. 480, Laws of 1847, it is provided that there shall hereafter be elected in each of the towns of this state, at the same time and in the same manner that other town officers are chosen, an officer to be denominated "Town Superintendent of common schools." It is his duty, on or before the first Monday of November after his election, to execute to the supervisor of his town and file with the town clerk, a bond, with one or more sufficient sureties, to be approved of by said supervisor by endorsement over his signature on said bond, in the penalty of double the amount of school money which his town received from all sources during the year preceding that for which he shall have been elected, conditioned for the faithful application and legal disbursement of all the school money coming into his hands during his term of office, and for the faithful discharge of all the duties of said office. In case such bond shall not be executed and filed within the time herein specified, the office of such Town Superintendent is to be deemed vacant, and such or any other vacancy is to be filled by any three Justices of the Peace of the same town, by a warrant under their hands and seals; and the persons so appointed are, (by the provisions of § 14, chap. 382, Laws of 1849,) to hold their offices until the first Monday of November following the next annual town meeting. The justices making such appointment are to cause their warrant to be filed with the town clerk, and to give immediate notice to the person appointed.

If there are less than three justices residing in the town in which such vacancy occurs, the resident justice or justices may associate with themselves one or more justices from any adjoining town. 1 Rev. St. 398, § 56.

Every town superintendent is required on the execution of his bond, as above provided, to enter upon the duties of his office on the *first Monday of November succeeding his election*, and is to hold his office *for two years* thereafter; and whenever the office of town superintendent shall be vacant for any cause, or before the time of the annual town meeting, shall be held by a person appointed by the Justices as above provided, the electors of the town at such town meeting are required to choose a town superintendent to fill such vacancy or to supercede such appointee; and the person so elected is to enter upon the duties of the office on the first Monday of November following his election, and to hold his office for the term of two years.

In the interim between the town meeting and the first Monday of November following, the office is to be filled by appointment by the Justices.

Town superintendents are declared by law to be ineligible to the offices of Trustee of School District, Supervisor, or Town Clerk.

The powers and duties formerly by law conferred upon the trustees of the Gospel and school lots in the several towns of the state, are, by the first section of chap. 186, Laws of 1846, vested in and to be exercised by town superintendents.

Town superintendents are entitled to receive $1,25 per day for every day actually and necessarily devoted by them, in their official capacity, to the service of the town in which they are elected, to be paid in like manner as other town officers are paid.

Town superintendents are required, immediately after the commencement of their official term, to report their names and post office address to the Department.

The various powers and duties appertaining to the office of Town Superintendents, may be arranged under the following heads:

1st. The formation and alteration of districts.

2d. The apportionment and payment of public money.

3d. The inspection and licensing of teachers, and the visitation and supervision of schools.

4th. The making and transmission of their annual reports.

5th. The collection of certain penalties and forfeitures.

6th. Miscellaneous duties under various provisions of law.

I. OF THE FORMATION AND ALTERATION OF SCHOOL DISTRICTS.

By the 43d section of the act of 1847, above referred to, it is provided that "in the erection or alteration of a school district, the trustees of any district to be affected thereby may apply to the supervisor and town clerk to be associated with the Town Superintendent; and their action shall be final unless duly appealed from. The compensation of the supervisor and town clerk, when thus associated, shall be the same as that of the Town Superintendent." The various remarks under this head will therefore be applicable as well to the action of the town supervisor, superintendent and clerk, when associated together by virtue of this provision, as to that of the Town Superintendent alone; although for the sake of brevity and simplicity the latter only is referred to.

It is proper, however, in this connection to advert to the general duties of the town clerk, in his capacity as clerk to the Town Superintendent, independently of the provision above cited. By the 32d section of the school act (No. 00) he is required "to receive and keep all reports made to the Town Superintendent from the trustees of school districts, and all the books and papers belonging to the Town Superintendent when required, and to file them in his office; to receive all his estimates and apportionments of school money, and to record the same in a book to be kept for that purpose; and to notify the Town Superintendent, upon receiving notice from the county clerk, that he has not made his annual report, for the purpose of making such report."

Consent of Trustees, and Notice of Alteration.

By the 45th section of the school act (No. 71) it is provided that "no alteration of any school district made without the consent of the trustees thereof, shall take effect until three months after notice in writing shall be given by the Town Superintendent, to some one or more of such trustees. *Nor shall any alteration or regulation of an organized school district be made to take effect between the first day of December in any one year, and the first day of May following.*"

As the principal portion of the inhabited territory of the state has already been sub-divided into school districts, every formation of a new district will, to a greater or less extent, involve some alteration in districts previously existing. The consent of a majority of the trustees, therefore, of each district affected by such alteration, or a written notice thereof, to some one of such trustees, is in all cases indispensable to the validity of the proceeding. In the absence of such consent, the order of the Town Superintendent is, to use a legal phrase, *inchoate*, or in *abeyance*, until the expiration of three months after service of the notice required by law; and the districts to be affected by the proposed alteration remain, for all district purposes, in their original condition, the same as though no action whatever had been had.

All alterations made between the first day of December in any year, and the first day of May ensuing, should specify on their face that they are to take effect on or after the first day of May, and if after at what time.

The law has not prescribed any specific time within which the notice of the alteration must be given, where the consent of trustees has been withheld; but it is obviously proper that such notice should be given at the time of the alteration, or as soon thereafter as may be practicable. A notice at any subsequent period would undoubtedly, however, be valid, and would amount to a republication of the order of the Town Superintendent; and at the expiration of three months from the service of such notice, the alteration would take effect. The consent of the trustees, when given, would appear from the record of the alteration, but in the absence of such proof, it may be established by other testimony.

Whenever any portion of the inhabitants or territory of one district is annexed to another existing district, the consent of a majority of the trustees of *each* district must be procured, or the notice required by law must be given.

The consent of trustees to a proposed alteration in their district may be given either verbally or in writing; and it has even been held that their *presence* at the time of alteration, with full knowledge of the fact of such alteration, amounts, in the absence of any *objection* on their part, to a consent.—*Com. School Dec.* 59.

Persons attached to a district without the consent of trustees, may be transferred to another district at any time prior to the expiration of three months, and such new transfer amounts to a virtual abandonment of the original order.

The consent of trustees to an alteration in their district must in all cases have reference to the specific alteration proposed, and can not be general and unlimited.—*Com. School Dec.* 30.

The provision requiring the consent of trustees to detach persons from their district, and holding them three months without such consent, was made for the benefit and protection of the trustees, to whose injury the alteration might operate. For instance, trustees might have made contracts and incurred responsibilities which would operate oppressively, if some of the most wealthy were detached before they had time to collect the tax. And to carry this intention into effect, the act should be benignly and favorably construed for the protection of the trustees.—*Id.*

When the supervisor and town clerk are associated with the Town Superintendent in the formation or alteration of any district, a majority of the Board may make the requisite order.

Notice for the organization of a new District.

Whenever any school district is formed in any town, it is the duty of the Town Superintendent, within twenty days thereafter, to prepare a notice in writing, describing such district, and appointing a time and place for the first district meeting, and to deliver such notice to a taxable inhabitant of the district, who is bound to notify every other inhabitant of the district, qualified to vote at district meetings, by reading the notice in the hearing of each such inhabitant, or in case of his absence from home, by leaving a copy thereof, or of so much thereof as relates to the time and place of such meeting, at the place of his abode, at least six days before the time of the meeting. In case such notice shall not be given, or the inhabitants of a district shall refuse or neglect to assemble or form a district meeting, when so notified; or in case any such district, having been formed and organized in pursuance of such notice, shall afterwards be dissolved, so that no competent authority shall exist therein, to call a special district meeting in the manner hereinafter provided; such notice must be renewed by the Town Superintendent, and served in the manner above described.—54—56. (Nos. 76—78.)

The notice here required to be served on *each voter* in the district by the inhabitant to whom the Town Superintendent delivers the notice prepared by him, need not contain the *description of the district* referred to in the 54th section. It is sufficient if it specify the time, place, and general object of the meeting. "It is necessary for the person notifying the inhabitants to have the district described, that he may know whom to notify. The inhabitant notified has no necessity for knowing who else is notified. The notice is to him as an individual. The same section defines the extent of this notice to individuals by saying, when the person is absent from home, he is to be warned by leaving at his place of abode a copy of the notice, *or of so much thereof as relates to the time and place of meeting.* This is clear and conclusive. It could not be necessary that a personal notice should be more full and particular than is required of a notice left in the absence of the person notified."—Per Flagg, *Sup't. Com. School Dec.* 18.

If in consequence of the refusal of the trustees of the district or districts, from which a new district is formed, to consent to the proposed alteration, such new district cannot go into operation until after the expiration of three months from the service of notice of such alteration, the notice for the first meeting must be deferred until the expiration of such time; or at least must specify a day subsequent thereto for the holding of such meeting.

Where a meeting has been held and officers chosen under a notice given by the Town Superintendent, in the mode prescribed by law, a second notice for such organization cannot be given under the pretence that the proceedings of such first meeting were invalid or irregular.—*Com. School Dec.* 176.

On the formation of a new district, if notice for the first district meeting is not given within twenty days, it may be given subsequent to the expiration of that period: the provision requiring the notice to be given within that time being *directory* merely.—*Id.*358.

By § 50 of the school act, as amended by chap. 382, Laws of 1849, it is provided that "when two or more districts shall be consolidated into one, the new district shall succeed to all the rights of property possessed by the districts of which it shall be composed, and when a district is annulled and portions thereof are annexed to other districts, the property of the district so annulled shall be sold by the town superintendent of the town in which the school house is located, at public auction to the highest bidder therefor, after at least five days public notice by notices posted in three or more public places in said town, one of which shall be within the district so annulled, and the proceeds of such sale shall be first applied so far as requisite, to the payment of any just debts due from the district so annulled, and the residue thereof shall be apportioned among the taxable inhabitants of the district so annulled in the ratio of their several assessments upon the last corrected assessment roll of the town or towns with which such district is located."

Where there are any moneys in the hands of the officers of a district that is or may be annulled, or belonging to such district, the Town Superintendent of common schools of the town may demand, sue for, and recover the same, in their name of office, and is required to apportion the same equitably between the districts to which the several portions of such annulled district may have been annexed, to be held and enjoyed as district property.—*Id.* § 52, (No. 74.)

The former provisions of law, authorizing the sale and apportionment of district property whenever a new district was formed from one or more districts possessed of a school house or other property, has been repealed: and no such sale or apportionment can take place except in the case of a dissolved district, as above specified.

Formation or alteration of Joint Districts.

By § 44, (No. 70) of the school act, it is provided that "whenever it may be necessary or convenient to form a district out of two or more adjoining towns, the Town Superintendents of *each* of such adjoining towns or the major part of them may form, regulate and alter such districts."

In accordance with the spirit of this provision, and of the adjudications under it, it is conceived that the assent of the Town Superintendent, either singly, or if the supervisors or town clerk are associated with him, of a majority of the officers of *each* of the towns from which a joint district is partly composed, is essential to the validity of any order forming or altering such joint district. In the formation of joint districts, the Town Superintendents, &c., represent their respective towns, and the rights of those whom they represent cannot be voted away by officers representing the inhabitants of another town. The principle has been settled by the decisions of Messrs. Flagg, Dix and Young, Superintendents, against the dissenting opinion of Mr. Spencer, that the law does not authorize the question of the formation or alteration of a joint district, to be settled by a joint ballot of the officers representing the several towns, from parts of which it is, or is proposed to be, composed. See *Com. School Dec.*, 23, 174.

The moment a single district becomes *joint*, the action of the proper officers of *all* the towns of which it is a part is indispensable to give validity to any alteration in its boundaries; and such alteration, whether its effect is to change a joint to a single district, or to continue the joint district, can be made only by the concurrence of *the representatives of each of the towns interested.* This construction is in entire accordance with the whole tenor of the Superintendent's decision; and if it is not clear from the language of § 44 that such is the true meaning of that section, all doubt on this point will be dispelled by reference to § 46, which provides for the case of a refusal on the part of the proper officers of one town to act with those of another, for the purpose of altering a joint district." Per Dix *Sup't. Com. School Dec.* 174; modified in conformity to the existing provisions of law in reference to the proper officers to form, regulate and alter districts. At pages 248 and 253 of the same volume, the same principle is again distinctly recognized and enforced by the same Superintendent. "The consent of the trustees of a joint district to an alteration does not authorize the proper officers of one town to make it without the concurrence of those of the others of which it may be composed. *Each town* of which the district is a part, is concerned in its preservation, and it is only with the consent of the official authority of *each town* that its boundaries can be enlarged or diminished, excepting when the proper officers of one town refuse or neglect to meet those of the others when their attendance has been required."

By § 46, (No. 72) above alluded to, it is provided that where the Town Superintendent of common schools of any town shall require in writing the attendance of the proper officers of any other town or towns, at a joint meeting, for the purpose of altering a school district formed from their respective towns, and a major part of the officers notified shall refuse or neglect to attend, those in attendance may, by a majority of votes, call a special district meeting of such district, for the purpose of deciding on such proposed alteration; and the decision of such meeting shall be as valid as if made by the proper authority of all the towns interested; but shall extend no further than to dissolve the district formed from such towns. The effect of such a dissolution would be to cause the inhabitants and territory of each of the towns from parts of which the joint district had been composed, to revert under the separate jurisdiction of the proper officers of the respective towns, who might make such disposition of them as they should deem most expedient and proper.

Single districts are frequently transformed into joint districts by operation of law, on the division of towns and counties, or the alteration of their boundaries. A district intersected by the line of division between a new town and the town from which it was taken, becomes a joint district, and is thereafter subject to the principles and provisions of law applicable to joint districts.

Although the joint action of the requisite legal authority of all the towns from portions of which a joint district is composed, is necessary to any alteration of such district, yet where such alteration involves the *dissolution* of the joint district, the powers of the joint board cease with the order for such dissolution, and the proper officers of each of the towns resume their jurisdiction over the inhabitants and territory belonging to their town. The co-operation of the other members of the joint board, in such subsequent proceedings, although unnecessary and irregular, would not, however, it is presumed, vitiate the proceedings.

In the formation or alteration of joint districts, a *joint board* must in all cases be formed. The officers of one town cannot concur in the proceedings of those of another, at a subsequent period. They have no power to act, either separately or by proxy. They can neither give their consent beforehand to what their colleagues may do, nor can they afterwards in any mode render that valid, which was before illegal and void.

General Principles applicable to the Formation and Alteration of Districts.

The great aim of the officers to whom this duty has been confided should be to form, as far as may be practicable, permanent and efficient districts, competent both in respect to taxable property and number of children, to sustain good schools for from eight to ten months of each year, and affording all requisite facilities for the regular attendance of all the children entitled to participate in the benefits of the school.

Whenever alterations may become necessary or expedient, the utmost care should be taken to secure the general co-operation of the inhabitants interested, and to avoid all those sources of contention and discord which are so fatal to the prosperity, harmony and efficiency of the district. It is better to submit to many temporary and local inconveniences, than to hazard the disastrous results which almost uniformly follow any general dissatisfaction with contemplated alterations, even though such alterations may upon the whole be judicious and advantageous. "The good sense of a district may be relied upon, to perceive ultimately its true interest, and the loss of time in attaining the desired end is unimportant when compared with the consequences of defeating the wishes of a decided majority," or even of a respectable minority "of a district."

School districts must be composed of contiguous territory; and it has been decided that when a person is set off from one district to another, and there are lands between the farm so set off and the district to which it is annexed, such intermediate territory passes to the latter.

In his annual report to the legislature for the year 1843, the Superintendent, (Col. YOUNG,) observes, "One of the most formidable obstacles to the efficiency of our common schools is believed to be the uncessary multiplication and subdivision of districts. In those portions of the state where the population is scattered over a large extent of territory, the convenience and accommodation of the inhabitants, require the formation of districts comprising a small amount of taxable property, applicable to the support of schools and a limited number of children. But where an opposite state of things exists, the interests of education will be most effectually promoted, by assigning to each district the greatest extent of territory compatible with securing to the children the requisite facilities for their regular attendance at the schools."

In a case coming before him on appeal, in 1835, Gen. DIX observes in reference to this subject: "Almost all the existing evils of the common school system have their origin in the limited means of the school district. The tendency is to subdivision and to a contraction of their territorial boundaries. This consequence must follow in some degree from the increase of population ; but the subdivision of school districts tends to advance in a much greater ratio. The average number of children in our school districts is about fifty-five. *No school district should number less than forty children between [four and twenty-one years] of age.* From the observations he has made, the Superintendent deems it due to the common school system, that no new district shall be formed with a much smaller number, unless peculiar circumstances render it proper to make it an exception to the general rule. In feeble districts, cheap instructors, poor and ill furnished school-houses, and a general languor of the cause of education are almost certain to be found."—*Com. School Dec.* 220.

II. APPORTIONMENT AND PAYMENT OF PUBLIC MONEY.

By subdivisions 5, 6 and 7 of § 8 of the school act (No. 33) it is made the duty of the Town Superintendents "To apply for and receive from the county treasurer, all moneys apportioned for the use of common schools in their town, and from the collector of the town, all moneys raised therein for the same purpose, as soon as such moneys shall become payable, or be collected, and to apportion the school moneys received by them, on the first Tuesday of April, in each year, among the several school districts, parts of districts, and neighborhoods separately set off, within their town, in proportion to the number of children residing in each, over the age of four and under that of twenty-one years, as the same shall have appeared from the last annual reports of their respective trustees. If they shall have received the school moneys of their town, and all the reports from the several school districts therein, before the first Tuesday in April, they shall apportion such moneys as above directed, within ten days after receiving all of the said reports and the said moneys." The practice of making *two divisions* of the public money among the districts in the course of the year, is contrary to the express provision of the statute. The sixth subdivision of section 8 (No. 33) makes it the duty of the Town Superintendent to apportion the school moneys received by him on the *first Tuesday of April* in each year ; and by the 7th subdivision of the same section, if he have received reports from all the districts *before* that day, he is to divide the money within ten days after receiving all the reports and the money.

The annual reports of the trustees of the several districts are, as will be seen hereafter under the appropriate head required to be made and transmitted to the Town Superintendent, between the first and fifteenth of January in each year; and the public money from all sources is payable immediately after its receipt by the county treasurer on the first of February. If, therefore, the reports of the respective trustees are made within the time prescribed by law, ample opportunity will be afforded to the Town Superintendent to point out all errors and deficiencies in them, and to enable the trustees either to make the necessary corrections or apply to the department for relief, before the apportionment is finally made. In making the apportionment, the Town Superintendent is first to assign to each district, from which the necessary report has been received, or which is entitled to share in the apportionment, its proportion of the public money received from all sources, according to the number of children between the ages of four and twenty-one, *designating the respective proportions of teachers' and library money* belonging to each district. The proportion of library money to be apportioned to each district, may be ascertained by setting apart five dollars out of each hundred *or five per cent of the whole amount apportioned to each district.* The teachers' money is to be paid over "on the written order of a majority of the trustees of each district, to the teachers entitled to receive the same." It will therefore be incumbent on the Town Superintendent to satisfy himself, both of the genuineness of the order and that the person presenting it has the certificate of the trustees that he is or was a teacher of the district, and duly qualified according to law. In order to entitle a district to its share of teachers' money, it must appear from its annual report, "that a school had been kept therein for at least six months during the year, ending at the date of such report, by a qualified teacher," *after obtaining a certificate of competency* from the proper authority ; that all the teachers' money received during the year has been expended in the payment of *such teacher ;* "*that no other than a duly qualified teacher had at any time during the year for more than one month been employed to teach the school in said district* ;" and such report must, in all other respects, be in accordance with law, and the requisitions and instructions of the Superintendent, made in pursuance of law. In other words, it must be in the form prescribed by the Superintendent, and must contain all the information required by law and by the department to be given.

The *library money* is to be paid over, to, or on the order of, a majority of the trustees, on its appearing from the annual report that "the library money received at the last preceding apportionment was duly expended according to law, (in the purchase of books suitable for a district library, or in the purchase of maps, globes, black-boards, or other scientific apparatus for the use of schools, in the cases and in the mode prescribed by law, or for teachers' wages, with the assent of the state superintendent, *on or before the first day of October subsequent to such apportionment.*" The report must uniformly be accompanied with a catalogue of the books or apparatus purchased since the last preceding catalogue, and must state accurately the number of volumes and their condition; and when the money has been expended in the purchase of apparatus, &c., or for teachers' wages, the authority under which such expenditure has been made, and a full and particular inventory of the articles purchased, must be specifically reported.

By chapter 257 of the Laws of 1829, in those counties where the distinction between town and county poor is abolished, the inhabitants of towns having any funds in the hands of their overseers of the poor, may appropriate all or any part of such funds to such purposes as shall be determined at an annual or special town meeting. If appropriated for the benefit of common schools, it is made a fund for that purpose, and is placed under the charge of the Town Superintendent of common schools of the town. The *interest* is to be applied "to the support of common schools." But the town may, at an annual meeting, direct the whole principal, as well as the interest, to be applied for the benefit of common schools. [*See vol.* 1, *2d ed. Rev. Statutes, page* 351, *and Com. School Dec., page* 418.]

The Town Superintendent will, therefore, be bound to distribute the interest, and the principal when directed by the town, equally among the districts. He cannot adopt a more just or convenient ratio than that established by the existing law in relation to the public money—the number of children above four and under twenty one years of age.

The purchase of district libraries would not be an application "to the support of common schools." They are not intended for the schools exclusively, or particularly, but for the benefit of all the inhabitants, and cannot be said to form any part of "the common schools." No part of the interest or principal of this town fund, therefore, can be distributed as "library money;" the whole must be apportioned and paid over as school money.

There are laws of a similar character respecting the gospel and school lots, which are so local and peculiar as not to justify any particular observations concerning them in this connection, except that none of these funds can properly be applied to the purchase of books.

In apportioning and paying the money in their hands to trustees of school districts, the Town Superintendents should bear in mind that the "teachers' money" and the "library money" are entirely independent of each other. The report of the trustees of school districts may entitle them to their "teachers' money," and yet they may not have complied with the conditions upon which they are authorized to receive the "library money." For instance, they may not have expended the latter in the purchase of books; and yet they may have fully complied with the law in regard to their schools. So they may be entitled to "library money" and yet not have had a school kept six months by a qualified teacher. In all such cases the money appropriated to the different objects, teachers or library, is to be distributed upon the reports relating to those objects *only*.

By § 15 of the act of 1841, (No. 147,) Town Superintendents are required to apportion and pay to the trustees of colored schools established in their town, according to the provisions of that section, a portion of the public money, according to the number of colored children between the ages of four and twenty-one years, appearing by the reports of the trustees to have been instructed in such schools for at least four months during the preceding year by a licensed teacher, and to deduct the amount so apportioned from the shares of the districts from which such children have respectively attended.

In all cases where the annual report of the trustees of a district shall not be found in substantial accordance with the law, or the forms or instructions prescribed by the Superintendent, it is the duty of the Town Superintendent to withhold from such district the share of teachers' or library money to which it would otherwise have been entitled; to direct the defaulting trustees to make immediate application to the department, setting forth under oath any excuse they may have for omitting to comply with the requisitions of law; and to retain the amount apportioned to such district and so withheld, to await the directions of the department in reference to its disposition. In case no directions are received, prior to the next succeeding apportionment, the Town Superintendent is to add the amount so retained to the fund for distribution the ensuing year.

By the second section of the act of 1841, (No. 39,) it is provided that "whenever an apportionment of the public money shall not be made to any school district, in consequence of any accidental omission to make any report required by law, or to comply with any other provision of law, or any regulation, the Superintendent of Common Schools may direct an apportionment to be made to such district, according to the equitable circumstances of the case, to be paid out of the public money on hand; or if the same shall have been distributed, out of the public money to be received in a succeeding year." And by the sixth section of chap. 177, Laws of 1839, (No. 161,) whenever any library money shall be withheld from any school district, the same may be distributed among other districts complying with such conditions, or may be retained and paid subsequently to the district from which the same was with held, as shall be directed by the Superintendent of common schools, according to the circumstances of the case.

By §§ 17 and 18 (No.'s 42 and 43) of the school act, "All moneys apportioned by the Town Superintendent to the trustees of a district, part of a district or separate neighborhood, which shall have remained in the hands of such Superintendent for one year after such apportionment, by reason of the trustees neglecting or refusing to receive the same, shall be added to the moneys next thereafter to be apportioned, and shall be apportioned and paid therewith in the same manner; aud in case any school moneys received by the Town Superintendent cannot be apportioned by him for the term of two years after the same are received, by reason of the non-compliance of all the school districts in the town with the provisions of this title, such moneys shall be returned by him to the county treasurer, to be by him apportioned and distributed, together and in the same manner with the moneys next thereafter to be received by him for the use of common schools."

If the Town Superintendent knows, or has good reason to believe, any district report to be erroneous or false, he may withhold the public money from the district, and submit the facts to the Superintendent.

If, after the time when the annual reports are required to be dated, and before the apportionment of the school moneys shall have been made by the Town Superintendent, a district shall be duly altered, or a new district be formed in the town, so as to render an apportionment founded solely on the annual reports unjust, as between two or more district of the town, the Town Superintendent is required by § 15 (No. 40) of the school act, to make an apportionment among such districts, according to the number of children in each, over the ages of four and under twenty-one years, ascertaining that number by the best evidence in his power; and by the first section of chap. 206 of the Laws of 1831, § 16 (No. 41) the same provision is extended to all cases where a school district shall have been formed at such time previous to the first day of January, as not to have allowed a reasonable time to have kept a school therein for the term of six months, such district having been formed out of a district or districts in which a school shall have been kept for six mouths, by a teacher duly qualified, during the year preceding the first day of January.

The apportionment of public money by the Town Superintendent can in no case be made prior to the first Tuesday in April, except where reports from all the districts and parts of districts in the town, and all the public moneys, have been received before that time; but under certain circumstances it may be made subsequently. The specification of time in the statute is not intended to limit the exercise of the authority of the Town Superintendent in this respect, but may be regarded as directory merely; and it has accordingly been held that if for any justifiable cause the apportionment is not made or completed on the day specified, it may be made at a subsequent period.

In all cases where school districts have complied substantially with the law, the trustees may be allowed to correct their reports, as to mere matter of form, at any time before the money is actually apportioned and paid. A district ought not to lose its money in consequence of a misconception of the law, or a mere clerical error on the part of some of its officers. The Town Superintendent should consider himself the guardian of the equitable rights of the districts, and when he discovers an error as to *form*, which, if not corrected, would deprive a district of its just share of public money, he should point it out to the trustees, to the end that it may be corrected, and the fair rights of the district secured.—*Per* FLAGG *and* DIX, *Sup'ts. Com. School Dec.* 36, 181.

By a regulation of the Superintendent of Common Schools made in pursuance of law, Town Superintendents are prohibited from paying over the share of library money apportioned to any district in the following cases:

1st. Where a catalogue of the title of all the books in the district library, purchased or obtained since the last preceding catalogue, with the number of volumes of each set or series, and the condition of such books, signed by the trustees and librarian, has not been delivered.

2d. Where the number of books belonging to the library is not stated in the annual report of the trustees.

3d. Where it does not clearly appear from such report that the whole of the library money paid to such district the preceding year has been expended within the time and in the mode prescribed by law; and if for the purchase of maps, globes or other school apparatus, or for teachers' wages, for what particular articles, and under what authority or resolution of the district.

4th. Whenever it appears that any portion of the library money of the preceding year has been expended in the purchase of any text book or any book *clearly improper* to be admitted into a district library. In cases where there may be room for an honest difference of opinion as to the admissibility of any book or books, purchased by the trustees, the Town Superintendent should include the district in the apportionment of library money, and refer the inhabitants aggrieved by such selection to their remedy by appeal.

III. THE INSPECTION AND LICENSING OF TEACHERS, AND THE VISITATION AND SUPERVISION OF SCHOOLS.

The Town Superintendent is, by virtue of his office, inspector of common schools of his town; and it is his duty "to examine all persons offering themselves as candidates for teaching common schools in such town." In making such examination it is his duty "to ascertain the qualifications of the candidate in respect to moral character, learning and ability." If he "shall be satisfied in respect to the qualifications of the candidate, he shall deliver to the person so examined a certificate signed by him, in such form as shall be prescribed by the Superintendent of Common Schools."

He may annul any such certificate given by him or his predecessor in office, when he shall think proper, giving at least ten days' previous notice in writing to the teacher holding it, and to the trustees of the districts in which he may be employed, of his intention to annul the same.

Whenever he shall deem it necessary, he may require a re-examination of all or any of the teachers in his town, (not holding State or county certificates or the diplomas of the State Normal School,) for the purpose of ascertaining their qualifications to continue as such teachers. The annulling of a certificate does not, however, disqualify the teacher to whom it was given, until a note in writing thereof, containing the name of the teacher, and the time when his certificate was annulled, shall be made by the Town Superintendent and filed in the office of the clerk of the town.

Where any school district is composed of a part of two or more towns, or any school-house shall stand on the division line of any two towns, the Town Superintendent of either town may examine into and certify the qualifications of any teacher offering to teach in such district, and may also in the same manner annul the certificate of such teacher.—§ 33—40, (Nos. 59—66) school act.

The duties and powers thus confided to the Town Superintendent are most important and involve great responsibility; and upon their proper fulfilment, depends in a very essential degree, the elevation and improvement of the district schools. If none but properly qualified teachers are permitted to find their way to our schools; if the certificate of the examining officer, and the sanction of his authority, are given only to those who are intellectually and morally fitted adequately to discharge the duties of instructors of youth, "apt to teach," competent to communicate instruction in the mode best adapted to develop the various faculties of the expanding mind, patterns alike of moral and social excellence; these elementary institutions will speedily become the fitting temples of science, the nurseries of virtue and the pride and boast of the state. Hitherto this duty has been deplorably neglected; and the disastrous conseqences are every where visible in the degradation of the district school, the substitute of private and select schools of every grade, the low estimation in which the profession of the teacher is held, and the miserable pittance—too often most costly in its utmost scantiness—which is reluctantly doled out to the needy and destitute adventurer. A thorough reform in this respect is imperatively demanded as well by public sentiment, as by a just regard to the paramount interests of education; and no consideration of temporary convenience to a particular district, of favor to individuals, or of regard to the prejudices or preferences of inhabitants or trustees, will, it is hoped hereafter be permitted in any case to sway the action of the certifying officer, or incline him, either to the right or the left, from the plain path of duty and obligation. A certificate should in no case, and under no circumstances, be granted, unless the candidate is found upon a careful examination, *well qualified to instruct* in all the ordinary branches usually taught in common schools—thoroughly versed in the *principles* of elementary science—capable of readily applying them to any given case, and able to communicate with facility, the results of his knowledge; and unless in addition to this, his character and demeanor are irreproachable, his habits exemplary, and his moral principles undoubted. In order as well to be assured that the impressions resulting from the examination were well founded, as to make himself acquainted with the condition and prospects of the schools, the Town Superintendent should, once at least during each term, *visit and inspect* the schools; and whenever practicable, should be accompanied by the trustees of the districts and such of the inhabitants as may be prevailed upon to attend. To afford every reasonable accommodation to those teachers desiring to offer themselves as candidates for examination, Town Superintendents should appoint a particular day and place in the town, and when the town is very large, in different sections of it, when they will be in readiness to examine teachers. Public notice of such appointment should be given. It is probable that this will bring together several applicants, and thus diminish the labors of the superintendent, particularly as this course will obviate the necessity of special examinations, as well as prevent the necessity of a re-examination during the year. In making such examinations, they should confine themselves to the subjects specified in the statute § 35, (No. 61,) and should ascertain the qualifications of the candidates in respect, 1st, to moral character; 2d, learning; and third, ability.

First.—They should require testimonials of moral character, from those acquainted with the applicant, which is to be either verbal or written, and the latter is to be preferred. This is not a matter to be neglected or slighted. Those to whom the training of our youth is to be committed, should possess such a character as will inspire confidence in the rectitude of their principles and the propriety of their conduct; and it is to be understood as a positive regulation of this department, that no license is to be granted, without entire satisfaction on this point. This must be understood to relate to moral character—to the reputation of the applicants as good citizens, free from the reproach of crime or immoral conduct. It does not extend to their belief, religious or political: but it may apply to their manner of expressing such belief or maintaining it. If that manner is, in itself, boisterous and disorderly, intemperate and offensive, it may well be supposed to indicate ungoverned passions, or want of sound principles of conduct, which would render its possessor obnoxious to the inhabitants of the district, and unfit for the sacred duties of a teacher of youth, who should instruct as well by example as by precept.

SECOND.—As to the learning of the applicants. It should appear from their examination that they are good spellers, distinct and accurate readers, write good and plain hands, can make pens and are well versed,

1st. In the definition of words:

2d. In arithmetic, mental and written:

3d. In geography, as far as contained in any of the works in ordinary use.

4th. In the history of the United States, of England, and of Europe generally:

5th. In the principles of English grammar: and,

6th. In the use of globes.

If they are found well acquainted with the other branches, a more slight knowledge of the 4th and 6th heads, as above enumerated, may be excused.

THIRD.—The ability of the applicants to teach. Mere learning without the capacity to impart it, would be of no use. The superintendents should satisfy themselves by general inquiries, and particularly by a thorough investigation of the applicants respectively, of their qualifications in this respect, of their tact in dealing with children, and especially of their possessing the unwearied patience and invariable good nature, so necessary to constitute useful teachers of youth.

Having satisfied themselves on these several points, the town superintendents will grant certificates in the usual form.

The certificates of qualification granted by Town Superintendents are to be in the form prescribed by the State Superintendent; to remain in force for one year only; are available only within the town for which they were granted, and may be annulled at any time by the officer granting them, or his successor, giving ten days notice in writing of intention to annul the same, to the teacher and trustees.

By § 41 and §42 of the school act, (Nos. 67, 68,) it is made the duty of the Town Superintendent to visit all such common schools, within his town, as shall be organized according to law, at least twice a year, and oftener if he shall deem it necessary. At such visitations, he is required to examine into the state and condition of such schools, both as respects the progress of the scholars in learning, and the good order of the schools, and may give his advice and direction to the trustees and teachers of such schools, as to the government thereof, and the course of studies to be pursued therein.

"If the opinions of the best and most experienced writers on primary education are not entirely fallacious, and if all the results of experience hitherto are not deceptive, the consequences of such a vigorous system of inspection will be most happy. The teachers and pupils will feel that they are not abandoned to neglect; the apprehension of discredit will stimulate them to the greatest effort; while the suggestions of the visitors will tend constantly to the improvement of the schools, and they will themselves be more and more enabled to recommend proper measures, from their better acquaintance with the subject."—*Instructions of Spencer, Sup't*, 1841.

A certificate cannot be annulled by the Town Superintendent until ten days' previous notice in writing has been given to the teacher and to the trustees of the district in which he has been employed, of the intention to annul the same. As the complaint must necessarily be stated, and its truth investigated, before any decision, it would be more convenient to the Town Superintendent, and more fair and just to the teacher, to apprise him of its nature in the notice of intention to annul.

Certificates of qualification granted by Town Superintendents to teachers must, in all cases, be in conformity to the form prescribed by the Superintendent of Common Schools. They cannot be granted upon the ground of ability to teach a particular school, for a particular term, or in a particular district. When granted in the form prescribed by the Superintendent, they authorize the holder to teach any school in the town for which they were granted, during any part of the year commencing at their date.

The examination of candidates for teachers should in all cases be thorough and strict, and no certificate should be granted unless the examining officer is satisfied as to all the qualifications required by law. "A certificate of qualification in any other form than that prescribed by the Superintendent is not a compliance with the statute; as for instance, that A. B. gave the examining officer good satisfaction in certain enumerated branches, and that his moral character is good. The law authorizes him to give a certificate in a certain event, and then it must be in the form specified. If he is satisfied as to the qualifications of the teacher in respect to moral character, learning and ability, he is bound to give him such a certificate as the Superintendent shall have prescribed. If he is not satisfied he should give him no certificate all. He is wholly unauthorized to take a middle course by *giving a qualified certificate.*" —*Per* DIX, *Sup't. Com. School Dec.* 236.

The certificate must also bear date on the day of examination, and cannot be ante-dated.

In cases where a school district is composed of parts of two or more towns, the Town Superintendent of the town *in which the school house is situated*, is exclusively authorized by Sec. 40, (No. 66,) to examine into and certify the qualifications of any teacher offering to teach in such joint district, and for sufficient causes to annul the certificate of such teacher. His jurisdiction in this respect cannot in any manner, or under any pretence, be interfered with by the superintendents of either of the other towns from which such joint district is partly composed.

The qualifications of teachers are left to the discrimination and judgment of the legal examiners. They must determine the degree of learning and ability necessary for a teacher. They ought to be satisfied that a certificate is given to those only whose learning and ability fit them in all respects to instruct common schools. In revising the school law, the revisers inserted a provision that no candidate for teaching should be deemed qualified, unless upon examination he should appear to be well instructed in reading, orthography, penmanship, English grammer, geography and arithmetic, including vulgar and decimal fractions." This provision, however, was stricken out by the legislature, and the whole matter is left discretionary.—*Com. School Dec.* 42.

In judging of the moral character of a candidate for teacher, if the examining officer knows of any serious imputation or defect of principle, it is his duty to refuse to certify. A certificate may be annulled for immoral habits generally, notwithstanding the teacher may perform all his duties during school hours.—*Id.* 46.

In relation to the moral character of the teacher, much is left to the discretion of the examining officer. He must be satisfied that it is good, because he has to certify to its correctness. On this point what would be satisfactory to one man might be unsatisfactory to another. Every person has a right to the enjoyment of his own religious *belief* without molestation: and the examining officer should content himself with inquiries as to the *moral character* of the teacher, leaving him to the same liberal enjoyment of his religious belief that he asks for himself. If, however, a person openly derides all religion, he ought not to be a teacher of youth. The employment of such a person would be considered a grievance by a great portion of the inhabitants of all the districts.—*Per* FLAGG, *Sup't. Id.* 60.

Neither the trustees nor the inhabitants of school districts are the judges of the qualifications of teachers. The law has confided the power of examining teachers to the officers expressly designated for that purpose; and its object was to secure the employment of competent persons. If the trustees or inhabitants are to determine what their district require, and the certifying officers are to be governed by their opinions and wishes, the officers themselves might as well be dispensed with. In his annual report to the legislature for the year 1835, the Superintendent of Common Schools (Gen. DIX) observes: "One of the most responsible and delicate trusts to be executed under the common school system is that of inspecting teachers and pronouncing upon their qualifications. If this is negligently conducted or with a willingness to overlook deficiencies, instead of insisting rigidly upon the requirements of the law, it is manifest that men without the necessary moral character, learning or ability, will gain a foothold in the common schools, and present a serious obstacle to the improvements of which they are susceptible. This would be an evil of the greatest magnitude, and there is no remedy for it but a strict inspection of the candidates. It has been the practice in some instances for the inspectors to have a reference to the *particular circumstances of the cases* in giving a certificate. Thus they have sometimes given an individual a certificate with a view to a *summer school,* in which the children taught are usually smaller and require less of the teacher, when the certificate would have been withheld, if it was asked with a view to qualify the teacher for a *winter school.* But it is obvious that such a distinction is wholly inadmissible. A certificate must be unconditional, by the terms of the law. The inspectors must be satisfied with the qualifications of the teacher "in respect to moral character, learning and ability;" and the certificate when once given is an absolute warrant for the individual to teach for a year, and to receive the public money, unless revoked before the expiration of the year, in which case it ceases to be operative from the date of its revocation. The standard of qualification for teachers, so far as granting certificates is concerned, is of necessity, arbitrary. The law does not prescribe the degree of learning or ability which a teacher shall possess, but virtually refers the decision of this important matter to the inspectors, who have not, neither should they possess the power of relaxing the general rule with reference to the circumstances of any particular case, by departing from the standard of qualification which they assume as their guide in others."—*Id.* 326.

1. The act does not *require* the superintendents to notify the trustees of their visits and invite their attendance. The superintendents should, however, give notice to the trustees of the districts, of the time when their schools will be visited. To enable them to comply with these provisions, they should make a previous arrangement of their visits, in reference to the means of traveling, so as to reach as many districts as possible in the shortest time. Having fixed the time for visiting the schools, they should at once give ample notice, by transmitting a copy of their arrangement to the trustees of the districts embraced within it, and request them to attend.

The inhabitants of the district, and particularly parents who have children attending the school, should be invited to be present at the inspection by the superintendent; and trustees of districts are hereby required, whenever they receive information of an intended visit, to communicate it as generally as possible to the inhabitants. Their attendance will afford an opportunity for the public addresses of the superintendents, herein suggested.

2. *Examination of the School.*—Preparatory to this, the superintendent should ascertain from the teacher the number of classes; the studies pursued by each; the routine of the school; the successive exercises of each class during each hour of the day; the play spells allowed, &c., and thus obtain a general knowledge of the school, which will be found greatly to facilitate his subsequent duties. Every superintendent is enjoined to call for and examine

the list of scholars in the book which the Statute requires the teacher to keep, in order that he may see whether the names are correctly and neatly entered. He will also examine the *day roll* and the *weekly roll*, which by the the succeding regulations, teachers are directed to preserve, and will ascertain by the proper enquiries, whether they are exact in entering all who are present.

The superintendent will then hear each class recite the ordinary lesson of the day. It will then be examined on the subjects of study. Generally it will be better to allow the teacher to conduct the exercises and examinations, as the pupils will be less likely to be intimidated, and an opportunity will be given of judging of the qualifications of the instructors.

To enable him to compare the school with itself at another time, and with other schools, and to comply with the regulations hereinafter contained, respecting the annual reports, the superintendent should keep notes of his observations, and of the information he obtains on all the subjects on which he is required to report; and he should particularly note any peculiarities which seem to require notice, in the mode of instruction, in the government and discipline of the school, and the appearance of the pupils, in respect to their cleanliness of person and neatness of apparel.

3. The superintendent will also examine the condition of the school house and its appurtenances; whether the room has the means of ventilation, by lowering an upper sash, or otherwise; whether it is sufficiently tight to protect the children from currents of air, and to keep them warm in winter; whether there is a supply of good water; the condition of the privies, and whether they are provided for both sexes; and the accommodations for physical exercise. Their attention will be given to the arrangement of the school room; whether the seats and desks are placed most conveniently for the pupils and teachers, and particularly whether backs are provided for the seats, a circumstance very important to the comfort and health of the children. They should also inquire whether blackboards and alphabetical cards, or any apparatus to assist learners are furnished.

The preceding topics of inquiry are suggested, rather as hints of the most important, than intended to embrace the whole field. The judgment and observation of the superintendents will discover many other subjects deserving their attention.

4. The superintendents will also inquire into the condition of the district, in relation to its ability to maintain a school; whether its interest and the convenience of its inhabitants can be promoted by any alterations, without iujury to others; and they will suggest whatever occurs to them, to the trustees.

In case of any gross deficiency or inconvenience, which the proper officers refuse or decline to remedy, the superintendents will note it in their annual reports to the county clerks.

5. They will also examine the district library, and obtain the information respecting it, hereinafter required to be stated in their reports.

Advising and consulting with the trustees and other officers of school districts.

This is made a special duty of the town superintendents by these instructions; they are to advise the trustees and other officers in relation to all their duties, and to recommend to them and the teachers the proper studies, discipline, and conduct of the school, the course of instruction to be pursued, and the elementary books to be used. The notes which the superintendents make during their inspection of the school, will much facilitate the discharge of this portion of their duty.

1. In regard to proper studies. If they find any important one omitted, or that pupils are hastened on without thoroughly understanding the preliminary or previous branches, they should point out the error and its consequences. For instance, they should urge the absolute necessity of children being thoroughly and frequently exercised in spelling, so that they make no mistakes in any words in common use. Without this it is impossible for them to be good readers. And in the exercise of reading, they should insist on clear and district articulation, more than any other quality; and generally the ability of the superintendent is relied upon to detect bad habits in the manner of reciting, erroneous ideas on the subject and superficial acquirements.

2. The *discipline* and *conduct* of the school. It can scarcely be necessary to remark on the importance of order and system in the schools, not only to enable the pupils to learn anything, but to give them those habits of regularity so essential in the formation of character. Punctuality of attendance, as well as its steady continuance should be enforced. Parents should be told how much their children lose, to what inconvenience they expose the teacher, and what disorder they bring upon the whole school, by not insisting upon the scholars being punctually at the school room at the appointed hour; and above all, they should be warned of the injurious consequences of allowing their children to be absent from school during the term. By being indulged in absences they lose the connection of their studies, probably fall behind their class, become discouraged, and then seek every pretext to play the truant. The habit of irregularity and insubordination thus acquired, will be apt to mark their character through life. Trustees should be informed that the omission of parents to require the regular and punctual attendance of their children will justify their exclusion, on account of the effect of such irregularity upon the other pupils.

The superintendents should also observe whether the teachers are careful to preserve the respect of their pupils, not only by maintaining their authority, but by a becoming deportment, both in the school room and out of it.

3. With regard to the *course of instruction*, the advice of the superintendents will often be of great value. The usual order has been found by long experience to be the best, viz: the alphabet, spelling, reading with definitions, arithmetic, geography, history and grammar. No child should be put to any study beyond his capacity, or for which he is not already prepared. English grammar particularly demands so much exercise of the intellect, that it ought to be delayed until the pupil has acquired considerable strength of mind.

4 *The books of elementary instruction.*—It is believed that there are none now in use in our schools that are very defective; and the difference between them is so slight, that the gain to the scholar will not compensate for the heavy expense to the parent, caused by the substitution of new books with every new teacher; and the capriciousness of change which some are apt to indulge on this subject, cannot be too strongly or decidedly resisted. Trustees of districts should look to this matter when they engage teachers.

One consequence of the practice is, the great variety of text books on the same subject, acknowledged by all to be one of the greatest evils which afflicts our schools. It compels the teacher to divide the pupils into as many classes as there are kinds of books, so that the time which might have been devoted to a careful and deliberate hearing of a class of ten or twelve, where all could have improved by the corrections and observations of the instructor, is almost wasted in the hurried recitations of ten or a dozen pupils in separate classes; while in large schools, some must be wholly neglected. Wherever the superintendents find this difficulty existing, they should not fail to point out its injurious consequences, and to urge a remedy by the adoption of uniform text books as speedily as possible. To accomplish this, let the trustees, under the advice of the teacher, inspectors and superintendents, determine what text books shall be used in each study, and require every child thereafter coming to the school to be provided with the designated books. This very desirable uniformity may, perhaps, be facilitated by exchanges between different districts, of the books that do not correspond with those in general use, for such as do. For instance, in one school the great majority of spelling books may be those of Webster with some of Marshall's, while the latter may predominate in another district in which there are also several of Webster's In such cases, an exchange of the different books between the two would obviously be mutually beneficial. The superintendents might assist in the execution of such an arrangement by noting the proportions of the various books in the different schools.

5. *The Erection of School Houses.*—It would be well for the town superintendents to give particular attention to this subject Whenever they learn that the building of a school house is contemplated, they should advise with the trustees respecting its plan. He must

be a superficial observer, who has not perceived how much the health of pupils, the order and discipline of a school, and the convenience of the teacher, depend upon the arrangements of the school room. This is not the place to state the best models. Information upon that point, collected with great care from Europe and America, has already been given, in the District School Journal, and in Mr. BARNARD's admirable volume on school architecture. Whenever repairs are about to be made to school houses, the superintendents should avail themselves of the occasion to recommend such improvement as may be desirable.

6. In their consultations with trustees and teachers, the superintendents should be especially careful to communicate their suggestions in a kind and friendly spirit, as the most likely means of success, and as the only mode of preserving those harmonious relations, which are essential to their own happiness as well as usefulness; and whenever they observe any thing in the mode of instruction, in the government or discipline of the school, or in any other point, which, in their judgment, requires correction, they will make it a point to intimate their views to the teacher in private, and never, on any occasion, suffer themselves to find fault with him in the presence of his pupils. Children cannot discriminate, and they will feel themselves at liberty to blame, when the example has been set by others. The authority of the teacher should be preserved entire while he remains. If his conduct is worthy of public censure, he should be at once dismissed, rather than be retained to become an object of the contempt of his scholars.

IV. ANNUAL REPORT OF THE TOWN SUPERINTENDENT.

By § 19 (No. 44) of the school act, and the succeeding sections, it is made "the duty of the Town Superintendent in each town, between the first day of July and the first day of August, in each year, to make and transmit to the county clerk, a report in writing bearing date on the first day of July, in the year of its transmission, and stating,

1. The whole number of school districts and neighborhoods, separately set off within their town:

2. The districts, parts of districts, and neighborhoods, from which reports shall have been made to him, or his immediate predecessors in office, within the time limited for that purpose:

3. The length of time a school shall have been kept in each of such districts or parts of districts, distinguishing what portion of that time the school shall have been kept by qualified teachers:

4. The amount of public moneys received in each of such districts, parts of districts and neighborhoods:

5. The number of children taught in each, and the number of children over the age of four and under twenty-one years, residing in each:

6. The whole amount of moneys received by him or his predecessors in office, during the year ending at the date of his report,

and since the date of his last preceding report; distinguishing the amount received from the county treasurer and from any other and what source:

7. The manner in which such moneys have been expended, and whether any and what part, remains unexpended, and for what cause:

8. The amount of money paid for teachers' wages, in addition to the public money paid therefor, in the districts, parts of districts and neighborhoods from which reports shall have been received by him or his immediate predecessors, in office, *with such other information as the Superintendent of Common Schools may from time to time require, in relation to the districts and schools within his town.*

Under this provision the Superintendent has required the following additional items of information to be comprised in such annual reports of the Town Superintendents:

1. The number of times the school in each district has been inspected by Town Superintendents, to be taken from the abstract furnished by the trustees:

2. The number of volumes in the library of each district, as returned by the trustees:

3. The whole number of school districts, the school houses of which are situated in their town:

4. The amount of money expended in each school district for teachers' wages, besides and beyond the public money apportioned to such district; that is they will condense from the reports of the trustees the amount paid by individuals, on rate-bills or otherwise, and the amount collected from any local funds.

5. The attendance of pupils in the several district schools for the following different terms, viz:

Those who attended less than two months;
" " two months and less than four;
" " four months and less than six;
" " six months and less than eight;
" " eight months and less than ten;
" " ten months and less than twelve;
" " twelve months;

6. The amount of taxes levied in the several districts of the town during the year reported for purchasing sites, building, hiring, repairing and insuring school houses, fuel, books, book-case, school apparatus and other purposes:

7. The number of select and private schools in their town, other than incorporated seminaries, and the average number of pupils therein, as stated in the reports of the trustees of the several districts:

8. They are also required to condense, from the reports of the several trustees, the number of schools for colored children taught in their town, specifying the districts in which such schools have been taught, the number of colored children, between the ages of

four and twenty-one attending such schools; and the amount of public money apportioned to the respective districts from which such children attended, specifying such districts.

The most common mistake committed by the Town Superintendents is in their report of moneys received by them, or their predecessors, since the date of the last report. They often confound this money with that received by *trustees* of districts, which is an entirely different item. This last item is received on the first Tuesday of April, and reported by the trustees on the first of January following, and is embodied in the report of the superintendent among the abstracts of the trustees' reports, in the columns headed "amount of money received in each district." But the money received by the Town Superintendents is that paid to them by the county treasurer and town collector *after* the first of January, and apportioned by them on or before the first Tuesday in April, and is not contained in the reports of the trustees.

In making their annual reports, the Town Superintendents should see that the several columns of their table are correctly footed, and the figures plainly and distinctly made.

Town Superintendents neglecting to make such report within the limited period, forfeit severally to their town, for the use of the common schools therein, the sum of ten dollars; and the share of school moneys apportioned to such town for the ensuing year, may, in the discretion of the Superintendent of Common Schools, be withheld, and be distributed among the other towns in the same county, from which the necessary reports shall have been received. When the share of school moneys apportioned to a town shall thus be lost to the town by the neglect of the Town Superintendents, the officer guilty of such neglect forfeits to his town the full amount, with interest, of the moneys so lost. It is the duty of the supervisor of the town, upon notice of such loss, from the Superintendent of Common Schools, or county treasurer, to prosecute without delay in the name of the town, for such forfeiture; and the moneys recovered are required to be distributed and paid by such supervisor to the several districts, parts of districts, or separate neighborhoods of the town, in the same manner as it would have been the duty of the Town Superintendent to have distributed and paid them, if received from the county treasurer.—§ 22, 23, 24. (No. 47, 48, 49.)

By § 15, of chap. 382, Laws of 1849, it is provided that "whenever it shall be satisfactorily proved to the State Superintendent that any county or town superintendent, or other school officers, has embezzled the public money, or any money coming into his hands for school purposes, or has been guilty of the wilful violation of any law, or neglect of duty or of disobeying any decision, order or regulation of the Department of Common Schools, the State Superintendent is authorised to remove such officer from such office, by an order under the seal of office of the Secretary of State.

V. PENALTIES AND FORFEITURES TO BE COLLECTED BY TOWN SUPERINTENDENTS.

By subdivision 8 of § 8, Rev. Stat. (No. 33,) the Town Superintendent is to sue for and collect by his name of office, all penalties and forfeitures imposed by the title relating to common schools, where no other provision is made; for the penalty of five dollars prescribed by § 57, (No. 79,) upon the refusal or neglect of any inhabitant of a district to serve the notice of the first meeting; the same penalty for altogether refusing to serve in a district office; and the penalty of ten dollars for neglecting to perform the duties of a district office, not having refused to accept the same; and for the penalty of $25, against Trustees neglecting or refusing annually to render an account of the moneys received by them, given by §130 (No. 150) of the school act.

He is also to prosecute for the penalty of twenty-five dollars imposed by §123 (No. 143,) upon every trustee who signs a false report, with the intent of obtaining an unjust proportion of the school moneys of the town. Justice to the several districts requires that the Town Superintendents should be vigilant in detecting such errors, and in applying the remedy provided by law in all cases where they arise from design.

The sums collected by him in suits for penalties, after deducting his costs and expenses, are to be added to the school moneys received by him during the year, and apportioned among the several districts.

VI. MISCELLANEOUS DUTIES.

By § 25, (No. 50,) and the succeeding sections, the Town Superintendent in each town is required to keep a just and true account of all school moneys received and expended by him during the year for which he shall have been chosen, and to lay the same before the board of auditors of the accounts of other town officers at the annual meeting of such board in the same year. Within fifteen days after the termination of his office he is required to render to his successsor in office a just and true account, in writing, of all school moneys by him received, before the time of rendering such account, and of the manner in which the same shall have been appropriated and expended by him; and the account so rendered is to be delivered by such successor in office to the town clerk, to be filed and recorded in his office. If, on rendering such account, any balance shall be found remaining in the hands of the Town Superintendent, the same is immediately to be paid by him to his successor in office. If such balance, or any part thereof, shall have been appropriated by the Town Superintendent to any particular school district, part of a district or separate neighborhood, and shall remain in his hands for the use thereof, a statement of such appropriation is required to be made in the account so to be rendered, and the balance paid to such successor in office, to be paid over by him, according to such appropriation. His successor in office may bring a suit in his name of office, for the recovery, with interest, of any unpaid balance of school moneys that shall appear to have been in the hands of any previous Town Superintendent on leaving his office, either by the accounts rendered by such Town Superintendent, or by other sufficient proof. In case of the death of such Town Superintendent, such suit may be brought against his representatives, and all moneys recovered are to be applied in the same manner as if they had been paid over without suit.

By § 30, the Town Superintendent of common schools in each town, has the powers and privileges of a corporation, so far as to enable him to take and hold any property transferred to him for the use of common schools in such town.

A mere *transfer* of vouchers or receipts, by a Town Superintendent, on the expiration of his official term, is not such an *account* as the law contemplates. There must be a *written statement* of the amount of moneys received, appropriated and expended by him; and this statement must be filed and recorded by the town clerk.—*Com. School Dec.* 189.

The written approbation of the Town Superintendent to be endorsed on the warrant is, by the 113th section of the act of 1843, (No. 133) made requisite to the validity of any second or subsequent renewal of a school district warrant for the collection of a tax list or rate bill. This approbation should be granted only where a satisfactory excuse is shown for the omission to collect the amount specified in the warrant within the time prescribed by law, and extended by one renewal. Taxes and rate bills should be promptly collected; and in ordinary cases sixty days affords ample time for this purpose; and further indulgence should in no case be granted excepting under special and peculiar circumstances.

By § 70 (No. 92) of the school act, it is provided that "no tax to be voted by any district meeting, for building, hiring or purchasing a school house shall exceed the sum of four hundred dollars, unless the Town Superintendent of common schools of the town in which the school-house is to be situated, shall certify in writing, his opinion that a larger sum ought to be raised, and shall specify the sum; in which case, a sum not exceeding the sum so specified shall be raised." And by §1 of chap. 44, Laws of 1831, Sec. 73, (No. 95,) "Whenever a school house shall have been built or purchased for a district. the site of such school house shall not be changed, nor the building thereon be removed, as long as the district shall remain unaltered, unless by the consent, in writing, of the Town Superintendents of Common Schools, of the town or towns within which such district shall be situated, stating that in their opinion such removal is necessary; nor then, unless *a majority of all the taxable inhabitants of said district to be ascertained by taking and recording the ayes and noes at a special meeting* called for that purpose, shall vote for such removal and in favor of such new site."

A majority of the taxable inhabitants who are legal voters in the district, *present and voting* at such special meeting is sufficient, in conjunction with the written certificate of the Town Superintendent to authorize a change of site in an altered district.

Town Superintendents are bound to furnish answers to all appeals brought from any of their proceedings.—*Com. School Dec.* 187.

Where a school district is established by the State Superintendent on appeal, Town Superintendents have no power to alter, modify or dissolve the same, without express authority from the State Superintendent; nor can they, without such authority, re-establish a district, or re-publish an order after their proceedings in the same matter have once been set aside on appeal.

Where any school district office is vacated by the death, refusal to serve, removal out of the district, or incapacity of any officer, and the vacancy occasioned thereby shall not be supplied by a district meeting, within one month thereafter, the Town Superintendent may appoint any person residing in the district to supply such vacancy, § 77 (No. 98.) If, however, the district, by election, fills the vacancy *after* the expiration of the month, and prior to the action of the Town Superintendent, such election is valid, and the Town Superintendent cannot subsequently make an appointment.—*Com. School Decisions*, 179.

By § 146 of the act of 1847, (No. 169) it is provided that "In any suit which shall hereafter be commenced against Town Superintendents of Common Schools, or officers of school districts, for any act performed by virtue of, or under color of, their offices, or for any refusal or omission to perform any duty enjoined by law, and which might have been the subject of an appeal to the Superintendent, no costs shall be allowed to the plaintiff in cases where the court shall certify that it appeared on the trial of the cause that the defendants acted in good faith. But this provision shall not extend to suits for penalties, nor to suits or proceedings to enforce the decisions of the Superintendent."

By § 6 of chap. 330 of laws of 1839, § 145, (No. 168) "Town Superintendents of common schools, and trustees and clerks of school districts, refusing or wilfully neglecting to make any report, or to perform any other duty required by law, or regulations or decisions made under the authority of any statute, shall severally forfeit to their town, or to their district, as the case may be, for the use of the common schools therein, the sum of ten dollars for each such neglect or refusal, which penalty shall be sued for and collected by the supervisor of the town, and paid over to the proper officers, to be distributed for the benefit of the common schools in the town or district to which such penalty belongs; and when the share of school or library money apportioned to any town or district, or any portions thereof, or any money to which a town or school district would have been entitled, shall be lost in consequence of any wilful neglect of official duty by any town superintendent of common schools, or trustees or clerks of school districts, the officers guilty of such neglect shall forfeit to the town or district the full amount with interest, of the moneys so lost; and they shall be jointly and severally liable for the payment of such forfeiture."

By § 72 (No. 94) It is provided that "in every case where a district embraces a part of more than one town, the town superintendents of the towns so in part embraced, upon application of the trustees of such districts, or of those persons liable to pay taxes upon real property therein, shall proceed to enquire and determine whether the valuation of real property upon the several assessment rolls of said towns are substantially just as compared with each other, so far as such district is concerned, and if determined not to be so, they shall determine the relative proportion of taxes that ought to be assessed upon the real property of the parts of such districts so lying in different towns, and the trustees of such district shall thereupon assess the proportion of any tax *thereafter to be raised* according to the determination of said superintendents until the same shall be altered by said superintendents until the same shall be altered by said superintendents upon like application, using the assessment rolls of the several towns to distribute the said proportion among the persons liable to be assessed for the same. In cases where two superintendents shall be unable to agree, they shall summon a superintendent from some adjoining town, who shall unite in such inquiry and determination."

Town superintendents are not within the class of public officers required by the Constitution to take the oath of office.

FORMS PRESCRIBED AND RECOMMENDED BY THE SUPERINTENDENT OF COMMON SCHOOLS FOR THE USE OF TOWN SUPERINTENDENTS.

1. FORM OF BOND TO BE GIVEN BY THE TOWN SUPERINTENDENT TO THE SUPERVISOR.

Know all men by these presents, that we A. B., C. D., and E. F., of the town of ——— in the county of ——— are held and firmly bound to J. K. Esq., Supervisor of said town, in the penal sum of [double the amount of school money received in said town from all sources during the preceding year,] to be paid to the said J. K. or his successor in office; to the which payment, well and truly to be made, we bind ourselves and our legal representatives, jointly and severally, firmly by these presents. Witness our hands and seals this ——— day of June, 1851.

Whereas, the said A. B. has been duly elected [or appointed] Town Superintendent of Common Schools for the said town of

———: Now therefore, the condition of this obligation is such, that if the said A. B. shall faithfully apply and legally disburse, all the school money which may come into his hands during his term of office as such Town Superintend nt, and faithfully discharge all the duties of said office, then this ob igation to be null and void; otherwise to remain in full force and virtue.

Signed sealed and delivered in presence of	A. B. [L. S.]
	C. D. [L. S.]
	E. F. [L. S.]

(Endorsement.) "I hereby approve of C D. and E. F. as sureties to the within bond." J. K.

2. FORM OF A RESOLUTION CREATING A NEW DISTRICT.

At a meeting, &c.

Resolved, That a new school district be formed, to consist of [the present Districts Nos. 1 and 2; or of the present District No. 1 and a part of District No 2; or parts of Districts No. 1 and No. 2, as the case may be.] which said new district shall be numbered [23,] and shall be bounded as follows: [on the north by the north tine of the town of *Trenton*: on the east by the easterly line of the farms and lots of land now occupied by *Thomas Jones, William Thomas,* &c.: on the south by the south line of lots No. 56, 57 and 58, as designated on the map of said town: and on the west by the westerly line of the farms and lots now occupiee by A, B, C, D, &c.]

The formation of the aforesaid district, involving an alteration of District No. [1 and No. 2,] the consent of the trustees of the said districts to such alteration has been presented to the Town Superintendent, and filed with the town clerk. [Or, if such consent has not been given, the following entry should be made: The formation of the aforesaid district, involving an alteration of districts No. 1 and 2, and the consent of the trustees of District No. 1 to such alteration not having been given, it is ordered that a notice in writing of the said alteration, signed by the Town Superintendent, be served on one of the trustees of the said district.] If the order is made between the first day of December, in any year, and the first day of May thereafter, the following clause should be added, viz: "This order will take effect on the first day of May next, [or on some subsequent day to be specified.]

2. The consent of the trustees of the altered districts may be given by endorsing it on a copy of the order, as follows:

We hereby consent to the alteration made in District No. 2, in the town of *Trenton*, by the order of which the within is a copy.

Dated, &c.

A. B.	*Trustees of district No. 1.*
C. D.	
E. F.	

This consent, like all other acts of trustees, should be given at a meeting of the whole, or a majority, when all have been notified to attend. The statute does not require it to be in writing; but it is advisable to prevent disputes, that a written consent should be filed with the town clerk.

3. FORM OF NOTICE TO TRUSTEES NOT GIVING THEIR CONSENT TO AN ALTERATION OF THEIR DISTRICT.

The Trustees of District No. 1, in the town of *Trenton* will take notice that an order was made this day by the Town Superintendent of Common Schools of the said town, of which the following is a copy, by which certain alterations in the said district are made, as will appear by the said order; and that such alterations will take effect after three months from the service of this notice. [If the expiration of the three months occur between the first day of December and May, then some day subsequent to the to the thirtieth of April should be specified.] Dated, &c.

G. H., *Town Superintendent of Common Schools of the town of* Trenton.

[Here insert copy of order of Town Superintendent.]

This notice may be served on any one of the trustees; and it will be found useful to have an acknowledgment of the service by the trustees receiving the notice, endorsed on a copy of it and, filed with the town clerk.

4. NOTICE OF THE FIRST MEETING IN A DISTRICT TO ORGANIZE.

This is required by law to be given within twenty days, after the formation of any district. If the consent of the trustees of the districts interested, has been given to the alterations covered by the order, then the notice should be for a day as early as may allow sufficient time for general information. But if it be necessary to give notice of the alterations to the trustees of any district, then the notice for the first meeting should specify a day subsequent to the expiration of three months after service of the notice of alteration, because the district cannot organize until after that time.

The notice may be in the following form:

To —— ——, a taxable inhabitant of District no 23, in the town of *Trenton*.

Thé town Superintendent of Common Schools of the town of *Trenton*, having by an order, of which the following is a copy, formed a new district in the said town to be numbered 23, consisting of the territory particularly specified in the said order; you are hereby required to notify every inhabitant of the said district qualified to vote at district meetings, to attend the first district meeting of the said district, which is hereby appointed to be held at the house of   in the said town, on the   day of   next, at 6 o'clock in the afternoon, by reading this notice in the hearing of each such inhabitant, or in case of his absence from home, by leaving a copy of this notice, or of so much thereof as relates to the time and place of such meeting, at least six days before the said time so appointed for the said meeting. Dated, &c.

A. B., *Town Superintendent of Common Schools of the town of* Trenton.

A copy of the order forming the district should be annexed to this notice, as the most convenient mode of describing the district, and most likely to prevent errors.

The inhabitant serving the notice should keep a memorandum of the names of the persons notified by him, specifying the manner of notifying, whether by reading or leaving a copy, or the substance of the notice, at the place of abode of any absent voter; and this memorandum, certified by him, should be delivered to the chairman or clerk of the district meeting and read, that it may be ascertained whether notice has been duly given so as to justify the voters in proceeding to the transaction of business; and the original notice and return should be filed with the district clerk, as evidence of the regularity of the organization.

7. FORM OF A RESOLUTION FOR THE ALTERATION OF A DISTRICT.

At a meeting of, &c.,

Resolved, That districts number 1 and number 2, in the said town, be altered as follows, viz: by setting off the farms and parcels of land occupied by *John Brown*, *Thomas Jones*, and *William Richards*, from District number one, in which they have heretofore been included to District number two; so that the east boundary of District number one shall be the easterly line of the farms and parcels of lands occupied by A. B. C. D. &c., and the westerly boundary of district number two shall be the westerly lines of the farms and parcels of land occupied by the said *John Brown*, *Thomas Jones* and *William Richards*; the said *John Brown* having consented to be set off as aforesaid. The written consent of the trustees of the said districts number one and two, having been presented to the Town Superintendent, is filed with the town clerk; [or, The consent of the trustees of the said districts respectively, (or of district No. 1 or 2, as the case may be,) not having been given to the said alteration, it is ordered that a notice in writing of such alteration signed by the Town Superintendent, be served on some one of the trustees of each of the said districts, (or of district No. 1 or 2.)]

In the above form, it will be seen that the new boundaries of the districts, caused by the alteration, are given. This is deemed very necessary in order to prevent all mistake or ambiguity, and to preserve a continual record of the actual bounds of the districts. If any of the persons set off consent to the alteration, it should be stated, so that the trustees may know whether he is taxable for building a school-house.

The consent of trustees to the alteration, and in case of their not consenting, the notices to them, will be as before given under the 2d and 3d heads.

8. PROCEEDINGS IN THE FORMATION OR ALTERATION OF A JOINT DISTRICT, FROM TWO OR MORE TOWNS.

The proceedings in the *formation* of a joint district will be in all respects similar to those previously given in relation to ordinary cases, with the following additions:

As there is no clerk assigned by law to the joint meeting, the officers present should sign the proceedings.

The caption should give the names of the towns to which the Town Superintendents belong; and the resolutions should be recorded in each of those towns.

9. FORM OF CERTIFICATE TO TEACHER BY TOWN SUPERINTENDENT.

I hereby certify that I have examined A. B. and do believe that he [or she] is well qualified, in respect to moral character, learning and ability, to instruct a common school in this town for one year from the date hereof.

Given under my hand at this day of 18

C. D., *Town Superintendent of Common Schools for the town of*

10. FORM OF INSTRUMENT ANNULLING A TEACHER'S CERTIFICATE.

Having enquired into certain complaints against A. B., heretofore licensed as a teacher of common schools of said town, and being of opinion that he, the said A. B., does not possess the requisite qualifications as a teacher, in respect to moral character, [or "in respect to learning," or "in respect to ability in teaching," as the case may be,] and having given at least ten days previous notice in writing to said teacher, and to the trustees of the district in which he is employed, of the intention so to do, I have annulled and hereby do annul the said certificate and license so granted as aforesaid.

Given under my hand this day ot 18

C. D., *Town Superintendent of Common Schools.*

As a note in writing, containing the name of the teacher, and the time when his certificate was annulled, must be filed in the town clerk's office, to give it effect, the most convenient and effectual mode of complying with the law, will be to make out, sign and file a duplicate of the instrument itself.

11. FORM OF THE ANNUAL REPORT OF THE TOWN SUPERINTENDENT OF COMMON SCHOOLS, TO BE MADE TO THE COUNTY CLERK.

I, A. B. Town Superintendent of common Schools of the town of in the county of in conformity with the statutes in relation to common schools, do report: that the number of entire school districts in said town, organized according to law, is [*eight*,] and that the number of parts of school districts in said town is [*five*] ; that the number of joint districts, the school-houses of which are situated wholly or partially in said town, is [*three*] ; that he number of entire districts from which the necessary reports have been made for the present year, within the time limited by law, is [*eight*,] and the number of parts of districts from which such reports have been made is [*five*.] That the number of schools for colored children taught by said town during the year aforesaid, for six months or upwards, by a duly qualified teacher, was [*two*.]

And I do further certify and report, that the whole amount of money received by me, or my predecessors in office, for the use of common schools, during the year ending on the date of this report, and since the date of the last report of said town, is $ of which sum the part received from the county treasurer is $ the part from is $ and that we have collected the sum of for penalties (*if any has been collected*) [*and if there be any other source from which any part has been received, here state it particularly*.] That the said sum of money has been appropriated to the several districts from which the necessary reports were received, for the purposes and in the proportion following, viz: the sum of $ for the payment of teachers' wages, and the sum of $ for the purchase of district libraries. That of the monies so apportioned, there has been paid over to or on the order of the trustees of the several districts entitled thereto, the sum of dollars and cents for teachers' wages, and dollars and cents of the library money; and that the balance of said monies so apportioned and not paid over, is now in my hands amounting in the aggregate to dollars and cents, and ready to be paid according to law. That the sum of $ was apportion by me to district No. for colored children in said district between the ages of four and 21 years, who have attended a school in district No. in said town, by a duly qualified teacher, for six months during the preceding year; and $ to district No. for colored children attending in said district; and that I have deducted the said several amounts from the sums by me apportioned to the said districts No. and respectively. And I further certify that during the year before mentioned, I have not collected any fines, penalties or forfeitures: [or, And I further certify that during the year before mentioned, I have collected a penalty of $25, imposed on A. B. a trustee of district No. in said town, for signing a false report; and that my costs and charges in such collection amounted to $; and the balance of such penalty was by me added to the school money received by me and apportioned as above mentioned.] That the school books most in use in the common schools of said town are the following, viz: [*here specify the principal books reported by the several trustees.*] And I further certify the tables following, to be true abstracts from the reports of the trustees of the several districts and parts of districts as aforesaid:

Districts and parts.	Districts & parts of districts from which reports have been made.	Whole length of time any school has been kept therein.		Length of time such school has been kept by licensed teachers.		Amount of money received by districts.			
						For teachers' wages		For Libraries.	
		Months,	Days.	Months.	Days.	Dols.	Cts.	Dols.	Cts.
No....	1	6	......	3	......	10	30.	5	15
	2	4	....	4	......	17	88.	8	94
DISTRICTS.	3	8	12	8	12	15	76.	7	88
	4	8	....	4	....	21	51.	10	76
	5	6	....	6	....	21	21.	10	62
	6	4	....	4	....	16	06.	8	04
	7	4	....	4	..... .	11	51.	5	76
	8	9	12	4	....	14	54.	7	27
PARTS OF DISTRICTS.	9	10	6	10	6	9	70.	4	85
	10	6	....	3	....	4	55.	2	27
	11	6	....	6	... ...	8	48.	4	24
	12	3	5	3	5	8	18.	4	09
	13	8	....	8	....	8	79.	4	39
Total,	13	83	35	65	23	168	47.	84	26

[*Continuation of Table on next page.*]

No of districts.	Number of volumes in district libraries.	Number of children taught.	Number of children who have attended less than 2 months.	Two months and less than four.	Four months and less than six.	Six months and less than eight.	Eight months and less than ten.	Ten months and less than twelve.	Twelve months.	Amount of taxes levied in the several districts during the year.									No. of children exempted on account of indigence of parents.	Amount raised to pay the expenses of such exemptions.	Number of children over 4 and under 21 years of age.	Number of times inspected by town superintendent.	Amount raised by rate bills for teachers wages.	Number of unincorporated select and private schools, in said district.	Average number of pupils attending said schools.	Number of children between 5 and 16 years taught in colored schools.	Amount of public money received on account of such schools.	Amount paid for teachers' wages in colored schools, besides public money.
										Purchasing school house sites.	Building school houses.	Hiring school houses.	Repairing school houses.	Insuring school houses.	Fuel.	Supplying deficiencies in rate bills.	Book case, purchase of books and school apparatus.	Other purposes.										
DISTRICTS.																												
PARTS OF DISTRICTS.																												

Dated at *Trenton*, this first day of July in the year of our Lord one thousand eight hundred and

A. B., *Town Superintendent of Common Schools.*

CHAPTER III.

POWERS AND DUTIES OF INHABITANTS OF SCHOOL DISTRICTS.

By § 65 (No. 87) of the school act, it is provided that " an annual meeting shall be held at the time and place previously appointed; and at the first district meeting, and at each annual meeting, the time and place of holding the next annual meeting shall be fixed."

Annual meetings need not be precisely one year apart. The time may be a few days or weeks more or less than a year, if the inhabitants think it necessary. For instance, an annual meeting held on the *first* Tuesday of October may be adjourned to the *second* Tuesday of October of the next year. The propriety of the act in every case must depend upon the circumstances attending it. No general rule as to the extent of the variation from a year can be laid down as applicable to all cases.—*Com. School Dec.* 289.

It is proper, however, to observe, that as by the act of 1843 one trustee only is hereafter to be annually elected, who holds his office for *three years*, and as in case of a vacancy, such vacancy is to be supplied only for the unexpired term left vacant, the variations in the time of holding the annual meeting ought not to exceed three or four weeks. The time from one annual meeting to another must always be considered and treated as one year.

By § 66 of the act of (No. 88,) " Whenever the time for holding annual meetings in a district, for the election of district officers shall pass without such election being held, a special meeting shall be notified by the clerk of such district to choose such officers; and if no such notice be given by him or the trustees last elected or appointed, within twenty days after such time shall have passed, any inhabitant of such district qualified to vote at district meetings, may notify such meeting in the manner provided by law in case of the formation of a new district; and the officers chosen at any such special meeting, shall hold their office until the time for holding the next annual meeting."

By § 67 of Laws of 1847, (No. 89,) " When the clerk, and all the trustees of a school district, shall have removed, or otherwise vacated their office, and where the records of a district shall have been destroyed or lost, or where trustees neglect or refuse to call meetings to choose trustees, the Superintendent of Common Schools shall have authority to order such meetings."

By § 68 (No. 90,) " When in consequence of the loss of the records of a school district, or the omission to designate the day for its annual meeting, there shall be none fixed, or it cannot be ascertained, the trustees of such district may appoint a day for holding the annual meeting of such district."

If an annual meeting is held at the time and place appointed at or adjourned from the annual meeting of the preceding year, the proceedings will be deemed valid, notwithstanding the omission of the clerk to give the notices prescribed by law.

Where the place and time of day for holding the annual meeting are not designated by the inhabitants, the usual place and time of day for holding such meetings will be understood, and the notices of the clerk should correspond thereto. When assembled, the inhabitants may adjourn to any other convenient place ; but the clerk cannot, in his notices for the annual meeting, designate any other than the usual place for holding such meeting, where the inhabitants at their last annual meeting omitted to specify any place. —*Com. School Dec.* 129, 141.

The law has not specified what number of inhabitants shall constitute a quorum for the transaction of business at a district meeting, annual or special: and accordingly the proceedings, if otherwise regular, will not be disturbed by reason of the paucity of attendance on the part of the inhabitants, where the notice has been fair and public, and there is no room for the allegation of surprise. A reasonable time, should, however, be allowed for the inhabitants to assemble, after which those in attendance may legally proceed to the transaction of any district business.

By § 69 (No. 91) it is provided that "a special meeting shall be held in each district whenever called by the trustees; and the proceedings of no district meeting, annual or special, shall be held illegal, for want of a due notice to all the persons qualified to vote thereat, unless it shall appear that the omission to give such notice was wilful and fraudulent."

This latter provision was intended for cases where through accident or mistake, the proper legal notice has not been given to *all who are entitled to it:* but it cannot be construed to extend to cases in which *no attempt* is made to give the notice required by law to *any* of the inhabitants. Where the clerk of a district undertakes to give a notice in the manner provided by the statute, and has failed, unintentionally, to serve such notice on all the persons entitled to receive it, or where such notice is imperfectly served, the proceedings of the meeting will not be *void* on that account. They may, however, be *set aside* on appeal, on showing sufficient cause.—*Com. School Dec.* 186, 223.

The law in terms, prescribes that the *object* for which a special meeting is called shall be stated in the notice for such meeting.

The opportunities afforded by the coming together of the inhabitants of each district, for deliberation and consultation in relation to their schools, and the various interests connected therewith, are calculated to exert a most beneficial influence in favor of education; to promote union, harmony and concert of action in the several districts; and to cement the ties of friendly social intercourse between those having a common interest in the moral and intellectual culture of their children. It is, therefore, of the utmost importance that they should not be neglected; that the inhabitants should be prompt and uniform in their attendance; and that the proceedings should be invariably characterized with that order, regularity dignity and decorum which can alone command respect and efficiently attain the objects to be accomplished. To secure as far as possible the attainment of these desirable ends, it is proposed in this place to examine the powers and duties of the inhabitants, when assembled in district meeting, the mode of proceeding the keeping of the minutes and records, the qualifications of voters, and some other subjects of general interest, connected with the proceedings of district meetings.

1. POWRRS AND DUTIES OF INHABITENTS WHEN ASSEMBLED IN DISTRICT MEETING.

These are particularly specified in § 62, (No. 84) of the act, and will be noticed in their proper order. They are, to appoint a moderator; to adjourn from time to time as occasion may require; to choose district officers at their first meeting upon the organization of the district, and as often as *vacancies* occur, by expiration of the term of office or otherwise; to designate a site for district school-houses; to lay such tax on the taxable inhabitants of the district as the meeting shall deem sufficient to purchase or lease a suitable site for a school-house, and to build, hire, or purchase such school-house, and to keep in repair and furnish the same with necessary fuel and appendages; and to repeal, alter and modify their proceedings from time to as occasion may require.

By the 10th section of the act of 1841, sub. 8. (No. 84,) the inhabitants are authorized, with the consent of the Town Superintendent of common schools, to designate sites for *two* or *more* school houses for their district, and to lay a tax for the purchase or lease thereof, and for the purchase, hiring or building of school houses thereon, and the keeping in repair and furnishing the same with necessary fuel and appendages.

This provision authorizing more than one site and school house, is intended for the accommodation of those districts that may be so peculiarly situated as to render a division inconvenient or not desirable. A banking or other corporation, or some manufacturing establishment liable to taxation, may thus be rendered beneficial to a large territory and a greater number of inhabitants, instead of having its contributions applied for the benefit of a few. And in populous places, it may often be convenient to have a school for very young children distant from that attended by those more advanced. In these and other cases, the districts should not hesitate to exercise the power given by this section. But they should in all cases obtain the *previous assent* of the Town Superintendent.

The same section authorizes the inhabitants, in their discretion and without the assent of the Town Superintendent, to levy a tax not exceeding twenty dollars in any one year, for the purchase of maps, globes, black-boards and other school apparatus. The principal facts in geography are learned better by the eye than in any other manner, and there ought to be in every school-room a map of the world, of the United States, of this state and of the county. Globes also are desirable, but not so important as maps. Large black-boards, in frames or plaster are indispensable to a well conducted school. The operations in arithmetic performed on them, enable the teacher to ascertain the degree of the pupils' acquirements, better than any result exhibited on slates. He sees the various steps taken by the scholar, and can require him to give the reason for each. It is in fact an exercise for the entire class; and the whole school, by this public process, insensibly acquires a knowledge of the rules and operations in this branch of study.

Cards containing the letters of the alphabet, or words, may be usefully hung up in the room. Indeed the whole apparatus provided by Mr. Holbrook and others, is eminently calculated to facilitate the acquisition of knowledge and to render it agreeable.

The amount of the tax which may be voted for the purchase or lease of sites for the district school-house, and for the repairs, furniture, fuel and appendages, is left wholly to the discretion of the district, and is unlimited by law: but no tax for building, hiring or purchasing a school house can exceed the sum of four hundred dollars, unless on the certificate of the Town Superintendent that a larger sum, specifying the amount, ought, in his opinion, to be raised; in which case a sum not exceeding the sum so specified, may be raised. § 70 (No. 92,) If the district under the act of 1841, raise a tax for building, hiring or purchasing *two* or *more* school-houses, a tax for *each* may be levied, to the amount of $400, without a certificate from the Town Superintendent.

Whenever a majority of all the taxable inhabitants who are legal voters of any school district, to be ascertained by taking and recording the ayes and noes of such inhabitants attending at any annual, special or adjourned school district meeting legally called or held, determine that the sum proposed and provided to build a school house, shall be raised by instalments; it is the duty of the trustees to cause the same to be levied, raised and collected, in equal annual instalments, in the same manner, and with the like authority that other school district taxes are raised, levied and collected, and to make out their tax list and warrant, for the collection of such instalments as they become payable according to the vote of the said inhabitants; but the payment or collection of the last instalment can not be extended beyond five years from the time such vote was taken; and no vote to levy any such tax can be reconsidered except at an adjourned general or special meeting to be held within thirty days thereafter, and the same majority is required for reconsideration as is required to levy such tax.

By § 71 (No. 93) and § 74 No. 96, the inhabitants are authorized, whenever the site of their school-house has been legally changed, to direct the sale of the former site or lot, and the buildings thereon, and appurtenances, or any part thereof, at such price and upon such terms as they shall deem most advantageous to the district.

By the 136th section of the act of 1847, (No. 155) it is provided that "whenever the number of volumes in the district library of any district numbering over fifty children between the age of four and twenty-one years, shall exceed one hundred and twenty-five; or of any district numbering fifty children or less, between the said ages shall exceed one hundred volumes, the inhabitants of the district qualified to vote therein, *may, at a special or annual meeting, duly notified for that purpose*, by a majority of votes, appropriate the whole or any part of the library money belonging to the district for the current year, to the purchase of *maps, globes, black-boards, or other scientific apparatus, for the use of the school,*" and in every district having the required number of volumes in the district library, and the maps, globes, black-boards and other apparatus aforesaid, the said moneys, *with the approbation of the State Superintendent* may be applied to the payment of teachers wages.

The object of this enactment is two-fold. It is designed in the first instance, to secure to every district at least one hundred volumes of suitable books for a district library; and to districts numbering over fifty children, one hundred and twenty-five; and in the second, to authorize the inhabitants of any district so supplied, when duly convened for that special pu pose, to appropriate so much of the library fund for the current year, as they may think proper, to the purchase of maps, globes, black-boards or scientific apparatus, for the use of the school, or to the payment of teachers wages when authorized by the State Superintendent. In the absence of any such appropriation, or whenever any balance remains unappropriated, the library money, or such unappropriated balance, must be applied to the purchase of books; and in any event,that money must be expended for the one or the other of these purposes, on or before the first day of October in each year. It is respectfully recommended to the inhabitants of those districts which are already supplied with the requisite number of books,and of others, whenever they shall reach the specified number, to avail themselves of the power thus conferred upon them, to supply their school with those useful articles of scientific apparatus which so materially conduce to the improvement of the pupils. Independently of this appropriation, no district should dispense with a black-board; and if suitable maps, globes and a few of the more simple means of illustrating the elementary truths of science, can be superadded, the library money for two or three years cannot perhaps be more advantageously appropriated. In the mean time, the books on hand can be generally read; and such additions to the library as the growing wants and increased intelligence of the district may require, can then be from time to time procured. The advice of the Town Superintendent may at all times be had as to the most proper and judicious appropriation of the fund for the purposes provided for by the section under consideration.

By the provision of the several acts relative to school district libraries, (No. 159 *et seq.*) the inhabitants of the several districts are authorized to lay a tax, not exceeding twenty dollars for the first year, and ten dollars for each subsequent year, for the purchase of a district library, *consisting of such books as they shall in their district meeting direct*, and such further sum as they may deem necessary for the purchase of a book-case.

These provisions, it will be observed, are entirely distinct from those which relate to the purchase of books with the public moneys provided by the act of 1838. They are confined to such books as are obtained by means of a district tax; and wherever the inhabitants do not choose to place the latter on the same footing with the former, the distinction should be carefully observed. The library directed to be purchased with the public money provided for that purpose, is to be selected by the *trustees;* the inhabitants have no direct control over such selection; and the rules and regulations for its government are to be prescribed by the Superintendent alone; while the library to be raised by *tax must* consist of such books as the inhabitants in districts meeting shall direct; and the rules and regulations for its management may be adopted at such meeting. Still, both classes of books may be placed upon substantially the same footing, by a general direction to the trustees as to the books to be purchased, and the adoption of the rules and regulations prescribed by the Superintendent.

By § 141 (No. 160,) the legal voters in any two or more adjoining districts,may,with the approbation of the Superintendent, *unite* their library moneys, as they shall be received or collected, and purchase a *joint library* for the use of the inhabitants of such districts, to be selected by the *trustees*, or such persons as they shall designate, and to be placed under the charge of a librarian to be appointed by them.

By section 143 of the same act, (No. 162) the legal voters in any district are authorized to direct the trustees to apply to the Superintendent to select and forward to the county clerk for the use of the district, a library.

By sub. 9 of § 82, (No. 103,) the power of inhabitants of districts to direct the division of the public (teacher's) money, into not exceeding four portions for each year, and to assign and apply one of such portions to each term taught during the year by a duly qualified teacher, is expressly recognized.

Where by reason of the inability to collect any tax, there shall be a deficiency in the amount raised, the inhabitants of the district in district meeting, are empowered to direct the raising of a sufficient sum to supply such deficiency, by tax.—§ 84, (No. 105.)

By § 46, (No. 72,) "If the Town Superintendent of common schools in any town, shall require in writing, the attendance of the Town Superintendents of any other town or towns, at a joint meeting for the purpose of altering a school district formed from their respective towns, and a major part of the Town Superintendents notified shall refuse or neglect to attend, the Town Superintendents attending, by a majority of votes, may call a special district meeting of such district, for the purpose of deciding on such proposed alteration; and the decision of such meeting shall be as valid as if made by the Town Superintendents of all the towns interested, but shall extend no further than to dissolve the district formed from such towns."

The powers conferred upon the inhabitants ot school districts must be strictly pursued, and can in no case be exceeded. No vote or proceeding of a district meeting can be legal, for which authority is not expressly or by necessary implication, to be derived from the statute.

2. CHANGE OF SITE OF SCHOOL HOUSE.

By § 73, (No. 95,) it is provided that "whenever a school-house shall have been *built* or *purchased* for a district, the site of such school-house shall not be changed, nor the building thereon be removed, as long as the district *shall remain unaltered*, unless by the consent, in writing, of the Town Superintendent of common schools, of the town or each of the towns within which such district shall be situated, stating that in their opinion such removal is necessary; *nor then*, unless a majority of all the taxable inhabitants of said district to be ascertained by taking and recording the ayes and noes at a special meeting of such district *called for that purpose*, shall be in favor of such new site."

This provision is designed to secure permanency in the location of the district school-house, while the circumstances under which it was so located remain substantially the same. But when an alteration has taken place in the district, *since such location*, either by the *addition* of new inhabitants, and the consequent annexation of new territory, from the adjoining districts, or by the *setting off* of a portion of the inhabitants and territory to some other district, then, the reason for the enactment failing, a change of site may be voted by a majority of the altered district, in the usual manner. When the new site is again established, either in this manner, or by a two-third vote, as provided in the section above quoted, and a house built the same principle again prevails. No further alteration can be made while the district remains substantially in the same condition as when the new site was fixed.

The *alterations* here referred to must be such as are made in the *territorial boundaries* of the district. Changes of residence by the inhabitants removing out of the district, or the removal of persons into it from other districts, cannot be deemed alterations within the meaning of the law, while the territory remains the same.

When the district has not been altered, and a change of site is proposed, the consent, in writing, of the Town Superintendent, as above specified is requisite, and in addition thereto, a vote of *a majority of the taxable inhabitants of the district who are legal voters, present and voting*, by ayes and noes. No taxable inhabitant who is not a *legal voter* of the district can vote therein on any question; nor is it necessary that a majority of all the taxable inhabitants or legal voters *residing in the district* should be obtained; but only of a majority of those *present and voting* at a meeting duly notified.—Per MORGAN Supt. April 1851.

Experience has shown that by far the most fertile sources of contention and difficulty in the various school districts, originate from the proceedings of the inhabitants connected with the change of the site of their school-house. Such a measure should, therefore, only be adopted when the convenience and accommodation of the inhabitants will be essentially promoted thereby; when the altered situation of the district imperatively requires a change; and even then, the full and hearty concurrence not merely of a clear and decided majority of the district, but of the inhabitants generally, should be secured, before any final decision is made. There must always be a portion of the inhabitants, residing at the extremities of the district, who will experience more or less inconvenience, at particular seasons of the year, in consequence of their distance from the school-house: but it is better that these partial inconveniences should be submitted to, than that they should be transferred to others and the whole district plunged into a contention respecting the site. But when, in consequence of the enlargement of the boundaries of the district, a change is indispensable, the inhabitants should come together in a conciliatory and friendly spirit, having no other object in view than the best interests of the district and the convenience of the greatest number: and their action should be deliberate and circumspect—reconciling, as far as possible, the interests of all, and rejecting every proposition calculated to sow the seeds of dissension or disturbance in any portion of the district:—bearing in mind that a mere numerical triumph, leaving a large minority dissatisfied and irritated, however gratifying to the successful party, for a time, is but a poor compensation for a divided and distracted district, and an embittered and hostile neighborhood.

By § 74, (No. 96,) it is provided that whenever the site of a school house shall have been changed as herein provided, the inhabitants of the district entitled to vote, lawfully assembled at any district meeting, shall have power by a majority of the votes of those present, to direct the sale of the former site or lot, and the buildings thereon, and appurtenances, or any part thereof, at such price, and upon such terms as they shall deem most advantageous to the district; and any deed duly executed by the trustees of such district, or a majority of them, in pursuance of such direction, shall be valid and effectual to pass all the estate or interest of such school district in the premises intended to be conveyed thereby, to the grantee named in such deed; and when a credit shall be directed to be given upon such sale, for the consideration money, or any part thereof, the trustees are authorized to take in their corporate name, such security by bond and mortgage, or otherwise, for the payment thereof, as they shall deem best, and to hold the same as a corporation, and account therefor to their successors in office and to the district, in the manner they are now required by law to account for moneys received by them; and the trustees of any such district for the time being, may in their name of office, sue for and recover the moneys due and unpaid upon any security so taken by them, or their predecessors in office, with interest and costs.

By § 75, (No. 97,) all moneys arising from any sale made in pursuance of the last preceding section, shall be appropriated to the payment of the expenses incurred in procuring a new site, and in removing or erecting a school house, or either of them, so far as such application thereof shall be deemed necessary.

3. DESIGNATION OF SITE OF SCHOOL-HOUSE.

When the site of a school-house is to be fixed, it should be designated with distinctness and precision. It is very common in many of the districts to vote a site in general terms, as at *or near* a particular spot, *between* two points, or by other equally vague descriptions; and in some instances, the precise location has been left to the discretion of the trustees, or of a committee appointed for that purpose. All this is directly contrary to law. The inhabitants in district meeting assembled, are to "*designate* a site for a district school-house," and this designation must be sufficiently explicit, and must be described by metes and bounds, or other known and permanent land marks, to enable the trustees to locate the site, and to contract for and receive a title to the same; and the best rule will be to make such a description as would be required in a deed of the premises.

4 BUILDING, HIRING, PURCHASING AND REPAIRING OF SCHOOL HOUSES, AND PROVIDING FURNITURE AND APPENDAGES.

When a tax is voted by the inhabitants of a district for building a school-house, it is important, not only that the specific amount to be raised should be stated, but if any portion of it is designed to be expended in the erection of other appurtenances, such as a wood-house, necessary, or fence that those purposes should be specifically set forth in the resolution. It would, in all cases, be desirable that a committee of the inhabitants, consisting of or including the trustees who are charged by law with the execution of the work, should be appointed, to digest and, under the advice of the Town Superintendent, mature a full plan for the building, appendages and appurtenances, together with a detailed estimate of the expense, and to submit the same at an adjourned meeting for the sanction and approval of the district.

From this proceeding many useful results would follow. The trustees would be placed in possession of all the information necessary to enable them sufficiently and systematically to discharge their duties, in contracting for and superintending the erection of the house ; an opportunity would be afforded of obtaining and comparing the best models of architecture, and the inhabitants would be enabled to discuss at their leisure the several plans submitted, and to consult their convenience, taste and accommodation in the several details.

The volume of "School Architecture," by the Hon. HENRY BARNARD, of Connecticut, will be found exceedingly valuable, in the construction or alteration of school-houses, and should, whenever practicable, be consulted.

The school-house, when built or purchased, should never be permitted to remain for any length of time out of repair. It is the duty of the trustees to keep it in repair, and the district should, whenever called upon, provide for the expense. They should also see that the school-rooms are properly furnished with fuel, prepared for use ; that all the necessary articles of furniture are provided; that the seats, desks and other fixtures are in good condition, and that the district library, the apparatus for the school, and all the other property of the district, is properly taken care of, and such articles as are wanted, promptly furnished. In other words, the district should exercise a constant supervision over its officers, and provide the means for an efficient discharge of their duties.

When it is supposed that more than four hundred dollars will be necessary to build, hire, or purchase a school-house, care should be taken to procure the certificate of the Town Superintendent *before* the tax is voted by the district, as such certificate seems by the act and has been held by the department to be indispensable, to authorize the vote. If there be a site and house, they should be sold, and the proceeds applied first to the purchase of the new site, and next to the building. And whatever sum is applicable to the erection or purchase of the school-house must, according to a decision of the department, go in reduction of the amount which the district may vote for a school-house.—(*Decisions, p.* 183.) Thus, if the former site and building sell for 200 dollars, and 50 dollars be applied to the procuring a new site, the remaining 150 dollars being applicable to the new house, the district cannot vote a tax of more than 250 dollars for the building, without the consent of the Town Superintendent.

The following will be a proper form of a resolution for raising a tax for the erection of a school-house:

The certificate of the Town Superintendent of common schools of the town of   having been obtained, that in his opinion a larger sum than four hundred dollars ought to be raised for building a school-house in the said district, namely, the sum of *six hundred* dollars, [or whatever the whole sum may be.]

Resolved, That the said sum of six hundred dollars be raised by tax upon the said district, for the purpose of building a school-house therein.

The resolution for the purchase of a site should be distinct, and may be in the following form :

Resolved, That the sum of fifty dollars be raised by tax upon the said district, for the purchase of the site for a new school-house heretofore designated by the legal voters thereof.

Either or both of the above taxes may be raised, but cannot be expended before a site is purchased and a legal title procured.

A tax having been voted to build a school-house, the tax list made out and a warrant issued, the collection of the tax cannot be suspended by vote of a district meeting.—*Com. School Dec.*, 68. But where no proceedings have been had in pursuance of such vote, it may be rescinded.—*Id.* 261.

Where a tax is voted in express terms, a direction subsequently given as to the time and manner of its collection, is void.—*Id.* 282.

Where the inhabitants of a school district authorize the trustees or any other person to select a site for a school-house, it is not a legal site until subsequently fixed by a vote of the inhabitants.—*Id.* 353.

Where the title to the site of a district school-house fails, a new site may be fixed by a majority vote, without the certificate of the Town Superintendent.—*Id.* 107, 132, 142, 195.

When the site of the school-house has been fixed, it may be changed by a majority of votes, at any time before the school-house is built or purchased.—*Id.* 182.

In voting a tax to purchse a site, a sufficient sum may be included to cover all necessary expenses in perfecting the title to the premises.

The fact that the site of a school-house is covered by a mortgage does not affect the validity of the proceedings of a school meeting, in voting to build upon it; although upon timely application the Superintendent might not permit the house to be constructed until the lien was removed.

Where the title to the site of a school-house consists of a lease of the ground so long as it shall continue to be used for the purposes of a district school, if the inhabitants appropriate the land to any other purpose, it reverts to the grantor.

A *contract* for the purchase of land intended to be occupied as the site for a school-house, is not strictly a lease, although the vendee may for some purposes be regarded as a tenant. Where such a contract is not *executed* by the performance of its conditions, it does not amount to a purchase. But where such conditions have been performed, the vendees have an equitable title, and the court of chancery would enforce the performance of the contract on the part of the vendor. A presumption in favor of such performance would, it seems, arise from the circumstance of long possession on the part of the district.

Where a school district has been altered, after the original establishment of its site, either by adding to or diminishing from its territory, so that the site is no longer central or convenient, such site may be changed by a vote of a majority of the inhabitants of the district, at any meeting, annual or special; but after such change has been effected, and a new site established, and a new house built or purchased, the site cannot again be changed until some further alteration occurs in the boundaries of the district, without the consent of the Town Superintendent and a majority of the voters of the district, in the mode prescribed by the 73d section of the school act. [No. 95.]

The costs and expenses of a bill in equity to perfect the title to the site of a school-house, held under an agreement by the owner to convey, may legally be defrayed by a tax to be voted by the district.—*Per* YOUNG, *Sup't.*

Where the inhabitants of a school district have, by a vote to that effect, authorized the trustees to go on and make repairs, or to do any other lawful acts involving an expenditure of money, they will be required to save the trustees harmless, if the latter have acted in good faith. But where trustees undertake to do any act which they are not by law authorized to do, in the absence of any directions on the part of the district, it is at their own peril. The inhabitants may ratify their proceedings by a subsequent vote; but if they do not choose to do so, the trustees are without remedy.—*Com. School Dec.* 41, 222.

A school-house built by subscription may, if under the control of the trustees, be kept in repair by a tax on the property of the district.—*Id.* 47.

There can be no partnership in the erection of a school-house, which will prevent the district from controlling it entirely for the purposes of the district school.—*Id.* 201, 290.

No more money can be legally expended on a school-house than is necessary for common school purposes. An additional room can not be provided for a select school.—*Id.* 203.

A tax should not be voted by the inhabitants of a district for repairing the school-house, where the district has no title to the site, and the owner has forbidden the repairs to be made.—*Id.* 60, 187.

Nor should a tax to build a school-house be imposed or expended until the district has acquired such an interest in the site as to be able to control the house.—*Id.* 168.

A tax cannot be raised to build a school-house on a site selected without legal authority.—*Baker* v. *Freeman*, 9 *Wendall*, 36.

Where a school-house is built by subscription, a tax may be voted for its purchase, if the district has title to the site on which it stands. —*Id.* 193.

The rule of law is, that the right of property in all permanent erections upon lands, resides in the owner of the soil. The latter is therefore the legal owner of a school-house erected without his permission on his land. But if such school-house was originally placed there *with* his permission, the district has a right to direct its removal.—*Per* YOUNG, *Supt.*

The inhabitants of a district may legally vote a tax to *enlarge* their school house, notwithstanding it may already have cost $400, without a certificate from the Town Superintendent.—*Id.*

Where a school house is so decayed as in the opinion of a majority of the district to be no longer suitable for the purposes of the school, a tax may be voted in the usual manner for building a new one on the same site.—*Per* SPENCER, *Sup't.*

Inhabitants of school districts cannot, by a vote to that effect, authorize the trustees to provide *fuel* in any other mode than those prescribed by law.—*Com. School Dec.* 264.

Nor can they dispose of any portion of the district property, unless in the cases and in the manner specifically pointed out by law.

Although the inhabitants of a district may direct the division of the teachers' money for the current year into portions, applicable to the respective school terms, they cannot so appropriate the money for the succeeding year: nor can they direct such division after its appropriation by the trustees on a specific contract with a teacher.

A tax may be levied in a school district to build a wood house and necessary.—*Com. School Dec.* 21.

Money cannot be raised by tax in a school district for *contingent* purposes.—*Id.* 233.

A tax to purchase a district library cannot be voted at a meeting of which no *notice* is required to be given: e. g. an adjourned meeting, where the adjournment is for a less period than one month. —*Id.* 286.

A tax cannot be laid to erect a building to be occupied *jointly* as a school house and a meeting house.—*Id.* 290.

When the whole amount of a tax raised for any additional purpose is not required for such purpose, the balance may be applied by vote of the district to any other authorized object.—*Id.* 315.

A tax cannot be voted for *arrearages* generally, or to reimburse trustees or other officers of the district for moneys expended by them, unless it appears by the vote that the money is to be applied to one of the objects for which taxes may by law be raised. —*Id.* 316.

A vote of the district is necessary to raise by tax the excess beyond $400 certified to be necessary for building a school-house. —*Id.* 339.

A tax may be voted for the erection of a *fence* around the school-house lot; and for a *bell.*

5. MODE OF PROCEEDING IN DISTRICT MEETING.

As a general rule, the punctual attendance of the inhabitants of the district should be secured by the organization of the meeting at the appointed hour, after making a fair allowance, say ten or fifteen minutes, for the variation of time-pieces; at the expiration of which time, those in attendance, whatever may be their number, should organize, by the appointment of a moderator. Any number of inhabitants, however small, are, as before observed, competent to the transaction of the business for which the meeting was called; but if there be only a very small number present, it will be advisable to adjourn the meeting. The clerk of the district, if present, will act as clerk of the meeting; and in case of his absence, any other inhabitant of the district may be designated by the meeting to act as clerk *pro tem.* The inhabitants will then proceed to the transaction of the business for which they were convened.

Where the officers of the district are to be chosen, the choice should be by ballot, separately for each office; and this mode of proceeding should never be dispensed with where there is reason to believe any difference of opinion exists as to the proper person to be chosen. Where no such difference of opinion exists, it is still better to regard the choice by ballot as the regular mode, and when dispensed with in any individual case, it should be done by express resolution. All other business of the meeting should be transacted by written resolutions, regularly put to vote in the customary manner; and where, for any reason, the result cannot be accurately ascertained, the numbers voting for or against any resolution should be determined by a count, or by ayes and noes. For this purpose it would be well for the clerk to have always in readiness a list of the legal voters of the district, with a series of columns attached, to designate the manner in which each person votes on any question that may be submitted. When the site is to be changed in a district that has not been altered, the law specifically requires the vote to be taken by ayes and nays. Such list may be in the following form.

Names of Voters.	On change of site of sch'l house.		On motion to build school house.		On resolut'n to raise tax of $150.		On resolut'n to raise tax for apparat.	
	Ayes.	Nays.	Ayes.	Nays.	Ayes.	Noes.	Ayes.	Noes.
John Morehouse,..	—		—		—			
Jacob Curtis,.......		—		—	—			
Thomas Budd,......	—		—		—			
William Carroll...		—		—		—		
Henry Beltis,.......	—		—			—	—	—
Frederick Hough...	—		—			—	—	—
	4	2	4	2	3	3	4	2

6. MODE OF KEEPING MINUTES AND RECORDS OF THE PROCEEDINGS.

The person acting as clerk should keep accurate minutes of the proceedings on loose sheets of paper; and before the meeting is finally adjourned these minutes should be read and approved by the meeting, and signed by the moderator and clerk, and afterwards transferred into the record book of the district. The following general form may be used for this purpose:

Form of Minutes to be kept by the District Clerk, of proceedings of District Meetings.

At a meeting of the legal voters of school district number in the town of held pursuant to adjournment, at on the day of 18 , [*or, if it be the annual meeting, say* "*at an annual meeting of, &c., held pursuant to appointment and public notice, at,*" *&c. Or if it be a special meeting, say,* "*at a special meeting of, &c., called by the trustees of said district, and pursuant to special notice, at, &c. on the day of, &c.,*] A B. was chosen moderator, and C. D. was present as district cler (or if the clerk be not present, say E. F. was appointed clerk pro. tem. the district clerk being absent.)

Resolved unanimously, (*or by a majority of voters present, as the case may be,*) [*here enter the proceedings of the district in the form of resolutions, and with as much precision and certainty as possible.*]

Where the subject of a change of site in an unaltered district has been under discussion, and a determination had by the district, in the manner prescribed by law, the proceedings should be particularly recorded, in the following form:

At a meeting of the legal voters of district No. in the town of held at the school house, in pursuance of notice to all the legal voters therein, on the day of 18 , A. B. was chosen moderator, and C. D. was present as district clerk, (or E. F. was appointed clerk *pro. tem.* the district clerk being absent.) The written consent of the Town Superintendent of common schools of the town having been read, stating that in his opinion the removal of the site of the school house in said district is necessary: And it having been moved and seconded that the present site of the school house in the said district be changed, and that the northeast corner of lot No. 10 in the said town, (or of the farm now occupied by A. B. on the N. E. corner, formed by the intersection of two certain roads, describing them,) be designated as the site of a school house for the said district, and the question taken by ayes and noes, it was carried, a majority of all those present at such special meeting voting for such removal, and in favor of such new site: Those who voted in the affirmative were John Morehouse, Thomas Budd, Wm. Carroll and Frederick Hough; those who voted in the negative, were Jacob Curtis and Henry Bettis.

Ayes 4 *Noes* 2.

[In stating the ayes and noes, the christian names of the voters, should be given.]

[Or, and the question being taken by ayes and noes, it was lost, a majority of all those present at the meeting not voting in favor thereof. The votes are then to be stated as before.]

After changing the site of the school house in the manner before prescribed, the voters of the district, at the same or any subsequent meeting, may pass a resolution, by a majority of those present, in the ordinary mode, directing the trustees to sell the house, according to No. 96 *ante*.

7. QUALIFICATIONS OF VOTERS.

Great difficulty has been heretofore experienced in ascertaining the requisite legal qualifications for voters in school district meetings. The act of 1847, has removed this difficulty by defining them particularly, and has pointed out the means of ascertaining the right of any individual to vote in such meetings, by a challenge, §59, 60, 61, (Nos. 81, 82, 83.)

The following general qualifications are required in all cases:

1. The voter must be a male.
2. Of full age, that is, twenty-one years old, or more.
3. He must be an actual resident of the district.

In addition to the above, the voter must possess *one or other* of the following qualifications:

4. He must be entitled by law to hold land in this state, and must own or hire real property in the district, subject to taxation for school purposes; *or*,
5. He must be authorized to vote at town meetings of the town in which the district, or part of a district is situated—and in addition thereto must have paid a rate bill for teachers' wages in the district within one year preceding, or must have paid a district tax within two years preceding, or must be owner of personal property liable to be taxed for school purposes in the district, exceeding fifty dollars in value, exclusive of what is exempt from execution.

Under the above 4th division are included two classes of persons—citizens owning or hiring real property, subject to taxation, and aliens not naturalized, who have filed the affidavit prescribed by § 16 of title 1, chap. 1, part 2, Rev. Stat. of their intention to become citizens, and of having taken the necessary incipient measures for that purpose, and who own or hire *real property* in the district subject to taxation for school purposes. It does not extend to those who have personal property, but neither own nor hire real property. The provision was intended to meet the case of residents, who although not entitled to vote at town meetings, may have a strong interest in the proceedings of district school meetings.

Any resident of the district, who owns *or hires* real estate *liable to taxation* in the district, whether he pays the tax on such property himself or not, and whatever may be its value, and whether he holds it by a written or verbal lease, (if for one year or less) is a legal voter, at any district meeting, even though he may not have resided either in the State or County for a sufficient length of time to enable him to vote at town meetings or elections.

In reference to the above 5th division, those "citizens of the several towns in this state, qualified by the constitution to vote for elective officers," are included, provided they possess the other requisite qualifications. Of course, persons claiming to vote at district meetings *under this qualification* must have been inhabitants of the state for one year, of the county for six months immediately preceding, and must then be actual residents of the town. To these must be added some one of the qualifications above specified in division 5. By § 60 and § 61, (Nos 82 and 83.) it is provided that "If any person offering to vote at any school district meeting, shall be challenged as unqualified by any legal voter in such district, the chairman presiding at such meeting shall require the person so offering, to make the following declaration: "I do declare and affirm that I am an actual resident of this school district, and that I am qualified to vote at this meeting." And every person making such declaration shall be permitted to vote on all questions proposed at such meeting; but if any person shall refuse to make such declaration, his vote shall be rejected.

"Every person who shall wilfully make a false declaration of his right to vote at a district meeting, upon being challenged as herein before provided, shall be deemed guilty of a misdemeanor, and punishable by imprisonment in the county jail for a term not exceeding one year, nor less than six months, at the discretion of the court; and any person voting at any district meeting without being qualified, shall, on conviction, be subject to a fine of ten dollars, to be sued for and recovered by the trustees of the district for its use, and with costs of suit, before any justice of the peace."

The proceedings of district meetings where illegal votes are alleged to have been given, will not be set aside, unless it is shown on appeal, 1st, that such votes were actually illegal; 2d, that they affected the result; and 3d, that they were legally challenged upon being offered, or that they were not at the time known to be illegal.

8. RECONSIDERATION OF PROCEEDINGS.

The inhabitants of school districts may reconsider and repeal, alter and modify their proceedings at any time before they have been carried into effect, either wholly or in part. But the intention to do so, should be explicitly set forth in the notice of the meeting called for that purpose. When, however, contracts have actually been entered into, liabilities incurred, or expenditures of money had, in the prosecution of any measure directed by the district, a reconsideration will not be sanctioned, as no means exists to indemnify those who may be losers thereby.

9. TAXES SHOULD BE SPECIFICALLY VOTED.

Where a tax is voted by the inhabitants for any purpose, the specific amount of the tax, and the particular purpose for which it is designed, should be fully and clearly stated. And where several objects of expenditure are to be provided for, the amount to be raised for each should be expressed in the resolution, in order that the district and the trustees may know the precise extent of their liability, and the mode of its application. There may be cases, however, where the necessary amount to be raised, cannot be ascertained with any approach to accuracy; and in such cases the district may direct the performance of specific acts by the trustees, or authorize them to incur such expenses as may be necessary to the accomplishment of a particular object to be specified; and the trustees are then authorized by §109, of the act of 1847, (No. 129,) to raise such amount by tax upon the district in the same manner as if the definite sum to be raised had been voted. This general delegation of authority should, however, be resorted to only in cases of necessity.

CHAPTER IV.

TRUSTEES OF SCHOOL DISTRICTS.

THESE officers are to be chosen by the inhabitants of the district entitled to vote, at their first meeting, and thereafter at any annual or special meeting legally convened, whenever there is a vacancy, by expiration of their term of office or otherwise. In case of the existence of a vacancy, by the death, refusal to serve, removal out of the district, or incapacity of the incumbent, unless such vacancy is supplied by a district meeting within one month thereafter, it is the duty of the Town Superintendent of common schools to appoint some person to supply such vacancy in which case the person so appointed holds his office for the unexpired term, § 63, (No 85.) The expiration of their term of office, also creates a vacancy; and if, for any reason, the annual meeting passes over without the election of officers, ample provision is made, (see § 66-68, (No. 88-90,) for the calling of a special meeting to supply such vacancy.

By § 79, (No. 100,) every person duly chosen or appointed to any such office, who without sufficient cause shall refuse to serve therein, shall forfeit the sum of five dollars; and every person so chosen or appointed, and not having refused to accept, who shall neglect to perform the duties of his office, shall forfeit the sum of ten dollars.

By § 80, (No 101,) "any person chosen or appointed to any such office, may resign the same by presenting his resignation to the Town Superintendent of the town where such officer shall reside, who is authorized for sufficient cause shown to him to accept the same, and the acceptance of such resignation shall be a bar to the recovery of either of the penalties mentioned in the preceding section. The Town Superintendent accepting the resignation shall give notice thereof to the clerk, or to one of the trustees of the school district to which the officer resigning shall belong."

By § 6 of the act of 1847, (No. 30,) "no Town Superintendent of common schools, shall be eligible to the office of trustee of a school district; and no person chosen a trustee, can hold the office of district clerk."

By § 63 of the act of 1847, (No. 85,) it is provided that "the trustees of each of the several school districts next hereafter to be chosen, shall be divided by lot into three classes, to be numbered one, two and three; the term of office of the first class shall be one year; of the second, two; of the third, three; and one trustee only shall thereafter annually be elected, who shall hold his office for three years, and until a successor shall be duly elected or appointed. In case of a vacancy in the office of either of the trustees, during the period for which he or they shall have been respectively elected, the person or persons chosen or appointed to fill such vacancy shall hold the office only for the unexpired term so becoming vacant."

This extension of the official term of trustees to three years, combined with the annual choice of one of their number, is a very important improvement of the system, securing as it does, uniformity, stability and harmony in the councils of the district, and preventing that ignorance of its previous arrangements and affairs, which has so frequently been found not only to paralyze the exertions of new trustees, but to involve them in pecuniary embarrassment and subject them to personal liability. On the accession of a new trustee, under the present arrangement, he will find two experienced colleagues already in office, conversant with all the affairs of the district, and able and willing to aid and co-operate with him in the discharge of his duties. All the deliberations and actions of the board under this arrangement, will partake of a greater uniformity, and become more systematic. Teachers will be likely to be retained for a longer period; contracts will be likely to be more promptly fulfilled, and taxes and rate bills to be more accurately made out and more speedily collected; and order and harmony will gradually succeed to the chaotic confusion and irregularity which have too generally characterized the records, the councils and the proceedings of trustees ignorant and careless of their duty, and anxious only to transfer the inextricable embarrassments of their district, unexplained and inexplicable, to their successors.

One important operation of the provision in question, will be as before observed, to prevent the district from changing the time of its annual meeting, thereby avoiding those frequent misunderstandings as to the period when officers of the district are to be chosen, from which so many profitless and vexatious controversies have arisen.

The duties of trustees may be arranged under the following general heads:

1. The receipt and application of public money.
2. The calling of annual and special meetings.
3. The assessment and collection of district taxes.
4. The purchase or lease of sites; building, hiring, or purchasing of school-houses, the repairing and furnishing such houses with necessary fuel and appendages, and their custody and safe-keeping;

and the sale of such sites and houses when no longer required for district purposes.

5. The employment of teachers, and their payment; and the making out and collection of rate-bills.

6. Their duties in reference to the district library.

7. The making of annual reports.

8. The accounting to their successors and the district, at the expiration of their term of office; and paying over balances on hand.

9. Suits by and against them.

10. Miscellaneous provisions.

I. THE RECEIPT AND APPLICATION OF PUBLIC MONEY.

By the 10th section of the school act of 1847, (No. 35,) it is made the duty of the Town Superintendent to pay over the proportion of teacher's money to which each district may be entitled on its annual report for the preceding year, "on the written order of a majority of the trustees of such district to the *teacher* entitled to receive the same."

This order may be in the following form:

A. B. Esq. Town Superintendent of common schools of the town of pay C. D. a teacher duly employed by us, and qualified according to law, fifteen dollars, that being the amount which he is entitled to receive, out of the funds in your hands, applicable to the payment of teachers' wages, and apportioned to our district. Dated at this day of 18

E. F. } Trustees
G. H. } District No.

Upon the day of the annual apportionment, or as soon as possible thereafter, the trustees should call upon the Town Superintendent, or send one of their number, or the clerk, with an order signed by them, or a majority of them, for the share of library money due their district. If the Town Superintendent withholds such money, without justifiable cause, it is the duty of the trustees to prosecute for the same.—§ 114, (No. 134.)

The teachers should, if possible, present their orders at the same time, so that all the public money belonging to the district may at once be paid over and duly receipted.

To entitle a district to its share of teachers' money, it must appear from its annual report "that a school had been kept therein for at least six months during the year, ending at the date of such report, by a qualified teacher," *after obtaining a certificate of competency* from the proper authority; that all the teachers' money received during the year has been expended in the payment of such teacher; "that no other than a duly qualified teacher had at any time during the year, for more than one month, been employed to teach the school in said district;" and such report must, in all other respects, be in accordance with law, and the requisitions and instructions of the Superintendent, made in pursuance of law. In other words, it must be in the form prescribed by the Superintendent, and must contain all the information required by law and by the department to be given.

There are two classes of cases in which relief may be sought for the refusal of the Town Superintendent to apportion or pay over public money to a district.

1st. Where it is supposed his decision is erroneous upon some question of fact, or some principle of law In such case the remedy is *by appeal* to the State Superintendent, in the manner prescribed by the regulations concerning appeals. The interest of the district, as well as of other districts, requires that the proceedings should be prompt, as an appeal stays further action by the Town Superintendent.

2d. Where there has been any accidental omission to comply with any provision of law or any regulation of the Superintendent, in consequence of which an apportionment of public money has not been made In such cases a general authority is given *to the State Superintendent*, by § 14 of the act of 1847, (No. 39,) to cause the apportionment to be made, on the equitable circumstances of the case, and a similar authority is given in relation to library money by the last clause of § 6 of the act of 1839, § 142. (No. 161.

These provisions are intended only for cases of accidental and unintentional omissions, and the authority given by them will not be exercised where there is a wilful disobedience of law, or a perverse and intended violation of any regulation.

Applications for relief in this class of cases should be made as soon as the omission is discovered, in order to prevent the inconvenience of correcting the apportionment after it has been acted upon ; and any unnecessary delay will in itself form a strong ground of declining to grant the relief desired.

The facts and circumstances on which the application is founded must be verified by affidavit.

APPLICATION OF SCHOOL MONEY RAISED BY OR BELONGING TO A TOWN.

If there are any other common school funds belonging to the town, arising from their poor-moneys, or from their gospel and school lots, any portion of which is received by the trustees of a joint district, they are to apply such portion exclusively for the benefit of the parents of the children attending the school belonging to the town owning such fund. And the trustees should be careful *not* to apply any part of the money in their hands, coming from the common school fund belonging to a town, to the purchase of a library, or to any other purpose than the support of common schools.

DIVISIONS OF TEACHERS' MONEY INTO PORTIONS.

By subdivision 9 of § 82, (No. 103,) trustees are authorized "to divide the public moneys received by them, whenever authorized by a vote of their district, into not exceeding four portions for each year; and to assign and apply one of such portions to each quarter or term, during which a school shall be kept in such district for the payment of the teachers' wages, during such quarter or term." Where no action is had on the subject by the district, trustees have the right to appropriate the public money in such proportions to the different terms as they may deem expedient. It is not essential that the public money should be paid exclusively for services rendered during the year in which it is received: if the whole amount received be applied during the year to the payment of the compensation of qualified teachers, it is immaterial whether such wages were earned wholly during that year, or in part the year previous. It is of frequent occurrence for teachers to commence their term in November or December, and end in the succeeding spring; and there is no impropriety or illegality in paying their wages for the whole term, wholly or in part, from the public money received after its close.

The teachers' money can be applied only to the benefit of such schools as are established by trustees of districts in pursuance of law.—*Com. School Dec.* 55.

Where any portion of the teachers' money is applied to the payment of the wages of a teacher not duly qualified, or is otherwise illegally appropriated, the trustees, under whose authority such expenditure is made, are personally liable to the district for the amount.—*Id.* 213.

ACCOUNT BOOKS.

Trustees are required by § 104 of the act of 1847, (No. 127,) to keep an account in a book to be provided for that purpose by them, from time to time, as shall be necessary, of all moneys received and paid out by them, in their official capacity; and a statement of all moveable property belonging to the district. This account and statement is to be entered at large and signed by them, at or before each annual meeting in their district. They should charge themselves on one page with the whole amount of money received by them, either from the Town Superintendent or on tax lists or rate bills, specifying particularly the source whence derived and the time when received; and on the opposite page credit themselves with the respective expenditures and payments, specifying particularly to whom, when paid, and for what purpose, and referring to the proper vouchers, on file, whenever practicable.

On another page they should make an accurate inventory of all the moveable property belonging to the district, such as the library of the district, stating the number of volumes and their condition, and giving a catalogue of the books, wherever a general reference cannot properly be made, as to the 1st, 2d, 3d, &c., series of the Harper Library, or Nos. 1, 2, 3, &c., of the Harper Library or

Family Library, &c., &c., and the furniture, appendages, and apparatus of the school-room, specifying each article. The whole to be followed by a certificate in the following form:

We, the subscribers, Trustees of District No. in the town *Trenton*, do hereby certify that the preceding, from page to page inclusive, contains a true and accurate account of all the moneys received by us for the use of said district, and of the expenditures thereof; and a correct statement and inventory of all the moveable property belonging to said district.

Dated this day of 18

A. B.
C. D   *Trustees.*
E. F.

LIBRARY MONEY.

The library money is to be paid over to, or on the order of, a majority of the trustees, on its appearing from the annual report that "the library money received at the last preceding apportionment was duly expended according to law, (in the purchase of books suitable for a district library, or in the purchase of maps, globes, black-boards or other scientific apparatus for the use of the schools, in the cases and in the mode prescribed by the late law, and which will be hereafter considered,&c.,) on or before the first day of October subsequent to such apportionment." The report must uniformly be accompanied with a catalogue of the books and apparatus, &c., purchased since the last preceding catalogue was furnished, and must state accurately the number of volumes, and their condition; and when the money has been expended in the purchase of apparatus, &c., the authority under which such expenditure has been made, and a full and particular inventory of the articles purchased, must be specifically reported.

II. THE CALLING OF ANNUAL AND SPECIAL MEETINGS.

Trustees have power to call special meetings of the inhabitants of their district liable to pay taxes, whenever they shall deem it necessary and proper. This power should be liberally exercised for the benefit of the district; and special meetings should be called by the trustees, whenever requested for a proper and legitimate purpose, by a respectable number of inhabitants. The trustees should act as a board, whenever such meetings are directed to be called; and they, or a majority of them, when all have been notified, may require the clerk of the district, either verbally or in writing, to give the necessary notices to the inhabitants. The object of the meeting should, in all cases, be specified in the notice. Where there is no clerk of the district, or he is absent or incapable of acting, any one of the trustees, designated by the board, may give the notices.

Where the time for holding the annual meeting has for any reason passed, without the election of officers, and neither the clerk nor acting trustees give the necessary notices for a special meeting, authorized by § 68 (No. 90,) within twenty days thereafter, any inhabitant of the district, qualified to vote, is authorized by § 66, (No. 88,) to notify such meeting in the manner provided by law, in case of the formation of a new district; and the officers chosen at any such special meeting hold their office until the next annual meeting.

III. ASSESSMENT AND COLLECTION OF DISTRICT TAXES.

This duty is one of the most difficult and perplexing devolved upon trustees; requiring for its proper and legal exercise a strict conformity to the statutes in form as well as substance. A careful examination and collation of their various provisions in this respect becomes indispensable. Any departure from the specific directions thus given is almost sure to subject the trustees to serious personal liability, for which no indemnity is provided, as well as to cause embarrassment and confusion in the affairs of the district generally.

In order to enable them to execute this portion of their duties with accuracy and ease, the several steps of the process will be distinctly and particularly pointed out; and such directions given as will, it is hoped, prevent all liability to error in its future performance.

I. GENERAL PROVISION.

The general duty of trustees under this head, is comprised in the 3d and 4th subdivisions of § 82, (No. 103,) and is as follows: "To make out a tax list of every district tax voted by any such meeting, (special, annual or adjourned,) containing the names of all the taxable inhabitants residing in the district at the time of making out the list, and the amount of tax payable by each inhabitant set opposite to his name and to annex to such tax list a warrant directed to the collector of the district, for the collection of the sums in such list mentioned.

2. TAX LIST WHEN TO BE MADE OUT.

By § 99, (No. 122,) "Every district tax shall be assessed, and the tax list thereof be made out by the trustees, and a proper warrant attached thereto, *within one month* after the district meeting in which the tax shall have been voted.

The reason of this provision is obvious. The inhabitants and property of school districts are constantly changing, and where a tax is voted for a specific purpose, it should be assessed only upon those for whose benefit it was voted. While the statute should, therefore, be strictly complied with whenever it can be, yet if a literal compliance is prevented by accident or unavoidable circumstances, the list may be made out after the expiration of the month or thirty days; as the statute is supposed to be directory, and similar to that in the case of the People vs. Allen, 6 Wendell, 486. The regulations of the Superintendent, on appeals, have allowed thirty days, within which any person aggrieved, in consequence of the proceedings of any district meeting, may appeal; and, as will hereafter be seen, twenty days' notice is required to be given by the trustees, in case a reduction is claimed, or an original assessment becomes necessary.

In the first case, if a copy of the appeal be served prior to the expiration of the month, and *before* the trustees have made their assessment, the time during which such appeal is pending is not to be computed as part of the month within which the tax list is to be made out, as the service operates as a stay of all proceedings in any way relating to or *consequent upon* the act complained of. Still the assessment, when made out, must have reference to the property of the district, as it existed at the expiration of the month. In the second case, the trustees should *make out* their tax list within the month, although they may not be able finally to *complete* it. They should, however, *within the first ten days* after the meeting at which the tax is voted, make out their assessment; so that if a reduction is claimed, or an original valuation is found to be necessary, they can give the twenty days' notice required by law, and complete their list by the expiration of the month.

Errors in tax lists and rate-bills have often been discovered after they were made out. If discovered within a month from the time the tax was voted, and nothing has been collected, the trustees may recall them, correct the error, and redeliver them to the collector. But after the expiration of the month, and after any tax had been, in whole or in part collected, they did not, previously to the act of 1839, (modified by the act of 1843,) possess the power of correction. In consequence they were exposed to prosecutions for slight and accidental errors which might have been easily corrected by parties who did not choose to take the more convenient and summary mode of appealing to the Superintendent. This is now effectually remedied by § 13 of the act referred to, (No. 133,) by which trustees may, with the approbation and consent of the state superintendent, correct and amend errors in making out any tax list or rate-bill which may be discovered prior to the expenditure of the amount therein directed to be raised, and may refund to any person any sum improperly collected in consequence of such error. By availing themselves of this provision, trustees may now protect themselves from vexatious suits. They need not wait for an appeal by any party aggrieved, but as soon as they become aware of the existence of any error, they should proceed at once to correct it, and to refund any amount improperly collected in consequence of such error.

3. HOW, AND UPON WHOM TO BE ASSESSED, AND FOR WHAT PROPERTY

Trustees are required by § 85 of the act of 1847, (No. 108.) to apportion taxes, "on all *taxable inhabitants* of the district, or *corporations* holding property therein." This provision includes, of course, all *actual residents* of the district; and is extended by § 87, (No. 110,) to "every person owning or holding any real property within any school district, who shall improve and occupy the same by his agent or servant," whether he resides in the district or not. They are also to apportion taxes "upon all real estate lying within the boundaries of such district, the owners of which shall be non-residents, and which shall be liable to taxation for town or county purposes, and shall be situated within three miles of the site of the school-house in such district." This includes *uncultivated and unimproved* lands owned by non-residents, and situated in the district; and is an extension of the power given by § 78 of the old act, which limited the lands of non-residents, subject to taxation, to those which were actually *cleared and cultivated.* The trustees may, in their discretion, omit to assess any tract or parcel of unoccupied non-resident land in their district, where the proportion of the tax payable therefor, would not amount to fifty cents. This provision is inserted to save the trouble of the subsequent proceedings rendered necessary in such cases, where so small a sum only can be finally collected.

The apportionment is also to be made according to the valuations of the taxable property which shall be owned or possessed by them, (the inhabitants of the district, &c. as aforesaid,) *at the time of making out such list;* within such district, *or partly within such district and partly in an adjoining district.*

Taking these provisions together, the following general principles may be deduced:

1. All the *actual inhabitants* of a district are taxable for the whole property, real and personal, owned or held by them *within the district.* Executors and administrators having *in their possession* or under their control the property of their testator or intestate, within the district are taxable therefor, in their representative capacity, *as* executors, &c.

2. They are also taxable for any real property owned by them, lying *partly within such district and partly in an adjoining district*—that is, for such property as *at the time of making out the tax list* is owned by them and intersected by the boundaries of the district. In this respect the old law is not substantially altered. Nor is it in any sense material when the *title* of the owner to the whole or any part of the land so intersected accrued, whether before or after the organization of the district, so that it belonged to him *at the time of making out the tax list,* and is *then* intersected by the boundaries of such district. In such case, no matter what may be the respective proportions of the land owned

in each district, the owner is taxable for the *whole farm or property belonging to him, and which is connected and occupied as one farm in the district where he resides, only;* and being so liable there, he cannot, of course, be taxed for the same property in any other district.

The principles of law applicable to the taxation of school district purposes, of real estate intersected by the boundary line between two districts, are these: Each inhabitant of a school district is taxable, under § 85 act of 1847, (No. 108,) in the district where he actually resides "according to the valuations of the taxable property which shall be owned or possessed by him, at the time of making out such list, within such district, or partly within such district and partly in an adjoining district." This principle has been repeatedly recognized and asserted; and the only difficulty consists in its practical application to a class of cases supposed to come within the purview of a series of decisions made by Superintendents FLAGG and DIX, confining its operation to the period of the organization of the district. At page 24 of the volume of "Common School Decisions," Mr. FLAGG says, "The principle is, that where a line between two districts runs through a man's farm, he shall be taxed for the whole of his farm, in the district where his house stands, or where he resides." And he observes that on this point the law is clear, and that such has been the construction given it. "The same principle," he adds, governs the town assessments;" the provision of law in this respect being that "whe1e the line between two towns divides any occupied lot or farm, the same shall be taxed in the town where the occupant lives, provided he or she lives on the lot." At page 69, however, of the same volume he lays down the rule in the following terms: "Where a person purchased a lot in an adjoining district, along side of his farm, it was decided that he was taxable for the lot purchased, in the district where it was situated. If his farm had been interesected by the district line *when the commissioners formed it*, then he would have been assessed for his whole farm in the district where his house was situated; but the lot purchased is a distinct lot, and *the lines of districts cannot be changed by individual purchases.*" The same doctrine is asserted in a subsequent decision made by Gen. DIX, at page 128 of the volume referred to. These two decisions have been repeatedly over-ruled by subsequent Superintendents, upon the ground that they establish a criterion by which to determine the liability of property to taxation, in the class of cases under consideration, not recognized by the statute, viz: intersection by the boundary line of the district, *at the time of the formation of the district*, instead of at the *time of making out the tax list.* The language of the statute, in this respect, seems to be clear and explicit: "In making out a tax list, the trustees of school districts shall apportion the same on all the taxable inhabitants of the district, or corporations holding property therein, according to the valuations of the taxable property which shall be owned or possessed by them, *at the time of making out such list,* within such district, or partly within such district and partly in an adjoining district."

The owner or occupant of a farm, therefore, situated partly in two adjoining districts, is taxable in the district where he actually resides, for the whole farm, *provided he occupies or improves the whole as one farm, either by himself, his agents, or servants.* So if the owner of a farm situated wholly in one district, purchases a piece of land adjoining his farm, in another, and occupies the whole as one farm, it is taxable only in the district where such owner resides.

If, however, there is a *tenant* on that portion of the farm situated in a different district from that of the owner's residence, such *tenant* is taxable in the district where he resides, for so much of the property as he rents or leases.

This rule of taxation in no respect interferes, as has frequently been supposed, and as seems to be inferred from the tenor of the above named decisions of Messrs. Flagg and Dix, with the *boundaries* of the respective districts. *They* remain unaltered and unaffected ; so that if that portion of a farm situated in a district other than that of the owner's residence, should again be sold to an inhabitant of the district in which it is situated, it would again become taxable in that district. The rule is one simply of *taxation :* and no more interferes with the territorial organization of districts, than does the corresponding principle applicable to town assessments, with the boundary lines of towns or counties. It is based upon the injustice and inexpediency of requiring an inhabitant of one district to contribute to the expense of supporting the schools in another, merely because a part of his farm extends beyond the boundary line of his district, and operating, as it does, equally in every district, furnishes a guide to trustees in the assessment of taxes, which relieves them from much embarrassment and labor, otherwise unavoidable, in determining as to the relative value of detached portions of the same farm situated on either side of the boundary line of their districts.

3. All non-resident owners of real estate in the district, who improve and occupy the same by their agents or servants, are by § 87, (No. 110,) taxable therein for the property so owned, improved and occupied, in the same manner as though they actually resided therein. This provision is also to be construed in connexion with those above referred to, and is applicable in its full extent only to cases where the property so occupied is wholly situated in the district. Where it is situated partly in the district where the owner actually resides, it is taxable only in that district. And where it is situated partly in two or more districts, in *neither* of which the owner resides, *each districts must tax such owner only for the part actually within its boundaries.* It is also to be borne in mind that this class of cases is distinct from that in which the land is occupied by a *tenant*—and also from that in which it is so occupied by a person working it under a contract for a share of the produce of

such land. In each of these cases the actual possessor is to be taxed in the same manner as though he were the owner. See § 86, (No. 109.) and § 88, (No. 111.)

4. All real estate situate in a district, within three miles of the school-house therein, and owned by non-residents, not included in either of the above class of cases, is also liable to taxation, and forms the subject of the directions contained in § 89 to 95 inclusive, in the act of 1847, (Nos. 112 to 118, both inclusive.)

5. *Land* in the district belonging to *corporations*, whether cultivated or not, is taxable for school district purposes. The provision in the act of 1847, in this respect, produces a material alteration of the law as it formerly stood, and renders turnpike, railroad and plank road corporations taxable for so much of the land owned by them as is situated within the respective school districts through which their roads pass. Such corporations and all others, are to be regarded as residents of the districts where their principal place of carrying on business is situated, and non-residents elsewhere.

By a decree of the Chancellor of this state, 4th vol. Paige's Chan. Rep. 384, it has been decided that railroad "companies, whose stock, or the principal part thereof, is vested in the lands necessary for their roads, and in their railways and other fixtures connected therewith, are taxable on that portion of their capital as real estate in the several towns or wards in which such real estate is situated." They are, of course, taxable in school districts for common school purposes, on so much of such real estate as is included within the boundaries of those districts.

In the decree referred to, it was also decided that such real estate "is to be taxed upon its actual value at the time of the assessment, whether that value is more or less than the original cost thereof."

In ascertaining the value of so much real estate as is included within the boundaries of a school district, the trustees must, from the necessity of the case, be guided by the best evidence which it is in their power to obtain. They should ascertain from the assessment roll of the town the aggregate value of so much of the real estate of the company as is within the town. They should then ascertain whether the proportion of that value, in respect to the railway included within their district, is equal to the value of the whole of the real estate of the company included within another district, in which the length of the railway is the same. This cannot always be the case, for within the boundaries of one school district the company will have a depot, while it has none in another district. Within one school district the railway may have a double, while in another it may have but a single track. All these circumstances must be ascertained and taken into consideration by the trustees. If the company has in a school district nothing but its railway, and has a depot within the same town, then the value of the depot should be deducted from the valution of the real estate of the company on the last assessment roll of the town, as preliminary to a valuation of that part of the railway which is within the boundaries of such district.—*Com. School Dec.* 350.

The same principles are, in the main, applicable to plank road corporations.

Banks are taxable for common school purposes.—*Id.* 87.

Associations formed under the *general banking law* are *corporations*, and as such are liable to taxation on their capital.—1 *Hill's Rep.* 616; 3 *id.* 389.

By chap. 327, Laws of 1846, "*rents reserved in any leases in fee*, or for one or more lives, or for a term of yea s exceeding twenty-one years, and chargeable upon lands in any town or ward," ar to be "assessed to the person or persons entitled to receive the same as *personal estate*, at a principal sum, the interest of which, at the legal rate per annum, shall produce a sum equal to such annual rents; and in case such rents are payable in any other thing except money, the value of such annual rents in money shall be ascertained by the assessors, and the same shall be assessed in manner aforesaid." Trustees of districts are to include this species of property in their tax lists; and if no property can be found on which to levy, and the tax remains unpaid, the collector should return accordingly, and the trustees apply to the County Treasurer, who is required to issue his warrant to the Sheriff of the County where any real or personal estate of the person upon whom such tax is imposed, may be found, for the collection thereof.

PROCEEDINGS IN CASE OF UNOCCUPIED AND UNIMPROVED NON-RESIDENT LANDS.

Where any real estate within a district, liable to taxation, is unoccupied, the trustees, at the time of making out their tax list, are required by § 89 of the act of 1847, (No. 112,) whenever they impose a tax on such property, "to make out and insert in such tax list a statement and description of every such lot, piece or parcel of land so owned by non-residents therein, in the same manner as required by law from town assessors, in making out the assessment rolls of their towns." If the tax is returned by the collector unpaid, upon receiving from him an account thereof, with the descriptions of the property, as directed to be made, and the amount of the tax, together with an affidavit of the fact of non-payment, and of due diligence used for the collection, the trustees are to credit him with the amount, § 90, (No. 113,) to compare the account so rendered with the original tax list, certify to its accuracy, and transmit it, together with the collectors affidavit and their certificate, to the county treasurer, § 91, (No. 114,) who is to pay the amount so returned out of any moneys in the treasury raised for contingent expenses. § 92, (No. 115.)

Such county treasurer is to lay the account, affidavit and certificate before the board of supervisors, who are to cause the amount of such unpaid taxes, with seven per cent in addition, to be levied on the lands of the respective non-residents liable to pay the same; which amount, when collected, is to be returned to the county treasurer, to reimburse the amount so advanced, with the expense of collection. § 93, (No. 116.)

Any person whose lands are included in any such account, may pay the tax assessed thereon to the county treasurer, at any time before the board of supervisors shall have directed the same to be levied. § 94, (No. 117.)

The same proceedings are to be had for the collection of the amount so directed to be raised by the board of supervisors, as are provided by law in relation to taxes on non-resident lands generally; and upon a return to the comptroller of the arrears uncollected the amount is to be paid on his warrant to the county treasurer, and the state is to collect the same in the manner prescribed by law in respect to arrears of county taxes upon lands of non-residents. § 95, (No. 118.)

To enable the trustees better to perform the duties thus devolving upon them, that part of the Revised Statutes referred to in § 89, (No. 112,) and which is applicable, is hereto annexed:

"§ 11. The lands of non-residents shall be designated in the same assessment roll, but in a part thereof separate from the other assessments, and in the manner prescribed in the two following sections.

"§ 12. If the land to be assessed be a tract which is subdivided into lots, or be part of a tract which is so subdivided, the assessors shall proceed as follows:

"1. They shall designate it by its name, if known by one, or if it be not distinguished by a name, or the name be unknown, they shall state by what other lands it is bounded:

"2. If they can obtain correct information of the subdivisions, they shall put down in their assessment rolls, and in a first column. all the unoccupied lots in their town or ward, owned by non-residents, by their numbers alone and without the names of their owners, beginning at the lowest number and proceeding in numerical order to the highest:

"3. In a second column, and opposite to the number of each lot, they shall set down the quantity of land therein liable to taxation:

"4. In a third column, and opposite to the quantity, they shall set down the valuation of such quantity:

"5. If such quantity be a full lot, it shall be designated by the number alone; if it be a part of a lot, the part must be designated by boundaries, or in some other way, by which it may be known.

"§ 13. If the land so to be assessed be a tract which is not subdivided, or if its subdivisions cannot be ascertained by the assessors, they shall proceed as follows:

"1. They shall enter in their roll the name or boundaries thereof, as above directed, and certify in the roll that such tract is not subdivided, or that they cannot obtain correct information of the subdivisions, as the case may be:

"2. They shall set down in the proper column the quantity and valuation as above directed:

"3. If the quantity to be assessed be the whole tract, such description by its name or boundaries will be sufficient; but if a part only is liable to taxation, that part or the part not liable must be particularly described:

"4. If any part of such tract be settled and occupied by a resident of the town or ward, the assessors shall except such part from their assessment of the whole tract, and shall assess it as other occupied lands are assessed."

The residue of the sections relates to the making of a map which is supposed not to be applicable to trustees of school districts; if a map is already on file, the trustees might refer to it in aid of their descriptions.

4. VALUATIONS OF PROPERTY, HOW ASCERTAINED, AND MODE OF PROCEEDING WHEN REDUCTION IS CLAIMED.

The valuations of taxable property are to be ascertained, as far as possible, from the last assessment roll of the town, and no person is entitled to any reduction in the valuation so ascertained, unless he gives notice of his claim to such reduction to the trustees of the district before the tax list shall be made out.—§ 96, (No. 119.)

The assessment roll of the town, when signed and certified according to the provisions of the 26th section of title 2, chap. 13, 1 Revised Statutes, is to be deemed the last assessment roll of the town. By § 27, of the same title, this roll is to be delivered to the supervisor of the town on or before the first day of September in each year, to be by him delivered to the board of supervisors at their next meeting.

According to the opinion of the supreme court in 7 Wendell, 89, the roll is then to be deemed completed, so that the trustees may use it as the basis of their tax list. It is true that it may afterwards be altered by the board of supervisors, by increasing or diminishing the aggregate valuation of real estate of the town to make it correspond with that of other towns. But it is obvious this will not affect the proportion between the inhabitants of the same town, so that an assessment apportioned on either roll would be the same, so far as the real estate is concerned. Should the proportions be varied when real and personal estates are assessed to the same person, yet under the decision referred to, the tax list made out upon the assessment roll as completed by the assessors *before* any variation made by the supervisors would be valid. If any change is made by them, a subsequent tax list should vary also in the same particulars. Generally, the roll completed by the assessors will be a guide, but the trustees cannot be safe without recurring to the roll after its correction by the supervisors, as it has been held by the supreme court in the case above referred to, and in other cases, that if the tax list is made upon an assessment roll that is not the last valid one, the trustees will be personally liable.

The question is often raised, how far, and to what extent, the last assessment roll of the town is to be followed in the valuations of trustees in levying taxes. It is to be adopted as the sole guide, where a valuation has actually been made by the assessors on property, the condition of which remains substantially the same. But where improvements have been made on real estate which has thereby actually been enhanced in value since the last assessment roll was completed, or where any material change has occurred in the situation of the property, it is obvious that the last assessment roll ceases to be a standard of valuation. So, where an inhabitant acquires or parts with personal property, since the assessment roll was made out. And it is to be recollected that trustees are bound to follow the last assessment roll as far as possible, only with reference to the *valuations* of property. Where it has changed hands, they are to put the assessment to the present owner, adopting the valuation of the town assessors. Where, for instance, one inhabitant sells his farm to another, the trustees, in levying a tax, are to assess the farm to the vendee, at the valuation of the town assessors, where no substantial improvement enhancing its value has occurred in the mean time ; reducing, if the circumstances require it, the valuation of his personal property, by the amount paid or secured to be paid as the consideration money of the purchase, and increasing by the same amount the valuation of the personal estate of the vendor. In either of these cases, however, as an original valuation by the trustees in part would become necessary, the proceedings prescribed by § 97, (No. 120,) would be requisite. But where a mere exchange of real estate is effected, no change in the valuations should be made, unless in the cases above specified, of substantial improvements or alterations ; the names of the respective persons liable, only, requiring to be changed.

Where a reduction is duly claimed, and where, for any reason, the valuation of taxable property cannot be ascertained from the last assessment roll of the town, the trustees are required by § 97, (No. 120,) to "ascertain the true value of the property to be taxed from the best evidence in their power, giving notice to the persons interested, and proceeding in the same manner as the town assessors are required by law to proceed in the valuations of taxable property." The proceedings to be had in such cases are specifically and particularly pointed out in the following extract from the Revised Statutes as amended by chap. 176, laws of 1851 relating to the assessment of taxes. Substituting the word "trustees" for "assessors," wherever it occurs, the directions there given will afford a perfect guide in all proceedings under section 97. It has been decided by the Superintendent, *p.* 319 *Decisions*, &c. that the notice may be given by posting it in three public places. It is to be given in *all cases of variation* from the town assessment roll.

"§ 6, [Act. of 1851.] Whenever any person on his own behalf, or on behalf of those whom he may represent, shall apply to the assessors of any town or ward to reduce the value of his real and personal estate, as set down in their assessment roll, it shall be the duty of such assessors to examine such person under oath, touching the value of his or their said real or personal estate, and after such examination they shall fix the value thereof, at such amount as they may deem just, but if such person shall refuse to answer any question to the value of his real or personal estate, or the amount thereof, the said assessors shall not reduce the value of such real or personal estate. The examination so taken shall be written, and shall be subscribed by the person examined, and shall be filed in the office of the town clerk of the town or city in which such assessment shall be made, and any person who shall wilfully swear falsely on such examination before the assessors, shall be deemed guilty of wilful and corrupt perjury.

"§ 7. The assessors of the several towns and wards of this State, shall have power to administer oaths to any person applying to them under the provisions of the sixth section of this act.

"§ 17, (R. S.) All real and personal estate liable to taxation, shall be estimated and assessed by the assessors at its full and true value, as they would appraise the same in payment of a just debt, due from a solvent debtor."

After completing the assessment roll, section 19 provides that the assessors "shall make out one fair copy thereof, to be left with one of their number. They shall also forthwith cause notices thereof to be put up at three or more public places in their town or ward."

"§ 4. (Act of 1851.) "Such notices shall set forth that the assessors have completed their assessment roll, and that a copy thereof is left with one of their number, at a place to be specified therein, where the same may be seen and examined by any person interested, until the third Tuesday of August; and that on that day the assessors will meet at a time and place also to be specified in such notice, to review their assessments. On the application of any person conceiving himself aggrieved, it shall be the duty of the said assessors on such day to meet, at the time and place specified, and hear and examine all complaints in relation to such assessments that may be brought before them; and they are hereby empowered, and it shall be their duty, to adjourn from time to time, as may be necessary, to hear and determine such complaints; but in the several cities of this State, the notices required by this section, may conform to the requirements of the respective laws regulating the time and place and manner for revising the assessments in said cities, in all cases where a different time, place and manner is prescribed by said laws from that mentioned in this act.

"§ 5. If the assessors shall wilfully neglect to hold the meeting specified in the last preceding section, each assessor so neglecting shall be liable to a penalty of twenty dollars, to be sued for and recovered before any court having jurisdiction thereof, by the supervisor of the town, for the use of the poor of the same town; and in case of such neglect to meet for review, any person aggrieved by the assessment of the assessors may appeal to the board of supervisors, at their next meeting, who shall have power to review and correct such assessment.

"§ 21. The assessor with whom such assessment roll is left shall submit the same, during the twenty days specified in such notice, to the inspection of all persons who shall apply for that purpose."

It will be observed, that under the provisions of the act of 1847, (No. 108, § 85,) it is no longer necessary that the *agent* or *servant* of the non-resident owner should *reside on*, or "improve and occupy" land situated within the boundaries of the district, in order to render such non-resident owner liable to taxation; provided such land is taxable for town and county purposes, and is situated within three miles of the site of the school-house of the district in which it lies.

A non-resident owner is taxable for land occupied by an *agent;* but not, if occupied by a *tenant.* If the person living on the premises rents the land as tenant, such tenant is liable to be taxed for the premises so occupied by him.—*Com. School Dec.* 27. The principle of this decision is fully sustained by the supreme court in the case of *Dubois* vs. *Thorne*, 7 Wendell, 518, in which a lessee of a non-resident owner was held liable for a tax for a part of a lot, and two sub-tenants for the parts occupied by them respectively. The court observed that the mere ownership of the property, without occupation by himself, his agent, or servant, was not sufficient to charge the non-resident owner with the tax. As the law now stands, however, such ownership will be sufficient in the absence of any occupation by a *tenant.*

A *saw-mill*, having an agent or servant in charge of it, is taxable to the non-resident owner.—*Com. School Dec.* 82. So a factory unoccupied, is taxable to the non-resident owner.—*Id.* 100.

Where there is a known error in the town assessment, the trustees may correct it in the district assessment. For instance, if a resident of a district should purchase or sell a lot after the town assessment had been made, the trustees would be required to vary the district assessment accordingly. But where there is no change in the property of the district, and the valuation is a matter of opinion merely, the trustees must be guided by the last assessment roll of the town, even though in their judgment such property, or any portion of it, is worth more or less than the estimate put upon it by the town assessors.—*Com. School Dec.* 3.

Alterations by the trustees from the last assessment roll of the town, by reason of improvements subsequently made, in consequence of which the property assessed has become enhanced in value, should be made only where such improvements are *complete.*—*Id.* 194.

In assessing taxes in joint districts, the last assessment roll in *each town* must be followed, with respect to the taxable property within it, notwithstanding the standard of valuation adopted by the assessors of the respective towns may be different.—*Id.* 315. But e e § 72, (No. 194,) Laws, &c.

Trustees cannot assess an individual for personal property if he has been taxed for none on the last assessment roll of the town, on the *supposition* that he may have more than his debts amount to. The assessment roll of the town settles the matter, and the trustees cannot vary the amount but from some *knowledge* of an alteration after that roll was made out, or to correct some known and acknowledged error.—*Id.* 342.

Where land owned by the same person is situated in different districts in the same town, but all included under one assessment by the town assessors, if all the land is of the same *description*, and was actually valued at the same rate per acre, without any variation on account of improvements or otherwise; or if it appears on the roll at what rates the separate parts were valued,then the valuation of the portion situated in any particular district may be ascertained by the trustees from such last assessment roll. But if the valuation by the town assessor was *general*, and if the land was of different degrees of quality or value, or if a dwelling-house or other improvements are situated in one district and none in another, a new and original assessment must, in such case, be made by the trustees, giving the notices, &c., and proceeding in the mode required by law.—*Per* SPENCER, *Supt. Jan.* 1841.

Unless a reduction is claimed, or some departure from the last assessment roll of the town becomes necessary, trustees are not required to give notice of the assessment of a tax.—*Com. School Dec.* 40.

Land purchased after a tax is voted, but before the tax list is made out, must be assessed to the purchaser if he resides in the district.—*Id.* 8.

Persons leasing specific portions of a lot are to be taxed for so much as they lease.—*Id.* 16.

Persons about to remove from a district must be included in a tax list, if they are actually inhabitants when the list is made out. —*Id.* 66.

A store and *lot* must be taxed in the district in which they are *situated*, but goods in a store are to be taxed in the district in which the *owner resides*. Real estate is taxable where it lies, and personal property where the owner resides.—*Id.* 71, 86.

Bridge companies are taxable in the district where the tolls are collected.—*Id.* 74.

If a person owns two farms and the district line separates them, and they are *separately occupied*, he is liable to be taxed for each farm in the district where it lies. But if they are occupied as one farm, the whole is taxable only in the district where the owner resides.—*Id.* 81. *And see ante.*

The general rule is, that where a new district is formed, and the line intersects a farm, the *whole farm* is to be taxed in the district where the owner resides. *Separate tenancies* are, however, exceptions to this rule. When a part of a farm is leased, it ceases to be an entire possession, and the part so leased must, with regard to taxation, be considered as following the residence of the lessee or tenant.—*Id.* 103.

The vendor of a farm remaining in possession is liable for taxes assessed on it.—*Id.* 83.

Trustees are bound to know the condition of the taxable property of their district, so that in assessing taxes no person shall be improperly taxed.—*Id.* 108.

The toll-house and gate of a turnpike or bridge company, including a lot no more than sufficient for the accommodation of the toll-gatherer, are necessary appendages to the franchise, and taxable as *personal estate* in the district where the principal office of the company, for the transaction of its business, is situated.—*Id.* 135.

Two or more taxes voted at the same time may be included in the same tax list.—*Id.* 158.

If a taxable inhabitant sells his farm and remains in the district, he is liable to be taxed on the amount of the purchase money paid, or secured to be paid, as personal property, and the purchaser is taxable for the farm, according to its assessed value on the last assessment roll of the town.—*Id.* 285, 342.

Trustees must include in a tax list every taxable inhabitant residing in the district at the time the list is made out.—*Id.* 109, 342.

If, before a tax is assessed, the trustees ascertain that the whole amount voted will not be required, they may make out a tax list for a smaller sum.—*Id.* 342.

If an inhabitant removes from a district before the end of one month after a tax is voted, and *before the tax list is delivered to the collector*, he cannot be included in it; the tax list, while remaining in the hands of the trustees, not being complete, except in cases where notice is required to be given in pursuance of law.—*Id.* 357, *as subsequently modified by* YOUNG, *Superintendent.*

A tenant is taxable, whether a householder or not, for land occupied and improved by him. He may *board out*, and yet, if he hire the lot and improve it, as a tenant, he is taxable for it.—*Id.* 155.

The temporary occupancy of a house on a farm, by a person hired to work it by the month, does not, however, constitute such a *tenancy* as to subject such occupant to taxation for the farm. He can be regarded only as *agent* for the owner.—*Per* DIX, *Superintendent*, 1837.

Where a person, assessed for a greater number of acres than his farm contains, omits to claim a reduction when the tax is assessed by the trustees, he will not be relieved subsequently on appeal.—*Com. School Dec.* 341.

Trustees, guardians, executors and administrators are taxable in their representative character, where they reside, for all the personal estate and property in their possession, or under their control, belonging to the *cestuique trust*, ward, testator or intestate, whom they represent. By § 10, 1 R. S. 391, a deduction is to be made by the assessors for debts due from the individual assessed, in his representative character, as specified in § 27, 2 R. S. 87. It is in the power of such trustees, guardians, executors or administrators to claim a reduction under the provisions of § 79 of the school act, above referred to; and to reduce the amount of such assessment by a specification of the value of the property. The question whether the real owners of the property are to be directly or indirectly benefitted by the expenditure of the tax assessed upon it, does not appear to have been one of the considerations in the provisions above referred to, for it is manifest that the personal property in the hands of a trustee, guardian, &c., in Buffalo, is liable to be taxed there, although the real parties in interest may live in Albany. After the administration of an estate in the hands of an executor or administrator, upon the rendition and settlement of a final account of his proceedings, the personal property is of course no longer liable to taxation where he resides; but so long as it is in his possession, or under his control, it is so liable.—*Id.* 157, 230.

PERSONS AND PROPERTY EXEMPT FROM TAXATION.

By § 89, (No. 121,) the trustees, in assessing a tax for *building* a school-house, are to exempt any person set off to their district, *without his consent*, from any other district, within four years preceding the assessment of such tax, who shall have actually paid within that period, in the district from which he was taken, under a lawful assessment therein, a district tax for the same purpose. The burden of proof in this case undoubtedly rests with the person claiming the exemption, as the trustees can have no official knowledge of the fact.

This exemption does not extend to taxes for *repairs*, or for any other purposes than building a school-house.

By § 4 of chap. 13, 1 R. S. 379, (2d edition,) the following property is declared to be exempt from taxation:

1. All property, real or personal, exempted from taxation by the Constitution of this state or of the United States:

2. All lands belonging to this state or to the United States:

3, Every building erected for the use of a college, incorporated academy or other [incorporated] seminary of learning; every building for public worship; every school-house, court-house and jail; and the several lots whereon such buildings are situated, and the furniture belonging to each of them:

4. Every poor-house, alms-house, house of industry, and every house belonging to a company incorporated for the reformation of offenders, and the real and personal property belonging to or connected with the same:

5. The real and personal property of every public library:

6. All stocks owned by the state or by literary or charitable institutions:

7. The personal estate of every incorporated company not made liable to taxation on its capital by law:

8. The personal property of every minister of the gospel or priest of any denomination; and the real estate of such minister or priest, when occupied by him; provided such real and personal estate do not exceed the value of $1,500. If such real and personal estate, *or either* of them, exceed the value of $1,500, that sum is to be deducted from the valuation of the property of such minister, and the residue is liable to taxation:

9. All property exempted by law from execution.

The land owned by a minister of the gospel, if *rented,* can be taxed to the tenant. It is exempt from taxation to a certain extent, only *when occupied by such minister.* If, however, the occupant is the *agent* merely of the minister, so as to render it necessary to make out the assessment against the latter as owner, the property is then exempt.

Land *occupied* by a minister of the gospel as *tenant,* has been held exempt to the amount of $1,500, under the provision above quoted.—*Com. School Dec.* 61.

6. WHEN TAXES MAY BE IMPOSED BY TRUSTEES WITHOUT BEING SPECIFICALLY VOTED.

By § 109 of the act of 1847, (No. 129,) "When the trustees of any school district are required or authorized by law, or by vote of their district, to incur any expense for such district, and when any expenses incurred by them are made by express provision of law a charge upon such district, they may raise the amount thereof by tax, in the same manner as if the definite sum to be raised had been voted by a district meeting, and the same shall be collected and paid over in the same manner."

By § 104 of the act of 1847, (No. 127,) the trustees are required to purchase two blank books, for the purposes specified in that section, and by sub. 1. of §81, (No. 102,) a book is to be provided for recording the proceedings of the district. The trustees will be justified in imposing a tax, or adding to the amount of any voted by the district, for the expenses of these books.

By § 105, as amended by chap. 382, Laws of 1849, "When the necessary fuel for the school of any district shall not be provided, by means of a tax on the inhabitants of the district *or otherwise,* it shall be the duty of the trustees of the district to provide the necessary fuel, and levy a tax upon the inhabitants of the district to pay for the same."

The inhabitants of the district sending to school may, *by voluntary arrangement,* furnish their respective proportions of fuel, according to the number of children and the length of time they send, but they cannot be *compelled* to do so *by a vote of the district;* and where no *tax* is voted for the supply of fuel, and no arrangement of this kind voluntarily entered into and carried into effect by those sending to school, it becomes the duty of the Trustees, under the above provision, to furnish the necessary fuel and to levy a tax upon the district therefor.

7. *Form of a District Tax List to raise any tax voted or charged on a District, and of a Warrant for its collection.*

List of Taxes apportioned by the Trustees of District No. in the town of Trenton, on the taxable inhabitants of the said district, and corporations holding property therein, and upon real estate lying within the boundaries of such district, the owners of which are non-residents thereof, for the purpose of raising the sum of laid and charged on the said district, according to law.

Names of inhabitants and Corporations.	Amount of Taxes.
James Thomas,.............	$6 00
The President, Directors and Company of the Bank of Utica	60 00
James Thomas, executor of the Estate of John Thomas, deceased,..................	50 00

Statement and description of unoccupied and unimproved Lands of non-residents of said district, upon which a tax has been imposed as above stated.

No. and descriptions of lots and parts of lots.	Quant. of land therein liable to taxation.	Valuation of such quantity.	Amount of tax.
No. 17,...........	10 acres.	$25 00	$0 75
Southwest quarter of lot No. 23,........	2½ "	6 00	50
Tract not subdivided,.	5 "	10 00	0 62½
Or,			
Tract, the subdivisions of which cannot be ascertained, bounded north by lot No. 17, south by north line of A. B., east by lot 15, and west by town line.	"	"	"

To the Collector of School District No. in the town of *Trenten*, in the county of *Oneida*.

You are hereby commanded to collect from each of the taxable inhabitants and corporations named in the foregoing list, and of the owners of the real estate described therein, the several sums mentioned in the last column of the said list, opposite to the persons and corporations so named, and to the several tracts of land so described, together with five cents on each dollar thereof for your fees, unless such amount is paid within two weeks from the receipt of this warrant, in which case you are to retain one per cent. only as your fees; and in case any person, upon whom such tax is imposed, shall neglect or refuse to pay the same, you are to levy the same by distress and sale of the goods and chattels of the person or corporation so taxed, in the same manner as on warrants issued by the board of supervisors to the collectors of towns; and you are to make a return of this warrant within thirty days after the delivering thereof to you; and within that time to pay over all moneys collected by virtue hereof, to the trustees of the said district, some or one of them; and if any tax on the real estate of a non-resident mentioned in the said list shall be unpaid at the time when you are required to return this warrant, you are to deliver to the trustees of the said district an account thereof, according to law.

Given under our hands this day of in the year one thousand eight hundred and forty

A. B.
C. D. } *Trustees.*
E. F.

By § 110 of the act of 1847, (No. 130,) it is not necessary for the trustees to affix their seals to any warrant.

8. WARRANTS FOR THE COLLECTION OF TAX LISTS AND RATE BILLS.

By various provisions of the school act (No. 131, 132,) it is provided that the warrant annexed to any tax list for the collection of a district tax or any rate bill for the payment of teachers' wages, shall command the collector, in case any person named in such list shall not pay the sum therein set opposite to his name on demand, to levy the same of his goods and chattels in the same manner as on warrants issued by the board of supervisors to the collectors of towns, except as hereinafter specified in relation to rate bills.

The time specified in any warrant, for its collection and return begins to run from the *delivery* of such warrant to the collector, and not from its date.—*Com. School Dec.* 286.

Where a warrant is signed by two trustees only, the presence or concurrence of the third will be presumed.—*Id.* 258.

Trustees in office only, can sign warrants.—*Id.* 275.

By § 112, 132, "If the sum or sums of money, payable by any person named in any tax list or rate bill, shall not be paid by him or collected by such warrant within the time therein limited, it may be lawful for the trustees to renew such warrant, in respect to such delinquent person; or in case such person shall not reside within their district, at the time of making out a tax list or rate bill, or shall not reside therein at the expiration of such warrant, and no goods or chattels can be found therein whereon to levy the same; the trustees may sue for and recover the same, in their name of office.

Such renewal should be made at the earliest practicable period after the expiration of the time specified for the collection in the original warrant. It is not, however, necessary that it should be made *prior* to the expiration of such original warrant.

Any second or subsequent renewal of such warrant must be with the written approbation of the Town Superintendent endorsed thereon.

Trustess may legally renew the warrants of their precessors in office.—*Com. School Dec.* 27.

Where a district meeting votes to renew a warrant and collect a tax, the trustees may regard it as an original vote, and issue a new warrant for its collection.—*Id.*

By §100, as amended by the act of 1849 (chap. 382,) it is made the duty of the trustees, after the expiration of the thirty days allowed by law to deliver the tax list and warrant to the collector of the district, "and such collector is hereby authorized and directed, upon receiving his warrant, for two successive weeks, to receive such taxes as may be voluntarily paid to him; and in case the whole amount shall not be so paid in, the collector shall proceed forthwith to collect the same. He shall receive for his services, on all sums paid in as aforesaid, one per cent, and upon all sums collected by him after the expiration of the time mentioned, five per cent; and in case a levy and sale shall be necessarily made by such collector, he shall be entitled to travelling fees at the rate of six cents per mile, to be computed from the school house in such district."

IV. DUTIES OF TRUSTEES IN RELATION TO THE PURCHASE, CUSTODY AND SALE OF SCHOOL-HOUSES AND SITES, THE REPAIR OF SCHOOL-HOUSES, AND FURNISHING THEM WITH NECESSARY FUEL AND APPENDAGES.

1. PURCHASE, REPAIR AND CUSTODY OF SCHOOL-HOUSE.

By sub. 5, of § 82 of the school act, (No. 103,) it is made the duty of trustees, and they are empowered "to purchase or lease a site for the district school-house, as designated by a meeting of the district; and to build, hire, or purchase, keep in repair and furnish such school house with necessary fuel and appendages, *out of the funds collected and paid to them for such purpose.*"

If trustees undertake to remove a school-house, buy a lot for a site, or do any other act which they are not by law authorized to do without a vote of the inhabitants of the district, it is at their own peril. The inhabitants may ratify their proceedings by a subsequent vote; but if they do not choose to do so, the trustees are without remedy.—*Com. School Dec.* 41, 222.

But where the inhabitants of a school district have, by a vote to that effect authorized their trustees to make repairs or do any other lawful act, involving an expenditure of money, they will be required to save them harmless, provided they have acted in good faith. The inhabitants may always limit a contemplated expenditure by voting a specific sum for the purpose. But if they neglect to do so, and give a general direction to the trustees to go on and make repair, &c., without restricting the amount to be expended, the Superintendent will, on the refusal of the inhabitants after the work is done, to indemnify them, for their reasonable and *bona fide* expenditures, order a tax to be levied for the amount.—*Id.* 222.

By sub. 6 of § 82, above referred to, it is provided that the trustees shall have the custody and safe-keeping of the district school-house."

Questions have frequently arisen, as to the extent of the power conferred by this last subdivision; and to what uses the school house should be confined by the trustees.

The general principle in relation to questions of this nature arising in the several school districts, is this; that it is the duty of the trustess to exercise such a general supervision over the care and management of the district school-house, as that the instruction of pupils in the school shall not be embarrassed by any use of the house other than for school purposes; and that the property of the district, and the furniture, books, and papers belonging to the school, or the pupils, shall not be injured or destroyed. Any use of the house in subordination to these restrictions, and not inconsistent with the main purposes for which it was designed, must be left to the determination and pleasure of those to whom it belongs, whose wishes and directions, in this respect,the trustees are bound to carry out. The school-house is the property of the district, and subject to its control, within the limitations of the law. The purpose for which it was erected must be pursued, and nothing can be suffered to interfere with that. But when that purpose is accomplished, there is neither reason nor law for prohibiting its application to any object of social or moral improvement which the majority of the inhabitants may sanction. Upon this principle, and subject to the restrictions and limitations referred to, it may be used, out of school hours, and when not wanted for any district purposes, for religious meetings, Sunday schools, lectures, debating societies, or any other moral, literary, or useful purpose, with the approbation of a majority of the district and the consent of the trustees, or any two of them.

Trustees cannot, however, allow *any part* of the district school house to be occupied for any other purpose than that of the district school, while such school is actually in progress.—*Com. School Dec.* 51.

Select or private schools will not be permitted to be kept in the district school-house.—*Id.* 119.

Except in extraordinary cases, schools must be kept in the district school house: and by §120 of the act of 1847, (No. 140,) "Whenever it shall be necessary, for the accommodation of the children in any district, the trustees may hire temporarily any room or rooms, for the keeping of schools therein; and the expense thereof shall be a charge on such district."

If there is no school-house in the district a school cannot be opened by the trustees until the inhabitants have designated the place.—*Com. School Dec.* 190.

2. SALE OF SCHOOL HOUSE AND SITE.

A very important branch of the duties incumbent upon trustees, is that which relates to the disposition of the school-house and site, when no longer required for district purposes. By §74, of the of act 1847, (No. 96,) the inhabitants of the district are authorized, whenever the site of the school-house has been legally changed, to direct the sale of the former site, together with the buildings and appurtenances, or any part thereof at such price and upon such terms as they shall deem most advantageous to the district. In this case the trustees act merely as the ministerial officers of the district, and are bound to carry out the directions of the inhabitants. They are to execute the necessary conveyances to the purchaser; and when a credit is directed to be given for any portion of the consideration money, they are to take, in their corporate name, such security, by bond and mortgage or otherwise, as they may think proper; to hold the same as a corporation, and account to their successors; and they are also authorized, in their name of office to sue for and recover the moneys due and unpaid upon any security so taken by them, or their predecessors, with interest and costs. They are by § 75 to apply the moneys arising from such sale to the expenses incurred in procuring a new site, and in removing or erecting a school-house, so far as such application shall be necessary.

V. THE EMPLOYMENT OF TEACHERS AND THEIR PAYMENT, AND THE MAKING OUT AND COLLECTING OF RATE BILLS.

1. CONTRACTS WITH TEACHERS.

By sub. 7 of § 82, No. 103, trustees are "to contract with and employ all teachers in the district."

The most fruitful source of difficulty in school districts, has been the looseness and irregularity with which these contracts have been made. In some districts the trustees are in the habit of agreeing to pay the teacher the whole amount of public money that should be received, be it more or less. This is unjust to the teacher or the district, and has almost always led to contention. The agreement should be to pay him a specific sum by the month or by the quarter, adequate to the value of his services. If the public money is not sufficient, the deficiency should be supplied by a rate-bill. It is not to be believed that any intelligent citizens will consider that sordidness to be economy, which prefers that their children should be brought up in ignorance, or instructed in error, rather than contribute the mere trifle which will secure them an education, sound and accurate, at least as far as it goes. When the rewards which other professions and avocations hold out to talent, knowledge and industry, are so liberal, how can it be expected that persons competent to the great business of instruction, should devote themselves to it for a compensation inadequate to their support?

If the public money should be more than sufficient to remunerate the teacher, the trustees should consider whether they may not establish another school, or a district department. A large amount of public money indicates a large number of children, and of course there will be the materials for a large school, or for more than one, especially if they are of a character to command respect and inspire confidence.

Should there be a surplus of public money, after paying a fair and just equivalent to the teachers who can be usefully employed, the district will always be relieved from the consequence of not expending the whole, upon application to the Superintendent.

It is the duty of trustees of a school district to have a school kept in the district school-house, wherever there are a number of children to attend sufficient to defray the expenses of a teacher: and if a portion of the public money has been assigned to each portion of the year, then it is their duty to have a school kept whenever the expense can be defrayed by the public money, and the rate-bills against those sending children to the school. This principle is applicable as well to summer as to winter schools. Trustees are bound to provide a school, whenever requested by any portion of the inhabitants of the district, able and willing, with the help of the public money or otherwise, to defray its expense: and in this respect they are not to be governed or controlled by any vote of the district. The very object and business of their office is to provide schools; and no district meeting can abridge their powers, or relieve them from the performance of their duty in this respect.—*Per* SPENCER, *Supt. on appeal.*

A practice prevails to a very considerable extent among the several school districts, of trustees' engaging with a teacher that he shall board with the parents of the children alternately. There is no authority for such a contract, and it cannot be enforced on the inhabitants. This compulsory boarding gives occasion to constant altercation and complaint, which often terminates in breaking up the school. The best arrangement is to give the teacher a specific sum and let him board himself. But there are some districts so destitute that it may afford the inhabitants considerable relief to be permitted to board the teacher. In such cases the object can be obtained in another way. Let the trustees contract with the teacher at a specific sum per month, or by the quarter, and they may then agree with him, that if he shall be afforded satisfactory board at the house of any of the inhabitants, he will allow whatever sum may be agreed on per week for such board, to be applied to his wages, and will give an order on the trustees for the amount, to the person with whom he boards: and the trustees may then accept such order from the inhabitants, as payment to that extent upon his tuition bill, and deduct it from the amount to be paid the teacher, after having paid him the whole of the public money.

It is strongly recommended that all contracts with teachers be made in writing, and a duplicate kept by each party. In no other way can justice be done to the parties in case of any dispute.

The power of the trustees to contract with and employ teachers, cannot be controlled by the inhabitants; although it should never be exercised, unless under very peculiar circumstances, in opposition to the known wishes of a decided majority of the district.

Contracts by trustees of school districts for teachers' wages are binding on them personally, individually and collectively, while they remain in office; and on their successors after the expiration of their term: and trustees who are not in office, as such, are no longer personally answerable on such contracts. See 7 *Wendell*, 181, 4 *Hill; Com. School Dec.* 191, 282.

A contract made by all the trustees of a district, but signed by two only, is binding upon all; and the presence or concurrence of the third will be presumed from the signature of the remainder. So two trustees may enter into a contract, in the absence of the third, if he was duly notified of a meeting for that purpose, or was consulted, and refused to act.—*Mc Coy* vs. *Comtree*, 9 *Wend.* 17. In short, so far as the rights of third persons are concerned, a contract made by a majority of the trustees will be regarded as *prima facie* valid and obligatory. The party with whom the contract has been entered into is not bound to enquire whether the requisite preliminary steps to authorize the majority to act without the presence or concurrence of the third trustee have been taken or not.

If a teacher's certificate is annulled, the trustees are at liberty to dismiss him, and to rescind their contract with him. They engage him as a qualified teacher, and the moment he ceases to be so, there is a failure of the consideration for the contract. If, however, the trustees continue him to the school after notice that his certificate has been annulled, it will be regarded as such a continuance of the contract that they will not be allowed at a subsequent period to dispute it.—*Com. School Dec.* 212.

2. MODE OF PAYING TEACHERS.

This is specifically provided for by § 82, (No. 103,) above referred to. By subdivision eight, the trustees are "to pay the wages of such teachers, when qualified, out of the moneys which shall come into their hands from town superintendents of common schools, so far as such moneys shall be sufficient for that purpose; and to collect the residue of such wages, excepting such sums as may have been collected by the teachers, from all persons liable therefor."

By subdivisions nine, ten, eleven, twelve, thirteen and fourteen, they are,

"To divide the public moneys received by them, whenever authorised by a vote of their district, into not exceeding two portions for each year, to assign and apply one of such portions to each term during which a school shall be kept in such district, for the payment of the teachers' wages during such quarter or term; and to collect the residue of such wages, not paid by the proportion of public money allotted for that purpose, from the persons liable therefor, as above provided.

"To exempt from the payment of wages of teachers, either wholly or in part, such indigent persons within the district as they shall think proper, in any one quarter or term, and the same shall be a charge upon such district:

"To certify such exemptions, and deliver the certificate thereof, to the clerk of the district, to be kept on file in his office:

"To ascertain, by examination of the school lists kept by such teachers, the number of days for which each person not so exempted, shall be liable to pay for instruction, and the amount payable by each person:

"To make out a rate-bill containing the name of each person so liable, and the amount for which he is liable, and to annex thereto a warrant for the collection thereof: and

"To deliver such rate-bill, with the warrant annexed, to the collector of the district, as directed by subdivision 14, of § 82, (No. 103,) and § 83, (No. 104.)

By § 84, of the same act, (No. 105,) "where by reason of the inability to collect any tax or rate-bill, there shall be a deficiency in the amount raised, the inhabitants of the district, in district meeting, shall direct the raising of a sufficient sum to supply such deficiency, by tax, or the same shall be collected by rate-bill, as the case may require."

In accordance with these several provisions, trustees of districts in making out their rate bills, will hereafter proceed as follows:

1. They will first ascertain the amount due to the teacher, under his contract, for the first quarter's services.

2. They will then apply so much of the public money as is applicable to the term, in diminution of such amount.

3. They will assess the balance upon each inhabitant who has sent to the school during the term, (including indigent persons) according to the number of children and of days sent by each, as appears by the verified list kept by the teacher, under the 104th section of the aforesaid act. (No. 127.)

4. They will then proceed to exempt, either wholly or in part, such indigent inhabitants as they may think proper for the payment of their proportion of such assessment, and certify the whole amount of such exemptions, and deliver the certificate thereof to the clerk of the district, to be kept by him.

5. They will then make out a rate bill against those exempted in part, for the balance remaining after such partial exemption, and against those not exempted either wholly or in part, for the collection of the amounts assessed against them respectively, and add their warrant, in the usual manner. Such warrants need not be under seal, and may be executed by the collector "in any other district or town, in the same manner, and with the like authority, as in the district for which he was chosen or appointed." (No. 126.)

6. The trustees will collect the amount of exemptions, as certified by them, by a tax, which they are authorized to impose upon all the taxable inhabitants of the district. They may immediately proceed to impose this tax; or they may add the amount to any tax thereafter imposed for district purposes, as may be most convenient.

Trustees should exercise a liberal discretion in making exemptions in behalf of indigent inhabitants, so that the charge for tuition shall in no case be burdensome: while on the other hand, they should never allow the consideration of the trifling amount of the general tax for such exemption when levied upon the whole taxable property of the district, to tempt them into an unnecessary exercise of the powers confided to them.

To illustrate this proceeding more fully, let us apply the several steps necessary to be taken in ordinary cases. Suppose a teacher employed for the usual term of four months at $20 per month. The public money, including local funds, belonging to the district, and applicable to the term, either by the decision of a district meeting, as above specified, or by the determination of the trustees, is $40: the amount due the teacher for his quarter's services is of course $80, of which the trustees pay him $40 at once, from the public money, and take his receipt therefor. They then call upon him for his list, kept and verified according to the provisions of § 104, (No. 127,) and after having ascertained from such list, the number of days' attendance for which each person sending to school is liable, they will proceed to assess the respective proportions of the remaining $40, from each, according to the whole number of days and children sent. Thus if one inhabitant has sent four children for 104 days, he will be charged for 416 days, and so on. Suppose upon adding up the whole number of days thus ascertained, the total is found to be 4,000, for the average attendance of 40 scholars for the whole term: the proportion of $40 due for one scholar for each day, would be one cent: and this multiplied by the number of days each scholar attended, would give his proportion: and by adding the proportions of each belonging to the same family, the amount due from each person sending to school is ascertained. The trustees then make out an assessment in the following form.

Form of Assessment.

Assessment containing the name of each person liable for teachers' wages in district No. in the town of Trenton, for the term ending on the day of 185 , and the amount for which each person is liable.

Names of inhabitants sending to school.	Whole No. of days sent.	Amount of school bill.
John Jackson,........................	104	$1 04
James Johnson,.......................	416	4 16
Timothy Warner,......................	312	3 12
Peter Barney,........................	50	50
Solomon Kinney,......................	54	54
William Jones,.......................	416	4 16
John Dye,............................	104	1 04
William Johnson,.....................	104	1 04
Thomas Jones,........................	520	5 20
John Radcliff,.......................	520	5 20
James Tunicliff,.....................	520	5 20
John Simons,.........................	520	5 20
Joseph Williams,.....................	360	3 60
	3,120	$40 00

The assessment should be signed by the trustees and filed with the district clerk.

The next step is to exempt such indigent persons as the trustees may think proper, from the payment of the sums set opposite to their names, either wholly or in part. Suppose Peter Barney to be exempted wholly, and Thomas Jones and John Radcliff each from the payment of one-half the amounts assessed to them; the trustees will first make out a certificate, to be filed with the clerk of the district in the following form:

3. CERTIFICATE OF EXEMPTION.

We, the undersigned, trustees of District No. in the town of Trenton, do certify, that we have this day exempted Peter Barney from the payment of any share of the wages of the teacher employed in said district for the term ending on the day of 18 and Thomas Jones and John Radcliff each from the payment of one half the amount assessed to them respectively, as their share of such wages.

Dated this day of
18

A. B.
C. D. } *Trustees.*
E. F.

They will then proceed to make out their rate bill and warrant in the following manner:

Form of Rate Bill and Warrant.

Rate bill, containing the name of each person liable for teachers' wages, in District No. in the town of Trenton, for the term ending on the day of 185 and the amount for which each person not exempted, either wholly or in part, from the payment of such amount, is so liable, with the fees of the collector thereon.

Names of inhabitants sending to school.	Whole number of days sent.	Amount of school bill.	
John Jackson,............	104	$1 04	
James Johnson,...........	416	4 16	
Timothy Warner,..........	312	3 12	
Solomon Kinney,..........	54	0 54	
William Jones,............	416	4 16	Paid to teacher.
John Dye,................	104	1 04	
William Johnson,..........	104	1 04	$3 paid to teacher.
Thomas Jones,............	520	2 60	
John Radcliff,............	520	2 60	
James Tunicliff,...........	520	5 20	
John Simon,..............	520	5 20	
Joseph Williams,..........	360	3 60	
	3,070	36 90	

To the Collector of School District No. in the town of Trenton, in the county of Oneida.

You are hereby commanded to collect from each of the persons in the annexed rate bill named, the several sums mentioned in the last column thereof, with five per cent for your fees, except on amounts paid in within two weeks after the receipt of this warrant at one per cent., and within thirty days after receiving this warrant to pay the amount so collected by you, into the hands of the trustees of said district, or one of them; and in case any person therein named shall neglect or refuse to pay the amount set opposite his name as aforesaid, you are to levy the same by distress and sale of the goods and chattels of such person, except such as are exempt by section twenty-two, article two, title five, chapter six, part three of the revised statutes from levy and sale under execution.

Given under our hands, this day of in the year of Lord one thousand eight hundred and

A. B.
C. D. } *Trustees.*
E. F.

There will still remain $3 10 of the amount due the teacher for his wages, being the amount of exemptions by the trustees; and this sum must be levied by tax on all the taxable inhabitants of the district and corporations holding property therein, in the same manner as though such amount had been actually voted by the district to be raised. If the teacher can wait upon the district, or the trustees choose to advance the money in its behalf, the amount may be added to the next tax that may be voted for district purposes. It should, however, be assessed within a reasonable time; and wherever the amount of exemptions is sufficient to warrant an immediate assessment, it should at once be levied. The trustees must exercise a sound discretion in this respect, with reference to the amount to be raised, and the probability of an early opportunity to add it to some district tax.

The following property when owned by any person being a house-holder is exempt from the operation of the collecter's warrant, on a *rate-bill*, viz:

"1. All spinning wheels, weaving looms and stoves put up, or kept for use in any dwelling house:

"2. The family bible, family pictures and school books used by or in the family of such person; and books not exceeding in value fifty dollars, which are kept and used as part of the family library:

"3. A seat or pew occupied by such person or his family, in any house or place of public worship:

"4. All sheep to the number of ten, with their fleeces and the yarn or cloth manufactured from the same; one cow, two swine, the necessary food for them; all necessary pork, beef, fish, flour, and vegetables actually provided for family use; and necessary fuel for the use of the family for sixty days:

"5. All necessary wearing apparel, beds, bedsteads and bedding for such person and his family; arms and accoutrements required by law to be kept by such person; necessary cooking utensils; one table; six chairs; six knives and forks; six plates; six teacups and saucers; one sugar dish; one milk-pot; one tea-pot and six spoons; one crane and its appendages; one pair of and-irons and a shovel and tongs:

"6. The tools and implements of any mechanic, necessary to the carrying on of his trade, not exceeding twenty-five dollars in value."

Sec. 22. *Chapter* 6. *Art.* 2. *Title* 5. *Part* 3. *Rev. Stat.*

Where a person agrees to pay for a certain number of scholars, he is entitled to the benefit of the public money in reduction of their school bills.—*Com. School Dec.* 83.

In making out rate-bills, inhabitants of districts can only be charged for so much time, as their children have actually attended school.—*Id.* 15.

All children attending the district school must be charged at the same rate for tuition, without regard to the studies pursued.—*Id.* 47.

A *resident* of a school district cannot be prosecuted by the trustees for the amount due on his rate-bill. The only remedy against him is by distress and sale of his goods and chattels.—*Id.* 254.

In the exercise of the power conferred upon the trustees, of exempting indigent inhabitants of their district from the payment of the whole or of portions of their rate-bills, the utmost liberality, compatible with justice to the district, should be indulged. Nothing can be more at variance with the benign spirit and intent of the school laws, than the compulsory distress and sale of articles of absolute necessity to an indigent family, for the purpose of satisfying the rate-bill for teachers' wages. And yet cases of this kind are frequently brought to the notice of the department. Every reasonable facility should be afforded to the children of the poor, for the attainment of all the blessings and advantages of elementary instruction: and this should never be permitted to become in any degree burdensome to their parents. Where any inhabitant of the district in indigent circumstances cannot meet the rate-bill for the payment of the teachers' wages, without subjecting himself to serious embarrassment, or his family to sensible deprivation, he should promptly and cheerfully be exonerated. A just feeling of pride may reasonably be expected to preclude any from availing themselves of this exemption, unless under the pressure of absolute necessity; and occasional abuses of the privilege so accorded, are productive of less disastrous results, than a prevailing impression among the indigent inhabitants of a district, that their children can partake of the advantages of common school education, only at a burdensome charge to themselves, and by a sacrifice of the ordinary necessities and comforts of their families.

Indigent persons may be exempted from the payment of school bills, whether there is public money to be applied to the term or not.—*Com. School Dec.* 56.

The exemption of indigent persons from the payment of the wages of teachers is a matter of discretion with the trustees, not regulated by any specific restrictions, but entrusted to them to be disposed of in good conscience, with a just regard to the rights of all concerned.—*Id.* 241.

Trustees are the sole judges of the ability of the persons residing within their respective districts to pay their school bills.—*Com. School Dec.* 254.

The wages of an unqualified teacher must be collected by rate-bill against those sending to school, in the same manner as though he held a certificate, provided he was duly employed by the trustees. —*Id.* 61, 76, 213.

The wages of two teachers, employed for different terms, or different portions of the same term, at different rates of compensation, cannot be included in one rate-bill.—*Id.* 168, &c.

Trustees cannot transfer to teachers the right of enforcing the collection of their wages. If the teacher agrees to collect his own wages, it is right that he should do so, to the extent of his ability; but in case of failure, the trustees alone can issue a rate-bill and warrant; and they should do so notwithstanding any agreement to the contrary with the teacher.—*Id.* 288 ; *Per* DIX, *Sup't.*

Trustees cannot include in a rate-bill any other object than the *wages* of the teacher under the contract made by them.

Where a person had from charitable motives, taken a poor family to reside with him, in his house, the children of which attended the district school, it was held that he was not liable for the tuition of such indigent children, unless they were sent to school by him under an express or implied contract to be responsible for such tuition ; and that if sent by their parents, or if they attended school of their own accord, the trustees should exempt the parents from payment of the tuition bill.—*Per* SPENCER, *Supt.* 1840.

A grandfather is not *prima facie* liable for the board or schooling of a grandchild. He may, however, *become* liable, in the same manner and to the same extent as any individual who has a youth residing with him whom he supports and suffers to go to school, without giving any particular directions on the subject. An implication would arise that it was by his assent. But the father or mother is *prima facie* liable : and some positive acts on the part of the grandfather must be shown, amounting to an assumption of liability on his part before he can be held responsible for the payment of tuition under such circumstances.—*Id.* 1841.

SCHOOLS FOR COLORED CHILDREN.

By § 147 of the act of 1847, (No. 179,) a school for colored children may be established in any district, with the approbation of the commissioners, which is to be under the charge of the trustees of the district in which such school is established. Trustees in their annual reports are also required particularly to specify the number of such children over four and under twenty-one years of age attending such school from different districts, naming such districts respectively, and the number from each attending for four months, and instructed by a duly qualified teacher, which report is to form the basis of an apportionment to such school, of a share of the public money.

The provisions contained in this section are more particularly applicable to those cities and large villages where no special legal provisions have been made for the instruction of colored children. The means provided, are it is true, altogether insufficient to meet the expense which must necessarily be incurred in the organization of these schools ; and inasmuch as the class of community for whose special benefit they are intended are generally unable to contribute to such expense, in any considerable degree, the object in view can seldom be fully attained, but through the efforts of charitable and benevolent individuals in the several districts, from which the colored schools are composed. These efforts have hitherto been paralyzed from the absence of any legal power to effect the necessary organization; and the provision now made was, doubtless, intended to supply that defect, and to furnish a nucleus around which the benevolent exertions of the friends of education and humanity might be concentrated. If, however, in any of the country districts, a colored school can be organized and efficiently kept up for the requisite length of time, it is hoped no efforts will be spared to carry into effect the provisions of the section. Colored children are entitled equally with all others, to the privileges and advantages of the district school; and wherever they can be grouped together in a separate school, under the charge of a competent teacher, they will be far more likely to derive the full benefits of such instruction as may be best adapted to their circumstances and condition, while at the same time, the disadvantages inseparable from their attendance at the district school, will be avoided.

Trustees have power, with the assent of the Town Superintendent, and by a vote of the inhabitants of their district, to purchase, hire or build a school-house or room for the accommodation of the colored children of their own and other adjoining districts; to supply the same with the necessary furniture, fuel and appendages; and to employ a competent teacher.

By § 104, of the act of 1847, (No. 127,) the trustees of each district are to provide a book, in which the teachers are to enter the names of the scholars attending school, and the number of days they shall have *respectively* attended, and also the number of times the school has been inspected by the Town Superintendents. This list is to be verified by the oath of the teacher.

None but children residing in a school district can of right be benefitted by the public money. Indeed, the trustees can exclude all children, except those who are residents of the district, from the school. But if such non-resident children are permitted by the trustees to attend the school, their parents should be apprised of the conditions on which they are received; and one of these conditions may be, that part of the public money shall be applied for their benefit. Where no such conditions however are exacted by the trustees, and such non-resident children are admitted on the application and responsibility of an inhabitant of the district, the trustees must make out the rate bill against such inhabitant in the usual manner.

Children of non-resident parents coming into a district and *boarding* for the purpose of attending school therein, are not entitled to any share of the public money in reduction of their rate bills; and their tuition, in such case, may be charged, in the first instance, to the person with whom they board; whose liability therefor can be discharged only by express notice to the trustees, that he declines being accountable for such tuition. Where, however, such children are *hired* to labor or service in the family of an inhabitant of the district, or are regarded and treated as *part of the family* of such inhabitant and not as mere temporary *boarders*, they are entitled to participate equally with the other children of the district, in the public money.—*Per* YOUNG, *Sup't.* 1842.

Trustees cannot refuse admittance in the school to any child whose residence is in the district, if such child complies with the reasonable and proper regulations of the school.—*Com. School Dec.* 47.

No child residing in a school district can be excluded from the school on account of the inability of the parents to pay his tuition.—*Id.* 119.

If a non-resident owner of taxable property in the district sends his children to the school in such district they should be permitted to attend, unless by their admission the school would become too crowded.—*Id.* 317.

All children residing in a district and attending the school, are entitled to participate in the public money, without reference to their ages.—*Id.* 34.

As a general rule, *all* under the age of twenty-one years, and of a proper age to be benefitted by instruction, are entitled to admission. There must, however, be some discretion vested in the trustees, in regard to such admission. Children having infectious diseases—idiots—infants—and persons over twenty-one, may undoubtedly be excluded; and colored children, where their attendance is obnoxious to the greater portion of the patrons of the school, especially in cases where schools have been established for their separate benefit, within a reasonable distance from their residence. —*Per* SPENCER, *Sup't.* 1841.

It is the duty of the trustees to co-operate with the teacher in the government of the school, and to aid him, to the extent of their power and influence, in the enforcement of reasonable and proper rules and regulations; but they have no right to dismiss a scholar, except for the strongest reasons; for example, such a degree of moral depravity as to render an association with other scholars dangerous to the latter, or such violent insubordination as to render the maintenance of discipline and order impracticable, in which case they may legally exclude him from the school, until such period as he may consent to submit to the reasonable rules and regulations of the teacher and trustees; and if after such exclusion he persists in attending, without permission from the Trustees, and contrary to their directions, he may be proceeded against as a trespasser.—*Per* DIX *and* MORGAN, *Sup'ts* 1837 *and* 1850.

VI. DUTIES OF TRUSTEES IN REFERENCE TO THE DISTRICT LIBRARY.

The trustees of each school district are constituted by law the trustees of the library. They are responsible for its preservation and care; and the librarian is subject to their direction, and may at any time be removed by them from office for wilful disobedience of such directions, or for any wilful neglect of duty, or even when they have reason to *apprehend* the loss of any books, or their injury or destruction by his misconduct. In case of such removal, or of a vacancy occurring from any cause, they are to supply such vacancy by appointment, until the next annual meeting of the district. They are personally liable to their successors for any neglect or omission in relation to the care and superintendence of the library, by which any books therein are lost or injured, to the full amount of such loss or injury, and their action in reference to its management, may be at any time controled by the department, on appeal.

By the 4th section of chap. 237, of the Laws of 1838, the sum of $55,000 from the annual revenue of the U. S. Deposit Fund, was required to be annually distributed "to the support of common schools, in like manner and upon the like conditions as the school moneys now are or shall hereafter be distributed, except that the *trustees* of the several districts shall appropriate the sum received to the purchase of a district library for the term of three years, (afterwards by § 6 of chap. 177, Laws of 1839, extended to five years,) and by the act of 1843, indefinitely, with the modifications therein expressed.

Trustees are, by this provision authorized to make the selection of the books for the library, as the application of the money is to be made by them.

The object of the law for procuring district libraries is to diffuse information, not only, or even chiefly, among children or minors, but among adults and those who have finished common school education. The books, therefore, should be such as will be useful for circulation among the inhabitants generally. They should not be children's books, or of a juvenile character merely, or light and frivolous tales and romances, but works conveying solid information which will excite a thirst for knowledge, and also gratify it, as far as such a library can. Works imbued with party politics, and those of a sectarian character, or hostility to the Christian religion, should on no account be admitted; and if any are accidentally received they should be immediately removed. Still less can any district be permitted to purchase school books, such as spelling books, grammars, or any others of the description used as text book in schools. Such an application of the public money would be an utter violation of the law. If any case of improper selection of books should come before the Superintendent, by appeal from any inhabitant, such selection would be set aside; and if it appeared from the reports, which according to these regulations must be made that such books had been purchased, the Town Superintendent will be bound to withhold the next year's library money from such district. These penalties and provisions will be rigidly enforced; for upon a faithful administration of the law the usefulness and the continuance of the system will depend. If the public munificence be abused it will unquestionably cease.

The selection of books for the district library, is devolved by law exclusively upon the trustees; and when the importance of this most beneficent and enlightened provision for the intellectual and moral improvement of the inhabitants of the several districts, of both sexes and all conditions, is duly estimated, the trust here confided is one of no ordinary responsibility. In reference to such selections, but two prominent sources of embarrassment have been experienced. The one has arisen from the necessity of excluding from the libraries all works having directly or remotely, a sectarian tendency, and the other, from that of recommending the exclusion of novels, romances and other fictitious creations of the imagination, including a large proportion of the lighter literature of the day. The propriety of a peremptory and uncompromising exclusion of those catch-penny, but revolting publications which cultivate the taste for the marvellous, the tragic, the horrible, and the supernatural—the lives and exploits of pirates, banditti and desperadoes of every description—is too obvious to every reflecting mind, to require the slightest argument. Unless parents desire that their children should pursue the shortest and surest road to ignominy, shame and destruction—should become the ready and apt imitators on a circumscribed scale, of the pernicious models which they are permitted and encouraged to study—they will frown indignantly on every attempt to place before their immature minds, works, whose invariable and only tendency is disastrous, both to the intellect and the heart.

The exclusion of works imbued to any perceptible extent with sectarianism, rests upon the great conservative principles which are at the foundation of our free institutions. Its propriety is readily conceded when applied to publications, setting forth, defending, or illustrating the peculiar tenets which distinguish any one of the numerous religious denominations of the day from the others. On this ground no controversy exists as to the line of duty. But it has been strongly argued that those "standard" theological publications which, avoiding all controverted ground, contain general expositions of Christianity—which assume only those doctrines and principles upon which all "evangelical" denominations of Christians are agreed, are not obnoxious to any reasonable censure, and ought not, upon any just principles, to be excluded from the school district library. There are two answers to this argument, either of which is conclusive. The one is, that the works in question, however exalted may be their merit, and however free from just censure, on the ground of sectarianism, are strictly *theological*, doctrinal or metaphysical; and therefore no more entitled to a place in the district library than works devoted to the professional elucidation of law, medicine, or any other learned professions. Their appropriate place is in the family, church or Sunday school library. The other answer is, that in every portion of our country are to be found conscientious dissenters from the most approved theological tenets of these commentators on Christianity; individuals who claim the right, either of rejecting Christianity altogether, (as the Jews,) or of so interpreting its fundamental doctrines, as to place them beyond the utmost verge of "evangelical" liberality; and this too, without, in any degree, subjecting themselves to any well-founded imputations upon their moral character as citizens and as men. The state, in the dispensation of its bounty, has no right to trample upon the honest convictions and settled belief of this or of any other class of its citizens against whose demeanor, in the various relations of society, no accusation can be brought; nor can it rightfully sanction the application of any portion of those funds to which they, in common with others, have contributed, to the enforcement of theological tenets to which they cannot conscientiously subscribe. Any work, therefore, which, departing from the inculcation of those great, enduring and cardinal elements of religion and morality which are impressed upon humanity as a part of its birth-right—acknowledged by all upon whom its stamp is affixed, however departed from in practice, and incorporated into the very essence of Christianity as its pre-eminent and distinctive principle—shall descend to a controversy respecting the subordinate or collateral details of theology, however ably sustained and numerously sanctioned, has no legitimate claim to a place in the school district library, nor can its admission be countenanced consistently with sound policy or enlightened reason.

The following general principles have been laid down in a special report on common school libraries, prepared under the direction of the department by Henry S. Randall, Esq., County Superintendent of common schools of Cortland county, and may be regarded as the settled principles of the department in reference to this class of books:

"1. No works written professedly to uphold or attack any sect or creed in our country, claiming to be a religious one, shall be tolerated in the school libraries.

"2. Standard works on other topics shall not be excluded, because they incidentally and indirectly betray the religious opinions of their authors.

"3. Works avowedly on other topics which abound in direct and unreserved attacks on, or defences of, the character of any religious sect; or those which hold up any religious body to contempt or execration, by singling out or bringing together only the darker parts of its history or character, shall be excluded from the school libraries.

"Is it said that under the above rules, heresy and error are put on the same footing with true religion—that Protestant and Catholic, orthodox and unorthodox, Universalist, Unitarian, Jew, and even Mormon, derive the same immunity? The fact is conceded; and it is averred that each is equally entitled to it, in a government whose very Constitution avows the principle of a full and indiscriminate religious toleration.

"He who thinks it hard that he shall not be allowed to combat, through the medium of the school libraries, beliefs, the sin and error of which are as clear to him as is the light in Heaven, will bear in mind that the library at least leaves him and his religious beliefs, in as good a condition as it found him. If it will not propagate his tenets, it will leave them unattacked. If he is not allowed to use other men's money to purchase books to assault their religious faiths, he is not estopped from expending his own as sees fit, in his private, or in his Sunday-school library—nor is he debarred from placing these books in the hands of all who are willing to receive them. His power of morally persuading his fellow men is left unimpaired; nor will he, if he has any confidence in the recuperative energies of truth—if he believes his God will ultimately give victory to truth—ask more. In asking, or condescending to accept the support of an earthly government, he admits the weakness of his cause, the feebleness of his faith. He leans on another arm than that which every page in the Bible declares all-sufficient. In what age of the world has any church entered into meretricious connexion with temporal governments, and escaped unsullied from the contact? Any approximation to such connexion, even in the minutest particular—any exclusive right or immunity given to one religious sect or another in the school library or elsewhere, is not only anti-religious, but anti-republican. As men we have the right to adopt religious creeds, and to attempt to influence others to adopt them; but as Americans, as legislators or officials dispensing privileges or immunities among American citizens, we have no right to know one religion from another. The persecuted and wandering Israelite comes here, and he finds no bar in our naturalization laws. The members of the Roman, Greek, or English church equally become citizens. Those adopting every hue of religious faith—every phase of heresy, take their place equally under the banner of the Republic—and no ecclesiastical power can snatch even 'the least of these' from under its glorious folds. Not an hour of confinement, not the amercement of a farthing, not the deprivation of a right or liberty weighing 'in the estimation of a hair' can any such power impose on any American citizen, without his own full an entire acquiescence."

With reference to the admission of novels, romances, and other works of the imagination, usually comprehended under the term "light reading," the proper course to be adopted cannot be better illustrated than by the following extracts from a report of the majority of a committee appointed by the Board of Commissioners of common schools of the city of Utica, understood to be from the pen of WILLIAM J. BACON, Esq., to examine the books in the school district library of the city, and to report, among other things, as to the character and tendency of any objectionable works they might discover therein.

"The importance of applying the funds provided by the state, with rigid regard to their appropriate object, is so weighty—and the temptations to misapply them, in consequence of a present prevailing fondness for light and equivocal literature, are so strong, that your committee deem it proper to enter somewhat into an examination of the principles which should govern those to whom is entrusted the responsible duty of making selections for school district libraries.

"A library for instruction is a very different thing from a library for amusement. The circulating library of a place of public resort for invalids or persons in pursuit of ease and pleasure, is essentially of a trifling character: the library of a college, or eminent public institute, is composed of graver and more elevated productions. While the book shelves of a light young man are filled with frivolous and amusing works, those of a student display the treasures of standard literature. School district libraries should not fall below the dignity of usefulness; in proportion as they do, they fail of fulfilling the true design of their institution.

"A consideration of the object of instituting these libraries will enable us to judge pretty correctly of the general character of books which should compose them; it is obviously, the information and improvement of the body of the people who can read, without reference to parties, sects, classes, callings, or professions. 'The primary object of their institution,' says the Superintendent who recommended it, 'was to disseminate works suited to the intellectual improvement of the great body of the people, rather than to throw into school districts for the use of young persons, works of a merely juvenile character.' It was, in the language of a succeeding Superintendent, 'to diffuse information—not only, or even chiefly, among children or minors—but among adults and those who have finished their common school education.' It was, in short, to provide a supplemental source of instruction to those on whom the common school has exhausted its more limited means.

"Improvement and information, then, form the main object of these libraries. It is only thus that they become the proper subjects of public munificence. Entertainment, simply as entertainment, is not to be regarded in making selections for the school district library. It is no part of our public policy to provide amusements for the people. In this particular we have improved not only on antiquity, but on many modern governments, by substituting, in the place of vain and wasteful public shows and frivolities, those more substantial and elevating subjects of public bounty, which consist in permanent and wise institutions, designed to fit our citizens for the proper discharge of their duties as members of a great community, whose duration and prosperity depend upon the knowledge and virtue of the people.

"We first teach the children of the republic to read, and to appreciate instruction. We lead them to thirst for information, and then seek to open the fountains which may satisfy that thirst. The common school is the first step in their advancement—the school district library is partially designed to be the second. It supplies information of a more varied and extensive sort—and if that information comes clothed in allurements of a virtuous, or entertainment of an innocent character, it is the more welcome on that account. These are mere incidents, however—when they appear alone, they want that substantial recommendation which is necessary to secure their introduction into the school district library. Books designed for amusement simply—to while away a vacant hour, and be forgotten like ephemera—are evidently no worthy occupants of the shelves of such a library. There is enough which is instructive and substantial to exhaust the public liberality, without squandering the well-meant beneficence of the state in transient and trivial publications, which amuse to-day and to-morrow are rubbish. 'The books, therefore,' says one of the Superintendents before quoted, 'should be such as will be useful among the inhabitants generally. They should not be children's books, or of a juvenile character, or light and frivolous tales and romances; but works conveying solid information, which will excite a thirst for knowledge, and also gratify it, as far as such a library can.'"

The following remarks from the annual report of the Superintendent of common schools, for the year 1844, will exhibit more fully the view taken of this branch of the subject by the department:

"There is reason to apprehend that the officers charged with the duty of selecting books for these libraries have too generally failed to appreciate the importance of a suitable provision for the intellectual and moral wants of the *children* of the district. Much misapprehension has existed on this subject, in consequence of the general prohibition, contained in the instructions heretofore communicated from this department, against the introduction into the school libraries of books of 'a *merely juvenile* character.' The true principles upon which the selections for these institutions should be made, may be clearly inferred, as well from the original design of the appropriation, as from the contemporaneous exposition of the Superintendent, under whose immediate auspices it was first carried into effect. The distribution of the fund provided for this purpose, was directed by the act under which it was supplied, to be made 'in like manner and upon the like condition as the school moneys are now or shall hereafter be distributed, except that the trustees of the several districts shall appropriate the sum received to the purchase of a district library.' The amount of library money, therefore, under this provision, to which each district became entitled, was in proportion to the *number of children* between the ages of five and sixteen, residing therein, compared with the aggregate number in all the districts, and not in proportion to the adult population merely, or the whole population combined. The primary object of the institution of district libraries, was declared in the circular of Gen. Dix accompanying the publication of the act of 1838, to be 'to disseminate works suited to the intellectual improvement of the great body of the people, rather than to throw into school districts for the use of the young, *books of a merely juvenile character*; and that by collecting a large amount of useful information, where it will be easily accessible, the influence of these establishments can hardly fail to be in the highest degree salutary to those who have finished their common school education, as well as to those who have not. The object in view will probably be best answered by having books suitable for all ages above ten or twelve years, though the proportion for those of mature age ought to be by far the greatest.' When it is considered that the foundations of education are laid during the period of youth, and that the taste for reading and study is, with rare exceptions, formed and matured at this period, if at all, the importance of furnishing an adequate supply of books, adapted to the comprehension of the immature but expanding intellect—suited to its various stages of mental growth, and calculated to lead it onward by a gradual transition, from one field of intellectual and moral culture to another, cannot fail to be appreciated. And even if the intellectual wants of many of the inhabitants of the districts, of more mature age, are duly considered, it admits of little doubt that a due proportion of works of a more familiar and elementary character than are the mass of those generally selected, would have a tendency not only to promote, but often to create that taste for mental pursuits which leads by a rapid and sure progression to a more extended acquaintance with the broad domains of knowledge. Those whose circumstances and pursuits in life, have hitherto precluded any systematic investigation of literary subjects, and who, if they possessed the desire, were debarred the means of intellectual improvement now brought within their reach, can scarcely be expected to pass at once to that high appreciation of useful knowledge, which the perusal of elaborate treatise on any of the numerous branches of science or metaphysics requires; and the fact brought to view by the annual reports of the County Superintendents, that by far the greater proportion of the inhabitants of the several districts neglect to avail themselves of the privileges of the library, indicates too general a failure, to supply these institutions with the requisite proportion of elementary books.

"In the selection of books for the district libraries, suitable provision should be made for every gradation of intellectual advancement; from that of a child, whose insatiable curiosity eagerly prompts to a more intimate acquaintance with the world of matter and of mind, to that of the most finished scholar, who is prepared to augment his stock of knowledge by every means which may be brought within his reach. The prevalence of an enlightened appreciation of the requirements of our people in this respect, has already secured the application of the highest grade of mental and moral excellence to the elementary departments of literature: and works adapted to the comprehension of the most immature intellect, and at the same time conveying the most valuable information to more advanced minds, have been provided—wholly free, on the one hand, from that puerility which is fit only for the nursery, and on the other, from those generalizations and assumptions which are adapted only to advanced stages of mental progress. A more liberal infusion of this class of publications, sanctioned by the approbation of the most experienced friends of education into our district libraries, would, it is confidently believed, remove many of those obstacles to their general utility, which otherwise are liable to be perpetuated from generation to generation."

It is the duty of the trustees to provide a plain and sufficient case for the library, with a good lock, if the district shall have neglected to do so. They are also to cause the books and case to be repaired as soon as may be, when injured; and to provide sufficient wrapping paper to cover their books, and the necessary writing paper to enable the librarian to keep minutes of the delivery and return of books. These are proper expenses for the preservation and repair of the books, and are to be defrayed by a tax on the district, which is to be added by the trustees to any tax voted by a district meeting. It is not necessary that the tax to defray these expenses should be voted by the inhabitants of the district; it is to be assessed and collected in the same manner as a tax for building or repairing a school-house, or to furnish it with necessary fuel and appendages.

The trustees of each school district are required, at the time of making their annual reports, to deliver to the Town Superintendent of common schools of their town, a catalogue containing the titles of all the books in the district library, not previously reported, with the number of volumes of each set or series, and the condition of such books, whether sound, or injured, or defaced. This catalogue must be signed by them and by the librarian.

Trustees are authorized by the regulations of the Superintendent in pursuance of law, to impose the following fines:

1st. For each day's detention of a book beyond the time allowed by the regulation, six cents, but not to be imposed for more than ten days' detention.

2d. For the destruction or loss of a book, a fine equal to the full value of the book, or of the set, if it be one of a series, with the addition to such value of ten cents for each volume. And on the payment of such fine, the party fined shall be entitled to the residue of the series. If he has also been fined for detaining such book, then the said ten cents shall not be added to the value.

3d. For any injury which a book may sustain after it shall be taken out by a borrower, and before its return, a fine may be imposed of six cents for every spot of grease or oil upon the cover or upon any leaf of the volume; for writing in or defacing any book not less than ten cents, nor more than the value of the book; for cutting or tearing the cover, or the binding, or any leaf, not less than ten cents, nor more than the value of the book.

4th. If a leaf be torn out, or so defaced or mutilated that it cannot be read, or if any thing be written in the volume, or any other injury done to it, which renders it unfit for general circulation, the trustees will consider it a destruction of the book, and will impose a fine accordingly, as above provided in case of loss of a book.

5th. When a book shall have been detained seven days beyond the twenty days allowed by the regulations, the librarian is to give notice to the borrower to return the same within three days. If not returned at that time, the trustees may consider the book lost or destroyed, and may impose a fine for its destruction in addition to the fines for its detention.

Previous to the imposition of any fine, two days' written or verbal notice is to be given by any trustee, or the librarian, or any other person authorized by either of them, to the person charged, to show cause why he should not be fined for the alleged offence or neglect; and if within that time good cause be not shown, the trustees must impose the fine herein prescribed. No other excuse for an extraordinary injury to a book, that is, for such an injury as would not be occasioned by its ordinary use should be received, except the fact that the book was as much injured when it was taken out by the person charged, as it was when he returned it. As such loss must fall on some one, it is more just that it should be borne by the party whose duty it was to take care of the volume, than by the district. Negligence can be prevented, and disputes avoided, only by the adoption of this rule. Subject to these general principles the imposition of all, or any of these fines, is *discretionary* with the trustees, and they should ordinarily be imposed only for *wilful* or *culpably negligent* injuries to books, or where the district actually sustains a loss, or serious injury. Reasonable excuses for the detention of the books beyond the twenty days, should in all cases be received.

The librarian is to inform the trustees of every notice given by him to show cause against the imposition of a fine; and they are to assemble at the time and place appointed by him, or by any notice given by them, or any one of them; and to hear the charge and defence. They are to keep a book of minutes, in which every fine imposed by them, and the cause, shall be entered and signed by them, or the major part of them. Such original minutes, or a copy certified by them, or the major part of them, or by the clerk of the district, is made conclusive evidence of the fact that a fine was imposed as stated in such minutes, according to the regulations.

It is the duty of trustees to prosecute promptly for the collection of all fines imposed by them. Fines collected for the detention of books, or for injuries to them, are to be applied to defray the expense of repairing the books in the library. Fines collected for the loss or destruction of any book, or of a set or series of books, are to be applied to the purchase of the same or other suitable books.

VII. ANNUAL REPORT OF TRUSTEES.

1. WHEN TO BE MADE, AND WHAT TO CONTAIN.

By section 116 of the act of 1847, (No. 136,) trustees are required to make and transmit their annual reports to the Town Superintendent, between the *first and fifteenth days of January* in each year. By § 115, (No. 137,) such report is to be dated on the first day of January, and must specify:

1. The whole time any school has been kept in their district during the year ending on the day previous to the date of such report, and distinguishing what portion of the time such school has been kept by qualified teachers:

2. The amount of moneys received from the Town Superintendent of common schools, during such year, and the manner in which such moneys have been expended:

3. The number of children taught in the district during such year, and the name and age of each child:

4. The name and age of each child residing in the district, on the last day of December previous to the making of such report, over theage of four years and under twenty-one years of age, (except Indian children, otherwise provided for by law,) and the names of the parents or other persons with whom such children shall respectively reside and the number of children residing with each.

5. The amount of money paid for teachers' wages, in addition to the public money paid therefor, the amount of taxes levied in said district for purchasing school-house sites, for building, hiring, purchasing, repairing and insuring school-houses, for fuel, for supplying deficiencies in rate-bills, for district libraries or for any other purpose allowed by law, and such other information in relation to the schools and the districts as the Superintendent of common schools may from time to time require.

By virtue of the authority conferred on the Superintendent, under this provision, they are also required to state in their annual reports,

1. The number of books belonging to their district library on the last day of December in each year:

2. The number of times the school in their district has been inspected and visited by the Town Superintendents, respectively, during the year reported:

3. The names of the several school books in use in the school in their district, during such year:

4. The number of pupils who have attended the school in said district for a term less than two months, during the said year; the number attending two, and less than four months; the number attending four and less than six months; the number attending six and less than eight months; the number attending eight and less than ten months; the number attending ten and less than twelve months; and the number attending twelve months:

5. The number of select and private schools in their district, other than incorporated seminaries, and the average number of pupils attending them during the preceding year:

6. The number of colored children between the ages of four and twenty-one years, attending any school for such children established in the district, and instructed therein at least six months by a teacher duly licensed, specifying the number attending from different districts, designating such districts, and the number from each, the amount of public money received from the Town Superintendent *for such schools*, during the year ending with the date of their report, and the amount paid for the compensation of such teacher, over and above the public money so received.

One of the most important items in the annual report of trustees is the number of children residing in the district between the ages of 4 and 21, as it affords the most sure and practical test of the progress of primary education. There is reason to believe, that the reports have heretofore been very inaccurate in this respect. Some difficulty has, it is true, been experienced in determining with the requisite precision, the children proper to be included within the boundaries of the several districts; but the specific provisions of the late act, § 118, (No. 138,) will, it is believed, remove every difficulty of this kind. By that section it is required that the reports shall include all children over 4 and under 21, who, at the date of the report, are *actually* in the district, composing part of the family of their employers, &c., residing at the time in the district, although such residence,—that is of the employers, parents, &c., be *temporary*. But children belonging to the family of a person who is an inhabitant of another district, are not to be included. If therefore a person who is not an inhabitant of some other district, resides temporarily in a given district, all the children belonging to his family are to be reported. The law embraces a class of persons who were not before enumerated in any district—those whose parents or employers had not gained a residence in the state.

Children attending an academy, are to be enumerated, only where their parents are actually residents of the district in which the academy is situated.—*Com. School Dec.* 58.

Trustees are expressly prohibited by law from including in their enumeration children supported at a county poor-house, § 117, (No. 137.)

The children of a man removing on the last day of December from one district to another, are to be enumerated in the district into which he moves. The enumeration is made with a view to the apportionment of the money for the succeeding year ; and it is proper that the money drawn upon the basis of that enumeration should as far as possible, go to the district in which the children enumerated are to reside, and in which the money received for their benefit is to be expended.—*Com. School Dec.* 216.

A man cannot, however, gain a *residence* in a place unless he goes there *with the intention of remaining.* Where, therefore, an inhabitant of a school district leaves such district with the whole or a portion of his family a few days previous to the last of December, and goes into another district, where after remaining a few days, he returns to the former district, his children are nevertheless to be enumerated by the trustees of the district to which he evidently belongs.—*Per* YOUNG, *Sup't.*

Form of a district report to be made by the Trustees to the Town Superintendent of Common Schools.

To the Town Superintendent of common schools of the town of

We, the trustees of school district number in said town, in conformity with the statutes relating to common schools, do certify and report,that the whole time any school has been kept in our district during the year ending on the date hereof, and since the date of the last report for the said district is, [*here insert the whole time any school has been kept in the district school-house, although for a part of that time it may have been kept by teachers not duly qualified,*] and that during said year and since the date of said last report such school has been kept by a teacher [*or teachers as the case may be,*] after obtaining a certificate of qualification, according to law, is [*here insert the time with precision:*] that the amount of money apportioned to our district by the Town Superintendent of common schools during the said year and since the date of the said last report, except library money, is [*here insert the whole amount, excepting library money, although it may have been received in whole or in part by predecessors in office,*] and that the said sum has been applied on our order to the payment of the compensation of teachers employed in the said district and licensed as the statute prescribes. [*If the amount apportioned has not been expended, the reason for such omission should be particularly specified.*] That the amount of library money received in our district from the Town Superintendent of common schools during said year and since the date of the said last report, is [*here insert the whole amount of library money, although it may have been received in whole or in part by predecessors in office,*] and that the said sum has been applied to the purchase of a library for the district, [*or to the purchase of a map of the State of New York, a terrestrial globe, a black-board, &c.*, (specifying particularly the articles purchased) *in pursuance of a vote of the district at a special meeting called and held according to law.*] That the number of volumes belonging to the district library and on hand on the last day of December last, is [*here insert the whole number of volumes.*] That the number of children taught in said district, during said year and since last report is [*here insert the same, not by conjecture, but by reference to the teachers' list, or other authentic sources.*] That of the said children (10) attended less than two months; (5) two months and less than four; (8) four months and less than six; (4) six months and less than eight; eight months and less than ten; ten months and less than twelve; twelve months. And that the number of children residing in our district on the last day of December last, who are over four and under twenty-one years of age, is [*here insert the number, taking in such as resided in the district on the last day of December, and who were then over four and under twenty-one years of age,*] and that the names of the parents, and other persons with whom such children respective reside, and the number residing with each are contained in schedule A. annexed.

[*If a colored school has been taught in the district the following should be added:*]

That the number of colored children between the ages of 4 and twenty-one years attending a school taught in our district during the year aforesaid, by a licensed teacher for at least six months, was [24;] of whom [10] resided in said district, [5] attending from district No. 5, [4] from district No. 7, [2] from district No. 6, and [3] from district No. 19. That the whole amount of public money received from the Town Superintendent of common schools of our town, during the year aforesaid, for the use of said colored school, was $ and that the said sum has been applied to the compensation of the teacher thereof; and that the amount paid to such teacher, over and above the public money so received, was $.]

And we further report, that our school has been visited by the Town Superintendent times, during the year preceding this report, and that the sum paid for teachers' wages, over and above the public moneys apportioned to said district, during the same year, amounts to $. [*Is to be filled with the sum total of all the school bills for the year,* after *applying the school money to the payment of such wages.*] That the school books in use in said district during said year, are the following, viz: [*Here specify the titles of all the text books used in the school during the several terms.* That there have been private or select schools, not incorporated, taught in said district during the year aforesaid, and that the average number of pupils in attendance therein was. [*Here state the number as near as can be ascertained.*]

Dated at the first day of January, in the year of our Lord one thousand eight hundred and

A. B.
C. D. } *Trustees.*
E. F.

Form of a District Report, where the district is formed out of two or more adjoining towns.

To the Town Superintendent of common schools of the town of

We, the trustees of school district number , formed partly out of said town, and partly out of the adjoining town of , do, in conformity with the statutes relating to common schools, certify and report,

That the school house in said district is situated in the town of . That the whole time any school has been kept in our district, during the year ending on the date thereof, and since the date of the last report for said district, is [*here insert the whole time any school has been kept in the district school-house, although for a part of that time it may have been kept by teachers duly qualified,*] and that the time during said year and since the date of said last report, such school has been kept by a teacher, [*or teachers, as the case may be,*] after obtaining a certificate of qualification according to law is [*here insert the time with precision.*] That the amount of money apportioned to our district by the Town Superintendents of common schools, during the said year, and since the date of the said last report, excepting library money, is [*here insert the whole amount excepting library money, although it may have been received in whole or in part by predecessors in office,*] and that of the said sum of money so as above stated to have been apportioned to our said district, to be applied to the payment of teachers' wages, the sum of was apportioned for and on account of that part of said district lying in the said town of and the sum of for and on account of the other part thereof lying and being in said town of and that the said sum has been applied, on our order, to the payment of the compensation of teachers employed in said district, and licensed as the statute prescribes. That the amount of library money received in our district from the Town Superintendent of common schools during said year, and since the date of said last report, [*here insert the whole amount of library money, although it may have been received in whole or in part by predecessors in office,*] that of the said sum of money so as above stated to have been received in our said district for the purchase of a district library the sum of was received for and on account of that part of said district lying in said town of and the sum of for and on account of the other part thereof lying and being in the said town of and that the said sum was, on or before the first day of October last, applied to the purchase of a library for the district, [*or to the purchase of maps, globes, &c.* (specifying the articles purchased) *in pursuance of a vote of the district at a special meeting called and held in the manner prescribed by law.*] That the number of volumes belonging to the district library and on hand on the last day of December last, is [*here insert the whole number of volumes.*] That the number of children taught in said district during said year, and since said last report, is [*here insert the same, not by conjecture, but by reference to the teachers' list or other authentic sources.*] That of the said children [10] attended less that two months, [8] two months and less than four, [6] four months and less than six, [8] six months and less than eight, [3] eight months and less than ten, ten months and less than twelve, twelve months. And that the number of children residing in our district on the last day of December last, who were over four and under twenty-one years of age, is [*here insert the number, taking in such as actually reside in the district on said day, and who were then over four and under twenty-one years of age,*] and that the names of the parents or other persons with whom such children respectively reside, and the number residing with each are contained in schedule A. annexed.

[*If a colored school has been taught in the district the following should be added :*]

That the number of colored children between the ages of 5 and 16 years attending a school taught in our district during the year aforesaid, by a licensed teacher for at least four months, (24,) of whom (10) reside in said district, (5) attended from district No. 5, (4) from district No. 7, (2) from district No. 6, and (3) from district No. 19. That the whole amount of public money received from the Town Superintendent of common schools of our town during the year aforesaid, for the use of said colored school, was $, and that the said sum has been applied to the compensation of the teacher thereof; and that the amount paid to such teacher over and above the public money so received, was $.] That of the said children, so as above stated to have been taught in our said district, the number belonging to that part of said district lying in said town of is , and that the number belonging to the other part thereof, lying in said town of is . That of the said children between the said ages of four and twenty-one years, so as above, stated to reside in our district, the number residing in that part of said district lying in said town of is , and that the number residing in the other part thereof, lying in said town of is .

And we do further report that our school has been inspected by the Town Superintendent during the past year [*once or twice, or not at all,* as the case may be.] That the sum paid for teachers' wages in said district, over and above the public money apportioned to said district, during the same year, amounts to $ cents, of which dollars cents, were paid by that part of the district lying in the town of and dollars cents, by that part lying in the town of

[*This blank is to be filed with the sum total of all the school bills for the year, which are made out after applying the school money to the payment of the teachers' wages.*]

That the school books in use in said district, during said year, are the following, viz: [*Here specify the title of all the text books used in the school during the several terms.*] That there have been private or select schools, not incorporated, taught in said district during the year aforesaid, and that the average number of pupils in attendance therein was [*here state the number as near as can be ascertained.*]

Dated at , this first day of January in the year of our Lord one thousand eight hundred and

A. B.
C. D. } Trustees.
E. F.

By § 145 of the act of 1847, (No. 168,) "Town Superintendents of common schools, and trustees and clerks of school districts, refusing or wilfully neglecting to make any report, or to perform any other duty required by law, or by regulations or decisions made under the authority of any statute, shall severally forfeit to their town, or to their district, as the case may be, for the use of the common schools therein, the sum of ten dollars for each such neglect or refusal, which penalty shall be sued for and collected by the supervisor of the town, and paid over to the proper officers, to be distributed for the benefit of the common schools in the town or district to which such penalty belongs; and when the share of school or library money apportioned to any town or district, or school, or any portions thereof, or any money to which a town or district would have been entitled, shall be lost in consequence of any wilful neglect of official duty by any Town Superintendent of common schools, or trustees or clerks of school districts, the officers guilty of such neglect shall forfeit to the town or district the full amount, with interest, of the moneys so lost; and they shall be jointly and severally liable for the payment of such forfeiture."

By § 123, of the school act, (No. 143,) "Every trustee of a school district, or separate neighborhood, who shall sign a false report to the Town Superintendent of common schools of his town, with the intent of causing such Town Superintendent to apportion and pay to his district or neighborhood, a larger sum than its just proportion of the school moneys of the town, shall, for each offence, forfeit the sum of twenty-five dollars, and shall also be deemed guilty of a misdemeanor."

By § 15 of chap. 382, of Laws of 1849, "Whenever it shall be satisfactorily proven to the State Superintendent that any county or town superintendent, or other school officer, has embezzled the public money, or any money coming into his hands for school purposes, or has been guilty of the wilful violation of any law, or neglect of any duty or of disobeying any decision, order or regulation of the Department of Common Schools, the State Superintendent is hereby authorised to remove such officer from such office, by an order under the seal of office of the Secretary of State."

VIII. TRUSTEES ACCOUNTING TO THEIR SUCCESSORS, PAYING OVER BALANCES AND DELIVERING PAPERS TO THEM.

By § 125, et. seq. of the school act, (No. 145, et. seq.,) "The trustees of each school district shall, once in each year, render to the district, at its annual meeting, a just and true account, in writing, of all moneys received by them respectively, for the use of their district, and of the manner in which the same shall have been expended; which account shall be delivered to the district clerk, and be filed and recorded by him. Any balance of such moneys, which shall appear from such account to remain in the hands of the trustees, or either of them, at the time of rendering the account, shall immediately be paid to some one or more of their successors in office. Every trustee who shall refuse or neglect to render such account, or to pay over any balance so found in his hands, shall, for each offence, forfeit the sum of twenty-five dollars.

"It shall be the duty of his successors in office, or of the Town Superintendent, to prosecute without delay, in their name of office, for the recovery of such forfeiture; and the moneys recovered shall be applied by them to the use and benefit of their district schools. Such successors shall also have the same remedies for the recovery of any unpaid balance in the hands of a former trustee, or his representatives, as are given to the Town Superintendent of Common Schools against a former Superintendent and his representatives; and the moneys recovered shall be applied by them to the use of their district, in the same manner as if they had been paid without suit. All bonds or securities taken by the trustees from the collector of their district, shall, on the expiration of their office, be delivered over by them to their successors in office."

IX. SUITS BY AND AGAINST TRUSTEES.

I. SUITS BY TRUSTEES.

By § 74, Laws of 1847, (No. 96,) trustees are authorized to sue for and recover the moneys due upon any security taken by them or their predecessors in office, on the sale of the school-house and site of their district, in the cases provided for by that section, with interest and costs.

By § 89, (No. 112,) trustees are authorized to prosecute for the amount due on a tax list or rate-bill, against non-residents of their district, where no goods or chattels can be found in the district whereon to levy.

By § 114, (No. 134,) they are directed, in case the moneys apportioned to their district are withheld by the Town Superintendent, to prosecute for the recovery thereof, with interest, or to pursue such other remedy for the recovery thereof as is or shall be given by law. This provision, it is supposed, is applicable only to cases of *illegal* detention in the hands of the Town Superintendent of money apportioned to a district, and not to the withholding of such money in consequence of the discovery of some illegality or informality in the reports from the districts. Where the right of the district to its share is incontestible, and the amount is still withheld for any reason, the trustees are directed to prosecute, and the proper remedy in such a case would be an action of assumpsit for money had and received to the use of the district or teacher against such Town Superintendent.

By § 128, (No. 148,) trustees are directed to prosecute their predecessors for the recovery of the forfeiture of twenty-five dollars, incurred by a refusal or neglect to account, or to pay over any balance due from them, on the expiration of their term of office, and to apply the money recovered to the use and benefit of their school; and by § 129, (No. 149,) they are authorized to prosecute for any unpaid balance in the hands of a former trustee, or his representatives, and directed to apply the amount recovered to the use of the district, in the same manner as if it had been paid without suit.

By § 102, (No. 125,) they are also authorized to prosecute for the recovery, with interest and costs, of all forfeitures incurred by a collector, and unpaid balances in his hands, and to apply the moneys recovered in the same manner as if paid without suit.

By § 61, (No. 83,) trustees are to prosecute for the recovery of the fine of ten dollars, with costs of suit, imposed upon any inhabitant, voting at any school district meeting, without being qualified.

2. SUITS AGAINST TRUSTEES.

It is conceived that an essential service may be rendered to officers connected with common schools, by informing them of some general principles to show the extent of their liability to suits by individuals.

Officers required by law to exercise their judgments are not answerable for mistakes of law, or mere errors of judgment, without any fraud or malice. *Jenkins vs. Waldron*, 11*th Johnson's Reports*, 114.

A public officer who is required by law to act in certain cases, according to his judgment or opinion, and subject to penalties for his neglect, is not liable to a party for an omission arising from a mistake or want of skill, if acting in *good faith*. *Seaman vs. Patten*, 2*d Caine's Reports*, 312.

But an officer entrusted by the common law or by statute, is liable to an action for *negligence* in the performance of his trust, or for *fraud* or neglect in the execution of his office. *Jenner vs. Joliffe*, 9 *John. Rep.* 381.

And an officer who commands an act to be done by issuing a warrant or other process, if he act without *jurisdiction* of the subject matter, or of the person, is liable as a trespasser. *Horton vs. Auchmoody*, 7 *Wendell*, 200. But if he have jurisdiction, errors in judgment do not subject him to an action.

Mere irregularities in proceedings will not render an officer having dscretionary powers, or acting as a judge, liable to a civil suit. There is a large class of cases, in which the remedy is only by plea to the proceedings or by writ of error.—*See Butler vs. Potter* 17 *Johns.* 145, *and Griffin vs. Mitchell*, 2 *Cowen's Rep.* 548.

The collector or other officer who *executes* process, has peculiar protection. He is protected, although the court or officer issuing such process have not, in fact, jurisdiction of the case; if on the face of the process, it appears that such court or officer had jurisdiction of the *subject matter*, and nothing appears in such process to apprise the officer but that there was jurisdiction of the person of the party affected by the process. *Savacool vs. Boughton*, 5 *Wendell's Reports*, 170.

A contract made by all the trustees, and signed by two, is binding; and where a contract is signed or a warrant issued by two trustees, the presence of the third will be presumed, until the contrary be shown. Two trustees can contract against the will of the third, if he was duly notified of a meeting of the trustees, or was consulted and refused to act.—*McKoy vs. Courtree*, 9 *Wendell*, 17.

When a district votes a tax to purchase a new site, and build a school-honse thereon, where the consent of the Town Superintendent had not been obtained for a change of the site, [the district not being an altered one,] the trustees are liable in trespass for making out a tax list and issuing a warrant for the collection of such tax; on the ground that the district had no authority to vote such a tax. *Baker vs. Freeman*, 9 *Wendell*, 36.

Trustees are not liable as trespassers for omitting to insert the names of all the taxable inhabitants in the tax list, where there is no evidence of bad faith on their part.—*Easton vs. Calendar*, 11 *Wendell*, 90.

Subordinate tribunals are not liable as trespassers for acts done growing out of an error of judgment.—*Ib.*

Trustees are liable in trespass for making out their tax list upon any other basis than the last assessment roll of the town, after it has been reviewed and finally settled by the assessors.—*Alexander vs. Hoyt*, 7 *Wend.* 89.

Inhabitants of a district must vote a precise and definite sum as a tax for building a school-house or any other purpose, and trustees will not be authorized to issue their warrant to levy a tax under a general vote.—*Robinson vs. Dodge*, 18 *Johns.* 351.

Trustees in office are liable on the contracts of their predecessors for the employment of teachers, personally, because they have the means of indemnifying themselves, and those who made the contract are not liable after the expiration of their term of office.—*Silver vs. Cumming*, 7 *Wendell*, 181.

The court intimate a distinction between those cases where the trustees are not to act unless money is previously raised, and those where it is to be collected subsequent to the performance of the work. In the first class of cases they are not to incur responsibilities beyond the means in their possession; they render themselves personally responsible, and their successors are not holden. The first class of cases would seem to include those only which are specified in sub. 5 of § 82, (No. 103,) and those in which blank books, maps, globes, black boards and other school apparatus may be procured by means of a previous tax. In these cases successors are supposed not to to be liable, unless money comes into their hands for the purpose.

In all other cases, it is supposed successors are liable on the contracts of their predecessors.

It is quite important to trustees to know that the decisions of this department have been, uniformly, that their costs in any suit cannot be paid by a vote of the district to levy a tax for that purpose, as the only purposes for which a tax can be voted are specified in the statutes, and this is not among them.

Questions respecting the liability of trustees for their joint acts and for the acts of each other are frequently presented. It becomes proper to state the grounds and limits of their responsibility in this respect, that they may be better enabled to guard against its consequences.

The object being to secure fidelity to the trust and to prevent negligence and fraud, the rules which govern in the cases of executors, guardians and other private trustees, must be applicable to officers holding a similar fiduciary relation to the public, and therefore the principles which have been settled in those cases by the courts, will be the guide in determining the extent of the liability of the trustees.

The general rule, as laid down by an eminent jurist, (Story on Equity Jurisprudence,) and sustained by the adjudged cases, is, that joint trustees are responsible only for their own acts, and not for the acts of each other, unless they have made some agreement by which they have expressly agreed to be bound for each other; or have, by their voluntary co-operation or connivance, enabled the other to accomplish an object in violation of the trust. This rule is exemplified in the following cases:

1. Where money has been received jointly, all are in general liable for its application, and a joint receipt is presumptive evidence of the fact that it came to the hands of all; but either may show that his joining in the receipt was formal or necessary, and that the whole of the money was in fact received by his compan-

ions. And if it was misapplied before there was a reasonable opportunity to control it, he would not be responsible.

2. When by any positive act, direction or agreement, of one joint trustee, the money is paid over and comes to the hands of the others, when it might and should have been otherwise controlled or secured by both, then each will be chargeable for the whole.

There is great difficulty in applying this rule to the case of trustees of common schools. The money for distribution cannot be in the hands of more than one; there are ordinarily no means of insuring a control over it by all, by depositing it in a bank or other place of security, and there is no authority by which any two trustees could require the third to give security for its faithful disbursement. One has as much right to its custody as another. The simple fact, therefore, that public money has been received by one and misapplied, cannot in itself render the others liable. It would seem therefore, that there should be some act of omission or commission on the part of the others to render them liable for the misconduct of their associate; and here the following rule seems better adapted to the case:

3. If one trustee wrongfully suffer the other to detain the trust money *a long time* in his own hands without security, or should lend it to him on his simple note, or should join with the other in lending it on sufficient security, in all such cases he would be held liable for any loss. Of course, a trustee who has connived at or been privy to an embezzlement of the trust money would be liable. And if it be mutually agreed between them that one shall have the *exclusive* management of one part of the trust property, and the other of another part, both would be liable for the acts of each.

Considering the equal rights and powers of each trustee, that the law has made no provision for requiring security from them, and the gross injustice of making an officer responsible for the misconduct of an associate over whom he has no control, they ought not to be held liable for each other's acts unless there be some evidence of participation or connivance, like those specified in the third class of cases above mentioned.

By section 108, of title 4, chap. 8, part 3, Rev. Stat., p. 476, vol. 2, 1st edition, [§ 112, p. 390, 2d edition, vol. 2,] it is provided that in suits against trustees of school districts, and other officers, "the debt, damages or costs recovered against them, shall be collected in the same manner as against individuals; and the amount so collected shall be allowed to them in their official accounts." It is presumed that this provision does not relate to actions for personal delinquences, but to those only which arise out of an official duty. As the recoveries are to be "allowed them in their accounts," it is implied that they may retain the amount of monies in their hands, and set off the sums recovered. But this cannot apply to the public school moneys, as those moneys are appropriated by law to specific purposes, and cannot be diverted to any other.

By § 146, of the act of 1847, (No. 169,) it is provided that "in any suit which shall hereafter be commenced against Town Superintendents of common schools, or officers of school districts, for any act performed by virtue of, or under color of, their offices, or for any refusal or omission to perform any duty enjoined by law, and which might have been the subject of an appeal to the Superintendent, no costs shall be allowed to the plaintiff in cases where the court shall certify that it appeared on the trial of the cause that the defendants acted in good faith. But this provision shall not extend to suits for penalties, nor to suits or proceedings to enforce the decisions of the Superintendent."

By § 1, of chap. 172, laws of 1847, as amended by chap. 388, laws of 1849, it is provided that "whenever a suit shall have been commenced, or shall hereafter be commenced against the trustees of a school district, in consequence of acts by them performed in pursuance of and by the direction of such district, for any act performed by virtue of, or under color of their office, and such suit shall have been finally determined, or whenever after the final determination of any suit commenced by or against any trustees or other officers of a school district, a majority of the taxable inhabitants of any school district shall so determine, it shall be the duty of the trustees to ascertain in the manner hereinafter described, the actual amount of all costs, charges and expenses paid by such officer, and to cause the same to be assessed upon and collected of the taxable inhabitants of said district, in the same manner as other taxes of said district are by law assessed and collected, and when so collected to pay the same over to the officer, by virtue of this act, entitled to receive the same; but this provision shall not extend to suits for penalties, nor suits or proceedings to enforce the decision of the superintendent.

By § 2. "Whenever any person mentioned in the first section of this act shall have paid any costs, charges or expenses as mentioned in said first section, he shall make out an account of such charges, costs and expenses so paid by him, giving the items thereof, and verify the same by his oath or affirmation; he shall serve a copy of said account so sworn to, upon the trustees of the district against which such claim shall be made, together with a notice in writing that on a certain day therein specified, he will present such account to the board of supervisors of the county in which such school district shall be situated, for settlement at some legal meeting of such board; and it shall be the duty of the officer upon whom such copy, account and notice shall be served, to attend at the time and place in such notice specified, to protect the rights and interests of such district upon such settlement.

§ 3. "Upon the appearance of the parties, or upon due proof of service of the notice and copy of account mentioned in the second section of this act, if the said board shall be of opinion that such account or any portion thereof ought justly to be paid to the claimant, such board may by an order to be made by a majority of all the members elected to the same, and to be entered in its minutes, require such account or such part thereof as such board shall be of opinion ought justly to be paid to the claimant, by such district to be so paid; but no portion of such account shall be so ordered to be paid which shall appear to the said board to have arisen from the wilful neglect or misconduct of the claimant. The account, with the oath of the party claiming the same, shall be prima facie evidence of the correctness thereof. The board may adjourn the hearing from time to time as justice shall seem to require.

§ 4. "It shall be the duty of the trustees of any school district, within thirty days after service of a copy of such order upon them to cause the same to be entered at length in the book of records of said district, and to issue to the collector of said district a warrant for the collection of the amount so directed to be paid, in the same manner and with the like force and effect as upon a tax voted by said district."

It will be perceived that two classes of cases are here alluded to. 1st. Where suits have been brought *against trustees*, in consequence of the performance of any official act by them, and such suits shall have been finally determined; in which case, the trustees may at once make out their account of costs, charges and expenses, verify the same, and present it to the Board of Supervisors, *without any action on the part of the district;* or they may, in their discretion, procure a vote of the district to that effect: and 2d, When suits have been brought *by or against* any trustees, or *other officers* of a school district, and such suits shall have been finally determined; in which case, (with the exception of suits brought *against* trustees, as above referred to,) a *vote of the district* is necessary to authorize an account of the costs, charges and expenses, to be made out, as provided by the second section, and laid before the Board of Supervisors. In both cases, no tax can be levied on the district for the amount of such costs, charges and expenses, except on the order of the Board of Supervisors, as specified in the third section.

IX. MISCELLANEOUS PROVISIONS APPLICABLE TO TRUSTEES.

1. SCHOOLS FOR COLORED CHILDREN.

By § 147, of the act of 1847, (No. 179,) a school for colored children may be established in any district, with the approbation of the Town Superintendent, which is to be under the charge of the trustees of the district in which such school is established. Trustees, in their annual reports, are also required particularly to specify the number of such children over four and under twenty-one years of age attending such school from different districts, naming such districts respectively, and the number from each attending for six months, and instructed by a duly qualified teacher, which report is to form the basis of an apportionment to such school, by the Town Superintendent, of a share of the public money Full and explicit instructions to Town Superintendents and trustees, and the necessary forms for reports in relation to these schools, will be found under the appropriate heads.

The provisions contained in this section are more particularly applicable to those cities and large villages where no special legal provisions have been made for the instruction of colored children. The means provided, are, it is true, altogether insufficient to meet the expense which must necessarily be incurred in the organization of these schools; and inasmuch as the class of community for whose special benefit they are intended is generally unable to contribute to such expense in any considerable degree, the object in view can seldom be fully attained, but through the efforts of charitable and benevolent individuals in the several districts from which the colored schools are composed. These efforts have hitherto been paralyzed by the absence of any legal power to effect the necessary organization; and the provision now made, was doubtless intended to supply that defect, and to furnish a nucleus around which the benevolent exertions of the friends of education and humanity might be concentrated. If, however, in any of the country districts, a colored school can be organized and efficiently kept up for the requisite length of time, it is hoped no efforts will be spared to carry into effect the provisions of the section. Colored children are entitled equally with all others, to the privileges and advantages of the district school: and wherever they can be grouped together in a separate school, under the charge of a competent teacher, they will be far more likely to derive the full benefits of such instruction as may be best adapted to their circumstances and condition, while at the same time, the disadvantages inseparable from their attendance at the district school, will be avoided.

By Chap. 228 of the laws of 1845, (Nos. 174–178,) it is provided that no person shall wilfully disturb, interrupt or disquiet any assemblage of persons met at any school district, with the assent of the trustees of the school district, for the purpose of receiving instruction in any of the branches of education usually taught in the common schools of this state, or in the science of music. Whoever shall violate the provisions of the foregoing section, may be tried before any justice of the peace of the county, or any mayor, alderman, recorder, or other magistrate of any city where the offence shall be committed; and upon conviction, shall forfeit a sum not exceeding twenty-five dollars, for the use and benefit of the school district in which such offence shall be committed. It shall be the duty of the trustees of any school district in which any such offence shall be committed, to prosecute such offender before any officer having cognizance of such offence. If any person convicted of the offence herein prohibited, shall not immediately pay the penalty incurred, with the costs of conviction, or give security, to the satisfaction of the officer before whom such conviction shall be had, for the payment of the said penalty and costs within twenty days thereafter, he shall be committed by warrant to the common jail of the county, until the same be paid, or for such term, not exceeding thirty days, as shall be specified in such warrant. It shall and may be lawful for any person who may be complained of for a violation of the provisions of this act, to demand of such magistrate that he may be tried by a jury. Upon such demand, it shall be the duty of such officer to issue a venire to the proper officer, commanding him to summon the same number of jurors, and in the same manner, and the said court shall proceed to empannel a jury for the trial of said cause, in the same manner and subject to all the rules and regulations prescribed in the act providing for the trials by jury in courts of special sessions."

2. BOND TO BE REQUIRED OF THE COLLECTOR.

Trustees are authorized by § 103, (No. 126,) to require of the collector of their district, before delivering to him any warrant for the collection of moneys, a bond with one or more sureties conditioned for the faithful performance of the duties devolved upon him as such collector.

It is strongly recommended to trustees to exact of the collector, the bond authorized under this section of the school law, before any warrant is placed in his hands. This practice will be attended with very little trouble, and will secure the district from all loss, and the trustees themselves from personal liability, in many instances. It will also secure the prompt collection of taxes and promote system and regularity in the financial affairs of the district.

Form of a Bond to be given by a District Collector.

Know all men by these presents, that we, A. B. and C. D., (the collector and his surety,) are held and firmly bound to E. F. and G. H. &c., trustees of school district number in the town of in the sum of (here insert a sum double the amount to be collected,) to be paid to the said E. F., G. H., &c., trustees as aforesaid, or to the survivor or survivors of them, or their successors; to the which payment, well and truly to be made, we bind ourselves, our heirs, executors and administrators, firmly by these presents. Sealed with our seals, and dated this day of 18 &c.

Whereas the above bounden A. B. has been chosen (or appointed, as the case may be,) collector of the above mentioned school district number in the town of in conformity to the statutes relating to common schools; now, therefore, the condition of this obligation is such that if he the said A. B. shall well and truly collect and pay over all moneys received by him as such collector and shall in all respects duly and faithfully execute all the duties of his office as collector of such district, then this obligation shall be void, otherwise to be in full force and virtue.

Signed, sealed and delivered, in the presence of

A. B. [L. S.]
C. D. [L. S.]

CHAPTER V.

DISTRICT CLERK.

The general duties of this officer are particularly specified in § 74 of the school act, (No. 102.) He is to keep, in a book to be provided by the district, a record of the proceedings of each annual and special meeting held in his district: to give notice of the time, place and object of such meetings in the manner prescribed by law, and to preserve all records, books and papers relating to the district, and deliver the same, on the expiration of his official term, to his successor.

By § 66 of the Laws of 1847, (No. 88,) he is to notify a special meeting for the election of officers, whenever the time for holding the annual meeting has passed without such election being held; and generally it his duty to give the necessary legal notices of a district meeting, whenever required to do so by a majority of the trustees. The purpose and object of such meetings should in all cases be set forth in general terms; and this is specially required by law, when a meeting is called for the purpose of changing the site and removing the school-house in an unaltered district. [See No. 95.] And also when a tax is to be levied for the purchase of books for a district library.

By § 69, (No. 91,) it is declared that "the proceedings of no district meeting, annual or special, shall be held illegal for want of a due notice to all the persons qualified to vote thereat, unless it shall appear that the omission to give such notice was wilful and fraudulent." But this provision will not exonerate a clerk from liability for gross neglect; nor will it sanction an intentional omission to give notice.

Notices of annual and special meetings must be given at least five days before the day on which such meetings are directed to be held; that is, the notices for a meeting to be held on *Saturday* for instance, must be given on or before the preceding *Monday*.

In the case of *annual* meetings, or special meetings which have been *adjourned* for a longer time than one month, a notice in writing, affixed in at least four public places in the district, is sufficient, but notices of *special* meetings must be personally served on each inhabitant of the district *liable to pay taxes,* (which includes, of course, every legal voter in the district,) "by reading the notice in the hearing of such inhabitant, or in case of his absence from home, by leaving a copy thereof, or so much thereof as relates to the time and place of such meeting, at the place of his abode. (§ 55, No. 77.)

Form of Notice for Annual Meeting.

Notice is hereby given, that the annual meeting for the election of officers in District No.   in the town of   , and for the transaction of such other business as the meeting may deem necessary, will be held at the school-house in said district on *Monday*, the day of at six o'clock, P. M.

Dated this day of

A. B., *District Clerk.*

Form of a Notice for an adjourned District Meeting, to be posted up in four public places in the District.

SCHOOL DISTRICT NOTICE.

Notice is hereby given, that a meeting of the freeholders and inhabitants of school district No. in the town of authorized by law to vote therein, will be held at on the day of next, [or instant, as the case may be,] at o'clock in the noon, pursuant to adjournment.

Dated this day of A. D. 18 .

A. B. *District Clerk.*

Form of a Notice for a Special District Meeting.

To the clerk of district number

The trustees of district number at a meeting held for the purpose, have resolved that a special meeting be called at the school-house, on the day of 18 at o'clock in the noon of that day, for the purpose of (*choosing a collector in the place of A. B., removed, or whatever the object of the meeting may be,*) and for the transaction of such other business as the meeting may deem necessary.

You will therefore notify each inhabitant of the district entitled to vote therein, by reading this notice in his hearing, or if he is absent from home, by leaving a copy of it, or so much as relates to the time and place of meeting, at the place of his abode, at least five days before such meeting.

Dated at this day of 18 .

A. B.
C. D. } *Trustees.*
E. F.

The district clerk of each school district in this state, is, by a regulation of the department, required within ten days after each annual or special meeting for the election of officers in his district, to forward to the town clerk, the names of the several officers elected at such meeting, and the offices to which they were respectively elected. The omission to do so, however in no respect invalidates the election or proceedings of the officers so chosen.

In pursuance of § 32, of the act of 1841, the District School Journal is forwarded by mail, to the clerk of each district, whose duty it is, by that section, to cause each volume to be bound at the expense of the district, and to deposit the same in the district library. He or one of the trustees is therefore bound to take the paper from the post-office, punctually, paying the postage, quarterly in advance: and the amount so paid, being an expenditure authorized by law, may be added by the trustees to any tax list thereafter made out for district purposes, and refunded to the clerk, or trustee paying it. Great care should be taken to secure the regular receipt and careful preservation of the numbers, which will be sent on the first of each month; and with this view, the clerk should stitch them together in covers, as soon as they arrive; and in no case permit them to be taken out of his custody, although any inhabitant of the district should be allowed free access to them, for the purpose of perusal, at all proper hours. The same precautions should be observed, and the same freedom of access and perusal allowed, in respect to the volume of Laws and Instructions, the volume of Common School Decisions and Laws heretofore published, and all other books, papers and documents belonging to the district, and placed under his official control.

They will observe that heavy penalties and forfeitures are incurred by them, under § 145 of the act of 1847, (No. 168,) for neglect of any duty devolved upon them by law; and that they are made individually responsible for any loss that may accrue to their district, in consequence of such neglect, or omission.

CHAPTER VI.

COLLECTORS OF SCHOOL DISTRICTS.

It is the duty of the collector of each district to collect and pay over to the trustees of his district, some or one of them, all moneys which he shall be required by warrant to collect, within the time limited by such warrant for its return, and to take the receipt of such trustee or trustees, for such payment.

When required by the trustees, such collector is to execute a bond with one or more sureties, for the due and faithful performance of his duty.

1. JURISDICTION OF THE COLLECTOR.

By § 103, of the act of 1847, (No. 126,) the jurisdiction of the collector in the execution of his warrant, extends to any other district or town in the same county, or in any other county in the case of a joint district composed of parts of two or more counties, "in the same manner, and with the like authority, as in the district for which he was chosen or appointed."

2. MODE OF PROCEEDING IN THE COLLECTION OF TAXES.

By various provisions of the school act collectors are authorized and required, in the execution of warrants, delivered to them for the collection of tax lists to collect the amount due from the respective persons named in such warrants, *in the same manner that collectors of towns are authorized to collect town and county taxes.* This is specifically pointed out by the following extracts from the 13th chapter of the first volume of the Revised Statutes, (pages 397, 398.)

"§ 1. Every collector, upon receiving the tax list and warrant, shall proceed to collect the taxes therein mentioned, and for that purpose shall call at least once on the person taxed, or at the place of his usual residence, if in the town or ward for which such collector has been chosen, and shall demand payment of the taxes charged to him on his property.

"§ 2. In case any person shall refuse or neglect to pay the tax imposed on him, the collector shall levy the same by distress and sale of the goods and chattels of the person who ought to pay the same, or of any goods and chattels in his possession, wheresoever the same may be found within the district of the collector; and no claim of property to be made thereto by any other person shall be available to prevent a sale.

"§ 3. The collector shall give public notice of the time and place of sale, and of the property to be sold, at least six days previous to the sale, by advertisements to be posted up in at least three public places in the town where such sale shall be made. The sale shall be by public auction.

"§ 4. If the property distrained shall be sold for more than the amount of the tax, the surplus shall be returned to the person in whose possession such property was when the distress was made, if no claim be made to such surplus by any other person. If any other person shall claim such surplus on the ground that the property sold belonged to him, and such claim be admitted by the person for whose tax the same was distrained, the surplus shall be paid to such owner; but if such claim be contested by the person for whose tax the property was distrained, the surplus moneys shall be paid over by the collector to the supervisor of the town, who shall retain the same until the rights of the parties shall be determined by due course of law."

"No replevin shall lie for any property, taken by virtue of any warrant for the collection of any tax, assessment or fine, in pursuance of any statute of this state."—*2d R. S. page* 522, *sec.* 4.

These provisions must, however, be subject to the action of congress, on a subject which by the Constitution is within its jurisdiction. The constitution in express terms gives to congress the power "to provide for organizing, arming and disciplining the militia."

By the act of congress of May 8, 1792, vol. 2, Laws of the U. S. 298,) every citizen enrolled in the militia is required to provide himself with the following accoutrements, viz: "a good musket or firelock, a sufficient bayonet and belt, two spare flints and a knapsack, a pouch with a box therein, to contain not less than twenty-four cartridges suited to the bore of his musket or firelock, each cartridge to contain a proper quantity of powder and ball; or with a good rifle, knapsack, shot pouch and powder horn, twenty balls suited to the bore of his rifle, and a quarter of a pound of powder:" and the commissioned officers are required to be armed with a sword or hanger, or espontoon; and it is declared that "every citizen so enrolled and providing himself with the arms, ammunition and accoutrements required as aforesaid, shall hold the same exempted from all suits, distresses, executions or sales for debt or *for the payment of taxes*."

By the laws of this state (chap. 6, part 3, title 5, § 22, vol. 2, R. S.) the "arms and accoutrements required by law to be kept by any person," as well as a variety of other articles therein specified, are exempt from *execution* but not from *distress from taxes*. The only exemption, therefore, from the operation of a collector's warrant on a *tax list*, arises under the act of Congress before quoted; and this can only be extended to the arms, ammunition and accoutrements therein specified.

In the collection of warrants on *rate-bills*, all property exempted by section 22 of article two, title five, chapter six of part three of the Revised Statutes, is exempt from levy and sale on such warrants. For the extent of such exemption see *ante* pages 215, 216.

The collector or other officer who *executes* process, has peculiar protection. He is protected, although the court or officer issuing such process, have not, in fact, jurisdiction of the case; if on the face of the process it appears that such court or officer had jurisdiction of the *subject matter*, and nothing appears in such process to apprise the officer but that there was jurisdiction of the person of the party affected by the process. *Savacool* vs. *Boughton*, 5 *Wendell's Reports*, 170.

By § 100, (No. 123,) of the school act, it is the duty of the collector, upon receiving his warrant, for two successive weeks to receive such taxes as may be voluntarily paid to him; and in case the whole amount shall not be so paid in, the collector shall forthwith proceed to collect the same. He shall receive for his services, on all sums paid as aforesaid, one per cent, and upon all sums collected by him after the expiration of the time mentioned, five per cent; and in case a levy and sale shall be necessarily made by such collector, he shall be entitled to travelling fees, at the rate of six cents per mile, to be computed from the school house in such district.

Where *trustees* receive payments on tax lists or rate-bills, they are regarded as receiving the same as the *agents* of *the collector;* and the latter is entitled to his percentage on the amount so received, and may legally collect it by virtue of his warrant. The collector is also entitled to his percentage on the amount paid by the trustees, notwithstanding no actual exchange of funds is made between the latter and the former.—*Per* YOUNG, *Superintendent* 1843.

A *teacher*, if otherwise eligible, may be collector; but he cannot charge a percentage on voluntary payments of his own wages.—*Id.*

Where a collector levies upon and sells property for the payment of a tax list and the owner of the property refuses to receive the excess beyond an amount sufficient to satisfy the warrant, the collector must retain the amount in his own hands, and rely upon his plea of tender.—*Com. Sch. Dec.*, 217.

In the execution of his warrant, the collector should aim to take property amply sufficient to satisfy the amount he is required to collect, and no more. He is not bound to take any particular article of property which may be offered: but if *at the request of the owner,* he were to take and sell property worth ten times the amount required to be raised, such request would constitute a valid answer to the charge of making an excessive distress.—*Id.* 219.

Where, by the neglect of a collector, moneys which might have been collected by him within the time limited, are lost to the district, he is liable for the amount, *whether he has given a bond to the trustees or not.* The bond is an additional security; but if it is not required of him, he is not released from any obligation which the law imposes on him.—*Id.* 308.

So, where a warrant runs out in his hands, he is answerable for any loss arising from his neglect, notwithstanding such warrant may have been afterwards renewed and delivered to his successor. —*Id.*

A trustee of a school district cannot hold the office of collector. The same objection is not applicable to the district clerk; although, as the law has created separate offices, it is better to carry out its intention strictly, by conferring them on different individuals.—*Id.* 142.

If the warrant annexed to a rate-bill, or tax list, is signed by a majority of the trustees, it is sufficient for the protection of the collector, *although the third trustee was not, in fact, present, or consulted.*—*Id.* 328.

Where a warrant is renewed by the trustees, the collector in office at the time of such renewal, must execute it.—*Id.* 47.

Where a warrant is issued for the collection of a tax which has not been legally assessed, according to the last assessment roll of the town, or otherwise, or where the trustees have included in the tax list persons not liable to be so included, such warrant is a protection to the collector, notwithstanding the trustees might be answerable in trespass.—*Id.* 282.

A collector cannot legally *sell* property after the expiration of his warrant, unless such warrant is renewed, notwithstanding a previous levy.—*Id.* 286.

Where the collector, in the execution of a warrant, receives money current at the time of its receipt, but which subsequently becomes depreciated or valueless, before payment to the trustees, the *district,* and not the collector, must lose the amount.—*Per* SPENCER, *Sup't*, 1841.

The collector can pay over money collected by him only to the trustees, or on their order.—*Per* DIX, *Sup't*, 1838.

Trustees have no power to indemnify a collector for improperly selling property under their warrant.—*Id.*

The *representatives of a deceased person* are not entitled to any delay in the payment of a rate-bill, or tax list, but are bound to pay on demand : and on refusal or neglect, the collector may proceed to sell any property found on the premises. By § 27, sub. 2, 2 R. S. 28, taxes of all kinds have preference to any other demand. —*Per* SPENCER, *Sup't*, 1840.

Where a collector levies upon property *out of his district*, he should put up notices of the sale of such property, as well in the district where the sale is to take place as in that of his residence. —*Per* YOUNG, *Sup't*, 1842.

CHAPTER VII.

LIBRARIAN.

This officer is to be chosen at the annual meeting of the district. In case the inhabitants neglect at such meeting to choose offices, the district clerk becomes *ex-officio* librarian, until the vacancy is filled by the trustees, or by the inhabitants, at their next annual meeting.

By section 137, Laws of 1847, (No. 156,) "The librarian of any district library shall be subject to the directions of the trustees thereof, in all matters relating to the preservation of the books and appurtenances of the library, and may be removed from office by them for wilful disobedience of such directions, or for any wilful neglect of duty."

By section 139, of the same act, (No. 158,) "A set of general regulations respecting the preservation of school district libraries, the delivery of them by librarians and trustees to their successors in office, the use of them by the inhabitants of the district, the number of volumes to be taken by any one person at any one time, or during any term, the periods of their return, the fines and penalties that may be imposed by the trustees of such libraries for not returning, losing or destroying any of the books therein, or for soiling, defacing or injuring them, may be framed by the Superintendent of common schools, and printed copies thereof shall be furnished to each school district of the state ; which regulations shall be obligatory upon all persons and officers having charge of such libraries, or using or possessing any of the books thereof. Such fines may be recovered in an action of debt in the name of the trustees of any such library, of the person on whom they are imposed, except such person be a minor ; in which case they may be recovered of the parent or guardian of such minor, unless notice in writing shall have been given by such parent or guardian to the trustees of such library, that they will not be responsible for any books delivered such minor. And persons with whom minors reside shall be liable in the same manner, and to the same extent, in cases where the parent of such minor does not reside in the district."

By § 141, (No. 160,) "The legal voters in any two or more adjoning districts may, in such cases as shall be approved by the town Superintendent of common schools, unite their library moneys and funds as they shall be received or collected, and purchase a joint library for the use of the inhabitants of such districts, which shall be selected by the trustees thereof, or by such persons as they shall designate, and shall be under the charge of a librarian to be appointed by them; and the foregoing provisions of this act shall be applicable to the said joint libraries, except that the property in them shall be deemed to be vested in all the trustees for the time being of the districts so united. And in case any such district shall desire to divide such library, such division shall be made by the trustees of the two district whose libraries are so united, and in case they cannot agree, then such division shall be made by three disinterested persons, to be appointed by the Superintendent of common schools.

By the regulations of the Superintendent made in pursuance of this provision, the librarian is required, whenever any library is purchased and taken charge of by him to make out a full and complete catalogue of all the books contained therein. At the foot of each catalogue he is to sign a receipt in the following form.

I, A. B., do hereby acknowledge that the books specified in the preceding catalogue have been delivered to me by the trustees of school district No.   in the town of   to be safely kept by me as librarian of the said district for the use of the inhabitants thereof, according to the regulations prescribed by the Superintendent of common schools, and to be accounted for by me according to the said regulations to the trustees of the said district, and to be delivered to my successor in office. Dated, &c.

A correct copy of the catalogue and receipt is then to be made to which the trustees are to add a certificate in the following form:

We the subscribers, trustees of school district No.   in the town of   do certify that the preceding is a full and complete catalogue of books in the library of the said district now in possession of A. B., the librarian thereof, and of his receipt thereon. Given under our hands this   day of   18

The catalogue having the librarian's receipt, is to be delivered to the trustees, and a copy having the certificate of the trustees, is to be delivered to the librarian for his indemnity.

Whenever books are added to the library, a catalogue with a similar receipt by the librarian is be delivered to to the trustees, and a copy with a certificate of the trustees that it is a copy of the catalogue delivered them by the librarian, is to be furnished to him. Every catalogue received by trustees is to be kept by them carefully among the papers of the district and to be delivered to their successors in office.

Whenever a new librarian shall be chosen, all the books are to be called in. For this purpose the librarian is to refuse to deliver out any books for fourteen days preceding the time so prescribed for collecting them together. At these periods, they must make a careful examination of the books, compare them with the catalogue, and make written statements in a column opposite the name of each book, of its actual condition, whether lost or present, and whether in good order or injured, and if injured, specifying in general terms, the extent of such injury. This catalogue, with the remarks, is to be delivered to the successors of the trustees, to be kept by them; a copy of it is to be made out, and delivered to the new librarian with the library, by whom a receipt in the form above prescribed is to be given, and to be delivered to the trustees. Another copy certified by them as before mentioned, is to be delivered to the librarian.

Trustees, on coming into office, are to attend at the library for the purpose of comparing the catalogue with the books. They are at all times when they think proper, and especially on their coming into office, to examine the books carefully, and note such as are missing or injured. For every book that is missing, the librarian is accountable to the trustees for the full value thereof, and for the whole series of which it formed a part: such value to be determined by the trustees. He is accountable also for any injury which a book may appear to have sustained, by being soiled, defaced, torn, or otherwise. And he can be relieved from such accountability only, by the trustees, on its being satisfactorily shown to them that some inhabitant of the district has been charged or is chargeable for the book so missing, or for the amount of the injury so done to any work. It is the duty of the trustees to take prompt and efficient measures for the collection of the amount for which any librarian is accountable.

The librarian must cause to be pasted in each book belonging to the library, a printed or written label, or must write in the first blank leaf of each book, specifying that the book belongs to the library of school district No.   in the town of   , naming the town and giving the number of the district; and he is on no account to deliver out any book which has not such printed or written declaration in it. He is also to cause all the books to be covered with strong wrapping paper, on the back of which is to be written the title of the book, and its number in large figures. As new books are added, the numbers are to be continued, and they are in no case to be altered; so that if a book be lost, its number and title must still be continued on the catalogue, with a note that it is missing.

The librarian must keep a blank book, that may be made by stitching together half a dozen or more sheets of writing paper. Let those be ruled across the width of the paper so as to leave five columns of the proper size for the following entries, to be written lengthwise of the paper; in the first column, the date of the delivery of any book to any inhabitant; in the second, the title of the book delivered, and its number; in the third, the name of the person to whom delivered; in the fourth, the date of its return; and in the fifth, remarks, respecting its condition, in the following form:

Time of delivery.	Title & No. Book.	To whom.	When returned.	Condition.
1839, June 10.	History of Va. 43.	T. Jones.	20th June.	Good.

As it will be impossible for the librarian to keep any trace of the books without such minutes, his own interest to screen himself from responsibility, as well as his duty to the public, will, it is to be hoped, induce him to be exact in making his entries at the time any book is delivered; and when it is returned, to be equally exact in noticing its condition, and making the proper minute.

A fair copy of the catalogue should be kept by the librarian, to be exhibited to those who desire to select a book; and if there be room, it should be fastened on the door of the case.

REGULATIONS CONCERNING THE USE OF THE BOOKS IN DISTRICT LIBRARIES PRESCRIBED BY THE SUPERINTENDENT OF COMMON SCHOOLS PURSUANT TO THE THIRD SECTION OF THE "ACT RESPECTING SCHOOL DISTRICT LIBRARIES," PASSED APRIL 15, 1839.

I. The librarian has charge of the books and is responsible for their preservation and delivery to his successor.

II. A copy of the catalogue required to be made out by Article III, and IV. of Regulations No. 1, is to be kept by the librarian, open to the inspection of the inhabitants of the district at all reasonable times. It will be found convenient to affix a copy of it on the door of the book-case containing the library.

III. Books are to be delivered as follows:

1st. Only to inhabitants of the district.

2d. One only can be delivered to an inhabitant at a time, and any one having a book out of the library must return it before he can receive another.

3d. No person upon whom a fine has been imposed by the trustees under these regulations, can receive a book while such fine remains unpaid.

4th. A person under age cannot be permitted to take out a book unless he resides with some responsible inhabitant of the district; nor can he then receive a book if notice has been given by his parent or guardian or the person with whom he resides, that they will not be responsible for books delivered such minor.

5th. Each individual residing in the district, of sufficient age to read the books belonging to the library, is to be regarded as an inhabitant, and is entitled to all the benefits and privileges conferred by the regulations relative to district libraries. Minors will draw in their own names, but on the responsibility of their parents or guardians.

6th. Where there is a sufficient number of volumes in the library to accommodate all residents of the district who wish to borrow, the librarian should permit each member of a family to take books, as often as desired, so long as the regulations are punctually and fully observed. But where there are not books enough to supply all the borrowers, the librarian should endeavor to accommodate as many as possible, by furnishing each family in proportion to the number of its readers or borrowers.

IV. Every book must be returned to the library within twenty days after it shall have been taken out, but the same inhabitant may again take it, unless application has been made for it, while it was so out of the library, by any person entitled, who has not previously borrowed the same book, in which case such applicant shall have a preference in the use of it. And where there have been several such applicants, the preference shall be according to the priority in time of their applications, to be determined by the librarian. Upon application to the Superintendent, the time for keeping books out of the library will be extended to a period not exceeding twenty-eight days, where sufficient reasons for such extentension are shown.

V. If a book be not returned at the proper time, the librarian is to report the fact to the trustees; and he must also exhibit to them every book which has been returned injured by soiling, defacing, tearing or in any other way, before such book shall again be loaned out, together with the name of the inhabitant in whose possession it was when so injured.

VI. The trustees of school districts being, by virtue of their office, trustees of the library, are hereby authorized to impose the following fines:

1st. For each day's detention of a book beyond the time allowed by these regulations, six cents, but not to be imposed for more than ten days' detention.

2d. For the destruction or loss of a book, a fine equal to the full value of the book, or of the set, if it be one of a series, with the addition to such value of ten cents for each volume. And on the payment of such fine, the party fined shall be entitled to the residue of the series. If he has also been fined for detaining such book, then the said ten cents shall not be added to the value.

3d. For any injury which a book may sustain after it shall be taken out by a borrower, and before its return, a fine may be imposed of six cents for every spot of grease or oil upon the cover, or upon any leaf of the volume; for writing in or defacing any book, not less than ten cents, nor more than the value of the book; for cutting or tearing the cover or the binding, or any leaf, not less than ten cents, nor more than the value of the book.

4th. If a leaf be torn out, or so defaced or mutilated that it can not be read, or if anything be written in the volume, or any other injury done to it, which renders it unfit for general circulation, the trustees will consider it a destruction of the book, and shall impose a fine accordingly, as above provided, in case of loss of a book.

5th. When a book shall have been detained seven days beyond the twenty days allowed by these regulations, the librarian shall give notice to the borrower to return the same within three days. If not returned at that time, the trustees may consider the book lost or destroyed, and may impose a fine for its destruction in addition to the fines for its detention.

VII. But the imposition of a fine for the loss or destruction of a book, shall not prevent the trustees from recovering such book in an action of replevin, unless such fine shall have been paid.

VIII. When, in the opinion of the librarian, any fine has been incurred by any person under these regulations, he may refuse to deliver any book to the party liable to such fine, until the decision of the trustees upon such liability be had.

IX. Previous to the imposition of any fine, two days' written or verbal notice is to be given by any trustee, or the librarian, or any other person authorized by either of them, to the person charged, to show cause why he should not be fined for the alleged offence or neglect; and if within that time good cause be not shown the trustees shall impose the fine herein prescribed. No other excuse for an extraordinary injury to a book, that is for such an injury as would not be occasioned by its ordinary use, should be received, but the fact that the book was as much injured when it was taken out by the person charged, as it was when he returned it. As such loss must fall on some one, it is more just that it should be borne by the party whose duty it was to take care of the volume, than by the district. Negligence can only be prevented, and disputes can only be avoided, by the adoption of this rule. Subject to these general principles the imposition of all, or any of these fines, is *discretionary* with the trustees, and they should ordinarily be imposed only for *wilful* or *culpably negligent* injuries to books, or where the district actually sustains a loss or serious injury. Reasonable excuses for the detention of the books beyond twenty days should in all cases be received.

X. It is the special duty of the librarian to give notice to the borrower of a book that shall be returned injured, to show cause why he should not be fined. Such notice may be given to the agent of the borrower who returns the book, and it should always be given at the time the book is returned.

XI. The librarian is to inform the trustees of every notice given by him to show cause against the imposition of a fine; and they shall assemble at the time and place appointed by him, or by any notice given by them, or any one of them; and shall hear the charge and defence. They are to keep a book of minutes, in which every fine imposed by them and the cause, shall be entered and signed by them, or the major part of them. Such original minutes, or a copy certified by them, or the major part of them, or by the clerk of the district, shall be conclusive evidence of the fact that a fine was imposed as stated in such minutes, according to these regulations.

XII. It shall be the duty of trustees to prosecute promptly for the collection of all fines imposed by them. Fines collected for the detention of books, or for injuries to them, are to be applied to defray the expense of repairing the books in the library. Fines collected for the loss or destruction of any book, or of a set or series of books, shall be applied to the purchase of the same or other suitable books.

XIII. These regulations being declared by law "obligatory upon all persons and officers having charge of such libraries, or using or possessing any of the books thereof," it is expedient that they should be made known to every borrower of a book. And for that purpose, a printed copy is to be affixed conspicuously on the case containing any library, or on one of such cases, if there be several; and the librarian is to call the attention to them of every person, on the first occasion of his taking out a book.

The offices of trustee and librarian are incompatible, and cannot be held by the same person.

CHAPTER VIII.

TEACHERS.

By § 104, (No. 129,) the trustees of each district are to provide a book, in which the teachers are to enter the names of the scholars attending school, and the number of days they shall have respectively attended, and also the number of times the school shall have been inspected by the town superintendent. This list is to be verified by the oath of the teacher.

The strict and faithful performance of this duty is highly important, not only to the district but to the teacher. It is the basis upon which the rate-bills are to be made out, and by which the sums to be paid by parents are to be ascertained. Error in these lists will therefore produce injustice. It has been held by this department, that the teacher is not entitled to call on the trustees for his wages, unless he furnishes them an accurate list of scholars, on which they can prepare the rate-bills and issue their warrant. Hence the teacher has a direct personal interest in the preservation of an accurate list, which he can verify by his oath.

For the purpose of executing this provision, the teacher will write the following heading or caption in his book, at the commencement of each quarter:

A list of the scholars who attended the district school of district No.   in the town of   during the quarter or term commencing the   day of   185 , and the number of days they respectively attended the same.

Time of entrance.	Name of scholar.	No. of days' attendance.	
Nov. 1, 1851,	John Thompson,	Seventy-eight,	78 days.
Dec. 1, "	Peter Barker,	Forty-three,	43 "
Dec. 4, "	James Thomas,	Forty,	40 "

At the time any pupil enters the schools, the teacher should immediately insert the date and the name of the scholar. At the close of the quarter, the whole number of days that each pupil attended is to be ascertained, from the check roll, and entered in the third column, in words at length, and also in figures, as in the above form.

Each teacher, at the commencement of every quarter, must provide a day or check roll, in which the name of every scholar is to be entered. It should be ruled so as to give six columns, corresponding to the number of days in the week. The number attending should be ascertained each half day, and pencil marks made in the column for the day opposite to the name of each one present. At the end of the week, the number of days each pupil has attended during the week should be summed up and entered on the weekly roll. Each half day's attendance should be noted, and two half days should be reckoned as one day. The pencil marks on the day roll may be obliterated, so that the same roll may be used during the quarter. The weekly roll should be formed in the same manner, so as to contain the names of the pupils, and thirteen columns ruled, corresponding to the number of weeks in the quarter. In each of these columns is to be entered the result of the daily check roll for each week, in the following form:

Weekly Roll.

Attendance of pupils in district school of district No.

Names of pupils.	1st week.	2d week.	3d week.	4th week.	5th week
J. Tho'n,	6 days.	4 days.	5 days.	6 days.	5½ days.

At the end of the quarter, the teacher will sum up the attendances of each pupil from this weekly roll, and enter the result in the book provided by the trustees as before mentioned, showing the whole number of days each scholar has attended during the quarter.

At the end of the list, the following oath or affirmation is to be written:

A. B., being duly sworn, (or affirmed) deposes, that the foregoing is a true and accurate list of the names of the scholars who attended the district school of district No.   in the town of   during the quarter commencing the   day of   185   , and the number of days they respectively attended.

This oath or affirmation is to be signed by the teacher, and certified by a justice of the peace, commissioner of deeds, judge of any court of record, town superintendent, or county clerk, to have been taken before him.

The teachers are also required to make an abstract of the lists for the use of the trustees, at the end of each quarter, showing the results exhibited under the following heads and in the following form:

Abstract of the attendance of scholars, at the district school of district No.   in the town of   during the quarter commencing the   day of   185   .

Of scholars who attended less than two months, there were
Of scholars who attended two months and less than four,
"   "   four months and less than six,
"   "   six months and less than eight,
"   "   eight months and less than ten,
"   "   ten months and less than twelve,
"   "   twelve months.

This abstract is to be signed by the teacher and delivered to the trustees.

In another part of the book provided by the trustees, and towards the end of it, the teacher will enter the days on which the school has been inspected, in the form of a memorandum, as follows:

Account of Inspections of the School in District No.   .

November 1, 1841. The school was inspected by *William Jones*, town Superintendent.

December 1, 1841. The school was inspected.

To this also an oath or affirmation of the correctness must be added, in the following form:

A. B., being duly sworn, (or affirmed) deposes, that the foregoing is a true account of the days on which the school in District No.   , in the town of   , was visited and inspected by the town superintendent, during the quarter commencing on the day of 185 .

Teacher.

Sworn (or affirmed) and subscribed this day of 185 , before me.

Teachers cannot demand payment of their wages until the collector has had thirty days to collect them.—*Com. School Dec.* 101.

A teacher may employ necessary means of correction to maintain order ; but he should not dismiss a scholar from school without consultation with the trustees.—*Id.* **145.**

If a teacher's certificate is annulled, the trustees are at liberty to dismiss him, and to rescind their contract with him. But if they continue him in school, after notice that his certificate has been annulled, it will be regarded as such a continuance of the contract, that they will not be allowed at a subsequent period to dispute it. —*Id* 212

Contracts by trustees for teachers' wages are binding upon successors in office.—*Id* 191, 282.

Teachers, though not, strictly speaking, ***inhabitants*** of the district where they are located, should be allowed to participate in all the privileges and benefits of the district libraries.—*Per* SPENCER, *Supt,* 1841.

The convenience and accommodation of many, if not of most of the inhabitants of the several districts, would be essentially promoted by placing the charge of the library, temporarily with the teacher, during the term of his or her employment, and depositing it in some convenient and safe place in the school-house. This arrangement can only be carried into effect by the concurrence of the trustees and librarian, and under their supervision. Generally, the teacher, not being an inhabitant of the district, cannot be chosen librarian. But where the trustees and librarian have sufficient confidence in the teacher and in the safety of the books, when left at the school-house, they will find this arrangement in many respects conducive to the convenience of the district.

The authority of the teacher to punish his scholars, extends to acts done in the school-room, or play-ground, only ; and he has no legal right to punish for improper or disorderly conduct elsewhere. —*Per* SPENCER, *Sup't.*

Teachers may open and close their schools with prayer, and the reading of the Scriptures, accompanied with suitable remarks ; taking care to avoid all discussion of controverted points, or sectarian dogmas.

Where a teacher is dismissed by the trustees for good cause, he can collect his wages only up to the period of his dismissal.

The teacher of a school has necessarily the government of it ; and he may prescribe the rules and principles on which such government will be conducted. The trustees should not interfere with the discipline of the school except on complaint of misconduct on the part of the teacher ; and they should then invariably sustain such teacher, unless his conduct has been grossly wrong.—*Per* SPENCER, *Sup't*

Where a teacher agrees to collect his own wages he will be concluded by such an agreement, and will not afterwards be permitted to call on the trustees to enforce the collection of any part of such bill by rate-bill.—*Id.*

Where a teacher contracts with the trustees of a district to teach their school for a given sum *per scholar*, he is entitled to *charge the trustees* that sum for each scholar attending the school during the quarter, without reference to the number of days' attendance ; provided such scholar has not been detained from school during the greater portion of the term, by illness or unavoidable casualty.— The *trustees* however, must graduate their *rate-bill against the inhabitants* sending to school, by the number of days attendance, to be ascertained from the verified list of the teacher.—*Per* YOUNG *Sup't.*

Schools may be kept on *Sunday* for the benefit of those persons who observe *Saturday* as holy time , and the teacher must be paid for that day by those who send to school.—*Com. School Dec.* 138.

The *holydays* on which a teacher may dismiss his school are such as it is customary to observe, either throughout the country or in particular localities ; among which may be enumerated the *Fourth of July*, Thanksgiving, Christmas, New-Year's, &c.—*Id.* 139.

The teacher may also, unless restrained by special contract to the contrary, dismiss his school on the afternoon of each Saturday, or the whole of each alternate Saturday, according to the particular custom of the district in that respect, or his own convenience and that of the inhabitants.—*Id.*

The practice of inflicting *corporal punishment* upon scholars, *in any case whatever*, has no sanction but usage. The teacher is responsible for maintaining good order, and he must be the judge of the degree and nature of the punishment required where his authority is set at defiance. At the same time he is liable to the party injured for any abuse of a prerogative *which is wholly derived from custom*—*Per* JOHN A. DIX, *Sup't. Common School Decisions*, 102.

CHAPTER IX.

APPEALS TO THE STATE SUPERINTENDENT.

The cases in which the courts will not entertain jurisdiction of complaints of erroneous proceedings under the school laws, and in which only a certiorari will ie, may be inferred from the decision of the Supreme court in the case of Easton and others, *vs* Calender, 11 Wend. 90. "The plaintiff below was not without his remedy. 1 R. S. 487, §110, 111 and the amendment of the law, 20th April 1830, provides "that any person conceiving himself aggrieved in consequence of any decision made by the Trustees of any district in paying any teacher ; or concerning any other matter under the present title," (which includes the whole of the school act,) "may appeal to the Superintendent of Common Schools, whose decision shall be final." This provision was intended for what it practically is, a cheap and expeditious mode of settling most, if not all, of the difficulties and disputes arising in the course of the execution of the law. A common law certiorari would no doubt lie from this court, to the trustees to bring up and correct any erroneous proceeding not concluded by an adjudication of the Superintendent, or in a case where his powers were inadequate to give the relief to which the party was entitled."

The passage of several acts of the Legislature renders necessary a revision of the regulations concerning appeals : And the following are therefore substituted for those heretofore established :

CASES IN WHICH APPEALS MAY BE MADE.

I. Where any decision has been made by any School District meeting.

This includes the whole class of cases, in which district meetings have the power to decide on any proposition or motion that may legally be made to them, under any section of the School Act.

II. Where any decision has been made by the Town Superintendent of Common Schools, or by him and the Supervisor and Town Clerk, in forming or altering, or in refusing to form or alter any School District, or in refusing to pay any school moneys to any district, and under the general provision, "concerning any other matter under the present title," appeals will also lie from the proceedings of such Town Superintendent in any erroneous distribution of public money, in paying it to any district not entitled, or more than it is authorized to receive ; and in fact any official decision, act or proceeding, and from a refusal to discharge any duty imposed by law, or the regulations of the Superintendent, or incident to the duties of his office.

III. Where any decision has been made by trustees of school districts in paying any teacher, or refusing to pay him, or in refusing to admit any scholar gratuitously into the school: And under the same general provision referred to, in improperly admitting any scholar gratuitously, in making out any tax list, or rate-bill, or in any act or proceeding whatever, which they undertake to perform officially ; and also for the refusal to discharge any duty enjoined by law, or any regulation of the Superintendent, or incident to the duties of their office.

IV. Where Town Superintendents have improperly granted or annulled a certificate or qualification to a teacher; or have refused to grant or annul such certificate; and where they have undertaken to perform any official act, or refused to discharge any duty imposed by law or under its authority, in the inspection of teachers and visitation of schools.

V. Where Clerks of Districts, Clerks of Towns, or other ministerial officers, refuse to perform any duty enjoined by the Common School Act.

VI. Where any other matter under the said act, shall be presented, either in consequence of disputes between districts respecting their boundaries, or any other subject; or in consequence of disputes between any officers charged with the execution of any duties under the laws concerning Common Schools, or disputes between them any other person relating to such duties or any of them.

Under the 140*th section "respecting School District Libraries,"* (*No.* 159.)

VII. Appeals may be made from any act or decision of trustees or school districts concerning the Libraries or the books therein, or the use of such books.

VIII. Any act or decision of the Librarian in respect to the Library.

IX. Any act or decision of any district meeting in relation to their school library.

X. Appeals also lies from the acts of Town Superintendents of Common Schools in withholding or paying over library money to any district.

BY WHOM APPEALS ARE TO BE MADE.

XII. The person aggrieved by the act complained of, only, can appeal. Generally every inhabitant of a district is aggrieved by the wrongful act or omission of a trustee or town superintendent, by which money or property is disposed of, or not secured for the benefit of the district. But no one is aggrieved by another being included in a tax list or rate-bill, although other inhabitants are by the omission of one who should be taxed; and appeals may be made by trustees, in behalf of their districts whenever they are aggrieved.

FORM AND MANNER OF PROCEEDING.

XIII. An appeal must be in writing and signed by the appellant. When made by the trustees of a district, it must be signed by all the trustees, or a reason must be given for the omission of any, verified by the oath of the appellant, or of some person acquainted with such reason.

XIV. A copy of the appeal, duly verified, and of all the statements, maps and papers intended to be presented in support of it, must be served on the officers whose act or decision is complained of, or some of them ; or if it be from the decision or proceeding of a district meeting, upon the district clerk or one of the trustees, whose duty it is to cause information of such appeal to be given to the inhabitants who voted for the decision or proceeding appealed from.

XV. Such service must be made within thirty days after the making of the decision, or the performance of the act complained of, or within that time, after the knowledge of the cause of complaint came to the appellant, or some satisfactory excuse must be rendered for delay.

XVI. The party on whom the appeal was served, must within ten days from the time of such service, answer the same, either by concurring in a statement of facts with the appellant, or by a separate answer. Such statement and answer must be signed by all the trustees, or other officers, whose act, omission or decision is appealed from, or a good reason on oath must be given, for the omission of the signature of any of them, verified by oath, and a copy of such answer must be served on the appellants, or some one of them.

XVII. So far as the parties concur in a statement no oath will be required to it. But all facts, maps or papers not agreed upon by them and evidenced by their signature on both sides, must be verified by oath.

XVIII. All oaths required by these regulations must be taken before a judge of a court of record, a commissioner of deeds, a justice of the peace, or a town superintendent.

XIX. A copy of the answer and of all the statements, maps and papers intended to be presented in support of it, must be served upon the appellants, or some one of them, within ten days after service of a copy of the appeal, unless further time be given by the state superintendent, on application, in special cases; but no replication or rejoinder shall be allowed, except by permission of the state superintendent, and in reference exclusively to matters arising upon the answer, and which may be deemed by such state superintendent pertinent to the issue: in which case such replication and rejoinder shall be duly verified by oath, and copies thereof served on the opposite party.

XX. Proof or admission of the service of copies of the appeal, answer and all other papers intended to be used on the hearing of such appeal, must in all cases, accompany the same.

XXI. When any proceeding of a district meeting is appealed from, and when the inhabitants of a district generally are interested in the matter of the appeal, and in all cases where an inhabitant might be an appellant, had the decision or proceeding been the opposite of that which was made or had; any one of more of such inhabitants may answer the appeal, with or without the trustees.

XXII. Where the appeal has relation to the alteration or formation of a school district, it must be accompanied by a map, exhibiting the site of the school house, the roads, the old and new lines of districts, the different lots, the particular location and distance from the school-houses, of the persons aggrieved; and their relative distance, if there are two or more school-houses in question. Also, a list of all the taxable inhabitants in the district or territory to be affected by the question; the valuation of the property taken from the last assessment roll, and the number of children between five and sixteen belonging to each person, distinguishing the districts to which they respectively belong.

XXIII. When the copy of the appeal is served, all proceedings upon or in continuation of the act complained of, or consequent in any way upon such act, must be suspended until the case is decided. So where any decision concerning the distribution of public money to one or more districts is appealed from, the town superintendent must retain the money which is in dispute until the appeal is decided. And where trustees have money in their hands claimed to belong to any person, or any other district, after the copy of an appeal is served on them in relation to such claim, they must retain such moneys to abide the result, and must not expend them so as to defeat the object of the appeal.

XXIV. Whenever a decision is made by the superintendent, and communicated to the town superintendent of common schools, respecting the formation, division or alteration of districts, he must cause the decision to be recorded in the office of the town clerk. All other decisions communicated to him, or to the trustees of districts, are to be kept among the official papers of the clerk of the town or district and handed over to his successors; and the district clerks are required to record all such as come to their hands in the district book kept by them.

NOTE.—By a clerical error in the engrossment of the 16th section of Chap. 382 of the laws of 1849, section 132 of Chap. 480, laws of 1847, conferring appellate jurisdiction on the State Superintendent of Common Schools, was inadvertently repealed. The Superintendent has, however, continued to entertain appeals in accordance with the regulations above inserted, *where such appeals have been submitted by the parties respectively*, to his decision. A bill correcting the error in the act of 1849, passed the Assembly at its last session, and was supposed to have passed the Senate, at the time of the passing of these sheets through the press, in consequence of which, the original section (132) relating to appeals was restored. As there can be little doubt that this section will be re-instated at the ensuing session of the Legislature, it has been deemed expedient to retain that portion of the instructions relating to appeals, with this explanatory note.

PART IV.

LOCAL LAWS AND REGULATIONS,

RESPECTING

COMMON SCHOOLS.

ALBANY.

[*Laws of* 1844, *Chap.* 128.]

§ 1. The mayor and recorder of the city of Albany, and the Regents of the University residing in said city, shall, without delay, appoint nine persons, residents of the city of Albany, to be denominated a Board of Commissioners of the District Schools of the city of Albany, who shall be divided by lot into three classes, to be numbered one, two and three: the term of office of the first class shall be one year, from the first day of June next; of the second, two; and of the third, three years from that day: and three commissioners shall thereafter annually be appointed by the said mayor and recorder of the city of Albany, and the regents of the university residing in said city, in place of those whose terms of office shall expire, who shall hold their office for three years, and until their successors be duly appointed. In case of a vacancy in the office of either of the commissioners, during the period for which he or they shall have been respectively appointed, the said mayor and recorder of the city of Albany and the regents of the university residing in the said city, shall fill such vacancy, and the person or persons so appointed to fill such vacancy, shall hold the office only for the unexpired term so becoming vacant.

§ 2. Any member of said board of commissioners may be removed, for cause, from office, by a vote of two-thirds of the persons authorized by the preceding section to appoint such commissioners; and any vacancy so made shall be filled in the manner already provided.

§ 3. The board of commissioners shall have power to appoint one of their number president of said board, who shall have the powers usually incident to such office; and said board shall have power, and it shall be their duty, to appoint a secretary to said board, who shall perform such duties as the said board from time to time may direct, and who shall receive therefor such compensation, not exceeding one hundred and fifty dollars annually, as the said board shall provide, out of any moneys remaining unexpended in the hands of said board.

§ 4. The board of commissioners shall have power, and it shall be their duty, to contract with and employ the teachers of the district schools of said city; to remove any teacher upon manifest neglect of duty, or upon violation of his or her contract; to appoint a collector for the said district schools; to make out rate bills and exempt indigent children therefrom; to select and introduce uniform class books into said schools; to supply indigent pupils with said class books, by using and appropriating for that purpose a portion of the library money, not exceeding three hundred dollars in any one year; to appropriate and use, for the purpose of keeping in repair the several libraries of said district schools, for increasing the same, and for purchasing maps and apparatus for said schools, a farther portion of said library money, not exceeding three hundred dollars annually; to provide for the instruction of the pupils of said district schools in vocal music, by appropriating a farther portion of said library money, not exceeding four hundred dollars annually; to secure, with whatever may remain unexpended of said library money, the education of such number of indigent pupils from said district schools, in either of the academies or in any normal school of said city, by paying for their tuition therein, as the common council of said city may sanction; but all children so educated shall have been members of said district schools for at least two years; and neither of such academies shall receive from the distribution of the literature fund, any sum for or on account of such pupils; and such academies shall, in their annual report to the regents of the university, state the number of such pupils taught therein; and no portion of said unexpended money shall be so appropriated until the ordinary expenses of said district schools for libraries and tuition are first satisfied; to visit the district schools as often as once a quarter; to hold a meeting of the board once a month, and at the quarterly meetings of said board to require the presence and reports of the several principal teachers of said schools; to make a semi-annual report of all the acts of said board to the common council, and to make and publish an annual report in two of the daily papers of said city; and generally to possess the powers, discharge the duties and be subject to all of the obligations of the several trustees and other school officers of the said city of Albany, as granted and imposed by the several acts now in force in relation to said district schools of said city.

§ 5. The board of commissioners shall have power, and it shall be their duty, to make such by-laws and regulations as may be necessary for the prosperity, good order and sound discipline of said district schools; for the security and preservation of the school-houses and other property belonging to said districts; and generally to carry into effect the provisions of the several school acts of said city; and when said by-laws and regulations are sanctioned by the persons authorized by this act to appoint said commissioners, they shall take effect, and not before.

§ 6. All school moneys whatsoever, belonging to said district schools, whether received from the State, raised by tax, or collected on school rates, shall be deposited with the Chamberlain of said city, until drawn, from time to time, by duly certified orders of said Board of Commissioners; and said orders shall set forth the object of each payment, and be signed by the officers of said board. Provided always, that nothing in this act shall be so construed as to authorize said board to incur any obligation that shall increase the taxes of said city.

[*Laws of* 1845. *Chap*. 245.]

§ 1. The Board of Commissioners of the Albany district schools are hereby authorized to apply any library money, not expended under the fourth section of the act entitled, "An Act amendatory to the several acts relating to district schools in the city of Albany," passed April 8, 1844, either to the payment of teachers' wages, or to the contingent expenses of the district schools of said city.

[*Laws of* 1837. *Chap.* 213.]

§ 9. The school buildings and lots on which the same are erected, now belonging to, or that may hereafter belong to any school district in said city of Albany, shall be exempt from all taxes or assessments.

[*Laws of* 1837. *Chap.* 358.]

§ 2. The Commissioners of common schools shall apportion annually, on the returns of qualified teachers, for the instruction of the children in the Albany Orphan Asylum for destitute children, their proportion of the public money for the support of schools; which money, when so apportioned and paid to the trustees of the district, shall be paid to such teachers for teachers' wages.

[*Laws of* 1837. *Chap.* 369.]

§ 9. The Supervisors of the county of Albany, at their annual meeting in each year, shall cause a sum of money, equal to twice the amount of the money apportioned to the city from the common school fund, together with collector's fees, to be raised, levied and collected in the same manner that other taxes are raised, levied and collected; and when so raised, to be paid to the Chamberlain, for the support of common schools in the city of Albany, to be apportioned and distributed, as now provided for by law.

§ 2. All moneys apportioned by the commissioners of common schools to the trustees of a district which shall have remained in the hands of the Chamberlain for one year after such apportionment, by reason of the trustees neglecting or refusing to receive the same, shall be added to the moneys next thereafter to be apportioned by the commissioners, and shall be apportioned and paid therewith and in the same manner.

§ 3. No school district now formed, or hereafter to be formed, east of Perry street, shall have power to hold a district school meeting, to vote a tax, or to do any act as a district meeting; nor shall have power to sell or dispose of the district property, without a legislative enactment.

AUBURN.

[*Laws of* 1850. *Chap.* 349.]

§ 1. Title eight of an act to incorporate the city of Auburn, passed March 21, 1848, is hereby repealed.

§ 2. The offices of the several trustees, clerks, collectors and librarians of school districts, in the city of Auburn, shall cease on the third Tuesday in April, one thousand, eight hundred and fifty, in like manner as if the same had expired by lapse of time. The inhabitants of said city, qualified to vote at school district meetings, shall assemble in their respective school districts on the day last mentioned, at the school house in such district, and choose one trustee and a clerk of the district, who shall hold their respective offices until the next annual district meeting in the district, for which they shall be respectively chosen, and until their successors shall have been severally chosen. Such annual district meeting shall hereafter be holden in the several districts in said city, on the second Monday in March in each year; and from and after the passage of this act, only one trustee shall be chosen annually in any school district in said city.

§ 3. The trustee elected in any district in said city, shall have the power and it shall be his duty, to call special meetings of the inhabitants of such districts liable to pay taxes, whenever he shall deem it necessary or proper to give notice of special, annual and adjourned meetings, in the manner prescribed in this act, if there be no clerk of the district, or he be absent or incapable of acting, or shall refuse or neglect to give such notice; to visit the schools kept in the district as often as once in each quarter, and to report the condition of the same, with such suggestions for the improvement thereof as he may deem proper, to the board of education hereinafter named, and to perform such other duties as may be from time to time imposed upon him by the said board of education.

§ 4. It shall be sufficient notice of an annual, special, adjourned or first district meeting, to affix such notice on the outer door of the district school house, if there be any, and to post a copy of the same in three other public places in such district—the affixing and posting of such notice to be done at least ten days before such meeting, and no other notice of any such meeting need be given.

§ 5. It shall be the duty of the clerk of each school district to record the proceedings of his district in a book to be provided for that purpose by the said board of education; to give notice in the manner provided in the last preceding section, of the time and place of every annual district meeting or special district meetings, when ordered by the trustees of the district, and of any adjourned district meeting, when the same shall be adjourned for a longer period than one month; to keep and preserve all records, books and papers belonging to his office, and to deliver the same to his successor in office.

§ 6. Any vacancy in the office of district clerk may be supplied by the trustee of the district in which such vacancy shall happen, but the person appointed to supply such vacancy shall hold the office only for the unexpired term.

§ 7. The term of office of the superintendent of common schools in said city shall cease on the third Tuesday of April, one thousand eight hundred and fifty, in the same manner as if the same had expired by lapse of time. The common council of said city, at the last regular meeting thereof, next preceding the third Tuesday of April next, shall appoint by ballot a superintendent of common schools, who shall hold his office until the second Monday of March, one thousand, eight hundred and fifty-two. The common council of said city, at the annual meeting thereof, held on the second Monday of March, 1852, and as often thereafter as the term of office of such superintendent of common schools shall expire, shall appoint a superintendent of common schools for said city, who shall hold his office for two years, and until a successor shall be appointed. The superintendent of common schools so appointed, shall possess all the powers and be subject to all the duties and responsibilities of superintendents of common schools in towns, so far as the same are applicable, except as otherwise provided in this act; in case of a vacancy in such office, the common council of said city shall supply the same by appointment, for the unexpired term.

§ 8. The common council of said city shall, at the last regular meeting thereof, next preceding the third Tuesday of April, one thousand eight hundred and fifty, appoint one school commissioner in each of the wards of said city, who shall be residents of the wards for which they are respectively appointed; immediately upon the appointment of such school commissioners, the city clerk shall, in the presence of the common council, divide them by lot into four classes, to be numbered one, two, three, four. The term of office of the first class shall expire on the first Monday succeeding the first Tuesday in April, 1851; the second class in one year thereafter; the third in two years, and the fourth in three years, and one commissioner only shall thereafter be annually appointed, who shall be appointed at the annnal meeting of the common council, held on Monday next succeeding the annual election, and who shall be a resident of the same ward with the school commissioner whose term of office shall then expire, who shall hold his office for four years, and until a successor shall be duly appointed In case of a vacancy in the office of either of the commissioners, the common council shall appoint a successor, who shall be a resident of the ward in which such vacancy shall occur, for the unexpired term.

§ 9. The trustees of the several school districts so elected, and the school commissioners so appointed, together with the mayor and superintendent of schools of said city, shall constitute and are hereby denominated the board of education for the city of Auburn. They shall meet on the first Tuesday of each and every month, and as much oftener as they shall from time to time appoint. A majority of the said board shall constitute a quorum for the transaction of business. The mayor shall be the president of such board and shall have power to call special meetings thereof, in the manner provided by law for calling special meetings of the common council. In the absence of the mayor, the said board shall appoint some other member to preside at such meetings, and perform the duties of the president. The superintendent of common schools shall be the clerk of such board; he shall attend the meetings and keep a record of the proceedings of the said board; he shall possess all the powers and be required to perform all the duties, in reference to the schools of said city, of town superintendents of common schools, except as otherwise in this act provided, and shall perform such other duties as the said board shall from time to time prescribe.

§ 10. The board of education shall fix the compensation of the superintendent of common schools, for his services as clerk of such board, not exceeding one hundred dollars per year, and for such other services as he may perform otherwise than as such clerk, he shall be entitled to the same compensation as provided by law for town superintendents of schools for similar services, and his account therefor shall be audited by such board and paid by the city treasurer, out of the moneys in this act specified as the common school fund, and not otherwise.

§ 11. The said board of education shall possess all the powers conferred by law upon town superintendents of common schools, as to the formation and alteration of school districts within said city, except that in arranging such districts, no territory without the limits of said city shall be included, nor shall any territory within said city belong to or be taxed in any school district of any adjoining town; and shall possess all the powers and be subject to all the duties and responsibilities of trustees of common schools in towns, as to the several common or district schools within said city, so far as the same are applicable, except as otherwise in this act provided, and shall have the custody of all the property, real and personal, belonging to or owned by the several school districts, and shall pay the compensation of the teachers of the said schools, and all other necessary and contingent expenses incurred in the support thereof; and shall appoint librarians to take charge of the several district libraries, who shall be subject to the control and hold their offices during the pleasure of such board; and shall have the power and it shall be their duty to pass such by-laws and ordinances for the regulation, government, control and management of the common schools in said city, and of the teachers and pupils of such schools, and of the officers of the several school districts in said city, and for the safe-keeping, disposition and management of the libraries, maps and apparatus appertaining to such schools, and to regulate the text books used in such schools, as they shall deem expedient; and said board may prescribe a penalty for a violation of any ordinance or by-law authorized by this act, not exceeding ten dollars; and any such penalty may be sued for and recovered with costs, in the name of the mayor and common council of the city of Auburn; and the said board may subject the parent or guardian of any minor, and the master or mistress of any apprentice or servant, to any such penalty for a violation of any such ordinance or by-law, by any such minor, apprentice or servant.

§ 12. All penalties collected by virtue of this act shall be paid to the city treasurer, and by him deposited to the credit of the common school fund.

§ 13. The clerk of the board of education shall keep a record of all by-laws and ordinances which shall be passed by said board, and the same shall be published and take effect, and be proved and read in evidence, in like manner as ordinances passed by the common council of the city of Auburn; a record or entry made by the said clerk at the time of the first publication of any ordinances, or a copy thereof duly certified by him, or the affidavit of the printer or publisher, shall be presumptive evidence of the publication thereof, in all courts and places.

§ 14. Whenever the inhabitants of any school district shall, by vote, determine to build a school-house, it shall be the duty of the said board of education to fix the site of the said school house, and determine the sum necessary to be raised for the purchase of such site and the building of said school house, and report the same to the common council, which sum shall in no case exceed the sum of three thousand dollars.

§ 15. It shall be the duty of the common council to levy and raise upon the said district the sum so reported, pursuant to the last section, in the same manner as the general taxes of the city are levied or raised, except that the same shall be collected on a separate warrant, and when the same shall be collected it shall be paid to the city treasurer, and deposited to the credit of the board of education; and no part thereof shall be appropriated by said board otherwise than for the purchase and improvement of such site and the erection of such school-house, with the appurtenances.

§ 16. The said board of education shall annually, on or before the first day of June, fix and determine, and certify and report to the common council, the amount of money which, when added to the money annually apportioned to the city of Auburn, or to the several school districts comprised therein, out of the funds belonging to the state, shall be necessary to defray the expenses of all the common or district schools in said city for the ensuing year, for fuel, furniture, school apparatus, repairs and insurance of school-house, teachers' wages and contingent expenses, and also to defray the expenses of a school for colored children, as hereinafter provided; and to pay the compensation of the clerk of the board of education, and the contingent expenses of such board. The amount so certified shall in no case exceed five times the amount which shall have been apportioned out of the funds belonging to the state as aforesaid, for the year next preceding.

§ 17. The common council of the said city shall annually levy and raise the amount of money so certified and reported by the board of education, and the said amount so to be raised shall be levied and collected at the same time and in the same manner as the other general taxes of the said city are levied and raised, and in addition thereto; but the warrant issued to the collector for the collection of such taxes shall specify what amount of such taxes shall be paid to the treasurer for general city purposes, and what part as a fund for the support of schools.

§ 18. All moneys levied and raised for the support of common schools, together with the public money received from the state, shall be paid to the treasurer of the city of Auburn, and shall by him be kept separate and distinct from the other moneys of said city, and shall be known and distinguished as the common school fund, and shall be paid out by the treasurer, only upon an order drawn upon him, and signed by the president and countersigned by the clerk of said board of education; and no such order shall be drawn except by virtue of a resolution of the board. Such order shall specify for what purpose the amount specified therein is to be paid, and the clerk of such board shall keep an accurate account, under the appropriate heads of expenditure, of all orders drawn on the treasury, in a check book, to be kept by him for that purpose.

§ 19. The board of supervisors of Cayuga county shall not have power to levy any tax upon the city of Auburn, for the support or on account of common schools.

§ 20. The said board of education shall exclusively audit all accounts and claims against any school district, or which have accrued on account of any district school in said city, and the payment of the same or of such parts thereof as shall be allowed by the said board, shall be made directly to such claimants by the city treasurer, out of the moneys belonging to the common school fund, upon the order of said board, as hereinbefore provided; but the aggregate of the expenditures and contracts of the said board during any year shall not exceed the amount of moneys which shall be subject to their order during the then current year.

§ 21. Whenever, from the annual estimate presented to the common council by said board of education, it shall appear that the expenses of any school district for the ensuing year, exclusive of teachers' wages, will exceed the sum of fifty dollars, the common council may, in their discretion, order the amount of such excess to be levied and assessed upon and collected from such district, in the manner hereinbefore provided for raising moneys to build a school house; and such moneys, when so collected, shall be paid to the city treasurer, and be by him placed to the credit of the said board of education, and shall by said board be expended solely for the benefit of such district.

§ 22. The said board of education shall have power to establish and cause to be kept in said city, a school for the instruction of colored children, as they shall deem expedient, and the said board shall have and exercise all the powers in relation to such school, of trustees of school districts in towns, so far as applicable.

§ 23. Whenever the said board of education shall determine to establish a school for the instruction of colored children, they shall make an estimate of the expense of erecting a suitable school-house therefor, and determine the site thereof, and report such proceedings to the common council.

§ 24. The common council shall have power to raise by general tax, in the manner hereinbefore provided, and on a separate warrant, or in addition to the general city tax, such sum as shall be necessary to purchase such site and build such school-house, not exceeding three thousand dollars; or, the said common council may refuse to raise such tax. In case the common council shall refuse to raise such tax, the said board of education shall have power to provide and lease a suitable room or building, for the accommodation of such school, but the annual expenditure for this purpose shall not exceed the sum of one hundred dollars—the same to be paid from the common school fund.

§ 25. All teachers of common schools in said city shall be employed by the city superintendent of common schools, and the trustees of the district for which such teacher or teachers shall be employed; but no appointment or employment of any such teacher shall be valid beyond the first regular meeting of the board of education thereafter, unless such appointment shall be approved by such board; and all contracts made with teachers by said superintendent and any trustee, shall be subject to the provisions of this act; and such contract shall cease to be binding on the rejection of such teacher by the board of education.

§ 26. The said board of education may remove any teacher for cause, to be specified in the minutes of the proceedings of the said board; and in case of any such removal, any contract with any such teacher shall cease, and another teacher shall be employed in the manner provided in the last preceding section.

§ 27. To the first annual estimate of school expenses presented by the board of education to the common council, the said board shall add the present indebtedness of every school district within said city, for any of the causes specified in section (16) sixteen of this act, or which may necessarily accrue therefor, previous to the time of presentation of such first estimate, and such additional amount shall be raised in like manner as the other moneys stated in said estimate, and shall be paid into and compose a part of the common school fund; and the said board shall assume and pay such indebtedness out of the monies so received.

§ 28. The said board of education shall annually publish in some newspaper in said city, a statement of the number of common schools in said city, and the number of pupils instructed therein, the total amount of moneys received for school purposes, with the sources thereof, and the expenditures on account of each school, specifying as near as may be the items of such expenditures.

§ 29. An appeal may be taken to the state superintendent of common schools from any proceeding of the said board of education, in the formation or alteration of any school district, in the same manner and for the same causes as appeals may be taken from the proceedings of town superintendents of common schools.

§ 30. All titles taken to real estate to be used for school purposes, with the exception of a site for a school house for colored children, shall be taken in the name of the trustees of the district in which such real estate shall be situated, in his official name; and any real estate now or hereafter owned by any school district, may be sold by the trustees of such district, upon a vote of the inhabitants of said district, and with the approval of the said board of education; and the avails of such real estate shall be paid to the city treasurer, and be by him placed to the credit of the board of education, and by said board appropriated exclusively to the benefit of such district.

§ 31. The treasurer and collector of the city of Auburn shall respectively, with their sureties, be liable on their official bonds for any default, delinquency, neglect or misconduct in the duties with which they may be respectively charged, under and by virtue of this act, in the same manner and with the like effect as for any other official default, delinquency, neglect or misconduct.

§ 32. All acts and parts of acts inconsistent with this act are hereby repealed.

§ 33. This act shall take effect immediately.

BROOKLYN.

[*Laws of* 1850. *Chap.* 143.]

§ 1. The common council of the city of Brooklyn shall, on the first Monday of February after this act becomes a law, appoint thirty-three persons, residents of said city, one of whom at least shall reside in each school district thereof, who together shall constitute a board of education. It shall then divide the said board into three equal classes, each class containing eleven members, and shall determine by lot their respective terms of office, so that the first class shall serve one year, the second two years, and the third three years. In each year thereafter, the said common council shall appoint eleven members of said board, care being had to preserve the representation of at least one member from each school district, whose term of office shall continue three years: and in case a vacancy shall at any time occur in said board, the said council shall supply the same. The persons so appointed shall be re-eligible, and shall hold office until their successors are appointed and shall have qualified.

§ 2. The board of education shall have the entire charge and direction of all the public schools of said city, and of the school moneys raised for the support of the same, and shall possess the powers and be subject to the general duties of trustees of common schools in this state, so far as the same are not impaired or affected by this act. It shall annually choose a presiding officer, make its own by laws, keep a journal of its proceedings, define the duties of its officers and committees, and prescribe such rules and regulations for instruction and discipline in the said public schools as are not inconsistent with the laws of the state; and all the provisions of the act relating to resignations and expulsions in the common council shall be applicable to the board of education.

§ 3. The whole city shall be a school district for all purposes of taxation as well for the purchase of school sites and the building and repairing of school houses, as for the annual support of schools; but shall be divided by the board of education into as many districts as there are schools, for the purpose of determining the limits within which children may attend such schools.

§ 4. The board of education shall have power to organize and establish schools for colored children, and such evening schools as it may, from time to time, deem expedient, and shall adopt the necessary rules for the government of the same. It may make use of the public school houses under its charge for such evening schools, and the expenses of said schools shall be paid out of the general fund, in the same manner as those of the other public schools. No person shall be prohibited from attending the evening schools on account of age.

§ 5. The board of education shall appoint a city superintendent of common schools, who shall, ex-officio, be the secretary of the board. In addition to such other duties as may be devolved upon him by the board, in the visitation and superintendence of the schools, he shall examine the qualifications of teachers and grant certificates, in such manner and form as may be prescribed by the state superintendent, which shall not be in force longer than a year, and may at any time be revoked by the board of education. He shall also make such annual and other reports of the condition of the schools and of other matters as may be required by law or by the said board. He shall be paid a salary out of the general fund, to be fixed by the board, and may be removed from office by the vote of a majority of all the members of the board of education.

§ 6. The treasurer of the city shall be, ex-officio, the treasurer of the board of education, and shall receive to the credit of said board, from the county treasurer, the amount of school money to which the city is entitled from the state appropriation, together with such amount as is raised by the board of supervisors to entitle the city to its distributive share of the school moneys of the state, and from the city collector the money raised by tax for the support of schools; and he shall disburse the same only by the order and upon the warrant of the board of education, drawn in favor of the person entitled to payment, signed by the presiding officer of the board, and countersigned by its secretary.

§ 7. The treasurer shall give such bonds for the faithful performance of his duty as the common council may require, and shall report monthly to the board of education his receipts and expenditures, with the balance remaining on hand to the credit of the board, and such other information in relation thereto as the board of education may, from time to time, require.

§ 8. The board of education shall provide for taking an annual census of all the children of the city, on the thirty-first day of December in each year, between the ages of five and sixteen years inclusive, which enumeration, with such statistical and other information as may be required by law, shall be included in the report of the city superintendent, required in a previous section.

§ 9. The board of education shall present, annually, on or before the first Monday in February, to the common council, an estimate of the money required to be raised in the ensuing year for the support of the schools, and for the purchase of school sites, as well as for the building and repairing of school-houses; and the common council shall determine what sums shall be raised for such purposes, respectively, in addition to the amount already required by law, in order to entitle the city to its distributive share of the state school money.

§ 10. The amount of money to be raised for the support of schools in any one year, exclusive of the sums required to purchase sites and to build and repair school-houses, as well as to entitle the city to its share of the state school money, shall not be less than one dollar and twenty-five cents, nor more than one dollar and seventy-five cents for each child between the ages of five and sixteen years within the city—as ascertained by the previous census, herein required to be taken on the thirty-first day of December in each year.

§ 11. The several amounts so determined by the common council to be raised as aforesaid, shall be levied upon all the taxable property of the city, in the same manner and at the same time as the taxes for city purposes, and shall be stated and sent to the board of county supervisors to be levied and collected accordingly.

§ 12. The board of supervisors, in their warrant to the collector, shall direct him to pay the amount so to be collected to the treasurer of the city, to the credit of the board of education, out of the first moneys collected.

§ 13. It shall be the duty of the first board of city assessors elected after this law shall take effect, to estimate the value of the school property of each school district as heretofore existing, and certify the same to the board of supervisors. The supervisors shall thereupon, proceed to equalize the said value by assessing the aggregate amount thereof upon the whole city, and crediting each school district on account of its general tax, with the value of its separate school property, and its special school taxes already laid and in progress of collection.

§ 14. The board of education shall determine the number and location of schools; but no expenditures for the purchase of ground or the erection of school-houses shall hereafter be made, unless the same shall have been approved of by the common council. Such approval shall be deemed to have been given when the tax therefor shall be approved by the common council, and levied by the supervisors; or it may be specially given upon the application of the board of education to make such expenditure, in anticipation of a tax to be levied in the ensuing year.

§ 15. The title of all the property now or hereafter to be required for school purposes, shall be vested in the board of education.

§ 16. The board of education shall determine whether any and what portion of the state appropriation and the county tax, designated as library money, shall be applied to the purchase of school libraries and apparatus, and the disposition thereof; and the residue of said money shall be applied to the payment of teachers' wages, or for the purchase of school books, and to no other purpose.

§ 17. The money raised for the purchase of school sites, and the building, repairing and furnishing of school-houses, shall be known as the "special school fund," and all other moneys as the "general school fund;" and it shall be the duty of the board of education to keep accurate accounts of its receipts and expenditures, distinguishing between those of a general and those of a special character; and it shall not be lawful to expend any portion of the moneys raised for the use of one of said funds, for the purposes of the other of said funds, but the expenditures shall be made in conformity with the appropriations under which the funds were levied and collected.

§ 18. The board of education shall make returns annually, to the common council, of its receipts and expenditures, specifying those on account of the general and special funds respectively, with such other details as the common council may from time to time require.

§ 19. No school in said city shall be entitled to any portion of the school moneys, in which the religious sectarian doctrine or tenets of any particular christian or other religious sect shall be taught or inculcated, or which shall refuse or prohibit visits or examinations by the city superintendent or members of the board of education of said city; provided that this section shall not be deemed to prohibit the use of the holy scriptures without note or comment.

§ 20. The schools of the asylum societies, in said city, shall participate in the distribution of the school moneys, in such manner that they shall respectively receive a sum in proportion to the number of children who shall have actually attended such school without charge during the preceding year, for which school moneys are raised; which sum shall be equal to the amount paid to any of the public schools in said city, in proportion to the number of children who shall have actually attended any such school during the said preceding year, actually orphans, or half orphans.

[*Laws of* 1851, *Chap.* 229.]

§ 15. The amount of money to be raised in any one year for the support of Common Schools in the city of Brooklyn, exclusive of the sums required to purchase sites, to build and repair school houses, and to entitle the city to its share of the State School money, shall be such sum as the said Common Council may deem necessary therefor, not to exceed the amount now allowed by law.

BUFFALO.

[*Laws of* 1843, *ch.* 122, *titles II and IX, as amended by ch.* 166, *laws of* 1849.]

TITLE II. § 11 and 22. The common council shall, on the second Tuesday of March in each year, or as soon thereafter as practicable, appoint by ballot, a city superintendent of common schools, who shall hold his office until the second Tuesday of the month of March next after such appointment, unless sooner removed or disqualified, and until his successor in office shall be appointed, and enter upon his duties.

[*Title IX—of Common and other Schools.*]

§ 1. The mayor and aldermen of the city of Buffalo, shall, by virtue of their offices, be commissioners of common schools in and for said city, and in common council shall perform all the duties of such commissioners, and shall possess all the rights, power and authority of commissioners (town superintendents) of common schools in the several towns in this state.

§ 2. The clerk of said city, shall be the clerk of the mayor and aldermen thereof, when acting as commissioners of common schools, and shall perform all the duties required of the town clerks of the several towns in the state, as clerks of the commissioners of common schools of such towns, and be subject to the same penalties for the neglect thereof.

§ 3. In all appropriations of public money for schools, or other purposes, the city of Buffalo shall be taken and considered as a town in the county of Erie, and shall be entitled to copies of laws in the same manner as other towns in said county; and all such moneys or books shall be paid or delivered to the common council.

§ 4. The common council may expend such portion as they may deem proper, of any library moneys hereafter received from the state, in binding and repairing the books in the city library, in purchasing maps and other apparatus for the schools, and in supplying indigent scholars in the schools under their charge, with necessary common school books, and other implements of learning.

§ 5. All the district schools organized within the city of Buffalo, shall be public, and free to all white children residing within the district, under the age of sixteen [21] years, and the common council, by a vote of two-thirds of all the aldermen elected, are hereby authorized to include in the general annual city tax authorized to be raised, under the third section of the fifth title of this act, such additional sum as, in their opinion, with the public school moneys for the year, will be sufficient to support their school system, and to defray the expenses of all the schools under their charge, except such of said expenses as may be raised by district tax. The moneys thus raised for school purposes, together with all moneys received from other sources for such purposes, shall constitute a separate fund, to be called the school fund, and a separate and distinct account thereof shall be kept by the proper officer or officers of the city; and the moneys of this fund shall not be appropriated or diverted to any other purpose whatever.

§ 6. The common council shall provide and maintain one or more free schools in the city for the colored children thereof; and may purchase one or more sites, and erect thereon, furnish and maintain all buildings necessary for such schools; and shall from time to time, raise all moneys necessary for these purposes, by general tax, in the manner provided by the last section.

§ 7. The common council shall have power, and it shall be their duty, whenever it may be necessary so to do,

1. To designate and purchase or lease, in each school district, a site or sites for the school-house or school houses therein, and to fence and improve the same as to them shall appear suitable and proper:

2. To build on such site or sites, or on any lot owned by such district, such school-house or school-houses and out houses as shall to them appear suitable and sufficient for such districts:

3. To complete, improve, enlarge or repair any district school-house, from time to time as they shall think proper, and to supply such school-houses, whenever they deem it expedient, with such school apparatus, books, furniture and appendages as they may direct; and to prescribe the course and extent of the studies to be pursued therein:

4. To order from time to time, a tax to be levied upon all the taxable property of any district, sufficient to pay all such sums as they may have expended or deem necessary to be expended in that district, for the purposes in this section above specified:

5. To make out a tax roll or list of every district tax ordered by them, within sixty days after such district tax shall be ordered, similar in form to the general assessment roll in said city, ascertaining the valuation of the property to be taxed as far as possible from the last assessment roll of said city; and no person shall be entitled to any reduction of the valuation of such property so ascertained, unless he shall give notice of his claim to such reduction to the city superintendent of common schools within ten days after the passage of the order to raise such tax; and when such valuation of taxable property cannot be ascertained from such assessment roll, the common council, or such superintendent, shall ascertain such valuation by the best means in their power. Such rolls may be delivered for collection to the collector of the district or to the city collector:

6. To make such by-laws and ordinances as they may deem necessary for the prosperity and good order and government of the common schools, and the security and preservation of the school-houses and other property belonging to the school districts, and to prescribe the duties and powers of the superintendent and of the several district clerks, trustees and collectors, in all cases not provided for by this act:

7. To require and take from the district collectors such security as they may deem adequate; if such security be not given by any such collector, they may remove him and appoint a successor:

8. To authorize and require the superintendent of common schools in said city to do any act or to perform any duty required of any trustee of a school district of said city, in case of any vacancy in the office of trustee, or of the neglect or refusal of such trustee to perform such duty:

9. To divide the district schools in said city into primary and higher departments or otherwise, whenever they shall deem such division desirable, and to prescribe regulations for the transfer of scholars from one department to the other, and also to direct the superintendent to provide suitable and sufficient instructors for each of the said departments.

§ 9. The superintendent of common schools of said city, shall be the executive officer of the common council to carry into effect all the provisions of this act, and the ordinances and orders of the said common council, in respect to common schools; and it shall be lawful for the said common council to assign to the said superintendent, the performance of any duty required of them, in respect to the common schools of said city; he shall, in respect to the common schools of said city, possess all the powers and authority, and be subject to the duties and obligations of the inspectors of common schools of the different towns of this state. He shall also have power, and it shall be his duty,

1. To have the care and custody, and provide for the safe keeping of district school-houses in said city:

2. To contract with and employ all teachers of the several district schools therein:

3. Under the direction of the common council, to contract for and superintend the building, enlarging, improving, furnishing and repairing of all school-houses ordered to be erected by the said common council, and the making of all repairs and improvements on and around the same:

4. In all cases where no other provision is made by this act, to supply the place and perform the several duties in respect to the several school districts in said city, required of the trustees of the several school districts in this state, by the general statutes relating to common schools:

5. To perform such other duties as may be from time to time imposed on him by the common council.

§ 10. The inhabitants of any school district entitled to vote at district meetings, when legally assembled in district meeting, shall have the same power as is now given by law to the inhabitants of the several school districts in the different towns in this state, except that there shall be but one trustee elected in each district; and that such meeting shall not possess the power to designate the site for a school-house, or to lay a tax to purchase or lease a site for a school-house, or to build, hire, or purchase a school-house for such district. The clerk and collector of such districts shall possess the powers and authority, and be subject to the same duties and obligations, as such officers in the several districts of this state except as herein otherwise provided.

§ 11. It shall be sufficient notice of any annual, special or adjourned district meeting, to publish such notice once in each week, for two successive weeks preceding the time of holding such meeting, in the city paper, and by affixing a copy of the same on the outer door of the district school-house, (if there be any,) and posting a copy of the same in three other public places in such district; the posting of said notice to be done at least ten days before such meeting; and no other notice of any such meeting need be given. The annual meetings of such district shall be held on the Monday preceding the last Tuesday in December in each year. The superintendent of the common schools for the said city, shall revise the proceedings of such meetings, and see that the proper records of such proceedings are made by the clerk in the book of district records, to be provided by the said superintendent, and kept by the clerk of such district for such purposes; and the said superintendent, and the mayor and aldermen of said city, and every taxable inhabitant of such district shall be permitted by the clerk, at all proper times, to examine the same.

§ 12. The trustee elected in any school district in said city shall have the power, and it shall be his duty,

1. To call special meetings of the inhabitants of such district, liable to pay taxes, whenever it shall be by him deemed necessary or proper:

2. To give notice of special, annual and adjourned meetings, in the manner prescribed in this act, if there be no clerk of the district, or he be absent or incapable of acting, or shall neglect or refuse to give such notice:

3. To visit the schools kept in the district as often as once in each quarter, and to report the condition of the same, with such suggestions for the improvement thereof as he may deem proper to the common council:

4. To perform such other duties as may be from time to time imposed upon him by the common council.

§ 13. The common council shall annually publish in the city paper a statement of the number of common schools in the said city; the number of pupils instructed therein, the year preceding; the several branches of education pursued by them, and the receipts and expenditures of each school, specifying the sources of such receipts, and the objects of such expenditure.

BUSHWICK.

[*Laws of* 1847, *chap.* 311.]

AN ACT *to provide for free schools in the town of Bushwick.*

Passed October 16, 1847, "three-fifths being present."

The People of the State of New-York, represented in Senate and Assembly, do enact as follows:

§ 1. The trustees of the several school districts in the town of Bushwick in the county of Kings shall annually, at least three weeks before their annual meeting, or of a special meeting to be called for that purpose, prepare an estimate of the amount which they shall deem necessary to pay the debts of such district, and for the support of common schools therein, for the ensuing year, exclusive of the moneys which they may be entitled to receive from the town superintendent, and including the sums required for the purchase of necessary furniture, apparatus and books, and for contingent expenses, and shall cause printed notices thereof to be posted for two weeks thereafter, in five or more of the most public places in said districts. They shall present such estimate at such meeting, when the inhabitants of such district then present, shall vote thereon for each item separately, and the same or so much thereof as shall be approved of by a majority of such inhabitants, shall be levied and raised by tax on such district, as now provided by law for raising a district school tax.

§ 2. When the trustees shall have completed the tax list, they shall deliver the same, to the superintendent of schools for said town, who shall issue his warrant to the collector of taxes of said town, returnable in thirty days, for the collection of the same, and take from such collector approved security for the performance of his duty; such warrant may be renewed from time to time. The moneys so collected shall be paid to said trustees, and by them appropriated to the purposes for which the same was voted, unless otherwise directed by a vote of the inhabitants, at their annual district school meeting, or a special meeting called for the purpose.

§ 3. The tax hereby imposed shall be a lien upon the lands taxed, to be enforced and collected by sale, in the manner that county taxes are, upon a return to be made by said collector to the treasurer of the county, of all unpaid taxes in said districts.

§ 4. This act shall take effect immediately.

CLYDE HIGH SCHOOL.

[*Laws of* 1834, *chap.* 175, *as amended by chap.* 268 *laws of* 1842.]

§ 1. School district number seventeen, in the town of Galen, in the county of Wayne, shall form a permanent school district, not subject to alteration by the Town Superintendent of Common Schools of the said town of Galen, and shall hereafter be known by the name of "The Clyde High School."

§ 2. The Trustees of the Clyde High School, shall be seven in number; and the first trustees shall be George Burrell, John Condit, Sylvester Clark, Cyrus Smith, Isaac Lewis, William S. Stow, and Calvin D. Tompkins; and shall hold their offices until the first annual meeting of said permanent school district, and until others are chosen.

§ 3. Said trustees are authorized to receive gifts, grants and donations, towards defraying the expenses of purchasing a site and building a suitable school-house for said high school.

§ 4. Said trustees, on receiving the sum of one thousand dollars, or having the said sum secured to be paid to them, by subscription or otherwise, shall have power to levy and cause to be raised by tax upon the taxable inhabitants of said permanent school district, a like sum of one thousand dollars; but no such tax shall be levied until said trustees shall have called a special meeting of the taxable inhabitants of said permanent school district, in manner now provided by law, for calling special school district meetings.

§ 5. Said trustees shall report in writing to said meeting, the amount of moneys received by them, the sum or sums secured to be paid to them, and the manner in which it is secured; and if the sum of one thousand dollars appears to be paid or is secured to be paid to said trustees, said meeting shall proceed to elect a clerk and collector for said high school, who shall hold their offices until the first annual meeting of said permanent school district, and until others are chosen.

§ 6. The trustees hereby appointed, and clerk and collector hereby directed to be chosen, shall be subject to the same penalties, and shall have the same powers, and perform the same duties, as like officers directed to be chosen by chapter fifteenth, title second, and article fifth of the revised Statutes, and all subsequent elections shall be held under that act.

§ 7. The trustees of said high school shall select a suitable site in the village of Clyde for the erection of their school-house; and shall contract for, and purchase the same, and thereon erect a school-house of sufficient size to accommodate such children as may be required to be educated in said permanent school district, and shall furnish the necesssary furniture and fixtures for the same.

§ 8 School districts fourteen and seventeen, or either of them, may sell their district property and pay the amount of money arising from such sale or sales, to the trustees of the Clyde High School.

§ 9. Said trustees on receiving such moneys, shall, if required by either district, deduct the amouut from that part of the tax hereby directed to be imposed on the taxable inhabitants of the individual district paying the same.

§ 10. The school money which school districts number fourteen and seventeen shall from time to time be entitled to receive from the commissioners of common schools in the town of Galen, shall be paid to the trustees of the Clyde High School; who shall be required to report to said commissioners in the same manner as other school districts are by law required to report.

§ 11. The trustees receiving such moneys, shall give their receipt for the same, and shall apply the money received, exclusively to the payment of the teachers employed by them; and it may be applied in such manner as to render the tuition of such poor children in said district as they may deem proper, gratuitous.

§ 12. It shall be the duty of the trustees of the said high school, to make an annual report to the superintendent of common schools, of the state and condition of the said school.

§ 13. The trustees shall have the general superintendence of all schools taught in said school-house, and shall employ as many teachers and assistants as they shall deem necessary, and shall direct the course of instruction, and regulate all the internal concerns of said school. [§ 2, act of 1842.] The trustees of said Clyde High School may frum time to time, rent or lease for scholastic purposes, such rooms or apartments in their school house, as in their judgment may not be required for the use of schools therein, established by them.

§ 14. This act shall take effect on the passage thereof; and the legislature may at any time alter, modify, or repeal this act.

COHOES.

[*Laws of* 1850. *Chap.* 341.]

AN ACT *to establish Free Schools in the village of Cohoes.*

Passed April 10, 1850, "three-fifths being present."

The People of the State of New-York, represented in Senate and Assembly, do enact as follows:

§ 1. The several school districts of the village of Cohoes, shall constitute one school district, and the schools therein shall be free to all children between the ages of five and twenty-one years, residing in such districts.

§ 2. There shall be erected in each district one or more school-houses.

§ 3. The title of the school-houses, sites, lots, furniture, books, apparatus and appurtenances, and all other school property in this act mentioned, shall be vested in the village of Cohoes, and the same while used or appropriated for school purposes shall not be levied upon or sold by virtue of any warrant or execution, nor be subject to taxation; and the said village, in its corporate capacity, shall be able to take, hold and dispose of any real or personal estate transferred to it by gifts, grants, bequest or devise, for the use of the common schools of said village.

§ 4. The trustees of said village may upon the recommendation of the board of education hereinafter mentioned, sell any of the school houses, lots, or sites, or any other school property now or hereafter belonging to said village. The proceeds of all such sales shall be paid to the treasurer of the village, and shall be expended under the direction of the board of education, for any school purpose.

§ 5. There shall be elected at the annual election in said village, to be held on the first Tuesday of March, 1851, in the same manner that other village officers are elected, from each of the districts in said village two trustees; the persons so elected shall be residents of the district for which they shall be elected, and shall within ten days after receiving notice of their election, take the oath of office prescribed by the Constitution of this State, and file the same with the village clerk.

§ 6. Within ten days after as in the last section mentioned, said trustees so elected from these districts shall meet in the office of the clerk of said village and shall determine by lot which of the two persons so elected for each district shall serve for the term of one year, and which for the term of two years.

§ 7. In each year thereafter there shall be elected in said village at the annual election, in the same manner, and under the same regulations as other village officers are elected, one trustee of common schools for each district, to supply the place of those whose terms are about to expire The term of office of all trustees elected pursuant to this act shall commence on the second Tuesday next after their election and shall continue two years.

§ 8. The trustees of said village shall fill all vacancies which may happen by death, resignation, or removal from the district in which each or any of the trustees of common schools were elected; the trustees so appointed shall hold their office until the second Tuesday succeeding the next annual election, and at each annual election there shall be elected a trustee to supply the place of any person so appointed, and the person thus elected shall serve out the unexpired term.

§ 9. Any trustee of common schools in said village may be removed from office for official misconduct, or neglect of duty, by the trustees of said village; but a written copy of the charges against said trustees shall be served upon him, and he shall be allowed an opportunity to refute any such charge of misconduct or neglect of duty before removal.

§ 10. The trustees of the several school districts of said village shall constitute a board to be styled the Board ot Education of the village of Cohoes, which shall be a corporate body in relation to all the powers and duties conferred upon them by virtue of this act; a majority of the board shall form a quorum. The first meeting of the board shall be held on the second Wednesday next after their election, and the annual meeting of the board thereafter, shall be on the second Wednesday next after their election. At the first meeting of the board and annually thereafter, at the annual meeting, they shall elect one of their number president of the board, and whenever he shall be absent a president pro tempore may be appointed. The said trustees shall receive no compensation for their services.

§ 11. The trustees of the several school districts now existing in said village, shall within thirty and not less than fifteen days preceding the time for holding their annual meetings, prepare estimates of the amount of money necessary to be raised in the district for continuing the several schools for the time intervening between the time of holding the annual meeting and the first day of March, 1851, when the present system shall be brought into use; and they are required within thirty days, and not less than fifteen days previous to the first day of March, 1851, to prepare an estimate of the amount of money necessary to be raised in the several districts for the ensuing year, to be submitted to the annual village meeting, which estimate shall be made out in items and passed upon, item by item, by the legal voters present, and adopted or rejected wholly or in part; the votes shall be taken by ayes and nays, or by ballot, if ordered by a majority of the voters entitled to vote for such taxes.

§ 12. It shall be the duty of said board of education, within thirty, and not less than fifteen days previous to the annual meeting, each year, to prepare an estimate of all sums necessary to be raised for all school purposes mentioned in this act, or deemed advisable by the board, and the specific sum necessary for each item in said estimate, and publish the same two weeks in one or more of the village papers, which shall be voted for, item by item, in the same manner as prescribed in the 11th section of this act.

§ 13. Said board of education shall appoint a clerk who may be one of their own number, who shall hold his office during the pleasure of the board, and whose compensation shall be fixed by them. The said clerk shall keep a record of the proceedings of the board, and perform such other duties as the board may prescribe; the said record or a transcript thereof, certified by the president and clerk, shall be received in all courts as prima facie evidence of the facts therein set forth, and such records and all the books, accounts, vouchers and papers of said board, shall at all times be subject to the inspection of the trustees of the village, or any committee thereof.

§ 14. The trustees of said village, shall have the power, and it shall be their duty to raise from time to time by tax, to be levied equally upon all the real and personal estate in said village, liable to taxation for the ordinary village taxes, or for town or county charges, such sum or sums of money as may be approved of at the annual village meeting, for any or all the following purposes:

1. To purchase, lease, or improve sites for school houses:

2. To build, purchase, lease, enlarge, alter, improve and repair school houses and their out houses and appurtenances:

3. To purchase, exchange, improve and repair school apparatus, books, furniture and appendages:

4. To procure fuel and defray the contingent expenses of the several schools and the board of education, and the expenses of the libraries of said village:

5. To pay the wages of teachers due, after the application of the public moneys which may by law be appropriated and provided for that purpose. Provided, nevertheless, that the tax to be levied as aforesaid and collected by this act shall be collected at the same time and in the same manner as other village taxes:

6. To pay the expenses of insuring all the school property of said village.

§. 15. All moneys to be raised pursuant to the provisions of this act, and all school moneys by law appropriated to, or provided for said village, shall be paid to the treasurer thereof, who, together with the sureties upon his official bond, shall be accountable therefor in the same manner as for other moneys of said village; the said treasurer shall be liable to the same penalties for any official misconduct in relation to said moneys as for any similar misconduct in relation to the other moneys of said village. The treasurer shall pay out all school moneys on the warrant of the board of education, signed by its president and clerk, and all accounts so paid shall be accompanied by the affidavit of the owner thereof, setting forth that the claims are reasonable, and that all the articles named were furnished by the direction of the legally appointed officers.

§ 16. The said board shall have power, and it shall be their duty,

1. To establish and organize in said village a system of education embracing such and so many schools (including the common schools now existing therein) as they shall deem requisite and expedient, and to alter and discontinue the same as may be found necessary.

2. To hire or cause to be hired school houses and rooms as they may find it necessary for the accommodation of the students in said village.

3. To alter, improve and repair school houses and appurtenances, as they may deem advisable.

4. To purchase, improve and repair school apparatus, books for indigent pupils, furniture and other necessary articles, including libraries.

5. To have the custody and safe keeping of the school houses, out houses, books, furniture and appendages.

6. To contract with and employ all teachers in said schools, and at their pleasure remove them.

7. To pay the wages of such teachers out of the moneys appropriated and provided by law for that purpose, so far as the same shall be sufficient, and the residue thereof from the moneys authorized to be raised for that purpose by section fourteen of this act, by tax upon said village.

8. To defray the necessary contingent expenses of the board, including an annual salary to the clerk, provided the account of such expenses shall first be audited and allowed by the board of trustees of said village.

9. To have in all respects the superintendence, supervision and management of the common schools in said village, and from time to time to adopt, alter, modify and repeal as they may deem expedient, rules and regulations for their organization, government and instruction, for the reception of pupils and their transfer from one school to another, and generally for the promotion of their good order, prosperity and public utility.

10. Whenever, in the opinion of the board, it may be advisable to sell any of the school houses, lots or sites, or any of the school property now or hereafter belonging to the village, to report the same to the trustees of the village.

11. Between the first day of July and the first day of August, in each year, to make and transmit to the county clerk or such other officer as may be designated by law in the year of its transmission, and stating,

1. The number of school houses in said village, and an account and description of all the common schools kept in said village during the preceding year and the time they have severally been taught.

2. The number of children taught in said schools respectively, and the number of children over the age of five years and under the age of sixteen [21] years, residing in said village on the first day of January of that year.

3. The whole amount of school moneys received by the treasurer of said village during the year preceding, distinguishing the amount received from the county treasurer from the village tax and from any other source.

4. The manner in which such money had been expended and whether any and what part remains unexpended, and for what cause.

5. The amount of money received as tuition fees from foreign pupils during the year, and the amount paid for teachers' wages in addition to the public moneys, with such other information relating to the common schools of said village as may from time to time be required by the state superintendent of common schools.

§ 17. It shall be the duty of each trustee to visit the schools in his district twice in each year, and the board of education shall provide that each of the schools in the village shall be visited by a committee of three or more of their number or by their clerk at least once in each term.

§ 18. The said board of education shall have power to allow the children of persons not resident within the village to attend any of the schools of said village under the care and control of said board upon such terms as said board shall by resolution prescribe, fixing the tuition which shall be paid therefor.

§ 19. It shall be the duty of such board in all their expenditures and contracts to have reference to the amount of moneys which shall be subject to their order during the then current year for the particular expenditure in question and not to exceed that amount.

§ 20. The said board of trustees shall be trustees of the school library or libraries in said village, and all the provisions of law which now are, or may hereafter be passed relative to district school libraries shall apply to said trustees, they shall also be vested with the same discretion as to the disposition of the moneys appropriated by any law of this State for the purchase of libraries which is therein conferred upon the inhabitants of school districts.

§ 21. The said board of education shall have the control of all the books and appurtenances belonging to the libraries of said village, shall appoint a librarian or librarians and regulate the drawing of books from said library.

§ 22. It shall be the duty of said board at least three weeks before the annual election of trustees in each year, to prepare and report to the village trustees true and correct statements of the receipts and disbursements under and in pursuance of the provisions of this act, during the preceding year, in which account shall be stated under appropriate heads,

1. The moneys raised by the village trustees under the fourteenth section of this act.

2. The school moneys received by the village treasurer from all sources.

3. The moneys received by the village trustees under the third section of this act.

4. All other moneys received by the treasurer subject to the order of the board, specifying the sources.

5. The manner in which such sums of money shall have been expended, specifying the amount paid under each head of expenditure; and the trustees of said village shall at least cause the same to be published in one or more of the newspapers published in said village, for two weeks before such election, and cause written or printed notices to be posted on each schoolhouse door.

§ 23. It shall be the duty of the clerk of said village, immediately after the election of any person as a trustee of common schools, to personally, or in writing, notify him of his election, and if any such person shall not, within ten days after receiving such notice of his election, take and subscribe the constitutional oath and file the same with the clerk of the said village, the trustees of said village may consider it a refusal to serve, and proceed to supply the vacancy occasioned by such refusal, and the persons so refusing shall forfeit and pay to the village treasurer, for the benefit of the contingent fund, a penalty of ten dollars.

§ 24. It shall be the duty of the several school districts in the village of Cohoes, on or before the first Tuesday in March, 1851, to transfer and convey to said village all school houses, sites, lots and all other school property of whatever name and description, and to place in care of the board of education, all school districts, records, account books, vouchers, contracts, papers, and other school property, and the said board shall settle all unsettled business of the several school districts or parts of districts now existing in said village.

§ 25. All laws or parts of laws conflicting with this act are hereby repealed.

§ 26. This act shall take effect immediately.

DELHI.

[*Laws of* 1851. *Chap.* 23.]

AN ACT *authorizing the election of three trustees and a district clerk in school district number sixteen, located in the village of Delhi.*

Passed Feb. 26, 1851, "three-fifths being present."

The People of the State of New-York, represented in Senate and Assembly, do enact as follows:

§ 1. At the first annual meeting of the trustees and inhabitants of the village of Delhi, after the passage of this act, it shall be the duty of the legal voters thereat to elect three persons legally qualified and inhabitants of said village, who shall be styled "trustees of the school district of said village," and also one person as district clerk of said district, and they respectively shall have all the powers over the said district, and shall discharge all the duties which by law are given to and enjoined upon trustees and district clerks of school districts.

§ 2. The trustees so chosen shall be divided by lot into three classes, to be numbered one, two and three, the term of office of the first class shall be one year, of the second, two, and of the third, three years, and one trustee only shall thereafter annually be elected, who shall hold his office for three years, and until a successor shall be duly elected or appointed. In case of a vacancy in the office of trustees during the period for which he or they shall have been respectively elected, the person or persons chosen or appointed to fill such vacancy, shall hold the office only for the unexpired term.

§ 3. The district clerk shall hold his office for one year, or until a successor shall be duly elected.

§ 4. So much of chapter one hundred and twelve, section ten, of an act entitled "An act to incorporate the trustees and inhabitants of Delhi and to invest them with certain powers," passed March sixteenth, eighteen hundred and twenty-one, as is inconsistent with the foregoing sections of this act, is hereby repealed.

§ 5. This act shall take effect immediately.

FLUSHING.

[*Laws of* 1848. *Chap.* 81, *as amended by Chap.* 117, *laws of* 1849.]

AN ACT *to establish free schools in district number five, in the town of Flushing.*

Passed March 10, 1848, "three-fifths being present."

The People of the State of New-York, represented in Senate and Assembly, do enact as follows:

§ 1. School district number five in the town of Flushing, in the county of Queens, shall form a permanent school district, and shall not be subject to alteration by the town superintendent of common schools for the town in which said district is situated.

§ 2. The said district shall be under the direction of a board to be styled "the board of education," which board shall consist of five members, three or more of whom shall constitute a quorum for the transaction of business; Effingham W. Lawrence, Edward E. Mitchell, Samuel B. Parsons, William H. Fairweather and Thomas Leggett, junior, shall compose the first board of education, and shall hold their offices from one to five years; that is to say, one shall go out of office in each year, and in the order in which their names stand recorded in this section.

§ 3 There shall be elected in each year in said district, one member of said board of education, who shall be a resident and taxable inhabitant of said district, and shall hold his office for five years; the said election shall take place at the annual meeting of said district, and the board of education shall appoint three suitable persons as inspectors of said election, and of all other elections provided for by this act, except as provided in section fourteenth of this act, within thirty days next preceding any such election; such elections shall be by ballot, and notice thereof shall be given, the same shall be held and conducted, the votes shall be canvassed, and the result of the election determined in the same manner as in the case of the annual election of other village officers.

§ 4. The said board of education may make all necessary by-laws for their government, they shall have the entire control and management of all the common schools within the said district and all the property belonging to the same, they shall have and possess within the said district, all the rights, powers, and authority of town superintendent of common schools. They may appoint a collector with all the powers and duties of a district collector, or may employ the town or village collector for that purpose, and such collector shall collect and pay over the school moneys assessed upon said district, to the treasurer of the board of education in the same manner and under the same conditions as is imposed by the laws of the town or village of which he is such collector. They shall require two of the members of said board to visit each school in said district at least once in each week, to render such assistance to the teachers, and advice to the pupils as maybe necesssry, and to see that the regulations are rigidly adhered to.

§ 5. The said board of education are hereby authorized and empowered to raise a sum not exceeding the sum of five thousand dollars, either by a tax on said district or by a loan, such loan to be secured by a mortgage upon the public school property of said district to be executed by said board in their official capacity.

§ 6. The said board of education in addition to the other taxes which they are hereby authorized to raise, may levy and collect a sum sufficient to pay interest on loans as the same becomes due, and whenever any part of the principal of such loans becomes due, they shall levy and collect an amount sufficient to pay the same, which sums when collected shall be paid over by said board in discharge of such principal and interest.

§ 7. The said board of education are hereby authorized and directed to levy and collect by tax in each year, upon all the taxable property in said district, such sum as may be necessary, not exceeding in amount one-fifth of one per cent. on the value of such taxable property, as the same shall be assessed by the assessors of the town of Flushing. And the said board shall add to the amount of any warrant for the collection of taxes such amount as they shall deem proper, as the collector's fees for collection, which compensation, however, shall in no case exceed five per cent. on the amount of any warrant.

§ 8. The town superintendent of common schools of the town of Flushing shall pay over to the treasurer of the board of education all the public moneys to which said district number five shall be entitled for school purposes.

§ 9. The said board of education shall call an annual district meeting at such time in the year as they may think proper, and shall submit thereto a full report in writing of their doings as such board ; and shall state therein the number and condition of the schools in said district under their charge, and the number of scholars attending the same, the studies pursued, the amount of moneys received from the State as well as the amount required in the district for school purposes and the expenditure of the same, and generally all the particulars relating to the schools in said district, which report shall immediately after it is made be published in a newspaper published in the town of Flushing for two weeks, and once in each week.

§ 10. The board of education shall have control and charge of the district school library in said district, they may employ a librarian, make such addition to the library, and such regulations in relation thereto, as they shall deem necessary.

§ 11. The school for the colored children under the charge of the female association, in the village of Flushing, may with the consent of said association, be taken under the charge of the board of education, and be organized as a district school, and be supported as the other schools in said district are under this act.

§ 12. Whenever the said board of education shall deem it necessary to erect one or more school houses in said district, they shall prepare an estimate showing the location proposed, the cost of the ground required, a plan of the building, with the estimated cost of the building and appurtenances, and shall submit the same to the electors of said district at a special meeting to be called for that purpose, in the same manner as other special meetings are required to be called, and if a majority of all the electors present at such meeting shall vote in favor of the same, then said board may proceed to erect said school house or houses in the manner proposed by said estimate, and if the sum authorized to be raised by section five of this act should be insufficient to pay the estimated cost of such buildings and ground, with the expense of grading and regulating the grounds, building the necessary out houses and fences, with the cost of necessary books, stationary and necessary apparatus for the school house and rooms, then the said board of education may raise a sum in addition to the sum mentioned in section five, and in the manner therein authorized, a sum not exceeding fifteen hundred dollars, and they are also authorized to levy and collect such amount as may be necessary topay the principal or interest of such additional sum as the same may become due in the same manner as is provided in section sixth of the said act.

§ 13. The said board of education may call special meetings of said district whenever they may deem it necessary: they shall give notice of the same by posting up a written or printed notice thereof, in at least four public places in said village, and by publishing the same in a newspaper published in the village of Flushing, at least one week previous to the time fixed for said meeting, which notice shall state the time and place of such meeting, and the purpose for which the same is called; and no business shall be transacted at any such special meeting, except that stated in the notice calling the same.

§ 14. [Provides for submitting the act for the approval of the legal voters of the district.]

§ 15. All laws and parts of laws inconsistent with this act are hereby repealed, so far as the same relate to district number five in the town of Flushing.

GLENS FALLS.

[*Laws of* 1851. *Chap.* 424.]

AN ACT *to unite the libraries of the common school districts of the village of Glens Falls.*

Passed July 9, 1851.

§ 1. The libraries of school districts number two, seven, eight, eighteen, nineteen, twenty, in the town of Queensbury, in Warren county, shall be united into one common library for the joint use of the inhabitants of the said districts, to be called the common school library of Glens Falls; and the library money which shall now be or may hereafter become due to the said districts, shall be paid over by the town superintendent to the directors of the said library, to be appointed as hereinafter mentioned, on the same terms and conditions as the said money is now paid over to the trustees of the school districts.

§ 2. On or before the last Monday in April, eighteen hundred and fifty-one, it shall be the duty of the board of trustees of the village of Glens Falls, to appoint three directors, who and whose successors shall be known as "the directors of the common school library of Glens Falls," who shall have the sole and exclusive control of the property and funds of said library. The said directors shall be divided by lot into three classes, numbered one, two and three, and the term of office of the first class shall be one year, that of the second class two years, and that of the third class three years; and on or before the last Monday in April in each year thereafter, one director shall be chosen, who shall hold his office for three years and until a successor shall be duly appointed. In the case of a vacancy in the office of any director during the period for which he shall have been chosen, the person to fill such vacancy shall hold the office only for the unexpired term of three years.

§ 3. It shall be the duty of the said directors,

1. To establish and organize on a proper basis the said "common school library."

2. To purchase books, exchange or cause to be repaired damaged books, sell any books they may deem useless or not suited to the library, and apply the proceeds to the purchase of other books for the said library, and to purchase maps and apparatus for the joint use of the school districts:

3. To have in all respects the superintendence, supervision and management of the said library and funds, and to adopt, modify and repeal as they may deem expedient, rules and regulations for the government, safe keeping and preservation of the same, and the promotion of its public utility, and to make and enforce proper penalties for the violation of its rules and regu-

4. On or before the last Monday in April in each year, to report to the trustees of the village of Glens Falls a statement of the books which they have purchased the preeeding year, together with an account of their expenses and disbursements, and such other matters connected with the condition of the said library as they shall deem proper :

5. And shall further perform all other duties not inconsistent with this act, and be subject to all the liabilities of the trustees of the school district libraries; but their expenditures are to have reference to the funds subject to their order during the current year.

§ 4. It shall also be the duty of the said directors annually to appoint a librarian, who shall be subject to all the requirements and perform all such duties not inconsistent with this act as are now required to be performed by the librarians of the school districts.

§ 5. The directors are empowered to pay the librarian a sum not exceeding twelve dollars per annum for his services, and may audit and allow other proper accounts and expenses necessary for the maintenance, support and proper conduct of the said library, to a sum not exceeding eight dollars per year ; and it shall be the duty of the trustees of the village to furnish suitable cases for the preservation of the said library, and of all additions to the same. All expenses incurred by the provisions of this section to be paid by the village corporation. But the said directors shall perform their services without compensation.

§ 6. The said directors shall have the same power and authority in regard to the prosecution and defence of all suits at law touching the property of the said library as are now possessed by trustees of school districts in relation to school district property; but all such suits shall be prosecuted or defended, and also all fines and penalties that may be imposed by the terms of this act, shall be collected in the name of the "common school library of Glens Falls ;" and this provision shall extend to all books which may be in the hands of individuals and not returned to the libraries of the respective school districts at the time of the passage of this act ; and all the rights and duties of the trustees with regard to such books, shall be vested in the said directors.

§ 7. The legislature may at any time alter or repeal this act.

§ 8. This act shall take effect immediately.

HUDSON.

[*Laws of* 1841. *Chap.* 350, *as amended by Chap.* 12, *laws of* 1843, *and Chap.* 132, *laws of* 1844.]

AN ACT *in relation to common schools in the city of Hudson.*

The People of the State of New-York, represented in Senate and Assembly do enact as follows :

§ 1. The members of the common council of the city of Hudson shall by virtue of their office be commissioners for common schools in and for said city, and in common council shall perform all the duties of such commissioners, and shall possess all the rights, powers and authority, and shall be subject to all the duties and obligations of commissioners of common schools [town superintendent] in the several towns of this state, and shall have power,

1. To divide the city into school districts of which there shall not be less than three in the compact part of the city.

2. They shall designate, purchase, or lease, or otherwise obtain, in eac school district, a site or sites for a school house or the school houses therein and shall fence or improve the same in such manner as to them shall appear suitable and proper.

3. They shall cause to be built or procured in each district such school house or school houses and out houses, as shall appear to them suitable and sufficient.

4. They shall complete, improve, enlarge or repair any district school house, from time to time, as they shall think proper; and they shall supply the district school houses, whenever they shall deem it expedient, with such school apparatus, books, furniture and appendages as they may think necessary.

5. They shall appoint, in the manner provided by them for the appointment of other officers of said city, three persons to be denominated a board of superintendents; of these three persons the one first chosen shall continue in office for three years; the one next appointed shall continue in office for two years, and the one last appointed shall continue in office for one year.

6. They shall have power, and it shall be their duty, to make such by-laws and ordinances as may be in their opinion necessary for the prosperity and good order and efficient government of the common schools, and the security and the preservation of the school houses, and other property belonging to the school districts; and to prescribe the duties and powers of the board of superintendents in all cases not provided for by this act.

7. They shall require and take from the superintendents and collectors such security as they shall deem expedient, and if such security is not given by any superintendent or collector, the said common council may declare his office forfeited, and appoint another superintendent or collector in his place.

8. They shall supply a vacancy produced in the board of superintendents from any cause; the person appointed to fill such vacancy shall continue in office during the unexpired remainder of the term for which his predecessor was chosen, and no longer, unless reappointed.

9. They shall divide the district schools in said city into primary and higher departments or otherwise, whenever they shall deem such division desirable; and they shall prescribe regulations for the transfer of scholars from one department to another, and they shall direct the board of superintendents to provide a sufficient number of suitable instructors for each of these departments.

§ 2. The clerk of said city by right of office shall be the clerk of the mayor and aldermen thereof when acting as commissioners of common schools, and he, as such clerk, shall perform all the duties in reference to said city, that the town clerks in the several towns in this state perform as clerks of common schools in such towns, and be subject to the same penalties for the neglect thereof,

§ 3. The board of superintendents of common schoools in the city of Hudson shall in respect to the common schools in said city, possess all the powers and be subject to all the duties and obligations of the inspectors of the common schools in the different towns in this state; it shall carry into effect all the ordinances and orders of the common council in respect to common schools; and it shall be lawful for the said common council to assign to said board any duty required of them, in respect to the common schools in said city. The said board shall be under the direction of the common council, and they shall have power, and it shall be their duty,

1, To contract for and superintend the building, enlarging, improving, furnishing and repairing of all school houses under the charge of said common mon council, and the making of all repairs and improvements on and around the same.

2. To provide for the safe keeping of the district school houses in said city.

3. To contract with and employ all the teachers in the several districts therein.

4. To prevent scholars resident in one district from attending a school in another district, and also to prevent scholars from going from one school to another in the same district, without having in both the above cases written permission so to do from the said board.

5. To select such books as they shall deem most suitable to be used as class books in the schools, and to establish an uniformity in all the schools in regard to the books used therein.

6. To visit each school as often as once in each quarter, and to report the condition of the same, with such suggestions for the improvement thereof, to the common council as they may deem advisable, which reports shall be published by the common council in two of the city papers.

7. To remove any teacher, on manifest neglect of duty, or upon his violating his contract; upon paying such teacher pro rata for the time he has been employed.

8. To pay the wages of all the teachers by orders on the common council as commissioners of common schools, so far as the public money in their hands, or the money raised by tax, as to be hereafter provided for, and the money paid over by the collector of the rate-bills, shall be sufficient for the purpose.

9. To make out rate-bills for the payment of teacher and contingent expenses, against the parent or guardian of each scholar, and expense of collection of the same, (except those exempted, as hereafter to be provided for,) which shall not however exceed two dollars per quarter for each scholar; and no bill shall be made out for less time than one quarter, and to annex thereto a warrant for the collection thereof.

§ 4. The said common council of the city of Hudson, shall appoint a collector or collectors for the purpose of collecting the rate bills, if any are made out by the board of superintendents; rate-bills shall be made out and levied upon the parents or guardians of children sent to the district schools, in the manner provided by law in respect to school districts, except such as shall procure a certificate of inability to pay the same, from the aldermen or assistant aldermen of the ward in which such parent or guardian resides.

§ 1. [Act of 1843.] The board of superintendents appointed or to be appointed under the act hereby amended, are hereby authorized to receive all the moneys intended for the support of common schools in and for the city of Hudson, and to expend the same as provided in said act.

§ 2. [Act of 1843.] It shall be the duty of the treasurer of the county of Columbia, and of the collectors of taxes in and for the city of Hudson, and of the collectors of rate-bills, under the provisions of the act hereby amended, to pay over directly to the said board of superintendents all the moneys that may come into the hands of said treasurer and said collectors respectively, intended for the benefit and support of common schools in said city.

§ 5. The said common council shall be authorized to borrow the sum of five thousand dollars for twenty years, at a rate of interest not exceeding six per cent. per annum, for the purpose of procuring suitable school houses for said city, with such appurtenances and improvements as may be deemed expedient.

§ 6. The Comptroller is hereby authorized to loan to the city of Hudson, the sum of five thousand dollars to be paid in twenty equal annual instalments, out of any moneys now or hereafter in the treasury of this state, belonging to the capital of the common school fund, on receiving from the chamberlain in behalf of the said city, a bond conditioned from him as treasurer of said city and his successor in office, to repay the said sum in twenty equal annual instalments, together with the annual interest on said loan from the time it was made, at the rate of six per cent. per annum, and which bond said chamberlain is hereby authorized to make and execute.

§ 7. The common council of said city are hereby authorized to raise by tax upon the real and personal property of said city, in the same manner as the general taxes of said city are levied and collected, the annual interest of the above mentioned loan, and to pay over the same in discharge of such interest; and also in each year in which an instalment of the above loan shall become due, to raise, levy and collect in the same manner, a sum equal to that instalment, and to pay over the same in discharge thereof, and the said common council shall also in the same manner raise, levy and collect such sum annually, not exceeding two hundred dollars, as may be necessary for repairs, furniture of said school buildings and contingent expenses.

§ 8. The supervisors of the county of Columbia, at their annual meeting in each year, shall cause a sum of money equal to four times the amount of money apportioned to the city of Hudson from the common school fund, together with the collector's fees, to be raised, levied and collected in the same manner that other taxes are raised, levied and collected, and when so raised to be paid to the board of superintendents for the support of common schools in said city.

§ 9. After the year one thousand eight hundred and fifty-three, the common council shall have it in their power to reduce, if they deem it expedient, the above sum to twice the amount apportioned to the city of Hudson, from the common school fund, and have recourse to the system of rate-bills as adopted in the several towns in this state, to supply deficiencies.

§ 1. [Act of 1844.] It shall be the duty of the board of superintendents of common schools of the city of Hudson, annually hereafter to appoint a librarian for the joint school district library in said city, who shall perform all the duties and be subject to all the restrictions and liabilities now required or imposed upon librarians in the several school districts of the state: and may be removed from office and a successor appoined by said superintendents for any wilful neglect of duty, and whenever they shall have reason to apprehend the loss of, or injury to any of the books belonging to such library, through his misconduct.

§ 2. [Act of 1844.] The common council of said city are hereby authorized and empowered, annually to appropriate such sum for the compensation o said librarian as they may deem expedient, not to exceed the sum of fifty dollars, which shall be raised, levied, and collected in the same manner as other city charges, and when so collected shall be paid over to the superintendents aforesaid, to be by them appropriated as specified in the first section of this act.

§ 10. All the general laws of this state relating to common schools and their officers, except as the same are modified by this act, shall extend to and include the schools established under this act, and the commissioners, inspectors and other officers having charge thereof or in any way connected therewith.

§ 11. All laws relating to the appointment of commissioners and inspectors of common schools in the city of Hudson, and the act entitled, "An act to authorize the raising of money for the support of the Lancaster school of the city of Hudson," passed May 11, 1835, and all other acts which conflict with this act, are hereby repealed.

§ 12. This act shall take effect immediately.

LANSINGBURGH.

[*Laws of* 1847. *Chap.* 336.]

AN ACT *to provide for a free school in district number one in the town of Lansingburgh.*

Passed October 26, 1847, "three-fifths being present."

The People of the State of New-York, represented in Senate and Assembly, do enact as follows:

§ 1. The trustees of school district number one in the town of Lansingburgh, in the county of Rensselaer, shall annually, at least three weeks before their annual meeting, prepare an estimate of the amount which they shall deem necessary to pay the debts of such district, and for the support of common schools therein, for the ensuing year, exclusive of the moneys which they may be entitled to receive from the town superintendent, and including the sums required for the purchase of necessary furniture, apparatus and books, and for contingent expenses, and shall cause printed or written notices thereof to be posted for two weeks thereafter, in five or more of the most public places in said district. They shall present such estimate at such annual meeting, when the inhabitants of such district, entitled to vote at school district meetings, then present, shall vote thereon, and the same having been approved of by a majority of such inhabitants, shall be levied and raised by tax on such district, as now provided by law for raising a district school tax.

§ 2. When the trustees shall have completed the tax list, they shall issue their warrant to the collector of taxes of said district, returnable in thirty days, for the collection of the same, and take from such collector approved security for the performance of his duty; such warrant may be renewed from time to time. The moneys so collected shall be paid to said trustees, and by them appropriated to the purposes for which the same was voted, unless otherwise directed by a vote of the inhabitants, at their annual district school meeting, or a special meeting called for the purpose.

§ 3. The tax hereby imposed shall be a lien upon the lands taxed, to be enforced and collected by sale, in the manner that county taxes are, upon a return to be made by said collector to the treasurer of the county, of all unpaid taxes in said district.

§ 4. This act shall take effect immediately.

LOCKPORT.

[*Laws of* 1847, *Chap.* 51, *Laws of* 1850. *Chap.* 77,]

AN ACT *in relation to common schools in the village of Lockport.*

Passed March 31, 1847, "three-fifths being present."

The People of the State of New-York, represented in Senate and Assembly, do Enact as follows:

§ 1. School districts numbers one, two, five, seven, eight, fifteen and sixteen, of Lockport, lying principally within the village of Lockport, are hereby consolidated for the purposes and to the extent in this act specified; and shall hereafter, for such purposes, and to such extent, form but one school district, to be called "The union school district of Lockport."

§ 2. Said seven school districts shall remain and continue separate and distinct, for the purposes and to the extent in this act specified: and shall be called "primary school districts," and numbered as follows:

Said district number one, shall form primary district number one;
Said district number two, shall form primary district number two;
Said district number seven, shall form primary district number three;
Said district number fifteen, shall form primary district number four;
Said district number eight, shall form primary district number five;
Said district number sixteen, shall form primary district number six; and
Said district number five, shall form primary district number seven.

Said districts shall not be subject to alteration except by the acts of the legislature, or by resolution of the board of education hereinafter created. The schools in said primary districts, shall be used as preparatory schools for the instruction of children until they arrive at a certain age, and attain a certain proficiency in learning; who shall then be transferred, upon the proper testimonials, into the union school hereinafter mentioned; the age, qualifications and testimonials, to be prescribed by the by-laws, rules and regulations of the board of education hereinafter created.

§ 3. Sullivan Caverno, residing in primary district number one;
William G. M'Master, residing in primary district number two;
Joseph T. Bellah, residing in primary district number three;
Silas H. Marks, residing in primary district number four;

Isaac C. Coulton, residing in primary district number five;

John S. Woolcott, residing in primary district number six; and

Edwin L. Boardman, residing in primary district number seven, are hereby appointed trustees in behalf of such districts respectively; and Nathan Dayton, Samuel Works, Jonathan L. Woods, Lyman A. Spaulding and Hiram Gardner, are hereby appointed trustees in behalf of said union district. The trustees so named, and their successors, to be chosen as hereinafter provided, are hereby constituted a corporation by the name of "The board of education for the village of Lockport."

§ 4. On the first Monday of September next, there shall be elected, in the manner that trustees of school districts are now elected, by each primary district, one trustee, (who shall be a resident of such primary district,) to fill the places of those named in the last section, in behalf of such districts respectively. On the first Monday of October next, there shall be elected in like manner, by a meeting of the persons qualified to vote for school district officers, residing within the bounds of said union district, five trustees, resident of said union district, to fill the places of those named in the last section, in behalf of said union district. Annually thereafter, on the days above specified for such elections, there shall in like manner, be elected four trustees to fill the places of those whose terms shall next thereafter expire, as hereinafter provided. The trustees named in the third section above, shall hold their offices until the first Monday of January next, and until their successors shall be chosen and enter upon the discharge of the duties of their offices respectively. Every officer elected under this act, shall enter upon the duties of his office on the first Monday of January next succeeding his election, and shall hold his office for the term hereinafter provided, and until his successor shall be elected, and shall enter upon the discharge of the duties of his office. Within ten days after any such election, the clerk of such district shall certify to said board of education, the names of the officers so elected.

§ 5. Within ten days after the first election of trustees of said union district, as provided in the last section, all the trustees so elected by said primary and union districts, or a majority of them, shall meet and cause the whole number of trustees so elected, to be divided into three classes; to be severally numbered first, second and third. The term of office of the first class, shall expire at the end of one year; of the second class, at the end of two years; and of the third class, at the end of three years from the first Monday of January next. There shall also be elected in each of said districts, at the time of so electing trustees, a clerk, who shall hold his office for one year, and until his successor be elected, and enter upon the duties of his office.

§ 6. There shall annually be appointed by said board of education, a collector, librarian, and treasurer of said union district; who shall each, within ten days after receiving notice in writing, of his appointment, and before entering upon the duties of his office, execute and deliver to said board of education, a bond in such penalty, and with such sureties as said board may require; conditioned for the faithful discharge of the duties of his office. In case such bond shall not be given within ten days after receiving such notice, such office shall thereby become vacated, and said board of education shall thereupon make an appointment to supply such vacancy.

§ 7 Notices for annual elections, and all other meetings of said districts, shall be given by said board of education, at least ten days before such election or meeting, by publishing such notice once in each of the newspapers printed in the village of Lockport; and if such notice be for an election or meeting of said union district, by posting the same on the door of the school-house in each primary district; if such notice be for an election or meeting of any primary district, then by posting such notice on the door of the school-house in such district.

§ 8. In case of a vacancy of any office mentioned in this act, occasioned by the death of such officer, his refusal to serve, removal out of the district for which he shall have been elected or appointed, his incapacity, or any cause other than the expiration of the term of office of persons elected, said board of education may make an appointment to fill such vacancy. The officer so appointed, shall hold his office for the unexpired term of the person, to supply whose place he shall be so appointed.

§ 9. Said board of education shall be a corporate body in relation to all the powers and duties conferred upon them by virtue of the provisions of this act; a majority of the board shall form a quorum.

§ 10. Said board of education shall possess all the powers and be subject to all the duties in respect to all of said school districts that the trustees of common schools now possess or are subject to; and such other powers and duties as are given or imposed by this act. The clerk, collector and librarian of said union district, shall possess all the powers, and be subject to all the duties in respect to said union district, that like officers of common schools now possess or are subject to, and such other powers aud duties as are given or imposed by this act. The offices of collector and librarian, and two of the trustees of each of the school districts hereby consolidated, shall be abolished from and after the time when said union school shall go into operation. In the mean time, such officers, and the several districts in district meetings, shall continue to discharge such ordinary powers and duties as said board of education may by resolution prescribe; but they shall not possess or exercise any right or power which may conflict with the provisions of this act, or impair the powers hereby intended to be conferred on said board of education, or in any way embarass the said board of education in the exercise of the powers, or in the discharge of the duties conferred or imposed upon said board, by the provisions of this act.

§ 11. Said board of education, shall, at its first meeting, and annually thereafter, at their meeting held next after the first of January, in each year, appoint one of their number president and another secretary. In the absence of either of such officers at any regular meeting of the board, a president or secretary may be appointed for the time being.

§ 12. The secretary shall keep a record of the proceedings of said board of education, which record, or a transcript therefrom, certified by the president and secretary, shall be received in all courts as presumptive evidence of the facts therein set forth.

§ 13. Each member of said board of education, and every other officer of said union district, before entering upon the duties of his office, shall take and subscribe the oath of office prescribed by the constitution of this state, and file the same with the secretary of said board.

§ 14. Said board of education shall have power, and it shall be their duty,

1. To establish and organize so many primary schools as they shall deem requisite and expedient, and to alter and discontinue the same;

2. To purchase or hire school houses, rooms, lots or sites for school houses, and to fence and improve them as they may think proper;

3. Upon such lots or sites, and upon any lot or site now owned by any primary district, to build, enlarge, alter, improve and repair school houses, out houses and appurtenances as they may deem advisable;

4. To purchase, exchange, improve and repair school apparatus, books, furniture and appendages, to provide fuel for the schools, and defray their contingent expenses, and the expenses of the library and salary of the librarian;

5. To have the custody and safe keeping of the school houses, out houses, apparatus, books, furniture and appendages, and see that the ordinances and by-laws of said board, in relation thereto, be observed;

6. To contract with and employ all teachers, in all the schools under their charge, and at their pleasure to remove them;

7. To pay the wages of such teachers out of the public money, and tuition fees to be received by them according to the provisions of this act, so far as the same shall be sufficient, and the deficiency, if any, out of the moneys to be raised for general purposes of education, under and virtue of the provisions of this act;

8. To fix the rate of tuition fees in said union school, subject to the limitations and restrictions hereinafter contained, and to designate some person or persons to whom the same may be paid previous to issuing the warrant for the collection thereof; and by a resolution of said board, to be recorded by the secretary, to exempt from the payment of the whole or any part of the tuition fees, such persons as they may deem entitled to such exemption, from indigence, or any other sufficient cause;

9. After the close of each quarter of said union school, to make out a rate-bill, containing the name of each person liable to pay tuition fees for tuition in said union school, who shall not have paid the same prior to making out such rate-bill, according to the provisions of the last preceding sub-division of this section, and the amount for which such person is liable, adding thereto a sum not exceeding five cents on each dollar for collector's fees, (which fees shall be fixed by said board, at the time of making out every rate-bill,) to annex thereto a warrant for the collection thereof, to be signed by the president of said board or a majority of the members thereof, and deliver the same to the collector, who shall collect the same in the same manner as collectors of school districts are by law authorized and required to execute like warrants issued by the trustees of common school districts; and who, in the execution of the same, shall be under the same protection, possess all the powers, and be subject to all the duties as such collectors now have, possess, and are subject to in respect to like warrants; and for this purpose, the jurisdiction of said board of education, and of said collector, shall extend to any other district or town, and to any resident of such other district or town, who may be liable for tuition in said union school, in the same manner and with the like authority, as to said union district, or residents of said union district;

10. To have in all respects the superintendence, supervision, management and control of all the schools mentioned or contemplated in, and by the provisions of this act; to prescribe the course of studies therein, the books to be used and establish an uniformity in respect to such course of studies and books; from time to time to adopt, alter, modify and repeal, as they deem expedient, rules, regulations and ordinances, for the organization, government and instructions of such schools, for the reception of pupils and their transfer from one school to another; for the promotion of their good order, prosperity and public utility; for the protection, safe keeping, care and preservation of school houses, lots, sites and appurtenances, and all other property connected with or appertaining to such schools;

11. To cause such rules, regulations, ordinances and by-laws to be published in such manner and form, as they may deem best calculated to give general information; to cause one copy thereof, together with a copy of this act to be kept in each of said schools, and such parts thereof as relate to such schools respectively, to be read therein, at least once during each quarter;

12. Said board of education shall in all respects be subject to the visitation and control of the superintendents of common schools of the town, county and state in the same manner as the common schools in this state are subject.

§ 15. Said board of education shall have power, and it shall be their duty, to raise from to time, by tax upon the real and personal estate within the bounds of said union district which shall be liable to taxation for the ordinary taxes of said village, or for town or county charges, such sums as may be determined by resolution of said board, to be necessary for any and all the purposes mentioned in the last preceding section, or to meet any deficiency arising from any cause connected with the subject of education in said village, to provide for which, power shall be given to said board by the provisions of this act, the laws relating to common schools, or the rules and regulations of the superintendent of common schools. Whenever any sum of money shall be needed by any primary district, for any of the objects in this or the last preceding section mentioned, except for teachers' wages, said board of education shall cause such amount to be assessed, levied and collected from the property of such district by the same warrant, in addition to, and in connection with the tax next to be raised for the general purposes of education, under and by virtue of the provisions of this act; making therefor a separate column in said tax list. The treasurer shall keep a separate account of all moneys so raised for such primary district, and said board of education shall, by orders on such specific fund, draw out such moneys only for such objects, and in favor of such primary district.

Said board of education shall, at the commencement of each year, make an estimate by the best means in their power, of the amount of money which will be needed for all the purposes of education, and other purposes provided for by this act, over and above the moneys to be received from the town superintendent, and from tuition fees, and shall cause the same to be raised by one assessment and warrant; and not more than two taxes for such purposes, shall ever be raised in one year.

The amount of money so to be raised in any one year, after the first year, shall not be less than the amount received in behalf of all said districts, from the town superintendent, for the year next preceding; nor more than four times that amount, unless such greater amount shall be authorized by a vote of the taxable inhabitants of said union district, at a regular meeting of such district.

§ 16. Said board of education shall have power, and it shall be their duty, forthwith to purchase a suitable lot, so situated as best to convene the whole of said union district, not to exceed, in cost, the sum of twenty-five hundred dollars, and procure a clear title thereof, to be vested, by deed, in said board of education; to cause said lot to be graded, fenced, and otherwise properly improved; to erect thereon a suitable and proper building or buildings, to be built of stone or brick, not to exceed in expense, the sum of eight thousand dollars, nor to cost less than five thousand dollars; furnish the same with all proper, useful and necessary furniture, apparatus and appendages; as soon as the building is in proper condition, employ a sufficient number of well qualified teachers, male and female, and cause a school to be commenced therein, to be called "The Lockport Union School," in which shall be taught only the higher branches of education.

The tuition fee in said union school, shall not exceed two dollars each, per quarter, for pupils whose parents or guardians reside within the territory of said union district; for all other pupils, said tuition fee shall not be less than two dollars, nor more than five dollars per quarter. No tuition fee shall thereafter be charged, nor any rate bill be made for tuition in the primary schools, but the same shall be free schools.

§ 17. Said board of education shall, as soon as practicable make an estimate of the amount of money, which, in their opinion, will be necessary for the purposes in the last section specified, and also for such purposes specified in section fourteen, of this act, as may be needed or required for the first year, and shall forthwith assess, levy and collect the same, by tax upon real and personal estate, as specified in section fifteen of this act. They shall, for this and all other taxes to be raised by them, make out a tax list, in the manner and form in which like tax lists are now made by trustees of school districts, so far as such form is applicable, annex thereto, a warrant in like form, signed by the president or a majority of the members of said board, and deliver the same to the collector; which, when so made and signed, shall be as effectual to all intents and purposes, as like tax lists and warrants, when made by the trustees of common school districts. Said board may, in respect to the collection of all taxes, conform to the provisions of the twenty-ninth, thirtieth and thirty-first sections of the one hundred and eightieth chapter of the Session Laws of one thousand eight hundred and forty-five, and require the collector to comply with the provisions of said sections, so far as the same are applicable. Said board may so far vary from the provisions of said sections, as to time and places, as to render them applicable, and may make such warrants returnable at sixty or ninety days, in their discretion, instead of thirty days, as now required by law, in respect to such warrants made by trustees of common school districts; but all property now exempt, by section twenty-two, title five, chapter six, part third of the Revised Statutes, from execution shall be exempt from all such warrants.

§ 18. All moneys to be raised by virtue of this act, and all moneys by law, appropriated to, or provided for said districts, shall be paid to the treasurer of said board, who together with the sureties upon his official bond, shall be accountable therefor, to said board of education. Said treasurer shall not pay out any of such moneys, except by resolution of said board, and upon an order drawn by the president and certified by the secretary, to be so drawn in pursuance of such resolution.

§ 19. Said board of education shall meet for the transaction of business, as often as once in each month, and may adjourn for any shorter time. Special meetings may be called by the president, or in his absence or inability to act, by the secretary or any other member of the board, as often as necessary, by giving personal notice to each member of the board, or causing a written or printed notice to be left at his last place of residence, at least twenty-four hours before the hour of meeting. No member of said board shall receive any pay or compensation for his services. It shall not be lawful for any member of said board, or any other officer of either of said districts, to become a contractor for building or making any improvement or repairs authorized by this act, or be in any manner, directly or indirectly, interested, either as principal, partner or surety in any such contract. All contracts, made in violation of this provision, shall be absolutely void, and the person so violating, shall forfeit the sum of fifty dollars; to be prosecuted for, and recovered by said board.

§ 20. Instead of the report now required by law to be made by trustees of school districts, to the town superintendent of common schools, the trustee so to be elected for each primary district, shall, within the time now required by law, make such report to said board of education, and shall therein embrace such other and further matters as may be required and prescribed by said board, or as such trustee may think the interests of such primary district or school may require. Said board of education shall, annually, between the first of January and the first of March, in each year, make to the town superintendent of common schools, a report, containing all such matters relating, as well to said Union district and Union school, as to said primary districts and their schools, as is now, or shall hereafter be required by law, or the regulations of the superintendent of common schools, to be reported to said town superintendent, and such other and further matters as they may deem advisable. Such report shall be received by said town superintendent, instead of the reports now required from each, of said seven districts. A copy of such report shall be filed with the secretary of said board.

§ 21. Said board of education shall, from time to time, appoint such, and so many members of their board, as they may deem proper, not less than three in number, a visiting committee; whose duty it shall be to visit said union school, and each of said primary schools, as often as once in each quarter; and make a report in writing to said board, showing the state and condition of each school, school-house, apparatus and appendages, and such other matters as said board may require of them, and such suggestions for the improvement of the same, as they may deem proper and advisable; such reports shall be filed and kept among the papers of said board. Such board may in their discretion, cause such reports, or any parts of the same, or the substance thereof, and any and all other matters relating to said schools, to be published in such form as they may deem advisable. They shall, at the close of each year, publish in one or more of the village newspapers, a report of the moneys received and expended by them, during the year, and such other matters as they deem advisable.

§ 22. Whenever, in the opinion of said board, the interests of any primary district, require the sale or exchange of the school lot therein, said board may cause such sale or exchange to be made, and hold the proceeds thereof, r the use and benefit of such primary district.

§ 23. The title of school-houses, sites, lots, furniture, books, apparatus and appurtenances, and all other school property in this act mentioned, shall be vested in said board of education; and the same, while used for, or appropriated to school purposes, shall be exempt from all taxes and assessments, and shall not be liable to be levied upon, or sold by virtue of any warrant or execution. Said board of education, in their corporate capacity, shall be able to take, hold and dispose of any real or personal estate, transferred to it by gift, grant, bequest or devise, for the use of said schools, or any or either of them. Provided, however, that said board shall not have power to sell, grant, dispose of or incumber, said union school lot.

§ 24. Every officer in this act mentioned, having at the time, the possession, custody, care, charge or control, of any property belonging to said schools, or any or either of them, or any money raised by the provisions of act, or provided by law for the purposes of education in said village, shall, at the expiration of his term, or whenever such officer shall resign, be removed from office, cease to act, or his office be otherwise vacated, transfer all such property, and pay over all such money to the board of education.

§ 25. Every resignation of officers appointed or elected under this act, shall be made to the board of education, and such resignation shall have no force or effect, nor in any degree excuse such officer from the discharge of his duties, until the same be accepted and approved by a resolution of said board.

§ 26. Any such officer may be removed from office for any official misconduct or neglect of official duty, by resolution of said board; two thirds of the members thereof concurring. Opportunity shall be given to every such officer to be heard in his defence, before any such resolution shall be adopted.

§ 27. Every person appointed or elected to any office mentioned in this act, who, without sufficient cause, shall refuse to serve therein, shall forfeit the sum of ten dollars; and every person so appointed or elected, and not having refused to accept, who shall neglect to discharge the duties of such office, shall forfeit the sum of twenty dollars to said board of education. It shall be the duty of said board of education, forthwith, to prosecute for all forfeitures and penalties under this act, and when recovered, to apply the same to the purposes of education in said village. All officers mentioned in this act, shall be deemed public officers, within the intent and meaning of section thirty-eight, of title six, of chapter one, part four of the Revised Statutes; and as such, liable to the penalty therein prescribed, in addition to the penalty in this section before provided.

§ 28. The several libraries of the said seven districts are hereby consolidated into one. Said board of education shall cause a suitable and proper room to be fitted up in said union school building, and furnished with necessary and suitable fixtures, furniture, apparatus and appendages, and transfer said library thereto, and put it under the charge of a librarian. They shall annually allow and pay to said librarian, such salary as in their opinion, shall be a fair and reasonable compensation for his services, but not to exceed the sum of fifty dollars in any one year. They shall pass such by-laws for the regulation and preservation of said library, and for the discharge of the duties of the librarian, as they may think necessary. The library money hereafter to be received in behalf of said districts, shall be paid by the town superintendent to the treasurer of said board. Said board shall expend such money entirely for the purchase of books and maps for the library.

§ 29. Lands of residents and non-residents of said districts may be sold by said board, for uncollected taxes assessed thereon for school purposes, by virtue of the provisions of this act, in the same manner, and by like proceedings as the trustees of said village adopt to sell lands for unpaid taxes assessed for village purposes, and such sales shall have the like effect as sales so made by the trustees of said village; or the lands of residents and non-residents of said districts, said board may cause to be returned to the county treasurer, in the same manner as trustees of common school districts are now authorized by law to return unoccupied and unimproved real estate of non-residents of their districts, for unpaid taxes assessed thereon. Said county treasurer shall pay to said board the amount of such taxes, out of any moneys in the county treasury raised for contingent expenses, and such proceedings in all respects, shall thereafter be had by said county treasurer, and the board of supervisors of the county of Niagara in relation to all lands so returned, as they are by law required to take in respect to unoccupied and unimproved lands of non-residents, when so returned by trustees of common school districts. But no lands shall be so sold or returned, until a reasonable effort shall have been made to collect such taxes by warrant, as provided in section seventeen of this act, and the collector shall have returned that he cannot collect the same.

§ 30. Said board of education may cause a school for colored children to be taught in said village, and include the expenses thereof in the amount so to be raised annually by tax, for contingent expenses and other purposes of education provided for in this act.

§ 31. Said board of education may organize in said union school, a department for the instruction of teachers, for such parts of the year, and under such rules and regulations, as they may by their by-laws adopt relative thereto.

§ 32. Said board of education, may at any time hereafter, whenever in their opinion the wants and interests of said schools shall require it, establish a class of so many schools intermediate said primary and union schools as they may deem advisable, to be called secondary schools, and for this purpose consolidate such and so many of said primary districts, as they may deem advisable, prescribe the tuition fees and course of studies therein, and so arrange and regulate the system of instruction in all of said schools, that the transfer of pupils shall thereafter be from the primary, directly into the secondary, and thence into the union school. And for this purpose, and for the organization, government and regulation of said secondary schools, said board shall have all such powers as are hereinbefore conferred upon them, in respect to said primary and union schools and their districts and property

[*Chap.* 77, *Laws of* 1850.]

§1. The provisions of the act entitled "An Act in relation to Common Schools in the village of Lockport," passed March 31, 1847, are not and shall not be deemed or adjudged to be or to have been affected, altered or impaired by the act entitled "An act establishing Free Schools throughout the State," passed March 26, 1849.

§ 2. "The board of education for the village of Lockport" is hereby authorized to increase the rates of tuition fees in the Union School under its charge, and to graduate the same according to the branches of instruction pursued.

§ 3. Said board of education is hereby authorized to appoint a superintendent of the schools under its charge, with such powers and duties and compensation as said board shall prescribe.

§ 4. From and after the first day of April next, so long as the common schools of this state shall be free, the said board of education shall cause each of the secondary schools under its charge to be taught by a competent male teacher, or a male and female teachers, and the usual common school studies shall be free; but for the time prior to the said first day of April next, said board may collect tuition fees for instruction therein, as well as in the Uuion school, as they have heretofore done; and such studies shall be taught in said Union school as said board may prescribe.

§ 5. Said board shall not raise by tax upon the property in the Union school district, any money for the salaries of teachers in the Union school district, which shall accrue after the first day of April next.

§ 6. The acts and doings of said board of education, in accordance with the provisions of their act of incorporation, since the act entitled "An act establishing free schools throughout the state," passed March 26, 1849, took effect are hereby ratified and confirmed.

§ 7. The public money which shall be apportioned to the districts included in the said Union school district, shall be paid to said board, and be applied by them to teachers' wages in the several schools in their charge in said district, in proportion to the average number of scholars pursuing common school studies in each of said schools. The annual report of receipts and expenditures required to be published by said board, shall specify all sums received, and from whom, and all persons to whom payments were made, and the general character of the demands paid.

Upon the application of said board of education to "the Regents of the University of the State of New York," said regents may acknowledge and declare said Union school to be an academy; and it shall thereafter be an academy, subject to, and to be governed by, the provisions of the act authorizing said Union school, and subject to such rules and regulations as said regents mayprescribe.

MEDINA.

[*Laws of* 1849. *Chap.* 286, *as amended by Chap.* 381 *Laws of* 1850.]

AN ACT *in relation to common schools in the village of Medina*

Passed April 9, 1849, "three-fifths being present."

The People of the State of New-York, represented in Senate and Assembly, do enact as follows:

§ 1. There shall hereafter be elected in school district number twelve, formed partly out of the town of Ridgeway and partly out of the town of Shelby, in the county of Orleans, and lying principally within the village of Medina, in the manner now provided by law, three trustees, who shall, respectively, hold their offices three years. Christopher Whaley, Silas M. Burroughs, John Ryan, Daniel Starr, Isaac W. Swan and Archibald Servoss, are hereby appointed trustees of said district, and shall, respectively, hold said office as follows, namely: the term of office of Christopher Whaley and Silas M. Burroughs shall expire at the same time that the term of office of Roswell Starr, as trustee of said district, shall expire. The term of office of John Ryan and Daniel Starr shall expire at the same time that the term of office of Isaac K. Burroughs, as trustee of said district, shall expire; and the term of office of Isaac W. Swan and Archibald Servoss shall expire at the same time that the term of office of Nathan Bancroft, as trustee of said district shall expire.

§ 2. The trustees of said district and their successors in office shall constitute a board of education for said district and for the purposes of this act in addition to the present powers and duties of trustees, are hereby constituted a body politic and corporate, by the name and style of "The board of education of the village of Medina," and said corporation shall have power to establish and organize a classical school in said village to be known by the name of "The Medina Academy," and such classical school shall be subject to all laws and regulations applicable to other incorporated academies of this state and shall be entitled to share in the distribution of the monies of the literature fund upon the same terms as other academies of this state; and the regents of the university shall recognize said academy as such as soon as the required sum of money shall be expended in buildings, and competent teachers employed therein.

§ 3. Said board of education shall appoint one of their number president of said board, who shall preside at the meetings of said board when present; when absent a president pro tempore shall be appointed in his stead. They shall also appoint one of their number secretary, who shall record all the acts doings and resolutions of said board; and in the absence of the secretary a secretary pro tempore shall be appointed to discharge such duties. They shall also appoint a collector, librarian, and treasurer of said district who shall respectively, hold their offices one year from their appointment, and until others are appointed in their places, unless sooner removed by said board; such collector, librarian and treasurer shall each, within ten days after notice of their appointment, in writing, and before entering upon the duties of their office, execute and deliver to said board of education a bond, in such penalty and with such sureties as said board may require, conditioned for the faithful discharge of the duties of his office. In case such bond shall not be given within ten days after receiving such notice, such office shall thereby become vacated, and said board of education shall thereupon make an appointment to supply such vacancy.

§ 4. The said board of education shall have power to fill any vacancy which may happen, by reason of the death or removal from the said district of any member of said board, and the officer so appointed shall hold his office for the unexpired time of the person to supply whose place he shall be so appointed.

§ 5. Said board of education shall possess all the powers, and be subject to all the duties in respect to said district, that the trustees of common schools now possess or are subject to, and such other powers and duties as are given or imposed by this act.

§ 6. The taxable inhabitants, of said district, at my annual, special or adjourned meeting legally held, may vote to raise such sum of money as they shall deem expedient for the purpose of purchasing a site and building a school house in said district, or for the purpose of purchasing any suitable building for such purpose, and direct the trustees to cause the same, to be levied and raised by instalments, and make out a tax for the collection of the same as often as such instalments shall become due; and the legal voters at any such meeting are authorised to fix the compensation for collecting and paying over to the said board of education the amount so levied.

§ 7. The inhabitants of said district shall have no power to rescind the vote to raise such sum of money, at any subsequent meeting, unless the same be done within ten days thereafter; nor shall they have power to reduce the amount of the same after the expiration of ten days from the time the tax was first levied, but may remit such sum as shall remain unappropriated after paying for the site and erection of the house or purchase of suitable building.

§ 8. The said board of education are hereby authorised to obtain by loan the whole or any part of the money legally voted by said district, and secure the payment of the same by their official bond.

§ 9. The Comptroller of this state is hereby authorised and directed to loan to the said board of education, such sum as the said board of education shall certify to said comptroller to have been voted by the inhabitants of said district, in pursuance of this act, not exceeding the sum of five thousand dollars, out of the moneys in the treasury belonging to the capital of the common School fund, and for the purpose of purchasing a site, and erecting or purchasing a suitable building for a school house in said district; and the money when loaned shall be charged upon the books of the comptroller to said district and the same shall be paid over to said board of education, to be applied by them for the purpose of purchasing a site and erecting or purchasing a school house for said district.

§ 10. The sum so loaned shall be paid to the comptroller of this state, in annual instalments thereafter as determined by the vote of said district raising such sum of money, with annual interest thereon.

§ 11. The said board of education are hereby authorised, and empowered to sell at public auction to the highest bidder, the school house and site thereof belonging to said district, by giving public notice to be posted in ten public places in said district, ten days previous to such sale, and apply the proceeds arising from such sale, towards purchasing a site and erecting a school house in said district, or to such other purpose, as said district shall direct; such sale may be made upon such terms of credit, as said board of education shall determine upon, and a bond and mortgage taken by said board for the whole or any part of the purchase money, or price for which said site and house may be sold and such bond and mortgage may be sold and assigned by said board at par, for money to be applied by them as herein provided.

§ 12. The said board of education, are hereby authorised and empowered to make such by-laws and regulations, as they may deem necessary to secure the prosperity, order and government of said school, and divide the same into primary and higher departments, and regulate the transfer of scholars from one department to the other, and provide suitable instructors for each department, direct what text books shall be used in the same, purchase fuel and other necessaries for the use of the school or schools in said district, and all contracts made by them in their official capacity, shall be binding upon them and their successors in office: to fix and regulate the terms of tuition fees in said primary and other higher branches in said school or schools, to sue for and collect in their corporate name, any sum of money due to said district: to receive and apply to the uses of said school or schools, or any department thereof, any gift, legacy, bequest or annuities, given or bequeathed to said board and apply the same, according to the instruction of the donor or testator to take and hold any real estate given or bequeathed to said board for the purposes of said school or schools, or any department thereof, and apply the same, or the interests or proceeds thereof, according to the terms and instructions of the donor or testator: to have in all respects the superintendence, supervision, management and control of said school or schools, or any department thereof, and to hire, pay and discharge any teacher or teachers, employed by them in said school or department thereof.

§ 13. Said board of education shall in all respects be subject to the restrictions and control of the superintendents of common schools, of the town, connty and state, in the same manner as the common schools in this state are subject.

§ 14. Said board of education shall have power and are hereby authorised to receive into said academy, and cause to be instructed therein any pupil or pupils residing in or out of said district, and to regulate and establish the terms of tuition fees of such resident or non-resident pupils; and said board of education shall have power to regulate the tuition fees and rates of charges for instruction in the higher English and classical departments of said academy, and shall have power to make such application of the money raised for the support of common schools in said district for the payment of teacher's wages as said board shall determine, and may divide and apportion the same in such manner as said board shall deem best to pay the salaries of teachers employed in said academy, or the elementary English schools connected therewith or maintained in said district under their supervision. The rates of tuition in the elementary English branches in the schools maintained in said district, shall be subject to the general laws relating to common schools, and after applying such portion of the money received in said district as said board shall determine towards the support of such elementary English departments, such sum, not to be less than one half of all the moneys received in said district for the support of common schools therein, the additional sum required to pay teacher's wages and provide fuel and other contingent expenses necessary to the support of such elementary schools, shall be estimated, assessed, collected and applied in the manner provided in chapter one hundred and forty and four hundred and four of the session laws of eighteen hundred and forty-nine, or in such other manner as shall be hereafter provided by law for the support of common schools.

§ 15. All moneys raised in said district for the purposes of said school, and all moneys to be received by such district from the common school fund or other source, shall be anually paid to the said board of education, and be applied by them for the uses of said school or schools according to law.

§ 16. The members of said board of education, before receiving any moneys belonging to said district, shall severally execute to the towu superintendent of common schools of the town of Ridgeway, their separate bonds with two sufficient sureties to be approved by said town superintendent, in a penalty at least double the amount to be expended by them, for the benefit of said school during the next ensuing year, conditioned that such trustee giving such bond, will faithfully account for the expenditure of all moneys, he shall receive for said district, and pay over the balance remaining in his hands at the time of the expiration of his office to the other trustees, and the district at any legal meeting thereof, may require the penalty of such bond to be increased, or additional security to be given by either or all the trustees, if they shall deem the same insufficient, and any trustee, treasurer of said district, or member of said board, who shall apply any moneys belonging to said district to his own use shall be deemed guilty of embezzlement.

§ 17. This act shall take effect immediately.

LODI AND OWEGO.

[*Laws of* 1846, *Chap.* 207.]

§ 1. The trustees of school district number one, formed from the towns of Persia and Perrysburgh, in the county of Cattaraugus, and the town of Collins, in the county of Erie, known as the "Lodi Union School District," are hereby authorized, if the inhabitants of said district shall, at any regular school district meetiug so direct, to make thereafter, and until the said inhabitants shall in like manner otherwise direct, separate and distinct rate-bills, for the payment of the wages of the teachers in the primary and in the higher departments of the school kept in the said district; provided that the manner in which such rate-bills shall be made, shall have been determined by such regular school district meeting aforesaid.

§ 2. The provisions of the preceding section of this act shall also apply to school district number one, in the village of Owego, in the county of Tioga, so far as the same shall be applicable to said district.

NEWTOWN.

[*Laws of* 1850. *Chapter* 60.]

AN ACT *to establish a free school in district number three in the town of Newtown.*

Passed March 16, 1850, "three-fifths being present."

The People of the State of New York, represented in Senate and Assembly, do enact as follows:

§ 1. School district number three in the town of Newtown, in the county of Queens, shall form a permanent school district, and shall not be subject to alteration by the town superintendent of common schools for the town in which said district is situated.

§ 2. The said district shall be under the direction of a board, to be styled "The Board of Education," which board shall consist of five members, three or more of whom shall constitute a quorum for the transaction of business. John B. Reboul, Daniel R. Remsen, Roe H. Smith, Nathaniel Filbey and Albert O. Wittemore shall compose the first board of education, and shall hold their office from one to five years, that is to say, one shall go out of office in each year, and in the order in which their names stand recorded in this section.

§ 3. At the annual meeting of said district in each year, there shall be elected, for five years, one member of said board of education, who shall be a resident and taxable inhabitant of said district. Said election, and all other elections provided for by this act, shall be held by three inspectors, who shall be appointed by the board of education at least thirty days preceding such election, and shall be by ballot, and conducted in the same manner as the annual election of village officers.

§ 4. The said board of education may make all necessary by-laws for their government; they shall have the entire control and management of all the common schools within the said district, and all the property belonging to the same; and they shall have and possess within the said district all the rights, powers and authority of town superintendent of common schools, and they shall provide for keeping a school in said district at least six months in each year, and as much longer as may be practicable. They may appoint a collector, with all the powers and duties of a district collector, or may employ the town or village collector for that purpose; and such collector shall collect and pay over the school moneys assessed upon said district, to the treasurer of the board of education, in the same manner and under the same conditions as is imposed by the laws of the town or village of which he is such collector. They shall require two of the members of said board to visit each school in said district at least once in each week, to render such assistance to the teachers and advice to the pupils as may be necessary, and to see that the regulations are rigidly adhered to.

§ 5. The said board of education are hereby authorized and empowered to raise a sum not exceeding one thousand dollars, by tax on said district, to be levied and collected in the same manner as taxes are authorized by law to be levied and collected in the towns of this state.

§ 6 The said board of education are hereby authorized and directed to levy and collect by tax, in each year, upon all the taxable property and inhabitants, such sum as may be necessary, not exceeding in amount one-fifth of one per cent. on the value of such taxable property, as the same shall be assessed by the assessors of the town of Newtown; and the said board shall add to their warrant for collection of such taxes, such amount as they may deem proper for fees for collection, not exceeding five per cent on the amount.

§ 7. The town superintendent of common schools of the town of Newtown shall pay over to the treasurer of the board of education all the public moneys to which said district number three shall be entitled, for school purposes.

§ 8. The said board of education shall call an annual district meeting at such time in the year as they may think proper, and submit thereto a full report in writing of their doings as such board; and shall state therein the number and condition of the schools in said district, under their charge, and the number of scholars attending the same; the studies pursued; the amount of moneys received from the state, as well as the amount raised in the district for school purposes, and the expenditure of the same, and generally all the particulars relating to the schools in said district; which report may, if the said board think proper, be published in pamphlet form, or in some news paper published in the county.

§ 9. The board of education shall have entire control and charge of the district library; they may employ a librarian, make such additions to the library and such regulations in relation thereto, as they may deem necessary or proper.

§ 10. A school for colored children may be organized as a district school, and be supported as the other schools in said district are under this act.

§ 11. Whenever the said board of education shall deem it necessary to erect one or more school-houses in said district, they shall submit the plans and estimated cost of such building to the electors of such district, at a special meeting called for that purpose, and if a majority of such electors present shall vote in favor of the same, the said board may proceed to erect said school-house or houses; and if the sums authorized to be raised by secti five and six of this act shall be insufficient to pay the cost of such building, then the said board may raise an additional sum not exceeding five hundred dollars, to be levied and collected as provided for in sections five and six of this act, to be expended in defraying such cost.

§ 12. The said board of education may call special meetings of said district whenever they may deem it necessary; and whenever a special meeting shall be called, notices of it shall be posted up in five public places in said district, at least one week previous to said meeting; and no business shall be transacted at such meetings except that stated in the notice calling the same.

§ 13. All laws and parts of laws inconsistent with this act are hereby repealed, so far as they relate to district number three in the town of Newtown, county of Queens.

§ 14. This act shall take effect immediately.

[*Laws of* 1851, *Chap.* 398.]

AN ACT *to amend an act entitled, "An act to establish a free school in district number three in the town of Newtown," passed March* 16, 1850

Passed July 8, 1851, "three-fifths being present."

The People of the State of New-York, represented in Senate and Assembly, do enact as follows:

§ 1. The fifth section of the act entitled "An act to establish a free school in district number three, in the town of Newtown," passed March 16, 1850, is hereby amended so as to read as follows:

§ 5. The said board of education are hereby authorized and empowered to raise a sum not exceeding one thousand dollars, by tax on said district, to be levied and collected in the same manner as taxes are authorized by law to be levied and collected in the towns of this state; and said board of education are also hereby authorized and empowered to raise the sum of three thousand and five hundred dollars by a loan, which sums are to be expended in the erection of a school-house in said district and furniture for the same; such loan to be secured by a bond and a mortgage upon the public school property of said district, which bond and mortgage shall be executed by said board of education in their official capacity, under their hands and a common seal to be provided by them. Said loan shall be paid off in annual instalments of five hundred dollars each, and the first of said instalments shall be paid in three years after the date of said bond and mortgage. Said board is also authorized and empowered to raise such additional sum, from time to time, by tax on said district, to be levied and collected in the same manner as taxes are authorized by law to be levied and collected in towns of this state, as may be necessary to pay the accruing interest on said loan and the said instalments thereof, and also such amount as they may deem proper for fees for collection, not exceeding five per cent. on the amount.

§ 2. The said board of education are hereby authorized to sell and convey the lot of land in Astoria in said district, which has heretofore been occupied as the school lot, and which is situated adjoining St. George Protestant Episcopal Church, and execute a conveyance therefor under their said corporate seal, and invest the proceeds of the sale in the purchase of another lot, or in the completion of said new school-house, as by the said board may be deemed most advisable for the interests of the said district.

§ 3. The words "sections five and six," wherever they occur in section eleven of the act hereby amended, shall be construed to mean section first of this act and section six of the act hereby amended.

§ 4. This act shall take effect immediately.

CITY AND COUNTY OF NEW YORK.

[*Laws of* 1851. *Chap.* 386.]

AN ACT *to amend, consolidate and reduce to one act, the various acts relative to the Common Schools of the city of New York.*

Passed July 3, 1851, "three-fifths being present."

The People of the State of New York, represented in Senate and Assembly, do enact as follows:

OF SCHOOL OFFICERS AND THEIR ELECTION.

§ 1. There shall be two commissioners, two inspectors and five trustees of common schools in each of the wards of the city of New-York, who shall be known as the "school officers" of the ward. At each general election there shall be elected in each ward of said city, one commissioner and one inspector, whose terms of office shall be two years, and one trustee, whose term of office shall be five years, to commence in each case on the first day of January next succeeding such election. But the terms of office of the school officers elect, and those now holding office, except those whose terms of office will expire on the first Monday of June next, are hereby extended to the first day of January next after the day on which they would otherwise have expired, respectively, and there shall be no election of school officers in 1852. The elections so held shall be subject to the same laws and regulations, in all respects, as those which govern the general elections in said city. The ballots for said school officers shall be endorsed "common schools," and deposited in a separate box to be provided therefor; and the said school officers, before entering upon the duties of their offices, shall severally take and subscribe the oath prescribed by the constitution of the state.

OF THE BOARD OF EDUCATION—ITS POWERS AND DUTIES.

§ 2. The commissioners of common schools, elected as aforesaid, shall constitute a board of education for the city and county of New-York; they shall meet on the second Wednesday of January in each year, for the purpose of organization; and thereafter for the transaction of business as often as they may determine. They shall elect one of their number president and shall appoint a clerk and assistant or assistants, whose compensation shall be fixed and paid by the board.

The board of education shall have power:

1st. To take and hold property, both real and personal, devised or transferred to it, for the purposes of public education in the city of New York:

2d. To appoint a superintendent of common schools for said city, as hereinafter provided:

3d. On the nomination of the school officers of any ward to fill vacancies in school offices, which may occur in such ward between the general elections:

4th. To establish new schools, as hereinafter provided:

5th. To draw from the moneys which shall be raised for the purposes of public education, such sums as may be required for the purpose of defraying the necessary incidental expenses of the board, and such further sums as may be required for the payment of the salaries of their clerk and assistant or assistants, and of the city superintendent of common schools:

6th. To visit and examine the schools, subject to the provisions of this act:

7th. To make rules of order and by-laws for the government of the board, its members and committees, and general regulations to secure proper economy and accountability in the expenditure of the school moneys:

8th. And, for the purposes of this act, the said board shall possess the powers and privileges of a corporation.

§ 3. It shall be the duty of the board of education,

1st. On or before the fifteenth day of November in each year, to report to the board of supervisors of the said city and county, an estimate of the amount over and above the sums specified in the fifteenth section of this act, which will be required during the year, for the purpose of meeting the current annual expenses of common school instruction; for erecting, purchasing, leasing and procuring sites for school-houses, and the fitting up and furnishing thereof, and the alterations in, the additions to, and repairs of, the school buildings of the ward schools; for the support of schools which shall have been organized since the last annual apportionment of the school moneys made by the board; for the support of evening schools, not exceeding the sum of fifteen thousand dollars in each year; for the support of the free academy, an annual sum not exceeding twenty thousand dollars; and such further sum or sums as may be necessary for any of the purposes authorized by this act; but the aggregate amount so reported shall not exceed the sum of four dollars for each pupil who shall have actually attended and been taught in the preceding year in the schools entitled to participate in the apportionment:

2d. To apportion all the school moneys which shall have been raised for the purposes of meeting the current annual expenses of public instruction, to each of the schools provided for by this act:

3d. To file with the chamberlain of said city, on or before the first Monday of April in each year, a copy of their apportionment, stating the amount apportioned to the ward schools, and to the trustees, managers and directors of the several schools enumerated in this act:

4th. To continue to furnish through the free academy, the benefit of education, gratuitously, to persons who have been pupils in the common schools of the said city and county for a period of time to be regulated by the board of education, not less than one year:

5th. To supervise, manage and govern said free academy, and, from time to time, make all needful rules and regulations therefor; fix the number and compensation of teachers and others to be employed therein; prescribe the preliminary examination, and the terms and conditions on which pupils shall be received and instructed therein and discharged therefrom; direct the course of studies therein, and provide in all things for the good government and management of the said free academy; and purchase the books, apparatus, stationery and other things necessary and expedient to enable the said free academy to be properly and successfully conducted, and to keep the said building or buildings properly repaired and furnished:

6th. To appoint annually a standing committee of not less than five persons of their number, who shall, subject to the control, supervision and approbation of the said board, constitute an executive committee for the care government and management of the said free academy, under the rules and regulations prescribed as aforesaid, whose duty it shall be, to make detailed reports to the said board of education, and, among other things, to recommend the rules and regulations which they deem necessary and proper for the said academy. The board of education may, at any regular meeting thereof, by a majority of all the members of said board, remove any or all the members of the said committee, and appoint another person or persons in the place of the member or members of the said committee so removed.

7th. To make and transmit annually on or before the first day of February in each year, to the common council of said city, and also to the secretary to the board of regents of the university of the state of New-York a report signed by the president and clerk of the said board of education, and dated on the first day of January, in the year of its transmission; which report shall state the names and ages of all the pupils instructed in such free academy during the preceding year, and the time that each was so instructed; a particular statement of the studies pursued by each pupil at the commencement of his instruction, and of his subsequent studies until the date of such report, together with the books such student shall have studied in whole or in part, and if in part what portion; an account or estimate of the cost of the library, philosophical and chemical apparatus, and mathematical or other scientific instruments belonging to such academy; the names of the instructors employed in said academy, and the compensation paid to each; what amount of moneys the board of education received, during the year for the purposes of such academy, and from what sources, specifying how much from each, and the particular manner, and the specific purpose for which such moneys have been expended; and such other information in relation to education in said academy, and the measures of the board in the management thereof, as the said common council or the regents of the university of the state of New-York may from time to time require:

8th. To provide evening schools for those whose ages or avocations are such as to prevent their attending the day schools established by law, in such of the ward school houses or other buildings used for school purposes, and in such other places in said city as they may, from time to time deem expedient:

9th. To furnish all necessary supplies or make regulation, for furnishing such supplies for the several schools under their care, but when such supplies are furnished by the board of education they shall be obtained by contract, proposals for which shall be advertised for the period of at least two weeks:

10th. To make and transmit between the fifteenth day of January and the first day of February in each year, to the clerk of the city and county of New-York, a report in writing, bearing date the first day of January in the year of its transmission, stating the whole number of schools within their jurisdiction, specially designating the schools for colored children; the schools or societies from whichreports shall have been made to the board of education within the timelimited for that purpose, the length of time such schools shall have been kept open; the amount of public money apportioned or appropriated to said schoolorsociety; the number taught in each school, the whole amount of money drawn from the city chamberlain for the purposes of public education during the year ending at the date of their report, distinguishingthe amount received from the general fund of the state from all other and what sources;the manner in which such moneys shall have been expended, and such otherinformation as the superintendent of common schools may from time to time require, in relation to common school education in the city and county of New-York.

§ 4. If the board of education shall neglect to make such annual report within the time limited, the share of school moneys apportioned to the city and county of New-York may, in the discretion of the superintendent of common schools, be withheld until a suitable report shall have been rendered.

§ 5. The clerk of the board of education shall have charge of the rooms, books, papers and documents of the board, and shall in addition to his duties as secretary of the board, perform such other clerical duties as may be required by its members or committees:

§ 6. All schools which have been organized under the act entitled "An act to extend to the city and county of New-York the provisions of the general act in relation to common schools, passed April 11, 1842," and the acts amending the same, or organized or adopted under this act, shall be called common schools ["ward schools,"] or ward primaries, and each class shall be numbered consecutively, according to the time of their organization or adoption, and all such schools shall be under the supervision and government of the commissioners, inspectors and trustees of the ward in which they are located.

POWERS AND DUTIES OF SCHOOL OFFICERS.

§ 7. It shall be the duty of the school officers, or a majority of them, in any ward:

1st. To certify to the board of education of the city and county of New York, whenever in their opinion it is necessary, to organize one or more additional schools in said ward, with the facts and circumstances showing such necessity, together with the character of the school buildings required, and the number and class of scholars who will probably attend such schools if organized, and to organize such schools as hereinafter provided:

2nd. To provide, under such rules and regulations as the board of education may establish, the necessary books, stationary, and other essentials necessary to organize and conduct any school in their ward;

3rd. To examine, ascertain and report to the board of education, and as frequently as may be, whether the provisions ofthis act in relation to the teaching of sectarian doctrines, or the use of sectarian books, shall have been violated; and

4th. To notify the board of education of any vacancy in the office of any school officer of their respective wards.

POWERS AND DUTIES OF COMMISSIONERS.

§ 8. It shall be the duty of the commissioners of common schools in the several wards:

1st. To attend all the meetings of the board of education; and if any commissioner shall refuse or neglect to attend any three successive stated meetings of the board, after having been personally notified to attend, and if no satisfactory cause of his non-attendance be shown, the board may declare his office vacant;

2nd. To transmit to the board of education all reports made to them by the trustees and inspectors of their respective wards;

3rd. To visit and examine all the schools entitled to participate in the apportionment;

4th. They shall be ex officio members of the board of trustees in their respective wards.

POWERS AND DUTIES OF INSPECTORS.

§ 9. It shall be the duty of the inspectors of common schools:

1st. To inspect and examine each of the schools in their respective wards, at least twice in each year, and oftener if necessary; and on or before the fifteenth day of October, in each year, to make and transmit to the board of education and to the trustees of the ward, a report in writing, in which they shall set forth the condition of the several school buildings in use in their ward, and whether any, and if any, what repairs, alterations or modifications of those buildings seem to them necessary;

2. Whether they are kept clean and in good order;

3. In what manner they are heated and ventilated, and how effectual the means used are in producing the result desired;

4. The studies pursued;

5. The progress of the classes in their different studies;

6. The punctuality of attendance of the scholars and teachers;

7. The order, attention and general appearance of the school;

8. The length of each morning and evening session, and the number and length of recesses allowed;

9. The number and qualifications of the teachers, and such other facts as in their opinion are important to insure the discipline or extend the usefulness of the schools;

10. In conjunction with the city superintendent of common schools, to license teachers for their respective wards; and

11. To examine and audit all accounts when duly certified by the trustees to be correct.

POWERS AND DUTIES OF TRUSTEES.

§ 10. It shall be the duty of the trustees of each ward and they shall have power:

1. To have the safe keeping of all the property belonging to the ward schools and the ward primaries in their respective wards;

2. Under such general rules and regulations as the board of education may adopt, to contract with and employ teachers in said schools, and make other contracts for conducting and managing their schools;

3. To procure, as may be necessary, blank books, in one of which a statement of the amounts of all moneys received and paid by the trustees, and of all moveable property belonging to each school shall de er tered at large and signed by such trustees; and in other books, the teacher shall enter the names and residence of the scholars attending school, and the number of days they shall have respectively attended; and also the days on which each school shall have been visited by the city superintendent and the school officers of the ward, or any of them, which entries shall be verified by the oath or affirmation of the principal teacher in such school. The said books shall be preserved by the trustees as the property of the schools, and shall be delivered to their successors;

4. To make, on or before the fifteenth day of January, in every year, and transmit to the board of education, a report in writing, dated on the first day of January, which shall be signed and certified by a majority of the trustees, which report shall state: the whole number of schools within their jurisdiction, especially designating the schools for colored children; the length of time each school shall have been kept open; the whole number of scholars over four and under twenty-one years of age, who shall have been taught, free of expense to such scholars, in their schools during the year preceding the first day of January, which number shall be ascertained by adding to the number of children on register at the commencement of each year, the number admitted during that year, which shall be considered the total for that year; the average number that has actually attended such schools during the year to be ascertained by the teachers' keeping an exact account of the number of scholars present every school time or half day, which being added together and divided by four hundred and sixty, or if less than a year, by the number of school sessions, shall be considered the average of attending scholars, which average shall be sworn or affirmed to by the teachers; a detailed statement of the amount of moneys received for their respective schools during the last year from the chamberlain of the city, and of the purposes for, and the manner in which the same shall have been expended; and a particular account of the state of the schools and of the property and affairs of each school under their care; and the titles of all books used, with such other information as the board of education shall require. A report in all respects similar shall be requred from the trustees, managers or directors of the corporate schools;

5. To hold as a corporation, all personal property vested in or transferred to them for school purposes in their respective wards; and

6. To render at the expiration of their respective terms of office, to their successors, a just and true account in writing, of all moneys received by them for school purposes, and of the manner in which the same shall have been expended, and to pay any balance which may remain in their hands, to their successors.

OF THE CITY SUPERINTENDENT.

§ 11. The board of education shall appoint a city superintendent of common schools for the city and county of New-York, who shall hold his office for two years, subject to removal by the board, on complaint for cause stated. He shall perform such duty, and be subject to such rules, and receive such salary, as may be prescribed by the board of education; but the salary shall not be increased or diminished during his term of office.

It shall be his duty specially:

1. To visit and examine all schools entitled to participate in the apportionment of the school moneys, as often in each year as the board of education may direct, and at least once in each year to notify the inspectors of common schools of the ward of the time appointed to visit the schools in such ward, and to invite such inspectors to visit with him the said schools, and, with such inspectors, if they, or any of them, shall attend at such visits, or, without their presence, at any time to enquire into all matters relating to the government, course of instruction, books, studies, discipline, and conduct of such schools, and the condition of the school-houses, and of the schools generally, and to advise and to counsel with the trustees in relation to their duties the proper studies, discipline, and conduct of the schools, the course of instruction to be pursued, and the books of elementary instruction to be used therein; and to examine, ascertain, and report to the board of education whether the provisions of the act in relation to religious sectarian teaching and books have been violated in any of the schools of the different wards of the city:

2. To examine, in conjunction with the inspectors of any ward, persons offering themselves as candidates for teachers of common schools, and to grant them certificates of qualification, in such form as shall be prescribed by the board of education; which certificates, when countersigned by one or more inspectors, shall be evidence of the qualifications of such teachers in every ward of the city and county: and

3. Generally, by all the means in his power, to promote sound education, elevate the character and qualifications of teachers, improve the means of instruction, and advance the interests of the schools committed to his charge.

§ 12. The city superintendent shall be subject to such general rules and regulations as the superintendent of common schools may prescribe; and appeals from his acts and decisions may be made to the superintendent in the same manner and with like effect, as in cases now provided by law, and he shall make annually to the superintendent of common schools, at such times as shall be appointed by him, a report in writing, containing the whole number of schools in the city and county, distinguishing the schools from which the necessary reports have been made to the board of education, by the commissioners, inspectors and trustees of common schools, and containing a certified copy of the reports of the board of education, to the clerk of the city and county, with such additional information as the superintendent of common schools may require.

§ 13. The office of county superintendent of common schools for the city and county of New-York is hereby abolished.

OF THE SUPPORT OF THE SCHOOLS.

§ 14. Whenever the clerk of the city and county shall receive notice from the superintendent of common schools of the amount of moneys apportioned to the county of New-York, for the support and encouragement of common schools therein, he shall immediately lay the same before the board of supervisors of the said county; and the chamberlain of the said city shall apply for, and receive the school moneys apportioned to the said county as soon as the same become payable, and place the same to the credit of the mayor, aldermen and commonalty of the city of New-York, for the benefit of public education therein.

§ 15. The said board of supervisors shall annually raise and collect by tax upon the inhabitants of the said city and county, a sum of money equal to the sum specified in such notice, at the time and in the same manner as the contingent charges of the said city and county are levied and collected; also a sum of money equal to one-twentieth of one per cent of the value of the real and personal property in the said city, liable to be assessed thereon, and pay the same into the city treasury, to be applied to the purposes of common schools in the said city; and the board of education shall apportion the money so raised to each of the schools hereafter provided for by this act, except the free academy, and the evening schools, according to the number of children over four and under twenty-one years of age, who were actual residents of the city and county of New-York at the time of their attendance on such schools, without charge, the preceding year; and the average shall be ascertained by adding together, the number of such children present at each morning and afternoon session, of not less than three hours, and dividing the sum by four hundred and sixty; and if any school shall have been organized since the last annual apportionment, the average shall be ascertained by dividing by a number corresponding to the actual number of morning and evening sessions, of not less than three hours each, held since the organization of such school; and the sum apportioned to any schools, other than the ward schools, shall be paid to the trustees, managers or directors of such schools, respectively, by drafts on the city chamberlain, to be signed by the president and clerk of said board, and made payable to the order of the treasurers of said trustees, managers, or directors.

§ 16. Said board of supervisors shall also raise and collect at the same time, and in the same manner, such additional sum or sums as the board of education, in pursuance of the provisions of the first subdivision of the third section of this act, shall have reported to be necessary for the purposes therein mentioned. Such moneys shall be paid into the city treasury, and shall, together with the amount apportioned to the ward schools, be paid by the chamberlain of the said city upon the drafts drawn on him by the board of education, signed by the president, and countersigned by the clerk of the board, and by the commissioners, or one of them, of the ward for which the money is to be paid, except such sums as shall be drawn pursuant to the fifth sub-division of the second section of this act, which shall be paid by said chamberlain, upon drafts drawn on him by said board, signed by the president and clerk, and countersigned by the chairman of the finance committee of said board, and all drafts shall be made payable to the person or persons entitled to receive the same.

§ 17. If any of the said newly organised ward schools, by reason of peculiar circumstances, shall be equitably entitled to a larger sum than they will receive under an apportionment made as aforesaid, then the board of education shall be authorised, and they are hereby required to make to such schools such further allowance out of the school moneys, as they, the board of education, shall deem just and proper.

§ 18. No school shall be entitled to, or receive any portion of the school moneys in which the religious doctrines or tenets of any particular christian, or other religious sect, shall be taught, inculcated or practiced, or in which any book or books, containing compositions favorable or prejudicial to the particular doctrines or tenets of any particular christian, or other religious sect, or which shall teach the doctrines or tenets of any other religions sect, or which shall refuse to permit the visits and examinations provided for in this act. But nothing herein contained shall authorise the board of education to exclude the Holy Scriptures, without note or comment, or any selections therefrom, from any of the schools provided for by this act; but it shall not be competent for the said board of education to decide what version, if any of the Holy Scriptures, without note or comment, shall be used in any of the schools: Provided that nothing herein contained shall be so construed, as to violate the rights of conscience as secured by the constitution of this state, and of the United States.

§ 19. If the school moneys apportioned to the common schools, agreeably to the previous section of this act, shall exceed the necessary and legal expenses of either of such schools, the board of education shall authorise the payment only of such sum or sums, as shall be sufficient to provide for such expenses, and any deficiency in the sums apportioned to meet the necessary and legal expenses of public education in the said schools, shall be supplied by the common council of the said city, and they are hereby authorised and directed to raise by loan, in anticipation of the annual tax, such sum or sums, as shall be necessary to meet such deficiency. And the board of education shall, in all cases, certify to the common council the cause of such deficiency, and that the same was unavoidable, and unless such certificate shall be made, the said common council may refuse to raise the sum required to meet such deficiency.

§ 20. In making the apportionment among the several schools, no share shall be allotted to any school from which no sufficient annual report shall have been received for the year ending on the last day of December, immediately preceding the apportionment.

§ 21. Whenever an apportionment of the public money shall not be made to any school, in consequence of any accidental omission to make any report required by law, or to comply with any other regulation or provision of law, the board of education may, in its discretion, direct an apportionment to be made to such school, according to the equitable circumstances of the case, to be paid out of the public money on hand, or if the same shall have been distributed, out of the public money to be received in a succeeding year.

OF THE SCHOOLS ENTITLED TO PARTICIPATE IN THE APPORTIONMENT.

§ 22. The schools of the Public School Society, the New-York Orphan Asylum School, the Roman Catholic Orphan Asylum School, the schools of the two Half-Orphan Asylums, the school of the Mechanic's Society, the school of the Society for the Reformation of Juvenile Delinquents in the city of New-York, the Hamilton Free School, the school for the Leake and Watt's Orphan House, the school connected with the Alms House of the said city the school of the Association for the benefit of Colored Orphans, the schools of the American Female Guardian Society, the schools of the society for the promotion of education among colored children, the schools organized under the act entitled, "An act to extend to the city and county of New-York, the provisions of the general act in relation to common schools, passed April 11, 1842," or an act to amend the same, passed April 18, 1843, or an act entitled an act more effectually to provide for common school education in the city and county of New-York, passed May 7, 1844, or any of the acts amending the same and including such normal schools for the education of teachers as the board of education may organize, and the normal school of the public school society for the education of teachers, and such schools as may be organized under the provisions of this act, shall be subject to the general supervision of the board of education, and shall be entitled to participate in the apportionment of the school moneys as provided for in this act, but they shall be under the immediate direction of their respective trustees, managers and directors, as herein provided.

OF NEW SCHOOLS.

§ 23. Whenever a majority of the school officers of any ward shall certify in writing to the board of education, that it is necessary to establish a school in said ward, with the facts and circumstances showing such necessity, together with the number and class of scholars who will probably attend such school if established; it shall be the duty of the board of education, without delay, to investigate the subject and determine the expediency of establishing such school in such ward applying for the same. Should the ward officers or any of them, deem themselves aggrieved by such decision, they may appeal to the state superintendent of common schools, who shall decide as to the propriety of the establishment of such school, and his decision, if adverse to the appellants, shall be binding for the term of one year.

§ 24. Upon a decision favorable to the establishment of a school or schools in any of the wards of the said city, it shall be lawful for the school officers of said ward to proceed to organize one or more schools, such as may be authorized by the board of education, and procure a school-house, by purchasing or hiring the same, or by procuring a site and erecting a building thereon, according to plans and specifications, and contracts which shall have been duly filed with and approved by the board of education, the erection of which said building, and the fitting up thereof, and the fitting up of any hired building, shall be done by contract, proposals for which shall be advertised for two weeks previous to deciding upon estimates thereon, unless such fitting up shall not exceed the sum of two hundred dollars; and the expense of establishing and organizing any school, as above mentioned, shall be levied and raised pursuant to the provisions of this act.

§ 25. The title to all school property, real and personal, purchased with any moneys derived from the distribution or apportionment of the school moneys, or raised by taxation in the city of New York, shall be vested in the mayor, aldermen and commonalty of said city, but no contract or contracts shall be made by the school officers of any ward for the purchase of any site, or for the erection or fitting up, or repairing of any building, when such repairs shall exceed in amount the sum of two hundred dollars, as authorised in this act, until a statement in writing of the amount required for that purpose shall have been presented to the board of education by said school officers, and, together with a copy of the working-drawings, plans, and specifications of the work to be done, pursuant to the provisions of this act, shall have been duly filed and approved of, as herein required, and an appropriation shall have been made by the board of education therefor.

§ 26. The trustees, managers and directors of any of the corporate schools entitled to participate in the apportionment of the school monies, may, at any time, convey their school houses and sites to the corporation o the city of New York, and transfer any of their schools to the board of education, on the terms and in the manner to be agreed upon and prescribed by the board of education, so as either to merge the said schools in the ward schools, or adopt them as ward schools; and the same shall then be ward schools, subject to all the rules, duties and liabilities, and enjoy the same rights, as if they had been originally established as ward schools. But nothing in this act shall take away from the Public School Society any rights which they have heretofore enjoyed, and the board of education are authorized to provide the Public School Society with all necessary moneys to make all proper repairs, alterations and improvements in the various school premises occupied by them.

OF THE DISCONTINUANCE OF SCHOOLS.

§ 27. Whenever, owing to any nuisance or other circumstance, in the immediate vicinity of any school, or to the small attendance of scholars therein, or other sufficient reason, it shall appear to the board of education necessary and proper to discontinue such school, in any of the wards of this city, the said board shall give notice to the trustees of said school of its intention to consider the propriety of such discontinuance; and in thirty days after such notice, may proceed to investigate the matter, and if a majority of the school officers of the ward shall consent to the same, and if the said board shall determine by a vote of a majority of all the members thereof, that it is proper to close the same, it shall be the duty of said board to withhold all moneys which may have been apportioned or appropriated for the support of said school, and the said school shall not thereafter participate in any subsequent apportionment of the school moneys. So soon as the same shall take effect, the comptroller of the city shall be notified thereof by the said board, and the said school-house and site may thereupon be used or disposed of, as a part of the general property of the city.

MISCELLANEOUS PROVISIONS.

§ 28. The common council of the city of New York are hereby authorized and directed to raise by loan, in anticipation of the taxes, when necessary, all moneys required for erecting, purchasing or leasing school-houses, and procuring sites therefor, and the fitting up and furnishing thereof, and for alterations in or additions to the present school-buildings, or required for any other of the purposes authorized by this act.

§ 29. All expenses incurred for the support of common schools in the respective wards, shall be certified by the trustees of common schools in such ward, or a majority of them, and delivered to the inspectors of said ward; and it shall be the duty of said inspectors to examine and audit the same, and upon said inspectors being satisfied of their correctness, to certify the same to the board of education. All bills audited and paid shall be filed with the board of education.

§ 30. No compensation shall be allowed to the commissioners, inspectors or trustees of common schools for any services performed by them, but the commissioners and inspectors shall receive their actual and reasonable expenses while attending to the duties of their office, to be audited and allowed by the board of education.

§ 31. Every school officer who shall refuse or neglect to render an account, or to pay over any balance in his hands, at the expiration of his term of office, shall for each offence forfeit the sum of fifty dollars, which sum, together with said unpaid balance, shall be sued for and collected by the board of supervisors, who shall prosecute without delay for the recovery of such forfeiture, together with the unpaid balance; and in case of the death of such school officer, suit may be brought against his representatives, and all monies recovered, after deducting expenses, shall be placed at the disposal of the board of education.

§ 32. Every school officer or teacher of a school or society, who shall wilfully sign a false report to the board of education, shall for each offence forfeit the sum of twenty-five dollars, and shall also be deemed guilty of a misdemeanor.

§ 33. The following shall be, substantially, the form of oath or affirmation to be made by the teacher:

"A. B., of the city of New-York, teacher of
No. department, being duly sworn or affirmed, declares and says, that to the best of (his or her) knowledge and belief, the average number of children, actual residents of the city and county of New York, at the time of attending said school, between the ages of four and twenty-one years, who attended said school or department, each school-time or half day, from the day of to the first day of January, was . Said average having been obtained by adding together the number of scholars present each school-time, or half day and dividing the total by four hundred and sixty, agreeably to the fifteenth section of this act."

§ 34. In any suit which shall hereafter be commenced against the commissioners or trustees of common schools, for any act performed by virtue of or under color of their offices, or for any refusal or omission to perform any duty enjoined by law, and which might have been the subject of an appeal to the superintendent, no costs shall be allowed to the plaintiff in cases where the court shall certify it appeared, on the trial of the cause, that the defendant acted in good faith. But this provision shall not extend to suits for penalties, nor to suits or proceedings to enforce the decisions of the superintendent of common schools.

§ 35. All children between the ages of four and twenty-one, residing in the city and county, shall be entitled to attend any of the common schools therein; and the parents, guardians or other persons having the custody or care of such children, shall not be liable to any tax, assessment or imposition for the tuition of any children, other than is hereinbefore provided.

§ 36. The free academy in the city of New-York shall be entitled to participate in the distribution of the income of the literature and other funds, in the same manner and upon the same conditions as the other academies of the state, and the regents of the university of the state of New-York shall pay annually to the board of education of the city and county of New-York, the distributive share of the said funds to which the said free academy shall by law be entitled,and which shall be applied and expended for library books for the said free academy.

§ 37. The clerk of the board of education is hereby authorized to administer oaths and take affidavits in all matters appertaining to the schools in the city and county of New-York, and for that purpose shall possess all the powers of a commissioner of deeds, but shall not be entitled to any of the fees or emoluments thereof.

§ 38. No school officer shall be interested in any contract, payments under which are to be made, in whole or in part, out of moneys derived from the school fund or raised by taxation for the support of common schools. No teacher employed in any of the schools entitled to participate in the apportionment of the school moneys, shall hereafter be eligible to the office of commissioner, inspector or trustee of common schools.

§ 39. The common council shall provide and furnish suitable rooms, for the meeting of the board of education, and for the transaction of its business.

§ 40. The act entitled, "An act to extend to the city and county of New York the provisions of the general act in relation to common schools," passed April 11th, 1842, and an act amending the same, passed April 18th, 1843; and the act entitled, " An act more effectually to provide for common school education in the city and county of New-York," passed May 7th, 1844, and the several acts amending the same, passed respectively on May 11th, 1847; March 27th, 1848; April 11th, 1849; and the act authorizing the board of education of the city of New-York to establish evening schools for the education of apprentices, and others, passed March 25th, 1848; and an act authorizing the board of education of the city and county of New-York to establish a free academy in caid city, passed May 7th, 1847, and all other acts and parts of acts inconsistent with or repugnant to the provisions of this act, are hereby repealed.

OSWEGO.

By chapter 116, laws of 1848, a city superintendent of common schools is authorized to be elected, who "shall have all the powers and perform all the duties, and be subject to all the liabilities and obligations of town superintendents of common schools in any town of the county of Oswego; and he shall also commence his term of office at the same time, and hold it for the same period as town superintendent." § 20.

By § 10 of the same act, as amended by the first section of chap. 182, laws of 1849, it is provided that "in case a vacancy, from any cause, shall happen in the office of superintendent of common schools, the common council may appoint, by ballot, a qualified person to fill such vacancy."

POUGHKEEPSIE.

[*Laws of* 1843. *Chap.* 211.]

AN ACT *to establish Free Schools in the village of Poughkeepsie.*

Passed April 18, 1843, by a two-third vote.

The People of the State of New-York, represented in Senate and Assembly, do enact as follows:

§ 1. The village of Poughkeepsie shall form a permanent school district, not subject to alteration by the commissioners of common schools for the town in which the said village is situated.

§ 2. There shall be elected in said district the first year, twelve commissioners of common schools, as soon after the passage of this act as the trustees of the village of Poughkeepsie can order an election, for the choice of said commissioners, after giving one week's notice in all the papers of the village, of the time and place of holding said election; the twelve commissioners then elected shall constitute, and are hereby denominated, the Board of Education for the village of Poughkeepsie. Four of the said board shall go out of office at the expiration of the first year, four at the expiration of the second year, four at the expiration of the third year—four persons being annually elected to supply their places, who shall hold their office in said board for three years. The annual election shall be held on the first Tuesday in June of each year.

§ 3. The trustees of the village of Poughkeepsie shall appoint inspectors of the said elections, and of all other elections to be held under this act, within thirty days next preceding the time of holding the same; and notice thereof shall be given in the same manner, and the same shall be held and conducted, the votes shall be canvassed, and the result of the election determined in the same manner as in the case of the annual election of other officers of the said village.

§ 4. In case of vacancy in the office of any such commissioners, or in case no person shall be elected thereto, by reason of two or more persons having an equal number of votes, the trustees shall appoint an inhabitant of the village to fill the same, and the person appointed shall hold his office until the next election of commissioners of common schools.

§ 5. Immediately after the election of the said board of education, they shall proceed, under the provisions of this law, to build and furnish one good and substantial school-house, containing two rooms, of sufficient capacity to accommodate not less than one hundred and twenty-five pupils each, and to rent five other rooms for primary schools; said primary schools to be opened for the reception of pupils by the first of May next ensuing, or as soon thereafter as practicable, and the other schools on or before the first of November next ensuing. Whenever the board may deem necessary, they shall have authority to establish other primary schools; and for the purpose of defraying the expenses of the five primary schools, and the schools to be kept in the building provided for in this section, for the first year after the passage of this act, the trustees of the corporation of the village of Poughkeepsie shall levy and raise the sum of fifteen hundred dollars.

§ 6. The trustees of the village of Poughkeepsie are hereby authorized and required to borrow on the bond of the corporation, at a rate of interest not exceeding seven per cent. per annum, for such a term of years as they may deem proper, the sum of three thousand dollars, for the purchase of a site and erection of a school-house, as is provided for in the preceding section; the money loaned to be payable in equal annual instalments of five hundred dollars per annum, after the expiration of the term of years for which it may be borrowed.

§ 7. It shall be the duty of the board of education to make to the trustees of the village of Poughkeepsie, who shall cause it to be published in at least two papers of the said village, an annual report, on or before the first Tuesday in February of each year, setting forth the number and condition of each school under their charge, and a detail of all the expenses during the past year, and all other particulars relating to the schools.

§ 8. In their annual report, the said board of education shall fix and determine, and certify the amount of money which, when added to the money annually apportioned to the said corporation, out of the funds belonging to the state, shall be necessary to support all the schools under their superintendence. The said amount shall in no case exceed four times the amount which shall have been apportioned out of the funds belonging to the state as aforesaid, for the year next preceding.

§ 9. On the day of the annual charter election of said village, the trustees shall state to the citizens the amount recommended by the board of education to be raised for the support of schools for the ensuing year, and the electors may vote the sum reported by said board, or any other amount they shall deem proper, not inconsistent with the preceding section.

§ 10. The trustees of said village shall annually levy and raise the amount of money so voted, at the same time and in the same manner as the other general taxes of the said village are levied and raised; and a separate column shall be provided in the general assessment rolls of the said village, in which shall be inserted by the village trustees the amount of tax assessed for the support of common schools.

§ 11. All moneys levied and raised for the support of common schools, together with the public moneys received from the state, shall be paid to the treasurer of the village of Poughkeepsie, and shall be kept by him in the same manner as other moneys of said village are kept, and shall be paid out by said treasurer from time to time, upon the resolution of the board of education, duly certified by the clerk thereof, and not otherwise.

§ 12. Whenever the said board of education shall deem an additional school-house necessary, they shall mention the same in their annual report, together with the location they propose for it, the cost of a lot for the building, a plan of the building and an estimate of the cost of it. And the electors of the village, at the annual election on the first Tuesday of June for four members of the board of education, as is hereinbefore provided for, shall vote by ballot for or against the erection of said school-house, under such regulations for conducting the election as the trustees of the village shall prescribe; and it shall not be lawful to erect said school-house until a majority of electors voting at such election shall decide in favor of it; and the cost of building and furnishing of said school-house shall in no case exceed the sum of three thousand dollars.

§ 13. Whenever the electors shall decide in favor of the erection of an additional school-house, it shall be the duty of the trustees of the village of Poughkeepsie to borrow on the bond of the village, at a rate of interest not exceeding seven per cent. per annum, the sum of three thousand dollars, for the erection of said school-house; but no part of said loan shall be payable in a less term than twelve years and then to be payable in equal annual instalments of five hundred dollars each. And all the loans authorized by this act, for the purchase of sites and erection of school-houses, shall not exceed the sum of twelve thousand dollars.

§ 14. The trustees of said village are hereby authorized to raise by tax upon the real and personal property of said village, in the same manner as the general taxes of said village are levied and collected, the annual interest of the above mentioned loan or loans, and to pay over the same in discharge of such interest; and also in each year in which an instalment of the above loan or loans shall become due, to raise, levy and collect, in the same manner, a sum equal to that instalment, and to pay over the same in discharge thereof.

§ 15. The said board of education, in addition to the powers and duties prescribed by this act, shall perform all the duties, and shall have and possess all the rights, powers and authority of commissioners of common schools in the several towns of this state, which shall not conflict with the provisions of this law.

§ 16. The said board of education shall have power to establish and cause to be kept, a school or schools in said village for the instruction of colored children.

§ 17. The said board of education, in addition to performing all the duties of commissioners of common schools, shall require three of their number to visit each school once a week, and render such assistance to the teacher and advice to the pupils as may be expedient.

§ 18. The said board of education shall make by-laws to regulate their proceedings, and shall have the entire control and management of all the common schools of the village, and the property connected therewith.

§ 19. The said board of education shall annually report to the commissioners of the town of Poughkeepsie, the number of children over the ages of five and under sixteen years, in said district.

§ 20. The commissioners of common schools of the town of Poughkeepsie shall pay over to the treasurer of said village the amount of the public money that said village is entitled to receive from the State.

§ 21. The said board of education shall have control of the district library, shall employ a librarian, and shall, from time to time, make such regulations respecting it as they shall deem necessary.

§ 22. The services of the board of education, designated by this act, shall be gratuitous, and any person elected a member of said board who shall refuse to serve, shall be liable to a penalty of twenty-five dollars, to be sued for and recovered by the trustees of the village, and the money to be applied to the purposes of education.

§ 23. The present Lancaster school may, with the consent of the trustees thereof and not otherwise, constitute one of the common schools in said village, and shall be conducted and supported as other schools under this act.

§ 24. All previous acts relating to common schools in the village of Poughkeepsie, conflicting with this act, shall be, and are, hereby repealed.

§ 25. This act shall not take effect unless approved by a majority of the legal voters of the village of Poughkeepsie, at a special election to be called for that purpose by the trustees of the village, within thirty days after the passage of this act, public notice of which shall be given in all the village papers, and by hand-bills, for at least one week before holding the election. The electors shall vote by ballot, the ballots having written or printed upon them the words "for free schools," or "against free schools;", and the election shall be conducted as the trustees of said village may prescribe, and they shall certify the result thereof; and if a majority of the said ballots shall be "for free schools," then this act shall take effect immediately.

ROCHESTER.

[*Chap.* 262, *laws of* 1850, *as amended by chap.* 389, *laws of* 1851.]

By § 9 of Title II, two Commissioners of Common Schools are required to be annually elected in each ward, on the first Tuesday in March.

"For the election of commissioners of common schools the electors of each ward shall deposit their ballots, containing the name of one person designated for the office; the two persons having the highest number of votes shall be declared to be elected; no ballot which contains more than one name shall be counted" § 17. By § 30. in case a vacancy shall occur in the office, "the Common Council may, in their discretion, fill such vacancy, by the appointment of a suitable person who is an elector, and if appointed for a ward or district, who is a resident of the ward or district for which he shall be appointed; and any officer appointed to fill a vacancy, if the office is elective, shall hold by virtue of such appointment, only until the first Monday of April next succeeding. If an elective officer whose office shall have become vacant, was one of a class, a successor for the unexpired term shall be elected at the next annual election."

By § 32 every person so elected or appointed to the office of commissioner, shall, before he enters on the duties of his office, and within five days after being notified of such election or appointment, take the oath of office prescribed by the constitution of the State, before some officer authorized to take affidavits to be read in courts of justice, and file the same with the clerk of the city; and by § 34 his neglect to do so, or if required by the common council, to execute an official bond or undertaking, the neglect to execute and file the same in manner and within the time prescribed by the common council, shall be deemed a refusal to serve.

TITLE VI—SCHOOLS AND BOARD OF EDUCATION.

§ 161. The several wards of the city of Rochester shall constitute one school district, for all purposes except as herein otherwise provided, and the schools therein shall be free to all children between the ages of five and sixteen [twenty-one] residing in such wards.

§ 162. The titles of the school houses, sites, lots, furniture, books, apparatus and appurtenances, and all other school property in this act mentioned, shall, within three months from the passage of this act, be transferred and conveyed by the trustees of the several school districts in the said city, to the said city of Rochester.

§ 163. The several school districts now in the city of Rochester shall, within three months from the passage of this act, deliver over to and place in the care of the board of education hereinafter mentioned, all school district records, account books, vouchers, contracts, papers and other school property; and the said school officers of the said city and the several school districts thereof shall continue in office until the unfinished business of said districts shall have been finally closed up and settled, not exceeding three months after the passage of this act, with all the power and duties now by law imposed upon them for the purpose of closing such unfinished business.

§ 164. The common council of said city may, upon the recommendation of the board of education hereinafter mentioned, sell any of the school houses, lots or sites, or any other school property now or hereafter belonging to said city, upon such terms as the said common council may deem reasonable. The proceeds of all such sales shall be paid to the city treasurer of the city, and shall be by the said common council again expended in the purchase, repairs or improvements of other school houses, lots, sites or school furniture, apparatus or appurtenances.

§ 165. The commissioners of common schools in said city shall constitute a board to be styled the "Board of Education of the city of Rochester," which shall be a corporate body in relation to all the powers and duties conferred upon them by virtue of this act; they shall meet on the first Monday of each and every month, and as much oftener as they shall from time to time appoint; a majority of the said board shall constitute a quorum for the transaction of business. The said board shall appoint one of their number president, who shall, when present, preside at all the meetings of said board, and shall have power to call special meetings of the board, in the manner described by this act for the calling of special meetings of the common council. In the absence of the president, the board shall appoint some other member to preside at such meetings and perform the duties of the president. No member of said board of education shall, during the period for which he was elected, be appointed to, or be competent to hold any office of which the emoluments are paid from the city treasury, or paid by fees directed to be paid by any act or ordinance of the board of education, or be directly or indirectly interested in any contract, as principal, surety, or otherwise, the expenses or consideration whereof are to be paid under any ordinance of the board of education.

§ 166. The said commissioners shall annually appoint a city superintendent of common schools, who shall hold his office during the pleasure of the board, and whose compensation shall be fixed by the said board; the said superintendent shall officiate as clerk of the board, and shall keep a record of the proceedings of the board, and perform such other duties as the board may prescribe. The said record or a transcript thereof, certified by the president and clerk, shall be received in all courts as prima facie evidence of facts therein set forth; and such records and all the books, accounts, vouchers and papers of said board shall at all times be subject to the inspection of the common council and of any committee thereof.

§ 167. The common council of said city shall have the power, and it shall be their duty to raise from time to time, by tax to be levied equally upon all the real and personal estate in said city which shall be liable to taxation for the ordinary city taxes or for city or county charges, such sum or sums of money as may be necessary or proper for any or all the following purposes:

1. To purchase, lease or improve sites for school houses.

2. To *build, purchase,* lease, enlarge, improve, alter and repair school houses and their out-houses and appurtenances.

3. To purchase, improve, exchange and repair school apparatus, books, furniture and appendages,

4. To procure fuel and defray the contingent expenses of the common schools.

5. To pay the wages of teachers due after the application of the public moneys which may by law be appropriated and provided for that purpose: provided, nevertheless, that the tax to be levied as aforesaid and collected by virtue of this act, shall be collected at the same time and in the same manner as other city taxes.

6. And the amount to be raised for teachers' wages and contingent expenses, in any one year, shall not be less than four nor more than five times the amount appropriated to said city from the common school fund of the State during the previous year. Nor shall the amount to be raised in any one year, to lease, alter, improve and repair school houses and their out-houses and appurtenances, exceed three thousand dollars. Nor shall the amount to be raised in any one year to purchase and improve sites, and build or enlarge school houses, exceed three thousand five hundred dollars each; and the common council of said city are authorized and directed, when necessary, to raise by loan, in anticipation of the taxes, the moneys so to be raised, collected and levied as aforesaid.

§ 168. All moneys to be raised pursuant to the provisions of this act, and all school moneys by law appropriated to, or provided for said city, shall be paid to the city treasurer thereof, who, together with their sureties upon his official bond, shall be accountable therefor in the same manner as for other moneys of said city. The said city treasurer shall be liable to the same penalties for any official misconduct in relation to the said moneys, as for any similar misconduct in relation to other moneys of said city.

§ 169. The said "board" shall have power, and it shall be their duty,

1. To establish and organize in the several wards of said city such and so many schools (including the common schools now existing therein) as they shall deem requisite and expedient, and to alter and discontinue the same.

2. To hire school houses and rooms and improve them as they may deem proper.

3. To alter, enlarge, and improve and repair school houses and appurtenances as they may deem advisable.

4. To purchase, exchange, improve and repair school apparatus, fnrniture and appendages, and to defray their contingent expenses.

5. To have the custody and safe keeping of the school houses, out-houses, fences, books, furniture and appendages, and to see that the ordinances of the common council in relation thereto be observed.

6. To contract with, license and employ all teachers in said schools and at their pleasure to remove them.

7. To pay the wages of such teachers out of the moneys appropriated and provided by law for the support of schools in said city, so far as the same shall be sufficient, and the residue thereof from the money authorised to be raised for that purpose by section 167 of this act, by tax upon said city.

8. To defray the necessary contingent expenses of the board including an annual salary to the superintendent.

9. To have in all respects the superintendence, supervision and management of the common schools in said city, and from time to time to adopt, alter, modify and repeal, as they may deem expedient, rules and regulations for their organization, government, visitation and instruction, for the reception of pupils and their transfer from one school to another, and generally for the promotion of their good order, prosperity, and public utility.

10. Whenever, in the opinion of the board it may be advisable to sell any of the school houses, lots, or sites, or any of the school property now or hereafter belonging to the city, to report the same to the common council.

11. To prepare and report to the common council such ordinances and regulations as may be necessary or proper for the protection, safe keeping, care and preservation of school houses, lots, and sites and appurtenances, and all the property belonging to the city connected with, or appertaining to the schools, and to suggest proper penalties for the violation of such ordinances and regulations; and annually on or before the first day of September on each year to determine and certify to said common council, the sums in their opinion necessary or proper to be raised under the 167th section of this act, specifying the sums required (for the year commencing on the first Monday of April thereafter) for each of the purposes therein mentioned and the reasons therefor.

12. Between the first day of January and the fifteenth day of January in each year, to make and transmit to the county clerk or such other officer as may be designated by law, a report in writing, bearing date the first day of January in the year of its transmission, and stating:

1. The number of school houses in said city, and an account and description of all of the common schools kept in said city during the preceding year, and the time they have severally been taught.

2. The number of children taught in said schools respectively, and the number of children over the age of five [four] years, and under the age of sixteen [21] years residing in said city on the last day of December previous.

3. The whole amount of school moneys received by the city treasurer of said city during the year preceding, distinguishing the amount received from the county treasurer from the city tax, and from any other source.

4. The manner in which such moneys had been expended, and whether any and what part remains unexpended and for what cause.

5. The amount of money received for tuition fees from foreign pupils during the year, and the amount paid for teachers' wages in addition to the public moneys, with such other information relating to the common schools of said city, as may from time to time be required by the state superintendent of common schools.

§ 170. The said board of education shall have power to allow the children of persons not resident within the city to attend any of the schools of said city under the care and control of said board, upon such terms as said board shall by resolution prescribe, fixing the tuition which shall be paid therefor.

§ 171. It shall be the duty of said board in all their expenditures and contracts to have reference to the amount of moneys which shall be subject to their order during the then current year, for the particular expenditure in question, and not to exceed that amount, and they shall apply the moneys levied, raised and received by them for the support of common schools in said city, in such a manner as shall secure equal educational advantages to all the children of said city over five andunder sixteen [21] years of age, by continuing the schools in each district an equal period as near as may be.

§ 172. The said board of commissioners shall be trustees of the school library or libraries in said city, and all the provisions of the law which now are or hereafter may be passed relative to district school libraries shall apply to the said commissioners. They shall also be vested with the same discretion as to the disposition of the moneys appropriated by any laws of this State for the purchase of libraries which is therein conferred upon the inhabitants of school districts. It shall be their duty to provide for the safe keeping of the libraries. The city superintendent shall be the general librarian. The board shall also appoint a librarian for each school, to have the care of the books and to superintend the letting out and return thereof. The several school librarians shall from time to time inform the general librarian of the state and condition of their libraries, and the said board or the general librarian under the direction or by resolution of the said board, may make all purchases of books for the libraries, and provide for their equitable distribution among the schools, and exchange or cause to be repaired, the damaged books belonging thereto, and also to sell any books which may be deemed useless, and apply the proceeds to the purchase of other books for said libraries.

§ 173. It shall be the duty of the said board, at least twenty days before the annual election for commissioners in each year, to prepare and report to the common council true and correct statements of the receipts and disbursements of money under and in pursuance of the provisions of this act, during the preceding year, in which account shall be stated under appropriate heads,

1. The moneys raised by the common council under the 167th section of this act:

2. The school moneys received by the city treasurer of the city:

3. The moneys received by the common council under the 167th section of this act:

4. All other moneys received by the city treasurer subject to the order of the board specifying the same and sources:

5. The manner in which such sums of money shall have been expended, specifying the amount paid under each head of expenditure. And the common council shall, ten days before such election, cause the same to be published in at least two of the newspapers published in said city.

§ 174. The common council of the said city shall have the power to pass such ordinances and regulations as the said board of education may report as necessary and proper for the protection, safe keeping, care and preservation of the school houses, lots, sites, appurtenances and appendages, libraries, and all necessary property belonging to or connected with the schools in said city, and to impose proper penalties for the violation thereof, subject to the restrictions and limitations contained in this act; and all such penalties shall be collected in the same manner that the penalties for the violation of the city ordinances are by law collected, and when collected shall be paid to the city treasurer of the city, and be subject to the order of the board of education in the same manner as other moneys raised pursuant to this act.

§ 175. It shall be the duty of the common council, within fifteen days after receiving the certificate of the commissioners required by the 169th section of this act, of the sums necessary or proper to be raised under the 167th section of this act, to determine and certify to said board of education the amount that will be raised by them for the year commencing on the first Monday of April thereafter, for the purposes mentioned in said 167th section, distinguishing between the amount to be raised for teachers' wages and contingent expenses, and the amount to be raised for the repair of school houses, which amounts shall be subject to the disposal of the board of education.

§ 176. All the moneys required, to be raised by virtue of this act or received by the said city for or on account of the common schools, shall be deposited for the safe keeping thereof with the city treasurer of said city to the credit of said board of education, and shall be drawn out in pursuance of a resolution or resolutions of said board by drafts drawn by the president and countersigned by the clerk of said board, payable to the order of the person or persons entitled to receive such moneys, and said city treasurer shall keep the funds authorized by this title to be received by him separate and distinct from any other fund which he is or may by law be authorized to receive.

§ 177. The real and personal estate in each of the school districts, numbers fourteen and sixteen, as at present existing shall be assessed toward defraying the expense of building a school house in each of said districts respectively as follows: Number fourteen, a sum not exceeding two thousand dollars, and number sixteen a sum not exceeding one thousand dollars, and the balance, which may be found necessary to complete the school houses in said districts fourteen and sixteen, respectively, shall be paid out of moneys authorized to be raised by section 167 of this act, to build and enlarge school houses.

§ 178. The said board of education shall have power to establish and cause to be kept, such number of schools in said city for the instruction of colored children, as they shall deem expedient.

§ 179. The said board of education shall possess all the power and be subject to all the duties and responsibilities of trustees of common schools in the towns, in respect to the school mentioned in the last preceding section, so far as the same are applicable; and shall pay the compensation of the teachers of the said schools, and all the other expenses thereof, out of the moneys raised by tax under this act, for the support of common schools; and until such schools for the instruction of colored children shall be so provided, it shall not be lawful to impose any tax upon the property of any colored person in said city, for the support of common schools.

§ 180. Whenever the said board of education shall determine to establish any schools for the instruction of colored children, they shall divide the said city into convenient districts for the accommodation of such children, and enter the boundaries thereof on their records; they shall make an estimate of the expense of erecting a suitable school house in each of said districts, and determine the sites thereof respectively, and report all their doings under this section, to the common council.

§ 181. The common council shall have power to raise by general tax, in the manner hereinbefore provided, and on a separate warrant, such sum as shall be necessary to build a school house in each of the said districts, or in as many of them as they may deem expedient, not exceeding in the aggregate the sum of five thousand dollars, or the said common council may refuse to raise such tax.

§ 182. In case the common council shall refuse to raise such tax, the said board of education shall have power to provide, and lease suitable rooms or buildings for the accommodation of such schools, or either of them; but the annual expenditure for this purpose shall not exceed the sum of five hundred dollars.

§ 183. It shall be the duty of the trustees of the Rochester Collegiate Institute to make the reports and returns which by law they are required to make, as trustees of a school district, to the said board of education.

SALEM.

[*Laws of* 1851. *Chap.* 206.]

§ 88. The board of trustees [of the village of Salem] aforesaid, shall, within twenty days after the passage of this act, appoint six commissioners of schools. The persons so appointed, shall, within five days after their appointment, take the oath of office prescribed by the constitution of this state for state officers, and file the same with the clerk.

§ 89. The board of trustees shall divide the said commissioners into three classes, to be denominated first, second and third, and shall designate to which class each person so appointed shall belong. The term of office of the first class shall expire on the last Monday in April next thereafter; of the second in one year; and the third, two years from the said last Monday in April.

§ 90. There shall be elected at the next annual election thereafter, two commissioners of schools, and each year thereafter the like number, to supply the places of those whose term is about to expire: such person so appointed or elected as aforesaid, shall hold their offices till successors shall be duly elected and qualified, and the term of office shall be two years, except when elected or appointed to fill a vacancy.

§ 91. The board of trustees may make appointments to fill vacancies, which may occur from any cause other than the expiration of the term of office of those elected. The commissioners so appointed shall hold their offices for the unexpired term of those, to supply whose places they are appointed.

§ 92. The president of the board of trustees, together with the said commissioners, shall constitute a board to be styled "The Board of Education of the village of Salem," and shall be a corporate body in relation to all the powers and duties conferred or imposed by law. In the absence of said president, such board may appoint one of their number to preside. A majority of such baard shall be a quorum. No member of such board shall receive any compensation for his services. The clerk of said village shall be clerk of said board.

§ 93. The clerk of said board of education shall keep a record of the proceedings thereof, and perform such other duties as the board may prescribe; such record or a transcript thereof, certified by such clerk under the seal of the said board, shall be presumptive evidence of the facts therein set forth; and such record, and all the books, accounts and proceedings of said board, shall be subject to the inspection of said board of trustees, and of any committee thereof. Such clerk shall also perform all the duties, and shall be vested with all the powers conferred or imposed by law on clerks of school districts in towns, so far as such laws may be applicable and can be applied to such village, and are not inconsistent with this act. He may appoint a deputy, who shall be vested with the same powers.

§ 94. The board of trustees aforesaid shall have power, and it shall be their duty, to raise from time to time by tax upon the taxable property and persons in such village, which shall be liable to taxation for county purposes, in addition to the amount now or hereafter to be provided by law for common schools in said village, such sums as may be determined and certified by said board of education to be necessary for any or all of the following purposes:

1. To purchase, lease, or improve sites for school houses and appurtenances.

2. To build, purchase, lease, enlarge, alter, improve and repair school houses, and their out houses, and appurtenances.

3. To purchase, exchange, improve and repair school apparatus, books, maps and charts, furniture and appendages; provided, however, that class or text books shall not be furnished for any scholars whose parent or guardian shall be able to furnish the same.

4. To procure fuel and defray the contingent expenses of schools and of the school library.

5. To pay teachers' wages.

6. To pay charges or expenses incurred by law or necessary to carry this act into effect, or to refund loans contracted by law, and to pay the interest thereon, or to pay such sums as shall be required to fulfil any contract duly made under the provisions of this act.

§ 95. The board of trustees shall cause the amount of such school tax to be added in a separate column, to the assessment roll for ordinary taxes in said village; and they shall cause the same to be assessed, levied and collected at the same time and by the same warrant, and in the same manner with the taxes raised for village purposes as aforesaid.

§ 96. All moneys raised for school purposes in said village and all belonging thereto, payable from other sources, shall be paid to the treasurer of said village, who together with the sureties on his official bond, shall be accountable therefor, in the same manner as for other moneys of the said village. The treasurer shall also be liable to the same penalties for any official misconduct in relation to such moneys, as for any similar misconduct in relation to other moneys of said village.

§ 97. The treasurer shall keep a separate account of all moneys in his hands or received for school purposes, to be called the "school fund." No payment shall be msde out of that fund, except upon orders duly drawn in pursuance of a resolution of said board of education, and certified by the clerk, and countersigned by the president of said board. The treasurer shall in his annual report, state fully the account of all receipts and disbursements from that fund during the year, and the balance, if any, in his hands. His account as to the school fund shall be examined by the board of education, annually, who shall report thereon to the trustees.

§ 98. The said board of education shall have power, and it shall be their duty:

1. To establish and organize such and so many schools in said village, including the common schools therein, as they shall deem requisite and expedient, and to alter and discontinue or change and consolidate the same.

2. To purchase or hire school houses and rooms and lots or sites for school houses, and to fence, improve and repair them as they shall judge expedient.

3. Upon such sites or lots, or upon any lots owned by said village, to build, enlarge, alter, improve and repair school houses, out houses and appurtenances, as they may deem advisable.

4. To purchase, exchange, improve and repair school apparatus, books for indigent pupils and for the school library, to provide fuel and lights, furniture and appendages for the schools, and defray their contingent expenses and the expenses of library.

5. To have the custody and safe-keeping of the school-houses and all the school property aforesaid, and to see that the ordinances of the board o trustees in regard thereto be observed, and to report to them any violation thereof.

6. To contract with, examine, license and employ all teachers in the schools either high or common, and in all branches or departments thereof, and at their pleasure to remove them.

7. To pay the wages of such teachers out of the school moneys which shall be appropriated and provided by the said village, so far as the same shall be sufficient, and the residue thereof from the money authorized to be raised by this act by tax as aforesaid.

8. To defray the necessary contingent expenses of the board of education, provided that the account of such expenses shall be first audited and allowed by the board of trustees.

9. To have, in all respects, the superintendence, supervision and management of the schools aforesaid, to adopt, alter, modify and repeal, as they may deem expedient, rules and regulations for their organization, government and instruction, for the reception of pupils and their transfer from one school to another, and generally for their good order, prosperity and public utility.

10. Whenever, in the opinion of the board of education, it may be advisable to sell any of the school-houses, lots or sites, to report the same to the board of trustees.

11. To prepare and report to the board of trustees such ordinances and regulations as may be necessary and proper for the protection, safe-keeping, care and preservation of property held for school purposes, and to suggest proper penalties for the violation thereof; and annually to determine and certify to said board the sums, in their opinion, necessary to be raised for the several school purposes specified in this act.

12. To provide for the payment to any adjoining school district, or any person or persons entitled thereto, of any sum on account of such person, or or any part of said district being or having been included or connected with territory not now included in said village.

13. Between the first day of July and the first day of August in each year, to make and file with the county clerk and with the clerk of said village, a report in writing, bearing date the first day of July in such year, and stating:

1. An account and description of all the schools kept in said village during the preceding year, and the time they have severally been taught.

2 The number of children taught in said school respective'y, and designating the number over five and under sixteen years of age, residing in said village on the first day of January in said year.

3. The whole amount of school moneys received by the treasurer of said village during the year preceding, designating the amount received from the county treasurer, from the village collector and from other sources, specifying the same.

4. The manner in which such moneys have been expended and whether any part remained unexpended with the amount and cause thereof.

5. The amount of moneys received for tuition fees from foreign pupils or others during the year; the amount paid for teachers' wages in the aggregate, and the amount over and above the public moneys, together with such other facts as relate to common schools as is required by law to be reported by town superintendents, or as said board of trustees shall deem necessary.

14. To establish, organize and maintain in said village, whenever in their opinion it shall be necessary a union or consolidated school, composed of primary and secondary schools and a high school, on such plan and under such discipline and management as they shall deem advisable; and in such case to prescribe the course of studies therein, and so arrange and regulate the system of instruction in each of said schools, that the transfer of pupils shall thereafter be from the primary, directly into the secondary and thence into the high school or otherwise as they shall deem advisable. And for the purposes aforesaid, said board shall be vested with all the powers and charged with all the duties and liabilities above specified in regard to schools generally.

And said board may organize and maintain primary, secondary or high schools, or either of them in, or cause the same to be taught in connection with the Washington academy on such terms and conditions, and for such time not exceding ten years, as shall be deemed expedient by and between said board of education and the trustees of such academy; such management shall, if made, be by contract duly executed by said parties, but no such contract shall be made without the assent of the board of trustees of said village; and in such case said board of education are vested with power to make such rules and regulations as they shall see fit as to the age or degree of scholarship required to enter said several departments, the compensation and payment therefor and other terms thereof, and the time of continuance therein.

§ 99. Such board of education shall have a standing committee, consisting of not less than three members, whose duty it shall be to visit said schools, and each department thereof, as often as twice every term, and to make report in writing to said board in regard thereto.

§ 100. The said board of education may permit children of persons not resident within said village, to attend said schools on such terms as they shall prescribe; and said board may, in the name of said village, sue for and recover of the father or mother, master or mistress, or other person under whose charge such child or children may be, all such sums as shall be so prescribed with costs of suit.

§ 101. The board of education shall be trustees of the district library or libraries in said village. All the provisions of law which now are or hereafter may be passed, relating to school district libraries, shall apply to the said commissioners and board of education, so far as the same are applicable and can be applied, and are not inconsistent with this act, in the same manner as if they were trustees of a school district composed of the said village. They shall be vested with the discretion as to the disposition of library moneys, which is by law conferred upon the inhabitants of school districts and they may consolidate the said libraries, or dispose of parts thereof, as deemed best. It shall be their duty to provide a library room or rooms, and the necessary furniture therefor, appoint a librarian, make all purchases of books, exchange or cause to be repaired all damaged books, and sell those deemed useless or of an improper character, and apply the proceeds to the purchase of others.

§ 102. No trustee of said village or member of said board of education shall be a contractor or be interested in any contract for building or making any erections or repairs authorized by this act, or furnishing materials therefor. All contracts made in violation hereof shall be void, so far as any benefit may be realized therefrom by the offender, and such person shall forfeit to said village fifty dollars, to be recovered by them before any court having cognizance of the same, with costs.

§ 103. The board of trustees of said village may pass such ordinances and regulations as they may deem necessary, or as shall be reported by said board of education, for the protection, safe keeping, care and maintenance of the school-house or other property connected with the schools or property held or occupied or used for school purposes, and to impose penalties for the violation thereof, subject to the restrictions contained in this act; and all such penalties shall be collected in the same manner as other penalties imposed by said board, and when collected shall be paid to the treasurer, to the credit of the school fund, and be subject to the order of the board of education.

104. Whenever the said board of education shall report to the trustees that it is advisable to sell any of the school property as aforesaid, the said trustees shall sell the same as soon as may be, and upon such terms as said trustees shall deem best. The proceeds of all such sales shall be paid to the treasurer, to the credit of the school fund.

§ 105. The title of the school house and other school property aforesaid, shall be vested in the trustees of the village of Salem; and the same, while used or kept for use for school purposes, shall not be levied on or sold by virtue of any process, or be subject to taxation for any purpose; nor shall the same be incumbered or in any way disposed of, except as authorized by this act. The said village, in its corporate capacity, may take, hold or dispose of any real or personal estate, transferred to it by gift, grant or devise, for the use or benefit of said schools, or any of them, and whether the same shall be transferred, given, granted or devised in terms to said village by its proper style, or by any other designation, or to any other designation, or to any person or persons, or body, or otherwise, for the use or benefit of said schools or either of them.

§ 106. The town superintendent of common schools of the town of Salem, in making the apportionment of school or library moneys among the several districts in said town, shall allot to said village such sum as shall be its proportion of such moneys, considering such village as a regular school district of said town, and the report of the board of education as the report of its trustees. Such superintendent shall allot to said village, in the apportionment to be made on the first Tuesday of April. 1851, such sum as school districts number eleven and twelve in said town would be entitled to, had said village not been consolidated into one district. All sums allotted as aforesaid shall be paid by said superintendent to the treasurer of said village, to the credit of the school fund aforesaid, at the same time and in the same manner as to trustees of school districts in said town.

§ 107. Said board of education shall between the first and fifteenth of January in each year, make and transmit a report in writing to the town superintendent of common schools of the town of Salem, bearing date on the first day of January in such year, and containing a statement of the name and age of each child residing in the said village, on the last day of December previous to the date of said report, over the age of five, and under that of sixteen years of age, except Indian children otherwise provided for by law; and the names of the parents or other persons with whom such children shall respectively reside, and the number of children residing with each. Such report shall be the only report required to be made in order to entitle such allotment as required in the last section. Said schools in said village, and said board of education, shall not in any other respect be bound to report to said superintendent; nor shall such schools, or the teachers thereof, be in anywise under his control or supervision.

§ 108. In case said board of education shall contract with the trustees of the Washington academy as authorized in this act, they are further empowered to lease from said trustees the academy building and grounds adjacent, or contract for the joint or several occupation of the same, or so much thereof, or such privileges therein, or appertaining thereto, on such conditions, and for such time not exceeding two years, as they shall deem advisable. And they may pay in advance to such trustees such gross sum for the rent thereof, for such term as being calculated with a proper rebate for the advance payment shall be deemed by said board, no more than a fair equivalent for the use and occupation thereof for the purposes required under this act. And such sum as shall be necessary for the purposes aforesaid, not exceeding one thousand dollars, may be loaned by the comptroller to said village out of any moneys belonging to the common school fund, on receiving from the board of trustees of said village, the bond of said village therefor, payable in five equal payments with annual interest. The moneys received thereon shall be paid to the treasurer to the credit of the school fund, and shall be drawn out in the same manner as other moneys in that fund; provided, however, that no such contract shall be made, nor any loan obtained by said board of education, without the previous assent of the board of trustees of said village. In case said loan shall be made, said trustees shall annually raise during each of said five years, by tax in the same manner, and at the same time as other village taxes are raised, such sum as over and above the expenses of collection, will pay the several instalments, so to grow due on such loan, with the interest.

§ 109. Any contract, lease or agreement made or executed by said board of education, with the trustees of the Washington academy under the provisions of this act, may be vacated, modified or renewed by the parties aforesaid, by and with the assent of the board of trustees of said village; provided no renewal thereof shall be made for a term exceeding ten years at any one time.

§ 110. All the property, real and personal, belonging to the districts, number eleven and twelve, shall be and is hereby transferred to and vested in the trustees of the village of Salem for school purposes; and they are authorized to take the same into their possession, and hold, use and occupy the same, and exercise the same powers in regard thereto, as if they had purchased the same for school purposes under this act; and the present trustees and officers of said districts are hereby required to deliver possession thereof, and of all books, papers and vouchers connected therewith to said board, and said board may sue for and recover the same with costs of suit of any person having the same or any part thereof.

§ 111. All debts and legal liabilities of said school districts number eleven and twelve, shall be audited, paid, satisfied and discharged by said board of education out of the school fund.

§ 112. Each and every of the schools established or maintained under this act, shall be free to the children of all residents of said village; provided however, that said board of education may cause the tuition fee to be charged and collected of the father or mother, master or mistress, or other person (in whose charge such pupil may be) residing in said village, of any pupil over sixteen years of age, or who shall pursue studies which said board shall deem should not be tuition free. For the purpose of collecting such fees, such board shall by general rules provide for the keeping of proper registers, in which shall be entered the name of every such pupil, and his father or mother, master or mistress, or other person in whose charge such pupil may be, the length of time such pupil shall attend such school, and the tuition fee chargeable therefor. Immediately previous to the issuing of the warrant for the collection of the annual village tax, said board of education shall cause to be presented to the board of trustees, an abstract from such registers containing a statement of names of every such father or mother, master or mistress, or other person residing in such village, from whom any sum or amount was due for such tuition fees, at the close of the term previous to the presentation of such lists. The annual tax list shall contain a column headed "tuition fees," in which shall be entered opposite the name of such person the amount so returned as aforesaid, which sum shall be included in the aggregate column to be collected under such warrant; and the same proceedings shall be had for the collection thereof as for other village taxes; and when collected the same shall be paid to the treasurer, to the credit of the school fund; but such return so made shall not include the name of any person who shall, in the opinion of the board, be in indigent circumstances; any person specified in such return may at any time before the collection of said tuition fee, apply to said board of education for a remission of the same; and if said board shall deem proper, they may by resolution duly passed remit the same in whole or in part, and the clerk shall certify such remission to the collector, and no further proceedings shall be had for the collection of the sum so remitted.

§ 113. Nothing in this act contained shall prevent the trustees of the Washington academy from receiving from the regents of the university any sum or allowance, for pupils pursuing classical studies therein, or for organizing and maintaining a teachers' department therein. And any pupil in any of the departments organized in said academy under the provisions of this act, pursuing such classical studies as are required by the regents aforesaid, in order to be entitled to an allowance, and being of sufficient age, shall be included in the returns of said trustees to said regents, and they shall be entitled to the same allowance for such pupil or pupils as for other classical pupils heretofore.

SCHENECTADY.

[*Laws of* 1829, *Chap.* 324.]

§ 1. The amount of monies allowed to the city of Schenectady, by the superintendent of common schools, shall be apportioned by the treasurer of the county of Schenectady, between the Schenectady Lancaster school society, and such common school districts and parts of districts as now are or hereafter may be organized without the bounds of the compact part of city of Schenectady, called the police; and in a ratio proportioned to the number of children over the age of five and under sixteen [21] years within such compact part, and the number of such children in such districts and parts of districts respectively, without such compact part

§ 2. The treasurer of the county of Schenectady shall pay the amount thus apportioned to the Schenectady Lancaster school society, to its treasurer, for the use of said society, and the amount thus apportioned to such school districts and parts of districts, to the commissioners of common chools for the several wards of the city of Schenectady.

§ 3. The commissioners of common schools for the several wards of the said city, shall distribute and pay to the trustees of such school districts and parts of districts, the amount so received by them from the county treasurer, in proportion to the number of children residing in each, over the age of five and under that of sixteen [twenty-one,] years, as the same shall have appeared from the last annual report of their respective trustees.

§ 4. The assessors of the several wards of the city of Schenectady, shall every year in their respective wards, take a census of the children between the ages of five and sixteen [twenty-one,] years, residing within the compact part of said city, and shall between the first day of May and the first day of October, in each year, make and transmit a report of the same to the clerk of the county of Schenectady.

§ 5. The reports required by law to be made by the trustees of the common school districts and parts of districts, without the bounds of the compact part of the city of Schenectady, to the commissioners of common schools, for the several wards of the said city, shall be verified by the affidavit of the said trustees.

§ 6. The monies received by the treasurer of the county of Schenectady, from taxes collected in said city, under the laws relative to common schools, shall be apportioned by him between such common school districts and parts of districts, without the bounds of the compact part of said city, and the Schenectady Lancaster school society, in the ratio proportioned to the amount of the assessments of the real and personal estates of the taxable inhabitants residing in such districts and parts of districts, and the assessments of all real estate situate therein and owned by persons residing out of such districts and parts of districts, and the amounts of the assessments of the real and personal estates of all the taxable inhabitants of the city, after deducting thereout the aggregate of the assessments last mentioned.

§ 7. The treasurer of the county of Schenectady shall pay the amount apportioned by virtue of the last preceding sections to the Schenectady Lancaster school society, to its treasurer, for the use of said society, and the amount apportioned under said sections to such school districts and parts of districts, to the commissioners of common schools for the several wards of said city, which amount so paid to the said commissioners shall be distributed and paid by them in the manner provided in the third section of this act.

§ 8. To enable the treasurer of said county to make the apportionment required by the sixth section of this act, the assessors of the several wards of the city of Schenectady shall annually, within the time limited in the fourth section of this act, for taking the census therein mentioned, make out and deliver to the treasurer of said county, an abstract from the assessment rolls of their respective wards, containing the names and the amounts of the assessments, of the real and personal estates of each of the taxable inhabitants residing in the said school districts or parts of districts, together with the amount of the assessments of all real estate situate therein, and owned by persons residing out of such districts or parts of districts.

§ 151. [Rev. St. Chap. 15, Art. 7, Title 2, Part 1.] The commissioners of schools of the city, shall divide that portion of the territory of the first and second wards of the city, not comprised within the bounds of the police, into such number of school districts as they may deem convenient, and may alter and regulate such districts according to the provisions of this title, and the provisions of this title shall apply to all districts so established.

§ 152. [Ditto.] It shall be the duty of the trustees of the Lancaster school society to make an annual report to the superintendent of common schools, in such form as shall be prescribed by him, of the state and condition of the schools for whose benefit the school moneys shall have been applied.

[*Laws of* 1839. *Chap.* 222.]

§ 14. It shall be lawful for the trustees of the Lancaster school society in the city of Schenectady, to cause to be taught in any school or schools established by them or placed under their charge by the mayor, recorder and aldermen of said city, within the bounds of the police of said city, all such branches of education as may by law be taught in any common school in this state; and that for teaching any such branches of education, it shall be lawful for said trustees to adopt such mode of instruction as shall seem to them best adapted to attain the end of rendering the benefits resulting from the school fund more extensively useful and beneficial to the inhabitants of said city.

§ 15. It shall be lawful for the common council of the city of Schenectady to expend, annually, any sum not exceeding five hundred dollars for the purposes of common schools and education generally throughout the city; and the said common council, for such purposes, may annually cause to be raised, by tax, any sum not exceeding five hundred dollars, in the same manner as the taxes for repairing highways and supporting the poor are raised in and by the twenty seventh section of the act entititled, "An Act relative to the city of Schenectady," passed April 29th, 1833.

SENECA.

[*Laws of* 1844. *Chap.* 175.]

§ 1. It shall be lawful for the trustees of school district number one, in the town of Seneca, in the county of Ontario, at the next annual meeting of the district after the passage of this act, to submit for the consideration of such meeting, a proposition, graduating the rates of tuition to be paid by scholars attending the different departments into which such school is now divided; if the same is approved, or shall be so amended as to be approved by a majority of those present qualified to vote in such meetings, such rates may be charged and collected, but they shall not be raised during the year next following their adoption.

§ 2. At any annual meeting of the district after such rates of tuition have been adopted, the same may be raised, reduced or entirely abolished, by a majority of such meeting.

SYRACUSE.

[*Laws of* 1848. *Chap.* 238.]

AN ACT *in relation to public schools in the city of Syracuse.*

Passed April 11, 1848, "three-fifths being present."

The People of the State of New-York, represented in Senate and Assembly, do enact as follows:

§ 1. There shall be appointed by the mayor and common council of the city of Syracuse, on the third Tuesday of April, eighteen hundred and forty eight, from each ward in said city, two commissioners of common schools for the said city, who shall be residents of the ward for which they are appointed. The persons so appointed shall, within ten days after their appointment take the oath of office prescribed by the constitution of this state, and file the same with the city clerk.

§ 2. Within ten days after their appointment, as in the last section mentioned, said commissioners shall meet at Market Hall in said city, and cause the said commissioners so chosen to be divided into two classes, to be denominated "first" and "second" classes. The term of office of the first class shall expire at the end of one year from the second Tuesday of March, eighteen hundred and forty-eight; of the second class at the end of two years from the said second Tuesday of March, eighteen hundred and forty eight.

§ 3. There shall, in like manner, in each year thereafter, be elected one commissioner of schools for each ward of said city, to supply the places of those whose term of office is about to expire; they shall hold their offices for two years, and until their successors are elected, and have taken the oath of office. The term of office of all commissioners elected pursuant to the provisions of this act, shall commence on the first Tuesday after their election. Said election shall take place at the time of the general charter election of said city in each and every year thereafter, and shall be subject to all the provisions in regard to said election, so far as the same may be applicable, as are contained in the charter of said city, passed on the 14th December, 1847

§ 4. The common council of said city may make appointments of commissioners of common schools to fill vacancies which may occur from any cause other than the expiration of the term of office of those elected. The commissioners so appointed shall hold their office for the unexpired term of those to supply whose places they were appointed

§ 5. Any commissioner of common schools in said city may be removed from office for official misconduct by the common council thereof, by a vote of two thirds of the members thereof, but said commissioner shall be allowed an opportunity to refute any such charge of misconduct, before removal.

§ 6. The commissioners of common schools in said city shall constitute a board, to be styled the "Board of Education of the city of Syracuse," which shall be a corporate body in relation to all the powers and duties conferred upon them by virtue of this act. A majority of the board shall form a quorum. At their first meeting after an election, they shall elect one of their number President, and whenever he shall be absent a president pro tempore may be appointed, but such president shall only have a casting vote. They shall also appoint a clerk and fix his compensation, and who shall hold his office during the pleasure of the board. The said commissioners shall receive no compensation for their services. They shall have the care of the gospel and school lands and securities taken therefor in said city.

§ 7. The clerk of said board shall keep a record of the proceedings thereof, and perform such other duties as the board may prescribe; which record, or a transcript thereof, certified by the president and clerk, shall be received in all courts as prima facie evidence of the facts therein set forth; and such records, and all the books and accounts of the said board, shall, at all times, be subject to the inspection of the common council and of any committee thereof.

§ 8. The common council of the said city shall have the power and it shall be their duty, to raise, from time to time, by tax upon the real and personal estate in said city which shall be liable to taxation for the ordinary city taxes, or for city or county charges, in addition to the amount of school monies now or hereafter appropriated or provided by law for common schools in said city, such sums as may be determined and certified by the said board of education to be necessary or proper for any or all of the following purposes:

1. To purchase, lease or improve sites for school-houses.

2. To build, purchase, lease, enlarge, alter, improve and repair school-houses, and their out-houses and appurtenances.

3. To purchase, exchange, improve and repair school apparatus, books, furniture and appendages, but the power herein granted shall not be deemed to the furnishing of class or text books for any scholar whose parent or guardian shall be able to furnish the same.

4. To procure fuel and defray the contingent expenses of the common schools, and the expenses of the district library of said city.

5. To pay the wages of teachers due after the application of the public moneys, which may, by law, be appropriated and provided for that purpose: Provided, nevertheless, that such tax shall not be laid oftener than once in each year:

6. Nor shall the amount to be raised for teachers' wages and contingent expenses in any one year be less than twice nor more than six times the amount of public money received during the previous year. Nor shall the amount to be raised in any one year for buying sites and erecting and repairing school-houses and the appurtenances, exceed one thousand five hundred dollars.

§ 9. The common council shall cause the amount of the tax at any time ordered to be raised in pursuance of this act, to be added to the amount which they are otherwise authorised by law to raise by tax in said city, and they shall cause the same, with the collector's fee thereon, to be assessed, levied and collected at the same time and by the same warrant, and in the same manner with the taxes raised for city expenses, under and by virtue of the act of incorporation of said city.

§ 10. All moneys to be raised pursuant to the provisions of this act, and all school moneys by law appropriated to or provided for said city, shall be paid to the treasurer of said city, who, together with the sureties upon his official bond shall be accountable therefor in the same manner as for other moneys of the said city: the said treasurer shall also be liable to the same penalties for any official misconduct in relation to the said moneys as for any similar misconduct in relation to other moneys of the city.

§ 11. After the passage of this act the treasurer of the said city shall not pay out any moneys in his hands received by the said city, either as school moneys or collected or received by virtue of any of the provisions of this act, excepting upon an order drawn upon him and signed by the president and clerk of said board of education, and no such order shall be drawn except by virtue of a resolution of the said board.

§ 12. The said board may cause a suit or suits to be prosecuted in the name of the city of Syracuse, upon the official bond of the treasurer or of any collector of said city for any default, delinquency or official misconduct in relation to the collection, safe keeping or payment of any moneys in this act mentioned.

§ 13. The said board shall have power and it shall be their duty,

1. To establish and organize such and so many schools in said city, (including the common schools now existing therein) as they shall deem requisite and expedient, and to alter and discontinue the same.

2 To purchase or hire school houses and rooms, and lots or sites for school houses, and to fence and improve them as they deem proper.

3. Upon such lots and upon any sites now owned by said city, to build, enlarge, alter, improve and repair school houses, out houses and appurtenances as they may deem advisable.

4. To purchase, exchange, improve and repair school apparatus, books for indigent pupils, furniture and appendages, and to provide fuel for the schools and defray their contingent expenses, and the expenses of the district library.

5. To have the custody and safe keeping of the school houses, out houses, books furniture and appendages, and to see that the ordinances of the common council in relation thereto be observed.

6. To contract with, license and employ all teachers in the common school and high school, and at their pleasure to remove them.

7. To pay the wages of such teachers out of the school moneys which shall be appropriated and provided in the said city, so far as the same shall be sufficient, and the residue thereof from the money authorised to be raised for that purpose by section eight of this act, by tax upon said city.

8. To defray the necessary contingent expenses of the board; including an annual salary to the clerk, provided that the account of such expenses shall first be audited and allowed by the common council.

9. To have, in all respects, the superintendence, supervision and management of the common schools in said city, and from time to time to adopt, alter, modify and repeal, as they may deem expedient, rules and regulations for their organization, government and instruction, for the reception of pupils and their transfer from one school to another, and generally for the promotion of their good order, prosperity and public utility.

10. Whenever, in the opinion of the board, it may be advisable to sell any of the school houses, lots or sites, or any of the school property now or hereafter belonging to the city, to report the same to the common council.

11. To prepare and report to the common council such ordinances and regulations as may be necessary or proper for the protection, safe keeping, care and preservation of school houses, lots and sites, and appurtenances, and all the property belonging to the city connected with or appertaining to the schools, and to suggest proper penalties for the violation of such ordinances and regulations; and annually to determine and certify to said common council the sums in their opinion necessary or proper to be raised under the eighth section of this act, specifying the sums required for each of the purposes therein mentioned, and the reasons therefor.

12. To provide for the payment to any adjoining school district the proper amount to which it may be entitled on account of such district, in whole or in part, having been connected with territory now included in the said city.

13. Between the first day of July and the first day of August in each year, to make and transmit to the county clerk a report in writing, bearing date the first day of July in the year of its transmission, and stating,

1. An account and description of all the common schools kept in said city during the preceding year, and the time they have been severally taught.

2. The number of children taught in said schools, respectively, the number of children over the age of five and under the age of sixteen, [21] residing in said city on the first day of January of that year.

3. The whole amount of school moneys received by the treasurer of said city during the year preceding, distinguishing the amount received from the county treasurer, from the city collector, and from any other source.

4. The manner in which such moneys had been expended, and whether any and what part remains unexpended and for what cause.

5. The amount of money received for tuition fees from foreign pupils during the year, and the amount paid for teachers' wages, in addition to the public moneys, with such other information as relates to the common schools of said city.

§ 14. Every school commissioner shall visit all the public schools at least four times each year during his official term; and the board of education shall provide that each of said schools shall be visited by a committe of three or more of their number at least once every term.

§ 15. The said board of education shall have power to allow the children of persons not resident within the city to attend any of the schools of said city under the care and control of said board, upon such terms as said board shall, by resolution, prescribe, fixing the tuition which shall be paid therefor.

§ 16. Any collector of the said city, and his sureties, shall be liable on his official bond for any default, delinquency, neglect or misconduct in the duties with which he may be charged under or by virtue of this act, in the same manner and with the like effect as for any other official default, delinquency, neglect or misconduct; and such collector shall be liable to the same penalties for any such official as for any similar misconduct in relation to any other duties of his office.

§ 17. It shall be the duty of the said board in all their expenditures and contracts, to have reference to the amount of moneys which shall be subject to their order during the then current year, for the particular expenditure in question, and not to exceed such amount.

§ 18. The said board of commissioners shall be trustees of the district library or libraries in said city, and all the provisions of law which now are or may hereafter be passed relating to district school libraries, shall apply to the said commissioners in the same manner as if they were trustees of a school district comprehending said city; they shall also be vested with the discretion as to the disposition of the moneys appropriated by any law of this state for the purchase of libraries, which is therein conferred upon the inhabitants of school districts. It shall be their duty to provide a library room or rooms and the necessary furniture therefor, and appoint a librarian or librarians, to make all purchases of books for the said library or libraries, and from time to time to exchange or cause to be repaired the damaged books belonging thereto; they may also sell any books which they may deem useless or of an improper character, and apply the proceeds to the purchase of other books for the said library or libraries.

§ 19. It shall be the duty of the said board, at least fifteen days before the annual election for commissioners in each year, to prepare and report to the common council true and correct statements of the receipts and disbursements of moneys under and in pursuance of the provisions of this act during the preceding year; in which account shall be stated under appropriate heads:

1. The moneys received by the common council under the eighth section of this act:
2. The school moneys received by the treasurer of the city from the county treasurer, and the collector of taxes for city and county charges in said city.
3. The moneys received by direct tax:
4. All other moneys received by the treasurer, subject to the order of the board specifying the sources:
5. The manner in which such sums of money shall have been expended, specifying the amount paid under each head of expenditure:

And the common council shall, ten days before such election, cause the same to be published in at least two of the newspapers published in said city.

§ 20. The said board shall be subject, from time to time, to the rules and regulations made by the state superintendent of common schools, so far as the same may be applicable to them, and not inconsistent with the provisions of this act.

§ 21. The common council of said city shall have the power, and it shall be their duty, to pass such ordinances and regulations as the said board of education may report as necessary and proper for the protection, safe-keeping, care and preservation of the school houses, lots, sites, and appurtenances, and all necessary property belonging to or connected with the schools in said city; and to impose proper penalties for the violation thereof, subject to the restrictions and limitations contained in the act to incorporate the said city; and all such penalties shall be collected in the same manner that the penalties for a violation of the city ordinances are by law collected, and when collected, shall be paid to the treasury of the city, and be subject to the order of the board of education, in the same manner as other moneys raised pursuant to the provisions of this act.

§ 22. Whenever the said board shall report to the common council that it is advisable to sell any of the school houses, lots or sites, or any of the school property now or hereafter belonging to the city, it shall be the duty of the common council to sell the same without unreasonable delay and upon such terms as the said common council may deem advisable. The proceeds of all such sales shall be paid to the treasurer of the city, and shall be subject to the order of the said board, to be expended by them in the purchase, leasing, repairs or improvements of other school houses, lots, school furniture, apparatus or appurtenances.

§ 23. The title of the school houses, sites, lots, furniture, books, apparatus and appurtenances, and all other school property in this act mentioned, shall be vested in the city of Syracuse; and the same while used for or appropriated for school purposes, shall not be levied upon or sold by virtue of any warrant or execution, nor be subject to taxation for any purpose whatever; and the said city, in its corporate capacity, shall be able to take, hold, and dispose of any real or personal estate transferred to it by gift, grant, bequest or devise, for the use of the common schools of the said city, whether the same shall be transferred in terms to said city, by its proper style, or by any other designation, or to any other designation, or to any person or persons or body, for the use of said schools.

§ 24. All moneys required to be raised by virtue of this act, shall, on being raised as herein provided, be deposited for the safe heeping thereof, with the treasurer of said city, to the credit of the said board of education, and shall be drawn out in pursuance of a resolution or resolutions of said board, by drafts drawn by the president and countersigned by the clerk of said board, payable to the order of the person or persons entitled to receive such moneys; and said treasurer shall keep the funds authorized by this act to be received by him, separate and distinct from any other fund which he is or may by law be authorized to receive.

§ 25. It shall be the duty of the said commissioners to ascertain and report to the common council of said city the amount of any and all indebtedness of each of the school districts within said city, and to whom due, and when and how payable; and the common council shall have the power, and it shall be their duty, in each year that any such indebtedness shall become due, or any portion thereof, to cause the amount so becoming due from any of said districts, to be assessed upon and collected from the taxable property within such districts, in the same manner as the taxes for contingent expenses are assessed and collected, for the use of the board of education, for the payment of such indebtedness.

§ 26. It shall be the duty of said commissioners, and they shall have power to procure a site within school district number sixteen (16) in the city of Syracuse, and cause to be erected thereon a suitable and proper school house, and cause a statement of the cost of such site and building to be laid before the common council of said city, who shall have power, and it shall be their duty to cause the sum of one thousand five hundred dollars to be assessed upon and collected from the taxable property within said district, in the same manner that the contingent expenses of said city are assessed and collected; and in case the said expenditure shall exceed the sum of fifteen hundred dollars, the said excess shall be collected from the city at large, for the use of the said commissioners for the purposes in this section specified.

§ 27. It shall be the duty of the clerk of said city immediately after the election of any person as a commissioner of common schools, to personally notify him of his election, and if any such person shall not within ten days after receiving such personal notice of his election, take and subscribe the constitual oath and file the same with the clerk of the said city, the common council may consider it a refusal to serve, and proceed to supply the vacancy occasioned by such refusal; and the person so refusing to serve shall forfeit and pay to the city treasurer, for the benefit of the tuition fund, a penalty of ten dollars.

§ 28. The present school officers of the school districts in the territory embraced in this act, shall continue in office until the unfinished business of said districts shall have been finally closed up and settled, with all the powers and duties now by law imposed upon them, for the purpose of closing up such unfinished business.

TROY.

[*Laws of* 1849. *Chap.* 198, *as amended by Chap.* 47, *laws of* 1851.]

AN ACT *to amend the charter of the city of Troy, and to provide for the establishment of free schools in said city.*

Passed April 4, 1849, "three-fifths being present."

§ 1. The several wards of the city of Troy shall constitute one school district, and the schools therein shall be free to all children, between the ages of five and sixteen [21] years, residing in such wards.

§ 2. There shall be erected in each of the said wards as hereinafter provided, one or more school houses of size and form sufficient to accommodate all the children between the aforesaid ages, residing in such wards. The purchase of sites for school houses shall be agreed upon in joint committee of three from each ward, hereinafter mentioned; and in case of disagreement the decision shall rest with the common council.

§ 3. The title of the school houses, sites, lots, furniture, books apparatus and appurtenances, and all other school property, in this act mentioned, shall be vested in the city of Troy, and the same while used or appropriated for school purposes, shall not be levied upon, or sold by virtue of any warrant or execution, nor be subject to taxation, for any purpose whatever, and the said city in its corporate capacity, shall be able to take, hold, and dispose of any real or personal estate, transferred to it by gift, grant, bequest or devise, for the use of the common schools of the said city, whether the same shall be transferred in terms to said city by its proper style, or by any other designation, or to any person or persons, or body, for the use of said schools.

§ 4. The common council of said city, may, upon the recommendation of the board of education hereinafter mentioned, sell any of the school houses, lots, or sites, or any other school property, now or hereafter, belonging to said city, upon such terms as the said common council may deem reasonable. The proceeds of all such sales shall be paid to the chamberlain of the city, and shall be by the said board of education again expended in the construction, repairs, or improvements of other school houses, lots, sites or school furniture, apparatus or appurtenances.

§ 5. There shall be elected at the annual charter election of said city, to be held on the first Tuesday of March, 1850, in the same manner as other ward officers are elected, from each of the 1st, 2d, 3d, 4th and 7th wards in said city, two persons, and from each of the 5th, 6th, and 8th wards thereof, one person, to be commissioners of common schools for said city. The persons so elected shall be residents of the ward for which they shall be elected, and shall within ten days after receiving notice of their election, take the oath of office prescribed by the constitution of this state, and file the same with the city clerk.

§ 6. Within ten days after their election, as in the last section mentioned, said commissioners so elected from those wards in which more than one commissioner is elected, shall meet in the office of the clerk of said city, and shall determine by lot which of the two persons so elected for each ward shall serve for the term ending on the second Tuesday of March, 1851, and which for the term ending on the second Tuesday of March, 1852.

§ 7. In each year, thereafter, there shall be elected in said city, at the annual charter election in the same manner, and under the same regulations, as other ward officers are elected, one commissioner of common schools for each ward, to supply the places of those whose terms are about to expire. The term of office of all commissioners elected pursuant to this act, shall commence on the Tuesday next after their election, and shall continue two years, except of those commissioners elected from the 4th, 6th and 8th wards, whose term of office will continue but one year.

§ 8. The common council of said city make may make appointment of commissioner of common schools to fill vacancies which may occur from any cause other than the expiration of the term of office of those elected, and the removal from the ward for which he was appointed or elected shall be deemed a resignation of his office by any commissioner. The commissioners so appointed shall hold their offices till the Tuesday succeeding the next annual election, and at each annual election there shall be elected a commissioner to supply the place of any person so appointed, and the person thus elected shall serve out the unexpired term.

§ 9. Any commissioner of common schools in said city, may be removed from office for official misconduct by the common council of said city, by a vote of two-thirds of the members thereof; but a written copy of the charges against said commissioner, shall be served upon him, and he shall be allowed an opportunity to refute any such charge of misconduct, before removal.

§ 10. The commissioners of common schools in said city, shall constitute a board, to be styled the "Board of Education of the city of Troy," which shall be a corporate body in relation to all the powers and duties conferred upon them by virtue of this act. A majority of the board shall form a quorum. The first meeting of the board shall be on the second Wednesday next after their election, and the annual meeting of the board, thereafter, shall be on the second Wednesday next after their election. At the first meeting of the board, and annually thereafter, at the annual meeting, they shall elect one of their number president of the board; and whenever he shall be absent, a president pro tempore may be appointed. The said commissioners shall receive no compensation for their services.

§ 11. The said commissioners shall appoint a clerk who may be one of their number, who shall hold his office during the pleasure of the board, and whose compensation shall be fixed by them. The said clerk shall keep a record of the proceedings of the board, and perform such other duties as the board may prescribe; the said record or a transcript thereof, certified by the president and clerk, shall be received in all courts as prima facie evidence of facts therein set forth; and such records and all the books, accounts, vouchers, and papers of said board shall at all times be subject to the inspection of the common council, and of any committee thereof.

§ 12. The common council of said city shall have the power, and it shall be their duty to raise from time to time by tax, to be levied equally upon all the real and personal estate in said city, which shall be liable to taxation for the ordinary city taxes, or for city or county charges, such sum or sums of money, as may be necessary or proper, for any or all the following purposes:

1. To purchase school houses, and also to purchase, lease or improve sites therefor.

2. To enable the board of education to build, lease, enlarge, alter, improve and repair school houses, and their out houses and appurtenances.

3. To purchase, exchange, improve and repair school apparatus, books, furniture and appendages; but the power herein granted, shall not be deemed to authorize the furnishing with class or text books any scholar whose parents or guardian shall be able to furnish the same.

4. To procure fuel and defray the contingent expenses of the common schools, and the expenses of the school libraries of said city.

5. To pay the wages of teachers due after the application of the public monies, which may by law be appropriated and provided for that purpose: Provided, nevertheless, that the tax to be levied, as aforesaid, and collected by virtue of this act, shall be collected at the same time, and in the same manner as other city taxes.

6. And the amount to be raised for teachers' wages and contingent expenses in any one year, shall not be less than twice, nor more than four times the amount apportioned to said city, from the common school fund of the state during the previous year, nor shall the amount to be raised in one year, after the 1st Tuesday in March, 1851, for purchasing sites and erecting and repair-

ing school houses exceed five thousand dollars. And the common council of said city are authorized and directed when necessary, to raise by loan in anticipation of the taxes, the moneys so to be raised, collected and levied as aforesaid.

§ 13. All moneys to be raised pursuant to the provisions of this act, and all school moneys by law appropriated to, or provided for said city, shall be paid to the chamberlain thereof, who together with the sureties upon his official bond, shall be accountable therefor, in the same manner as for other moneys of said city; the said chamberlain shall be liable to the same penalties for any official misconduct in relation to the said moneys, as for any similar misconduct in relation to other moneys of said city.

§ 14. The said board shall have power, and it shall be their duty,

1. To establish and organize, in the several wards of said city, such and so many schools, (including the common schools now existing therein) as they shall deem requisite and expedient, and to alter and discontinue the same.

2. To build, lease, or contract for the occupation and use of school houses and rooms, and to improve the same as they may deem proper.

3. To alter, improve and repair school houses and appurtenances as they may deem advisable.

4. To purchase, exchange, improve and repair school apparatus, books for indigent pupils, furniture and appendages, and to defray their contingent expenses, and the expense of the school libraries.

5. To have the custody and safe keeping of the school houses, out houses, books, furniture and appendages, and to see that the ordinances of the common council in relation thereto be observed.

6. To contract with, license, and employ all teachers in said schools, and at their pleasure to remove them.

7. To pay the wages of such teachers out of the moneys appropriated and provided by law, for the support of schools in said city, so far as the same shall be sufficient, and the residue thereof, from the money authorized to be raised for that purpose by section twelve of this act, by tax upon said city.

8. To defray the necessary contingent expenses of the board, including an annual salary to the clerk, provided the account of such expenses shall first be audited and allowed by the common council.

9. To have in all respects the superintendence, supervision, and management of the common schools in said city, and from time to time to adopt, alter, modify and repeal, as they may deem expedient, rules and regulations for their organization, government and instruction, for the reception of pupils, and their transfer from one school to another, and generally for the promotion of their good order, prosperity and public utility.

10. Whenever, in the opinion of the board it may be advisable to sell any of the school houses, lots, or sites, or any of the school property, now or hereafter belonging to the city, to report the same to the common council.

11. To prepare and report to the common council, such ordinances and regulations as may be necessary or proper for the protection, safe keeping, care and preservation of school houses, lots and sites and appurtenances, and all the property belonging to the city, connected with or appertaining to the schools, and to suggest proper penalties for the violation of such ordinances and regulations; and annually, on or before the first day of February in each year, to determine and certify to said common council, the sums in their opinion necessary or proper, to be raised under the twelfth section of this act, specifying the sums required for the year commencing on the first of March thereafter, for each of the purposes therein mentioned, and the reasons therefor.

12. Between the first day of July, and the first day of August, in each year, to make and transmit to the county clerk, or such other officer as may be designated by law, a report in writing bearing date the first day of July, in the year of its transmission, and stating,

1. The number of school houses in said city, and an account and description of all the common schools kept in said city during the preceding year, and the time they have severally been taught.

2. The number of children taught in said schools respectively, and the number of children over the age of five years, and under the age of sixteen [21] years, residing in said city, on the first day of January, of that year.

3. The whole amount of school moneys received by the chamberlain of said city during the year preceding, distinguishing the amount received from the county treasurer, from the city tax, and from any other source.

4. The manner in which such moneys had been expended, and whether any and what part remains unexpended, and for what cause.

5. The amount of money received for tuition fees from foreign pupils during the year, and the amount paid for teachers' wages in addition to the public monies, with such other information relating to the common schools of said city, as may from time to time be required by the state superintendent of common schools.

§ 15. It shall be the duty of each commissioner to visit the schools in his ward twice in each year; and the board of education shall provide that each of the schools in the city shall be visited by a committee of three, or more of their number, or by their clerk, at least once in each term.

§ 16. The said board of education shall have power to allow the children of persons not resident within the city to attend any of the schools of said city under the care and control of said board, upon such terms as said board shall by resolution prescribe, fixing the tuition which shall be paid therefor.

§ 17. It shall be the duty of said board, in all their expenditures and contracts, to have reference to the amount of moneys which shall be subject to their order, during the then current year, for the particular expenditure in question, and not to exceed that amount.

§ 18. The said board of commissioners shall be trustees of the school library or libraries in said city, and all the provisions of law which now are or hereafter may be passed relative to district school libraries, shall apply to the said commissioners; they shall also be vested with the same discretion as to the disposition of the moneys appropriated by any law of this state, for the purchase of libraries which is therein conferred upon the inhabitants of school districts. It shall be their duty to provide a library room, or rooms, in the several school houses in said city, and the necessary furniture therefor. The clerk of said board shall be the general librarian. The board shall also appoint a librarian for each school, to have the care of the books, and to superintend the letting out and return thereof. The several school librarians shall from time to time, inform the general librarian of the state and condition of their libraries, and the said board or the general librarian, under the direction and by resolution of the said board, may make all purchases of books for the libraries, and provide for their equitable distribution among the schools, and exchange or cause to be repaired the damaged books belonging thereto, and also sell any books which may be deemed useless, or of improper character, and apply the proceeds to the purchase of other books for said libraries.

§ 19. It shall be the duty of said board, at least fifteen days before the annual election for commissioners in each year, to prepare and report to the common council, true and correct statements of the receipts and disbursements of moneys under and in pursuance of the provisions of this act, during the preceding year; in which account shall be stated under appropriate heads:

1. The monies raised by the common council under the twelfth section of this act:

2. The school moneys received by the chamberlain of the city, from the county treasurer, distinguishing between the sum received from the state and the sum raised upon the city by the board of supervisors:

3. The moneys received by the common council under the third section of this act:

4. All other moneys received by the chamberlain subject to the order of the board, specifying the sources.

5. The manner in which such sums of money shall have been expended, specifying the amount paid under each head of expenditure:

And the common council shall, ten days before such election, cause the same to be published in at least two of the newspapers published in said city.

§ 20. The common council of said city shall have the power to pass such ordinances and regulations as the said board of education may report as necessary and proper for the protection, safe keeping, care and preservation of the school houses, lots, sites, appurtenances and appendages, libraries, and all necessary property belonging to, or connected with the schools in said city; and to impose proper penalties for the violation thereof, subject to the restrictions and limitations contained in the act to incorporate the said city; and all such penalties shall be collected in the same manner that the penalties for the violation of the city ordinances are by law collected, and when collected, shall be paid to the chamberlain of the city, and be subject to the order of the board of education, in the same manner as other moneys, raised pursuant to the provisions of this act.

§ 21. It shall be the duty of the common council, within fifteen days after receiving the certificate of the commissioners required by the fourteenth section of this act, of the sums necessary or proper to be raised under the twelfth section of this act, to determine and certify to said board of education the amount that will be raised by them for the year commencing on the 1st of March thereafter, for the purposes mentioned in said twelfth section, distinguishing between the amount to be raised for teachers' wages and contingent expenses, and the amount to be raised for the repair of school houses, which amounts shall be subject to the disposal of the board of education.

§ 22. All the moneys required to be raised by virtue of this act, or received by the said city, for or on account or the common schools, except such sums as are raised for the purchase of sites for school houses, shall be deposited for the safe keeping thereof, with the chamberlain of said city, to the credit of said board of education, and shall be drawn out in pursuance of a resolution or resolutions of said board, by drafts drawn by the president and countersigned by the clerk of said board, payable to the order of the person or persons entitled to receive such moneys; and said chamberlain shall keep the funds authorized by this act to be received by him, separate and distinct from any other fund, which he is, or may by law be authorised to receive.

§ 23. It shall be the duty of the clerk of said city, immediately after the election of any person as a commissioner of common schools to personally or in writing, to notify him of his election, and if any such person shall not within ten days after receiving such notice of his election, take and subscribe the constitutional oath, and file the same with the clerk of the said city, the common council may consider it a refusal to serve, and proceed to supply the vacancy occasioned by such refusal; and the person so refusing, shall forfeit, and pay to the city chamberlain, for the benefit of the tuition fund, a penalty of ten dollars.

§ 24. It shall be the duty of the several school districts in the city of Troy, within three months from the passage of this act, to transfer and convey to said city all school houses, sites, lots, and all other school property of whatever name and description, and to place in the care of the board of education, all school district records, account books, vouchers, contracts, papers, and other school property, and the said school officers of the said city and the several school districts thereof, shall continue in office until the unfinished business of said districts shall have been finally closed up and settled, not exceeding three months after the passage of this act, with all the power and duties now by law imposed upon them, for the purpose of closing such unfinished business.

§ 25. The common council of the city of Troy shall, on the third Thursday of April, 1849, appoint from each ward in said city commissioners of common schools for said city, corresponding in number with the aldermen elected from said wards, who shall hold their office until the second Tuesday of March,

1850; the said persons so appointed shall be residents of the ward for which they shall be appointed, shall during the time of their appointment constitute said board of education, and possess the same power and privileges, perform the same duties, and be subject to the same regulations as the commissioners to be elected under this act. Their first meeting shall be on the first Wednesday after their appointment.

§ 26. The said commissioners so appointed, shall, in addition to the other duties required of them by this act, on or before the first day of June, 1849, determine and certify to the common council in the manner designated by the fourteenth section of this act, the sums necessary and proper to be raised by said city for the purposes mentioned in said twelfth section, for the year commencing on the 1st of March, 1849. The said common council shall, within fifteen days after receiving said certificate, determine and certify to said commissioners in the manner specified in the twenty-first section, the amounts that will be raised by them, which amounts shall in like manner be subject to the disposal of said commissioners.

§ 27. All previous acts and parts of acts inconsistent herewith, are hereby repealed.

[*Chap.* 353, *laws of* 1850, *as amended by chap.* 366 *laws of* 1851.]

§ 1. It shall be lawful for the board of education of the city of Troy, and the said board is hereby authorized, to discharge all the duties and exercise all the powers belonging to the office of town superintendent of common schools by law, in relation to the formation of joint school districts out of parts of said city, and parts of adjoining towns, and also in the erection of separate school districts, as hereinafter provided, in either the fifth, sixth, and seventh wards of said city.

§ 2. Whenever it may become necessary or convenient to form a joint district out of parts of said city and of any adjoining town, the board of education may depute any member of said board or the clerk thereof, to meet with the superintendent of such adjoining town, and the proceedings of such member of said board, or the clerk thereof, and such town superintendent, in conformity with the statute, duly certified under their hands, in forming, regulating and altering any such districts, shall be valid and conclusive, when approved by said board at any meeting regularly convened.

§ 3. The said board of education may, in its discretion, upon the written application of at least two-thirds of the inhabitants, entitled by law to vote in school district meetings, residing within the territory to be included therein, erect separate school districts, and from time to time regulate and alter the same, in either the fifth, sixth and seventh wards of said city. Such separate school districts, when so erected, and the joint districts provided for in the second section of this act, when so formed, shall severally enjoy all the rights and privileges and be subject to all the duties and liabilities of school districts legally formed in the several towns of this state, and shall be no longer under the care and government of said board of education.

§ 4. It shall be the duty of the trustees of all such joint and separate districts as shall be formed and erected in pursuance of this act, to make to the board of education of said city, all the reports and returns which are or may be by law required in the several towns of this state to be made to the town superintendents thereof. It shall be the duty of the said board of education to apportion to each of the parts of such joint districts lying within said city, and to each of such separate districts, from all the public school moneys that shall thereafter be apportioned and paid to the city, whether the same shall be received from the state school moneys or from the taxes directed by law to be levied and collected for that purpose, the just proportion of such moneys according to the number of children residing within such parts of said joint districts as shall lie within said city, and within said separate districts, between the ages of five and sixteen years inclusive, making the whole number of such children residing within the city the basis for such apportionment, as the same shall appear from the last reports thereof.

§ 5. It shall be the duty of the board of supervisors of the county of Rensselaer, from and after the passage of this act, to direct that all the moneys levied and collected on the inhabitants of the city of Troy for common school purposes, whether the same shall be levied and collected as county taxes or otherwise, shall be paid over by the receiver of taxes for said city, to the chamberlain thereof, for the sole use and benefit of the free public schools within said city, and it shall be the duty of the board of education to apply all such moneys to the support of the free schools of said city in conformity to law.

[*Chap.* 366, *laws of* 1851.]

§ 2. Every ward in the city of Troy, and each portion of a ward in which a public school is now, or may hereafter, be maintained, shall constitute a school district, under the supervision and direction of the board of education of said city.

UTICA.

[*Laws of* 1842, *chap.* 137, *as amended by chap.* 131, *laws of* 1844. *Chap.* 184, *Title X, laws of* 1848, *and chap.* 66, *laws of* 1850.]

AN ACT *in relation to common schools in the city of Utica.*

Passed April 7, 1842, by a two-third vote.

The People of the State of New-York, represented in Senate and Assembly, do Enact as follows :

§ 1. At the next annual election for city officers to be held in the city of Utica, there shall be elected six commissioners of common schools for the said city, who shall be elected in the same manner as justices of the peace, supervisors and constables are elected in said city pursuant to the act incorporating said city.

§ 2. Within ten days after their election, the persons so elected shall take and subscribe the oath of office prescribed by the constitution, and file the same with the clerk of said city ; and they or a majority of them shall thereupon meet and cause the whole number of commissioners so chosen to be divided into three classes, to be severally numbered first, second and third. The term of office of the first class shall expire at the end of one year, of the second class at the end of two years, and of the third class at the end of three years ; but each class shall continue in office until their successors are elected, and have taken the oath of office.

§ 3. At every annual election for city officers in said city after the next, there shall in like manner be elected two commissioners of common schools, to supply the places of those whose term of office is about to expire ; they shall hold their office for three years, and until their successors are elected, and have taken the oath of office. The term of office of all commissioners elected pursuant to the provisions of this act, shall commence on the first Monday after the first Monday in March next succeeding their election.

§ 4. The common council of said city may make appointments of commissioners of common schools, to fill vacancies which may occur from any cause other than the expiration of the term of office of the person elected. The commissioners so appointed, shall hold their office for the unexpired term of those to supply whose places they are appointed.

§ 5. Any commissioner of common schools in said city may be removed from office for official misconduct, by the common council thereof, by a vote of two-thirds of the members thereof.

§ 6. The commissioners of common schools in said city shall constitute a board t be styled the "Commissioners of Common Schools in the city of Utica," which shall be a corporate body in relation to all the powers and duties conferred upon them by virtue of this act; a majority of the board shall form a quorum. At their first meeting after each annual city election, they shall elect one of their number chairman, and whenever the chairman shall be absent from a meeting of the board, they may appoint a chairman pro tempore; they shall also elect a clerk who shall hold his office during the pleasure of the board; the said commissioners shall receive no compensation for their services.

§ 7. The clerk of said board shall keep a record of the proceedings thereof, which record, or a transcript therefrom, certified by the chairman and clerk, shall be received in all courts as prima facie evidence of the facts therein set forth; and such records, and all the books, papers, and accounts of the said board, shall at all times be subject to the inspection of the common council, and of any committee thereof.

§ 8. The common council of the said city shall have the power, and it shall be their duty, to raise from time to time by tax upon the real and personal estates in said city, which shall be liable to taxation for the ordinary city taxes, or for town or county charges, such sums as may be determined and certified by the said board of of commissioners, to be necessary or proper for any or all of the following purposes;

1. To purchase, lease or improve sites for school houses:

2. To build, purchase, lease, enlarge, alter, improve and repair school houses and their out houses and appurtenances:

3. To purchase, exchange, improve, and repair school apparatus, books, furniture and appendages:

4. To procure fuel and defray the contingent expenses of the common schools, and the expenses of the district library of said city, and the contingent expenses of said board of commissioners including the salary of the clerk of said board, aad to meet any deficiency which shall occur in the payment of the wages of teachers of the said schools, after applying to the payment thereof, the school moneys appropriated and provided in said city, and the tuition fees which shall be collected as hereinafter provided; which shall be in addition to the amount of school moneys now or hereafter appropriated or provided by law, for common schools in said city; provided, nevertheless, that such tax shall not be laid oftener than once in each year; and that the whole amount to be raised shall not in any one year exceed the sum of three thousand dollars.

§ 9. The common council shall cause the amount of the tax at any time ordered to be raised in pursuance of the last section, to be added to the amount which they are otherwise authorized by law to raise by tax in said city, and they shall cause the same, with the collectors' fees thereon, to be assessed, levied and collected at the same time by the same warrant, and in the same manner with the taxes raised for city expenses, under and by virtue of the forty-fourth section of the act to incorporate said city.

§ 10. All moneys to be raised pursuant to the provisions of this act, and all school moneys by law appropriated to or provided for said city, shall be paid to the treasurer of the said city, who together with the sureties upon his official bond, shall be accountable therefor in the same manner as for other moneys of the said city; the said treasurer shall also be liable to the same penalties for any official misconduct in relation to the said moneys, as for any similar misconduct in relation to the other moneys of the city.

§ 11. After the passage of this act the treasurer of the said city shall not pay out any moneys in his hands received by the said city, either as school moneys, or collected or received by virtue of any of the provisions of this act, excepting upon an order drawn upon him, and signed by the chairman and clerk of the said board of commissioners, and no such order shall be drawn except by virtue of a resolution of the board.

§ 12. The said board may cause a suit or suits to be prosecuted in the name of the city of Utica, upon the official bond of the treasurer, or of any collector of the said city, for any default, delinquency or official misconduct in relation to the collection, safe keeping or payment of any moneys in this act mentioned.

§ 13. The said board shall have power, and it shall be their duty:

1. To establish and organize such and so many common schools in said city, (including the common and free schools now existing therein) as they shall deem requisite and expedient, and to alter and discontinue the same.

2. To purchase or hire school houses, and rooms and lots or sites for school houses, and to fence and improve them as they deem proper.

3. Upon such lots or sites, and upon any sites now owned by said city, to build, enlarge, alter, improve and repair school houses, out houses and appurtenances as they may deem advisable.

4. To purchase, exchange, improve and repair school apparatus, books, furniture and appendages, and to provide fuel for the schools, and defray their contingent expenses and the expenses of the district library.

5. To have the custody and safe keeping of the school houses, out houses, apparatus, books, furniture and appendages, and to see that the ordinances of the common council in relation thereto be observed.

6. To contract with and employ all teachers in the common schools and at their pleasure to remove them.

7. To pay the wages of such teachers out of the school moneys which shall be appropriated and provided in the said city, so far as the same shall be sufficient, and the residue thereof from the tuition fees they shall be authorized to collect or receive as herein provided; and in case the said school moneys and tuition fees shall be insufficient to pay such wages, then to pay the deficiency out of the moneys to be raised by the common council of said city in pursuance of the eighth section of this act.

8. To fix the rate of tuition fees in said schools at a sum not exceeding two dollars per term, which shall be a period of not less than eleven weeks, and to designate a person or persons to whom the same may be paid previous to issuing a warrant for the collection thereof, and to exempt from the payment of the whole or any part of the tuition fees, such persons as they may deem entitled to such exemption, for indigence or any other sufficient cause, and cause a list of the persons so exempted, with the extent of their exemption, to be kept by the clerk of the board.

9. To defray the necessary contingent expenses of the board, including an annual salary to the clerk, which shall not exceed one hundred dollars, provided that the account of such expenses shall first be audited and allowed by the common council.

10. After the end of each school term to make out a rate bill containing the name of each person liable to pay tuition fees, who shall not have paid them (prior to the making out of such rate bill) to the person or persons designated by the board for that purpose, and the amount for which such person is liable, addding thereto a sum not exceeding five cents on each dollar of the sum due, for collector's fees, and to annex to such rate bill a warrant for the collection thereof.

11. To deliver such rate bill, with the warrant annexed, to one of the collectors of taxes of said city, who shall execute the same in like manner and with like e ect, with the other warrants for the collection of taxes placed in his hands; or in [illegible] discretion, to deliver the same to a collector to be appointed by said board of commissioners, who shall, if required by said board, execute to said commissioners in their corporate capacity, a bond, with one or more sureties, to be approved by said commissioners, or a majority of them, which bond, as to its penalty and conditions, shall be the same as is by law required to be executed by the collectors of school districts; and the said board of commissioners shall have the same power and authority in regard to said bond and the collection thereof, as the trustees of school districts have by law, in regard to the bonds given by collectors of school districts; and the said collector shall have the same power in the execution of said warrant, that the collectors of taxes of said city have by virtue of this act.

12. To have in all respects the superintendence, supervision and management of the common schools in said city, and from time to time to adopt, alter, modify and repeal, as they may deem expedient, rules and regulations for eir organization, government and instruction, for the reception of pupils and

their transfer from one school to another, and generally for the promotion of their good order, prosperity and public utility.

13. Whenever, in the opinion of the board, it may be advisable to sell any of the school houses, lots or sites, or any of the school property now or hereafter belonging to the city, to report the same to the common council.

14. To prepare and report to the common council such ordinances and regulations as may be necessary or proper for the protection, safe keeping, care and preservation of school houses, lots, sites and appurtenances, and all the property belonging to the city, connected with, or appertaining to the schools and to suggest proper penalties for the violation of such ordinances and regulations; and annually to determine and certify to the said common council the sums in their opinion necessary or proper to be raised under the eighth section of this act, specifying the sums required for each of the several purposes therein mentioned.

15. To unite with the commissioners of schools of any adjoining town, and form, regulate and alter any district out of any portion of the said city and such town, whenever they shall deem it necessary and proper to do so, in which case, so far as such district or districts are concerned, and said board shall, during the existence of such districts, have the same powers and duties which the commissioners of schools in towns have.

16. Between the first day of July and the first day of August in each year, to make and transmit to the county clerk a report in writing, bearing date the first day of July in the year of its transmission, and stating,

1. The whole number of districts separately set off within the said city, in pursuance of subdivision fifteen of this section:

2. An account and description of all the common schools kept in said city during the preceding year, and the time they have severally been taught:

3. The number of children taught in the said schools respectively, and the number of children over the age of five and under sixteen [21] years residing in the city on the first day of January of that year:

4. The whole amount of school moneys received by the treasurer of the said city during the preceding year, distinguishing the amount received from the county treasurer, from the town collector, and from any other and what source:

5. The manner in which such moneys have been expended, and whether any and what part remains unexpended, and for what cause:

6. The amount of money received for tuition fees during the year, and the amount paid for teachers' wages, in addition to the public moneys with such other information as the superintendent of common schools may from time to time require.

§ 14. All persons collecting or receiving tuition fees pursuant to the designation, or the warrant of the said board, shall be liable for all moneys thus collected or received by them in the same manner as collectors are for moneys received by them for taxes, and any collector of the said city, and his sureties shall be liable upon his official bond, for any default, delinquency, neglect or misconduct, in the duties with which he may be charged under or by virtue of this act, in the same manner and with the like effect as for any other official default, delinquency, neglect or misconduct; and such collector shall also be liable to the same penalties for any such official misconduct as for any similar misconduct in relation to any other duties of his office.

§ 15. The warrant annexed to any rate bill pursuant to the provisions of this act, shall be under the hands of the commissioners, or a majority of them, and shall command the collector to collect from every person in such rate bill named, the sum therein set opposite his name, and in case any person so named, shall not pay such sum on demand to levy the same, together with the fees of said collector, by distress and sale of goods and chattels of the person who ought to pay the same, or of any goods and chattels in his possession, wheresoever the same may be found in the city of Utica, and to make return of such warrant to the treasurer of said city, within thirty days after the delivery thereof.

§ 16. Such warrants shall have the like force and effect as warrants issued by the boards of supervisors to the collectors of towns, and the collectors of the said city are authorized to collect the amount due from any person or persons in the said city, in the same manner and with the same power that collectors of a school district have for the collection of tax or rate bills issued by the trustees of school districts.

§ 17. The board of commissioners shall possess the same powers which the trustees of school districts have for the collection of tuition fees, which shall not be collected by the warrant issued by them with rate bills, and subject to the same regulations; and they may in like manner as the trustees of school districts, correct and amend errors in making out any rate bill, and refund to any person any sum improperly collected in consequence of such error.

§ 18. It shall be duty of the said board in all their expenditures and contracts to have reference to the amount of moneys which will be subject to their order during the then current year, for the particular expenditures in question.

§ 19. The said board of commissioners shall be the trustees of the district library in said city, and all the provisions of the act entitled, "An act respecting the School District Libraries," passed April 15, 1839, and all other laws which now are or may hereafter be passed relating to district school libraries, shall apply to the said commissioners in the same manner as if they were trustees of a school district comprehending the said city; they shall also be vested with the discretion as to the disposition of the moneys appropriated by the fourth section of chapter two hundred and thirty-seven, of the Statues of eighteen hundred and thirty-eight, which is therein conferred upon the inhabitants of school districts. It shall be their duty to provide a library room and the necessary library, furniture, and appoint a librarian, to make all purchases of books for the said library, and from time to time to exchange or cause to be repaired damaged books belonging thereto; they may also sell any books which they deem useless, or of improper character, and apply the proceeds to the purchase of other books for the said library.

§ 106. [Title X, chap. 184, laws of 1849.] The board of commissioners of common schools may from the moneys received by them for the school district library, defray the contingent expenses of the library and the salary of the librarian, and apply such portion of it as they may deem proper to the payment of teachers' salaries.

§ 20. It shall be the duty of said board, at least fifteen days before the annual election for city officers in each year, to prepare and report to the common council true and correct statements of the receipts and disbursements of moneys under and in pursuance of the provisions of this act during the preceding year; in which account shall be stated under appropriate heads,

1. The moneys raised by the common council under the eighth section of this act:

2. The school moneys received by the treasurer of the city from the county treasurer and the collector of taxes for town and county charges in said city:

3. The moneys received for tuition fees:

4. Alll other moneys received by the treasurer subject to the order of the board, specifying the sources:

5. The manner in which such moneys shall have been expended, specifying the amount paid under each head of expenditure;

And the common council shall, ten days before the said election cause the same to be published, with the statement required to be published by the thirty-third section of the act to incorporate the said city.

§ 21. The said board shall be subject to the rules and regulations from time to time made by the superintendent of common schools so far as the same may be applicable to them, and not inconsistent with the provisions of this act.

§ 22. The common council of said city shall have the power, and it shall be their duty to pass such ordinances and regulations as the said board of commissioners may report as necessary and proper for the protection, safe keeping, care and preservation of the school houses, lots, sites, and appurtenances, and all the necessary property belonging to or connected with the schools in said city; and to impose proper penalties for the violation thereof, subject to the restrictions and limitations contained in the act to incorporate the said city; and all such penalties shall be collected in the same manner that the penalties for violation of the city ordinances are by law collected; and when collected shall be paid to the treasurer of the city, and be subject to the order of the board of commissioners, in the same manner as other moneys raised pursuant to the provisions of this act.

§ 23. Whenever the said board shall report to the common council that it is advisable to sell any of the school houses, lots or sites, or any of the school property now or hereafter belonging to the city, it shall be the duty of the common council to sell the same without unreasonable delay, and upon such terms as the said council may deem advisable. The proceeds of all such sales shall be paid to the treasurer of the city, and shall be subject to the order of the said board, to be expended by them in the purchase, leasing, repairs or improvements of other school houses, lots, school furniture, apparatus or appurtenances.

§ 24. The title of the school houses, sites, lots, furniture, books, apparatus and appurtenances, and all other school property herein before in this act mentioned, shall be vested in the city of Utica; and the same while used for or appropriated for school purposes shall not be liable to be levied upon or sold by virtue of any warrant or execution, nor be subject to taxation or assessment for any purpose whatsoever; and the said city in its corporate capacity shall be able to take, hold and dispose of any real or personal estate, transferred to it by gift, grant, bequest or devise for the use of common schools of the said city, whether the same shall be transferred in terms directly to said city by its proper style, or by any other designation or to any other designation, or to any person or persons or body, for the use of said schools.

§ 25. All former acts and parts of acts in relation to common and free schools in the said city, inconsistent with the provisions of this act are hereby repealed.

[*Chap.* 66, *Laws of* 1850.]

§ 1. The board of school commissioners of the city of Utica shall annually prepare an estimate of the amount of money necessary to be raised in the said city, for the then ensuing year, for the payment of teachers' wages, exclusive of the public money and the money required by law to be raised by the county and town by the act establishing free schools throughout the state, and present the same to the board of supervisors of Oneida county, (at their annual meeting,) who shall cause the same to be levied and collected from the said city in the same manner as other town taxes; but the sum to be raised by virtue of this section, shall not in any year exceed twice the sum apportioned to the city from the state school moneys.

§ 2. The said board of commissioners shall appoint a superintendent of common schools for the city, to hold his office during the pleasure of the board, and to perform such duties in the care and oversight of the schools in the city as it may charge him with. He shall be paid such compensation for his services as the board shall from time to time determine, which shall be audited and allowed, as other town charges are in the said city.

WILLIAMSBURGH.

[*Laws of* 1851, *Chap.* 171.]

AN ACT *in relation to common schools in the city of Williamsburgh.*

Passed April 14, 1851, "three-fifths being present."

The People of the State of New-York, represented in Senate and Assembly, do enact as follows:

§ 1. The trustees of common schools in the city of Williamsburgh, holding office at the passage of this act, whose term, under the provisions of chapter one hundred and eighty-one, laws of eighteen hundred and forty-four, would expire in May, eighteen hundred and fifty-two, shall hold office until the first Monday in January, eighteen hundred and fify-two, and no longer. The trustees so holding office, whose term would expire in May, eighteen hundred and fifty-three, shall hold office until the first Monday in January, eighteen hundred and fifty-three, and no longer. And the trustees who shall be elected at the annual district meetings in May, eighteen hundred and fifty-one, shall hold office until the first Monday in January, eighteen hundred and fifty-four, and no longer.

§ 2. At each annual election for charter officers hereafter to be held in said city, there shall be chosen in each ward, one trustee of common schools, whose term of office shall commence on the first Monday in January next succeeding his election, and continue three years. All persons qualified to vote for members of the common council in said city, shall be entitled to vote for school trustees, and the election shall be conducted in the manner prescribed by law for other elections; provided, that a separate box shall be provided in each election district, to receive the votes of electors for said trustees, and that the ballots used in such election, shall be endorsed "school." Vacancies in the office of school trustee shall be filled at the election next succeeding their occurrence; but persons chosen to fill the same, shall hold office only for the residue of the term broken by the occurrence of such vacancy. All persons shall be eligible to the said office, who may be eligible by law to the common council.

§ 3. The three school trustees of each ward, in office at the same time, shall manage and control the common schools of such ward, in conformity to the provisions of this act, and the laws of this state.

§ 4. The trustees of common schools of the several wards of said city, shall in joint meeting, form a board of education. The said board shall have the general supervision of the schools of said city, and shall have power to make such rules for determining the qualifications of teachers in said schools, and ensuring uniformity of books and school discipline, as they may deem best for the interests of education. The said board shall maintain schools for colored children, and shall have power to establish, manage, and control evening schools, using for such purpose, such school house or school-houses as they may elect; and when the same may appear to be demanded by the wants of the people, they may establish, manage and control an academy or high school. The board of education shall make its own by-laws, not inconsistent with the laws of this state; and shall choose from their own number, annually, a president, and also a clerk, who shall keep a faithful record of the proceedings of the board.

§ 5. The several boards of school trustees shall by or before the first Monday of March in each year, prepare and file with the city clerk, a detailed estimate of the necessary expenses of conduc ing the schools in their wards respectively for the year commencing on the first day of May following, specifying in such estimate, the amount necessary for teachers' wages, for books, for maps, and other school apparatus, for fuel, for ordinary repairs of school houses, for contingent expenses, for salary of librarian, for the maintenance and moderate increase of the libraries, for furniture, for deficiencies of previous appropriations. The board of education shall in like manner, file with the city clerk, an estimate of the amounts necessary for their contingent expenses, and for conducting the schools for colored children, evening schools, and academy maintained by them, specifying the branches of appropriations and the amounts necessary for each as in the case of the ward schools.

§ 6. The city clerk shall within ten days after the period named in the preceding section issue notice to the members of the school board of finance to meet at an appointed time and place within ten days after the date of his notice. The school board of finance shall accordingly meet and consider the estimates submitted to them as hereinafter provided, adjourning from time to time as they may see fit; provided, that they shall make a final decision respecting said estimates previous to the first Monday of May. The said school board of finance shall have power to reduce, reject, or increase the sums named in the said estimates as they may think reasonable and expedient; and having determined upon the amount necessary, in their opinion, for the proper management and support of the schools in each ward, they shall file a statement under the hands of their president and clerk, with the trustees thereof, setting forth in detail said necessary amount, and the particular purposes for which said money shall be used. Having determined upon the amount necessary for the proper management and support of the schools for colored children, the evening schools, and the academy maintained by the board of education, and for the contingent expenses of said board, they shall file a statement thereof, similarly detailed, with the president of the board of education. They shall also file duplicates of said statements with the city comptroller and city treasurer.

§ 7. The gross amount of money which the said school board of finance shall so certify to be necessary for school purposes, less any balance of previous appropriations for such purposes remaining unexpended in the treasury and the amount of the distributive share of state school money to which the said city shall be entitled, and including a sufficient amount to entitle the city to such distributive share, shall be added by the common council of the said city to the amount of taxes to be levied by them for the year, upon the real and personal property of the city; and shall be paid with other monies raised by tax, to the city treasurer. The treasurer shall disburse the same only by the order and on the warrant of the school trustees of the several wards, or of the board of education by its president and clerk, as the case may be, drawn in favor of the person entitled to payment, and specifying the particular purpose to which the money is to be applied. The treasurer shall honor such drafts only so far as the specific appropriations by the school board of finance shall allow.

§ 8. The school board of finance shall consist of the mayor of the city the members of the city board of finance, who are not members of the common council and the trustees of common schools. The board shall choose a president from its own number. The city clerk shall be the clerk of said board, and shall keep a faithful record of its proceedings, entering the yeas and nays on every vote upon an appropriation. A majority of the school trustees, with a majority of the members of the board, shall be a quorum for the transaction of business, but a less number may adjourn from time to time.

§ 9. When the purchase of real estate, or the erection of an edifice for school or academy purposes may be decided by the board of education to be necessary, they shall file the vote by which such decision shall have been made, including an estimate of the extreme amount of money necessary for such purchase or erection, with the city clerk who shall lay the same at its next meeting before the common council of the said city. If said common council after due deliberation, shall also determine the same to be expedient, the said common council shall lay before the people, at the next election, the question whether they approve of the proposed erection or purchase; and if a majority of the ballots cast for and against such proposition shall prove to be in favor thereof, the said common council shall take measures to carry the same into effect. And for this purpose the said common council shall have power to add the necessary amount to the annual taxes, provided that they may at their discretion, divide such amount into yearly instalments, and make temporary loans in anticipation thereof.

§ 10. The title of the property now held by the several school districts of the town of Williamsburgh, and of all real estate and buildings purchased and erected under this act, shall vest in the city of Williamsburgh; and no such property shall be sold or otherwise diverted from use for educational purposes, without the recommendation or consent of the board of education. In case of such sale or diversion, the value of such property shall be applied to the purchase or erection of other property for educational purposes, or to the reduction of taxes for school purposes, as may be recommended by the board of education.

§ 11. If by any unforseen casualty, damage shall occur to the buildings held by the city for educational purposes, beyond the amount properly appropriated for repairs of such buildings, the common council shall cause such damage to be repaired, and make special appropriations therefor. If such damage occur by fire, and is covered by insurance, the treasurer shall collect the insurance; and the amount appropriated by the common council to pay for repairs of damage to buildings, less the amount, if any, received on account of insurance in case said damage occur by fire, shall be added by the common council to the annual taxes next to be levied by them.

§ 12. The city comptroller shall cause to be and keep insured, all buildings held by the city for school purposes, for a sufficient amount, in a company or companies of good standing; and the expense of such insurance, if upon a ward school house, shall be paid by the warrant on account of contingent expenses of the school trustees of the ward in which such school house is situated; and if upon a building used for a school for colored children, or for an academy, by the warrant on same account of the board of education.

§ 13. The office of superintendent of common schools for the town of Williamsburgh, is hereby abolished. The sums to which the schools of said city shall be entitled by the laws of this state, and which would be paid to such superintendent for distribution, shall be paid to the treasurer of the city of Williamsburgh.

§ 14. The president of the board of education, shall make frequent visitations of the schools and academy, if such there be, of said city, reporting from time to time to the board their condition, and the measures necessary in his opinion, to improve their efficiency and usefulness.

§ 15. The common schools of the city of Williamsburgh, shall be free to all children of said city, between the ages of five and sixteen years inclusive; provided, that a separate school or schools for colored children shall be maintained by the board of education. The said board shall prescribe the terms of admission to the evening schools and to the city academy, if any shall be established under this act; but they shall not make the payment of any money for entrance or tuition necessary to such admission.

§ 16. The office of district clerk is hereby abolished. The books and papers in the hands of the clerks of the several school districts of said city at the expiration of the year one thousand eight hundred and fifty-one, shall be placed in the hands of the school trustees of the corresponding wards. The said trustees shall keep correct records of their proceedings, and have the custody of all the papers and records relating to their several wards, except the deeds and muniments of title to the real estate held for school purposes, which shall be deposited with the city comptroller.

§ 17. The term of office of the librarians of the several school districts of the town of Williamsburgh, shall expire on the first Monday in January, one thousand eight hundred and fifty-two; and the school trustees of each ward shall annually thereafter appoint a librarian. The said trustees shall continue to maintain a public library, which shall be free to all inhabitants of the ward exercising the same powers in regard to them with which they are now by law invested. The public money designated as "library money," shall with other public money as provided by section thirteen of this act be paid to the city treasurer; but so much only of such library money shall be appropriated to the purchase of library books or school apparatus as may be required by the trustees of the several wards and authorized by the school board of finance as provided in section five and section six of this act.

§ 18. The monies paid or payable under chapter 181, laws of eighteen hundred and forty-four, to the trustees of the several school districts of the said city before the first day of May, eighteen hundred and fifty-two, shall continue to be held and disbursed by them until that time. The said trustees shall then render to the city comptroller a full and correct account of their receipts and disbursments for the previous year, and shall pay over to the city treasurer any school monies remaining in their hands.

§ 19. The common council of the city of Williamsburgh shall provide for the payment of loans lawfully made by the several school districts, so far as the same shall not be paid by appropriations made previous to the first day of May, eighteen hundred and fifty-two. And for this purpose they shall have power to add the necessary amount to the annual taxes of said city.

§ 20. The said common council shall have power to borrow money temporarily in anticipation of taxes for school purposes as for other purposes.

§ 21. The board of assessors for said city for the year eighteen hundred and fifty-two shall estimate the value of the real estate of said city held for school purposes in each ward, deducting therefrom the amount of indebtedness due or chargeable upon such property on the first day of May, eighteen hundred and fifty-two, and shall determine the ratio which said value bears to the whole assessed valuation of the real and personal property in such ward. They shall file with the city comptroller a statement of such value and ratio; and if such ratio shall vary in the several wards, the common council of said city shall gradually, at their discretion, so discriminate in levying the taxes upon the several wards, that each shall as near as may be, bear a just proportion according to its assessed valuation of the expenses of the property already purchased and erected for school purposes.

§ 22. The board of education shall provide for taking an annual census of all the children of the on the thirty-first day of December in each year, between the ages of five and sixteen years inclusive, which enumeration with all other information now required by law of school trustees and town superintendents, they shall cause to be forwarded to the state superintendent of common schools. The expense of such enumeration shall be paid by their warrant out of monies appropriated to their use for contingent expenses.

§ 23. For the purposes of all acts which have been or may be passed by the legislature of this state, providing for an equal division of public money among the school districts of this state, the city of Williamsburgh shall be deemed to contain as many school districts as school houses.

§ 24. No officer elected or appointed under this act shall receive any compensation for his services, except the librarian.

§ 25. Chapter 181, laws of eighteen hundred and forty-four, and all other acts and parts of acts inconsistent with the provisions of this act, are hereby repealed.

§ 26. This act shall take effect on the first Monday in January, eighteen hundred and fifty-two, except as herein otherwise provided.

WILLIAMSVILLE.

[*Laws of* 1846, *Chap.* 119.]

§ 1. The trustees of the school district at the village of Williamsville, in the town of Amherst and county of Erie, are hereby authorized, if the inhabitants of said district shall at any regular school district meeting so direct to make thereafter, and until the said inhabitants shall in like manner otherwise direct, separate and distinct rate bills, for the payment of the wages of the teachers in the primary and higher department of the schools kept in the said district, in such manner to collect on account of scholars attending each department, such balance as may be justly due for the wages of the teacher or teachers in that department, after the application to that purpose of such share of the public moneys as shall be apportioned to each department by such trustees, by giving to each such proportion of the whole sum applicable to the payment of teachers' wages in both departments, as the number of scholars who shall have attended such department during the time for which such rate bill is to be made, shall bear to the whole number of scholars attending both of such departments during the same period.

INDIAN SCHOOLS.

Laws of 1846, *Chap.* 114; *Laws of* 1847, *Chap.* 238.

AN ACT *to provide for the education of children of the Onondaga Indians in the county of Onondaga, and the children of the other Indians residing in this state.*

Passed April 30, 1846.

The People of the State of New-York, represented in Senate and Assembly, do enact as follows:

§ 1. The agent of the Onondaga Indians in the county of Onondaga, appointed under the authority of this state, is hereby authorised, with the consent of the chiefs of the said tribe of Onondaga Indians, to cause to be built and furnished a good and sufficient school house on the Onondaga reservation, at an expense not exceeding three hundred dollars, for the accommodation of the Indian children residing on such reservation; and to organize a school therein, and the sum of three hundred dollars is hereby appropriated for the payment of the expense of erecting and furnishing said school-house.

§ 2. The sum of two hundred and fifty dollars annually is hereby appropriated for the term of five years, for the payment of the wages of a teacher or teachers, and of the other expenses of maintaining such school.

§ 5. The sums appropriated by the first and second sections of this act shall be paid from time to time to the said agent of the Onondaga Indians on his giving to the people of this state and filing with the state superintendent of common schools, a bond with satisfactory sureties, to be approved by such superintendent conditioned for the proper and faithful expenditure of all moneys paid to him, or which shall come into his hands by virtue of this act, and for the rendering to such superintendent annually in the month of October, a just and true account of all his receipts and expenditures, under the provisions of this act.

§ 7. The sum of two hundred and fifty dollars is also hereby appropriated for the building and furnishing a school house on the lands of the St. Regis Indians, in this state; and the further sum of two hundred dollars per year, for the term of five years, is hereby appropriated for the payment of wages of a teacher of the school, to be kept in said school house, and for the payment of the other expenses of said school. The moneys appropriated by this section shall be paid from time to time to the agent of the said St. Regis Indians, on his giving to the people of this state, and filing with the state superintendent of common schools, a bond with satisfactory sureties, to be approved by such superintendent, conditioned for the proper and faithful expenditure within this state, of all moneys paid to him, and which shall come into his hands by virtue of this act, and for rendering to the said superintendent annually, in the month of October, a just and true account of all his receipts and expenditures by virtue of this act.

§ 8. The sums hereby appropriated shall be paid out of the income of the United States deposit fund; and the last two of the several annual payments herein provided for, shall not be paid for the Indians residing on either of the said reservations, unless the Indians on such reservation shall, before such payment in each year, pay into the hands of the persons authorised to receive and expend the moneys appropriated by this act, at least twenty per cent. of the sum authorised to be paid annually for the maintenance of the school on such reservation; nor shall any of the said annual payments except the first, be made unless the state superintendent of common schools shall have satisfactory evidence that a school has been kept in said school house for the term of at least six months during the preceding year; such twenty per cent. shall be expended by such commissioner for the support and maintenance of the school or schools on the reservation, occupied by the Indians paying the same.

§ 9. The schools organized and established by virtue of this act, shall be subject to the visitation and inspection of the superintendent of common schools of the town and county where the same shall be situated.

AN ACT *making appropriations for building and furnishing school houses, and providing for the education of the children of Indians, residing on the Cattaraugus and Allegany reservations.*

Passed May 7, 1847, "three-fifths being present."

The People of the State of New York, represented in Senate and Assembly, do enact as follows:

§ 1. The sum of three hundred dollars is hereby appropriated for the building and furnishing a school house on the Cattaragus reservation, and the like sum of three hundred dollars is hereby appropriated for the building and furnishing a school house on the Allegany reservation; such school houses to be for use, accommodation and education of the Indian children residing on the said reservations.

§ 3. The sums appropriated by this act. and all appropriations made, or that hereafter may be made for the education of the children of Indians residing on the Cattaraugus and Allegany reservations, shall be paid out of the income of the United States deposite fund, to Chester How, or his successor, on his executing to the people of this state, and filing with the superintendent of common schools, a bond in the penalty of two thousand dollars, with such sureties as shall be approved by the said superintendent, conditioned for the faithful expenditure of, and accounting for all moneys which shall be received by him under this act; and he shall, annually, in the month of October, render an account to the comptroller, of all receipts and expenditures by him.

§ 4. The appropriations made for the education of Indian children residing on said reservations, for eighteen hundred and forty-eight, and thereafter, shall not be expended by the said commissioner, until the chiefs of the Indians residing on said reservations shall pay to the said commissioner, twenty per cent. of the sums so appropriated, respectively, in each year, to be applied by him to the maintenance of the said schools; nor shall the sums so appropriated be paid to the said commissioner unless the superintendent of common schools shall have satisfactory evidence that schools have been kept on the said reservations, respectively, for at least six months during the preceding year.

§ 5. In case the said Chester Howe shall decline to accept the trust hereby conferred, or to execute the bond hereby required, or in case of his death, inability or resignation, the comptroller of this state may appoint some fit and proper person or persons to supply such vacancy, who, upon executing the bond herein required, shall be entitled to receive and expend the moneys hereby appropriated, and shall account for the same in the manner and upon the conditions herein provided.

§ 6. The schools established under this act, shall be subject to the visitation and inspection of the county and town superintendents of common schools, of the county and town in which they shall be kept.

[*Chap.* 164, *Laws of* 1831, *Revived by Chap.* 39, *Laws of* 1848.]

AN ACT *for the relief of the Shinecock tribe of Indians.*

Passed April 19, 1831.

§ 1. The superintendent of common schools shall in every year hereafter apportion from school moneys, the sum of eighty dollars in addition to the amount to which the county of Suffolk is now entitled by law; which sum shall be paid on the first day of February in every year on the warrant of the comptroller to the treasurer of said county.

§ 2. The treasurer of said county shall apply for and receive the said sum as soon as the same becomes payable, and shall hold the same subject to the order of the town superintendent of common schools of the town of Southampton, whose duty it shall be to receive and expend the same in the payment of the wages of a competent school teacher or teachers, to be by them employed in instructing the children between the ages of five and sixteen years, belonging to the Shinecock tribe of Indians residing in said town.

§ 3. The said town superintendent shall hereafter include in the annual report, a statement of the length of time that a school has been taught in pursuance of this act; the number of children taught in said school; the manner in which such moneys have been expended; and whether any and how much remains unexpended, and for what cause, and shall pay such balances if any, to their successors in office, to be by them expended as herein before provided.

[*Laws of* 1851, *Chap.* 243.]

AN ACT *to provide for the education of the children of the Tuscarora Indians, in the county of Niagara.*

Passed June 20, 1851, "three-fifths being present."

The People of the State of New-York, represented in Senate and Assembly, do enact as follows:

§ 1. The sum of two hundred dollars a year, for the term of two years is hereby appropriated for the support of a school or schools to be kept for the education of the children of the Tuscarora Indians, on the Tuscarora Reservation, in the county of Niagara.

§ 2. The sum appropriated by first section of this act shall be paid by the treasurer on the warrant of the Comptroller, as the same may from time to time be wanted, out of the income of the United States Deposite Fund to William Mount Pleasant, on his executing and giving to the people of this State and filing with the Superintendent of common schools a bond with satisfactory sureties, to be approved by the county Judge of the county of Niagara, by an endorsement of such approval upon said bond, conditioned for the faithful expenditure of all moneys paid to him, or which shall come into his hands by virtue of this act and for rendering to said superintenden annually in the month of October, a just and true account of all his receipts and disbursements by virtue of this act.

§ 3. It shall be the duty of the said William Mount Pleasant to whom the money is from time to time paid by virtue of this act, to expend the same in the payment of teachers for the education of the children of the Indians on the Reservation aforesaid.

[*Laws of* 1851, *Chap.* 361.]

AN ACT *to provide for the education of the children of the Tonawanda Indians in the county of Genesee.*

Passed July 1, 1851. "by a two-third vote."

The People of the State of New York represented in Senate and Assembly, do enact as follows:

§ 1. The sum of two hundred dollars a year, for two years, is hereby appropriated for the support of a school or schools to be kept for the education of the children of the Tonawanda Indians, on the Tonawanda reservation, in the county of Genesee.

§ 2. The sum appropriated by the first section of this act shall be paid by the treasurer, on the warrant of the comptroller, as the same may from time to time be wanted, out of the income of the United States deposite fund, to William Parker, on his executing and giving to the people of this state and filing with the superintendent of common schools a bond with satisfactory sureties, to be approved by the county judge, of the county of Genesee, by an endorsement of such approval upon said bond, conditioned for the faithful expenditure of all moneys paid to him, or which shall come into his hands by virtue of this act, and for rendering to said superintendent annually, of the month of October, a just and true account of all his receipts and disbursements by virtue of this act.

§ 3. It shall be the duty of the said William Parker, to whom the money is from time to time paid by virtue of this act, to expend the same in the payment of teachers for the education of the children of the Indians on the reservation aforesaid.

§ 4. This act shall take effect immediately.

DISTRICT SCHOOL JOURNAL.

[*Laws of* 1841 *Chap.* 260, *as amended by* § 17 *of Chap.* 132, *Laws of* 1843.]

§ 32. The superintendent of common schools, from year to year, shall be authorised to subscribe for so many copies of any periodical published at least monthly in this state, exclusively devoted to the cause of education, and not partaking of a sectarian or party character, as shall be sufficient to supply one copy to each organized school district in the state; in which periodical, the statutes relating to common schools, passed at the present, or any future session of the Legislature, and the general regulations and decisions of the superintendent made pursuant to any law, shall be published gratuitously. The said periodical shall be sent to the clerk of each district, whose duty it shall be to cause each volume to be bound, at the expense of the district, and the same shall be preserved in the district library for the use of the district. The expense of said subscription, not exceeding twenty-eight hundred dollars annually, shall be paid out of the surplus income arising from the moneys deposited with this state, by the United States.

STATE NORMAL SCHOOL.

[*Laws of* 1844, *Chap.* 311.]

AN ACT *for the establishment of a Normal School.*

Passed May 7, 1844.

The People of the State of New York represented in Senate and Assembly do enact as follows:

§ 1. The treasurer shall pay on the warrant of the comptroller, to the order of the superintendent of common schools from that portion of the avails of the literature fund appropriated by chapter two hundred and forty one of the laws of one thousand eight hundred and thirty-four, to the support of academical departments for the instruction of teachers of common schools, the sum of nine thousand six hundred dollars; which sum shall be expended under the direction of the superintendent of common schools, and the regents of the university, in the establishment and support of a normal school for the instruction and practice of teachers of common schools in the science of education and in the art of teaching, to be located in the county of Albany.

§ 2. The sum of ten thousand dollars shall, after the present year, be annually paid by the treasurer on the warrant of the comptroller, to the superintendent of common schools, from the revenue of the literature fund, for the maintenance and support of the school so established, for five years, and until otherwise directed by law.

§ 3. The said school shall be under the supervision, management and government of the superintendent of common schools and the regents of the university. The said superintendent and regents shall from time to time, make all needful rules and regulations, to fix the number and compensation of teachers and others to be employed therein, to prescribe the preliminary examination and the terms and conditions on which pupils shall be received and instructed therein, the number of pupils from the respective cities and counties, conforming as nearly as may be to the ratio of population, to fix the location of the said school, and the terms and conditions on which the grounds and buildings therefor shall be rented, if the same shall not be provided by the corporation of the city of Albany, and to provide in all things for the good government and management of the said school. They shall appoint a board consisting of five persons, of whom the said superintendent shall be one, who shall constitute an executive committee for the care, management and government of the said school under the rules and regulations prescribed as aforesaid, whose duty it shall be from time to time to make full and detailed reports to the said superintendent and regents, and among other things to recommend the rules and regulations which they deem necessary and proper for the said school.

§ 4. The superintendent and regents shall annually transmit to the legislature a full account of their proceedings and expenditures of money under this act, together with a detailed report by said executive committee of the progress, condition and prospects of the school.

[*Laws of* 1850, *Chap.* 89.]

§ 1. The treasurer shall pay on the warrant of the comptroller to the order of the state superintendent of common schools, from the general fund, a sum not exceeding one thousand dollars per year for the support and education of ten Indian youth in the State Normal School.

§ 2. The selection of such youth shall be made by the state superintendent of common schools from the several Indian tribes located within the state; and in making such selection, due regard shall be had to a just participation in the privileges of this act by each of the said several tribes, and if practicable, reference shall also be had to the population of each of said tribes in determining such selection.

§ 3. Such youths shall not be under sixteen years of age, nor shall any of such youths be supported or educated at said Normal School for a period exceeding three years.

§ 4. The executive committee of the State Normal School shall be the guardians of such Indian youths, during the period of their connection with the school, and shall pay their necessary expenses, not exceeding one hundred dollars per year for each pupil to be defrayed out of the money appropriated by the first section of this act.

§ 5. The Indian pupils selected in pursuance of this act, and attending said Normal School, shall enjoy the same privileges of every kind, as the other pupils attending said school, including the payment of travelling expenses, not exceeding ten dollars to each pupil.

TEACHERS' INSTITUTES.

[*Laws of* 1847, *Chap.* 361.]

AN ACT *for the establishment of teachers' institutes.*

Passed November 13, 1847, "three-fifths being present."

The People of the State of New York, represented in Senate and Assembly, do enact as follows:

§ 1. The treasurer shall pay, on the warrant of the comptroller, to the order of the several county treasurers of this state, the several sums of money hereinafter mentioned, not exceeding sixty dollars annually to any one county, from the income of the United States deposite fund, to be expended for the use and benefit of teachers' institutes as hereinafter provided.

§ 2. Whenever a majority of town superintendents of common schools in any county in this state unite in a recommendation, and file with the county clerk thereof a certificate, signifying their desire that a teacher's institute should be organized in such county, for the instruction and improvement of common school teachers for such county, it shall thereupon be the duty of such clerk forthwith to appoint three town superintendents of the county, and notify them of their appointment, to constitute an advisory committee, to make the necessary arrangements for organizing and managing such institute, and such clerk shall also immediately give such public notice in such manner as he may deem most proper to the teachers of common schools of the county, and to others who may desire to become such, specifying a time and place when and where the teachers may meet and form such institute.

§ 3. Whenever any institute shall have been organized as herein provided, it shall be the duty of said committee, and they shall have power to secure two or more suitable persons to lecture before such institute upon subjects pertaining to common school teaching and discipline, and various educational subjects which may be deemed calculated to qualify common school teachers, and to elevate the profession of teaching and to improve common schools; and said committee shall keep an accurate account in items, of the necessary expenses of such institute in procuring said lecturers, and otherwise, and shall verify said account by affidavit, and deliver the same to the county treasurer, to be audited by and filed with him when application shall be made to such treasurer, as hereinafter provided.

§ 4. Whenever any county treasurer shall receive satisfactory evidence that not less than fifty, or in counties of under thirty thousand population, then not less than thirty teachers and individuals intending to become teachers of common schools within one year, shall have been in regular attendance on the instructions and lectures of the institute in the county during at least ten working days, he shall audit and allow the account which shall be presented to him by the committee as aforesaid, and shall pay over to said committee the amount so audited and allowed, not exceeding sixty dollars in any one year, to be disbursed by said committee in paying the expenses incurred by the institute as aforesaid.

§ 5. Every such committee shall annually transmit to the state superintendent of common schools, a catalogue of the names of all persons who shall have attended such institute, with such other statistical information and within such time as may be prescribed by said state superintendent.

§ 6. This act shall take effect immediately.

LIBRARY MONEYS.

[*Laws of* 1851. *Chap.* 425.]

AN ACT *to amend the act entitled, "An act to establish free schools throughout the State."*

Passed July 9, 1851.

The People of the State of New-York, represented in Senate and Assembly, do enact as follows:

§ 1. The Act entitled, "An act to establish free schools throughout the State," passed April 12, 1851, shall not be so construed as to prevent or prohibit the distribution and application of library money, in the manner heretofore prescribed by law.

§ 2. Nothing in this act contained, shall be so construed as to require the board of supervisors of each county, to raise a sum of money for library purposes, equal to the sum which it will receive from the state.

§ 3. This act shall take effect immediately.

WEBSTER'S DICTIONARY.

[*Laws of* 1851. *Chap.* 449.]

AN ACT *to authorize the Superintendent of Common Schools to purchase Webster's Unabridged Dictionary for the Common School Districts of this State.*

Passed July 9, 1851.

The People of the State of New-York, represented in Senate and Assembly, do enact as follows:

§ 1. The state superintendent of common schools shall cause notice to be given, by circular, to one or more of the trustees of the several school districts in this state, on or before the first day of December next, which circular shall state the terms, and the funds out of which the same is to be paid; that Websters Unabridged Dictionary will be purchased by him, for each of the school districts in this state, entitled to participate in the distribution of public moneys for the support of common schools: provided such district shall notify the town superintendent of common schools of their respective towns, in writing, to be signed by a majority of the trustees of any school district that said Dictionary is wanted by the district giving such notice: such notice to be delivered to such town superintendent before the first day of January next.

§ 2. The town superintendent of common schools in each of the towns in this state, shall, on or before the fifteenth day of January next, make out and deliver to the county clerk, a complete list of all the school districts in their several towns: stating the number of such districts, and shall annex to the number of each desiring to purchase Webster's Unabridged Dictionary, that such district desires to purchase said dictionary, and shall file a copy of such list in the office of the town clerk of their respective towns, on or before the fifteenth day of January next.

§ 3. The county clerk of each of the several counties of this State, shall transmit such lists on or before the first day of February next, to the state superintendent of common schools.

§ 4. The state superintendent of common schools is authorized to purchase of the publishers of Webster's Quarto Unabridged Dictiouary, such number of said work as shall be sufficient to supply all the said school districts in the state which shall be found reported upon such lists as desire to purchase the same; such Dictionaries shall be the latest edition of Webster's Quarto Unabridged Dictionary, print ed on superior paper, well bound in leather, and in all respects perfect; the price to be paid shall not exceed four dollars per volome; and shall be paid for out of the public monies which shall be apportioned to the several school districts of the state for which the same shall be purchased, one half thereof in the year 1852 and one half thereof in the year 1853, and the contract for such purchase of the said publishers shall provide for such terms of payment, and the number of Dictionaries so purchased shall be delivered to the state superintendent of common schools, before the first day of April, 1852, and shall be by him delivered to the town superintendent of common schools of the respective towns, before the first day of May, 1852.

§ 5. The said town superintendent shall deliver such Dictionary to the trustees of each of the said several districts in their respective towns for which they shall be purchased as soon thereafter as shall be practicable, and shall retain in his hands the sum of two dollars out of the library monies apportioned to such districts in the year eighteen hundred and fifty-two, and such sum out of the library monies, to be apportioned to such district in the year eighteen hundred and fifty-three, as shall be sufficient to pay the balance of the purchase price of such Dictionary, not exceeding the sum of two dollars, and shall deposite the same immediately thereafter with the treasurer of their respective counties, and take a receipt for the same and deliver such receipt to the county clerk of their respective counties, to be forwarded by such county clerk to the state superintendent of common schools.

§ 6. The monies so deposited with the treasurers of the respective counties shall be subject to the order of the state superintendent of common schools, and shall be by him received and paid to the publishers of said Dictionaries upon his contract for the same.

§ 7. Such dictionary shall be kept in the libraries of the librarians of the several school districts of this state, during the time there shall be no school taught in said district, and subject to the same rules that are applicable to other books in school district libraries; and during the time a school shall be taught therein the said dictionary shall be under the control of the teacher for the time being, and be kept and used in said school.

PROCEEDINGS OF SCHOOL DISTRICTS UNDER ACT OF 1849.

[*Laws of* 1851. *Chap.* 500.]

AN ACT *to legalize the acts of the several School Districts of the State, providing for the support of Common Schools.*

Passed July 10, 1851.

The People of the State of New York, represented in Senate and Assembly do enact as follows:

§ 1 All the acts of the several school districts of this state, providing for the raising of moneys by tax, for the support of common schools therein, during the years, one thousand eight hundred and forty-nine, one thousand eight hundred and fifty, and prior to the first day of May, one thousand eight hundred and fifty-one; and all the acts of the trustees of said districts, providing for the raising of moneys by tax, for the support of common schools in said districts, for the term of four months during each of said years, prior to the first day of May, 1851, so far as the same are in accordance with the act of March 26, 1849, entitled "An act establishing free schools throughout the state," and the acts amendatory thereof, are hereby declared legal and valid.

§ 2. Nothing in this act shall be construed to affect any suits which have been commenced against any trustee, or other officers of said districts, during said years, nor affect or impair any rights of action now existing.

§ 3. This act shall take effect immediately.

ERRATUM.

Page 342, Paragraph VII "Annual Report of Trustees," in the 4th line substitute "§ 116, (No. 136") for "§ 115, (No. 137.")

In Subdivisions 3 and 4 of same head strike out the words "the name and age of each child," so as to make the same conformable to the lawat page 122.

TO TRUSTEES AND TOWN SUPERINTENDENTS.

This volume is to be regarded as the property of the district or town to which it is sent, and of the Trustees or Town Superintendent *in their official capacity* : and is to be delivered, at the expiration of their official term, to their successors in office. When not required for present use by the trustees, it should be deposited with the District Clerk.

THE END.

INDEX.

A.

B.

Page.

C.

D.

Page.

E.

F.

G.

Page.

H.

I.

J.

L.

M.

N.

O.

P.

Q.

R.

S.

T.

U.

V.

W.

NOTE TO PAGE 187.

SINCE the passage of these sheets through the press, the Superintendent has decided that inhabitants of school districts may legally vote a tax not exceeding $400, for building, hiring or purchasing a school house, under § 70, (No. 92,) without the certificate of the Town Superintendent, *in addition to* the avails arising from, the sale of the former site and house of the district; thereby over-ruling the decision of Gen. Dix, at page 183, of the volume of Common School Decisions.

www.ingramcontent.com/pod-product-compliance
Lightning Source LLC
LaVergne TN
LVHW020106110826
845151LV00001B/79